THE OFFICIAL

A GUIDE BOOK OF
UNITED STATES COINS

PROFESSIONAL EDITION

R. S. YEOMAN

SENIOR EDITOR
KENNETH BRESSETT

RESEARCH EDITOR
Q. DAVID BOWERS

VALUATIONS EDITOR
JEFF GARRETT

Second Edition

Fully Illustrated Catalog and
Retail Valuation List—Federal U.S. Coinage

A Guide Book of United States Coins™
THE OFFICIAL RED BOOK OF UNITED STATES COINS™
PROFESSIONAL EDITION

THE OFFICIAL RED BOOK and
THE OFFICIAL RED BOOK OF UNITED STATES COINS
are trademarks of Whitman Publishing, LLC.

www.whitman**books**.com

ISBN: 0794831583
Printed in the United States of America.

© 2011 Whitman Publishing, LLC
3101 Clairmont Road • Suite G • Atlanta, GA 30329

OCG™ Collecting Guide   WHITMAN™

Collect all the books in the Bowers Series. *A Guide Book of Morgan Silver Dollars • A Guide Book of Double Eagle Gold Coins • A Guide Book of United States Type Coins • A Guide Book of Modern United States Proof Coin Sets • A Guide Book of Shield and Liberty Head Nickels • A Guide Book of Flying Eagle and Indian Head Cents • A Guide Book of Washington and State Quarters • A Guide Book of Buffalo and Jefferson Nickels • A Guide Book of Lincoln Cents • A Guide Book of United States Commemorative Coins • A Guide Book of United States Tokens and Medals • A Guide Book of Gold Dollars • A Guide Book of Peace Dollars • A Guide Book of the Official Red Book of United States Coins • A Guide Book of Franklin and Kennedy Half Dollars*

For a complete listing of numismatic reference books, supplies,
and storage products, visit Whitman Publishing online at
www.whitmanbooks.com

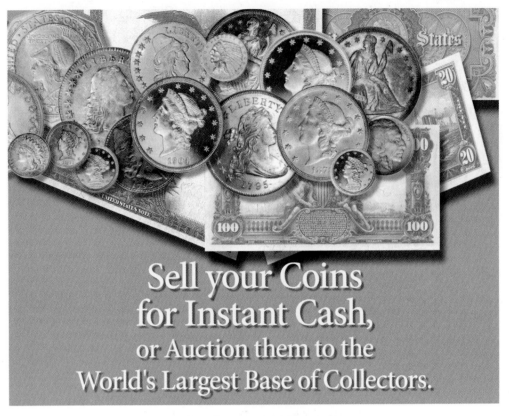

CONTENTS

CONTENTS

CONTENTS

CONTRIBUTORS TO THE SECOND EDITION

Senior Editor: Kenneth Bressett. Research Editor: Q. David Bowers. Valuations Editor: Jeff Garrett.

Special Consultants: Philip Bressett and Ben Todd.

Special credit is due to the following for service and data in this book. The Harry W. Bass Jr. Foundation, Jack Beymer, Larry Briggs, Roger W. Burdette, *Coin World,* John W. Dannreuther, Bill Fivaz, Kevin Flynn, Heather Grant, Ash Harrison, Matt Kleinsteuber, Chris McCawley, Jim McGuigan, Charles Moore, Numismatic Guaranty Corporation of America (NGC), Dick Osburn, Mark Salzberg, Rick Snow, J.T. Stanton, Anthony Swiatek, and Troy Thoreson.

Special photo credits are due to the following. Al Adams, Ira & Larry Goldberg Coins & Collectibles, Tom Mulvaney, the Smithsonian Institution, Stack's Rare Coins, and the U.S. Mint.

Contributors to the regular edition of the* Guide Book of United States Coins *include the following.

Gary Adkins
John Albanese
Mark Albarian
Dominic Albert
Buddy Alleva
Jeff Ambio
Richard S. Appel
Richard M. August
Richard A. Bagg
Mitchell A. Battino
Lee J. Bellisario
Jack Beymer
Stewart Blay
Mark Borckardt
Q. David Bowers
Kenneth Bressett
Philip Bressett
Larry Briggs
Roger W. Burdette
John Burns
H. Robert Campbell
J.H. Cline
Elizabeth Coggan
Alan Cohen
Gary Cohen
James H. Cohen
Steve Cohen
Frank J. Colletti
Columbus–America
   Discovery Group
Steve Contursi
Adam Crum
Raymond Czahor
Charles Davis
Tom DeLorey
Sheridan Downey
Steven Ellsworth
John Feigenbaum
George B. Fitzgerald
Bill Fivaz
George Fuld
Mike Fuljenz
Chuck Furjanic
Jeff Garrett
John Gervasoni
Dennis M. Gillio

Ronald J. Gillio
Ira M. Goldberg
Lawrence Goldberg
Kenneth M. Goldman
James C. Gray
J.R. Grellman
Tom Hallenbeck
James Halperin
John Hamrick
Ash Harrison
Steven Hayden
Brian Hendelson
Gene L. Henry
John W. Highfill
Karl D. Hirtzinger
Charles Hoskins
Jesse Iskowitz
Steve Ivy
James J. Jelinski
Larry Johnson
Robert W. Julian
Donald H. Kagin
Bradley S. Karoleff
Richard Kelly
George F. Kolbe
John Kraljevich
David W. Lange
G.J. Lawson
Richard A. Lecce
Robert Lecce
Julian M. Leidman
Stuart Levine
Kevin Lipton
Denis W. Loring
Andy Lustig
Dwight N. Manley
Arnold Margolis
J.P. Martin
David McCarthy
Chris McCawley
Robert T. McIntire
Harry Miller
Lee S. Minshull
Scott P. Mitchell
Michael C. Moline
Eric P. Newman

Casey Noxon
Paul Nugget
Nancy Oliver
Mike Orlando
John M. Pack
Joseph Parrella
Robert M. Paul
William P. Paul
Joel Rettew Jr.
Joel Rettew Sr.
Robert Rhue
Greg Rohan
Len Roosmalen
Maurice Rosen
P. Scott Rubin
Paul Rynearson
Mary Sauvain
Gerald Scherer Jr.
Cherie Schoeps
Richard J. Schwary
Neil Shafer
Robert W. Shippee
Roger Siboni
James A. Simek
Craig Smith
Rick Snow
Lawrence R. Stack
David M. Sundman
Anthony J. Swiatek
Steve Tanenbaum
Anthony Terranova
Troy Thoreson
Ben Todd
Jerry Treglia
Frank Van Valen
Mark R. Vitunic
Holland Wallace
Fred Weinberg
Weimar White
John Whitney
Douglas Winter
David Wnuck
John Wright
Mark S. Yaffe

INTRODUCTION

Numismatics, in its purest sense, is the study of items used as money. Today in the United States, as around the world, the term embraces the activities of a diverse community of hobbyists, historians, researchers, curators, and others who collect and study coins, tokens, paper money, and similar objects.

Since 1946 the *Guide Book of United States Coins* has served this community as the preeminent annual reference for coin specifications, mintages, values, photographs, and other information important to collectors and students. With more than 22 million copies in print since the first edition, the *Guide Book* (popularly known as "the Red Book") is well established as the most popular reference in numismatics—not to mention one of the best-selling nonfiction books in the history of American publishing. (In 1964 the 18th edition of the Red Book ranked no. 5 on the national sales lists, at 1.2 million copies—higher than Dale Carnegie's *How to Win Friends and Influence People* at no. 6, and John F. Kennedy's *Profiles in Courage* at no. 9.)

Building on this strong foundation, Whitman Publishing launched the Professional Edition of the *Guide Book of United States Coins,* an expanded and enlarged volume intended to serve especially the intermediate to advanced coin collector, the professional coin dealer or auctioneer, the researcher, and the investor. Its combination of more photographs, detailed higher-grade valuations, listings of additional varieties and rare early Proof coins, certified-coin population data, auction records, and other resources provides a wealth of information on every coin type ever made by the U.S. Mint. The Professional Edition is not an exhaustive study of die varieties, though it does expand (with close-up photographs, valuations, and chart notes) on the regular edition's coverage of such coins. Rather, it is a handy single-source guide that educates its users in auction and certification trends, retail valuations, and similar aspects of the marketplace.

The Professional Edition is not a substitute for the regular-edition *Guide Book of United States Coins*. The regular edition includes information not found here, including grading instructions and valuations for lower-grade coins, an introductory overview of the history of U.S. coinage, stories of coins from treasures and hoards, and coverage of colonial and early American coins and tokens; private and territorial gold; Hard Times tokens; Civil War tokens; Confederate coins; Hawaiian, Puerto Rican, and Philippine coins; Alaskan tokens; misstrikes and errors; numismatic books; and other topics.

HOW TO USE THIS BOOK

The *Guide Book of United States Coins, Professional Edition,* covers all federal U.S. coin series, from copper half cents to gold double eagles, plus classic commemoratives (1892–1954), Proof and Mint sets, and bullion. Readers will find the following information:

Denomination introductions. Each coinage denomination is discussed first in an overview of its history, major design types and subtypes, and general collectability by type. (The trade dollar is treated as its own denomination, separate from other dollar coins.) A second essay gives the reader a more in-depth analysis of specializing in that denomination. *These sections encapsulate decades of numismatic research and market observation, and they should be read in conjunction with the charts, photographs, and other information that follow.*

Type-by-type studies. Within each denomination, each major coin type is laid out in chronological order. As in the regular-edition Red Book, the type's designer and its specifications (weight, composition, diameter, edge treatment, and production facilities) are given. Each coinage design is pictured either at actual size or enlarged (in the latter case, along with a notation on the scale of enlargement).

Each type section includes summary text on the type's history; aspects of its striking, sharpness, and related characteristics; and its market availability. Grading guidelines and advice are included for the grades covered in the coin type's data charts. For most series, the grades start at the high end of those covered by the regular-edition Red Book, and include more and higher Mint State levels. (Readers interested in detailed guidelines for lower circulated grades may consult *Grading Coins by Photographs: An Action Guide for the Collector and Investor,* which covers grades About Good through Mint State, as well as Proofs.)

The data charts include these elements:

Mintages. Mintage data is compiled from official Mint records whenever possible, and in other cases from more than 60 years of active numismatic research. In instances where the Mint's early records are in question or have been proven faulty, the official numbers are provided and further information is given in chart notes. For some early Proof coins for which no official mintage records exist, an estimated mintage, or the number of coins known in collections, is given. For modern issues (usually those minted within the past five years), the Mint has released production and/or sales numbers that are not yet officially finalized; these are given in italics.

Note that Mint reports are not always reliable for estimating the rarities of coins. In the early years of the Mint, dies of previous years often were used until they became worn or broken. Certain quantities reported, particularly for gold and silver coins, cover the number of pieces struck and make no indication of the quantity that actually reached circulation. Many issues were deposited in the Treasury as backing for paper currency and later were melted.

Gold coins struck before August 1, 1834, are rare today, because from 1821 onward (and at times before 1821) the gold in the coins was worth more than their face values, so they were struck as bullion and traded at a premium. Many were exported and melted for their precious-metal value.

Mintage figures shown for 1964 through 1966 are for coins bearing those dates. Some of them were struck in more than one year and at various mints, both with and without mintmarks. In recent years, mintage figures reported by the Mint have been revised several times and remain uncertain as to precise amounts.

Mintage figures shown in italics are estimates based on the most accurate information available. Numismatic research is constantly ongoing, and listed figures are sometimes revised, when new information becomes available.

Certified Populations. For each circulation-strike coin, a summary is provided of (1) the number of coins certified, (2) the average grade, on a 1–70 scale, of those coins graded, and (3) the percentage of coins certified in Mint State.

For early (generally pre-1916) Proof coins, certified populations are summarized as (1) the number of coins certified, and (2) the level of the finest Proof known.

For later Proofs, certified populations are summarized as (1) the number of coins certified, and (2) the average Proof level.

These summaries provide the collector and investor with working data useful in comparing coins offered for sale or bid.

Certified population data are provided courtesy of Numismatic Guaranty Corporation of America (NGC), one of the nation's leading professional third-party grading firms.

It should be noted that for most coins, especially rare dates and varieties, the number certified actually represents the quantity of *submissions,* rather than the number of individual coins submitted. For example, a particular 1916-D dime that is submitted for certification five times would be counted the same as five individual coins. Such resubmissions can sometimes result in numbers close to or higher than a coin's entire mintage.

Note, too, that the grade number assigned to a "slabbed" (graded and encapsulated) coin does not tell anything about the quality of that particular coin's planchet, the strength of its strike, whether it has been cleaned or dipped, or its overall eye appeal. Such factors are important to a coin's value. Two rare coins of the same date and variety, each with the same amount of surface wear and graded MS-63, will find different values in the marketplace if one is eye-pleasing and well struck, and the other is dull and poorly struck.

Valuations. Coin values shown in the Professional Edition are retail prices compiled from data and market observations provided by dealers, auctioneers, and other market observers, under the direction and analysis of Valuations Editor Jeff Garrett. The values reflect typical auction and retail prices seen for *professionally certified* coins. The valuations of professionally certified coins, as listed in this book, often are higher than what collectors normally pay for non-certified ("raw") coins.

The coin market is so active in some categories that values can easily change after publication. Values are shown as a guide and are not intended to serve as a price list for any dealer's stock.

A dash appearing in a valuations column indicates that coins in that grade exist even though there are no current retail or auction records for them. The dash does not necessarily mean that such coins are exceedingly rare. Italicized numbers indicate unsettled or speculative (estimated) values. A number of listings of rare coins lack valuations or dashes in certain grades, indicating that they are not available, or not believed to exist, in those grades.

For wholesale pricing, the *Handbook of United States Coins* (popularly called the Blue Book, and published since 1942), by R.S. Yeoman, contains average prices dealers nationwide will pay for U.S. coins. It is obtainable through most coin dealers, hobby shops, bookstores, and the Internet.

There is some overlap in the grades valued in the regular edition of the *Guide Book of United States Coins* and those valued in the Professional Edition. In some cases their values are different. This is because the regular edition and the Professional Edition are published six months apart, and the market can change in that time.

Auction Records. A recent auction record is provided for every coin, some exceptions being coins that are too common to sell individually at auction. Each record indicates:

the price paid for the coin (including any fees)

the grade of the coin

the date (month and year) of the auction

This combination of data gives valuable market information for each coin. It also serves as a springboard for further research. Many auction firms have online archives of coins sold, or else their auction catalogs can be studied using the information provided.

ABBREVIATIONS USED IN THIS BOOK

BN—Brown; descriptive of the coloration or toning on certain copper coins

RB—Red and brown; descriptive of the mixture of mint red and brown coloration or toning on a copper coin

RD—Red; descriptive of the mint red color on an untoned copper coin

CAC—Abbreviation found in the auction-record listings; indicates that the coin listed met the grading standards of the Certified Acceptance Corporation (CAC offers the opinion of its staff of professional numismatists that independently graded coins are "solid" for their assigned grades. Such coins bear a green CAC label on their certification slabs.)

TransRev—Transitional Reverse

Cert—Certified population

Avg—Average grade (on a 1–70 scale)

%MS—Percentage of coins certified in Mint State

Ltrd—Lettered

Lg—Large

Med—Medium

Sm—Small

Ltrs—Letters

Rev—Reverse

Obv—Obverse

DblDie—Doubled die

Horiz—Horizontal

D/D—D Over D; a slash between words or letters represents an overdate or overmintmark

Dt—Date

RPD—Repunched Date

Var—Variety

FS—Full Steps

SMS—Special Mint Set

Cam—Cameo

DC—Deep Cameo

DCam—Deep Cameo

Knbd—Knobbed-Top

Inv—Inverted

FBL—Full Bell Lines

TripDie—Tripled Die

QuintDie—Quintupled Die

DMPL—Deep Mirror Prooflike

Mintmk—Mintmark

Sq—Square

Ex.—extremely

FB—Full Bands

Var—Variety

Horiz—Horizontal

FH—Full Head

RPM—Repunched Mintmark

UCam—Ultra Cameo

INVESTING IN RARE COINS

As with the regular edition of the *Guide Book of United States Coins,* those who edit, contribute to, and publish the Professional Edition advocate the collecting of coins for pleasure and educational benefits. A secondary consideration is that of investment, the profits of which are usually realized over the long term based on careful purchases.

Use Common Sense

The rare-coin market combines some aspects of commodity trading with peculiarities seen more often among markets such as those for fine art, real estate, cut gemstones, and similar investments and collectibles. Armed with knowledge, an investor can have a very rewarding experience in rare coins. An uneducated investor can just as easily see substantial losses.

The regular edition of the *Guide Book of United States Coins* includes this bit of guidance, which bears repeating here: "The best advice given to anyone considering investing in rare coins is to use common sense." Any collector with common sense would think twice about buying a silver dollar at a flea market for less than its silver value. A common-sense collector who is offered a $5,000 coin from an "unsearched estate," or from a non-specialist who claims to know nothing of its provenance, would refuse it at $1,000—at least until a diligent examination was possible, and only with an iron-clad return policy and guarantee of authenticity. Profitable investment requires careful selection of qualified dealers (e.g., those professionally credentialed by groups such as the Professional Numismatists Guild and the International Association of Professional Numismatists), and educated evaluation of the coins offered for sale.

Learn About Grading

In the past, coin grading was very subjective, and grade descriptions were far from universal. One dealer's "Choice Extremely Fine" might have been another's "About Uncirculated," and adjectives such as *gem* and *brilliant* varied in meaning from collector to collector. Today grading is still a subjective art striving to be an exact science, but progress has been made. The hobby's guidelines have been clearly standardized in systems such as the Official American Numismatic Association Grading Standards for United States Coins, and explored further in illustrated books such as *Grading Coins by Photographs.* Today there are professional certification services such as NGC, PCGS, ICG, and ANACS that grade and authenticate coins, encapsulating them in sealed "slabs" with their grades noted. These are third-party firms, so called because they are neither buyer nor seller of the coins graded (which guarantees a professional level of impartiality).

Learn About What You're Buying

In addition to carefully vetting professional dealers, examining potential purchases for authenticity, and studying the art and science of grading, an investor can profit by *learning* about coins. Each coin type has a cultural history that provides useful collecting/investing knowledge. For example, Morgan dollars often were stored by the Treasury in the thousands (and millions), so a bag of 1,000 Mint State dollars is not unheard of. On the other hand, the purchaser of a seemingly original bag of Mint State Indian Head cents would likely be left holding a few pounds of counterfeit copper coins. Similarly, each coin type has a typical strike, surface quality, and related characteristics; knowledge of these features can help reveal fakes and lower-than-average-quality specimens. The investor who knows that a certain coin type is rarely encountered in a certain high grade is more alert to potential opportunities. Conversely, if a type is common in high grades, the savvy investor will pass on an average or below-average coin and wait for the sharpest, most attractive one he can find, knowing that time and the marketplace are on his side.

For these reasons, even if you consider yourself more *investor* than *collector,* it is recommended that you read every section of the Professional Edition that covers the coin series you're interested in. The data charts provide one level of information, the denomination introductions another, the type summaries and grading guides yet others; combined, they offer a well-rounded education that prices alone cannot provide.

Understand the General Market

Coin values rise when (1) the economic trend is inflationary and speculators turn to tangible assets as a hedge, or when the number of collectors increases, while coin supplies remain stationary or decrease through attrition or melting; (2) dealers replace their stocks of coins only from collectors or other dealers, who expect a profit over what they originally paid; (3) speculators attempt to influence the market through selective buying; or (4) bullion (gold and silver) prices rise.

Coin values decline when (1) changes in collecting habits or economic conditions alter demand for certain coins; (2) speculators sell in large quantities; (3) hoards or large holdings are suddenly released and cannot be quickly absorbed by the normal market; or (4) bullion (gold and silver) prices decline.

Learn From the Experts

A rich numismatic world is available to the investor and collector who seek to learn. Weekly newspapers such as *Coin World* and *Numismatic News* cover the hobby and its markets from many angles, as do a variety of monthly magazines. Auction sale results, new U.S. Mint products, convention activities, market reports, and other information await the interested reader.

Web sites such as WhitmanCoinCollecting.com, NumisMaster.com, and CoinFacts.com gather and present information from authoritative sources.

Organizations such as the American Numismatic Association (ANA) and the American Numismatic Society (ANS), as well as dozens of specialized groups focused on particular coins or series, offer resources and connections to collectors worldwide.

Every major American city and many smaller cities have coin shops where experienced dealers can be consulted for advice and opinions.

Coin shows are another venue for learning from seasoned collectors and investors. The ANA mounts three popular shows annually, in different cities. Whitman Coin and Collectibles Expo (www.WhitmanExpo.com) hosts shows yearly in Baltimore and Philadelphia. Florida United Numismatists (FUN) organizes two shows in the winter and summer each year. All of these shows, and dozens of other local and regional conventions, offer opportunities to talk to other collectors and investors, meet market experts, listen to presentations, and examine hundreds of coins, tokens, and medals.

Books are another means of learning from the hobby's experts. Every collector and investor should have at least a basic numismatic library of standard references. In addition, nearly every specialty in American coins has one or more books devoted to greater in-depth exploration. Numismatic publishing has experienced a renaissance in recent years, making valuable knowledge more affordable and readily available than ever before. One book essential to the investor's understanding of the rare-coin market is a 672-page volume written by the "dean of American numismatics," Q. David Bowers. The *Expert's Guide to Collecting and Investing in Rare Coins* covers topics such as determining coin prices and values; focusing on rarity; quality and value for the smart buyer; coin market fads, trends, and cycles; making of the modern market for rare coins; predicting the rare coin market; techniques of smart buying and bidding; protecting your investment; and more.

In the long run, coin collectors—even those who seek mainly to profit financially from the hobby—are simply custodians of the relics they collect. Again, the regular edition of the *Guide Book of United States Coins* gives sound advice: "Those who treat rare coins with the consideration and respect they deserve will profit in many ways, not the least of which can be in the form of a sound financial return on one's investments of time and money."

AN OVERVIEW OF HALF CENTS

Building a type set of the six different major designs in the half cent series can be a challenging and rewarding pursuit. The first design, with Liberty Head facing left with pole and cap, minted only in 1793, is scarce in all grades and will be the most difficult to locate. However, hundreds exist of this American classic, and many are fairly attractive.

The second type, with a *large* Liberty Head facing right with pole and cap, made only in 1794, is scarce with good eye appeal. Most are dark and rough. The next type, the *small* Liberty Head facing right, with pole and cap, is scarce, but enough are on the market that a collector can find a specimen without difficulty.

The Draped Bust half cents, struck from 1800 to 1808, are easily available as a type, including in higher grades. The Classic Head (1809–1836) and Braided Hair (1840–1857) are plentiful as types.

For the earlier half cent types there is ample opportunity for connoisseurship, for quality often varies widely, and every coin is apt to have a different appearance and "personality," even within the same grade.

FOR THE COLLECTOR AND INVESTOR: HALF CENTS AS A SPECIALTY

Collecting half cents by dates and major varieties has been a popular niche specialty for a long time. Among the key issues in the series are the 1793; 1796 With Pole to Cap; 1796 Without Pole to Cap (the most famous of all the rarities); 1802, 2 Over 0 With Reverse of 1800 (a single leaf at each side of the wreath apex, rare but somewhat obscure); 1831; and the Proof-only issues of 1836, 1840 through 1848, Small Date, and 1852.

As there are so many Proof varieties, and each of these is rare as well as expensive, many collectors opt to acquire only the circulation strikes. However, the Proofs are not nearly as expensive as one might think, probably because with so many different dates and varieties needed to complete a collection the prospect is daunting to many buyers. Proofs of most dates are available in both original and restrike forms. Although this rule is not without exceptions, the original strikings of the 1840–1848 and 1849 Small Date half cents are usually described as having the Large Berries reverse, while restrikes are of the Small Berries reverse (within the Small Berries issues there are two dies—one with diagonal die striae below RICA and the other with doubling at the ribbon wreath). Assembling Proofs by reverse varieties is a somewhat arcane pursuit.

For an exhaustive study of die varieties of circulation strikes and Proofs, *Walter Breen's Encyclopedia of United States Half Cents, 1793–1857,* is definitive. Roger S. Cohen Jr.'s study, *American Half Cents, The "Little Half Sisters,"* gives detailed information on circulation strikes, but omits Proofs.

Die varieties are especially abundant among half cents of the first several types, 1793 to 1808. The year 1804 offers a panorama of dies, some of which have been studied as to *die states,* referring to the progression of use of a die as it develops wear, cracks, etc. Varieties of 1795 exist with and without the pole to the liberty cap, the without-pole being the result of a die being relapped (reground to dress the surface), during which process the pole was removed. On the other hand, the 1796 Without Pole half cent was the result of a die-engraving error—the diecutter forgot to add it. Some half cents of 1795 and 1797 were struck on planchets cut from copper tokens issued by the New York City firm of Talbot, Allum & Lee. Upon close inspection, some of the design details of the tokens can still be seen.

One curious and readily available variety of the 1828 half cent has 12 stars instead of the standard 13. However, in choice Mint State the 12-stars issue becomes a rarity, for, unlike the 13-stars issue, none were ever found in hoards.

The Early American Coppers Club is a special-interest group emphasizing copper half cents and large cents. Its journal, *Penny-Wise,* provides much research, social, and collecting news and information.

RECOMMENDED READING

Bowers, Q. David. *Whitman Encyclopedia of Half Cents and Large Cents,* Atlanta, GA, 2011.
Breen, Walter. *Walter Breen's Encyclopedia of United States Half Cents 1793–1857,* South Gate, CA, 1983.
Cohen, Roger S., Jr. *American Half Cents—The "Little Half Sisters"* (2nd ed.), 1982.
Fivaz, Bill, and Stanton, J.T. *The Cherrypickers' Guide to Rare Die Varieties* (5th ed., vol. I), Atlanta, GA, 2009.
Manley, Ronald P. *The Half Cent Die State Book, 1793–1857,* United States, 1998.

LIBERTY CAP, HEAD FACING LEFT
(1793)

Designer probably Henry Voigt; weight 6.74 grams; composition, copper; approx. diameter 22 mm; edge: TWO HUNDRED FOR A DOLLAR.

Cohen-4, Breen-4.

History. Among U.S. coinage, the Liberty Cap, Head Facing Left, design belongs to the small class of one-year-only types. Its design was inspired by Augustin Dupré's Libertas Americana medal. The Liberty Cap dies often are credited to Joseph Wright, who also cut the dies for the related cent, but were more likely done by Henry Voigt.

Striking and Sharpness. Good-quality copper was used in these half cents, so they often are found light brown and on fairly smooth planchets. Unlike in later types, the borders on both sides are raised beads; certain of these beads can be weak, though this is not the norm. Some varieties are lightly defined at HALF CENT on the reverse, due to a combination of striking and shallow depth of letters in the die. This feature cannot be used in assigning a grade, as in lower grades (up to and including VG-8) these words may be completely missing.

Availability. Most half cents of 1793 are AG-3 to F-12. EF and AU examples are rare, and MS very rare (most being MS-60 to 63). Market grading is often liberal. Early American Coppers Club (EAC) "raw" grades often are lower than those of the certification services.

AG-3 (About Good). *Obverse:* The portrait is visible only in outline. LIBERTY is weak but usually fully discernible. 1793 is weak, and the bottoms of the digits may be worn away. *Reverse:* (Grading at AG-3 is usually done by the reverse.) Parts of the wreath are visible in outline form, and all but a few letters are gone.

G-4, 6 (Good). *Obverse:* The eye position can be discerned, though the portrait is worn smooth and is seen only in outline form. LIBERTY is complete. 1793 is complete, but may be weak. *Reverse:* (The reverse is key in assigning Good grades; it shows more evidence of wear than does the obverse.) Extensive wear is seen overall. From half to two-thirds of the letters in UNITED STATES OF AMERICA and the fraction numerals are worn away.

VG-8, 10 (Very Good). *Obverse:* Although the eye can be seen, the portrait is well worn. The hair tips at the right show separation. Border beads are worn away, and the border blends into the field in most if not all of the periphery. LIBERTY and 1793 are bold. *Reverse:* The wreath, bow, and lettering are seen in outline form, and some leaves and letters may be indistinct in parts. Border beads are worn away, and the border blends into the field in most if not all of the periphery.

F-12, 15 (Fine). *Obverse:* The hair details are mostly worn away, with about one-third visible, mainly at the edges. Border beads are weak or worn away in areas. *Reverse:* The wreath leaves are worn flat, but their edges are distinct. HALF CENT may be missing on variety B-1, C-1 (also true in lower grades). Border beads are weak or worn away in areas.

VF-20, 30 (Very Fine). *Obverse:* At VF-20, wear on the portrait has reduced the hair detail to indistinct or flat at the center; at VF-30 there is slightly more detail. The thin, more-or-less horizontal ribbon near the top of the hair is distinct. The border beads are blended together, with many blurred or missing. No luster is evident. *Reverse:* At VF-20 the leaf details are nearly completely worn away; at VF-30 there is slight detail in the leaves at VF-30. The border beads are blended together, with many indistinct. Some berries in the sprays may be worn away (though on strong strikes they can be evident in grades down to Good). No luster is evident. HALF CENT, while fully legible, may be weak on certain coins (such as B-1, C-1) in which this feature was shallowly cut into the dies.

EF-40, 45 (Extremely Fine). *Obverse:* Wear is seen on the portrait overall. The separation of the hair strands on the highest part is reduced or eliminated. The cheek is slightly flat on the highest part. Some leaves retain some detail, especially where they join the stems. At EF-40, luster is minimal or non-existent; at 45, luster may survive in traces in protected areas. *Reverse:* Wear is seen on the highest wreath and ribbon areas and the letters. Luster is minimal, but likely more noticeable than on the obverse, as the fields are protected by the designs and lettering.

AU-50, 53, 55, 58 (About Uncirculated). *Obverse:* (Grading at the AU level is done mainly by viewing the obverse.) Friction is seen on the higher parts, particularly on the rounded cheek and on the higher strands of the hair. Friction and scattered marks are in the field, ranging from extensive at AU-50 to minimal at AU-58. Luster may be seen in protected areas, minimal at AU-50, but sometimes extensive at AU-58. Border beads, if well struck, are separate and boldly defined. *Reverse:* Friction is seen on the higher wreath leaves and (not as easy to discern) on the letters. The fields, protected by the designs, show friction, but not as noticeably as on the obverse. At AU-55 and 58 little if any friction is seen. The reverse may have original luster, toned brown, minimal on lower About Uncirculated grades, sometimes extensive at AU-58. Border beads, if well struck, are separate and boldly defined.

MS-60 to 65 (Mint State). *Obverse:* In MS-60 and 61, some slight abrasions can be seen on the higher areas of the portrait. Luster in the field is incomplete, particularly in the center of the open areas. At MS-63, luster is complete, with no abrasions evident. In higher levels, the luster is deeper, and some original mint color may be seen. *Reverse:* In MS-60 and 61, some abrasions are seen on the higher areas of the leaves. Generally, luster is complete in all MS grades, as the open areas are protected by the lettering and wreath. Otherwise, same comments apply as for the obverse.

	Mintage	Cert	Avg	%MS	F-12	VF-20	EF-40	EF-45	AU-50	MS-60BN	MS-63BN	Recent Auction Record
1793	35,334	124	37.2	11	$8,000	$12,500	$23,000	$25,500	$38,000	$65,000	$95,000	$46,000, MS-60BN, May-10

LIBERTY CAP, HEAD FACING RIGHT
(1794–1797)

1794—Designer Robert Scot; weight 6.74 grams; composition copper; approx. diameter 23.5 mm; edge: TWO HUNDRED FOR A DOLLAR. 1795—Designer John Smith Gardner; weight 6.74 grams; composition copper; approx. diameter 23.5 mm; edge: TWO HUNDRED FOR A DOLLAR. 1795–1797 (thin planchet)— Weight 5.44 grams; composition copper; approx. diameter 23.5 mm; edge: plain (some 1797 are either lettered or gripped).

Cohen-4, Breen-6.

History. The design of the half cent changed in 1794 to a depiction, by Robert Scot, of Miss Liberty facing right. A smaller-headed portrait was used from 1795 on.

Striking and Sharpness. Half cents of 1794 usually are dark, with rough surfaces, and of low aesthetic quality. Most 1795s are on high-quality planchets, smooth and attractive, this being truer of the later plain-edge type than the early thick-planchet issue. Striking can be weak in areas. Often the dentils are incomplete on one or both sides. Many Small Head coins, particularly of 1795 to 1797, have very little detail on the hair, even in higher grades. Half cents of 1796 vary in quality; higher-grade pieces usually are attractive. Half cents of 1797 are usually seen in low grades and on poor planchets; striking varies widely, but is usually weak in areas. Dentils can be weak or can be prominent in various circulated grades, down to the lowest; on certain varieties of 1795 they are prominent even on well-worn coins.

Grades must be assigned carefully, and expertise is recommended—combining knowledge of a given die variety and its relief or sharpness in the die, with observations of actual circulation wear. Grades of certified coins can vary widely in their interpretations.

Availability. As a general type, this issue is scarce, but available. Most are in lower grades, but VF and EF coins appear in the market with regularity.

G-4, 6 (Good). *Obverse:* The portrait is worn smooth and is seen only in outline form, although the eye position can be discerned. LIBERTY and the date are complete, although the date may be weak. Dentils are gone on some, but not all, die varieties. *Reverse:* Extensive wear is seen overall. From half to two-thirds of the letters in UNITED STATES OF AMERICA, and the fraction numerals, are worn away. Certain shallow-relief dies may have letters missing.

VG-8, 10 (Very Good). *Obverse:* The portrait is well worn, although the eye can be seen, and the hair tips at the left show separation. Border dentils are worn away on some issues (not as much for 1795). The border blends into the field in most if not all of the periphery. LIBERTY and the date are bold. *Reverse:* The wreath, bow, and lettering are seen in outline form. Some leaves and letters may be indistinct in parts. Border dentils are worn away, and the border blends into the field in most if not all of the periphery. In certain die varieties and die states, especially of 1797, some letters may be very weak or missing.

F-12, 15 (Fine). *Obverse:* The hair details are mostly worn away, with about one-third visible, mainly at the edges. Border dentils are weak or worn away in areas. *Reverse:* The wreath leaves are worn flat, but their edges are distinct. Border dentils are weak or worn away in areas.

VF-20, 30 (Very Fine). *Obverse:* Wear on the portrait has reduced the hair detail to indistinct or flat at the center. The border dentils are blended together, with many indistinct. No luster is seen. *Reverse:* At VF-20 the leaf details are nearly completely worn away; at VF-30, there is slight detail. The border dentils are blended together, with many indistinct. No luster is seen. The sharpness of details depends on the die variety. Half cents of 1797 require special care in their study.

EF-40, 45 (Extremely Fine). *Obverse:* Wear is seen on the portrait overall, with reduction or elimination of some separation of hair strands on the highest part. This varies by die variety; some are better delineated than others. The cheek shows light wear. Luster is minimal or nonexistent at EF-40, and may survive in traces in protected areas (such as between the letters) at EF-45. *Reverse:* Wear is seen on the highest wreath and ribbon areas and the letters. Luster is minimal, but likely more noticeable than on the obverse, as the fields are protected by the designs and lettering. Sharpness varies depending on die variety; certain issues of 1794 and 1797 are lighter.

AU-50, 53, 55, 58 (About Uncirculated). *Obverse:* (Grading at AU is mainly done by viewing the obverse.) Friction is seen on the higher parts, particularly the center of the portrait. Friction and scattered marks are in the field, ranging from extensive at AU-50 to minimal at AU-58. Luster may be seen in protected areas, minimal at AU-50, but sometimes extensive on an AU-58 coin. Knowledge of the die variety is important; for certain shallow-relief dies (such as 1797) an About Uncirculated coin may appear to be in a lower grade. *Reverse:* Friction is seen on the higher wreath leaves and (not as easy to discern) on the letters. The fields, protected by the designs, show friction, but not as noticeably as on the obverse. At AU-55 and 58 little if any friction is seen. The reverse may have original luster, toned brown, minimal on lower AU grades, sometimes extensive on higher.

MS-60 to 70 (Mint State). *Obverse:* In MS-60 and 61, there are some traces of abrasion on the higher areas of the portrait. Luster in the field is incomplete, particularly in the center of the open areas. At MS-63, luster is complete, with no abrasions. At higher levels, the luster is deeper, and some original mint color may be seen. At MS-65 there are some scattered contact marks and possibly some traces of fingerprints or discoloration, but these should be minimal and not distracting. Above MS-65, a coin should approach perfection. *Reverse:* In the lower ranges some abrasions are seen on the higher areas of the leaves. Generally, luster is complete in all ranges, as the open areas are protected by the lettering and wreath. Otherwise, the same comments apply as for the obverse.

1794, Normal Head   **1794, High-Relief Head**   **1795, With Pole**   **1795, Punctuated Date**   **1795, No Pole**

1796, "Dr. Edwards" Copy   **1797, 1 Above 1**   **1797, Low Head**

	Mintage	Cert	Avg	%MS	VG-8	F-12	VF-20	EF-40	AU-50	MS-60BN	MS-63BN	Recent Auction Record
1794, All kinds	81,600											$6,900, AU-50, Apr-10
1794, Normal Head		20	36.2	10	$785	$1,450	$2,500	$5,500	$10,000	$20,000	$35,000	
1794, High-Relief Head		13	37.9	8	825	1,500	2,750	5,750	11,000	20,000	35,000	$1,150, F-12, Jan-10
1795, All kinds	139,690											$8,625, AU-55, Mar-10
1795, Lettered Edge, With Pole		9	39.8	22	800	1,500	2,750	5,750	10,500	16,500	24,000	
1795, Lettered Edge, Punctuated Date		4	14.5	0	800	1,500	2,750	6,000	12,000	25,000	40,000	$2,185, VF-25, Mar-10
1795, Plain Edge, Punctuated Date		4	42.5	25	625	1,000	1,775	4,500	8,500	12,500	20,000	$1,610, VG-10, Sep-09
1795, Plain Edge, No Pole (a)		24	29.3	0	625	950	1,775	4,500	8,500	12,500	20,000	$891, F-15, Jun-10
1796, With Pole (b)	1,390	16	43.6	50	25,000 (c)	35,000	56,000	80,000	100,000	185,000		$18,732, VG-8, Aug-09
1796, No Pole	*	1	62.0	100	45,000 (d)	75,000	150,000	—	—	500,000		$74,750, Fine, May-09
1797, All kinds	127,840											
1797, 1 Above 1, Plain Edge					625	950	1,800	3,800	6,000	13,000		$4,600, EF-45, Jun-10
1797, Plain Edge, Low Head		2	5.5	0	800	2,000	3,500	12,500	—	—	—	$1,610, F-12, Jun-08
1797, Plain Edge		36	29.1	11	650	1,250	3,000	6,000	8,000	15,000		$1,725, F-12, Feb-10
1797, Lettered Edge		3	12.7	0	2,750 (e)	6,000	15,000	30,000	60,000			$41,400, VF-25, Sep-08
1797, Gripped Edge					55,000 (f)	70,000	—	—	—			$23,000, AG-3, Feb-01

* Included in number above. **a.** Many of this date/variety were struck on cut-down cents (coins that had been rejected for circulation by Mint workers), or on planchets cut from English-made Talbot, Allum & Lee tokens (see the *Whitman Encyclopedia of Colonial and Early American Coins*). **b.** The deceptive "Dr. Edwards" struck copy of this coin has a different head and larger letters, as pictured (see the *Whitman Encyclopedia of Half Cents and Large Cents* for more information). **c.** Value in G-4 is $15,000. **d.** Value in G-4 is $30,000. **e.** Value in G-4 is $1,500. **f.** Value in G-4 is $22,500.

DRAPED BUST
(1800–1808)

Designer Robert Scot; weight 5.44 grams; composition copper; diameter 23.5 mm; plain edge.

Cohen-13, Breen-10.

History. By the turn of the century the Draped Bust design was already familiar to Americans, from its use on cents and silver coins. The motif was introduced to the half cent in 1800, and was used through 1808.

Striking and Sharpness. Striking varies. Weakness is often seen at the center of the obverse and on the wreath leaves on the reverse. Planchet quality is often porous and dark for 1802, 1803, 1807, and 1808 due to the copper stock used.

Availability. As a type, Draped Bust half cents are available in any grade desired, up to and including Mint State, the latter usually dated 1806 (occasionally 1800 and, less often, 1804). The year 1804 includes many different die varieties and die states. Apart from aspects of strike, cherrypicking for planchet quality is essential for 1802, 1803, 1807, and 1808.

G-4, 6 (Good). *Obverse:* The portrait is worn smooth and is seen only in outline form, although the eye position can be discerned. LIBERTY and the date are complete, although the date may be weak. The border blends into the field more extensively than in VG, but significant areas are still seen. *Reverse:* Extensive wear is seen overall. From half to two-thirds of the letters in UNITED STATES OF AMERICA and the fraction numerals are worn away.

VG-8, 10 (Very Good). *Obverse:* The portrait is well worn, although the eye can be seen, as can hints of hair detail (some at the left shows separation). Curls appear as mostly solid blobs. Border dentils are worn away on most varieties, and the rim, although usually present, begins to blend into the field. LIBERTY and the date are bold. *Reverse:* The wreath, bow, and lettering are seen in outline form. Some leaves and letters may be indistinct in parts. The border may blend into the field on some of the periphery.

F-12, 15 (Fine). *Obverse:* The hair details are mostly worn away, with about one-third visible, mainly at the edges. Border dentils are weak or worn away in areas. *Reverse:* The wreath leaves are worn flat, but their edges are distinct. HALF CENT may be missing on variety B-1, C-1 (also true of lower grades). Border dentils are weak or worn away in areas.

VF-20, 30 (Very Fine). *Obverse:* Wear on the portrait has reduced the hair detail to indistinct or flat at the center. The border dentils are blended together, with many indistinct. No luster is seen. *Reverse:* The leaf details have slight detail at VF-30, and are nearly completely worn away at VF-20. The border dentils are blended together, with many indistinct. No luster is seen.

EF-40, 45 (Extremely Fine). *Obverse:* Wear is seen on the portrait overall, with reduction or elimination of some separation of hair strands on the highest part. The cheek shows light wear. Luster may survive among the letters of LIBERTY at EF-45, and is minimal or nonexistent at EF-40. *Reverse:* Wear is seen on the highest wreath and ribbon areas, and the letters. Luster is minimal, but likely more noticeable than on the obverse, as the fields are protected by the designs and lettering.

AU-50, 53, 55, 58 (About Uncirculated). *Obverse:* Friction is seen on the higher parts, particularly the hair. Friction and scattered marks are in the field, minimal at AU-58 to extensive at AU-50. Luster may be seen in protected areas, more at AU-58, minimal at AU-50. At AU-58 the field may retain some luster, as well. The luster is lesser in area and in "depth" than on the reverse. *Reverse:* Friction is evident on the higher wreath leaves and (not as easy to discern) on the letters. The die variety should be checked. The fields, protected by the designs, show friction, but not as noticeably as on the obverse. At AU-55 and 58, little if any friction is seen. The reverse may have original luster, toned brown, often extensive at AU-58, and minimal at lower AU grades.

MS-60 to 70 (Mint State). *Obverse:* In MS-60 and 61, some slight abrasions can be seen on the higher areas of the portrait. Luster in the field is incomplete, particularly in the center of the open areas, which on this type are very extensive. At MS-63, luster should be nearly complete, and no abrasions evident. In higher levels, the luster is complete and deeper and some original mint color may be seen. MS-64 coins may have some slight discoloration or scattered contact marks. An MS-65 or higher coin has full, rich luster; no marks visible except under magnification; and a blend of brown toning or nicely mixed (not stained or blotchy) mint color and natural brown toning. *Reverse:* In lower MS grades some abrasions are seen on the higher areas of the leaves. Generally, luster is complete in MS, as the open areas are protected by the lettering and wreath. Sharpness of the leaves can vary by die variety. Otherwise, the same comments apply as for the obverse.

1st Reverse (Style of 1800)   2nd Reverse (Style of 1803)   1803, Regular   1803, Widely Spaced 3   1804, Plain 4   1804, Crosslet 4

Stems to Wreath   Stemless Wreath   1804, "Spiked Chin"   1805, Medium 5   1805, Small 5   1805, Large 5

1806, Small 6   1806, Large 6   1808, 8 Over 7   1808, Normal Date

	Mintage	Cert	Avg	%MS	VF-20	EF-40	AU-50	MS-60BN	MS-63BN	MS-63RB	MS-65BN	Recent Auction Record
1800	202,908	132	50.5	39	$300	$700	$1,000	$2,000	$3,500	$5,000	$13,000	$1,380, AU-58, Jun-10
1802, 2 Over 0, Reverse of 1800	*	2	3.0	0	60,000 (a)	—	—					$35,938, VG-8, May-09
1802, 2 Over 0, Second Reverse	20,266	27	9.4	0	12,000 (b)	30,000	—					$1,553, G-6, Jun-10
1803	*	95	38.7	18	325	950	1,350	2,750	6,400	8,000	18,000	$374, VF-25, Jun-10
1803, Widely Spaced 3	92,000	21	40.0	10	325	950	1,450	2,950	6,600	8,250	19,000	$661, EF-40, Dec-09
1804, All kinds	1,055,312											
1804, Plain 4, Stems to Wreath		6	38.7	0	450	1,250	2,000					$748, VF-30, Sep-09
1804, Plain 4, Stemless Wreath		98	50.2	22	190	350	650	1,200	2,750	3,500	7,500	$489, EF-45, May-10
1804, Crosslet 4, Stemless		37	57.6	51	190	350	650	1,200	2,750	3,500	7,500	$2,760, MS-63BN, Jan-10

* Included in number below. **a.** Value in G-4 is $22,000; in VG-8, $34,000; in F-12, $45,000. **b.** Value in G-4 is $700; in VG-8, $1,700; in F-12, $4,000.

	Mintage	Cert	Avg	%MS	VF-20	EF-40	AU-50	MS-60BN	MS-63BN	MS-63RB	MS-65BN	Recent Auction Record
1804, Crosslet 4, Stems		79	50.0	20	$190	$350	$650	$1,200	$2,750	$3,500	$7,500	$1,093, AU-58, May-10
1804, "Spiked Chin"		236	47.1	18	235	400	750	1,750	3,500	4,500	9,000	$865, AU-53, Mar-10
1805, All kinds	814,464											
1805, Medium 5, Stemless		29	44.3	17	200	385	700	1,250	2,875	3,750	7,600	$345, VF-35, Mar-10
1805, Small 5, Stems		5	17.6	0	7,500 (c)	12,000	25,000					$54,625, VF-30, Jan-10
1805, Large 5, Stems		12	41.0	0	200	385	800	1,600	3,750			$1,668, AU-58, Jun-10
1806, All kinds	356,000											
1806, Small 6, Stems		14	34.8	0	1,600	3,250	8,500	12,000				$4,313, AU, Jul-09
1806, Small 6, Stemless		59	52.3	27	175	325	675	1,000	2,750	3,250	6,750	$1,955, MS-62BN, Mar-10
1806, Large 6, Stems		52	56.3	54	175	325	675	1,000	2,750	3,250	7,000	$3,450, MS-61RD, Feb-10
1807	476,000	165	43.3	9	200	500	1,000	2,000	3,750			$1,035, AU-55, Jun-10
1808, All kinds	400,000											
1808, 8 Over 7		25	22.3	0	1,500	4,250	10,000					$10,063, AU-53, Apr-10
1808, Normal Date		17	33.2	0	200	500	1,100	2,500	5,000			$173, VF-20, Dec-09

c. Value in G-4 is $850; in VG-8, $1,500; in F-12, $4,000.

CLASSIC HEAD
(1809–1836)

Designer John Reich; weight 5.44 grams; composition copper; diameter 23.5 mm; plain edge.

Breen-3.

History. The Classic Head design (by Mint engraver John Reich) made its first appearance on the half cent in 1809, a year after it was adopted for the one-cent coin. A very similar motif of Miss Liberty was used on the half eagles of the 1830s.

Striking and Sharpness. Coins of 1809 to 1811 usually have areas of light or incomplete striking. Grading coins of the early years requires special care and expertise. Sometimes coins as high as MS appear "blurry" in areas, due to the dies and striking. Those of later years are often found well struck and are easier to grade. Areas to check include the dentils and rims on both sides, the star centers and hair detail on the obverse, and the leaf detail on the reverse.

Availability. As a type this issue is easily enough found, although 1811 is scarce and 1831 and 1836 are notable rarities. MS coins from old hoards exist for certain of the later dates, particularly 1828, 1833, and 1835, but often have spotting, and many seen in the marketplace are cleaned or recolored. Care is advised. Although 1809–1811 half cents are often seen with extensive wear, those of the 1820s and 1830s are not often seen less than VF, as they did not circulate extensively.

G-4, 6 (Good). *Obverse:* The portrait is worn smooth and is seen only in outline form. Much of LIBERTY on the headband is readable, but the letters are weak. The stars are bold in outline. Much of the rim can be discerned. *Reverse:* Extensive wear is seen overall. Lettering in UNITED STATES OF AMERICA ranges from weak but complete to having perhaps a third of the letters missing. HALF CENT is usually bold.

VG-8, 10 (Very Good). *Obverse:* The portrait is well worn, although the eye and ear can be seen, as can some hair detail. The border is well defined in most areas. *Reverse:* The wreath, bow, and lettering are seen in outline form, and some leaves and letters may be indistinct in parts. The border is well defined in most areas.

F-12, 15 (Fine). *Obverse:* The hair details are fewer than in VF, but many are still present. Stars have flat centers. *Reverse:* The wreath leaves are worn flat, but their edges are distinct.

VF-20, 30 (Very Fine). *Obverse:* Wear on the portrait has reduced the hair detail, but much can still be seen. *Reverse:* The wreath details, except for the edges of the leaves, are worn away at VF-20, and have slightly more detail at VF-30.

EF-40, 45 (Extremely Fine). *Obverse:* Wear is seen on the portrait overall, with reduction or elimination of some separation of hair strands. The cheek shows light wear. Luster may survive among the letters of LIBERTY at EF-45, but is minimal or nonexistent at EF-40. *Reverse:* Wear is seen on the highest wreath and ribbon areas and the letters. Luster is minimal, but likely more noticeable than on the obverse, as the fields are protected by the designs and lettering.

AU-50, 53, 55, 58 (About Uncirculated). *Obverse:* Friction is seen on the higher parts, particularly the cheek and hair (under magnification). Friction and scattered marks are in the field, from minimal at AU-58 to extensive at AU-50. Luster may be seen in protected areas, minimal at AU-50 with more at AU-58. At AU-58 the field may retain some luster as well. *Reverse:* Friction is seen on the higher wreath leaves and (not as easy to discern) on the letters. Half cents of 1809 to 1811 require special attention. The fields, protected by the designs, show friction, but not as noticeably as on the obverse. At AU-58 and 55, little if any friction is seen. The reverse may have original luster, toned brown, often extensive at AU-58, minimal on lower AU grades.

MS-60 to 70 (Mint State). *Obverse:* In MS-60 and 61, some slight abrasions can be seen on the portrait, most evident on the cheek, as the hair details are complex. Luster in the field is complete or nearly complete. At MS-63, luster should be complete, and no abrasions are evident. In higher levels, the luster is complete and deeper, and some original mint color may be seen. MS-64 coins may have some slight discoloration or scattered contact marks. An MS-65 or higher coin has full, rich luster, with no marks visible except under magnification, and has a nice blend of brown toning or nicely mixed (not stained or blotchy) mint color and natural brown toning. Coins dated 1809 to 1811 may exhibit significant weakness of details due to striking (and/or, in the case of most 1811s, porous planchet stock). *Reverse:*

In the lower MS grades, some abrasions are seen on the higher areas of the leaves. Mint luster is complete in all MS grades, as the open areas are protected by the lettering and wreath. Sharpness of the leaves can vary by die

variety. Otherwise, the same comments apply as for the obverse. Coins dated 1809 to 1811 may exhibit significant weakness of details due to striking (and/or, in the case of most 1811s, porous planchet stock).

1809, Small 0 Inside 0   1809, Triple Punched 9   1809, Normal Date   1811, Wide Date   1811, Close Date

1828, 13 Stars   1828, 12 Stars

	Mintage	Cert	Avg	%MS	F-12	VF-20	EF-40	AU-50	MS-60BN	MS-63BN	MS-63RB	Recent Auction Record
1809, All kinds	1,154,572											
1809, Small o Inside 0		7	36.3	0	$90	$150	$375	$750	$1,000	$1,500		$805, EF-40, Jul-09
1809, Repunched 9 (a)		148	51.4	23	100	150	375	750	1,100	2,000	$3,000	$518, AU-55, May-10
1809, Normal Date		55	52.6	44	80	100	140	250	700	1,250	2,000	$7,475, MS-65BN, Mar-10
1810	215,000	64	46.3	22	120	240	550	1,000	1,900	3,000	6,000	$633, EF-45, Jan-10
1811, All kinds	63,140											
1811, Wide Date		2	19.0	0	1,300	2,200	6,500	8,000	11,500	15,000		$4,025, VF-35, May-09
1811, Close Date		2	30.0	0	1,250	2,100	6,000	7,500	9,000	12,500		$1,495, F-15, Jan-10
1811, Rev of 1802, Unofficial Restrike (extremely rare)		5	63.8	100			—	—	15,000	20,000	25,000	$23,000, MS-64BN, Sep-08
1825	63,000	183	54.1	33	80	90	175	325	800	1,500	3,500	$690, MS-61BN, Mar-10
1826	234,000	207	55.8	43	80	90	150	300	600	900	1,200	$8,338, MS-65BN, Mar-10
1828, All kinds	606,000											
1828, 13 Stars		77	57.6	57	70	100	120	180	350	575	1,025	$446, MS-63BN, Jun-10
1828, 12 Stars		164	53.7	29	70	120	250	400	1,300	1,800	3,700	$345, EF-45, Jun-10
1829	487,000	232	58.0	59	70	100	140	220	400	650	1,500	$6,325, MS-65RB, Mar-10

a. Formerly called 9 Over Inverted 9, "but now known not to have an inverted digit" *(Whitman Encyclopedia of Half Cents and Large Cents).*

	Mintage	Cert	Avg	%MS	AU-50	MS-60BN	MS-63BN	MS-63RB	MS-65BN	MS-65RB	MS-65RD	Recent Auction Record
1832 (a)	51,000	226	58.0	53	$175	$300	$500	$1,500	$1,900	$3,750		$334, AU-58, Feb-10
1833 (a)	103,000	446	60.9	78	175	300	450	750	1,250	2,300	$7,500	$1,093, MS-65BN, Jun-10
1834 (a)	141,000	420	59.3	65	175	300	450	750	1,250	2,300	5,000	$242, AU-58, May-10
1835 (a)	398,000	769	59.8	71	175	300	450	750	1,250	2,300	5,000	$518, MS-64BN, Jun-10

a. The figures given here are thought to be correct, although Mint records report these quantities for 1833 through 1836 rather than 1832 through 1835.

Proof Classic Head Half Cents

PF-60 to 70 (Proof). Proof half cents of 1831 and 1836 are rare; these dates were also restruck at the Mint around 1858 or 1859, and later. Carefully study any coin offered as a Proof; some prooflike circulation strikes (especially 1833) have been certified as Proofs. Blotchy and recolored

Proofs are often seen. Probably fewer than 25 of the Proofs of this type are truly pristine and problem-free. *Obverse and Reverse:* Proofs that are extensively hairlined or have dull surfaces (common among many issues except for 1831 and 1836) are graded PF-60 to 62 or 63. This also applies to arti-

ficially toned and recolored coins. To qualify as PF-65 or higher, hairlines should be microscopic, and there should be no trace of friction. Surfaces should be prooflike or fully mirrored, without dullness.

1831, Original **1831, Restrike** **Reverse, 1831–1836** **Reverse, 1840–1857**

	Mintage	Cert	Finest	PF-40	PF 50	PF-60BN	PF-63BN	PF-63RB	PF-65BN	PF-65RB	Recent Auction Record
1831, Original (a)	2,200	4	PF-65	$50,000	$60,000	$75,000	—				$69,000, PF-60BN, Jul-09
1831, Restrike, Large Berries (Reverse of 1836)	25–35	11	PF-67	—	2,500	6,000	$11,000	$15,000	$20,000	$30,000	$16,100, PF-65BN, Jun-08
1831, Restrike, Small Berries (Reverse of 1840–1857)	10–15			—	6,000	10,000	20,000	30,000	40,000		$63,250, PF-66BN, Jul-09
1832	10–15	1	PF-64	1,500	2,000	5,000	10,000	14,000	18,000	21,000	$46,000, PF-64BN, Aug-09
1833	25–35	13	PF-65	1,500	2,000	5,000	6,000	8,500	10,500	13,000	$5,175, PF-64BN, May-09
1834	25–35	11	PF-66	1,500	2,000	5,000	6,000	9,000	11,000	13,000	$10,350, PF-64RB CAC, Mar-09
1835	15–20	2	PF-64	1,500	2,000	5,000	6,000	8,000	10,500	13,000	$7,475, PF-64RB, Jan-09
1836, Original	140–240	13	PF-66	1,750	2,500	6,000	8,000	10,000	12,500	15,000	$7,475, PF-64RB, Jan-09
1836, Restrike (Reverse of 1840–1857)	8–15	2	PF-65	2,000	3,000	9,000	17,000	25,000	30,000	35,000	

a. Beware of altered date.

BRAIDED HAIR
(1840–1857)

Designer Christian Gobrecht; weight 5.44 grams; composition copper; diameter 23 mm; plain edge.

History. The Braided Hair half cent debuted in 1840, a year after the same design was introduced on copper cents. There was scant commercial demand for this denomination, so only Proofs were struck from 1840 to 1848 and in 1852. (In 1849 both Proofs and circulation strikes were made.) Ultimately the half cent was discontinued by the Act of February 21, 1857. After that point the coins were rapidly withdrawn from circulation, and by 1860 virtually all had disappeared from commerce.

Striking and Sharpness. Many if not most Braided Hair half cents are well struck, and nearly all are on good planchet stock. Check these points for sharpness: the dentils on both sides; the star centers and hair detail on the obverse; and the leaf detail on the reverse.

Availability. Because Braided Hair half cents were not struck for circulation until 1849 and they did not circulate after the 1850s, they never acquired extensive wear. Most coins grade EF-40 and finer. Lower grades are sometimes seen, but are not in demand.

VF-20, 30 (Very Fine). *Obverse:* Wear is more extensive than in EF. Some of the strands of hair are fused together. The center radials of the stars are worn nearly completely away. *Reverse:* The leaves show more extensive wear, with details visible at the edges, and only minimally and not on all leaves. The lettering shows smooth, even wear.

EF-40, 45 (Extremely Fine). *Obverse:* Wear is more extensive on the portrait than at AU, including the cheek, hair, and coronet. The star centers are worn down slightly. Traces of luster are minimal, if at all existent. *Reverse:* The centers of the leaves are well worn, with detail visible only near the edges of the leaves and nearby, with the higher parts worn flat. Letters show significant wear. Luster, if present, is minimal.

AU-50, 53, 55, 58 (About Uncirculated). *Obverse:* Wear is evident on the cheek, the hair above the forehead, and the tip of the coronet. Friction is evident in the field. In AU-50 wear is evident on the portrait; less so at 53, 55, and 58. Wear is seen on the stars, but is not as easy to discern as it is elsewhere. At AU-50 there is either no luster or only traces of luster close to the letters and devices. At AU-58, luster may be present except in the center of the fields. *Reverse:* Wear is most evident on the highest areas of the leaves and the ribbon bow. Luster is present in the fields. At AU-50 there is either no luster, or only traces of luster, close to the letters and devices. In higher AU grades wear is less, and luster increases.

MS-60 to 70 (Mint State). *Obverse:* In MS-60 and 61, some slight abrasion can be seen on the portrait, most evidently on the cheek. Also check the tip of the coronet. Luster in the field is complete, or nearly so. At MS-63, luster should be complete, and no abrasions evident. At higher levels, the luster is complete and deeper, and some original mint color may be seen. Mint frost on this type is usually deep, sometimes satiny, but hardly ever prooflike. MS-64 coins may have some slight discoloration or scattered contact marks. An MS-65 or higher coin has full, rich luster; no contact marks visible except under magnification; and a nice blend of brown toning or nicely mixed (not stained or blotchy) mint color and natural brown toning. *Reverse:* In the lower MS grades some abrasions are seen on the higher areas of the leaves. Mint luster is complete in all MS grades, as the open areas are protected by the lettering and wreath.

1849, Small Date (Proof Only)   1849, Large Date

	Mintage	Cert	Avg	%MS	EF-40	AU-50	MS-60BN	MS-63BN	MS-63RB	MS-65BN	MS-65RB	Recent Auction Record
1849, Large Date	39,864	205	59.8	72	$150	$240	$500	$700	$1,200	$2,100	$2,700	$748, MS-63BN, May-10
1850	39,812	153	59.6	69	150	240	500	700	1,500	2,300	2,800	$719, MS-63BN, Mar-10
1851	147,672	534	60.6	75	100	165	275	450	550	925	2,000 (a)	$377, MS-63BN, Jun-10
1853	129,694	724	62.4	87	100	165	275	450	550	925	1,650	$431, MS-64BN, May-10
1854	55,358	551	62.5	89	100	165	275	450	550	925	1,650	$1,495, MS-64RD, Mar-10
1855	56,500	853	62.8	91	100	165	275	450	550	900	1,550	$546, MS-64BN, Jun-10
1856	40,430	275	61.5	82	125	180	325	500	575	1,250	1,800	$863, MS-64RB, May-10
1857	35,180	448	62.0	86	180	260	400	650	750	1,750	2,400	$3,220, MS-64RD, Jun-10

a. Value in MS-65RD is $4,000.

Proof Braided Hair Half Cents

PF-60 to 70 (Proof). Only Proofs—not circulation strikes—were made for the half cent issues of 1840 to 1848, 1849 Small Date, and 1852. All were restruck at the Mint. Generally, the quality of these Proofs is very good, with excellent striking of details and nice planchet quality. Both originals and restrikes use the reverse of 1840–1857.

Originals have Large Berries in the wreath. This is the style used to strike half cents in the year indicated on the dies, for inclusion in Proof sets or for sale to numismatists. Until First Restrikes were made, circa 1856, Original die pairs for some dates were used to make a small number of restrikes. Some of these probably cannot be differentiated today from Original strikings.

First Restrike half cents have Small Berries, the NT of CENT is slightly doubled, and there is doubling of the wreath ribbon. This was the die used to strike Proof 1856 half cents for inclusion in sets of that year. Accordingly, it is sometimes called the Reverse of 1856.

Second Restrike half cents have Small Berries, and diagonal file marks over RICA of AMERICA. Likely, these were made from about the spring of 1859, or later, and continued in production in occasional batches for a decade or more. These are on planchets that are more or less within range of the normal weight of 84 grains.

Obverse and Reverse: PF-60 to 62 coins show a profusion of hairlines and a general dullness of the fields. Hairlines decrease until at PF-65 and 66 they show only under high magnification. At PF-67 no hairlines are seen, the fields are deeply mirrorlike, and there is no evidence of friction. Typical color for an undipped Proof ranges from light or iridescent brown to brown with some traces of mint color. Except for issues in the 1850s, Proofs are nearly always BN or, less often, RB. The rare Proofs of the 1840s are sometimes seen with light wear and can be classified using the AU and EF guidelines, except in place of "luster" read "Proof surface."

Proof Braided Hair Half Cent
Breen-1.

Large Berries   **Small Berries**

	Est Mintage	Cert	Finest	PF-63BN	PF-63RB	PF-65BN	PF65RB	Recent Auction Record
1840, Original	125–150	10	PF-66	$6,500	$7,500	$9,250	$13,000	$7,475, PF-62BN, Aug-06
1840, Restrike	21–25	8	PF-66	6,500	7,500	9,250	13,000	$48,875, PF-65RB, Mar-10
1841, Original	150–250	21	PF-66	5,500	7,500	8,750	13,000	$17,825, PF-66BN Star, Apr-10
1841, Restrike	15–19	7	PF-66	5,500	7,500	8,750	13,000	$8,625, PF-66BN, Jun-08
1842, Original	120–180	4	PF-65	7,000	9,000	10,000	14,500	$13,200, PF-64, Oct-87
1842, Restrike	35–45	10	PF-67	5,500	7,500	8,750	13,000	$20,700, PF-65RB, Apr-10
1843, Original	125–200	7	PF-65	5,500	7,500	8,750	13,000	$5,463, PF-63BN, Jan-10
1843, Restrike	37–44	8	PF-65	5,700	6,750	8,750	13,000	$6,900, PF-64BN, May-09
1844, Original	120–180	9	PF-65	6,000	8,500	9,000	14,000	$4,888, PF-50, May-08
1844, Restrike	21–26	2	PF-66	5,750	8,500	8,750	14,000	$5,463, PF-63BN, Oct-09
1845, Original	110–170	2	PF-66	6,000	8,500	9,250	14,000	$18,400, PF-62BN, Apr-08
1845, Restrike	20–24	8	PF-67	5,400	8,000	9,000	14,000	$8,050, PF-63BN, Mar-10
1846, Original	125–200	8	PF-66	6,000	8,000	9,000	14,000	$16,100, PF-64BN, Aug-08
1846, Restrike	19–24	7	PF-66	5,750	8,500	8,750	14,000	$8,913, PF-63BN, Feb-07
1847, Original	200–300	10	PF-66	6,000	8,500	9,250	14,000	$12,650, PF-64BN, Jan-07
1847, Restrike	33–44	15	PF-67	5,400	7,750	8,250	13,000	$6,900, PF-64BN, Jan-06

	Est Mintage	Cert	Finest	PF-63BN	PF-63RB	PF-65BN	PF-65RB	Recent Auction Record
1848, Original	150–225	4	PF-65	$6,250	$8,500	$9,250	$14,000	$10,350, PF-64, Sep-03
1848, Restrike	40–47	12	PF-66	5,600	7,500	8,250	13,000	$17,250, PF-64BN, Mar-10
1849, Original, Small Date	70–90	5	PF-65	5,500	7,500	10,000	25,000	$12,850, PF-65BN, Jan-07
1849, Restrike, Small Date	30–36	5	PF-66	5,300	9,250	9,500	14,500	$7,475, PF-65BN, Jul-08
1850	10–20	8	PF-66	5,750	9,500	10,250	14,500	$5,463, PF-65BN, Jun-10
1851	10–20			8,000	15,000	20,000	25,000	
1852, Original	225–325	1	PF-65	—				
1852, Restrike	110–140	31	PF-66	4,750	9,000	9,000	14,500	$6,325, PF-64BN, May-09
1854	10–20	3	PF-65	4,250	7,500	7,200	11,500	$8,050, PF-65RB, Apr-06
1855	40–60	17	PF-66	4,250	7,500	7,200	11,500	$3,738, PF-64BN, May-09
1856	50–75	20	PF-66	4,250	7,500	7,200	11,500	$4,025, PF-64BN, Mar-10
1857	75–100	41	PF-66	4,250	7,000	7,000	10,000	$4,600, PF-64BN, Apr-10

AN OVERVIEW OF LARGE CENTS

Collecting one each of the major types of 1793–1857 copper cents can be a fascinating challenge. Early varieties were struck from hand-engraved dies, often on copper planchets of uncertain quality. It was not until 1836 that steam power was used to run coining presses at the Mint. All earlier issues were made by hand, by two men tugging on the weighted lever arm of a small screw-type press. As might be expected, this resulted in many variations in striking quality.

The first cents of 1793, the Chain varieties, are found with two major differences: AMERI. on the reverse, and the later version with AMERICA spelled out in full. These early issues have been highly desired from the beginning days of the numismatic hobby in America, and remain in the limelight today.

Wreath cents of 1793 occur with the edge displaying a vine and bars motif and also with lettering ONE HUNDRED FOR A DOLLAR. Liberty Cap cents of the 1793–1796 years have lettered edges (ONE HUNDRED FOR A DOLLAR) used in 1793, 1794, and part of 1795, and plain edges for most 1795 coins and all of 1796.

The Draped Bust type commenced partway through 1796 and was continued through 1807. This span includes the notably rare 1799, 9 Over 8 overdate and the 1799 as well as the somewhat rare 1804. Many interesting die varieties occur in this type, particularly with regard to errors on the reverse. The Classic Head cent, designed by John Reich, was introduced in 1808, and was continued through 1814. In 1815 no cents of this date were produced. Then in 1816 the Matron Head commenced, a new motif with a new reverse as well. With modifications this was continued through 1839, in which year the Braided Hair design by Christian Gobrecht made its appearance. Cents were made continually through January 1857 and then discontinued.

FOR THE COLLECTOR AND INVESTOR: LARGE CENTS AS A SPECIALTY

For the enjoyment of copper cents 1793–1857 it is possible to go *far* beyond a type set. Today, varieties of the 1793–1814 cents are generally collected by Sheldon numbers (S-1, S-2, etc.), given first in *Early American Cents* and, later, in its revision, *Penny Whimsy.* Building upon this foundation, *Walter Breen's Encyclopedia of Early United States Large Cents, 1793–1814,* gives more information on this date range than available in any other single source.

Among dates and major varieties in the early range of the series, the 1793 Chain AMERI., Chain AMERICA, Wreath, and Liberty Cap issues, the 1799 (far and away the rarest date in the series), and the 1804 are key issues, each a part of an extensive series of more than 300 die varieties through and including 1814.

The most popular way to collect large cents is by basic varieties, mainly dates, overdates, and major varieties. Sometimes, a particular date is selected as a specialty for collecting die varieties by Sheldon numbers.

Generally, grades from Good to VF are popular objectives for the early series from 1793 to 1814, and for some varieties no better coins exist. EF, AU, and Mint State coins are available and are more likely to be sought by collectors of basic dates and major varieties, rather than by specialists seeing long runs of Sheldon numbers. Type-set collectors are also important in the market for high-grade pieces, where sights can be set high as there are fewer varieties to obtain. Accordingly, as a type-set collector one may aspire to own an AU or Mint State cent of the 1796–1807 Draped Bust type. However, for a specialist in die varieties, who wants to acquire more than 100 different specimens from this date range, such high grades might not be feasible to acquire.

Collecting cents of the later dates by basic varieties is an interesting pursuit, and one that is quite attainable in such grades as EF, AU, or even MS-60, most dates after the 1820s being readily available for relatively inexpensive prices. Key issues among 1816–1857 cents include 1823, 3 Over 2; 1823; 1824, 4 Over 2; 1839, 9 Over 6; and a few others. Collecting Braided Hair cents toward the end of the series, 1839 to 1857, is least expensive of all, and most major varieties can be obtained in such grades as MS-60 to MS-63, with lustrous brown surfaces, for reasonable figures.

RECOMMENDED READING

Bowers, Q. David. *Whitman Encyclopedia of Half Cents and Large Cents,* Atlanta, GA, 2011.

Breen, Walter. *Walter Breen's Encyclopedia of Early United States Cents, 1793–1814,* Wolfeboro, NH, 2001.

Fivaz, Bill, and Stanton, J.T. *The Cherrypickers' Guide to Rare Die Varieties* (5th ed., vol. I), Atlanta, GA, 2009.

Grellman, J.R. *Attribution Guide for United States Large Cents, 1840–1857* (3rd ed.), Bloomington, MN, 2002.

Newcomb, H.R. *United States Copper Cents, 1816–1857,* New York, 1944 (reprinted 1983).

Noyes, William C. *United States Large Cents, 1793–1794,* Ypsilanti, MI, 2006.

Noyes, William C. *United States Large Cents, 1793–1814,* Bloomington, MN, 1991.

Noyes, William C. *United States Large Cents, 1795–1797,* Ypsilanti, MI, 2007.

Noyes, William C. *United States Large Cents, 1816–1839,* Bloomington, MN, 1991.

Penny-Wise, official publication of Early American Coppers, Inc.

Sheldon, William H. *Penny Whimsy* (1793–1814), New York, 1958 (reprinted 1965, 1976).

Wright, John D. *The Cent Book, 1816–1839,* Bloomington, MN, 1992.

FLOWING HAIR, CHAIN REVERSE
(1793)

Designer Henry Voigt; weight 13.48 grams; composition copper; approx. diameter 26–27 mm; edge: bars and slender vine with leaves.

Sheldon-1.

AMERI. in Legend

AMERICA in Legend

Vine-and-Bars Edge

History. The first U.S. cents intended for circulation were struck at the Mint in Philadelphia from February 27 through March 12, 1793. These were of the Flowing Hair design, with a Chain reverse. Several varieties were struck, today attributed by Sheldon numbers. The first, or Sheldon-1, had AMERICA abbreviated as AMERI. A contemporary account noted that Miss Liberty appeared to be "in a fright," and that the chain motif on the reverse, 15 links intended to symbolize unity of the states in the Union, was an "ill omen" for a land of liberty; accordingly, the design was used for only a short time. The rims on both sides are raised, without dentils or beads.

Striking and Sharpness. The details of Miss Liberty's hair are often indistinct or missing, including on many higher-grade specimens. For all grades and varieties, the reverse is significantly sharper than the obverse. The portrait of Miss Liberty is shallow and is often weak, especially on the S-1 variety (which is often missing the date). Note that early copper coins of all kinds may exhibit "tooling" (engraving done outside the Mint in order to simulate details that were worn away or weakly struck to begin with). These old coppers also have sometimes been burnished, to smooth out areas of porosity. These alterations are considered to be damage, and they significantly decrease a coin's value.

Availability. Demand is higher than supply for all varieties, with fewer than 1,000 or so surviving today. Most are in lower grades, from Fair-2 to VG-8. Even heavily worn coins (still identifiable by the chain device) are highly collectible. VF and EF coins are few and far between, and AU and MS are very rare.

G-4, 6 (Good). *Obverse:* The portrait is worn smooth and is seen only in outline form, although the eye position can be discerned. LIBERTY may be weak. The date is weak, but the tops of the numerals can be discerned. *Reverse:* The chain is fully visible in outline form. Central lettering is mostly or completely readable, but light. Peripheral lettering is mostly worn away.

VG-8, 10 (Very Good). *Obverse:* The portrait is well worn, although Miss Liberty's eye remains bold. Hair detail is gone at the center, but is evident at the left edge of the portrait. LIBERTY is always readable, but may be faded or partly missing on shallow strikes. The date is well worn, with the bottom of the numerals missing. *Reverse:* The chain remains bold, and the center letters are all readable. Border letters may be weak or incomplete. The rim is smooth in most areas.

F-12, 15 (Fine). *Obverse:* The hair details are mostly worn away, with about one-third visible, that being on the left. The rim is distinct on most specimens. The bottoms of the date digits are weak or possibly worn away. *Reverse:* The chain is bold, as is the lettering within the chain. Lettering around the border shows extensive wear, but is complete. The rim may be flat in areas.

VF-20, 30 (Very Fine). *Obverse:* More wear is seen on the portrait than at EF, with perhaps half or slightly more of the hair detail showing, mostly near the left edge of the hair. The ear usually is visible (but might not be, depending on the sharpness of strike). The letters in LIBERTY show wear. The rim remains bold (more so than on the reverse). *Reverse:* The chain shows more wear than in EF, but is still bold. Other features show more wear and may be weak in areas. The rim may be weak in areas.

EF-40, 45 (Extremely Fine). *Obverse:* The center of the portrait is well worn, with the hair visible only in thick strands, although extensive detail remains in the hair tips at the left. No luster is seen. Contact marks are normal in the large expanse of open field. *Reverse:* The chain is bold and shows light wear. Other features show wear, as well—more extensive in appearance, as the relief is lower. The fields show some friction, but not as much as on the obverse.

AU-50, 53, 55, 58 (About Uncirculated). *Obverse:* Light wear is seen on the highest areas of the portrait. Little if any luster is seen in the large open fields at AU-50 and 53, with some seen at 55, and some more at 58. Scattered marks are normal and are most evident in the field. At higher levels, some vestiges of luster may be seen among the letters and numerals, and between the hair tips. *Reverse:* Light wear is most evident on the chain. The letters show wear, but not as extensive. Luster may be seen at AU-55 and 58, usually slightly more on the reverse than on the obverse. Generally, the reverse grades higher than the obverse.

MS-60 to 70 (Mint State). *Obverse:* In MS-60 and 61, some slight abrasions can be seen on the higher areas of the portrait. The large open field shows light contact marks and perhaps a few nicks. At MS-63 the luster should be complete, although some very light abrasions or contact marks may be on the portrait. At MS-64 or higher—nearly impossible for a Chain cent—there is no sign of abrasion anywhere. Mint color is not extensive on any known MS coin, but traces of red-orange are sometimes seen around the rim and devices on both sides. *Reverse:* In low MS grades some abrasions are seen on the chain links. There is some abrasion in the field. At MS-63, luster should be unbroken. Some abrasion and minor contact marks may be evident. In still higher grades, luster is deep and there is no sign of abrasion.

	Mintage	Cert	Avg	%MS	G-4	VG-8	F-12	VF-20	EF-40	AU-50	MS-60BN	Recent Auction Record
1793, Chain, All kinds	36,103											
1793, AMERI. in Legend		28	23.6	11	$10,000	$17,000	$28,000	$45,000	$75,000	$165,000	$300,000	$368,000, AU-58, Sep-09
1793, AMERICA, Periods		8	32.5	13	7,000	13,000	18,500	37,000	55,000	95,000	210,000	$33,350, VF-20, Jan-10
1793, AMERICA, No Periods		3	17.0	0	7,000	12,000	17,500	35,000	52,000	85,000	195,000	$18,400, F-12, Jan-10

FLOWING HAIR, WREATH REVERSE
(1793)

Designer Henry Voigt; weight 13.48 grams; composition copper; approx. diameter 26–28 mm; edge: vine and bars, or lettered ONE HUNDRED FOR A DOLLAR followed by either a single or a double leaf.

Sheldon-6.

Vine-and-Bars Edge

Lettered Edge (ONE HUNDRED FOR A DOLLAR)

History. Between April 9 and July 17, 1793, the U.S. Mint struck and delivered 63,353 large copper cents. Most of these, and perhaps all, were of the Wreath type, although records do not specify when the design types were changed that year. The Wreath cent was named for the new reverse style. Both sides have raised beads at the border, similar to the style used on 1793 half cents.

Striking and Sharpness. These cents usually are fairly well struck, although high-grade pieces often exhibit some weakness on the highest hair tresses and on the leaf details. (On lower-grade pieces these areas are worn, so the point is moot.) Planchet quality varies widely, from smooth, glossy brown to dark and porous. The lettered-edge cents are often seen on defective planchets. Consult Sheldon's *Penny Whimsy (1793–1814)* and photographs to learn the characteristics of certain varieties. The borders have raised beads; on high-grade pieces these are usually very distinct, but they blend together on lower-grade coins and can sometimes be indistinct. The beads are not as prominent as those later used on the 1793 Liberty Cap cents.

Availability. At least several thousand examples exist of the different varieties of the type. Most are in lower grades, from AG-3 to VG-8, although Fine and VF pieces are encountered with regularity. Choice EF, AU, and finer coins see high demand. Some in MS have been billed as "specimen" or "presentation" coins, although this is supposition, as no records exist.

VG-8, 10 (Very Good). *Obverse:* The hair is well worn toward the face. Details at the left are mostly blended together in thick strands. The eye, nose, and lips often remain well defined. Border beads are completely gone, or just seen in traces, and part of the rim blends into the field. LIBERTY may be slightly weak. The 1793 date is fully visible, although there may be some lightness. Scattered marks are more common than on higher grades. *Reverse:* The wreath, bow, and lettering are seen in outline form, and some leaves and letters may be indistinct in parts. Most of the berries remain visible, but weak. Border beads are worn away, and the border blends into the field in most if not all of the periphery.

F-12, 15 (Fine). *Obverse:* The hair details are mostly worn away, with about one-third visible, mainly at the edges. Beads are weak or worn away in areas. Scattered light scratches, noticeable contact marks, and the like are evident. Light porosity or granularity is common. *Reverse:* The wreath leaves are worn flat, but their edges are distinct. Border beads are weak or worn away in areas.

VF-20, 30 (Very Fine). *Obverse:* Wear on the hair is more extensive than at EF, and varies depending on the die variety and sharpness of strike. Two-thirds or so of the hair is visible. More beads are blended together, the extent of which depends on the striking and variety. Certain parts of the rim are smooth, with beads scarcely visible at all. No luster is seen. The date, LIBERTY, and hair ends are bold. *Reverse:* The leaf details are nearly completely worn away at VF-20, with slight detail at VF-30. The border beads are blended together, with many indistinct. Some berries in the sprays are light, but nearly all remain distinct. No luster is seen.

EF-40, 45 (Extremely Fine). *Obverse:* More extensive wear is seen on the high parts of the hair than at AU, creating mostly a solid mass (without detail of strands) of varying width in the area immediately to the left of the face. The cheek shows light wear. Luster is minimal or nonexistent at EF-40, and may survive in traces in protected areas (such as between the letters) at EF-45. *Reverse:* Wear is seen on the highest wreath and ribbon areas, and the letters. Luster is minimal, but likely more noticeable than on the obverse, as the fields are protected by the designs and lettering. Some of the beads blend together.

AU-50, 53, 55, 58 (About Uncirculated). *Obverse:* Friction is seen on the highest areas of the hair (which may also be lightly struck) and the cheek. Some scattered marks are normal in the field, ranging from more extensive at AU-50 to minimal at 58. *Reverse:* Friction is seen on the higher wreath leaves and (not as easy to discern) on the letters. The fields, protected by the designs (including sprays of berries at the center), show friction, but not as noticeably as on the obverse. At AU-55 and 58, little if any friction is seen. Border beads, if well struck, are separate and boldly defined.

MS-60 to 70 (Mint State). *Obverse:* On MS-60 and 61 coins there are some traces of abrasion on the higher areas of the portrait, most particularly the hair. This area can be lightly struck, so careful inspection is needed for evaluation, not as much in MS (as other features come into play), but in higher circulated grades. Luster in the field is incomplete at lower MS levels, but should be in generous quantity. At MS-63, luster should be complete, and no abrasion evident. At higher levels, the luster is deeper, and some original mint color may be seen. At MS-65 there might be some scattered contact marks and possibly bare traces of fingerprints or discoloration. Above MS-65, a coin should approach perfection. *Reverse:* In the lower MS grades some abrasion is seen on the higher areas of the leaves. Generally, luster is complete in all grades, as the open areas are protected by the lettering and wreath.

Regular Sprig

Strawberry Leaf

	Mintage	Cert	Avg	%MS	VG-8	F-12	VF-20	EF-40	AU-50	MS-60BN	MS-63BN	Recent Auction Record
1793, Wreath, All kinds	63,353											
1793, Vine/Bars Edge		147	33.7	14	$2,800	$4,800	$7,250	$12,500	$24,750	$55,000	$115,000	$50,313, AU-58, Jan-10
1793, Lettered Edge		13	31.7	8	3,500	5,000	7,500	15,500	30,000	80,000	140,000	$4,830, VG-10, Jun-10
1793, Strawberry Leaf † *(4 known)*		1	12.0	0	400,000	870,000						$218,500, G-4, Sep-09

† Ranked in the *100 Greatest U.S. Coins* (third edition).

LIBERTY CAP
(1793–1796)

1793–1795 (thick planchet)—Designer Joseph Wright; weight 13.48 grams; composition copper; approx. diameter 29 mm; edge: ONE HUNDRED FOR A DOLLAR followed by a single leaf. 1795–1796 (thin planchet)—Designer John Smith Gardner; weight 10.89 grams; composition copper; approx. diameter 29 mm; plain edge.

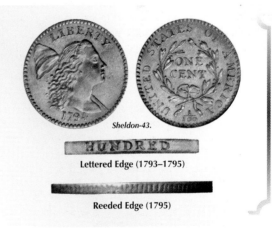

Sheldon-43.

Lettered Edge (1793–1795)

Reeded Edge (1795)

History. The Liberty Cap design was created in the summer of 1793 by artist and engraver Joseph Wright, who is also believed by some to have designed the 1793 half cent. On the cent, Miss Liberty faces to the right, rather than to the left (as on the half cent). Liberty Cap cents of 1793 have raised beaded borders. Other issues have dentils. Cents of 1794 and some of 1795 are on thick planchets with the edge lettered ONE HUNDRED FOR A DOLLAR, while those made later in 1795, and in 1796, are on thinner planchets and have a plain edge.

Striking and Sharpness. The depth of relief and striking characteristics vary widely, depending on the variety. Points to check are the details of the hair on Miss Liberty, the leaf details on the wreath, and the dentils on both sides. Generally, the earlier, thick-planchet issues are better strikes than are the thin-planchet coins. Plain-edge 1795 cents often have low or shallow rims. To determine the difference between lightness caused by shallow dies and lightness caused by wear, study the characteristics of the die variety involved (see in particular the reverses of 1793, S-13, and 1793, S-12/S-15).

Availability. Cents of this type are readily available, although those of 1793 are rare and in great demand, and certain die varieties of the other dates are rare and can command high prices. Typical grades range from AG upward to Fine, VF, and, less often, EF. Attractive AU and MS coins are elusive, and when found are usually dated 1795, the thin planchet variety.

G-4, 6 (Good). *Obverse:* The portrait is worn smooth and is seen only in outline form, although the eye and nose can be discerned. LIBERTY and the date are complete, although the date may be weak. Dentils are gone on varieties struck with low or shallow rims. *Reverse:* Extensive wear is seen overall. From half to two-thirds of the letters in UNITED STATES OF AMERICA and the fraction numerals are worn away. Certain shallow-relief dies may have letters missing. Darkness, porosity, and marks are common.

VG-8, 10 (Very Good). *Obverse:* The hair is more worn than in Fine, with detail present only in the lower areas. Detail can differ, and widely, depending on the dies. Border dentils are worn away on some issues (not as much for 1793 and 1794 coins), and the border blends into the field in areas in which the rim was low to begin with, or in areas struck slightly off center. LIBERTY and the date are bold. *Reverse:* The wreath, bow, and lettering are seen in outline form, and some leaves and letters may be indistinct in parts. Border dentils are worn away, and the border blends into the field in most if not all of the periphery. In certain die varieties and die states, some letters may be very weak, or missing.

F-12, 15 (Fine). *Obverse:* The hair details are mostly worn away, with about one-third visible, mainly at the lower edges. Border dentils are weak or worn away in areas, depending on the height of the rim when the coin was struck. *Reverse:* The wreath leaves are worn flat, but their edges are distinct. Border dentils are

weak or worn away in areas. In Fine and lower, planchet darkness and light porosity are common, as are scattered marks.

VF-20, 30 (Very Fine). *Obverse:* Wear on the portrait has reduced the hair detail to indistinct or flat at the center, and on most varieties the individual strands at the left edge are blended together. *Reverse:* The leaf details are nearly completely worn away at VF-20, and with slight detail at VF-30. Some border letters may be weak, and ditto for the central letters (on later varieties of this type). The border dentils are blended together with many indistinct. No luster is seen. The sharpness of details depends on the die variety.

EF-40, 45 (Extremely Fine). *Obverse:* For most varieties, the center of the coin shows wear or a small, flat area. Other hair details are strong. Luster is minimal or nonexistent at EF-40, and may survive in traces in protected areas (such as between the letters) at EF-45. *Reverse:* Wear is seen on the highest wreath and ribbon areas and the letters. Luster is minimal, but likely more noticeable than on the obverse, as the fields are protected by the designs and lettering. Sharpness varies depending on the die variety but is generally shallower than on the obverse, this being particularly true for many 1795 cents.

AU-50, 53, 55, 58 (About Uncirculated). *Obverse:* Very light wear is evident on the highest parts of the hair above and to the left of the ear. Friction is seen on the cheek and the liberty cap. Coins at this level are usu-

ally on smooth planchets and have nice eye appeal. Color is very important. Dark and porous coins are relegated to lower grades, even if AU-level sharpness is present. *Reverse:* (Grading at the AU level is mainly done by viewing the obverse, as many reverses are inherently shallow from lower-relief dies.) Very light wear is evident on the higher parts of the leaves and the ribbon, and, to a lesser extent, on the lettering. The reverse may have original luster, toned brown, varying from minimal (at lower AU grades) to extensive.

MS-60 to 70 (Mint State). *Obverse:* In MS-60 and 61 there are some traces of abrasion on the higher areas of the portrait. Luster is incomplete, particularly in the field. At MS-63, luster is complete, and no abrasion evident. At higher levels, the luster is deeper, and some original mint color may be seen on some examples. At MS-65 there may be some scattered contact marks and possibly some traces of fingerprints or discoloration, but these should be very minimal and not at all distracting. Generally, Liberty Cap cents of 1793 (in particular) and 1794 are harder to find with strong eye appeal than are those of 1795 and 1796. Mint State coins of 1795 often have satiny luster. Above MS-65, a coin should approach perfection, especially if dated 1795 or 1796. Certified MS cents can vary in their strictness of interpretation. *Reverse:* In the lower MS grades some abrasion is seen on the higher areas of the leaves. Generally, luster is complete in all grades, as the open areas are protected by the lettering and wreath. Often on this type the reverse is shallower than the obverse and has a lower rim.

Head of 1793 (1793–1794)
Head in high, rounded relief.

Head of 1794 (1794)
Well-defined hair; hook on lowest curl.

Head of 1795 (1794–1796)
Head in low relief; no hook on lowest curl.

1795, "Jefferson Head"

Beaded Border (1793)

Dentil Border (1794–1796)

1794, Normal Reverse

1794, Starred Reverse

	Mintage	Cert	Avg	%MS	VG-8	F-12	VF-20	EF-40	AU-50	MS-60BN	MS-63BN	Recent Auction Record
1793, Liberty Cap	11,056	12	11.6	0	$10,000	$15,500	$38,000	$74,000	$160,000			$506,000, AU-53, Sep-09
1794, All kinds	918,521											
1794, Head of 1793		9	18.0	11	2,800	4,000	9,000	24,000	40,000	$90,000	$175,000	$3,738, F-12, Nov-09
1794, Head of 1794		132	34.9	5	500	800	1,500	3,500	5,750	11,500	25,500	$1,610, VF-20, Feb-10
1794, Head of 1795		17	33.6	12	600	1,000	1,900	4,750	10,000	39,000	85,000	$1,840, VF-25, Jan-10
1794, Starred Reverse †		6	14.5	0	18,000	35,000	62,000	240,000	550,000			$20,700, VG-8, Dec-09
1794, No Fraction Bar		3	44.0	67	650	1,000	2,200	6,000	13,500	38,000	75,000	$2,875, F-12, Sep-09
1795, Lettered Edge	37,000	29	42.9	24	525	950	2,000	5,000	7,000	11,000	24,000	$40,250, MS-65RB, Jan-10
1795, Plain Edge	501,500	128	34.6	16	425	650	1,350	3,000	6,000	8,200	20,000	$5,175, AU-53, Jan-10
1795, Reeded Edge (7 known)					800,000 (a)	1,250,000						$1,265,000, VG-10, Sep-09
1795, "Jefferson Head" (b)					30,000	50,000	100,000	250,000				$94,875, VF-20, Sep-09
1795, "Jefferson Head,"												
Ltrd Edge (b) (3 known)					50,000	100,000	250,000					
1796, Liberty Cap	109,825	82	30.0	16	600	1,200	2,400	5,500	11,500	25,000		$1,840, F-15, Jan-10

† Ranked in the *100 Greatest U.S. Coins* (third edition). **a.** Value in G-4 is $110,000. **b.** The "Jefferson Head" is not a regular Mint issue, but a design struck privately in an attempt to win a federal coinage contract.

DRAPED BUST
(1796–1807)

Designer Robert Scot; weight 10.89 grams; composition copper; approx. diameter 29 mm; plain edge.

Sheldon-258.

History. The Draped Bust cent made its debut in 1796, following a coinage of Liberty Cap cents the same year. The motif, from a drawing by Gilbert Stuart, was first employed on certain silver dollars of 1795. (Its use on half cents did not take place until later, in 1800.) In 1798 Miss Liberty's head was slightly modified in design.

Striking and Sharpness. Most Draped Bust cents were struck on high-quality planchets. (This high planchet quality is less predictable for varieties of 1796, and almost never present for those of 1799 and 1800.) Detail sharpness differs by die variety. Weakness, when present, is usually on the hair behind the forehead, on the leaves in the upper part of the wreath, and among the dentils. However, a weak strike can show up in other areas as well. Many if not most Draped Bust cents are imperfectly centered, with the result that dentils can be bold on one side of a die and light or even missing on the opposite side; this can occur on obverse as well as reverse. Typically this does not affect value. Certain Draped Bust cents of 1796 have semi-prooflike surfaces. Those of 1799 often have rough or porous surfaces and are found in lower grades.

Availability. As a type, Draped Bust cents are readily available, although the 1799, 9 Over 8, and 1799 are the keys to the series, and the 1804 is elusive. A different scenario evolves when considering engraving errors, repunched dates, and recut letters and numerals; many of these varieties are very difficult to locate. The eye appeal of these rarities usually is below par. Other years are generally available in high grades, VF and finer, well struck (except for some reverse leaves, in instances), on high-quality planchets, and with excellent eye appeal. Dark and porous coins are plentiful among coins graded below VF. True MS coins tend to be MS-60 to 63, when found.

VF-20, 30 (Very Fine). *Obverse:* Wear on the portrait has reduced the hair detail greater than at EF, especially to the left of the forehead. The rolling curls are solid or flat on their highest areas, as well as by the ribbon behind the hair. The border dentils are blended together, with many indistinct. No luster is seen. *Reverse:* The leaf details are nearly completely worn away at VF-20, and with slight detail at VF-30. The border dentils are blended together, with many indistinct. No luster is seen.

EF-40, 45 (Extremely Fine). *Obverse:* Wear is seen on the portrait overall, with reduction or elimination of some separation of hair strands on the highest part. By the standards of the Early American Coppers society, if the "spit curl" in front of Liberty's ear is missing, the coin is not EF. The cheek shows more wear than on higher grades, and the drapery covering the bosom is lightly worn on the higher areas. Often weakness in the separation of the drapery lines can be attributed to weakness in striking. Luster is minimal or nonexistent at EF-40, and may survive in among the letters of LIBERTY at EF-45. *Reverse:* Wear is seen on the highest wreath and ribbon areas, and on the letters. Luster is minimal, but likely more noticeable than on the obverse, as the fields are protected by the designs and lettering. Most or nearly all of the "ribbing" (veins) in the leaves is visible (striking plays a part, and some leaves may be weak even in higher grades).

AU-50, 53, 55, 58 (About Uncirculated). *Obverse:* Friction is seen on the higher parts, particularly the hair and the cheek. Friction and scattered marks are in the field, ranging from more extensive at AU-50 to minimal at 58. Luster may be seen in protected areas, minimal at AU-50, more visible at 58. At AU-58 the field may retain some luster as well. In many instances, the luster is smaller in area and lesser in "depth" than on the reverse of this type. *Reverse:* Friction is seen on the higher wreath leaves and (not as easy to discern) on the letters. The die variety should be checked. The fields, protected by the designs, show friction, but not as noticeably as on the obverse. At AU-55 and 58, little if any friction is seen. The reverse may have original luster, toned brown, minimal on lower AU grades, often extensive at AU-58.

MS-60 to 70 (Mint State). *Obverse:* In MS-60 and 61, some slight abrasion can be seen on the higher areas of the portrait, especially the cheek, and the hair behind the forehead. Luster in the field is incomplete, particularly in the center of the open areas, which on this type are very open, especially at the right. At MS-63, luster is nearly complete, and no abrasions evident. In higher levels, the luster is complete and deeper, and some original mint color should be seen. MS-64 coins may have some slight discoloration or scattered con-

tact marks. An MS-65 or higher coin has full, rich luster; no marks visible except under magnification; and a nice blend of brown toning or nicely mixed (not stained or blotchy) mint color and natural brown toning. *Reverse:* In the lower MS grades some abrasions are seen on the higher areas of the leaves. Generally, luster is complete in all MS grades, as the open areas are protected by the lettering and wreath. Sharpness of the leaves can vary by die variety. Otherwise, the same comments apply as for the obverse.

Reverse of 1794 (1794–1796)
Note double leaf at top right;
14–16 leaves on left, 16–18 leaves on right.
(Shown 1.5x actual size)

Reverse of 1795 (1795–1798)
Note single leaf at top right;
17–21 leaves on left, 16–20 leaves on right.
(Shown 1.5x actual size)

Reverse of 1797 (1796–1807)
Note double leaf at top right;
16 leaves on left, 19 leaves on right.
(Shown 1.5x actual size)

1796, LIHERTY Error

1797, Wreath With Stems

1797, Stemless Wreath

Style 1 Hair
Found on all coins of 1796 and 1797, many
1798 varieties, and 1800, 1800 Over 1798.
(Shown 1.5x actual size)

Style 2 Hair
Found on coins of 1798–1807.
Note the extra curl near shoulders.
(Shown 1.5x actual size)

1798, 8 Over 7

1799, 9 Over 8

1799, Normal Date

1800, 1800 Over 1798

1800, 80 Over 79

1800, Normal Date

1801, Normal Reverse

1801, 3 Errors: 1/000, One Stem,
and IINITED

1801, Fraction 1/000

1801, 1/100 Over 1/000

1802, Normal Reverse

1802, Fraction 1/000

1802, Stemless Wreath

1803, Small Date

1803, Large Date

Note that Small Date varieties have a blunt 1 in the date, and Large Date varieties have a pointed 1 and noticeably larger 3.

1803, Small Fraction

         1803, Large Fraction

1803, 1/100 Over 1/000

1803, Stemless Wreath

1804, Broken Dies
Sheldon-266c.

Unofficial 1804 "Restrike"
Breen-1761, Pollock-6050.

Small 1807, 7 Over 6, Blunt 1

Large 1807, 7 Over 6, Pointed 1

1807, Small Fraction

1807, Large Fraction

1807, "Comet" Variety
Note the die break behind Miss Liberty's head.

	Mintage	Cert	Avg	%MS	VF-20	EF-40	AU-50	MS-60BN	MS-63BN	MS-63RB	MS-65BN	Recent Auction Record
1796, Draped Bust, All kinds	363,375											
1796, Reverse of 1794		12	18.1	0	$2,500	$5,500	$10,000	$18,000	$26,500	$42,500	$72,500	$3,738, VF-30, May-09
1796, Reverse of 1795		9	26.7	11	2,500	5,250	11,000	19,500	30,000	50,000	80,000	$32,200, AU-55, Sep-09
1796, Reverse of 1797		8	21.5	13	2,000	4,000	6,500	8,500	14,000	22,500	23,000	$6,325, VF-35, Jun-10
1796, LIHERTY Error		5	39.0	20	4,800	12,000	30,000	60,000	85,000	100,000	125,000	$29,900, EF-40, Sep-09
1796, Stemless Reverse *(3 known)*					(a)							
1797, All kinds	897,510											
1797, Gripped Edge, 1796 Reverse		4	35.8	0	1,000	3,500	7,750	26,000				$15,525, AU-50, Jun-10
1797, Plain Edge, 1796 Reverse		3	9.0	0	1,200	4,000	8,000	26,500				$14,375, EF-45, Sep-09
1797, 1797 Reverse, With Stems		52	31.6	15	950	2,000	3,500	5,750	11,750	16,500	21,500	$16,100, MS-65BN, Jan-10
1797, 1797 Reverse, Stemless		12	28.2	8	1,600	6,000	23,000	50,000				$2,990, VF-39, Jan-10
1798, All kinds	1,841,745											
1798, 8 Over 7		10	21.2	0	4,000	8,500	20,000					$10,350, AU-53, Sep-09
1798, Reverse of 1796		6	21.5	0	1,900	6,500	9,000	20,000	35,000	—		$13,225, AU-55, Sep-09
1798, Style 1 Hair		42	24.8	5	600	2,200	4,750	10,000	17,750	28,500		$5,175, AU-53, Jan-09
1798, Style 2 Hair		108	30.7	1	575	1,950	3,500	8,350	16,500	27,500		$805, VF-20, Jun-10
1799, 9 Over 8	(b)	4	9.8	0	28,000	75,000	200,000	400,000				$368,000, EF-45, Sep-09
1799, Normal Date	(b)	7	19.1	14	26,000	65,000	200,000	400,000				$21,850, VF-25, Jan-10
1800, All kinds	2,822,175											
1800, 1800 Over 1798, Style 1 Hair		9	33.8	11	1,000	3,850	7,000	10,000	14,000	30,000		$1,035, VF-20, Dec-09

a. Value in AG-3 is $10,000; in G-4, $22,000. **b.** Included in the "1798, All kinds" mintage.

Chart continued on next page.

	Mintage	Cert	Avg	%MS	VF-20	EF-40	AU-50	MS-60BN	MS-63BN	MS-63RB	MS-65BN	Recent Auction Record
1800, 80 Over 79, Style 2 Hair		6	40.3	17	$600	$2,200	$4,000	$8,000	$25,000	$40,000		$2,185, EF-40, Sep-09
1800, Normal Date		39	34.6	18	550	1,900	3,000	6,250	11,500	17,500		$4,025, AU-50, Sep-09
1801, All kinds	1,362,837											
1801, Normal Reverse		31	22.8	3	450	1,250	3,000	7,500	14,500	25,000		$518, VF-30, Aug-09
1801, 3 Errors: 1/000, One Stem, and IINITED		11	26.9	18	2,300	7,500	13,000	35,000	115,000			$12,075, AU-53, Sep-09
1801, Fraction 1/000		20	25.2	5	550	2,000	4,250	11,000	28,500			$1,438, VF-25, Jan-10
1801, 1/100 Over 1/000		2	37.5	50	800	2,200	6,000	14,000	25,000	57,500		$920, F-15 CAC, Jan-10
1802, All kinds	3,435,100											
1802, Normal Reverse		83	36.5	5	375	1,000	1,900	4,500	8,750	16,000	$27,500	$1,208, EF-45, Jun-10
1802, Fraction 1/000		14	40.8	21	500	1,700	3,000	7,200	15,500	25,000	42,500	$920, VF-35, Jan-10
1802, Stemless Wreath		26	30.6	8	450	1,400	2,750	6,300	13,500	22,500	38,500	$1,265, EF-45, Jun-10
1803, All kinds	3,131,691											
1803, Small Date, Small Fraction		74	34.5	7	350	1,000	1,450	3,000	8,500	17,000	27,500	$1,064, EF-40, Feb-10
1803, Small Date, Large Fraction		49	34.4	10	350	1,000	1,450	3,000	8,500	17,000	27,500	$417, VF-20, Feb-10
1803, Large Date, Small Fraction		1	3.0	0	30,000	85,000						$25,300, VG-10, Jan-10
1803, Large Date, Large Fraction		5	44.0	20	1,500	4,000	14,000					$3,565, VF-25, Sep-09
1803, 1/100 Over 1/000		11	36.1	9	750	2,200	4,900	7,750	18,000	30,000	65,000	$4,140, VF-35, Sep-09
1803, Stemless Wreath		4	48.8	50	750	2,200	4,700	7,250	17,000	30,000	65,000	$2,875, VF-35, Sep-09
1804 (c)	96,500	53	20.7	2	6,500	15,000	40,000	130,000	660,000			$143,750, AU-55, Jun-10
1804, Unofficial Restrike of 1860 (d)		76	61.0	87		850	900	1,200	1,450	2,000	1,700	$1,265, MS-62BN, Dec-09
1805	941,116	86	42.7	17	375	1,100	2,500	5,250	15,000			$690, VF-25, Jun-10
1806	348,000	48	39.7	17	600	2,000	3,750	8,750	28,000			$2,415, VF-25, Jan-10
1807, All kinds	829,221											
1807, Small 1807, 7 Over 6, Blunt 1		3	9.0	0	21,000	45,000	150,000					$25,300, VG-10, Sep-09
1807, Large 1807, 7 Over 6, Pointed 1		47	28.1	15	425	1,200	2,300	5,850	23,500			$1,840, EF-45, Oct-09
1807, Small Fraction		2	8.0	0	500	1,700	3,000	6,000	19,500			$33,350, EF-45, Sep-09
1807, Large Fraction		9	26.1	0	425	1,100	2,300	4,600	16,500			$19,550, MS-63BN, Sep-09
1807, "Comet" Variety		12	40.8	25	850	2,600	4,100	10,500	25,500			$54,000, MS-64BN CAC, Jan-10

c. All genuine 1804 cents have a crosslet 4 in the date and a large fraction. The 0 in the date is in line with the 0 in OF on the reverse. **d.** Discarded Mint dies were used, circa 1860, to create "restrikes" (actually novodels or fantasies) of the scarce 1804 cent for collectors. These combine two unrelated dies: an altered 1803 die was used for the obverse, and a die of the 1820 cent for the reverse. The resulting coins cannot be confused with genuine 1804 cents.

CLASSIC HEAD
(1808–1814)

Designer John Reich; weight 10.89 grams; composition copper; approx. diameter 29 mm; plain edge.

Sheldon-281.

History. The Classic Head design, by U.S. Mint assistant engraver John Reich, debuted in 1808. This cent type was minted through 1814. The quality of the coins' copper was poor during the War of 1812; the hostilities had ended the importation of high-quality planchets from England.

Striking and Sharpness. Striking sharpness varies, but often is poor. The cents of 1809 are notorious for having obverses much weaker than their reverses. Points to look for include sharpness of the dentils (which are often mushy, and in *most* instances inconsistent), star centers (a key area), hair details, and leaf details. Classic Head cents often are dark and porous due to the copper stock used.

Availability. Examples are readily available in grades from well worn to VF and EF, although overall quality often leaves much to be desired. AU and MS coins are elusive. Grading numbers do not mean much, as a connoisseur might prefer a high-quality EF-45 to a poorly struck MS-63. Overall eye appeal of obverse and reverse is often sub-par, a characteristic of this type.

VF-20, 30 (Very Fine). *Obverse:* Wear on the portrait has reduced the hair detail, especially on the area to the right of the cheek and neck, but much can still be seen. *Reverse:* The wreath details, except for the edges of the leaves and certain of the tips (on leaves in lower relief), are worn away at VF-20, and with slightly more detail at VF-30.

EF-40, 45 (Extremely Fine). *Obverse:* Wear is seen on the portrait overall, but most hair detail still is present. The cheek shows light wear. Luster is minimal or non-existent at EF-40, and may survive in among the letters of LIBERTY at EF-45. *Reverse:* Wear is seen on the highest wreath and ribbon areas and the letters. Leaf veins are visible except in the highest areas. Luster is minimal, but likely more noticeable than on the obverse, as the fields are protected by the designs and lettering.

AU-50, 53, 55, 58 (About Uncirculated). *Obverse:* Friction is seen on the higher parts, particularly the cheek. The hair will have friction and light wear, but will not be as obvious. Friction and scattered marks are in the field, ranging from more extensive at AU-50 to minimal at AU-58. Luster may be seen in protected areas, minimal at AU-50, but more visible at AU-58. At AU-58 the open field may retain some luster, as well. *Reverse:* Friction is seen on the higher wreath leaves and on the letters. Fields, protected by the designs, show some friction. At AU-55 and 58 little if any friction is seen. The reverse may have original luster, toned brown, minimal on lower AU grades, often extensive at AU-58.

MS-60 to 70 (Mint State). *Obverse:* In MS-60 and 61, some slight abrasions can be seen on the portrait, most evidently on the cheek, as the hair details are complex.

Luster in the field is complete or nearly complete; the field is not as open on this type as on the Draped Bust issues. At 63, luster should be complete, and no abrasion evident. In higher levels, the luster is complete and deeper, and some original mint color may be seen. MS-64 coins may have some slight discoloration or scattered contact marks. An MS-65 or higher coin has full, rich luster; no marks visible except under magnification; and a nice blend of brown toning or nicely mixed (not stained or blotchy) mint color and natural brown toning. Incomplete striking of some details, especially the obverse stars, is the rule. *Reverse:* In the lower MS grades, some abrasion is seen on the higher areas of the leaves. Mint luster is complete in all MS grades, as the open areas are protected by the lettering and wreath. Sharpness of the leaves can vary by die variety. Otherwise, the same comments apply as for the obverse.

1810, 10 Over 09

1810, Normal Date

1812, Small Date

1812, Large Date

1811, Last 1 Over 0

1811, Normal Date

1814, Plain 4

1814, Crosslet 4

	Mintage	Cert	Avg	%MS	VF-20	EF-40	AU-50	MS-60BN	MS-63BN	Recent Auction Record
1808	1,007,000	63	41.0	25	$600	$1,750	$3,250	$7,000	$14,500	$17,250, MS-63BN, Jan-10
1809	222,867	45	36.6	11	1,400	3,750	7,500	11,500	22,500	$9,200, MS-61BN, Sep-09
1810, All kinds	1,458,500									
1810, 10 Over 09		26	32.6	19	600	1,550	2,600	8,000	15,000	$5,463, AU-55, Jan-10
1810, Normal Date		22	38.7	18	600	1,450	2,500	8,000	16,500	$3,220, EF-45, Feb-10
1811, All kinds	218,025									
1811, Last 1 Over 0		17	36.1	18	1,750	5,200	10,000	25,000	55,000	$3,450, VF-35, Jan-10
1811, Normal Date		47	34.2	21	1,000	2,100	5,250	10,000	20,000	$14,950, MS-64BN, Jun-10
1812, All kinds	1,075,500									
1812, Small Date		15	40.3	7	575	1,450	2,350	5,250	10,500	$2,990, AU-53, Jan-10
1812, Large Date		17	34.8	6	575	1,450	2,350	5,250	10,500	$9,200, MS-63BN, Jan-10
1813	418,000	107	42.2	15	600	1,700	2,700	6,000	12,000	$3,450, AU-58, Feb-10
1814, All kinds	357,830									
1814, Plain 4		28	50.1	29	550	1,400	1,950	4,300	9,250	$2,070, AU-55, Jan-10
1814, Crosslet 4		28	34.9	21	550	1,400	1,950	4,600	9,750	$2,760, AU-53, Jan-10

Matron Head (1816–1836)
Newcomb-1.

Matron Head Modified (1837–1839)
Newcomb-5.

LIBERTY HEAD: MATRON HEAD (1816–1836) AND MATRON HEAD MODIFIED (1837–1839)

Matron Head: Designer Robert Scot or John Birch; weight 10.89 grams; composition copper; approx. diameter 28–29 mm; plain edge.

Matron Head Modified: Designer Christian Gobrecht; weight 10.89 grams; composition copper; diameter 27.5 mm; plain edge.

History. The term *Matron Head* describes cents of 1816 to 1836 (none were struck in 1815). Engraver Christian Gobrecht experimented with various "Matron Head Modified" portraits in the later 1830s.

Striking and Sharpness. Planchet quality is generally very good for Liberty Head cents. Color tends to be lighter on coins of the 1830s than on earlier dates. Striking can vary. Points to check include the obverse stars (in particular), the highest hair details, and the leaves on the reverse. Dentils can range from sharp to weak, and centering is often irregular. The reverse design is essentially the same as that used on the Classic Head of 1808 to 1814, and can be graded the same way. This motif stood up to circulation particularly well.

Availability. As a type, Liberty Head cents are easily available. The scarcest date by far is 1823 (and the related 1823, 3 Over 2 overdate). Cents of 1816 to 1820 (particularly 1818 and 1820) are readily available in MS. Other MS coins are generally scarce, although those of the 1830s are more readily available than those of the teens and 1820s. Circulated examples exist in approximate relationship to their mintages. Planchet quality and striking sharpness vary in all grades.

EF-40, 45 (Extremely Fine). *Obverse:* Wear is seen on the portrait overall, but most hair detail is still present, except in higher areas. The cheek shows light wear. Luster is minimal or nonexistent at EF-40, and may survive in among the letters of LIBERTY at EF-45. *Reverse:* Wear is seen on the highest wreath and ribbon areas, and on the letters. Leaf veins are visible except in the highest areas. Luster is minimal, but likely more noticeable than on the obverse, as the fields are protected by the designs and lettering.

AU-50, 53, 55, 58 (About Uncirculated). *Obverse:* Friction is seen on the higher parts, particularly the cheek. The hair has friction and light wear, usually most notable in the general area above BER (LIBERTY).

Friction and scattered marks are in the field, ranging from extensive at AU-50 to minimal at 58. Luster may be seen in protected areas, minimal at AU-50, more visible at 58. At AU-58 the field may retain some luster as well. *Reverse:* Friction is seen on the higher wreath leaves and on the letters. Fields, protected by the designs, show friction. At AU-55 and 58 little if any friction is seen. The reverse may have original luster, toned brown, minimal on lower AU grades, often extensive at AU-58.

MS-60 to 70 (Mint State). *Obverse:* In MS-60 and 61, some slight abrasions can be seen on the portrait, most evidently on the cheek, which is very prominent. Check higher areas of the hair, particularly the top and back of Liberty's head, but do not confuse with lightness of strike. Luster in the field is complete or nearly complete. At MS-63, luster should be complete, and no abrasion is evident. In higher levels, the luster is complete and deeper, and some original mint color may be seen. MS-64 coins may have some minimal discoloration or scattered contact marks. An MS-65 or finer coin will have full, rich luster; no marks visible except under magnification; and a nice blend of brown toning or nicely mixed mint color and natural brown toning. *Reverse:* In lower MS some abrasion is seen on the higher areas of the leaves. Mint luster is complete in all MS grades, as the open areas are protected by the lettering and wreath. Sharpness of the leaves can vary by die variety. Otherwise, the same comments apply as for the obverse.

1817, 13 Stars

1817, 15 Stars

1819, 9 Over 8

1819, Large Date

1819, Small Date

1820, 20 Over 19
Note the 1 under the 2.

1820, Large Date
Note the plain-topped 2.

1820, Small Date
Note the curl-topped 2.

1823, 3 Over 2

Unofficial 1823 "Restrike"
Newcomb-3, Breen-1823, Pollock-6220.

1824, 4 Over 2

1826, 6 Over 5

**Date Size, Through 1828
(Large, Narrow Date)**

**Date Size, 1828 and Later
(Small, Wide Date)**

**Large Letters
(1808–1834)**
*Note the size and proximity
of individual letters.*

**Medium Letters
(1829–1837)**
*Note the isolation of the let-
ters, especially of STATES.*

**1834, Large 8, Large Stars,
Large Reverse Letters**
Newcomb-6.

**1834, Large 8, Large Stars,
Medium Reverse Letters**
Newcomb-5.

**1834, Large 8, Small Stars,
Medium Reverse Letters**
Newcomb-3.

**1834, Small 8, Large Stars,
Medium Reverse Letters**
Newcomb-1.

**1835, Large 8, Large Stars,
Matron Head**

**1835, Small 8, Small
Stars, Matron Head**

1835, Matron Head
Shown 1.5x actual size.

1835, Head of 1836
Shown 1.5x actual size.

**Medium Letters
(1829–1837)**

**Small Letters
(1837–1839)**

1837
Note the plain hair cords.

1837, Head of 1838
*Note the slim bust and
the beaded hair cords.*

1839, 1839 Over 1836
Note the closed 9 and the plain hair cords.

1839, Silly Head
Note the prominent lock of hair at the forehead.

1839, Booby Head
Note the shoulder tip. Also note the absence of a line under CENT.

	Mintage	Cert	Avg	%MS	EF-40	AU-50	MS-60BN	MS-63BN	MS-63RB	MS-65BN	MS-65RB	Recent Auction Record
1816	2,820,982	216	58.9	68	$190	$300	$500	$700	$1,150	$1,700	$3,100	$11,213, MS-64RB, Jun-10
1817, All kinds	3,948,400											
1817, 13 Stars		137	57.3	66	135	225	450	600	900	1,550	2,600	$8,625, MS-63BN, Jun-10
1817, 15 Stars		35	52.1	29	500	900	2,500	3,600	8,000	20,000	40,000	$2,415, EF-45, Jun-10
1818	3,167,000	567	60.4	82	135	225	450	600	925	1,600	2,800	$4,888, MS-66RB, Jun-10
1819, All kinds	2,671,000											
1819, 9 Over 8		70	55.8	50	240	350	750	1,300	2,500	4,000		$2,185, MS-64BN, Jun-10
1819, Large Date		18	46.4	28	140	300	475	700	1,250	2,000		$483, EF-45, Jun-10
1819, Small Date		74	56.2	69	140	300	475	700	1,250	2,000		$2,300, MS-64BN, Jun-10
1820, All kinds	4,407,550											
1820, 20 Over 19		23	48.1	43	335	550	1,000	1,600	2,750	4,500	10,500	$5,290, MS-64BN, Jun-10
1820, Large Date		77	59.0	78	175	250	400	600	825	1,250	2,000	$863, MS-64BN, Jun-10
1820, Small Date		25	53.4	60	250	450	900	1,200	2,000	2,800	4,200	$2,128, MS-64BN, Jun-10
1821	389,000	71	41.1	13	1,200	2,300	7,750	11,000	27,000			$24,150, MS-63BN, Jun-10
1822	2,072,339	131	52.1	36	275	550	1,000	1,750	3,000	4,900	12,000	$3,450, MS-64BN, Jun-10

	Mintage	Cert	Avg	%MS	EF-40	AU-50	MS-60BN	MS-63BN	MS-63RB	MS-65BN	MS-65RB	Recent Auction Record
1823, 3 Over 2	(a)	53	25.6	0	$2,200	$4,250	$12,000	—				$8,338, AU-58, Jun-10
1823, Normal Date	(a)	25	27.2	8	3,500	6,000	14,000	—		$115,000	$250,000	$9,775, VF-35, Jun-10
1823, Unofficial Restrike (b)		57	63.3	96	500	900	1,250	$1,450	$1,600	1,750	2,200	$2,530, MS-63BN, Jun-10
1824, All kinds	1,262,000											
1824, 4 Over 2		24	41.7	17	1,200	2,500	6,000	10,000	20,000	35,000		$1,668, VF-35, Jun-10
1824, Normal Date		37	51.3	30	500	850	2,400	4,000	5,000	8,000		$3,680, MS-62BN, Jun-10
1825	1,461,100	102	52.5	40	325	650	*2,000*	2,750	4,700	7,500		$2,875, MS-63BN, Jun-10
1826, All kinds	1,517,425											
1826, 6 Over 5		13	52.7	38	900	1,500	2,800	5,300	7,500	19,000		$604, VF-25, Jun-10
1826, Normal Date		87	53.7	45	250	450	900	1,400	2,650	3,100		$1,955, MS-63BN, Jun-10
1827	2,357,732	135	52.1	42	225	425	775	1,400	2,500	3,500		$2,070, MS-63BN, Jun-10
1828, All kinds	2,260,624											
1828, Large Narrow Date		55	51.9	35	200	400	800	1,750	2,800	4,250	10,000	$1,150, MS-64BN, Jun-10
1828, Small Wide Date		11	53.9	64	275	650	1,950	3,500	5,500	20,000		$2,300, MS-63BN, Jun-10
1829, All kinds	1,414,500											
1829, Large Letters		26	50.3	46	185	385	650	1,500	3,000	5,200	12,000	$6,900, MS-64BN, Jun-10
1829, Medium Letters		11	45.5	27	750	2,400	6,250	10,500	12,500	16,000	25,000	$5,750, EF-45, Jun-10
1830, All kinds	1,711,500											
1830, Large Letters		57	53.0	49	190	300	550	1,000	1,900	2,700	3,600	$207, VF-35, Jun-10
1830, Medium Letters		3	46.3	33	2,000	4,000	13,000	25,000			50,000	$3,335, VF-30, Jun-10
1831, All kinds	3,359,260											
1831, Large Letters		68	53.4	54	140	250	375	700	1,150	1,800	3,400	$1,668, MS-64BN, Jun-10
1831, Medium Letters		32	53.5	53	175	300	425	800	1,250	1,900	3,500	$1,150, MS-64BN, Jun-10
1832, All kinds	2,362,000											
1832, Large Letters		24	58.0	63	140	250	375	650	1,000	1,700	3,000	$805, MS-62BN, Jun-10
1832, Medium Letters		18	59.3	61	140	250	375	650	1,000	1,700	3,000	$4,600, MS-64BN, Jun-10
1833	2,739,000	188	56.5	56	140	250	375	650	1,000	1,700	3,000	$5,290, MS-64RB, Jun-10
1834, All kinds	1,855,100											
1834, Lg 8, Stars, and Rev Ltrs		9	43.2	11	550	1,000	2,200	4,000	7,000	8,000		$3,335, MS-62BN, Jun-10
1834, Lg 8 and Stars, Med Ltrs		4	54.0	25	3,200	6,000	9,500	11,000	15,000	20,000		$7,188, EF-45, Jun-10
1834, Lg 8, Sm Stars, Med Ltrs		22	54.3	36	140	240	350	625	925	1,400	2,600	$5,750, MS-65RB, Jun-10
1834, Sm 8, Lg Stars, Med Ltrs		49	57.3	55	140	240	350	625	925	1,400	2,600	$1,035, MS-64BN, Jun-10
1835, All kinds	3,878,400											
1835, Large 8 and Stars		9	49.4	33	225	400	750	1,400	2,250	2,100	4,000	$8,625, MS-65BN, Jun-10
1835, Small 8 and Stars		31	50.0	32	175	375	475	675	1,400	1,400	2,600	$1,840, MS-63BN, Jun-10
1835, Head of 1836		76	54.5	45	125	250	350	550	900	1,200	1,800	$3,565, MS-63BN, Jun-10
1836	2,111,000	140	59.1	66	125	250	350	550	900	1,200	1,800	$1,495, MS-64BN, Jun-10
1837, All kinds	5,558,300											
1837, Plain Cord, Medium Letters		116	60.4	72	125	250	350	550	775	1,200	2,300	$483, MS-63BN, Jun-10
1837, Plain Cord, Small Letters		17	56.2	71	125	250	375	600	825	1,500	2,600	$1,006, MS-64BN, Jun-10
1837, Head of 1838		54	59.8	72	110	200	325	500	775	1,200	1,800	$1,898, MS-64BN, Jun-10
1838	6,370,200	605	59.4	71	120	225	335	575	925	1,300	2,150	$1,093, MS-63RB, Jun-10
1839, All kinds	3,128,661											
1839, 1839 Over 1836, Plain Cords		35	11.3	0	9,000	18,000	60,000	90,000	150,000	235,000		$22,425, EF-45, Jun-10
1839, Head of 1838, Beaded Cords		64	58.6	58	110	225	325	550	1,000	1,450	2,000	$1,380, MS-65BN, Jun-10
1839, Silly Head		82	56.6	65	200	400	850	1,200	2,200	2,700	3,800	$1,208, MS-63BN, Jun-10
1839, Booby Head		152	57.3	64	150	300	675	1,100	2,150	2,350	3,200	$1,438, MS-64BN, Jun-10

a. Included in "1824, All kinds" mintage. **b.** The unofficial 1823 "restrikes" (actually novodels or fantasies) were made at the same time (around 1860) and by the same people as those of 1804. The coins were made from a discarded obverse die of 1823 and an 1813 reverse die—both heavily rusted, producing surface lumps. Most examples have both dies cracked.

Proof Liberty Head, Matron Head, Large Cents

PF-60 to 70 (Proof). Proofs were made for cents from 1817 onward. Often, coins called "Proofs" are only partially mirrorlike, and sometimes the striking is casual, e.g., with weakness on certain of the stars. Complicating the situation: all but one of the same die pairs were also used to make circulation strikes. Many misattributions were made generations ago, some of which have been perpetuated. True Proofs with deeply mirrored surfaces are in the small minority. *Obverse and Reverse:* Proofs that are extensively hairlined or have dull surfaces, this being characteristic of many issues (exceptions, when found, are usually dated in the 1830s), are graded PF-60 to 62 or 63. Artificially toned and recolored coins may be graded lower. To qualify as PF-65 or higher, hairlines should be microscopic, and there should be no trace of friction. Surfaces should be prooflike or, better, fully mirrored and without dullness.

Proof Liberty Head, Matron Head,
Modified, Large Cent

	Est Mintage	Cert	Finest	PF-60BN	PF-63BN	PF-64BN	PF-65BN	Recent Auction Record
1817	2–3	1	PF-63	$29,000	$35,000	*$45,000*	$75,000	$48,300, PF-66, Jul-05
1819, 9 Over 8	2–3	1	PF-64	24,000	30,000	40,000	*60,000*	$32,200, PF-64BN, Jun-05
1820	8–15	5	PF-64	35,000	50,000	40,000	60,000	$46,000, PF-64, Nov-08
1821	4–6	3	PF-66	19,000	24,000	34,000	50,000	$48,875, PF-65, Feb-09
1822	4–6	5	PF-64	35,000	55,000	*65,000*		$25,300, PF-63, Mar-04
1823	2–3	1	PF-65	50,000	65,000	95,000		
1823, 3 Over 2	5–8	3	PF-65	45,000	60,000	80,000		$80,500, PF-64BN, Nov-08
1827	5–8	3	PF-64	17,500	20,000	*25,000*		$20,125, PF-64, Mar-04
1828	2–3	1	PF-65					
1829	2–3	1	PF-64	16,500	20,000	27,000		$54,625, PF-64RB, Jul-08
1829, Bronzed	10–15	6	PF-66	15,000	18,000	25,000	36,000	$23,000, PF-64BN, Jul-08
1830	2–3	1	PF-64				185,000	$16,500, PF-64, Nov-88
1831	10–20	9	PF-65	12,000	14,500	24,500	45,000	$12,650, PF-64BN, Sep-09
1832	2–4	1	PF-64					
1834	6–8	3	PF-66		52,000			$51,750, PF-63BN, Jan-08
1836	6–8	4	PF-66			20,000	*35,000*	
1837	8–12	5	PF-66	25,000	30,000			$20,700, PF-63, Mar-04
1838	10–20	7	PF-66	10,500	12,500	19,500	33,000	$29,900, PF-65, Feb-09

LIBERTY HEAD: BRAIDED HAIR
(1839–1857)

*Designer Christian Gobrecht; weight 10.89 grams;
composition copper; diameter 27.5 mm; plain edge.*

History. Christian Gobrecht's Braided Hair design was introduced in 1839. It loosely following the design he had created for the 1838 gold eagle. On issues of 1839 through part of 1843, Miss Liberty's portrait is tilted forward, with the left tip of her neck truncation over the 8 of the date. For most issues of 1843 and all later dates her head is larger and aligned in a more vertical position, and the tip of her neck is over the first digit of the date. The reverse lettering was made larger beginning in 1844. The net result is that cents after 1843 are less delicate in appearance than are those of earlier dates. These coins were made in large quantities, except for their final year. They remained in circulation in the United States until the late 1850s, not long enough to be worn down to very low grades. (Some circulated in the eastern part of *Canada* through the 1860s, accounting for many of the more worn examples seen today.)

Striking and Sharpness. Sharpness can vary. On the obverse, the star centers can be weak, especially for dates in the 1850s, and,

less often, there can be lightness on the front of the coronet and the hair. On the reverse the leaves can be light, but most are well struck. The dentils can be mushy and indistinct on either side, this being particularly true of dates in the early and mid-1850s. Flaky or laminated planchets can be a problem, again among coins of the 1850s, in which tiny pieces of metal fall away from the surface, leaving areas in the field that interrupt the luster on MS coins.

Availability. All dates of Braided Hair cents are readily available, with the 1857 somewhat less so (it was minted in January 1857 in low quantity; seemingly not all were released). The delicate-featured issues of 1839 to 1843 are becoming more difficult to find in EF or finer grades without surface problems. Cents dated in the 1850s are usually seen in VF or higher grades. Certain die varieties attributed by Newcomb numbers can be scarce or rare. For issues in the 1850s the differences can be microscopic, thus limiting their numismatic appeal and making them unattributable unless in high grades. Hoards were found of some dates, particularly 1850 to 1856, making MS coins of these years more readily available than would otherwise be the case. MS-64 RD or higher coins with *original* color range from scarce to very rare for dates prior to 1850,

but those of the 1850s are seen regularly (except for 1857). Coins below VF-20 are not widely collected and, for many issues, are too worn to attribute by die variety.

EF-40, 45 (Extremely Fine). *Obverse:* Wear is more extensive on the portrait than at AU, including the cheek, the hair above the ear, and the coronet. The star centers are worn down slightly (if they were sharply struck to begin with). Traces of luster are minimal, if at all existent. *Reverse:* The centers of the leaves are well worn, with detail visible only near the edges of the leaves and nearby, with the higher parts worn flat. Letters show significant wear. Luster, if present, is minimal.

AU-50, 53, 55, 58 (About Uncirculated). *Obverse:* Wear is evident on the cheek, the hair above the ear, and the tip of the coronet. Friction is evident in the field. At AU-58, luster may be present except in the center of the fields. As grade goes up to AU-58, wear becomes less evident on the cheek. Wear is seen on the stars, but is

not as easy to discern as it is elsewhere and, in any event, many stars are weakly struck. At AU-50 there will be either no luster or only traces of luster close to the letters and devices. *Reverse:* Wear is most evident on the highest areas of the leaves and the ribbon bow. Luster is present in the fields. As grade goes up from AU-50 to 58, wear increases and luster decreases. At AU-50 there is either no luster or just traces close to the letters and devices.

MS-60 to 70 (Mint State). *Obverse:* In MS-60 and 61, some slight abrasions can be seen on the portrait, most evidently on the cheek. Check the tip of the coronet and the hair above the ear, as well. Luster in the field is complete or nearly so. At MS-63, luster should be complete, and no abrasion evident. If there is weakness on

the hair it is due to light striking, not to wear; this also applies for the stars. In higher levels, the luster is complete and deeper, and some original mint color may be seen. Mint frost on this type is usually deep, sometimes satiny, but hardly ever prooflike. MS-64 coins may have some slight discoloration or scattered contact marks. An MS-65 or higher coin will have full, rich luster; no marks visible except under magnification; and a nice blend of brown toning or nicely mixed (not stained or blotchy) mint color and natural brown toning. *Reverse:* In the lower MS grades some abrasion is seen on the higher areas of the leaves. Mint luster is complete in all MS grades, as the open areas are protected by the lettering and wreath. The quality of the luster is the best way to grade both sides of this type.

1840, Large Date	**1840, Small Date**	**1840, Small Date Over Large 18**	**1842, Small Date**	**1842, Large Date**

Small Letters (1839–1843)   **Large Letters (1843–1857)**

Head of 1840 ("Petite Head," 1839–1843)
Shown 1.5x actual size.

Head of 1844 ("Mature Head," 1843–1857)
Shown 1.5x actual size.

1844, 44 Over 81   **1847, 7 Over "Small 7"**   **1851, 51 Over 81**

These are not true overdates, but are three of the more spectacular of several date-punch blunders of the 1844–1854 period. The so-called overdates of 1844 and 1851 each have the date punched upside down, then corrected normally.

1846, Small Date
Note the squat date and the closed 6.

1846, Medium Date
Note the medium date height and the ball-top 6.

1846, Tall Date
Note the vertically stretched date and the open-mouthed 6.

1855, Upright 5's

1855, Slanting 5's

1855, Knob on Ear

1856, Upright 5

1856, Slanting 5

1857, Large Date

1857, Small Date

	Mintage	Cert	Avg	%MS	EF-40	AU-50	MS-60BN	MS-63BN	MS-63RB	MS-65BN	MS-65RB	Recent Auction Record
1839	(a)	36	59.8	69	$110	$265	$400	$650	$850	$2,250	$4,000 (b)	$2,300, MS-64BN, Aug-09
1840, All kinds	2,462,700											
1840, Large Date		55	61.0	67	85	200	300	500	1,150	1,200	2,500	$460, AU-58, Jan-10
1840, Small Date		38	58.6	58	85	200	300	500	1,150	1,200	2,500	$805, MS-63BN, Feb-10
1840, Small Date Over Large 18		4	52.3	75	200	400	900	1,600	1,950	2,200	3,500	$1,156, AU-50, May-06
1841, Small Date	1,597,367	92	59.3	67	125	250	450	950	1,200	1,650	2,600 (c)	$3,450, MS-65RB CAC, Feb-10
1842, All kinds	2,383,390											
1842, Small Date		25	59.7	60	85	220	375	650	1,300	2,100	3,250 (d)	$748, MS-60, Jan-10
1842, Large Date		57	61.0	75	85	150	300	500	850	1,700	2,850 (e)	$4,945, MS-65RB, Jan-10
1843, All kinds	2,425,342											
1843, Petite, Small Letters		99	60.5	78	85	160	300	450	875	1,650	2,600	$1,187, MS-64BN, Jan-10
1843, Petite, Large Letters		34	57.5	65	210	320	825	1,500	1,850	2,200	3,500	$805, MS-63BN, Feb-09
1843, Mature, Large Letters		19	58.5	68	150	275	550	900	1,500	2,000	3,000	$506, EF-45, Jan-10
1844, Normal Date	2,398,752	35	59.3	60	85	160	300	500	950	1,400	2,500	$4,888, MS-64RB, Jan-10
1844, 44 Over 81	*	24	50.4	42	225	500	1,200	2,600	3,250	4,500		$1,265, MS-61BN, Feb-09
1845	3,894,804	207	60.1	75	75	130	225	375	750	1,100	2,450	$2,530, MS-64RB, Jan-10
1846, All kinds	4,120,800											
1846, Small Date		144	60.4	80	75	130	225	350	750	1,200	1,900	$633, MS-63BN, Feb-10
1846, Medium Date		15	61.8	87	85	150	250	400	900	1,350	2,550	$322, MS-62BN, May-09
1846, Tall Date		24	54.0	67	150	225	450	900	1,200	1,650	2,900	$414, EF-45, Jan-10
1847	6,183,669	254	60.7	73	75	130	225	350	600	900	1,800	$1,725, MS-65BN CAC, Mar-10
1847, 7 Over "Small 7"	*	16	56.3	63	150	350	850	1,250	1,500	1,850	2,750	$437, VF-30, Jan-10
1848	6,415,799	541	58.6	67	75	130	225	350	600	925	1,850	$2,875, MS-66RB, Jun-10
1849	4,178,500	322	57.7	61	85	150	250	450	1,000	1,200	2,450	$920, MS-64BN, Mar-10
1850	4,426,844	768	62.2	87	55	115	180	230	350	650	1,175 (f)	$949, MS-66BN, Jun-10
1851, Normal Date	9,889,707	298	61.7	82	55	115	180	230	350	650	1,175 (g)	$759, MS-64RB, Feb-10
1851, 51 Over 81	*	79	58.7	72	200	250	500	1,000	1,250	1,600	2,650	$805, AU-55, Jan-10
1852	5,063,094	1,008	61.7	82	55	115	180	230	350	635	1,150 (f)	$3,220, MS-67RB, Jan-10
1853	6,641,131	1,608	61.9	83	55	115	180	230	350	635	1,150 (h)	$489, MS-64RB, Jun-10
1854	4,236,156	827	60.7	76	55	115	180	230	350	650	1,200 (g)	$633, MS-65BN , Jun-10
1855, All kinds	1,574,829											
1855, Upright 5's		129	62.2	84	55	115	180	230	350	635	1,100 (f)	$1,265, MS-66RB, Jun-10
1855, Slanting 5's		35	62.5	83	60	120	200	275	650	1,250	1,800 (i)	$1,955, MS-67BN Star, Jan-10
1855, Slanting 5's, Knob on Ear		80	59.6	64	110	225	360	525	1,250	2,150		$949, MS-62BN, Jan-10
1856, All kinds	2,690,463											
1856, Upright 5		90	63.0	86	60	125	205	270	365	675	1,150 (h)	$354, MS-64BN, Feb-10
1856, Slanting 5		153	61.3	81	60	125	205	270	365	675	1,150 (h)	$230, MS-63BN, Feb-10
1857, All kinds	333,546											
1857, Large Date		439	60.3	74	200	300	400	750	1,000	1,200	2,000	$1,610, MS-65BN CAC, Feb-10
1857, Small Date		65	61.4	78	200	310	430	800	1,100	1,500	2,350	$863, MS-64BN, Feb-10

* Included in number above. **a.** Included in the "1839, All kinds" mintage. **b.** Value in MS-65RD is $7,000. **c.** Value in MS-65RD is $4,500. **d.** Value in MS-65RD is $7,500. **e.** Value in MS-65RD is $7,250. **f.** Value in MS-65RD is $3,400. **g.** Value in MS-65RD is $3,500. **h.** Value in MS-65RD is $3,300. **i.** Value in MS-65RD is $3,750.

Proof Liberty Head, Braided Hair, Large Cents

PF-60 to 70. Except for 1841, Proof Braided Hair cents before 1855 range from rare to very rare. Those from 1855 to 1857 are seen with some frequency. Most later Proofs are well struck and of nice quality, but there are exceptions. Most pieces from this era that have been attributed as Proofs actually are such, but beware of deeply toned "Proofs" that really are prooflike, or circulation strikes with polished fields, recolored. *Obverse and Reverse:* At PF-65 and 66 hairlines show only under high magnification, and at PF-67 none are seen. The fields usually are deeply mirrorlike on issues after 1843, sometimes less so on earlier dates. Striking should be sharp, including the stars (unlike the situation for many Proofs of the Matron Head type). There is no evidence of friction. In lower grades, hairlines are more numerous, with a profusion at PF-60 to 62, and there is also a general dullness of the fields. Typical color for an undipped coin ranges from light or iridescent brown to brown with some traces of mint color. Except for issues after 1854, Proofs are nearly always BN or, less often, RB.

Proof Liberty Head, Braided Hair, Large Cent

	Est Mintage	Cert	Finest	PF-60BN	PF-63BN	PF-64BN	PF-65BN	Recent Auction Record
1840	15–20	8	PF-65			$10,500	$18,000	$17,250, PF-65, Nov-08
1841	30–50	23	PF-66			9,500	14,500	$8,050, PF-65RB, Jun-09
1842	10–20	5	PF-65			11,000	18,000	$10,925, PF-64RB, Oct-06
1843	10–20	8	PF-66			11,000	18,000	$11,500, PF-63BN, Jan-06
1844	10–20	6	PF-65				65,000	$63,250, PF-65RD, Aug-08
1845	8–12	3	PF-65			14,500	22,000	$21,850, PF-65, Nov-08
1846	8–12	2	PF-66			14,500	22,000	$17,250, PF-64RB, Jun-09
1847	8–12	1	PF-64			14,500	22,000	$13,800, PF-64RB, Aug-06
1848	15–20	9	PF-66				29,000	$21,850, PF-66RB, May-09
1849	6–10	3	PF-65		$8,500	14,500	22,000	$21,850, PF-64RD, Jan-10
1850	6–10	3	PF-66			22,500	28,000	$32,200, PF-65, Nov-08
1852	4–6	1	PF-65				45,000	
1853	4–6	1	PF-64			12,500	15,000	
1854	4–6	5	PF-66		8,500	15,000	20,000	$7,475, PF-64BN, Feb-09
1855	15–20	8	PF-65			8,750	17,000	$5,175, PF-64BN, May-09
1856, Large Date	40–60	17	PF-66			7,000	12,500	$7,188, PF-64RB CAC, Nov-09
1857, Large Date	100–150	33	PF-66			7,000	12,500	
1857, Small Date	15–20	5	PF-66			8,000	13,000	$7,188, PF-64BN, May-09

Note: Numismatic anachronisms dated 1868 were struck in nickel and in copper, featuring the large cent design last used in 1857. These likely were quietly and unofficially sold by Mint employees to collectors. They are classified as Judd-610 and 611 in *United States Pattern Coins.*

AN OVERVIEW OF SMALL CENTS

On May 25, 1857, the new small-diameter Flying Eagle cent made its debut. Designed by Chief Engraver James B. Longacre, the obverse featured a flying eagle, copied after Christian Gobrecht's silver dollar of 1836. The reverse showed an agricultural wreath enclosing the denomination. Problems developed with striking the pieces up properly, and in 1859 a new motif, the Indian Head cent, was introduced. With several variations this design was continued through 1909. In that year the Lincoln Wheat Ears cent was introduced. The series was continued for many years, until 1959, when the Memorial Reverse type was introduced, continuing the same Lincoln portrait on the obverse. Then in 2009 several different reverses were introduced to commemorate the 200th anniversary of the birth of Lincoln and in 2010 a new reverse to symbolize Lincoln's preservation of the Union.

Forming a type set of small cents is done easily enough, although the first two issues, the 1857–1858 Flying Eagle cent and the 1859 Indian Head with laurel wreath reverse, can be expensive in higher grades. Striking quality is a consideration for all small cents from 1857 to the end of the Indian Head series in 1909, but enough exist that finding a needle-sharp piece is simply a matter of time. Lincoln cents are easy enough to find sharply struck, though some varieties are more difficult to find this way than others.

FOR THE COLLECTOR AND INVESTOR: SMALL CENTS AS A SPECIALTY

Flying Eagle and Indian Head cents often are collected together by specialists, who usually aspire to add the pattern 1856 Flying Eagle to the series. Proof Flying Eagle and Indian Head cents form a separate specialty and are widely collected. The Flying Eagle and Indian Cent Collectors Society welcomes aficionados of these series. Its journal, *Longacre's Ledger,* serves as a forum for new discoveries, market information, and the exchange of ideas.

One of the foundations of American numismatics is the collecting of Lincoln cents, 1909 to date. Collectors have a wide variety of folders, albums, and holders to choose from; these have a tradition dating back to the 1930s, when R.K. Post of Neenah, Wisconsin, launched his "penny boards" (made for him by Whitman Publishing Co., which later acquired the rights), and Wayte Raymond marketed a series of "National" album pages. Today, a search through pocket change might yield coins dating back to 1959, the first year of the Lincoln Memorial reverse, before which date even high-mintage issues are hardly ever seen. A generation ago it was possible to find cents from 1909 onward. However, key issues such as 1909-S V.D.B. (the most famous of all "popular rarities" in the U.S. series), 1914-D, 1924-D, 1926-S, 1931-S, and 1955 Doubled Die eluded most enthusiasts.

Lincoln cents can be collected casually, or a specialty can be made of them. A dedicated enthusiast may want to secure one each in a grade such as MS-65, also taking care that each is sharply struck. There are quite a few issues, including Denver and San Francisco varieties from about 1916 to the late 1920s, that are plentiful *except* if sharply struck (with full hair detail on the Lincoln portrait, no tiny marks on Lincoln's shoulder, and sharp details and a smooth field on the reverse). With the Mint's rollout of four new reverse designs in 2009, and another in 2010, the Lincoln cent promises to intrigue another generation of Americans and continue to bring new collectors to the hobby.

RECOMMENDED READING

Bowers, Q. David. *A Buyer's and Enthusiast's Guide to Flying Eagle and Indian Head Cents,* Wolfeboro, NH, 1996.

Bowers, Q. David. *A Guide Book of Lincoln Cents,* Atlanta, GA, 2008.

Fivaz, Bill, and Stanton, J.T. *The Cherrypickers' Guide to Rare Die Varieties* (5th ed., vol. I), Atlanta, GA, 2009.

Lange, David W. *The Complete Guide to Lincoln Cents,* Wolfeboro, NH, 1996.

Snow, Richard. *Flying Eagle and Indian Cent Attribution Guide 1856–1909* (2nd ed.), Tuscon, AZ, 2010.

Snow, Richard. *A Guide Book of Flying Eagle and Indian Head Cents* (2nd ed.), Atlanta, GA, 2009.

Steve, Larry, and Flynn, Kevin. *Flying Eagle and Indian Cent Die Varieties,* Jarretteville, MD, 1995.

Taylor, Sol. *The Standard Guide to the Lincoln Cent,* Anaheim, CA, 1999.

Wexler, John, and Flynn, Kevin. *The Authoritative Reference on Lincoln Cents,* Rancocas, NJ, 1996.

FLYING EAGLE
(1857–1858)

Designer James B. Longacre; weight 4.67 grams; composition .880 copper, .120 nickel; diameter 19 mm; plain edge. All coined at Philadelphia Mint.

Shown 1.5x actual size

History. Large copper cents became increasingly expensive to produce, and during the 1850s the U.S. Mint experimented with smaller versions. Finally a new design and format were chosen: the Flying Eagle cent, of smaller diameter and 4.67 grams' weight (compared to nearly 11). Many patterns were made of this design in 1856, and restrikes were extensive, with the result that many numismatists collect the 1856 cent along with the regular series. Distribution of the new cents for circulation commenced on May 25, 1857. Problems resulted from striking the design properly, and the motif was discontinued in 1858. The coins remained in circulation until the early 1900s, by which time any found in pocket change were well worn.

Striking and Sharpness. The heavy wreath on the reverse was opposite in the dies (while in the press) from the head and tail of the eagle on the obverse, and, accordingly, many Flying Eagle cents were weakly struck in these areas. Today, this lightness of strike is most visible at each end of the eagle and on the wreath, particularly the higher areas, and on the vertical separation at the middle of the ribbon knot. Striking weakness is most obvious (especially for novice collectors) on the eagle's tail feathers. Many Flying Eagle cents, however, are quite well struck.

Availability. As a type the Flying Eagle cent is easy to find, although some varieties, such as 1856 and 1858, 8 Over 7, range from scarce to rare. Most are seen in worn grades. In MS, many are in the marketplace, although dipping, cleaning, and recoloring (causing staining and spotting) have eliminated the majority from consideration by connoisseurs.

EF-40, 45 (Extremely Fine). *Obverse:* Wear is more extensive than at AU, especially on the eagle's breast and the top of the closest wing. Wear also shows on the other wing in the area below OF. Marks may be more extensive in the field. The wear is slightly greater at EF-40 than at EF-45, although in the marketplace these two grades are not clearly differentiated. *Reverse:* More wear shows on the higher areas of the wreath, but most detail still is present. There may be tinges of luster in protected areas, more likely at EF-45 than at 40.

AU-50, 53, 55, 58 (About Uncirculated). *Obverse:* At AU-50, light wear is seen on the breast of the eagle, the top edge of the closest wing, and, less so, on the head. As both the head and tail tip can be lightly struck, these are not reliable indicators of grade. Luster is present in traces among the letters. At higher AU levels the evidence of wear diminishes. An AU-58 coin has nearly full luster, but friction is seen in the fields, as are some marks. *Reverse:* At AU-50, light wear is seen on the ribbon bow and the highest areas of the leaves. Some luster is seen (more than on the obverse). Friction is evident, as are some marks, but these will not be as distracting as those on the obverse, as the heavy wreath and lettering are more protective of the reverse field. In higher grades, wear is less, and at AU-58 nearly full—or even completely full—luster is seen.

MS-60 to 70 (Mint State). *Obverse:* Contact marks, most obvious in the field, are evident at MS-60, diminishing at 61, 62, and higher. The eagle, the feathers of which usually hide marks, shows some evidence as well. At MS-65 or finer there is no trace of friction or rubbing. A few tiny nicks or marks may be seen, but none are obvious. Although in practice this is not always consistent, at MS-66 and higher there should be no staining or other problems, and the coin should have good eye appeal overall. *Reverse:* Check the higher parts of the wreath for slight abrasions at MS-60 to 62. Otherwise, the above guidelines apply.

1857, Reverse 25¢ Clash
FS-01-1857-901.

1857, Obverse $20 Clash
FS-01-1857-403.

1858, 8 Over 7
FS-01-1858-101.

1858, Large Letters

1858, Small Letters

Shown 2x actual size.

	Mintage	Cert	Avg	%MS	EF-40	AU-50	MS-60	MS-63	MS-64	MS-65	MS-66	Recent Auction Record
1856 † (a)	2,000				$12,000	$13,500	$16,000	$22,000	$30,000	$55,000		$71,875, MS-65, Jan-10
1857	17,450,000	2,218	60.1	83	150	200	350	725	1,250	3,500	$9,000	$2,530, MS-65, Mar-10
1857, Obv 50¢ Clash (b)	*	n/a	n/a	n/a	230	450	800	1,050				$1,628, MS-64, Apr-09
1857, Rev 25¢ Clash (c)	*	29	47.4	45	200	400	850	2,750				
1857, Obv $20 Clash (d)	*	9	19.3	0	2,100	5,000	15,000					

* Included in number above. † Ranked in the *100 Greatest U.S. Coins* (third edition). **a.** Actually a pattern, but collected along with the regular issue since it shares the same design. See *United States Pattern Coins*, 10th edition. **b.** The obverse die was clashed with the obverse die of a Liberty Seated half dollar. This is most evident through AMERICA. **c.** The reverse die was clashed with the reverse die of a Liberty Seated quarter dollar. The outline of the eagle's head is evident above ONE. **d.** The obverse die was clashed with the obverse die of a Liberty Head double eagle.

Chart continued on next page.

	Mintage	Cert	Avg	%MS	EF-40	AU-50	MS-60	MS-63	MS-64	MS-65	MS-66	Recent Auction Record
1858, All kinds	24,600,000											
1858, Lg Ltrs		852	58.0	75	$150	$200	$350	$725	$1,250	$3,500	$9,000	$1,150, MS-64, Jun-10
1858, 8 Over 7 (d)		135	51.1	53	875	1,450	4,000	10,000	20,000	45,000		$8,625, MS-63, Jun-10
1858, Sm Ltrs		859	57.1	73	150	200	350	725	1,250	3,500	9,000	$2,530, MS-65, Feb-10

* Included in regular 1857 mintage. **d.** The flag of the upper-right corner of a 7 can be seen above the second 8 in the date. There is a raised triangular dot in the field above the first 8. Late-die-state specimens are worth considerably less than the values listed, which are for early die states.

Proof Flying Eagle Cents

PF-60 to 70 (Proof). Proof 1856 Flying Eagle cents are the most plentiful of the available dates, surviving from perhaps 2,000 to 2,500 or more struck for sale to collectors beginning in 1859. Proofs of 1857 are very rare. Proofs of 1858 are rare, but significantly more readily available than those of 1857. A first-class Proof should have a fully and deeply mirrored field on both sides, except for those of 1856, which are usually a combination of mirrorlike and grainy in character. Note that some prooflike Mint State coins have wrongly been called Proofs. Quality is a challenge, and problem-free examples are in the minority. *Obverse and Reverse:* PF-65 coins have very few hairlines, and these are visible only under a strong magnifying glass. At PF-67 and higher there should be no evidence at all of hairlines or friction. PF-60 coins can be dull from repeated dipping and cleaning. (Proofs are without hairlines when struck; any hairlines on a Proof were caused by abrasive cleaning.) At PF-63 the mirrorlike fields should be attractive, with no rubbing, and with hairlines minimal (best seen when the coin is held at an angle to the light). PF-64 coins are even nicer.

Proof Flying Eagle Cent

	Est Mintage	Cert	Finest	PF-60	PF-63	PF-64	PF-65	PF-66	Recent Auction Record
1856	1,500	367	PF-67	$15,000	$20,000	$25,000	$35,000		$15,525, PF-64, Jun-10
1857	485	31	PF-66	5,000	8,500	13,500	25,000		$18,400, PF-65Cam, Jan-10
1858, Large Letters	100	34	PF-67	5,000	8,500	13,500	25,000		$31,050, PF-67Cam, Feb-10
1858, Small Letters	200	23	PF-66	5,000	8,850	13,500	25,000		$7,705, PF-63 CAC, Mar-10

INDIAN HEAD
(1859–1909)

Variety 1 (Copper-Nickel, Laurel Wreath Reverse, 1859): Designer James B. Longacre; weight 4.67 grams; composition .880 copper, .120 nickel; diameter 19 mm; plain edge. All coined at Philadelphia Mint.

Copper-Nickel, Laurel Wreath Reverse, Without Shield (1859 Only)

Variety 2 (Copper-Nickel, Oak Wreath With Shield, 1860–1864): Designer James B. Longacre; weight 4.67 grams; composition .880 copper, .120 nickel; diameter 19 mm; plain edge. All coined at Philadelphia Mint.

Copper-Nickel, Oak Wreath Reverse, With Shield (1860–1864)

Variety 3 (Bronze, 1864–1909): Designer James B. Longacre; weight 3.11 grams; composition .950 copper, .050 tin and zinc; diameter 19 mm; plain edge; mints: Philadelphia, San Francisco.

Bronze, Oak Wreath Reverse, With Shield (1864–1909)

History. After nearly a dozen varieties of patterns were made in 1858, in 1859 the Indian Head was adopted as the new motif for the cent. The reverse of the 1859 coin illustrates an olive (or laurel) wreath. In 1860 this was changed to a wreath of oak and other leaves with a shield at the apex, a design continued through the end of the series in 1909. From 1859 through spring 1864 cents were struck in copper-nickel, the alloy used earlier for Flying Eagle cents. In 1864 a new bronze alloy was adopted.

Indian Head cents remained in circulation through the 1940s, but were rarely seen by the early 1950s. In the 1930s, when Whitman and other coin boards and folders became widely available for collectors, many key dates were picked out of circulation. The typical grade for the scarce issues of the 1870s was Good or so, and the 1908-S and 1909-S could be found in VF.

Striking and Sharpness. The strike on Indian Head cents can vary widely. On the obverse the points to check include the details at the tips of the feathers and the diamonds on the ribbon. The diamonds *cannot* be used as a grading marker, and the feather tips can be used only if you have familiarity with how sharp the coin was struck to begin with. In general, the reverse is usually sharper, but check the leaf and shield details. On many bronze cents beginning in the 1870s the bottom of N (ONE) and tops of EN (CENT) are light, as they were in the dies (not factored when grading).

Check the dentils on both sides. Generally, copper-nickel cents of the early 1860s are candidates for light striking as are later issues in the bronze format, of the 1890s onward.

Availability. In worn grades Indian Head cents are available in proportion to their mintages, in combination with survival rates being higher for the later issues. The low-mintage 1909-S was saved in larger quantities than the higher-mintage 1877, as an example. MS coins survive as a matter of chance, with those of 1878 and before being much scarcer than those of 1879 and later, and some of the 1900s being readily available. Collectors who wanted single pieces often bought Proofs. Many if not most higher-grade MS coins have been dipped or recolored, unless they are a warm orange-red color with traces of natural brown. The search for quality among bronze cents is particularly challenging. Some tiny toning flecks are to be expected on many coins, and as long as they are microscopic they can often be ignored (except in grades on the far side of MS-65). A set of MS-65 coins in RB or RD can be formed quickly, but one with *original* color, sharp strike, and excellent eye appeal may take several years.

In the late 1930s, many 1878–1909 Proof Indian Head cents began to be released from several estate hoards. These had vivid violet and blue iridescent toning from being stored for decades in tissue paper. They are highly sought-after today.

EF-40, 45 (Extremely Fine). *Obverse:* Wear is more extensive than at AU, but all of LIBERTY is very clear. Wear is seen on the hair above and below the ear, on the central portion of the ribbon, and on the feather tips. Overall the coin is bold. Scattered marks are normal for this and lower grades, most often seen on the cheek and in the field. *Reverse:* The higher-relief parts of the leaves and ribbon bow show light wear, but details are sharp in lower areas. Some tiny lines in the vertical stripes in the shield may be blended. Scattered marks may be present, but on all grades they are usually fewer on the reverse than on the obverse.

AU-50, 53, 55, 58 (About Uncirculated). *Obverse:* At AU-50, wear is most noticeable on the hair above the ear, on the central portion of the ribbon, on the curl to the right of the ribbon, and near the feather tips, although the last is not a reliable indicator due to striking. Luster is present, but mostly in protected areas. At AU-53 and 55, wear is less. At AU-58 friction is evident, rather than actual wear. Luster, toned brown, is nearly complete at AU-58, but may be incomplete in the field. *Reverse:* At AU-50, light wear is seen on the ribbon and the higher-relief areas of the leaves, while the lower areas retain their detail. Some luster may be present in protected areas. At AU-53 and 55, wear is less and luster is more extensive. An AU-58 coin has nearly full luster and shows only light friction.

MS-60 to 70 (Mint State). *Obverse:* Contact marks, most obvious in the field, are evident at MS-60, diminishing at MS-61, 62, and higher. This abrasion is most noticeable on copper-nickel cents; on bronze issues, it blends in with the background. Liberty's cheek and the field show some evidence as well. Typical color is BN, occasionally RB at MS-63 and 64, unless dipped to be RD. At MS-65 or finer there is no trace of abrasion. A few tiny nicks or marks may be seen, but none are obvious. At MS-67 and finer the coin will approach perfection. Check so-called RD coins for originality. A theoretically perfect MS-70 will have no marks at all, even under a strong magnifier. Although in practice this is not always consistent, at MS-66 and higher there should be no staining or other problems, and the coin should have good eye appeal overall. *Reverse:* Check the high parts of the wreath for abrasion. Otherwise the above comments apply.

1860, Pointed Bust

1860, Rounded Bust

1863, Doubled-Die Reverse
FS-01-1863-801.

1864, No L

1864, With L

1865, Die Gouge in Headdress
FS-01-1865-1302.

1865, Doubled-Die Reverse
FS-01-1865-1801.

1869, 9 Over 9
FS-01-1869-301.

Shallow N

Bold N

1870, Doubled-Die
Reverse
FS-01-1870-801.

1873, Close 3

1873, Open 3

1873, Doubled LIBERTY
FS-01-1873-101.

1875, Dot
Reverse

1880, Doubled-Die
Obverse, Reverse Clash
FS-01-1880-101.

1882, Misplaced Date
FS-01-1882-401.

1886, Variety 1
*The last feather points
between the I and the C
in AMERICA.*

1886, Variety 2
*The last feather points
between the C and the A
in AMERICA.*

1887, Doubled-Die Obverse
FS-01-1887-101.

1891, Doubled-Die Obverse
FS-01-1891-101.

1888, Last 8 Over 7
FS-01-1888-301.

1894, Doubled Date
FS-01-1894-301.

COPPER-NICKEL COINAGE

	Mintage	Cert	Avg	%MS	EF-40	AU-50	MS-60	MS-63	MS-64	MS-65	MS-66	Recent Auction Record
1859	36,400,000	1,370	60.5	81	$110	$200	$250	$600	$1,200	$3,500	$5,000	$2,185, MS-65, Jun-10
1860, Rounded Bust	20,566,000	869	62.7	90	65	100	185	250	425	1,200	3,200	$2,990, MS-66, Feb-10
1860, Pointed Bust	*	100	60.8	89	90	150	290	575	1,150	2,200	10,000	$1,121, MS-64, Mar-10
1861	10,100,000	748	62.4	87	110	175	275	300	500	1,100	3,000	$2,990, MS-66, Jun-10
1862	28,075,000	1,303	62.7	92	45	70	100	175	360	1,000	3,000	$431, MS-64, Mar-10
1863	49,840,000	1,670	62.6	92	45	70	100	175	360	1,000	3,000	$322, MS-64, Feb-10
1863, DblDie Rev (a)	*	2	62.5	100	200	375	450	950	2,000	3,000		
1864, Copper-Nickel	13,740,000	1,005	62.7	92	90	135	175	300	500	1,600	4,300	$109, AU-55, Feb-10

* Included in number above. **a.** Strong doubling is evident on the right leaves of the wreath, and, to a lesser degree, on the upper left leaves.

BRONZE COINAGE

	Mintage	Cert	Avg	%MS	AU-50	MS-60BN	MS-63BN	MS-64RB	MS-64RD	MS-65RB	MS-65RD	Recent Auction Record
1864, Bronze, All kinds	39,233,714											
1864, No L		7	61.3	57	$90	$115	$150	$225	$400	$375	$825	$834, MS-65RD, Feb-10
1864, With L		992	56.5	66	375	425	600	950	1,800	1,700	5,000	$633, MS-64BN, Feb-10
1865	35,429,286	775	63.3	94	65	90	150	250	550	500	1,750	$1,265, MS-65RB, Feb-10
1865, Die Gouge in Headdress	*				500	750	1,200					
1865, DblDie Reverse	*	6	53.5	67	*1,100*	2,200	5,500					$2,185, MS-61BN, Mar-10
1866	9,826,500	685	59.9	79	250	290	380	775	1,950	1,500	5,250	$1,840, MS-66RB CAC, Jun-10
1867	9,821,000	690	58.5	78	275	300	400	850	2,000	1,600	6,000	$8,050, MS-65RD, May-10
1868	10,266,500	597	59.8	80	220	250	360	600	1,150	900	3,000	$1,150, MS-66RB, Mar-10
1869	6,420,000	652	54.7	69	500	550	700	1,250	2,150	1,800	4,500	$2,530, MS-64RD CAC, Feb-10
1869, 9 Over 9	*	231	47.6	49	800	900	1,100	1,500	2,200	2,000		$1,265, MS-65BN CAC, Jun-10
1870, Shallow N (a)	5,275,000	593	55.8	69	500	550	900	1,000	1,500	1,500		$1,265, MS-64RD CAC, Oct-09
1870, Bold N (a)	*				450	500	850	900	1,200	1,200	4,300	$1,265, MS-65RB, Mar-10
1870, DblDie Reverse	*	6	64.2	100	750	850	1,000	1,300	2,500	2,500		$1,380, MS-64 CAC, Feb-10
1871, Shallow N (a)	3,929,500	619	54.4	65	650	775	950	1,100	2,700	2,600		$51,750, MS-66RD, Jun-08
1871, Bold N (a)	*				525	550	800	1,250	2,550	2,350	7,250	$1,783, MS-65RB, Mar-10
1872, Shallow N (a)	4,042,000	703	51.7	57	700	950	1,250	2,150	4,700	4,500		$978, MS-62RB, Feb-10
1872, Bold N (a)	*				650	750	1,100	1,750	4,500	3,200	13,000	$5,635, MS-64RD, Mar-10

* Included in number above. **a.** Cents dated 1869 and earlier have a shallow N in CENTS. Those dated 1870, 1871, or 1872 have either shallow N or bold N. Those dated 1873 to 1876 all have the bold N. Circulation strikes of 1877 have the shallow N, while Proofs have the bold N.

	Mintage	Cert	Avg	%MS	AU-50	MS-60BN	MS-63BN	MS-64RB	MS-64RD	MS-65RB	MS-65RD	Recent Auction Record
1873, All kinds	11,676,500											
1873, Close 3		196	59.5	76	$235	$425	$550	$800	$1,850	$2,250	$7,500	$1,265, MS-64RB, Jun-10
1873, Doubled LIBERTY		103	46.6	40	4,500	7,500	13,500			47,500		$5,463, MS-61BN, Sep-09
1873, Open 3		289	59.3	74	190	250	325	485	1,200	1,275	4,300	$1,294, MS-65RB, Mar-10
1874	14,187,500	598	61.7	85	150	225	250	375	690	625	3,750	$748, MS-64RD, Mar-10
1875	13,528,000	593	61.3	87	160	235	260	360	1,000	750	2,700	$138, AU-55, Feb-10
1875, Dot Reverse (a)	*						—					
1876	7,944,000	534	60.3	81	240	300	380	625	1,200	925	2,550	$460, MS-63BN, Mar-10
1877 (b)	852,500	1,781	27.0	17	3,000	3,500	4,500	8,000	9,000	11,000	22,000	$920, VG-10, Jun-10
1878	5,797,500	520	61.2	87	275	325	380	500	925	950	2,200	$1,840, MS-65RD, Jan-10
1879	16,228,000	634	63.1	95	80	90	120	235	435	425	1,300	$1,156, MS-67BN, Mar-10
1880	38,961,000	570	63.7	98	60	80	130	225	450	350	1,300	$4,198, MS-66RD CAC, Mar-10
1880, DblDie Obv, Rev Clash (c)	*	6	64.0	100	400	750	1,500	1,750	2,100	2,000	2,900	
1881	39,208,000	608	63.5	98	35	60	90	215	325	315	1,150	$1,006, MS-65RD, Mar-10
1882	38,578,000	607	63.7	97	35	60	90	215	325	315	1,350	$104, MS-63BRB, Feb-10
1882, Misplaced Date (d)	*	3	64.3	100	450	875	1,700	3,000		6,000		
1883	45,591,500	602	63.8	98	35	60	90	215	325	315	1,150	$1,265, MS-67RB, Jun-10
1884	23,257,800	554	63.8	98	40	75	120	260	450	450	1,650	$920, MS-65RD, Mar-10
1885	11,761,594	492	63.4	93	80	110	200	335	550	650	2,100	$2,300, MS-65RD, Jun-10
1886, All kinds	17,650,000											
1886, Variety 1		210	59.7	74	175	200	250	475	1,150	975	4,000	$403, MS-64RB, Mar-10
1886, Variety 2		341	60.9	79	220	325	500	1,150	2,550	2,900	12,500	$1,265, MS-64RB CAC, Mar-10
1887	45,223,523	455	63.0	96	28	55	80	190	475	575	1,600	$322, MS-65RB, Feb-10
1887, DblDie Obverse	*	21	42.2	24	490	1,000	2,500	3,500		8,000		$431, MS-64RB, Mar-10
1888	37,489,832	569	61.8	93	27	65	125	365	650	725	2,250	$12,075, EF-40 CAC, Jul-09
1888, Last 8 Over 7	*	7	49.0	29	16,500	22,500	33,000					$1,173, MS-65RD, Mar-10
1889	48,866,025	602	62.9	95	27	60	80	180	460	400	2,000	$253, MS-64RB, Jan-10
1890	57,180,114	533	63.6	98	27	60	80	180	410	400	1,150	$805, MS-65RD, Mar-10
1891	47,070,000	604	63.3	97	27	60	80	180	400	385	1,100	
1891, DblDie Obverse	*	9	45.7	33	450	775	1,150					$518, MS-65RD, Mar-10
1892	37,647,087	564	63.5	98	27	60	80	185	385	375	1,100	$99, MS-64BN, Feb-10
1893	46,640,000	668	63.8	98	27	60	80	170	375	255	950	$6,900, MS-66RD, Jan-10
1894	16,749,500	554	63.2	95	65	80	115	200	350	380	1,075	$1,840, MS-62BN, Jan-10
1894, Doubled Date	*	72	52.6	61	350	575	1,150	2,200	4,800	3,700	9,000	$863, MS-65RD, Mar-10
1895	38,341,574	687	63.8	98	25	40	65	140	260	200	800	$230, MS-64RD, Feb-10
1896	39,055,431	505	63.8	98	25	40	65	140	260	220	925	$1,265, MS-65RD CAC, Jan-10
1897	50,464,392	607	63.1	96	25	40	65	125	260	200	925	$62, MS-63RB, Mar-10
1898	49,821,284	658	63.6	98	25	40	65	115	230	195	575	$437, MS-65RD, Feb-10
1899	53,598,000	1,135	64.1	98	25	40	65	115	210	195	460	$1,093, MS-67RB CAC, Jan-10
1900	66,831,502	713	63.7	97	20	38	55	90	185	170	460	$1,093, MS-67RB, Mar-10
1901	79,609,158	1,207	63.8	98	20	38	55	90	185	170	440	$12,650, MS-67RD, Feb-10
1902	87,374,704	1,194	63.4	97	20	38	55	90	185	170	485	$116, MS-64RB, Feb-10
1903	85,092,703	1,075	63.3	96	20	38	55	90	185	170	440	$89, MS-64RB, Mar-10
1904	61,326,198	895	63.5	97	20	38	55	90	185	170	460	$161, MS-65RB, Feb-10
1905	80,717,011	1,109	63.4	97	20	38	55	90	185	170	490	$322, MS-66BN, Mar-10
1906	96,020,530	1,231	63.1	96	20	38	55	90	185	170	440	$403, MS-65RD, Dec-09
1907	108,137,143	1,300	63.0	96	20	38	55	90	185	170	440	$100, MS-64RB, Mar-10
1908	32,326,367	1,170	63.7	98	20	38	55	90	185	170	440	$1,150, MS-64RD, Mar-10
1908S	1,115,000	1,495	51.9	59	250	290	385	600	1,150	850	2,200	$403, MS-65RD, Feb-10
1909	14,368,470	1,590	63.5	98	30	45	65	95	190	175	440	$13,800, MS-66RD, Jun-10
1909S	309,000	1,759	43.5	43	900	1,000	1,200	1,475	1,900	2,400	4,600	

* Included in number above. **a.** In 1875, Mint officials suspected a longtime employee was stealing Indian Head cents. They secretly modified a reverse die by making a small gouge in the N in ONE, and then put the die into production one morning. Later that morning the suspect employee was called aside. He was asked to empty his pockets, revealing 33 of the marked cents. At first he insisted his son gave him this pocket change, but when confronted with the secretly marked die, he admitted his guilt. He tendered his resignation, disgraced, after more than 50 years of service to the Mint. The market value for this variety is not yet reliably established. **b.** Beware the numerous counterfeits and altered-date 1877 cents. The latter typically are altered from 1875- or 1879-dated cents. **c.** Doubling is visible on the obverse in higher grades, as a very close spread on LIBERTY. The primary diagnostic, though, is the misaligned die clash evident on the reverse, with obvious reeding running from the upper-right leaf tip, through the E of ONE, and down to the very top of the N of CENT. **d.** The bases of at least four 1s are evident within the beads of the necklace.

Proof Indian Head Cents

PF-60 to 70 (Proof). Proof Indian Head cents were made of all dates, 1859 to 1909. The 1864 bronze variety with a tiny L (for designer James B. Longacre) on the ribbon is a rarity, with only about two dozen known. Generally, Proofs are sharp strikes until the 1890s, when some can be weak. On bronze coins tiny carbon flecks are typical, but should be microscopic. The majority of Proofs have been dipped, and many bronze pieces have been retoned. Most undipped coins are either rich brown, or red and brown. Extra value can be found in BN and RB—investors typically don't buy them, instead preferring RD coins, most of which have actually been dipped.

Proofs are generally designated BN if the surfaces are mainly brown or iridescent, or have up to perhaps 30% original mint

red-orange color. RB is designated if the surface is a mixture of red-orange and brown (best if blended together nicely, but often with patches of mint color among brown areas). RD designates a coin with original mint-red orange, always blending to slight natural brown toning unless the coin has been dipped. Likely, any RD coin with even a few hairlines has been cleaned (or at least mishandled) at one time; in most such cases, the RD is not original. Certification services take no notice of this. For this reason, a connoisseur will prefer a BN PF-63 coin with no hairlines to a PF-65 or 66 RD coin with some hairlines. The BN coin can always be dipped and cleaned (though this is not advised).

Proof copper-nickel Indian Head cents of 1859 to 1864 need no letters to indicate

color. As a general rule, these survive in higher grades and with greater eye appeal, as they stayed "brilliant" and did not need dipping. Moreover, when such pieces were cleaned and acquired hairlines, they tended to be fewer than on a bronze coin, due to the very hard nature of the copper-nickel alloy.

Obverse and Reverse: PF-60 coins can be dull from repeated dipping and cleaning and are often toned iridescent colors. At PF-63 the mirrorlike fields should be attractive, and hairlines should be minimal; no rubbing is seen. PF-64 coins are even nicer. At PF-65 there are very few hairlines, visible only under strong magnification. At PF-67 or higher there should be no evidence of hairlines or friction; such a coin is fully original (not cleaned).

Proof Indian Head Cent

	Est Mintage	Cert	Finest	PF-63	PF-64	PF-65	PF-66	Recent Auction Record
1859	800	179	PF-67	$1,400	$2,500	$4,500	$7,900	$4,505, PF-66, Mar-10
1860, Rounded Bust	1,000	55	PF-68	900	1,600	2,750	6,000	$6,325, PF-66 CAC, Jan-10
1861	1,000	77	PF-66	1,300	3,150	6,750	9,500	$805, PF-62, Jul-09
1862	550	306	PF-68	725	1,050	1,850	2,800	$805, PF-62, Feb-10
1863	460	133	PF-67	725	1,100	2,250	4,300	$1,150, PF-64 CAC, Feb-10
1864, Copper-Nickel	370	145	PF-67	750	1,250	2,400	4,500	$6,613, PF-66Cam CAC, Jan-10

	Mintage	Cert	Finest	PF-63BN	PF-63RB	PF-64RB	PF-64RD	PF-65RD	PF-66RD	Recent Auction Record
1864, Bronze, No L	150+	113	PF-67	$500	$1,000	$1,750	$2,900	$7,500		$4,313, PF-65RD, Jul-09
1864, Bronze, With L	20+	6	PF-66		24,000	45,000	95,000			$109,250, PF-64RD, Jul-08
1865	500+	134	PF-67	375	500	600	1,850	6,500		$886, PF-64RB, Mar-10
1866	725+	108	PF-67	400	500	600	2,000	4,400	$7,000	$2,530, PF-66RB CAC, Jun-10
1867	625+	171	PF-67	400	500	600	1,850	4,300	6,750	$1,451, PF-66RB CAC, Mar-10
1868	600+	114	PF-67	375	415	550	1,300	4,650	15,000	$489, PF-64RB, Mar-10
1869	600+	150	PF-67	380	550	650	1,150	2,650		$1,441, PF-64RDCam CAC, Mar-10
1870, Shallow N	1,000+	158	PF-66	425	650	725	1,000	2,500		$2,185, PF-64RD CAC, Feb-10
1870, Bold N	*			325	385	525	925	1,900	3,800	
1871, Shallow N	960+	179	PF-66	500	750	875	1,200	2,350	7,500	$1,150, PF-65RB, Feb-10
1871, Bold N	*			325	500	600	950	2,150	3,750	
1872, Bold N (a)	950+	203	PF-66	400	600	700	1,900	4,300	6,400	$1,265, PF-65RB, Feb-10
1873, Close 3	1,100+	213	PF-66	265	325	550	775	2,050	8,300	$1,898, PF-65RD, Mar-10
1874	700	140	PF-67	250	300	400	675	2,100	3,750	$3,680, PF-66RD CAC, Mar-10
1875	700	165	PF-67	250	300	500	1,600	4,500	11,500	$2,013, PF-66RB, Mar-10
1876	1,150	188	PF-67	250	325	450	725	1,900	4,600	$2,415, PF-65RD CAC, Feb-10
1877	900	241	PF-67	2,500	3,500	4,000	5,500	10,500	15,000	$5,750, PF-65RB, Jun-10
1878	2,350	284	PF-67	235	285	450	575	1,000	1,800	$978, PF-65RD, Mar-10
1879	3,200	334	PF-68	150	215	325	425	890	1,650	$920, PF-66RB, Mar-10
1880	3,955	356	PF-67	150	185	325	425	865	1,650	$334, PF-64RB, Feb-10

* Included in number above. **a.** Proofs of 1872 were struck only with the bold N, not the shallow N.

	Mintage	Cert	Finest	PF-63BN	PF-63RB	PF-64RB	PF-64RD	PF-65RD	PF-66RD	Recent Auction Record
1881	3,575	350	PF-68	$150	$185	$325	$400	$865	$1,600	$1,495, PF-66RD, Jun-10
1882	3,100	338	PF-67	150	185	325	500	1,000	2,150	$1,150, PF-65RD, Jan-10
1883	6,609	504	PF-67	150	185	325	500	1,200	3,000	$219, PF-63RB, Jan-10
1884	3,942	440	PF-68	150	185	325	400	900	1,550	$920, PF-66RB, Mar-10
1885	3,790	407	PF-68	150	185	325	450	1,200	1,950	$403, PF-65BN, Mar-10
1886, All kinds	4,290									
1886, Variety 1		88	PF-67	150	200	325	575	1,800	3,100	$207, PF-64BN, Dec-09
1886, Variety 2		63	PF-67	350	475	690				$1,725, PF-65RB, Feb-10
1887	2,960	276	PF-67	150	185	300	950	3,300	9,000	$920, PF-66RB, Jan-10
1888	4,582	237	PF-67	150	185	315	1,100	3,300	9,000	$299, PF-65BN, Aug-09
1889	3,336	239	PF-66	150	185	315	500	1,750	3,750	$748, PF-65RB, Feb-10
1890	2,740	224	PF-66	150	185	315	500	1,650	2,350	$374, PF-65RB, Feb-10
1891	2,350	246	PF-67	150	185	315	575	1,375	3,800	$753, PF-65RB, Mar-10
1892	2,745	262	PF-67	150	185	315	450	875	1,750	$6,555, PF-67RD CAC, Mar-10
1893	2,195	225	PF-67	150	185	315	500	1,100	2,600	$1,265, PF-66RD, Mar-10
1894	2,632	251	PF-67	150	185	325	465	1,000	2,450	$477, PF-64RD, Mar-10
1895	2,062	234	PF-67	160	205	315	450	835	1,550	$834, PF-65RD CAC, Jan-10
1896	1,862	193	PF-66	150	185	300	450	1,350	3,250	$259, PF-64BN, Mar-10
1897	1,938	222	PF-67	150	185	300	450	1,200	2,200	$481, PF-65RB, Mar-10
1898	1,795	233	PF-67	150	185	300	425	800	1,675	$854, PF-66RB, Mar-10
1899	2,031	221	PF-67	150	185	300	425	800	1,500	$1,380, PF-66RD, Jan-10
1900	2,262	212	PF-68	140	185	300	425	825	1,500	$748, PF-65RD, Jan-10
1901	1,985	251	PF-68	140	185	285	400	800	1,500	$5,175, PF-66RD CAC, Jun-10
1902	2,018	246	PF-68	140	185	285	425	775	1,475	$5,060, PF-66RD Cam CAC, Jun-10
1903	1,790	222	PF-68	140	185	285	400	775	1,700	$1,495, PF-65RD CAC, Jan-10
1904	1,817	211	PF-67	140	185	285	475	950	1,600	$403, PF-64RD, Mar-10
1905	2,152	213	PF-67	140	185	285	425	800	1,850	$6,325, PF-67RD, Jan-10
1906	1,725	185	PF-67	140	185	285	425	800	1,800	$403, PF-64RD, Mar-10
1907	1,475	183	PF-67	140	185	285	425	875	2,300	$2,013, PF-66RD, Jan-10
1908	1,620	239	PF-67	140	185	285	425	800	2,750	$288, PF-64BN, Feb-10
1909	2,175	219	PF-67	140	185	285	425	1,250	3,500	$288, PF-64RB, Mar-10

LINCOLN, WHEAT EARS REVERSE
(1909–1958)

Variety 1 (Bronze, 1909–1942): Designer Victor D. Brenner; weight 3.11 grams; composition .950 copper, .050 tin and zinc; diameter 19 mm; plain edge; mints: Philadelphia, Denver, San Francisco.

Variety 1, Bronze (1909–1942)

Variety 2 (Steel, 1943): Weight 2.70 grams; composition steel, coated with zinc; diameter 19 mm; plain edge.

Variety 2, Steel (1943)

Variety 1 Resumed (1944–1958): 1944–1946—Weight, 3.11 grams; composition .950 copper, .050 zinc; diameter 19 mm; plain edge. 1947–1958—Weight 3.11 grams; composition .950 copper, .050 tin and zinc; diameter 19 mm.

Variety 1 Resumed, Bronze (1944–1958)

Continued on next page.

History. The Lincoln cent, designed by Victor David Brenner, was first released on August 2, 1909. The earliest issues had Brenner's initials (V.D.B.) on the reverse; this was soon discontinued. In 1943, during World War II, zinc-coated steel was used for planchets, as copper was needed for the war effort. The Philadelphia, Denver, and San Francisco mints all produced these coins, but not in all years.

Striking and Sharpness. As a rule, Lincoln cents of 1909 through 1914 are fairly well struck. From 1915 through the end of the 1920s, many are weak, with Denver Mint coins particularly so. Issues of the 1930s onward are mostly well struck. With many different die pairs used over a long period of time, striking quality varies. On the obverse, check for details in Lincoln's hair and beard. Also check the lettering and the inner edge of the rim. *Tiny marks on the shoulder of Lincoln indicate a weak strike there;* this area cannot be used to determine *wear* on high-grade coins. (During striking, there was not enough die pressure to fill this, the deepest point of the obverse die; therefore, stray marks on the raw

planchet remain evident in this spot.) On the reverse check the wheat stalks, letters, and inner rim. A weak strike will usually manifest itself on the O of ONE (the area directly opposite Lincoln's shoulder). Coins struck from overused or "tired" dies can have grainy or even slightly wavy fields on either side.

Availability. Cents of 1909 are easily found in MS; later dates are scarcer, although Philadelphia varieties were made in higher quantities and are more often seen. Beginning in the early 1930s, bank-wrapped rolls of Mint State cents were saved in large quantities (starting mainly in 1934, though the low-mintage 1931-S was also hoarded). Dates after this time all are plentiful, although some more so than others, and there are a number of scarce and rare varieties. The demand for scarcer Lincoln cents and higher-grade issues is intense, resulting in a strong market. Many Mint State coins before the 1930s have been dipped and recolored, this being particularly true of pieces listed as RD. Others are stained and blotchy. See the Indian Head cents commentary for similar situations.

AU-50, 53, 55, 58 (About Uncirculated). *Obverse:* Slight wear shows on Lincoln's cheekbone to the left of his nose, and also on his beard. At AU-55 or 58 there may be some hints of mint red-orange. Most coins in AU are BN, but often are not qualified by color. *Reverse:* Slight wear is evident on the stalks of wheat to the left and right. Otherwise, the same standards apply as for the obverse.

MS-60 to 70 (Mint State). *Obverse and Reverse:* At MS-65 and higher, the luster is rich on all areas,

except perhaps the shoulder (which may be grainy and show original planchet surface). There is no rubbing, and no contact marks are visible except under magnification. Coins with full or nearly full mint orange-red color can be designated RD; those with full or nearly full brown-toned surfaces can be designated BN; and those with a substantial percentage of red-orange and of brown can be called RB. Ideally, MS-65 or finer coins should have good eye appeal, which in the RB category means nicely blended colors, not stained or blotched. Below MS-65, full RD coins become scarce,

and at MS-60 to 62 are virtually non-existent, unless they have been dipped. Copper is a very active metal, and influences such as slight abrasions, contact marks, and so on that define the grade also affect the color. The official American Numismatic Association grading standards allow for "dull" and/or "spotted" coins at MS-60 and 61, as well as incomplete luster. In the marketplace, interpretations often vary widely. BN and RB coins at MS-60 and 61 tend to be more attractive than (dipped) RD coins.

Designer's initials, V.D.B.
(1909 Reverse Only)

No V.D.B. on Reverse
(1909–1958)

V.D.B. on Shoulder
(Starting 1918)

Mintmark
Location

1909-S, S Over
Horizontal S
FS-01-1909S-1502.

1917, Doubled-Die
Obverse
FS-01-1917-101.

1922, No D
FS-01-1922-401.
Shown 1.5x actual size.

1922, Weak D

1934, Doubled-Die
Obverse
FS-01-1934-101.

1936, Doubled-Die Obverse
FS-01-1936-101.

1943-D, Boldly Doubled
Mintmark
FS-01-1943D-501.

1944-D, D Over S
FS-01-1944D-511.

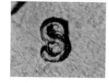
1946-S, S Over D
FS-01-1946S-511.

1951-D, D Over S
FS-01-1951D-512.

1955, Doubled-Die Obverse
FS-01-1955-101.
Shown 2x actual size.

1955, Doubled-Die Obverse,
Closeup of Date

1956-D, D Above
Shadow D
FS-01-1956D-508.

1958, Doubled-Die Obverse
FS-01-1958-101.

	Mintage	Cert	Avg	%MS	MS-63BN	MS-64BN	MS-64RB	MS-64RD	MS-65RB	MS-65RD	MS-66RD	Recent Auction Record
1909, V.D.B.	27,995,000	7,479	63.3	96	$30.00	$40.00	$65.00	$100.00	$100	$195	$340	$1,955, MS-67RD CAC, Jun-10
1909S, V.D.B. † (a)	484,000	5,457	48.1	51	1,800.00	2,200.00	2,450.00	3,300.00	3,400	5,250	14,000	$13,800, MS-66RD, Jun-10
1909	72,702,618	1,159	63.5	97	20.00	27.00	45.00	90.00	80	160	375	$3,220, MS-67RD, Jun-10
1909S	1,825,000	1,747	46.6	56	365.00	405.00	460.00	535.00	625	1,050	2,950	$2,990, MS-66RD, Jun-10
1909S, S Over Horiz S	*	329	57.3	81	370.00	420.00	480.00	585.00	725	1,250	3,000	$1,265, MS-65RD, Jun-10
1910	146,801,218	816	64.2	98	25.00	50.00	55.00	70.00	140	230	775	$10,350, MS-67RD, Jun-10
1910S	6,045,000	814	62.4	92	120.00	140.00	225.00	325.00	400	625	2,650	$13,800, MS-67RD, Jun-10
1911	101,177,787	459	64.1	99	50.00	65.00	100.00	180.00	150	360	1,750	$12,650, MS-67RD, Jun-10
1911D	12,672,000	568	60.6	84	125.00	195.00	310.00	465.00	650	1,450	6,350	$3,738, MS-66RD, Jun-10
1911S	4,026,000	526	58.9	77	235.00	335.00	465.00	600.00	900	2,600	17,500	$16,100, MS-66RD, Jun-10
1912	68,153,060	469	63.7	97	50.00	65.00	100.00	150.00	200	425	1,400	$16,100, MS-67RD, Jun-10
1912D	10,411,000	404	61.0	84	240.00	275.00	335.00	700.00	700	1,950	13,500	$9,200, MS-66RD, Jun-10
1912S	4,431,000	477	58.7	78	255.00	290.00	345.00	750.00	1,000	3,500		$2,313, MS-65RD, Jun-10
1913	76,532,352	496	63.8	98	55.00	70.00	100.00	150.00	175	400	1,900	$25,300, MS-67RD, Jun-10
1913D	15,804,000	427	61.2	88	175.00	225.00	375.00	525.00	700	2,150	6,300	$4,313, MS-66RD, Jun-10
1913S	6,101,000	414	59.1	79	225.00	325.00	635.00	1,375.00	1,275	5,300	37,500	$2,888, MS-65RD, Jun-10
1914	75,238,432	465	62.1	93	70.00	85.00	140.00	290.00	240	450	4,200	$7,475, MS-66RD, Jun-10
1914D (b)	1,193,000	2,480	27.9	16	3,300.00	4,150.00	5,450.00	6,500.00	8,200	18,400	40,000	$27,600, MS-66RD, Jun-10
1914S	4,137,000	389	52.2	57	460.00	550.00	1,025.00	1,950.00	2,400	8,150	50,000	$4,600, MS-65RD, Jun-10
1915	29,092,120	427	63.0	94	110.00	130.00	160.00	275.00	265	875	1,800	$13,800, MS-67RD, Jun-10
1915D	22,050,000	616	62.4	92	120.00	145.00	215.00	365.00	425	1,200	9,400	$6,900, MS-66RD, Jun-10
1915S	4,833,000	324	57.8	76	235.00	385.00	1,150.00	1,750.00	2,700	5,000	25,500	$12,650, MS-66RD, Jun-10
1916	131,833,677	595	63.8	97	35.00	42.50	57.00	75.00	95	300	725	$3,220, MS-67RD, Jun-10
1916D	35,956,000	550	61.9	91	150.00	175.00	300.00	550.00	775	2,850	13,500	$18,400, MS-66RD, Jun-10
1916S	22,510,000	543	61.1	88	175.00	225.00	575.00	1,750.00	1,550	7,500	19,000	$7,475, MS-65RD, Jun-10
1917	196,429,785	539	62.1	95	32.00	35.00	42.50	165.00	140	425	1,350	$6,900, MS-67RD, Jun-10
1917, DblDie Obv	*	46	36.1	20	5,750.00				15,000			$24,150, MS-66RD, Jun-10
1917D	55,120,000	457	61.1	88	125.00	165.00	375.00	635.00	750	2,750	13,800	$1,725, MS-66BN, Jun-10
1917S	32,620,000	344	61.8	90	160.00	225.00	575.00	1,800.00	1,275	14,000		$10,925, MS-65RD, Jun-10
1918	288,104,634	379	63.7	97	27.00	30.00	40.00	140.00	175	330	1,950	$12,650, MS-67RD CAC, Jun-10
1918D	47,830,000	334	61.3	86	140.00	200.00	425.00	825.00	1,200	3,500		$4,313, MS-65RD, Jun-10
1918S	34,680,000	404	61.3	84	160.00	325.00	500.00	2,200.00	1,400	11,500		$9,200, MS-65RD, Jun-10
1919	392,021,000	550	63.7	97	28.00	32.00	45.00	135.00	120	230	435	$6,038, MS-68RD, Jun-10
1919D	57,154,000	441	62.6	93	110.00	125.00	170.00	450.00	650	2,600	6,250	$5,463, MS-66RD, Jun-10
1919S	139,760,000	490	61.5	90	115.00	275.00	390.00	1,700.00	1,100	7,500		$7,590, MS-65RD, Jun-10
1920	310,165,000	493	64.2	99	28.00	34.00	42.50	65.00	95	220	800	$12,650, MS-67RD, Jun-10
1920D	49,280,000	359	61.8	90	110.00	130.00	195.00	450.00	525	2,050		$17,250, MS-66RD, Jun-10
1920S	46,220,000	370	61.9	88	185.00	300.00	350.00	1,900.00	2,250	11,500		$7,475, MS-65RD, Jun-10
1921	39,157,000	406	63.8	97	80.00	82.50	90.00	130.00	190	330	1,850	$9,775, MS-67RD, Jun-10
1921S	15,274,000	512	59.5	75	190.00	375.00	550.00	1,850.00	1,150	11,500		$10,638, MS-65RD, Jun-10
1922D	7,160,000	959	46.3	59	165.00	190.00	265.00	530.00	465	2,350	9,500	$11,500, MS-66RD CAC, Jun-10
1922, No D (c)	*	1,983	20.1	3	30,000.00							$37,375, MS-64RB, Jun-10
1922, Weak D (c)	*	168	16.5	6	1,000.00		6,000.00					$324, MS-61BN, Dec-08

* Included in number above. † Ranked in the *100 Greatest U.S. Coins* (third edition). **a.** Many counterfeits exist—some die struck, some made by adding an "S" to a Philadelphia coin. **b.** Many counterfeits exist, including crude fakes, sophisticated die-struck forgeries, and altered 1944-D cents (the latter, unlike an authentic 1914-D cent, will have the designer's initials, V.D.B., on the shoulder). **c.** 1922 cents with a weak or completely missing mintmark were made from extremely worn dies that originally struck normal 1922-D cents. Three different die pairs were involved; two of them produced "Weak D" coins. One die pair (no. 2, identified by a "strong reverse") is acknowledged as having struck "No D" coins. Weak D cents are worth considerably less. Beware of fraudulently removed mintmark.

Chart continued on next page.

	Mintage	Cert	Avg	%MS	MS-63BN	MS-64BN	MS-64RB	MS-64RD	MS-65RB	MS-65RD	MS-66RD	Recent Auction Record
1923	74,723,000	462	64.0	99	$30.00	$40.00	$70.00	$120.00	$155	$360	$1,050	$1,495, MS-67RD, Jun-10
1923S	8,700,000	294	59.3	72	390.00	500.00	1,400.00	3,450.00	2,700	16,100	30,000	$6,900, MS-65RD, Jun-10
1924	75,178,000	296	63.8	97	50.00	60.00	77.50	135.00	110	350	2,000	$3,738, MS-66RD, Jun-10
1924D	2,520,000	668	51.7	56	350.00	450.00	750.00	1,650.00	1,600	10,350		$1,035, MS-65BN, Jun-10
1924S	11,696,000	340	58.6	75	225.00	325.00	740.00	3,400.00	2,000			$2,301, MS-65RB, Jun-10
1925	139,949,000	655	64.6	99	20.00	26.00	50.00	70.00	75	135	370	$1,725, MS-67RD, Jun-10
1925D	22,580,000	482	62.7	94	90.00	140.00	265.00	525.00	875	3,500	60,000	$5,463, MS-65RD, Jun-10
1925S	26,380,000	345	60.7	86	200.00	250.00	575.00	5,000.00	3,600	18,000		$1,035, MS-65RB, Jun-10
1926	157,088,000	861	64.9	100	18.00	24.00	35.00	50.00	65	110	300	$978, MS-67RD, Jun-10
1926D	28,020,000	336	62.3	92	125.00	160.00	275.00	650.00	750	3,550		$4,026, MS-65RD, Jun-10
1926S	4,550,000	585	56.9	62	325.00	1,000.00	2,700.00	11,500.00	5,000	90,000		$6,342, MS-64RD, May-10
1927	144,440,000	589	64.2	98	20.00	25.00	37.50	80.00	40	130	400	$1,035, MS-67RD, Jun-10
1927D	27,170,000	421	63.0	95	85.00	125.00	185.00	375.00	575	2,100		$489, MS-65RB, Jun-10
1927S	14,276,000	300	61.7	89	140.00	190.00	375.00	1,350.00	1,850	7,750		$8,050, MS65RD, Jun-10
1928	134,116,000	614	64.4	99	13.00	19.00	33.00	67.50	70	120	375	$1,495, MS-67RD, Jun-10
1928D	31,170,000	370	63.4	95	80.00	100.00	155.00	250.00	245	1,350	6,500	$6,325, MS-66RD, Jun-10
1928S	17,266,000	257	62.7	92	100.00	160.00	300.00	750.00	850	4,600	25,500	$4,600, MS-65RD, Jun-10
1929	185,262,000	754	64.7	99	14.00	22.00	33.00	42.50	45	105	300	$920, MS-67RD, Jun-10
1929D	41,730,000	255	63.6	98	37.00	43.00	80.00	210.00	155	600	3,500	$3,738, MS-66RD, Jun-10
1929S	50,148,000	546	63.8	98	29.00	37.50	60.00	110.00	185	450	3,200	$4,600, MS-66RD, Jun-10
1930	157,415,000	2,288	65.5	100	10.00	13.00	16.00	20.00	22	43	105	$276, MS-67RD, Jun-10
1930D	40,100,000	509	64.5	98	28.00	30.00	34.00	37.00	40	105	800	$253, MS-66RD, Jun-10
1930S	24,286,000	1,359	65.0	100	12.00	14.00	19.00	38.00	29	90	385	$167, MS-66RD, Jun-10
1931	19,396,000	452	64.8	100	35.00	39.00	42.00	65.00	90	125	400	$2,185, MS-67RD, Jun-10
1931D	4,480,000	544	61.7	79	70.00	85.00	125.00	225.00	250	950	3,900	$863, MS-65RD, Jan-10
1931S	866,000	2,557	58.9	79	195.00	210.00	240.00	300.00	315	525	1,850	$1,898, MS-66RD, Jun-10
1932	9,062,000	534	65.0	99	28.00	31.00	34.00	45.00	48	105	265	$3,220, MS-67RD, Jun-10
1932D	10,500,000	306	64.6	98	28.00	32.50	42.00	62.00	60	145	525	$1,840, MS-67RD, Jun-10
1933	14,360,000	518	65.2	100	30.00	31.00	38.00	57.00	55	110	300	$3,881, MS-67RD, Jun-10
1933D	6,200,000	872	65.0	99	25.00	26.00	28.00	80.00	85	135	425	$4,025, MS-67RD, Jun-10
1934	219,080,000	1,553	65.9	100	7.00	10.00	11.00	16.00	16	37	59	$4,025, MS-68RD, Jun-10
1934, DblDie Obv (d)	*				250.00		350.00					
1934D	28,446,000	773	65.1	99	20.00	24.00	27.00	33.00	48	62	160	$5,175, MS-67RD, Jun-10
1935	245,388,000	1,564	65.7	99	6.00	9.00	12.00	20.00	28	33	42	$138, MS-67RD, Mar-10
1935D	47,000,000	1,167	65.9	100	8.00	11.00	14.00	21.00	35	39	54	$167, MS-67RD, Jun-10
1935S	38,702,000	650	65.1	99	17.00	20.00	23.00	37.50	40	60	275	$10,925, MS-67RD, Jun-10
1936	309,632,000	2,232	65.8	99	4.00	4.50	5.00	7.00	14	35	45	$230, MS-67RD, Jan-10
1936, DblDie Obv	*	107	50.4	51	300.00							$11,500, MS-66RD, Jun-10
1936D	40,620,000	1,491	66.1	100	4.50	5.00	6.00	9.00	16	21	65	$2,530, MS-68RD, Jun-10
1936S	29,130,000	1,095	65.7	100	7.00	8.00	9.00	11.00	17	25	115	$4,169, MS-67RD, Jun-10
1937	309,170,000	3,397	66.2	100	4.00	4.50	5.00	6.00	9	15	27	$403, MS-67RD Secure CAC, Jun-10
1937D	50,430,000	2,256	66.3	100	8.00	8.50	9.00	9.50	12	17	33	$8,625, MS-68RD, Jun-10
1937S	34,500,000	1,274	66.1	100	9.50	10.00	10.50	12.00	15	22	55	$633, MS-67RD, Jun-10
1938	156,682,000	1,425	66.2	100	9.00	9.50	10.00	10.50	12	16	34	$89, MS-66RD, Feb-10
1938D	20,010,000	1,741	66.2	100	9.00	10.00	10.50	11.00	13	17	35	$3,594, MS-68RD, Jun-10
1938S	15,180,000	2,306	66.2	100	8.00	9.00	10.00	11.00	14	21	42	$374, MS-67RD, Jan-10
1939	316,466,000	2,510	66.1	100	3.00	3.50	4.00	5.00	8	14	32	$219, MS-67RD, Jan-10
1939D	15,160,000	1,377	66.2	100	6.00	7.00	8.00	10.50	13	18	37	$161, MS-67RD, Jan-10
1939S	52,070,000	2,783	66.2	100	5.00	6.00	7.00	9.00	11	16	31	$253, MS-67RD, Jan-10
1940	586,810,000	1,712	66.2	100	3.00	3.50	4.00	5.00	8	14	24	$178, MS-67RD, Jun-10
1940D	81,390,000	1,144	66.3	100	5.00	5.50	6.00	7.00	9	15	25	$150, MS-67RD, Jun-10
1940S	112,940,000	2,088	66.2	100	5.00	5.50	6.00	7.00	9	15	29	$196, MS-67RD, Mar-10
1941	887,018,000	2,244	65.9	99	3.50	4.00	4.50	5.00	8	14	23	$276, MS-67RD, Jan-10
1941D	128,700,000	1,582	66.5	100	6.00	6.50	7.00	10.00	11	15	30	$109, MS-67RD, Jan-10
1941S	92,360,000	2,229	66.3	100	6.00	6.50	7.00	10.00	11	15	28	$127, MS-67RD, Feb-10
1942	657,796,000	1,644	66.1	100	3.00	3.50	4.00	5.00	8	14	26	$230, MS-67RD, Feb-10
1942D	206,698,000	2,307	66.2	100	3.00	3.50	4.00	5.00	8	14	29	$161, MS-67RD, Jan-10
1942S	85,590,000	1,761	66.0	99	11.00	12.00	12.50	13.50	13	17	32	$138, MS-67RD, Feb-10

* Included in number above. **d.** The remains of a secondary 3 and 4 are evident below the primary digits.

	Mintage	Cert	Avg	%MS	AU-50	MS-63	MS-65	MS-66	MS-67	MS-68	Recent Auction Record
1943	684,628,670	6,153	66.2	100	$0.50	$2.50	$8	$35	$90	$750	$62, MS-66, Feb-10
1943, Bronze † (a)	*	8	56.6	25	110,000.00						$60,375, VF-30, Sep-07
1943, Silver (a)	*				3,000.00						$4,313, AU-58, Mar-10
1943D	217,660,000	5,344	66.4	100	0.75	3.00	10	35	90	800	$2,300, MS-68, Jun-10
1943D, Boldly Doubled Mintmark	*	25	64.1	100	60.00	100.00	1,400	2,500	11,000		$10,063, MS-67, Jun-10
1943S	191,550,000	5,453	66.1	100	1.00	6.00	20	50	135	1,750	$184, MS-67, Jun-10

* Included in number above. † Ranked in the *100 Greatest U.S. Coins* (third edition). **a.** In 1943 a handful of cents were accidentally struck on old bronze and silver planchets, instead of the intended steel planchets. Today about a dozen are known to exist. Numerous regular steel cents have been plated with copper as novelties or with intent to deceive; their true nature is easily revealed with a magnet.

	Mintage	Cert	Avg	%MS	MS-63RB	MS-64RB	MS-64RD	MS-65RB	MS-65RD	MS-66RD	MS-67RD	Recent Auction Record
1944	1,435,400,000	2,202	66.0	100	$1.00	$2.00	$3	$5	$12	$25	$65	$74, MS-67RD, Dec-09
1944D	430,578,000	2,521	65.8	98	0.85	1.00	2	4	10	26	85	$184, MS-63RB, Jun-10
1944D, D Over S	*	220	56.1	63	450.00	500.00	900	650	2,500	9,200		$1,495, MS-65RD, Jun-10
1944S	282,760,000	2,818	66.2	100	0.85	1.00	2	4	13	27	110	$141, MS-67RD, Feb-10
1945	1,040,515,000	1,444	66.0	100	0.85	1.00	2	2	8	20		$127, MS-67RD, Dec-09
1945D	266,268,000	2,149	66.1	100	0.85	1.00	2	2	9	27	140	$94, MS-67RD, Dec-09
1945S	181,770,000	2,529	66.3	100	0.85	1.00	2	2	9	24	95	$89, MS-67RD, Mar-10
1946	991,655,000	903	65.6	100	0.60	0.85	2	2	14	175		$10,063, MS-67RD, Mar-10
1946D	315,690,000	1,332	66.2	100	0.60	0.85	2	2	10	23	300	$345, MS-67RD, Jan-10
1946S	198,100,000	2,226	66.0	100	0.60	0.85	2	2	9	24	135	$69, MS-67RD, Jan-10
1946S, S Over D	*	13	59.4	77	225.00							$374, MS-64RD, Jun-10
1947	190,555,000	790	65.5	100	1.00	2.00	4	3	20	175		$115, MS-66RD, Jun-10
1947D	194,750,000	1,156	66.0	100	0.60	0.85	2	2	10	29	650	$575, MS-67RD, Jan-10
1947S	99,000,000	1,593	66.2	100	0.85	1.00	2	2	10	27	175	$184, MS-67RD, Jan-10
1948	317,570,000	648	65.7	100	0.85	1.00	2	2	15	190		$59, MS-66RD, Aug-09
1948D	172,637,500	902	65.8	100	0.60	0.85	2	2	11	31	1,000	$161, MS-67RD, Mar-10
1948S	81,735,000	1,650	66.2	100	1.00	2.00	3	3	9	25	140	$69, MS-67RD, Feb-10
1949	217,775,000	573	65.8	100	1.00	2.00	3	3	19	175		$184, MS-66RD, Feb-10
1949D	153,132,500	857	65.8	100	1.00	2.00	3	3	12	42		$21, MS-66RD, Sep-09
1949S	64,290,000	2,065	66.1	100	2.00	3.00	4	4	16	38	200	$207, MS-67RD, Jan-10
1950	272,635,000	681	65.9	100	0.85	1.00	2	2	20	125	3,100	$59, MS-66RD, Dec-09
1950D	334,950,000	1,048	65.8	100	0.60	0.85	2	2	17	34		$184, MS-66RD, Aug-09
1950S	118,505,000	1,186	66.1	100	0.85	1.00	2	2	13	35		$2,530, MS-68RD, Jun-10
1951	284,576,000	529	65.8	100	0.70	0.90	2	2	25	150		$69, MS-66RD, Dec-09
1951D	625,355,000	1,283	65.8	100	0.60	0.85	2	2	9	24	750	$719, MS-67RD, Jan-10
1951D, D Over S	*	14	64.3	100	100.00	125.00	150					$62, MS-64RD, Feb-10
1951S	136,010,000	817	66.0	100	1.00	2.00	3	3	11	38	600	$575, MS-67RD, Jan-10
1952	186,775,000	687	65.9	100	1.00	2.00	3	3	17	160	4,500	$805, MS-67RD, Jan-10
1952D	746,130,000	1,434	65.8	100	0.75	0.90	2	2	9	24		$184, MS-67RD, Dec-09
1952S	137,800,004	998	66.2	100	2.00	3.00	4	4	13	31	490	$489, MS-67RD, Jan-10
1953	256,755,000	637	65.6	100	0.50	0.75	1	1	18	115		$47, MS-66RD, Dec-09
1953D	700,515,000	1,362	65.8	99	0.50	0.75	1	1	11	29		$40, MS-66RD, Feb-10
1953S	181,835,000	1,238	66.0	100	0.60	0.85	2	2	12	40	300	$94, MS-67RD, Dec-09
1954	71,640,050	720	65.4	100	0.60	0.85	2	2	27	60		$150, MS-66RD, Sep-09
1954D	251,552,500	2,020	66.0	100	0.50	0.75	1	1	10	55		$1,955, MS-67RD, Jan-10
1954S	96,190,000	4,383	66.0	100	0.50	0.75	1	1	8	15		$104, MS-67RD, Mar-09
1955	330,958,200	1,061	65.2	97	0.35	0.50	1	1	19	45		$30, MS-66RD, Sep-09
1955, DblDie Obv †	*	2,536	59.4	53	3,200.00 (a)	4,900.00	*8,600*	*13,500*	*34,500*			$32,200, MS-65RD, Jun-10
1955D	563,257,500	2,295	65.7	99	0.35	0.50	1	1	9	21		$276, MS-67RD, Jan-10
1955S	44,610,000	8,522	66.2	100	0.85	2.00	3	3	8	18	105	$26, MS-66RD, Mar-10
1956	420,745,000	1,608	65.9	100	0.35	0.50	1	1	13	50		$30, MS-66RD, Sep-09
1956D	1,098,201,100	2,290	65.7	99	0.30	0.50	1	1	9	25	3,450	$253, MS-67RD, Feb-10
1956D, D Above Shadow D (b)	*	91	63.3	90	35.00							
1957	282,540,000	1,765	65.9	100	0.30	0.50	1	1	15	42		$35, MS-66RD, Aug-09
1957D	1,051,342,000	2,840	65.7	100	0.30	0.50	1	1	9	29		$376, MS-67RD, Jan-10
1958	252,525,000	2,117	65.8	100	0.30	0.50	1	1	9	29	450	$20, MS-65RD, Dec-09

* Included in number above. † Ranked in the *100 Greatest U.S. Coins* (third edition). **a.** Value in EF-45 is $1,800; in AU-50, $1,950; in AU-55, $2,100; in MS-60BN, $2,300; in MS-63BN, $2,550; in MS-64BN, $3,750; in MS-65BN, $5,000. Varieties exist with doubling that, while still strong, is weaker than that pictured; these command premiums, but are not nearly as valuable. Note that many counterfeit 1955 Doubled Die cents exist. On authentic pieces, there is a faint die scratch under the left horizontal bar of the T in CENT. **b.** The remains of a totally separated D mintmark are evident in the field below the primary D.

Chart continued on next page.

	Mintage	Cert	Avg	%MS	MS-63RB	MS-64RB	MS-64RD	MS-65RB	MS-65RD	MS-66RD	MS-67RD	Recent Auction Record
1958, DblDie Obv *(3 known)* (c)	**				—							
1958D	800,953,300	4,139	65.9	100	$0.30	$0.50	$1	$1	$8	$24		$489, MS-67RD, Jan-10

** Included in regular 1958 mintage. **c.** No specimens have been reported being found in circulation, wheat cent bags, Uncirculated rolls, "or other means that would lead to credibility of a true accidental release from the mint" (*Cherrypickers' Guide to Rare Die Varieties*, fifth edition, volume I).

Proof Lincoln, Wheat Ears Reverse, Cents

PF-60 to 70 (Matte Proof). Matte Proof Lincoln cents of a new style were made from 1909 to 1916. These have minutely matte or pebbled surfaces caused by special treatment of the dies. The rims are square and sharp. Such pieces cannot easily be told from certain circulation strikes with similar borders. Expert verification is recommended. Certified holders usually list these simply as "Proof," not "Matte Proof." Most are brown, or brown with tinges of red. Nearly all full "red" coins have been dipped or recolored. Generally, Proofs below 63 are unattractive and are not desired by most collectors. *Obverse and Reverse:* At Matte PF-65 or higher there are no traces of abrasion or contact marks. Color will

range from brown (BN)—the most common— to brown with significant tinges of mint red-orange (RB), or with much mint color (RD). Some tiny flecks are normal on coins certified as PF-65 but should be microscopic or absent above that. Coins in the PF-60 to 63 range are BN or sometimes RB—almost impossible to be RD unless dipped. Lower-grade Proofs usually have poor eye appeal.

PF-60 to 70 (Mirror Proof). Mirror-finish Proofs were made from 1936 to 1942 and again from 1950 to 1958. Proofs of this era are mostly from dies polished overall (including the portrait), although some later issues have frosted

("cameo") portraits. Quality can be a problem for the 1936 to 1942 issues. Check for carbon spots and recoloring. Proofs of later dates are easy to find. Generally, Proofs below 63 are unattractive and are not desired by most collectors. *Obverse and Reverse:* PF-65 and higher coins are usually RB (colors should be nicely blended) or RD, the latter with bright red-orange fading slightly to hints of brown. Some tiny flecks are normal on coins certified as PF-65 but should be microscopic or absent above that. PF-60 and 61 coins can be dull, stained, or spotted but still have some original mint color. Coins with fingerprints must be given a low numerical grade. Lower-grade Proofs usually have poor eye appeal.

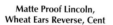

Matte Proof Lincoln, Wheat Ears Reverse, Cent

Mirror Proof Lincoln, Wheat Ears Reverse, Cent

	Mintage	Cert	Avg	PF-63RB	PF-64RB	PF-65RB	PF-65RD	PF-66RB	PF-66RD	PF-67RD	Recent Auction Record
1909, V.D.B. (a)	1,194	50	65.1	$8,000	$15,000						$37,375, PF-65RD, Jun-10
1909	2,618	214	64.6	500	950	$1,500	$2,900	$3,000	$4,900		$3,220, PF-66RD, Jun-10
1910	4,118	223	64.3	475	925	1,475	2,050	3,000			$17,250, PF-67RD, Jun-10
1911	1,725	172	64.4	475	900	1,600	3,600	2,500	9,800		$6,325, PF-67RB, Jun-10
1912	2,172	194	64.3	475	875	1,500	5,200				$5,750, PF-65RD, Jun-10
1913	2,983	287	64.6	475	825	1,450	2,500	3,450	5,200		$2,300, PF-65RD, Jun-10
1914	1,365	156	64.8	475	825	1,450	2,300	3,750	5,500		$4,025, PF-67RB, Jun-10
1915	1,150	114	64.9	475	825	1,450	2,300	3,750	5,750		$6,900, PF-67BN, Jun-10
1916	1,050	87	64.8	1,400	2,300	3,500	10,500				$10,350, PF-67RB, Jun-10
1917, Matte (b)	unknown										
1936	5,569	630	64.0	200	485	1,000	2,200	3,950			$6,325, PF-66RD T2, Jun-10
1937	9,320	724	64.4	65	90	155	350	850	900		$13,225, PF-67RDCam, Jun-10
1938	14,734	817	64.6	60	80	140	165	425	2,250		$2,530, PF-67RD, Jun-10
1939	13,520	843	64.7	55	70	120	155	400	1,250		$1,323, PF-67RD, Jun-10
1940	15,872	814	64.5	45	60	110	150	375	2,000		$4,888, PF-67RD, Jun-10
1941	21,100	826	64.4	40	55	100	135	370	375		$18,400, PF-67RD, Jun-10
1942	32,600	1,243	64.1	41	58	105	145	370	625		$2,760, PF-66RDCam, Jun-10
1950	51,386	934	65.3				70		90	$750	$633, PF-68RD, Jun-10
1951	57,500	800	65.5				65		85	225	$1,955, PF-67Cam, Jan-10
1952	81,980	752	65.9				55		75	130	$2,530, PF-67RDCam, Jun-10
1953	128,800	1,040	66.2				30		40	100	$2,070, PF-67RDCam, Mar-10
1954	233,300	968	66.3				20		30	60	$374, PF-68RDCam, Jan-10
1955	378,200	1,487	66.9				18		30	50	$50, PF-67RD, Feb-10
1956	669,384	1,031	66.8				17		25	30	$748, PF-68RDCam, Jun-10
1957	1,247,952	1,202	66.8				17		25	30	$84, PF-69RD, Feb-10
1958	875,652	1,159	66.8				15		20	27	$920, PF-68Cam, Feb-10

a. Of the 1,194 coins reported struck, an estimated 400 to 600 were issued. **b.** No early references (pre-1960s), Mint records, or reliable market listings have been found to confirm the existence of true 1917 Proofs. "Examples seen have had nice matte-like surfaces, sometimes on just one side, but have lacked the vital combination of broad, flat rims on both sides and a mirror Proof edge (when viewed edge-on from the side)" (*A Guide Book of Lincoln Cents*). The leading certification services do not recognize Proofs of this year.

LINCOLN, MEMORIAL REVERSE
(1959–2008)

Copper Alloy (1959–1982): Designer Victor D. Brenner (obverse), Frank Gasparro (reverse); mints: Philadelphia, Denver, San Francisco. 1959–1962—Weight 3.11 grams; composition .950 copper, .050 tin and zinc; diameter 19 mm; plain edge. 1962–1982—Weight 3.11 grams; composition .950 copper, .050 zinc.

Copper-Plated Zinc (1982 to date): Weight 2.5 grams; composition copper-plated zinc (core: .992 zinc, .008 copper, with a plating of pure copper; total content .975 zinc, .025 copper).

Copper Alloy
(1959–1982)

Copper-Plated Zinc
(1982–2008)

History. In 1959 a new cent design, by Frank Gasparro, was introduced. In 1969, the dies were modified to strengthen the design, and Lincoln's head was made slightly smaller. In 1973, the dies were further modified, and the engraver's initials (FG) were enlarged. In 1974 the initials were reduced slightly. During 1982 the dies were modified again and the bust, lettering, and date were made slightly smaller. The Lincoln Memorial reverse was used until 2009, when a switch was made to four new reverse designs honoring the bicentennial of Abraham Lincoln's birth. Lincoln Memorial cents were struck at the Philadelphia, Denver, and San Francisco mints, with the latter in smaller numbers. Partway through 1982 the bronze alloy was discontinued in favor of copper-coated zinc.

Striking and Sharpness. Striking varies and can range from "sloppy" to needle sharp. On the obverse, check Lincoln's hair and beard (although the sharpness of this feature varied in the dies; for more information see *A Guide Book of Lincoln Cents* [Bowers, 2008]). Tiny marks on the shoulder of Lincoln indicate a weak strike there. On the reverse the sharpness can vary, including on the tiny statue of Lincoln and the shrubbery. On the reverse there can be light striking on the steps of the Memorial, and at IBU and M (E PLURIBUS UNUM). The quality of the fields can vary, as well. Some early copper-coated zinc cents, particularly of 1982 and 1983, can have planchet blisters or problems.

Availability. Coins in this series are plentiful for standard dates and mintmarks.

MS-60 to 70 (Mint State). *Obverse and reverse:* At MS-65 and higher, the luster is rich on all areas, except perhaps the shoulder (which may be grainy and show original planchet surface). There is no rubbing, and no contact marks are visible except under magnification. Coins with full or nearly full mint orange-red color can be designated RD; those with full or nearly full brown-toned surfaces can be designated BN; and those with a substantial percentage of red-orange and of brown can be called RB. Ideally, MS-65 or finer coins should have good eye appeal, which in the RB category means nicely blended colors, not stained or blotched. Below MS-65, full RD coins become scarce, and at MS-60 to 62 are virtually non-existent, unless they have been dipped. Copper is a very active metal, and influences such as slight abrasions, contact marks, and so on that define the grade also affect the color. The official American Numismatic Association grading standards allow for "dull" and/or "spotted" coins at MS-60 and 61, as well as incomplete luster. In the marketplace, interpretations often vary widely. BN and RB coins at MS-60 and 61 tend to be more attractive than (dipped) RD coins.

1960, Large Date

1960, Small Date

1960-D, D Over D, Large Over Small Date
FS-01-1960D-101.

1969-S, Doubled-Die Obverse
FS-01-1969S-101.

1970-S, Small Date
(High 7)

1970-S, Large Date
(Low 7)

1970-S, Doubled-Die Obverse
FS-01-1970S-101.

1972, Doubled-Die Obverse
FS-01-1972-101.

1980, Doubled-Die Obverse
FS-01-1980-101.

1982, Large Date   **1982, Small Date**

1983, Doubled-Die Reverse
FS-01-1983-801.

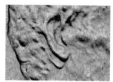

1984, Doubled Ear
FS-01-1984-101.

1992, Normal   **1992, Close AM**

1995, Doubled-Die Obverse
FS-01-1995-101.

1997, Doubled Ear
FS-01-1997-101.

1999, Normal   **1999, Wide AM**

	Mintage	Cert	Avg	%MS	MS-63RB	MS-65RD	MS-66RD	MS-67RD	Recent Auction Record
1959	609,715,000	815	65.6	100	$0.20	$0.30	$37	$450	$150, MS-67RD, Dec-09
1959D	1,279,760,000	679	65.7	100	0.50	0.55	25	375	$30, MS-66RD, Aug-09
1960, Large Date (a)	586,405,000	861	65.2	100	0.20	0.30	30		$40, MS-66RD, Aug-09
1960, Small Date (a)	*	831	65.5	100	3.00	7.00	38		$47, MS-66RD, May-09
1960D, Large Date (a,b)	1,580,884,000	559	65.2	99	0.20	0.30	29		$150, MS-67RD, Nov-09
1960D, Small Date (a)	*	987	65.6	99	0.20	0.30	31	1,850	$32, MS-66RD, Sep-09
1960, D/D, Sm Over Lg Date	*	216	64.3	99					
1961	753,345,000	496	64.7	99	0.15	0.30	50		$28, MS-66RD, Aug-09
1961D	1,753,266,700	671	65.5	99	0.15	0.30	100		$116, MS-66RD, Apr-09
1962	606,045,000	437	65.5	100	0.15	0.30	50		$299, MS-66RD, Dec-09
1962D	1,793,148,140	320	65.4	98	0.15	0.30	120		$253, MS-66RD, Apr-09
1963	754,110,000	472	65.3	99	0.15	0.30	60		$99, MS-66RD, Nov-09
1963D	1,774,020,400	438	65.2	100	0.15	0.30	575		$920, MS-66RD, Dec-09
1964	2,648,575,000	481	65.0	99	0.15	0.30	75		$127, MS-66RD, Dec-09
1964D	3,799,071,500	332	65.6	99	0.15	0.30	42		$79, MS-66RD, Dec-09
1965 (c)	1,497,224,900	287	65.9	100	0.20	0.50	27		$161, MS-67RD, Dec-09
1966 (c)	2,188,147,783	186	65.7	99	0.20	0.50	60		$56, MS-67RD, Dec-09
1967 (c)	3,048,667,100	157	65.5	99	0.20	0.50	90		$84, MS-66RD, Dec-09
1968	1,707,880,970	199	65.5	100	0.25	0.60	33		$35, MS-66RD, May-09
1968D	2,886,269,600	328	65.4	99	0.15	0.40	27		$127, MS-67RD, Dec-09
1968S	258,270,001	452	65.5	99	0.15	0.40	29		$34, MS-66RD, Oct-09
1969	1,136,910,000	259	65.7	100	0.35	0.70	55		$74, MS-66RD, Dec-09
1969D	4,002,832,200	279	65.5	100	0.15	0.30	28		$40, MS-66RD, Dec-09
1969S	544,375,000	394	64.1	92	0.15	0.50	65		$276, MS-66RD, Jan-10

* Included in number above. **a.** The alignment of the 1 and 9 in the date can be used for a quick determination of Large versus Small Date. *Large Date:* the top of the 1 is significantly lower than the top of the 9. *Small Date:* the tops of the 1 and 9 are at the same level. **b.** A variety once called 1960-D, Large Date, D Over Horizontal D has been disproved as such, and is now considered simply a triple-punched D. **c.** Values and auction records for Special Mint Set coins are listed with the Proofs for this type.

	Mintage	Cert	Avg	%MS	MS-63RB	MS-65RD	MS-66RD	MS-67RD	Recent Auction Record
1969S, DblDie Obv (d)	*	11	57.9	36	$75,000.00				$46,000, MS-64RB, Jun-10
1970	1,898,315,000	250	65.4	100	0.30	$0.65	$25	$250	$27, MS-66RD, May-09
1970D	2,891,438,900	217	65.4	100	0.15	0.30	70	1,350	$59, MS-66RD, Dec-09
1970S, All kinds	690,560,004								
1970S, Sm Dt (High 7)		465	64.7	100	25.00	55.00	240		$276, MS-66RD, Jan-10
1970S, Lg Dt (Low 7)		670	64.7	97	0.20	0.50	30		$47, MS-64R, Sep-09
1970S, DblDie Obv		7	62.4	71					$10,350, MS-64RD, Dec-08
1971	1,919,490,000	330	65.6	100	0.25	0.60	25		$31, MS-66RD, May-09
1971D	2,911,045,600	146	65.4	100	0.20	0.50	24	850	$42, MS-66RD, May-09
1971S	525,133,459	262	65.2	97	0.20	0.50	50		$56, MS-66RD, Dec-09
1972	2,933,255,000	371	65.3	97	0.15	0.30	32		$51, MS-66RD, Apr-09
1972, DblDie Obv (e)	*	2,204	64.4	99	400.00	550.00	950	5,500	$5,750, MS-67RD, Jun-10
1972D	2,665,071,400	156	65.2	97	0.15	0.30	28		$31, MS-66RD, May-09
1972S	376,939,108	197	64.9	98	0.25	0.75	78	1,500	$92, MS-66RD, May-09
1973	3,728,245,000	276	65.8	100	0.15	0.30	37	600	$37, MS-66RD, May-09
1973D	3,549,576,588	221	65.7	100	0.15	0.30	37		$48, MS-66RD, May-09
1973S	317,177,295	125	65.0	98	0.25	0.85	200		$374, MS-66RD, Aug-09
1974	4,232,140,523	224	65.9	100	0.15	0.30	27	175	$25, MS-66RD, May-09
1974D	4,235,098,000	182	65.7	100	0.15	0.30	23	100	$184, MS-67RD, May-09
1974S	409,426,660	82	64.9	100	0.25	0.75	100	900	$127, MS-66RD, May-09
1975	5,451,476,142	287	65.8	100	0.15	0.30	29	150	$29, MS-66RD, May-09
1975D	4,505,275,300	137	65.7	100	0.15	0.30	28	350	$14, MS-66RD, May-09
1976	4,674,292,426	147	66.1	99	0.15	0.30	27	55	$51, MS-67RD, May-09
1976D	4,221,592,455	92	65.4	100	0.15	0.30	35	900	$21, MS-66RD, May-09
1977	4,469,930,000	140	65.8	100	0.15	0.30	55	130	$127, MS-66RD, Jun-09
1977D	4,194,062,300	63	65.3	98	0.15	0.30	90	1,000	$174, MS-66RD, May-09
1978	5,558,605,000	92	65.7	100	0.15	0.30	80	625	$851, MS-67RD, Aug-09
1978D	4,280,233,400	55	65.2	100	0.15	0.30	75	425	$19, MS-66RD, May-09
1979	6,018,515,000	544	66.7	100	0.15	0.30	19	70	$23, MS-67RD, Nov-09
1979D	4,139,357,254	101	65.4	100	0.15	0.30	60		$78, MS-66RD, Jan-10
1980	7,414,705,000	66	65.4	100	0.15	0.30	27	125	$299, MS-67RD, Jul-09
1980, DblDie Obv	*	227	61.8	79	225.00	350.00			$253, MS-65RD, Sep-08
1980D (f)	5,140,098,660	121	65.3	99	0.15	0.30	40	400	$42, MS-66RD, May-09
1981	7,491,750,000	71	65.1	97	0.15	0.30	35	125	$31, MS-66RD, May-09
1981D	5,373,235,677	99	65.5	98	0.15	0.30	40	225	$184, MS-67RD, Aug-09
1982, Large Date	10,712,525,000	96	64.9	99	0.20	0.35	25	55	$127, MS-63RD, Jul-09
1982, Small Date	*	114	65.3	100	0.30	0.50	45		$69, MS-63RD, Jul-09
1982D	6,012,979,368	103	65.3	99	0.15	0.30	23	35	$127, MS-67RD, Jul-09
1982, Zinc, Lg Date	(g)	285	66.6	100	0.35	0.50	35	60	$44, MS-67RD, Feb-10
1982, Zinc, Sm Date	(g)	341	66.6	100	0.50	0.85	37		$299, MS-66RD, Dec-09
1982D, Zinc, Lg Date	(g)	208	66.5	100	0.20	0.40	25		$27, MS-66RD, Apr-09
1982D, Zinc, Sm Date	(g)	215	66.3	100	0.15	0.30	15		$27, MS-66RD, Apr-09
1983	7,752,355,000	170	65.7	98	0.15	0.30	18	45	$89, MS-67RD, Aug-09
1983, DblDie Rev (h)	*	637	65.0	98	250.00	385.00	535	1,300	$719, MS-67RD, Jun-10
1983D	6,467,199,428	180	66.8	100	0.15	0.30	15	31	$31, MS-67RD, May-09
1984	8,151,079,000	142	65.9	99	0.15	0.30	15	35	$115, MS-68RD, May-09
1984, Doubled Ear	*	424	65.7	99	175.00	230.00	350	425	$690, MS-68RD, Jun-10
1984D	5,569,238,906	130	66.4	100	0.15	0.30	15	35	$42, MS-67RD, May-09
1985	5,648,489,887	444	66.5	100	0.15	0.30	15	35	$30, MS-67RD, Aug-09
1985D	5,287,339,926	215	67.0	99	0.15	0.30	15	29	$44, MS-68RD, Aug-09
1986	4,491,395,493	164	66.5	100	0.15	0.30	15	35	$37, MS-67RD, May-09
1986D	4,442,866,698	178	66.8	100	0.15	0.30	15	35	$86, MS-68RD, May-09
1987	4,682,466,931	258	66.8	100	0.15	0.30	14	29	$374, MS-68RD, Dec-09
1987D	4,879,389,514	362	66.6	100	0.15	0.30	15	32	$1,035, MS-68RD, Dec-09

* Included in number above. **d.** Beware of specimens that exhibit only strike doubling, as opposed to a true doubled die; these are worth only face value. See appendix A of the *Cherry-pickers' Guide to Rare Die Varieties*, fifth edition, volume I. **e.** Several less dramatically doubled varieties exist; these command premiums over the normal coin but are worth considerably less than the variety pictured. Counterfeits of the 1972 doubled die are frequently encountered. **f.** A variety previously listed in the *Cherrypickers' Guide* as a 1980-D, D Over S, has since been delisted from that catalog. It should command no premium. **g.** Included in the mintage of the corresponding copper-alloy cent. **h.** All reverse lettering is strongly doubled, as are the designer's initials and portions of the Lincoln Memorial.

Chart continued on next page.

	Mintage	Cert	Avg	%MS	MS-63RB	MS-65RD	MS-66RD	MS-67RD	Recent Auction Record
1988	6,092,810,000	122	66.4	98	$0.15	$0.30	$20	$40	$50, MS-67RD, May-09
1988D	5,253,740,443	201	66.8	100	0.15	0.30	14	25	$24, MS-67RD, May-09
1989	7,261,535,000	248	66.6	100	0.15	0.30	14	25	$50, MS-67RD, Aug-09
1989D	5,345,467,111	221	66.4	100	0.15	0.30	14	31	$32, MS-67RD, Aug-09
1990	6,851,765,000	158	66.7	100	0.15	0.30	19	36	$31, MS-67RD, May-09
1990D	4,922,894,533	220	66.9	100	0.15	0.30	14	25	$64, MS-68RD, May-09
1991	5,165,940,000	153	66.8	100	0.15	0.30	14	25	$23, MS-67RD, May-09
1991D	4,158,446,076	181	66.9	99	0.15	0.30	14	25	$109, MS-68RD, Dec-09
1992	4,648,905,000	362	66.9	100	0.15	0.30	14	25	$15, MS-67RD, Aug-09
1992, Close AM (i)	*	1	55.0	0					
1992D	4,448,673,300	194	66.6	98	0.15	0.30	14	25	$34, MS-68RD, Jun-09
1992D, Close AM (i)	*	5	63.6	100					
1993	5,684,705,000	190	66.8	100	0.15	0.30	14	25	$59, MS-68RD, Jun-09
1993D	6,426,650,571	308	66.9	100	0.15	0.30	14	25	$84, MS-68RD, Oct-09
1994	6,500,850,000	162	66.5	99	0.15	0.30	14	25	$51, MS-67RD, May-09
1994D	7,131,765,000	168	66.8	99	0.15	0.30	15	27	$299, MS-68RD, Jul-09
1995	6,411,440,000	265	66.7	100	0.15	0.30	15	30	$38, MS-67RD, Sep-09
1995, DblDie Obv	*	16,808	67.3	100	35.00	45.00	90	200	$345, MS-68RD, Jun-10
1995D	7,128,560,000	196	66.8	98	0.15	0.30	15	35	$42, MS-67RD, May-09
1996	6,612,465,000	174	66.8	100	0.15	0.30	12	18	$127, MS-68RD, Aug-09
1996, Wide AM (i)	*								
1996D	6,510,795,000	262	66.8	100	0.15	0.30	12	18	$50, MS-68RD, May-09
1997	4,622,800,000	123	66.6	100	0.15	0.30	15	42	$42, MS-67RD, May-09
1997, Doubled Ear	*				275.00	500.00			
1997D	4,576,555,000	178	66.7	99	0.15	0.30	14	30	$29, MS-67RD, May-09
1998	5,032,155,000	103	66.3	97	0.15	0.30	12	18	$18, MS-67RD, May-09
1998, Wide AM (i)	*	224	65.4	99		10.00			
1998D	5,225,353,500	136	66.8	100	0.15	0.30	17	57	$518, MS-68RD, May-09
1999	5,237,600,000	197	65.3	100	0.15	0.30	13	30	$322, MS-68RD, Aug-09
1999, Wide AM (i)	*	84	64.5	95		500.00			$207, MS-65RD, Jan-10
1999D	6,360,065,000	179	66.9	99	0.15	0.30	12	25	$69, MS-68RD, Aug-09
2000	5,503,200,000	503	65.9	100	0.15	0.30	12	25	$40, MS-67RD, Aug-09
2000, Wide AM (i)	*	657	65.8	100	3.00	5.00	25		$18, MS-66RD, May-09
2000D	8,774,220,000	164	66.8	100	0.15	0.30	12	25	$64, MS-68RD, May-09
2001	4,959,600,000	74	66.8	100	0.15	0.30	11	18	$29, MS-68RD, May-09
2001D	5,374,990,000	161	67.0	100	0.15	0.30	11	18	$42, MS-68RD, May-09
2002	3,260,800,000	95	67.3	100	0.15	0.30	11	16	$138, MS-69RD, Aug-09
2002D	4,028,055,000	111	67.3	100	0.15	0.30	12	19	$150, MS-69RD, Aug-09
2003	3,300,000,000	229	67.0	100	0.15	0.30	11	16	$64, MS69RD, May-09
2003D	3,548,000,000	129	66.3	100	0.15	0.30	10	15	$21, MS-68RD, Aug-09
2004	3,379,600,000	121	66.8	100	0.15	0.30	10	20	$389, MS-69RD, Jan-10
2004D	3,456,400,000	100	66.4	100	0.15	0.30	10	18	$57, MS-68RD, May-09
2005	3,935,600,000	2,523	67.2	100	0.15	0.30	10	25	$53, MS-69RD, Jun-09
2005D	3,764,450,500	2,452	66.9	100	0.15	0.30	20	40	$42, MS-67RD, May-09
2006	4,290,000,000	1,388	67.0	100	0.15	0.30	10	18	$23, MS-67RD, May-09
2006D	3,944,000,000	1,177	66.7	100	0.15	0.30	13	25	$21, MS-67RD, May-09
2007	3,762,400,000	398	66.5	100	0.15	0.30	16	30	$39, MS-67RD, May-09
2007D	3,638,800,000	297	66.1	100	0.15	0.30	16	33	$42, MS-67RD, May-09
2008	2,558,800,000	157	67.1	100	0.15	0.30	12	18	$21, MS-67RD, May-09
2008D	2,849,600,000	141	66.7	100	0.15	0.30	15	31	$31, MS-67RD, May-09

* Included in number above. **i.** Varieties were made using Proof dies, which have a wide space between the A and the M in AMERICA. The letters nearly touch on other circulation-strike cents after 1993.

Proof Lincoln, Memorial Reverse, Cents

PF-60 to 70 (Proof). All Proof Lincoln Memorial cents are of the mirror format, usually with cameo or frosted contrast between the devices and the fields. High quality is common. Special Mint Set (SMS) coins were struck in lieu of Proofs from 1965 to 1967 and in some instances closely resemble Proofs. *Obverse and Reverse:* PF-65 and higher coins are usually RB (colors should be nicely blended) or RD, the latter with bright red-orange fading slightly to hints of brown. Some tiny flecks are normal on coins certified as PF-65 but should be microscopic or absent above that. PF-60 and 61 coins can be dull, stained, or spotted and still have some original mint color. Coins with fingerprints must be given a low numerical grade. Lower-grade Proofs usually have poor eye appeal. Generally, Proofs below PF-64 are not desired by most collectors.

Proof Lincoln, Memorial Reverse, Cent

1971-S, Proof, Doubled-Die Obverse	1979-S, Type 1 ("Filled" S)	1979-S, Type 2 ("Clear" S)	1981-S, Type 1 ("Filled" S)	1981-S, Type 2 ("Clear" S)

1990-S, No S, Proof
Shown 1.5x actual size.

1999-S, Normal   1999-S, Close AM

	Mintage	Cert	Avg	PF-65RD	PF-67RD	PF-67Cam	PF-68DC	Recent Auction Record
1959	1,149,291	1,235	67.0	$3.00	$22	$55	$865	$633, PF-69Cam, Jan-10
1960, Large Date	1,691,602	1,261	67.0	2.00	26	45	435	$1,640, PF-69RDUCam, Jan-10
1960, Small Date	*	722	66.8	22.00	37	75		$115, PF-68RD, Feb-10
1961	3,028,244	1,610	67.0	1.50	23	40	400	$115, PF-69Cam, Jun-09
1962	3,218,019	1,937	67.2	1.50	10	15	115	$22, PF-69RDUCam, Aug-09
1963	3,075,645	2,377	67.3	1.50	10	14	55	$690, PF-69DCam, Jan-10
1964	3,950,762	3,678	67.7	1.50	10	11	23	$230, PF-69DCam, Jan-10
1965, SMS	2,360,000	745	65.9	11.00	55			$460, MS-65Cam, Jun-10
1966, SMS	2,261,583	904	66.5	10.00	25			$74, MS-68RD SMS, Dec-09
1967, SMS	1,863,344	1,042	66.6	11.00	42			$1,840, MS-67RDCam SMS, Jan-10
1968S	3,041,506	624	67.2	1.00	12	16	50	$50, PF-68DCam, Oct-09
1969S	2,934,631	729	67.2	1.00	11	13	33	$31, PF-68DCam, May-09
1970S, All kinds	2,632,810							
1970S, Sm Dt (High 7)		254	66.7	40.00	55	150		$374, PF-68Cam, Feb-10
1970S, Lg Dt (Low 7)		673	66.9	1.00	15	25	65	$62, PF-68Cam, Sep-09
1971S	3,220,733	907	67.0	1.00	18	30	120	$161, PF-68DCam, Aug-09
1972S	3,260,996	442	67.3	1.00	15	20	35	$16, PF-68Cam, Aug-09
1973S	2,760,339	171	67.5	1.00	13	16	30	$50, PF-69DCam, Sep-09
1974S	2,612,568	198	67.3	1.00	13	16	30	$66, PF-69DCam, Feb-10
1975S	2,845,450	392	67.2	3.50	13	16	30	$109, PF-69DCam, Aug-09

* Included in number above.

Chart continued on next page.

	Mintage	Cert	Avg	PF-65RD	PF-67RD	PF-67Cam	PF-68DC	Recent Auction Record
1976S	4,149,730	635	67.2	$3.20	$13	$16	$30	$368, PF-69DCam, May-09
1977S	3,251,152	214	67.9	2.50	13	16	30	$42, PF-69DCam, Sep-09
1978S	3,127,781	333	67.3	2.50	13	16	30	$75, PF-69DCam, May-09
1979S, Type 1 ("Filled" S)	3,677,175	471	68.3	5.00	11	13	17	$920, PF-70DCam, Jan-10
1979S, Type 2 ("Clear" S)	*	392	67.7	6.00	17	20	30	$26, PF-66DCam, Dec-09
1980S	3,554,806	710	68.4	2.50	10	11	15	$94, PF-70DCam, Oct-09
1981S, Type 1 ("Filled" S)	4,063,083	750	68.2	3.00	10	11	15	$84, PF-70DCam, Oct-09
1981S, Type 2 ("Clear" S)	*	470	67.8	25.00	30	40	55	$265, PF-69UCam, Sep-09
1982S	3,857,479	390	68.1	2.50	10	11	15	$138, PF-70DCam, Sep-09
1983S	3,279,126	432	68.4	3.00	10	11	15	$115, PF-70DCam, Oct-09
1984S	3,065,110	396	68.9	4.00	10	11	15	$127, PF-70DCam, Sep-09
1985S	3,362,821	481	68.9	5.00	11	12	15	$138, PF-70DCam, Sep-09
1986S	3,010,497	375	68.9	7.00	11	12	15	$40, PF-70DCam, Dec-09
1987S	4,227,728	621	68.9	5.00	10	11	13	$69, PF-70DCam, Jan-10
1988S	3,262,948	381	68.9	9.00	11	12	13	$115, PF-70DCam, Jan-10
1989S	3,220,194	483	68.9	9.00	11	12	13	$150, PF-70DCam, Dec-09
1990S	3,299,559	718	69.0	5.00	10	11	13	$115, PF-70DCam, Dec-09
1990, Proof, No S	(a)	36	67.8	5,000.00	5,250	5,750	6,000	$14,950, PF-69DCam, Jun-10
1991S	2,867,787	696	69.1	12.00	13	14	16	$62, PF-70DCam, Jan-10
1992S	4,176,560	1,467	68.9	5.00	10	11	12	$59, PF-70DCam, Jan-10
1993S	3,394,792	1,389	68.8	9.00	10	11	12	$30, PF-70DCam, Dec-09
1994S	3,269,923	1,138	68.9	9.00	11	12	13	$56, PF-70DCam, Jan-10
1995S	2,797,481	1,211	69.0	9.00	11	12	13	$22, PF-70DCam, Dec-09
1996S	2,525,265	1,031	69.0	4.50	9	10	12	$26, PF-70DCam, Dec-09
1997S	2,796,678	1,007	69.1	10.00	12	13	14	$546, PF-70DCam, Jan-10
1998S	2,086,507	1,154	68.9	9.00	10	11	12	$115, PF-70DCam, Dec-09
1998S, Close AM (b)	*	13	68.2					$1,380, PF-69RDCam, Feb-10
1999S	3,347,966	4,821	69.0	6.00	9	10	12	$30, PF-70RDCam, Oct-09
1999S, Close AM (b)	*	167	68.3	90.00	125	200	275	$863, PF-69RDCam, Feb-10
2000S	4,047,993	3,619	69.1	4.00	7	8	11	$109, PF-70DCam, Feb-10
2001S	3,184,606	3,215	69.1	4.00	7	8	11	$46, PF-70UCam, Oct-09
2002S	3,211,995	3,495	69.1	4.00	7	8	11	$26, PF-70DCam, Oct-09
2003S	3,298,439	6,414	69.1	4.00	7	8	11	$59, PF-70DCam, Dec-09
2004S	2,965,422	3,894	69.1	4.00	7	8	11	$127, PF-70DCam, Feb-10
2005S	3,344,679	9,477	69.1	4.00	7	8	11	$32, PF-70UCam, Dec-09
2006S	3,054,436	4,009	69.2	4.00	7	8	11	$130, PF-70DCam, Dec-09
2007S	2,259,847	3,778	69.1	4.00	7	8	11	$69, PF-70UCam, Feb-10
2008S	1,998,108	2,415	69.1	4.00	7	8	11	$109, PF-70DCam, Dec-09

* Included in number above. **a.** An estimated 100 to 250 Proofs of 1990 were struck without the S mintmark (apparently from a circulation-strike die, without a mintmark, which had been given a mirror finish). This error escaped the notice of at least 14 people during die preparation and coining. **b.** Varieties were made in the circulation-strike style, with the A and the M in AMERICA nearly touching each other. On normal Proofs the two letters have a wide space between them.

LINCOLN, BICENTENNIAL
(2009)

Designers Victor D. Brenner (obverse), Richard Masters (Birth and Early Childhood reverse), Charles Vickers (Formative Years reverse), Joel Iskowitz (Professional Life reverse), and Susan Gamble (Presidency reverse); weight 2.5 grams; composition of regular-issue coins, copper-plated zinc (core: .992 zinc, .008 copper, with a plating of pure copper; total content .975 zinc, .025 copper); composition of special coins included in collector sets, .950 copper, .005 tin and zinc; diameter 19 mm; plain edge; mints: Philadelphia, Denver, San Francisco.

Birth and Early Childhood

Formative Years

Professional Life

Presidency

History. The one-cent coins issued during 2009 pay unique tribute to President Abraham Lincoln, commemorating the bicentennial of his birth and the 100th anniversary of the first issuance of the Lincoln cent. Four different reverse designs were issued by the Mint, each representing a major aspect of Lincoln's life. The obverse retained the traditional profile portrait of previous years.

The reverse designs, released quarterly throughout 2009, are: Birth and Early Childhood (designer, Richard Masters; sculptor, Jim Licaretz); Formative Years (designer and sculptor, Charles Vickers); Professional Life (designer, Joel Iskowitz; sculptor, Don Everhart); and Presidency (designer, Susan Gamble; sculptor, Joseph Menna).

The coins issued for general circulation were made of the exact same copper-plated composition used in the cent since 1982. Special versions struck for inclusion collector sets were made of the same alloy as the first Lincoln cents of 1909—95 parts copper and 5 parts tin and zinc.

Striking and Sharpness. Striking is generally sharp. The quality of the fields can vary. Some 2009 cents, even from original rolls and bags, have surface marks that look like water spots.

Availability. Cents of this year were minted in large quantities. They are readily available in the numismatic marketplace, and are starting to be seen more frequently in circulation.

MS-60 to 70 (Mint State). Obverse and reverse: At MS-65 and higher, the luster is rich on all areas. There is no rubbing, and no contact marks are visible except under magnification. Coins with full or nearly full mint orange-red color can be designated RD; those with full or nearly full brown-toned surfaces can be designated BN; and those with a substantial percentage of red-orange and of brown can be called RB. Ideally, MS-65 or finer coins should have good eye appeal, which in the RB category means nicely blended colors, not stained or blotched. Below MS-65, full RD coins become scarce, and at MS-60 to 62 are virtually non-existent, unless they have been dipped. Regarding the special copper coins issued in collector sets: copper is a very active metal, and influences such as slight abrasions, contact marks, and so on that define the grade also affect the color.

2009, Extra Finger

	Mintage	Cert	Avg	%MS	MS-63RB	MS-65RD	MS-66RD	MS-67RD	Recent Auction Record
2009, Birth and Early Childhood	284,400,000	14,905	66.0	100	$0.15	$0.30	$12	$20	
2009D, Birth and Early Childhood	350,400,000	6,380	66.3	100	0.15	0.30	12	20	
2009, Formative Years	376,000,000	28,168	66.0	100	0.15	0.30	12	20	
2009D, Formative Years		4,000	66.4	100	0.15	0.30	12	20	
2009, Professional Life		18,623	66.2	100	0.15	0.30	12	20	
2009D, Professional Life		3,287	66.7	100	0.15	0.30	12	20	
2009, Presidency		5,654	66.3	100	0.15	0.30	12	20	
2009D, Presidency		2,634	66.8	100	0.15	0.30	12	20	

Proof Lincoln Bicentennial Cents

PF-60 to 70 (Proof). All Proof Lincoln Bicentennial cents are of the mirror format, usually with cameo or frosted contrast between the devices and the fields. High quality is common. *Obverse and Reverse:* PF-65 and higher coins are usually RB (colors should be nicely blended) or RD, the latter with bright red-orange fading slightly to hints of brown. Some tiny flecks are normal on coins certified as PF-65 but should be microscopic or absent above that. PF-60 and 61 coins can be dull, stained, or spotted and still have some original mint color. Coins with fingerprints must be given a low numerical grade. Lower-grade Proofs usually have poor eye appeal. Generally, Proofs below PF-64 are not desired by most collectors.

Proof Lincoln Bicentennial Cents

Mintage	Cert	Finest	PF-65RD	PF-67RD	PF-67Cam	PF-68DC	Recent Auction Record
2009S, Birth and Early Childhood	11,040	69.1	$4	$7	$8	$11	
2009S, Formative Years	10,917	69.1	4	7	8	11	
2009S, Professional Life	10,942	69.1	4	7	8	11	
2009S, Presidency	11,150	69.1	4	7	8	11	

LINCOLN, SHIELD REVERSE (2010 TO DATE)

Designers Victor D. Brenner (obverse) and Lyndall Bass (reverse); weight 2.5 grams; composition copper-plated zinc (core: .992 zinc, .008 copper, with a plating of pure copper; total content .975 zinc, .025 copper); diameter 19 mm; plain edge; mints: Philadelphia, Denver, San Francisco.

History. Symbolically capping the life story told by the Lincoln Bicentennial cents of 2009, today's cents feature a reverse design "emblematic of President Lincoln's preservation of the United States as a single and united country." This is the seventh reverse used on the Lincoln type since 1909.

The shield motif was designed by U.S. Mint Artistic Infusion Program Associate Designer Lyndall Bass, and engraved by Mint Sculptor-Engraver Joseph Menna. It was unveiled during the launch ceremony for the fourth and final 2009 Bicentennial cent, held at the Ulysses S. Grant Memorial at the Capitol Building in Washington, DC, November 12, 2009.

In addition to a new reverse design, the Shield Reverse cents feature a modern update of Victor David Brenner's original portrait for the 1909 Lincoln cent.

Striking and Sharpness. Striking is generally sharp.

Availability. Cents of this design are minted in large quantities. They are readily available in the numismatic marketplace, and are starting to enter circulation through normal distribution channels.

MS-60 to 70 (Mint State). *Obverse and reverse:* At MS-65 and higher, the luster is rich on all areas. There is no rubbing, and no contact marks are visible except under magnification. Coins with full or nearly full mint orange-red color can be designated RD; those with full or nearly full brown-toned surfaces can be designated BN; and those with a substantial percentage of red-orange and of brown can be called RB. Ideally, MS-65 or finer coins should have good eye appeal, which in the RB category means nicely blended colors, not stained or blotched. Below MS-65, full RD coins become scarce, and at MS-60 to 62 are virtually nonexistent, unless they have been dipped.

	Mintage	Cert	Avg	%MS	MS-63RB	MS-65RD	MS-66RD	MS-67RD	Recent Auction Record
2010		5,818	65.4	100	$0.15	$0.30	$10	$18	
2010D		1,392	65.5	100	0.15	0.30	10	18	

Proof Lincoln, Shield Reverse, Cents

PF-60 to 70 (Proof). All Proof Lincoln, Shield Reverse, cents are of the mirror format, usually with cameo or frosted contrast between the devices and the fields. High quality is common. *Obverse and Reverse:* PF-65 and higher coins are usually RB (colors should be nicely blended) or RD, the latter with bright red-orange fading slightly to hints of brown. Some tiny flecks are normal on coins certified as PF-65 but should be microscopic or absent above that. PF-60 and 61 coins can be dull, stained, or spotted and still have some original mint color. Coins with fingerprints must be given a low numerical grade. Lower-grade Proofs usually have poor eye appeal. Generally, Proofs below PF-64 are not desired by most collectors.

Proof Lincoln, Shield Reverse, Cents

	Mintage	Cert	Finest	PF-65RD	PF-67RD	PF-67Cam	PF-68DC	Recent Auction Record
2010S		n/a	n/a	$4	$7	$8	$11	

An Overview of Two-Cent Pieces

The two-cent piece was introduced in 1864. Made in bronze, it was designed by Chief Engraver James B. Longacre, and was the first circulating United States coin to bear the motto IN GOD WE TRUST. At the time, coins were scarce in circulation, and silver and gold issues were entirely absent. It was felt that the two-cent piece would prove to be very popular as a companion to the Indian Head cent. However, the introduction of the nickel three-cent piece in 1865 negated much of this advantage, the production of two-cent pieces declined, and by 1873, when the denomination was discontinued, their only coinage consisted of Proofs for collectors.

A full "type set" of the two-cent piece consists of but a single coin. Most available in Mint State are the issues of 1864 and 1865, often seen with original mint orange color fading to natural brown. Proofs are available for all years.

For the Collector and Investor: Two-Cent Pieces as a Specialty

Two-cent pieces can be collected advantageously by date and variety. A basic display consists of an 1864 Large Motto, 1864 Small Motto (rare), 1873 Close 3, and 1873 Open 3, the last two being available only in Proof format. Some specialists opt to include just one of the 1873 varieties.

Collectors should select both circulation strikes and Proofs with care, for the number of truly choice *original* (unprocessed, undipped, not retoned) coins is but a small percentage of the whole. As a type, though, the two-cent piece is readily available for collecting.

Several specialized studies of two-cent pieces have been published over a long span of years, the first of significance being "Two-Cent Pieces of the United States," by S.W. Freeman, published in *The Numismatist,* June 1954.

Recommended Reading

Fivaz, Bill, and Stanton, J.T. *The Cherrypickers' Guide to Rare Die Varieties* (5th ed., vol. I), Atlanta, GA, 2009.
Flynn, Kevin. *Getting Your Two Cents Worth,* Rancocas, NJ, 1994.
Leone, Frank. *Longacre's Two Cent Piece Die Varieties and Errors,* College Point, NY, 1991.

TWO-CENT PIECES, 1864–1873

Designer James B. Longacre; weight 6.22 grams; composition .950 copper, .050 tin and zinc; diameter 23 mm; plain edge. All coined at Philadelphia Mint.

History. The two-cent piece, struck in bronze like the new Indian Head cents, made its debut under the Mint Act of April 22, 1864. Coins of all kinds were scarce in circulation at the time, due to hoarding. The outcome of the Civil War was uncertain, and Americans desired "hard money." Many millions of two-cent pieces were struck in 1864, after which the mintage declined, due to once-hoarded Indian Head cents becoming available again and to the new nickel three-cent coins being introduced in 1865. Continually decreasing quantities were made through 1872, and only Proofs were struck in the coin's final year, 1873.

Striking and Sharpness. Points to check for sharpness on the obverse include WE in the motto, the leaves, and the horizontal shield lines. On the reverse check the wreath details and the border letters. Check the dentils on both sides. Most coins are quite well struck.

Availability. Most MS coins are dated 1864 or 1865, after which the availability declines sharply, especially for the issue of 1872. Among 1864 coins most seen are of the Large Motto variety. Small Motto coins are elusive. Coins with much or nearly all *original* mint red-orange color are rare for the later years, with most in the marketplace being recolored.

AU-50, 53, 55, 58 (About Uncirculated). *Obverse:* WE shows light wear, this being the prime place to check. The arrowheads and leaves also show light wear. At AU-50, level wear is more noticeable. At 53 and 55, wear is less. At 58, friction is evident, rather than actual wear. Luster, toned brown, is nearly complete at 58, but may be incomplete in the field. *Reverse:* At AU-50, light wear is seen on the ribbon and the higher-relief areas of the leaves and grains, while the lower areas retain their detail. Some luster may be present in protected areas. At 53 and 55, wear is lesser and luster is more extensive. An AU-58 coin has nearly full luster and shows only light friction.

MS-60 to 70 (Mint State). *Obverse and Reverse:* At MS-65 and higher, the luster is rich on all areas. There is no rubbing, and no contact marks are visible except under magnification. Coins with full or nearly full mint orange-red color can be designated RD (the color on this is often more orange than red), those with full or nearly full brown-toned surfaces can be designated BN, and those with a substantial percentage of red-orange and of brown can be called RB. Ideally, MS-65 or finer coins have good eye appeal, which in the RB category means nicely blended colors, not stained or blotched, the latter problem mostly with dipped and irregularly retoned coins. Below MS-65, full RD coins become scarce, although MS-64 RD coins can be attractive. These usually have more flecks and tiny spots, while the color remains bright. At MS-60 to 62, RD coins are virtually non-existent, unless they have been dipped. The Official American Numismatic Association grading standards allow for "dull" and/or "spotted" coins at MS-60 and 61 as well as incomplete luster. MS-60 to 63 BN coins can be fairly attractive if not spotted or blotched, but those with hints of color usually lack eye appeal.

1864, Small Motto　　**1864, Large Motto**　　**1865, Plain 5**　　**1865, Fancy 5**

1867, Doubled-Die Obverse
FS-02-1867-101.

1869, Doubled-Die Obverse
FS-02-1869-101.

	Mintage	Cert	Avg	%MS	MS-60BN	MS-63BN	MS-63RB	MS-64BN	MS-64RD	MS-65RB	MS-65RD	Recent Auction Record
1864, Sm Motto (a)	*	166	64.6	100	$1,200	$1,500	$1,850	$2,000	$2,900	$3,750	$10,500	$3,220, MS-65BN CAC, Jun-10
1864, Lg Motto (b)	19,847,500	2,879	62.9	94	100	160	175	200	600	465	1,500	$2,760, MS-66RD, Jun-10
1865 (c)	13,640,000	1,921	62.6	93	100	160	175	200	600	465	1,500	$184, MS-63BN, Mar-10
1866	3,177,000	389	61.8	88	100	160	175	240	750	550	2,450	$1,380, MS-66RB, Feb-10
1867	2,938,750	428	62.0	91	120	175	210	250	1,000	650	3,250	$863, MS-65RB, Jun-10
1867, DblDie Obv (d)	**	35	50.6	46	1,000	1,500	2,250	2,500				$748, AU-55, May-09
1868	2,803,750	422	62.1	91	150	225	290	375	1,200	1,150	4,000	$518, MS-65RB, Jan-10
1869	1,546,500	358	61.3	87	160	225	290	375	1,200	1,150	3,500	$1,610, MS-65RB CAC, Jan-10
1869, DblDie Obv	**				600	900	1,000	1,250	2,250			
1870	861,250	299	60.7	86	250	300	450	575	1,750	1,500	4,500	$2,300, MS-64RD, Jun-10
1871	721,250	396	61.4	85	285	375	460	800	2,000	1,700	5,500	$748, MS-65BN CAC, Jun-10
1872	65,000	181	42.6	43	2,000	2,500	3,000	3,200	10,000	10,500	23,000	$460, VG-8, Jun-10

* Included in number below. ** Included in number above. **a.** The Small Motto is distinguished by a wider D in GOD, and the first T in TRUST nearly touching the ribbon crease at left. **b.** The Large Motto is distinguished by a narrow D in GOD, and a 1 mm gap between the first T in TRUST and the ribbon crease. **c.** Varieties show the tip of the 5 either plain or fancy (curved). **d.** This variety is somewhat common in low-end circulated grades, but is considered rare in EF and AU, and very rare in MS.

Proof Two-Cent Pieces

PF-60 to 70 (Proof). The 1864 Small Motto Proof is a great rarity, with fewer than two dozen estimated to exist. Coins of 1873 were made only in Proof format, of the Close 3 and Open 3 styles. Proofs of most dates are easily enough acquired. Very few have original color. Do not overlook the many nice brown and red-and-brown pieces on the market (some investors acquire only "red" copper coins, leaving many great values among others). Refer to the comments under Proof Indian Head cents. *Obverse and Reverse:* PF-60 two-cent pieces can be dull from repeated dipping and cleaning and are often toned iridescent colors or have mottled surfaces. At PF-63, the mirrorlike fields should be attractive, and hairlines should be minimal, most easily seen when the coin is held at an angle to the light. No rubbing is seen. PF-64 coins are even nicer. PF-65 coins have very few hairlines, visible only under strong magnification. At any level and color, a Proof with hairlines likely has been cleaned. At PF-67 or higher there should be no evidence at all of hairlines or friction; such a coin is fully original (not cleaned). As a general rule, Proofs of 1873 are of very high quality but, unless dipped or cleaned, are nearly always toned light brown.

Proof Two-Cent Piece

	Est Mintage	Cert	Finest	PF-64BN	PF-64RB	PF-65RB	Recent Auction Record
1864, Small Motto *(20–30 known)* †	*	8	PF-66	$21,000	$30,000	$47,000	$48,875, PF-64RD, Aug-07
1864, Large Motto	100+	123	PF-67	750	1,500	2,750	$4,600, PF-66RB, Jan-10
1865	500+	144	PF-67	525	550	1,200	$6,325, PF-66RDCam, Jun-10
1866	725+	148	PF-66	525	550	1,200	$575, PF-63RB, Feb-10
1867	625+	186	PF-67	525	600	1,200	$4,313, PF-65RD CAC, Dec-09
1868	600+	171	PF-67	525	635	1,200	$2,530, PF-66RB CAC, Jun-10
1869	600+	216	PF-67	550	650	1,250	$2,070, PF-65RD, Oct-09
1870	1,000+	236	PF-67	650	700	1,275	$633, PF-64BN, Mar-10
1871	960+	250	PF-67	875	900	1,300	$1,093, PF-64RD, Feb-10
1872	950+	303	PF-67	950	1,150	1,800	$3,450, PF-66RB, Feb-10
1873, Close 3	600	242	PF-67	2,750	3,000	3,500	$2,990, PF-64BN, Jun-10
1873, Open 3 (Restrike)	500	103	PF-66	2,500	2,750	3,000	$35,938, PF-66RD, Jan-10

* Included in number below. † Ranked in the *100 Greatest U.S. Coins* (third edition).

AN OVERVIEW OF THREE-CENT PIECES

SILVER THREE-CENT PIECES

The silver three-cent piece or *trime* is one of the more curious coins in American numismatics. The rising price of silver in 1850 created a situation in which silver coins cost more to produce than their face value. Mintages dropped sharply and older pieces disappeared from circulation. In 1851 a solution was provided by the three-cent piece. Instead of being made with 90% silver content, the quantity was set at 75%. Accordingly, the coins were worth less intrinsically, and there was no advantage in melting them. Large quantities were made through 1853. In that year, the standards for regular silver coins were changed, and other denominations reappeared on the marketplace, making the trime unnecessary. Mintages dropped beginning in 1854, until 1873, when production amounted to just 600 Proofs for collectors.

Of the three varieties of trimes, Variety 2 (1854–1858) is at once the scarcest and, by far, the most difficult to find with a sharp strike. In fact, not one in 50 Variety 2 coins is needle sharp. Curiously, when such pieces are found they are likely to be dated 1855, the lowest-mintage issue of the type. Trimes of the Variety 1 design (1851–1853) vary widely in striking, but can be found sharp. Variety 3 coins (1859–1873) often are sharp.

Mint State coins are readily found for Variety 1 and are usually in grades from MS-60 to 63 or so, although quite a few gems are around with attractive luster. Sharply struck gems are another matter and require some searching to find. Mint State Variety 2 trimes are all rare, and when seen are apt to be miserably struck and in lower grades. Variety 3 coins are readily found in Mint State, including in MS-65 and higher grades.

Proofs were made of all years, but not in quantity until 1858, when an estimated 210 were struck. For all dates after 1862, high-grade Proofs are much more readily available today than are Mint State coins. Circulated examples are available of all three varieties. While extensively worn coins of Variety 1 are available, most Variety 2 coins are Fine or better and most Variety 3 pieces are VF or better.

FOR THE COLLECTOR AND INVESTOR: SILVER THREE-CENT PIECES AS A SPECIALTY

Trimes cover a fairly long span of years and embrace several design types, but comprise no "impossible" rarities. Accordingly, it is realistic to collect one of each Philadelphia Mint coin from 1851 to 1873 plus the 1851-O. There are two overdates in the series, 1862, 2 Over 1 (which is distinct and occurs only in circulation strike format), and 1863, 3 Over 2 (only Proofs, and not boldly defined), which some specialists collect and others ignore. A curious variety of 1852 has the first digit of the date over an inverted 2.

Typically, a high-grade set includes Mint State examples of all issues 1851 through 1857 and Proofs after that date. As noted, Variety 2 trimes usually are very poorly struck, save the occasionally encountered sharp 1855. As an example, a specialist in the series who found an 1856 with needle-sharp details, at three times the regular market price, might be well advised to buy it. After 1862, Mint State coins are rare for most dates. The formation of a choice Mint State set 1851 through 1872 plus a Proof 1873 would be a formidable challenge.

A set of circulated coins can be gathered through and including 1862, after which such pieces become very rare. Most later dates will have to be acquired on a catch-as-catch-can basis, perhaps by acquiring impaired Proofs for certain of the years.

NICKEL THREE-CENT PIECES

Nickel three-cent pieces were introduced in 1865 to help fill the need for coins in circulation. At the time, silver and gold issues were hoarded, and were available only at a premium. The nickel three-cent piece joined the Indian Head cent and the new (as of 1864) two-cent piece. The coin proved to be very popular in its time, and millions were struck. In 1866 the nickel five-cent piece was introduced, after which time the demand for the nickel three-cent piece diminished somewhat. However, pieces were made in quantity until 1876. In that year silver coins again returned to circulation, and mintages for the nickel three-cent piece dropped sharply. Only Proofs were made in 1877 and 1878. In later years, mintages ranged from small to modest, except for 1881.

Mint State coins are readily available for the early years, although many if not most have weak striking in areas or are from clashed dies. Pristine, sharp Mint State coins on the market are mostly of later years, in the 1880s, where such pieces are the rule, not the exception.

FOR THE COLLECTOR AND INVESTOR: NICKEL THREE-CENT PIECES AS A SPECIALTY

Nickel three-cent coins are interesting to collect by date sequence from 1865 to 1889. Varieties are provided by the 1873, Close 3 and Open 3 and the 1887, 7 Over 6 overdate. A set of Mint State coins is considerably more difficult to form than a run of Proofs. A hand-selected set of well-struck coins MS-65 or finer could take several years to complete.

Among Proofs, the rarest year is 1865, probably followed by the "perfect date" (not overdate) 1887. Proofs of the 1860s and early 1870s are scarce in PF-65 with excellent strike and eye appeal. Proofs of the last decade of coinage are much more readily available and are usually choice.

SILVER THREE-CENT PIECES (TRIMES) (1851–1873)

Variety 1 (1851–1853): Designer James B. Longacre; weight 0.80 gram; composition .750 silver, .250 copper; diameter 14 mm; plain edge; mints: Philadelphia, New Orleans.

Variety 1 (1851–1853)
Shown 2x actual size.

Variety 2 (1854–1858): Designer James B. Longacre; weight 0.75 gram; composition .900 silver, .100 copper; diameter 14 mm; plain edge. All coined at the Philadelphia Mint.

Variety 2 (1854–1858)
Shown 2x actual size.

Variety 3 (1859–1873): Designer James B. Longacre; weight 0.75 gram; composition .900 silver, .100 copper; diameter 14 mm; plain edge. All coined at the Philadelphia Mint.

Variety 3 (1859–1873)
Shown 2x actual size.

History. In 1850 Americans began hoarding their silver coins, as the flood of gold from California made silver disproportionately valuable. To provide a small coin for commerce, the Mint introduced the silver three-cent piece, or *trime.* These were .750 fine (as opposed to the standard .900 fineness), and contained less than 3¢ of metal, so there was no incentive to hoard or melt them. Three different designs were made, Variety 1 of which was struck from 1851 to 1853. These coins were popular in their time and circulated widely. These are distinguished from the other two designs by having no outline or frame around the obverse star. The Act of February 21, 1853, reduced the amount of silver in other denominations (from the half dime to the half dollar, but not the dollar), which discouraged people from hoarding them. The tiny trime lost the public's favor, and mintages decreased.

In 1854 the design was changed considerably, creating Variety 2, which was made through 1858. The alloy was modified to the standard for other issues and the weight was lightened. A raised border was added to the obverse star plus two line frames around it. On the reverse an olive branch was placed above the III and a bundle of arrows below it. This new motif proved to be very difficult to strike up properly.

In 1859 the design was modified again, creating Variety 3. Demand for the denomination continued to be small, and after 1862 very few were made for circulation, as silver coins were hoarded by the war-weary public and began to trade at a premium. Under the Coinage Act of 1873 the trime was discontinued, and

that year only Proofs were struck. Also in that year, nearly the entire production of non-Proof coins of 1863 to 1872 was melted.

Striking and Sharpness. On the Variety 1 obverse the tiny shield at the center of the star often lacks certain details. On the reverse check the details and strength of the III. On both sides check the rims. Needle-sharp coins are in the minority. Sharpness of strike has been nearly completely overlooked in the marketplace.

Trimes of Variety 2 are usually poorly struck, with some or all of these characteristics: obverse lettering weak in places; frames around the star of inconsistent strength or missing in certain areas; shield weak in places; reverse stars irregular and poorly formed; olive branch and arrows weak in areas; weak or irregular rims. Now and then a sharp 1855 is found.

Most Variety 3 trimes are sharply struck. Points to look for include full outlines around the star, full shield on the star, and full leaf details and sharp stars.

Availability. Circulated examples of the Variety 1 trimes are plentiful. MS coins are often seen, although the 1851-O is scarce in MS and high circulated grades. Most MS coins are lustrous and attractive, especially at 63 and above. Circulated Variety 2 coins are scarce in all grades, particularly so at MS-64 and higher. With a needle-sharp strike, MS-65 and higher are *rarities.* Among Variety 3 trimes, circulated coins of the years 1859 to 1862 are easy to find. All later dates range from scarce to rare in circulation-strike format. MS-63 and better coins 1865 and later are very rare.

EF-40, 45 (Extremely Fine). *Obverse:* More wear is seen than at AU, most noticeable on the ridges of the star arms, this in addition to more wear on the frames (Varieties 2 and 3). Luster is absent, or seen only in traces. *Reverse:* More wear is seen on the C ornament and III. On Variety 2 and Variety 3 more wear is seen on the leaves and arrows.

AU-50, 53, 55, 58 (About Uncirculated). *Obverse:* Light wear is most obvious on the star arms and shield

on Variety 1, and on the points of the frames on Varieties 2 and 3. At AU-50, luster is evident, but only on part of the field. At 58 luster is nearly complete. *Reverse:* Light wear is seen on the C ornament and III. On Varieties 2 and 3, light wear is seen on the leaves and arrows.

MS-60 to 70 (Mint State). *Obverse and Reverse:* At MS-60, some abrasion and very minor contact marks are evident, most noticeably on the obverse star and the

C ornament on the reverse. At MS-63, abrasion is hard to detect except under magnification. An MS-65 coin has no abrasion. Luster should be full and rich (not grainy). Coins above MS-65 have fewer marks as perfection is approached.

1852, 1 Over Inverted 2
FS-3S-1852-301.

1853, Repunched Date
FS-3S-1853-301.

1854, Repunched Date
FS-3S-1854-301.

1862, 2 Over 1
FS-3S-1862-301.

	Mintage	Cert	Avg	%MS	EF-40	AU-50	MS-60	MS-63	MS-64	MS-65	MS-66	Recent Auction Record
1851	5,447,400	1,013	63.3	95	$80	$150	$175	$275	$425	$725	$1,100	$920, MS-66, Jul-10
1851O	720,000	380	61.8	84	150	220	350	650	1,200	2,900	5,000	$1,208, MS-64, Jun-10
1852, 1 Over Inverted 2 (a)	*				775	950	1,150	1,425	1,700	1,950		
1852	18,663,500	1,224	62.5	92	70	145	170	275	425	725	1,100	$3,220, MS-67, Jun-10
1853	11,400,000	605	62.2	90	70	145	170	275	425	725	1,350	$1,380, MS-66 CAC, Jun-10
1853, RPD (b)	**				100	200	260	300	650	1,000		$322, MS-64, Jan-03
1854	671,000	293	61.1	82	110	220	350	650	1,300	2,500	5,500	$2,185, MS-65, Mar-10
1854, RPD (c)	**				185	325	500	800	1,750	3,500		$219, AU-55, Jul-05
1855	139,000	117	58.7	68	190	300	550	1075	2,600	6,500	13,500	$3,220, MS-64, Mar-10
1856	1,458,000	264	60.8	79	110	250	280	600	1,275	3,150	8,500	$2,539, MS-65, Mar-10
1857	1,042,000	284	62.6	90	110	250	280	600	1,275	2,500	4,500	$2,990, MS-66, Mar-10
1858	1,603,700	471	62.3	85	110	250	280	600	1,275	2,500	4,500	$1,610, MS-64, Apr-10
1859	364,200	248	62.9	92	80	150	175	275	500	1000	1,650	$805, MS-64, Jun-10
1860	286,000	241	61.4	81	80	150	175	275	500	1000	1,650	$542, MS-64, Feb-10
1861	497,000	692	62.9	88	80	150	175	275	500	1000	1,400	$4,313, MS-67, Jul-10

* Included in number below. ** Included in number above. **a.** An inverted 2 is visible beneath the primary 1. "A secondary date punch was obviously punched into the die in an inverted orientation and then corrected after some effacing of the die" (*Cherrypickers' Guide to Rare Die Varieties,* fifth edition, volume I). **b.** Secondary digits are visible to the north of the primary 1 and 8. This repunched date can be detected on lower-grade coins. **c.** Secondary digits are visible to the west of the primary digits on the 8 and 5.

	Mintage	Cert	Avg	%MS	EF-40	AU-50	MS-60	MS-63	MS-64	MS-65	MS-66	Recent Auction Record
1862, 2 Over 1 (d)	*	282	64.0	94	$80	$150	$180	$350	$600	$1000	$1,500	$1,495, MS-66, Jun-10
1862	343,000	961	63.7	94	80	150	165	250	435	875	1,300	$546, MS-64, May-10
1863	21,000	77	64.2	96	435	550	650	1,000	1,300	2,100	2,900	$2,760, MS-66, Apr-10
1864	12,000	88	64.3	93	435	550	650	1,000	1,300	2,100	2,900	$4,313, MS-67, Apr-10
1865	8,000	90	62.4	89	450	575	675	1,100	1,400	2,200	3,200	$1,725, MS-62, Apr-10
1866	22,000	72	62.8	89	425	480	630	950	1,300	2,100	3,200	$2,530, MS-66, Jul-10
1867	4,000	40	62.7	90	450	500	650	1,000	1,750	2,700	6,500	$1,156, MS-62, Feb-09
1868	3,500	32	59.8	81	450	500	650	1,300	2,150	5,250	11,000	$3,881, MS-64 CAC, May-09
1869	4,500	44	63.6	95	450	500	650	1,300	1,900	2,500	4,900	$2,070, MS-64, Feb-09
1870	3,000	84	62.1	85	450	500	650	1,250	1,850	4,100	6,250	$4,888, MS-66, Dec-09
1871	3,400	142	64.5	94	450	500	650	1,000	1,400	1,950	2,500	$1,898, MS-66 Star CAC, Jul-10
1872	1,000	41	62.5	93	500	600	1000	1,800	2,400	4,850	11,000	$2,760, MS-63, Oct-09

* Included in number below. **d.** A secondary 1 is evident beneath the 2 of the date. "This overdate is believed to be due more to economy (the Mint having used a good die another year) than to error. Circulated examples are about as common as the regular-dated coin" *(Cherrypickers' Guide to Rare Die Varieties).*

Proof Silver Three-Cent Pieces

PF-60 to 70 (Proof). A few Proofs were made in the early 1850s and are great rarities today. After 1857, production increased. Most are needle sharp and have mirrored surfaces, although some of the late 1860s and early 1870s can have slightly grainy or satiny lustrous surfaces.

Striking quality varies. Lint marks and surface problems are not unusual. Careful examination is recommended. *Obverse and Reverse:* Proofs that are extensively cleaned and have many hairlines, or that are dull and grainy, are lower level, such as PF-60 to 62. These are difficult to verify as Proofs.

For a trime with medium hairlines and good reflectivity, a grade of PF-64 is assigned, and with relatively few hairlines, PF-65. PF-66 should have hairlines so delicate that magnification is needed to see them. Above that, a Proof should be free of such lines.

Proof Silver Three-Cent Piece
Shown 2x actual size.

	Mintage	Cert	Finest	PF-63	PF-64	PF-65	Recent Auction Record
1851	(1–2 known)			—			
1852	(1 known)			—			
1854	25–35	9	PF-65	$13,000	$16,000	$30,000	$12,765, PF-63, Mar-10
1855	30–40	22	PF-66	5,000	8,500	13,500	$9,775, PF-64, Oct-08
1856	40–50	22	PF-67	3,600	5,750	13,500	$5,463, PF-64, Oct-09
1857	60–80	32	PF-67	3,300	4,500	9,500	$8,740, PF-66, Oct-09
1858	300+	102	PF-68	2,350	4,000	6,750	$6,325, PF-65 CAC, Jun-10
1859	800	101	PF-67	525	800	1,700	$1,840, PF-65, Dec-09
1860	1,000	72	PF-68	525	950	3,300	$1,265, PF-64, Jun-10
1861	1,000	95	PF-68	525	800	1,550	$805, PF-64, Jun-10
1862	550	134	PF-67	525	800	1,600	$3,450, PF-66Cam CAC, Jul-10
1863, So-Called 3 Over 2	*			1,500	2,500	5,500	$3,738, PF-62, May-07
1863	460	120	PF-68	600	850	1,350	$748, PF-63, Apr-10
1864	470	163	PF-68	600	850	1,350	$4,025, PF-67, Apr-10
1865	500	149	PF-68	600	850	1,350	$1,495, PF-64, Apr-10
1866	725	193	PF-68	600	850	1,350	$1,093, PF-64Cam, Jul-10
1867	625	251	PF-68	600	800	1,300	$1,093, PF-65, Jul-10
1868	600	247	PF-67	600	800	1,250	$1,840, PF-66, Jul-10
1869	600	175	PF-68	600	800	1,300	$1,208, PF-65, Jul-10
1869, So-Called 9 Over 8, Pf only	**			1,500	2,500	5,000	$834, PF-61, Apr-02
1870	1,000	222	PF-68	600	875	1,400	$2,185, PF-65Cam, Jul-10
1871	960	205	PF-67	600	800	1,300	$1,093, PF-65, Jul-10
1872	950	219	PF-68	600	800	1,325	$1,265, PF-64Cam, Jun-10
1873, Close 3, Proof only	600	364	PF-67	1,600	1,800	2,400	$4,025, PF-66 CAC, Jun-10

* Included in number below. ** Included in number above.

NICKEL THREE-CENT PIECES (1865–1889)

Designer James B. Longacre; weight 1.94 grams; composition .750 copper, .250 nickel; diameter 17.9 mm; plain edge. All coined at Philadelphia Mint..

Shown 2x actual size.

History. The nickel three-cent coin debuted in the final year of the Civil War, 1865. The American public was still hoarding silver coins (a situation that would continue until 1876), including the silver three-cent piece. The highest-denomination coin in circulation at the time was the recently introduced two-cent piece. After 1875, when silver coins circulated once again, the three-cent denomination became redundant and mintages dropped. The last pieces were coined in 1889.

Striking and Sharpness. On the obverse check the hair and other portrait details. On the reverse the tiny vertical lines in the Roman numeral III can be weak. Check the dentils on both sides of the coin. Among circulation strikes, clashed dies are common, particularly for the earlier high-mintage years. Generally, coins of the 1860s and 1870s have weakness in one area or another. Many if not most of the 1880s are well struck.

Availability. Circulated examples of dates from 1865 to the mid-1870s are readily available. MS coins, particularly from the 1860s, are easily found, but often have areas of weakness or lack aesthetic appeal. MS coins of the 1880s are readily found for most dates (except for 1883, 1884, 1885, and 1887), some of them probably sold as Proofs. Many Proofs of the era had slight to extensive mint luster.

EF-40, 45 (Extremely Fine). *Obverse:* More wear is seen on the cheek and the hair to the right of the face and neck than at AU. The hair to the right of the coronet beads shows light wear. *Reverse:* The wreath still shows most detail on the leaves. Some wear is seen on the vertical lines within III (but striking can also cause weakness). Overall the reverse appears to be very bold.

AU-50, 53, 55, 58 (About Uncirculated). *Obverse:* Light wear is seen on the portrait, most notably on the upper cheek and on the hair to the right of the face. Mint luster is present in the fields, ranging from partial at AU-50 to nearly complete at AU-58. All details are sharp, unless lightly struck. *Reverse:* Light wear is seen on the top and bottom horizontal edges of the III and the wreath. Luster is partial at AU-50, increasing to nearly full at AU-58. All details are sharp, unless lightly struck.

MS-60 to 70 (Mint State). *Obverse and Reverse:* Mint luster is complete in the obverse and reverse fields.

Lower grades such as MS-60, 61, and 62 can show some evidence of abrasion. This is usually on the area of the hair to the right of the face (on the obverse), and on the highest parts of the wreath (on the reverse). Abrasion can appear as scattered contact marks elsewhere. At MS-63, these marks are few, and on MS-65 they are fewer yet. In grades above MS-65, marks can be seen only under magnification.

1866, Doubled-Die Obverse
FS-3N-1866-101.

	Mintage	Cert	Avg	%MS	EF-40	AU-50	MS-60	MS-63	MS-64	MS-65	MS-66	Recent Auction Record
1865	11,382,000	1,469	61.3	87	$40	$65	$125	$160	$225	$525	$1,100	$1,006, MS-66, Mar-10
1866	4,801,000	551	62.1	90	40	65	125	160	225	525	1,500	$518, MS-65 CAC, Jan-10
1866, DblDie Obv (a)	*	4	39.3	25	150	250	350	450	600	900		
1867	3,915,000	433	61.3	85	40	65	125	160	225	625	1,550	$1,731, MS-66 CAC, Mar-10
1868	3,252,000	418	61.4	88	40	65	125	160	225	525	950	$1,035, MS-66 CAC, Jun-10
1869	1,604,000	320	61.3	88	40	65	135	185	250	700	1,275	$1,610, MS-66, Feb-10
1870	1,335,000	321	62.2	90	40	65	140	185	250	725	1,450	$173, MS-63, Oct-09
1871	604,000	185	62.6	91	40	65	140	185	250	750	1,500	$863, MS-65 CAC, Feb-10
1872	862,000	123	62.3	89	40	65	150	190	345	950	2,100	$2,070, MS-66, Feb-10
1873, Close 3	390,000	67	62.0	84	40	65	150	190	425	1,150	2,750	$127, MS-61, Mar-10
1873, Open 3	783,000	51	60.0	84	40	65	140	175	600	4,250		$4,888, MS-65 CAC, Jan-10
1874	790,000	139	60.9	88	40	65	150	190	350	1,200	2,500	$299, MS-64, Mar-10
1875	228,000	192	63.8	97	45	80	175	225	300	800	1,500	$196, MS-62, Dec-09
1876	162,000	93	60.5	85	50	110	200	250	500	1,500	2,500	$1,265, MS-65 CAC, Jun-10
1879	38,000	132	61.7	86	110	150	275	400	500	850	1,200	$127, EF-45, Nov-09
1880	21,000	169	61.3	88	160	180	325	350	450	850	1,350	$2,300, MS-67, Feb-10
1881	1,077,000	468	61.0	81	40	65	125	185	250	650	1,000	$1,610, MS-66 Secure, Jun-10
1882	22,200	68	57.1	69	200	250	325	400	600	1,000	2,750	$6,325, MS-67, Dec-09
1883	4,000	33	58.7	67	300	350	375	800	1,750	4,500	15,000	$403, EF-40, Sep-09
1884	1,700	21	52.1	43	550	600	800	1,100	2,000	4,500	15,000	$23,000, MS-65, Jun-08
1885	1,000	29	60.9	86	650	675	900	1,100	1,500	2,500	10,000	$29,900, MS-66 CAC, Jan-10
1887	5,001	91	58.0	75	350	400	475	500	1,000	1,500	2,250	$1,725, MS-66, Mar-10
1887, 7 Over 6 (b)	*				425							$403, PF-50, Feb-06
1888	36,501	233	62.3	84	75	120	250	350	500	850	1,250	$978, MS-66, Feb-10
1889	18,125	181	61.4	81	150	190	250	400	600	850	1,350	$334, MS-63, Jan-10

* Included in number above. **a.** Moderate doubling is visible on AMERICA and on portions of the hair. "The dies clashed midway through the obverse's life. Mid- and late-die-state coins exhibit the clash marks and die cracks as progression occurs. This variety has proven extremely scarce" (*Cherrypickers' Guide to Rare Die Varieties,* fifth edition, volume I). **b.** Faint evidence of the underlying 6 are seen on both lower sides of the 7. Secondary images are visible to the east of the primary 1 and both 8s.

Proof Nickel Three-Cent Pieces

PF-60 to 70 (Proof). Proofs were struck of all dates and can be found easily enough in the marketplace. One of the rarest is 1865, the vast majority of which have a repunched date. Another is the 1887 (regular, not over-date) with a production of about 1,000 coins. Proofs of the years 1865 to 1876 can be difficult to find as true gems, while later Proofs nearly all are gems. Proofs from 1878 onward often have satiny or frosty fields, rather than mirrored surfaces, and resemble circulation strikes. *Obverse and Reverse:* PF-60, 61, and 62 coins show varying amounts of hairlines in the field, decreasing as the grade increases. Fields may be dull or cloudy on lower-level pieces. At PF-65, hairlines are visible only under magnification and are very light; the cheek of Miss Liberty does not show any friction or "album slide marks." Above PF-65, hair-lines become fewer, and in ultra-high grades are nonexistent, this meaning that the coin has never been wiped or abrasively cleaned. Blotched, deeply toned, or recolored coins are sometimes seen from PF-60 through 65 or even 66 and should be avoided; these are seen less often than on contemporary Proof nickel *five-cent* pieces.

Proof Nickel Three-Cent Piece
Shown 2x actual size.

1887, 7 Over 6, Proof
FS-3N-1887-302.

	Mintage	Cert	Finest	PF-64	PF-65	PF-66	Recent Auction Record
1865	500+	184	PF-67	$3,000	$6,500	$11,000	$10,350, PF-67Cam, May-10
1866	725+	265	PF-67	500	1,350	1,950	$2,300, PF-66Cam CAC, Jun-10
1867	625+	266	PF-67	550	1,350	2,000	$2,185, PF-66Cam CAC, Jun-10
1868	600+	243	PF-67	550	1,250	1,950	$1,265, PF-64Cam, Feb-10
1869	600+	343	PF-67	450	950	1,450	$2,300, PF-67Cam Star, Jan-10
1870	1,000+	303	PF-67	450	1,450	1,850	$1,495, PF-65Cam, Feb-10
1871	960+	318	PF-67	450	1,100	1,450	$834, PF-65, Mar-10
1872	950+	390	PF-67	425	850	1,250	$690, PF-65Cam CAC, Jan-10
1873, Close 3	1,100+	400	PF-67	425	950	1,350	$1,265, PF-66 CAC, Jun-10
1874	700+	299	PF-67	425	750	1,250	$1,840, PF-67Cam Star, Dec-09
1875	700+	225	PF-67	425	1,250	1,850	$920, PF-65, Mar-10
1876	1,150+	345	PF-67	425	900	1,300	$2,990, PF-66UCam, Jun-10
1877, Proof only	510+	410	PF-68	2,500	3,750	5,000	$4,025, PF-66, Jun-10
1878, Proof only	2,350	626	PF-68	900	1,050	1,200	$2,185, PF-67Cam CAC, May-10
1879	3,200	850	PF-68	400	600	800	$713, PF-66 CAC, Mar-10
1880	3,955	866	PF-68	400	600	800	$633, PF-65Cam, Feb-10
1881	3,575	909	PF-68	400	600	800	$1,236, PF-67 CAC, Feb-10
1882	3,100	908	PF-68	400	600	800	$920, PF-66, Mar-10
1883	6,609	1,363	PF-68	400	600	800	$633, PF-66, Mar-10
1884	3,942	1,033	PF-68	400	600	800	$518, PF-65, Mar-10
1885	3,790	854	PF-68	400	600	800	$1,035, PF-67, Feb-10
1886, Proof only	4,290	927	PF-68	425	650	850	$662, PF-66, Mar-10
1887	2,960	312	PF-67	450	950	1,100	$5,750, PF-67, Feb-10
1887, 7 Over 6 (a)	*	422	PF-68	600	800	1,000	$2,070, PF-67, Jun-10
1888	4,582	963	PF-67	400	600	800	$3,450, PF-67Cam, Feb-10
1889	3,436	947	PF-68	400	600	800	$721, PF-66 CAC, Mar-10

* Included in number above. **a.** Strong remnants of the underlying 6 are evident on either side of the lower portion of the 7, with the 1 and both 8s clearly repunched. This Proof overdate is relatively common; note that the regular date can be valued higher than the variety.

AN OVERVIEW OF NICKEL FIVE-CENT PIECES

Five-cent pieces made of nickel were introduced in 1866, in an era in which the silver half dime as well as other silver denominations were not seen in circulation. More than a dozen designs and their variations have graced the "nickel" in the past 140-plus years.

While Shield nickels of both types are slightly scarce in upper Mint State levels, they are within the financial reach of most collectors. Proofs are available of each type, but the 1866–1867 With Rays and the 1913 Buffalo Variety 1 issues are rare.

The quality of strike presents a challenge across the various types of nickel five-cent pieces, most particularly with the 1866–1867 With Rays, for there are fewer possibilities from which to choose. Although 1913–1938 Variety 2 Buffalo nickels are often poorly struck, there are enough sharp ones that finding a choice example should present no great challenge for the collector.

FOR THE COLLECTOR AND INVESTOR: FIVE-CENT PIECES AS A SPECIALTY

Shield nickels of the 1866–1883 era are often collected by date sequence. A full set includes 1866 and 1867 With Rays plus 1867 to 1883 Without Rays. In addition, there is the 1879, 9 Over 8 over-date, which is found only in Proof format but is readily available (constituting perhaps a third or so of the Proof mintage of 3,200 for the 1879 year) and the 1883, 3 Over 2 (scarce, and available only as a circulation strike).

Circulation strikes are available of all Shield nickel dates, 1866 to 1883, except 1877 and 1878, which were made only in Proof format. A set of Proofs can be completed except for the 1867 With Rays, which is exceedingly rare in Proof, with an estimated population of fewer than two dozen coins. Most 1878 Proofs are frosty and appear not much different from Mint State, but as only Proofs were made this year, they are called Proofs.

In circulated grades, Shield nickels are available in proportion to their mintage figures. The dates 1879 to 1881 had high Proof mintages (in the context of Proof figures), but low circulation-strike mintages, and thus they are key dates in the latter format. In other words, a gem MS-65 1880 Shield nickel (16,000 coined, but few were saved, as collectors acquired Proofs instead) is exceedingly rare today. In the same year 3,955 Proofs were struck, all were preserved by collectors and dealers, and today the Proof 1880 is one of the most plentiful dates.

Liberty Head nickels of the 1883 Without CENTS (or "No CENTS") type are plentiful in Mint State and also in Proof. Later dates With CENTS, through 1912, are generally available in proportion to their mintages. The 1885 and 1886 are considered to be key dates. Proofs are readily collectible, although pristine high-quality specimens can be hard to find. The 1912-D and 1912-S are scarce. In 1913 an estimated five Liberty Head nickels were privately made, and today stand as famous rarities.

Among Buffalo nickels, 1913 to 1938, the different dates and mints can be collected easily enough in circulated grades, although certain issues such as 1913-S Variety 2, 1921-S, and 1926-S are on the scarce side. An overdate, 1918-D, 8 Over 7, is a rarity at all grade levels. Curious varieties are provided by the very rare 1916 Doubled Date, the scarce 1937-D, 3-Legged (one of the forelegs of the bison was inadvertently filed off of the die), and the fascinating and readily available 1938-D, D Over S overmintmark.

In choice or gem Mint State most branch-mint Buffalo nickels, 1914–1927, are fairly scarce, and some are quite rare. Most branch-mint coins of the 1920s are lightly struck in one area or another, with the 1926-D being particularly infamous in this regard. Sharply struck examples of such varieties are worth much more than lightly struck ones, although the grading services take no particular note of such differences. Matte Proofs of dates 1913 to 1916 were struck, and mirror-finish Proofs were made in 1936 and 1937. These exist today in proportion to their mintages.

Jefferson nickels from 1938 to date are readily collectible in Mint State and Proof format. Many otherwise common varieties can be very rare if sharply struck.

RECOMMENDED READING

Bowers, Q. David. *A Guide Book of Buffalo and Jefferson Nickels,* Atlanta, GA, 2007.

Bowers, Q. David. *A Guide Book of Shield and Liberty Head Nickels,* Atlanta, GA, 2006.

Fivaz, Bill, and Stanton, J.T. *The Cherrypickers' Guide to Rare Die Varieties* (5th ed., vol. I), Atlanta, GA, 2009.

Fletcher, Edward L., Jr. *The Shield Five Cent Series,* Ormond Beach, FL, 1994.

Lange, David W. *The Complete Guide to Buffalo Nickels,* Virginia Beach, VA, 2006.

Nagengast, Bernard. *The Jefferson Nickel Analyst* (2nd ed.), Sidney, Ohio, 1979.

Peters, Gloria, and Mahon, Cynthia. *The Complete Guide to Shield and Liberty Head Nickels,* Virginia Beach, VA, 1995.

Wescott, Michael. *The United States Nickel Five-Cent Piece,* Wolfeboro, NH, 1991.

SHIELD
(1866–1883)

Designer James B. Longacre; weight 5 grams; composition .750 copper, .250 nickel; diameter 20.5 mm; plain edge. All coined at Philadelphia Mint.

Variety 1, Rays Between Stars
(1866–1867)

Variety 2, Without Rays
(1867–1883)

History. The nickel five-cent piece was introduced in 1866. At the time, silver coins (except the trime) did not circulate in the East or Midwest. The new denomination proved popular, and "nickels" of the Shield type were made continuously from 1866 to 1883. All 1866 nickels have rays between the stars on the reverse, as do a minority of 1867 issues, after which this feature was dropped. In 1877 and 1878 only Proofs were made, with no circulation strikes. The design, by Chief Engraver James B. Longacre, is somewhat similar to the obverse of the two-cent piece. Some Shield nickels were still seen in circulation in the 1930s, by which time most had been worn nearly smooth.

Striking and Sharpness. Sharpness can be a problem for Shield nickels in the 1860s through 1876, much less so for later years. On the obverse the horizontal shield stripes, vertical stripes, and leaves should be checked. The horizontal stripes in particular can be blended together. On the reverse the star centers can be weak. Check all other areas as well. Die cracks are seen on *most* circulation-strike Shield nickels, and do not affect value.

Availability. Circulated coins generally are available in proportion to their mintage quantities (exceptions being the 1873 Open 3 and Close 3 varieties, which tend to be elusive in all grades despite their relatively high mintage). MS coins are similarly available, except that 1880 is a rarity. Those dated 1882 and 1883 are plentiful.

EF-40, 45 (Extremely Fine). *Obverse:* Nearly all shield border and leaf detail is visible. Light wear is seen on the shield stripes (but the horizontal stripes can be weakly struck). *Reverse:* More wear is seen on the numeral 5 than at AU. The radial lines in the stars (if sharply struck to begin with) show slight wear. The field shows more wear.

AU-50, 53, 55, 58 (About Uncirculated). *Obverse:* Light wear is seen on the outside edges of the leaves, the frame of the shield, and the horizontal stripes (although the stripes can also be weakly struck). Mint luster is present in the fields, ranging from partial at AU-50 to nearly complete at 58. All details are sharp, unless lightly struck. *Reverse:* Light wear is seen on the numeral 5, and friction is seen in the field, identifiable as a change of color (loss of luster). Luster is partial at AU-50, increasing to nearly full at 58. All details are sharp, unless lightly struck.

MS-60 to 70 (Mint State). *Obverse and Reverse:* At MS-60 some abrasion and very minor contact marks are evident, most noticeably on high points of the shield on the obverse and the field on the reverse. Sometimes light striking on the shield and stars can be mistaken for light wear, and marks on the numeral 5 on the reverse can be from the original planchet surface not struck up fully. At MS-63 abrasions are hard to detect except under magnification. An MS-65 coin has no abrasion. Luster should be full and rich (not grainy). Coins above MS-65 have no marks that can be seen by the naked eye. Higher-grade coins display deeper luster or virtually perfect prooflike surfaces, depending on the dies used.

1866, Repunched Date
Several varieties exist.

1873, Close 3   1873, Open 3

1873, Close 3, Doubled-Die Obverse
*Several varieties exist. Pictured are FS-05-1873-101 (left)
and FS-05-1873-102 (right).*

1883, 3 Over 2
*Several varieties exist, as well as pieces with a recut 3.
Pictured are FS-05-1883-301 (left) and FS-05-1883-305 (right).*

	Mintage	Cert	Avg	%MS	EF-40	AU-50	MS-60	MS-63	MS-64	MS-65	MS-66	Recent Auction Record
1866, Rays	14,742,500	1,311	61.8	86	$160	$240	$275	$425	$750	$1,850	$4,350	$3,450, MS-66, Jun-10
1866, Repunched Date (a)	*	20	51.0	45	260	365	575	950	1,900			$6,900, MS-64, Jun-10
1867, Rays	2,019,000	458	61.3	81	190	285	375	485	850	3,100	7,500	$409, MS-63, Feb-10
1867, No Rays	28,890,500	660	62.4	89	60	110	140	225	350	725	1,850	$2,530, MS-66, Jun-10
1868	28,817,000	645	62.6	90	60	110	140	225	350	725	1,850	$345, MS-64, Jun-10
1869	16,395,000	397	62.9	92	60	110	140	225	350	725	1,850	$276, MS-63, Dec-09
1870	4,806,000	175	61.0	87	80	135	200	275	425	1,400	2,900	$276, MS-63, Mar-09
1871	561,000	77	60.6	86	250	300	400	625	875	1,775	3,850	$2,645, MS-65 CAC, Feb-10
1872	6,036,000	192	62.5	89	110	150	225	300	425	1,250	3,250	$207, MS-62, Jan-10
1873, Close 3	436,050	41	63.1	93	140	200	325	585	950	2,100	5,500	$2,530, MS-65, Jul-09
1873, Close 3, DblDie Obv (b)	*	12	55.5	50	425	675	900	1,500	2,000	3,500		$489, AU-53, Oct-08
1873, Open 3	4,113,950	64	61.8	89	100	140	210	300	500	1,600	5,000	$1,725, MS-65 CAC, Dec-09
1874	3,538,000	128	62.3	88	110	140	210	300	500	1,500	3,350	$276, MS-63, Dec-09
1875	2,097,000	127	62.5	91	130	180	240	360	525	1,700	3,450	$230, AU-68, Oct-09
1876	2,530,000	219	63.1	95	125	160	230	320	425	1,350	3,500	$920, MS-65, Feb-10
1879	25,900	65	60.6	82	700	750	900	1,000	1,450	2,350	3,750	$690, F-12, Feb-10
1880	16,000	31	49.9	29	1,300	1,850	4,000	7,500	15,000	37,500	60,000	$40,250, MS-65, Jun-10
1881	68,800	123	52.0	61	600	775	850	1,050	1,350	1,950	2,900	$2,530, MS-65, Jun-10
1882	11,472,900	806	61.4	91	65	110	150	200	275	575	1,250	$546, MS-65, Feb-10
1883	1,451,500	1,348	63.0	91	65	110	150	200	300	650	1,300	$3,105, MS-67 CAC, Jan-10
1883, 3 Over 2 (c)	*	81	59.6	63	850	1,200	1,450	1,850	2,750	8,000	15,000	$3,738, MS-64, Jun-10

* Included in number above. **a.** There are at least five similar, very strong repunched dates for 1866; the values shown are typical for each. **b.** There are several varieties of 1873, Close 3, Doubled-Die Obverse. The values shown are representative of the more avidly sought varieties; others command smaller premiums. **c.** Several varieties exist. For more information, see the *Cherrypickers' Guide to Rare Die Varieties*, fifth edition, volume I. "Beware of 1882 Shield nickels with a filled-in blobby 2, as these are very frequently offered as 1883, 3 Over 2. This is possibly the single most misunderstood coin in all U.S. coinage." (Howard Spindel, communication to Q. David Bowers, quoted in *A Guide Book of Shield and Liberty Head Nickels*)

Proof Shield Nickels

PF-60 to 70 (Proof). Proof Shield nickels were struck of all dates 1866 to 1883, including both varieties of 1867. Fields range from deeply mirrorlike to somewhat grainy in character to mirror-surface, depending on a given year. Many of 1878, a date struck only in Proof format, have *lustrous* surfaces or prooflike surfaces combined with some luster, resembling a circulation strike. While most Proofs are sharp, some have weakness on the shield on the obverse and/or the star centers on the reverse. Lint marks or tiny recessed marks from scattered debris on the die faces are sometimes encountered, especially on issues of the 1870s, but not factored into the grade in commercial certification unless excessive. *Obverse and Reverse:* PF-60, 61, and 62 coins show varying amounts of hairlines in the reverse field in particular, decreasing as the grade increases. Fields may be dull or cloudy on lower-level pieces. At PF-65, hairlines are visible only under magnification and are very light and usually only on the reverse. Above PF-65, hairlines become fewer, and in ultra-high grades are nonexistent, this meaning that the coins have never been wiped or abrasively cleaned. At PF-65 or better, expect excellent aesthetic appeal.

Proof Shield Nickel
Shown 1.5x actual size.

	Mintage	Cert	Finest	PF-63	PF-64	PF-65	PF-66	Recent Auction Record
1866, Rays	600+	260	PF-67	$2,250	$2,750	$3,500	$5,500	$4,313, PF-66Cam, Jun-10
1867, Rays †	25+	29	PF-66	34,500	45,000	65,000	85,000	$54,050, PF-65, Mar-10
1867, Without Rays	600+	241	PF-67	475	1,400	2,250	4,500	$1,725, PF-65Cam, Jan-10
1867, Without Rays, Pattern Rev (a)	21–30 known			2,000	3,500	6,000		$1,495, PF-63, Sep-09
1868	600+	196	PF-67	385	525	1,100	1,800	$1,121, PF-65Cam, Jan-10
1869	600+	299	PF-67	385	525	850	1,400	$1,029, PF-66, Mar-10
1870	1,000+	283	PF-67	385	525	850	1,400	$1,093, PF-66 CAC, Jan-10
1871	960+	281	PF-67	425	575	900	1,500	$978, PF-66Cam, Jan-10
1872	950+	322	PF-67	385	500	700	1,000	$546, PF-65, Jun-10
1873, Close 3	1,100+	326	PF-67	385	500	700	1,000	$2,013, PF-66Cam CAC, Jun-10
1874	700+	255	PF-67	385	525	725	1,100	$1,035, PF-66, Feb-10
1875	700+	267	PF-67	425	575	1,200	2,000	$311, PF-63, Mar-10
1876	1,150+	347	PF-68	385	525	725	1,100	$3,220, PF-66UCam, Feb-10
1877, Proof only	510+	360	PF-67	2,600	3,000	3,950	4,900	$4,025, PF-65, Jun-10
1878, Proof only	2,350	549	PF-67	1,900	2,250	2,750	3,500	$2,185, PF-66Cam, Jun-10
1879	3,200	494	PF-68	385	525	675	925	$3,220, PF-67 CAC, Jun-10
1879, 9 Over 8 (b)	*			400	650	750	1,000	$1,955, PF-67 CAC, Feb-10
1880	3,955	781	PF-68	385	525	675	850	$633, PF-62, Feb-10
1881	3,575	757	PF-68	385	525	675	850	$2,185, PF-67 CAC, Mar-10
1882	3,100	836	PF-68	325	425	625	800	$1,495, PF-67Cam, Jun-10
1883	5,419	1,024	PF-68	325	425	625	800	$805, PF-65Cam Star, Dec-09

* Included in number above. † Ranked in the *100 Greatest U.S. Coins* (third edition). **a.** These pattern coins (Judd-573) were struck from regular Without Rays dies. Two slightly different reverse varieties exist; they are valued the same. For more information, see *United States Pattern Coins*, 10th edition. **b.** This variety is confirmed only with Proof finish, although Breen mentions two circulation strikes and further mentions that there are "at least two varieties" *(Walter Breen's Complete Encyclopedia of U.S. and Colonial Coins)*. In the *Guide Book of Shield and Liberty Head Nickels*, Bowers discusses research and theories from Breen, DeLorey, Spindel, and Julian, noting that the variety's overdate status is "not determined."

Variety 1, Without CENTS
(1883 Only)

Variety 2, With CENTS
(1883–1912)

Mintmark is on the reverse,
to the left of CENTS.

LIBERTY HEAD
(1883–1912)

Designer Charles E. Barber; weight 5 grams; composition .750 copper, .250 nickel; diameter 21.2 mm; plain edge; mints: Philadelphia, Denver, San Francisco.

History. Liberty Head nickels were popular in their time, minted in large quantities most years, and remained in circulation through the 1940s, by which time most were worn down to grades such as AG-3 and G-4. Stray coins could still be found in the early 1950s. Serious numismatic interest in circulated examples began in the 1930s with the popularity of Whitman and other coin boards, folders, and albums. Many of the scarcer dates were picked from circulation at that time. The five known 1913 Liberty Head nickels were not an authorized Mint issue, and were never placed into circulation.

Striking and Sharpness. Many Liberty Head nickels have areas of light striking. On the obverse, this is often seen at the star centers, particularly near the top border. The hair above the forehead can be light as well, and always is thus on 1912-S (the obverse die on this San Francisco issue is slightly bulged). On the reverse, E PLURIBUS UNUM can vary in sharpness of strike. Weakness is often seen at the wreath bow and on the ear of corn to the left (the kernels in the ear can range from indistinct to bold). Even Proofs can be weakly struck in areas. Mint luster can range from minutely pebbly or grainy (but still attractive) to a deep, rich frost. Some later Philadelphia coins show stress marks in the field, particularly the obverse, from the use of "tired" dies. This can be determined only by observation, as "slabbed" grades for MS coins do not indicate the quality of the luster or surfaces.

Availability. All issues from 1883 to 1912 are readily collectible, although the 1885 (in particular), 1886, and 1912-S are considered to be key dates. Most readily available are well-worn coins in AG-3 and G-4. As a class, VF, EF, and AU pieces are very scarce in relation to demand. MS coins are generally scarce in the 1880s, except for the 1883 Without CENTS, which is plentiful in all grades. MS pieces are less scarce in the 1890s and are easily found for most 20th-century years, save for 1909, 1912-D, and 1912-S, all of which are elusive.

EF-40, 45 (Extremely Fine). *Obverse:* Nearly all hair detail is visible, save for some lightness above the forehead. The stars show radial lines (except for those that may have been lightly struck). The appearance overall is bold. *Reverse:* The wreath shows most detail on the leaves. The dentils are bold inside the rim.

AU-50, 53, 55, 58 (About Uncirculated). *Obverse:* Light wear is seen on the portrait and on the hair under LIB. Mint luster is present in the fields, ranging from partial at AU-50 to nearly complete at 58. All details are sharp, unless lightly struck. *Reverse:* Light wear is seen on the V, the other letters, and the wreath. Luster is partial at AU-50, increasing to nearly full at 58. All details are sharp, unless lightly struck.

MS-60 to 70 (Mint State). *Obverse and Reverse:* Mint luster is complete in the obverse and reverse fields. MS-60, 61, and 62 can show some evidence of abrasion, usually on the portrait on the obverse and highest parts of the wreath on the reverse, and scattered contact marks elsewhere. At MS-63 these marks are few, and at MS-65 they are fewer yet. In grades above MS-65, marks can only be seen under magnification.

1899, Repunched Date,
Early Die State

1899, Repunched Date,
Late Die State

FS-05-1899-301.

1900, Doubled-Die Reverse
FS-05-1900-801.

1913 Liberty Head Nickel
Shown 2x actual size.

	Mintage	Cert	Avg	%MS	EF-40	AU-50	MS-60	MS-63	MS-64	MS-65	MS-66	Recent Auction Record
1883, Without CENTS	5,474,300	5,882	63.8	96	$12	$14	$35	$50	$70	$195	$400	$403, MS-66 CAC, Feb-10
1883, With CENTS	16,026,200	765	62.9	93	85	120	150	200	285	575	1,150	$920, MS-66, Jun-10
1884	11,270,000	339	61.7	89	85	130	190	300	400	1,500	3,400	$1,955, MS-66 CAC, Jun-10
1885	1,472,700	450	36.8	41	1,350	1,700	2,000	2,700	5,000	8,000	16,000	$1,955, AU-55, Jun-10
1886	3,326,000	394	41.3	48	700	825	1,000	2,200	3,200	6,500	11,000	$29,325, MS-66 CAC, Feb-10
1887	15,260,692	385	63.0	95	75	110	140	195	325	900	1,800	$1,035, MS-65 CAC, Feb-10
1888	10,167,901	271	62.0	92	175	220	275	340	450	1,225	3,000	$1,265, MS-65 Secure CAC, Jun-10
1889	15,878,025	492	63.9	98	75	120	140	175	325	700	2,200	$920, MS-66, Jan-10
1890	16,256,532	256	63.3	96	65	110	160	200	350	1,200	2,300	$1,150, MS-66, Mar-10
1891	16,832,000	334	63.6	97	65	110	160	200	300	825	1,700	$127, MS-62, Mar-10
1892	11,696,897	345	63.4	97	65	110	140	160	300	1,000	3,000	$3,450, MS-66 CAC, Jun-10
1893	13,368,000	366	63.5	98	65	110	135	160	300	875	2,850	$150, MS-63, Jan-10
1894	5,410,500	258	62.0	91	240	300	350	425	550	1,200	2,100	$2,185, MS-66, Jan-10
1895	9,977,822	283	63.4	98	70	110	140	200	440	2,000	4,900	$4,888, MS-66, Jan-10
1896	8,841,058	250	63.1	95	90	150	190	265	450	2,100	6,000	$9,775, MS-66, Jan-10
1897	20,426,797	360	63.1	96	45	70	100	160	260	850	2,600	$253, MS-64, Feb-10
1898	12,530,292	352	63.3	96	45	75	150	185	290	1,000	2,000	$1,840, MS-66, Jan-10
1899	26,027,000	608	63.5	96	30	60	90	130	200	500	950	$920, MS-66, Mar-10
1899, Repunched Date (a)	*				85	150	190	240	550	800		$150, MS-63, Apr-02
1900	27,253,733	680	63.7	97	30	60	90	135	210	525	975	$4,600, MS-67 CAC, Jun-10
1900, DblDie Rev (b)	*	3	61.3	67	110	160	235	310	465	875		
1901	26,478,228	643	63.5	98	28	55	75	125	200	500	1,100	$978, MS-66, Feb-10
1902	31,487,561	630	63.5	97	28	55	75	125	200	500	1,050	$138, MS-63, Feb-10
1903	28,004,935	682	63.7	97	28	55	75	125	200	500	950	$978, MS-66, Jan-10
1904	21,403,167	568	63.5	97	28	55	75	125	200	500	950	$99, MS-63, Feb-10
1905	29,825,124	713	63.3	96	28	55	75	125	200	485	950	$978, MS-66 CAC, Jun-10
1906	38,612,000	515	62.8	93	28	55	75	125	210	575	2,250	$2,300, MS-66, Jan-10
1907	39,213,325	496	62.9	94	28	55	75	125	210	725	1,400	$805, MS-65, Feb-10
1908	22,684,557	441	62.8	93	28	55	75	125	210	825	3,500	$150, MS-63, Feb-10
1909	11,585,763	328	62.8	91	32	70	95	140	275	975	2,200	$1,955, MS-66 CAC, Jun-10
1910	30,166,948	507	62.9	93	28	45	70	100	185	525	2,850	$109, MS-63, Feb-10
1911	39,557,639	1,041	63.4	96	28	45	70	100	185	485	950	$360, MS-65, Feb-10

* Included in number above. **a.** "The loop of a 9, or possibly (but unlikely) an 8, is evident within the lower loop of the second 9. Some specialists believe this to be an 1899/8 overdate. However, we feel it is simply a repunched date, with the secondary 9 far to the south of the primary 9 at the last digit" (*Cherrypickers' Guide to Rare Die Varieties*, fifth edition, volume I). **b.** Doubling on this very popular variety is evident on all reverse design elements, including the V, with a stronger spread on the lower quadrant of the reverse.

	Mintage	Cert	Avg	%MS	EF-40	AU-50	MS-60	MS-63	MS-64	MS-65	MS-66	Recent Auction Record
1912	26,234,569	857	62.8	95	$28	$45	$70	$100	$185	$500	$1,350	$1,610, MS-66 CAC, Feb-10
1912D	8,474,000	656	62.3	93	85	175	300	385	525	1,650	3,650	$3,680, MS-66, May-10
1912S	238,000	774	41.8	57	850	1,400	1,750	2,000	3,000	5,500	14,000	$5,175, MS-65, Jun-10
1913 † (c)	(5 known)						3,750,000					

† Ranked in the *100 Greatest U.S. Coins* (third edition). **c.** An estimated five 1913 Liberty Head nickels (four circulation-strike and one Proof) were struck under irregular circumstances at the Mint. Some researchers consider them all to be Proofs. They were dispersed and are now held in various public and private collections.

Proof Liberty Head Nickels

PF-60 to 70 (Proof). Proof Liberty Head nickels were struck of all dates 1883 to 1912, plus both varieties of 1883. The fields range from deeply mirrorlike to somewhat grainy character to mirror-surface, depending on a given year. While most Proofs are sharp, some have weakness at the star centers and/or the kernels on the ear of corn to the left of the ribbon bow. These weaknesses are overlooked by the certification services. Generally, later issues are more deeply mirrored than are earlier ones. Some years in the 1880s and 1890s can show graininess, a combination of mint luster and mirror quality. Lint marks or tiny recessed marks from scattered debris on the die faces are sometimes encountered, but not factored into third-party–certified grades unless excessive. *Obverse and Reverse:* PF-60, 61, and 62 coins show varying amounts of hairlines in the field, decreasing as the grade increases. Fields may be dull or cloudy on lower-level pieces. At PF-65, hairlines are visible only under magnification and are very light; the cheek of Miss Liberty does not show any abrasion or "album slide marks." Above PF-65, hairlines become fewer, and in ultra-high grades are nonexistent, this meaning that the coins have never been wiped or abrasively cleaned. At PF-65 or finer, expect excellent aesthetic appeal. Blotched, deeply toned, or recolored coins can be found at most Proof levels from PF-60 through 65 or even 66, and should be avoided. Watch for artificially toned lower-grade Proofs colored to mask the true nature of the fields.

Proof Liberty Head Nickel
Shown 1.5x actual size.

	Mintage	Cert	Finest	PF-63	PF-64	PF-65	PF-66	Recent Auction Record
1883, Without CENTS	5,219	885	PF-67	$300	$400	$775	$1,050	$328, PF-64, Mar-10
1883, With CENTS	6,783	649	PF-68	250	350	650	900	$587, PF-66, Mar-10
1884	3,942	719	PF-68	225	325	525	725	$978, PF-66Cam, Jun-10
1885	3,790	725	PF-68	1,250	1,400	1,700	2,100	$8,913, PF-68, Jun-10
1886	4,290	722	PF-67	550	675	800	1,000	$805, PF-66, Feb-10
1887	2,960	526	PF-67	225	325	525	725	$476, PF-65, Mar-10
1888	4,582	707	PF-67	225	325	525	725	$4,888, PF-67Cam, Feb-10
1889	3,336	551	PF-68	225	325	525	725	$489, PF-65 CAC, Mar-10
1890	2,740	412	PF-68	225	325	575	1,150	$288, PF-64, Mar-10
1891	2,350	425	PF-68	225	325	575	1,150	$299, PF-64Cam, Mar-10
1892	2,745	464	PF-68	225	325	525	800	$3,220, PF-67Cam Star, Jun-10
1893	2,195	414	PF-68	225	325	525	800	$1,725, PF-66Cam CAC, Mar-10
1894	2,632	415	PF-68	225	325	525	1,000	$4,313, PF-67Cam Star, Jun-10
1895	2,062	394	PF-68	225	325	525	1,000	$748, PF-65Cam, Jan-10
1896	1,862	380	PF-67	225	325	525	900	$299, PF-64, Feb-10
1897	1,938	431	PF-69	225	325	525	725	$299, PF-64, Feb-10
1898	1,795	379	PF-68	225	325	525	875	$489, PF-65, Jan-10
1899	2,031	415	PF-67	225	325	525	725	$3,738, PF-67 CAC, Jan-10
1900	2,262	425	PF-68	225	325	525	725	$518, PF-65Cam, Mar-10
1901	1,985	469	PF-68	225	325	525	725	$1,725, PF-67Cam, Mar-10
1902	2,018	428	PF-68	225	325	525	725	$1,121, PF-67, Feb-10
1903	1,790	504	PF-68	225	325	525	725	$4,025, PF-67Cam, Jan-10
1904	1,817	402	PF-67	225	325	550	900	$253, PF-64, Feb-10
1905	2,152	403	PF-68	225	325	525	775	$288, PF-64, Feb-10

Chart continued on next page.

	Mintage	Cert	Finest	PF-63	PF-64	PF-65	PF-66	Recent Auction Record
1906	1,725	403	PF-68	$225	$325	$525	$750	$3,220, PF-67Cam CAC, Jan-10
1907	1,475	331	PF-67	225	325	525	775	$5,463, PF-67 Star CAC, Feb-10
1908	1,620	398	PF-68	225	325	525	775	$1,725, PF-66Cam, Feb-10
1909	4,763	1,239	PF-68	225	325	525	700	$725, PF-64DCam, Mar-10
1910	2,405	632	PF-68	225	325	525	725	$490, PF-65, Mar-10
1911	1,733	536	PF-68	225	325	525	750	$1,610, PF-67 Star, Jun-10
1912	2,145	533	PF-68	225	325	525	775	$253, PF-64, Feb-10
1913 † (a)	(5 known)	4	PF-66	3,750,000				$3,737,500, PF-64, Jan-10

† Ranked in the *100 Greatest U.S. Coins* (third edition). **a.** An estimated five 1913 Liberty Head nickels (four circulation-strike and one Proof) were struck under irregular circumstances at the Mint. Some researchers consider them all to be Proofs. They were dispersed and are now held in various public and private collections.

INDIAN HEAD OR BUFFALO
(1913–1938)

Designer James Earle Fraser; weight 5 grams; composition .750 copper, .250 nickel; diameter 21.2 mm; plain edge; mints: Philadelphia, Denver, San Francisco.

Variety 1, FIVE CENTS
on Raised Ground (1913)

Mintmark position is below FIVE CENTS.

Variety 2, FIVE CENTS
in Recess (1913–1938)

Mintmark position is below FIVE CENTS.

History. The Indian Head nickel five-cent piece today is almost universally known as the "Buffalo" nickel, after the American bison on the reverse. The design made its debut in 1913. James Earle Fraser, a sculptor well known in the private sector, was its creator. The obverse features an authentic portrait of a Native American, modeled as a composite from life, with three subjects posing. Unlike any preceding coin made for circulation, the Buffalo nickel had little in the way of open, smooth field surfaces. Instead, most areas on the obverse and reverse were filled with design elements or, especially on the reverse, an irregular background, as on a bas-relief plaque.

Soon after the first coins were released, it was thought that the inscription FIVE CENTS, on a high area of the motif, would wear too quickly. The Mint modified the design to lower the ground under the bison, which had been arranged in the form of a mound (on what became known as Variety 1). The flat-ground design is called Variety 2.

Striking and Sharpness. Most circulation-strike Buffalo nickels are poorly struck in one or more areas, and for many Denver and San Francisco issues of the 1920s the striking is very poor. However, enough sharp strikes exist among common dates of the 1930s that one can be found with some patience. Certification services do not reflect the quality of strike on their labels, so examine carefully. The matter of striking sharpness on Buffalo nickels is an exceedingly important aspect for the connoisseur (who might prefer, for example, a sharply struck coin in AU-58 over a fully

lustrous MS example with much shallower detail). Points to check on the obverse include the center of the coin, especially the area immediately above the tie on the braid. On the reverse check the fur on the head of the bison, and the fur "line" above the bison's shoulder on its back. On both sides, examine the overall striking of letters and other details.

Availability. Among circulated varieties of standard dates and mintmarks, availability is in proportion to their mintages. Among early issues the 1913-S, Variety 2, is the scarcest. The date wore away more quickly on the Variety 1 coins than on the modified design used from later 1913 through the end of the series. In the 1920s the 1926-S is the hardest to find. Collectors sought Buffalo nickels from circulation until the 1960s, after which most were gone. By that time the dates in the teens were apt to have their dates completely worn away, or be AG-3 or G-4. Among MS nickels, the issues of 1913 were saved in quantity as novelties, although 1913-S, Variety 2, is slightly scarce. Philadelphia Mint issues are readily available through the 1920s, while MS-63 and finer mintmarked issues from 1914 to 1927 can range from scarce to rare. From 1931 to 1938, all dates and mintmarks were saved in roll quantities, and all are plentiful today. Many Buffalo nickels in MS are very rare if with Full Details, this being especially true for mintmarked issues after 1913, into the early 1930s. Sharpness of strike is not noted on certification holders, but a connoisseur would probably rather own a Full Details coin in MS-65 than an MS-66 or higher with a flat strike.

EF-40, 45 (Extremely Fine). *Obverse:* More wear than at AU is seen on the cheek (in particular) and the rest of the face. The center of the coin above the braid is mostly smooth. Other details are sharp. *Reverse:* More wear is evident than at AU. The tip of the horn is well defined on better strikes. The shoulder, flank, and hip show more wear. The tip of the tail may be discernible, but is mostly worn away.

AU-50, 53, 55, 58 (About Uncirculated). *Obverse:* Light wear is seen on the highest area of the cheek, to the left of the nose, this being the most obvious checkpoint. Light wear is also seen on the highest-relief areas of the hair. Luster is less extensive, and wear more extensive, at AU-50 than at higher grades. An AU-58 coin will have only slight wear and will retain the majority of luster. *Reverse:* Light wear is seen on the shoulder and hip, these being the key checkpoints. Light wear is also seen on the flank of the bison and on the horn and top of the head. Luster is less extensive, and wear more extensive, at AU-50 than at higher grades. An AU-58 coin will have only slight wear and will retain the majority of luster.

MS-60 to 70 (Mint State). *Obverse and Reverse:* Mint luster is complete in the obverse and reverse fields, except in areas not fully struck up, in which graininess or marks from the original planchet surface can be seen. MS-60, 61, and 62 can show some evidence of abrasion, usually on the center of the obverse above the braid, and on the reverse at the highest parts of the bison. These two checkpoints are often areas of light striking, so abrasion must be differentiated from original planchet marks. At MS-63 evidences of abrasion are few, and at MS-65 they are fewer yet. In grades above MS-65, a Buffalo nickel should be mark-free.

1913, Variety 1, 3-1/2 Legged
FS-05-1913-901.

1914, 4 Over 3
FS-05-1914-101.

1916, Doubled-Die Obverse
FS-05-1916-101.

1916, Missing Designer's Initial
FS-05-1916-401.

1918, Doubled-Die Reverse
FS-05-1918-801.

1918-D, 8 Over 7
FS-05-1918D-101.

1935, Doubled-Die Reverse
FS-05-1935-501.

1936-D, 3-1/2 Legged
FS-05-1936D-901.

1937-D, 3-Legged
FS-05-1937D-901.

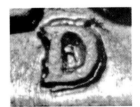

1938-D, D Over S
FS-05-1938D-511.

	Mintage	Cert	Avg	%MS	EF-40	AU-50	MS-60	MS-63	MS-64	MS-65	MS-66	Recent Auction Record
1913, Variety 1	30,992,000	6,211	64.5	98	$25	$35	$45	$60	$75	$150	$300	$16,100, MS-68, Jun-10
1913, Var 1, 3-1/2 Legged **(a)**	*				420	540	720	1,200	3,600	10,800	18,000	$10,350, MS-64, Apr-09
1913D, Variety 1	5,337,000	1,739	63.6	94	42	70	75	80	115	275	550	$2,185, MS-67, Jun-10
1913S, Variety 1	2,105,000	1,172	62.2	89	90	110	130	180	260	625	1,200	$4,888, MS-67, Jun-10

* Included in number above. **a.** The reverse die was heavily polished, possibly to remove clash marks, resulting in a die with most of the bison's front leg missing.

Chart continued on next page.

	Mintage	Cert	Avg	%MS	EF-40	AU-50	MS-60	MS-63	MS-64	MS-65	MS-66	Recent Auction Record
1913, Variety 2	29,857,186	1,462	63.4	94	$22	$30	$40	$80	$100	$310	$875	$3,450, MS-67, Jun-10
1913D, Variety 2	4,156,000	808	57.4	70	235	260	300	400	575	1,100	2,000	$5,175, MS-67, Jun-10
1913S, Variety 2	1,209,000	1,117	53.3	59	600	750	1,000	1,300	2,000	3,500	6,000	$9,788, MS-67, Jun-10
1914	20,664,463	1,179	60.3	86	35	45	60	85	145	420	900	$3,450, MS-67 CAC Star, Jun-10
1914, 4 Over 3 (b)	*				875	1,500	2,300	6,000	8,500	19,500		$978, AU-50, Jun-10
1914D	3,912,000	829	56.3	69	325	400	450	550	650	1,450	2,300	$2,128, MS-66, Jun-10
1914S	3,470,000	1,170	60.0	79	90	160	200	450	525	1,800	4,250	$13,800, MS-67, Jun-10
1915	20,986,220	1,181	63.5	93	25	45	60	90	125	300	600	$4,025, MS-67, Jun-10
1915D	7,569,000	741	60.3	72	130	160	270	350	475	1,600	3,600	$2,760, MS-66, Jun-10
1915S	1,505,000	567	53.9	66	400	500	650	1,000	1,350	2,600	4,500	$3,738, MS-66, Jun-10
1916	63,497,466	1,635	63.0	93	14	25	50	85	105	300	750	$4,313, MS-67, Jun-10
1916, DblDie Obv (c)	*	82	40.8	13	16,000 (d)	34,000	62,500	140,000	225,000	325,000		$4,025, G-4, Jun-10
1916, Missing Initial (e)	*				200	280	375	600				$575, MS-64, Apr-06
1916D	13,333,000	954	61.3	82	90	120	175	260	450	1,750	7,500	$7,188, MS-66, Jun-10
1916S	11,860,000	722	61.2	80	90	125	190	275	465	1,900	3,500	$3,220, MS-67, Jun-10
1917	51,424,019	784	63.0	92	16	35	60	150	210	475	700	$3,220, MS-67, Jun-10
1917D	9,910,000	682	57.7	71	150	275	350	750	950	2,300	8,750	$7,188, MS-66, Jun-10
1917S	4,193,000	510	52.7	61	200	375	450	1,150	1,800	3,850	7,750	$40,250, MS-67, Jun-10
1918	32,086,314	490	62.5	91	32	50	125	325	450	1,200	2,350	$14,950, MS-67 Star, Jun-10
1918, DblDie Rev (f)	*	3	44.0	33	1,450 (g)	2,300	3,500	7,000				
1918D, 8 Over 7 † (h)	**	542	20.2	9	9,500	12,500	35,000	60,000	75,000	265,000		$12,650, AU-55, Jun-10
1918D	8,362,000	508	51.8	59	225	350	450	1,300	1,450	3,500	7,400	$6,900, MS-66, Jun-10
1918S	4,882,000	475	56.6	71	200	325	550	2,000	4,550	23,500	125,000	$29,900, MS-66, Jun-10
1919	60,868,000	962	63.3	94	15	32	55	125	200	475	925	$10,925, MS-67, Jun-10
1919D	8,006,000	496	51.6	50	260	350	600	1,500	2,400	5,700	13,500	$10,350, MS-66, Jun-10
1919S	7,521,000	584	52.7	54	260	375	625	1,850	3,500	13,000	100,000	$2,645, MS-64, Jun-10
1920	63,093,000	704	63.4	95	14	30	65	140	225	650	1,275	$8,625, MS-67, Jun-10
1920D	9,418,000	553	54.0	66	275	325	600	1,575	1,800	5,000	75,000	$1,093, MS-63, Jan-10
1920S	9,689,000	601	54.4	64	175	300	600	1,850	3,700	24,000	45,000	$32,200, MS-66, Jun-10
1921	10,663,000	599	63.4	92	50	75	150	320	380	725	1,200	$3,738, MS-67, Jun-10
1921S	1,557,000	761	33.8	27	950	1,200	1,800	2,200	2,700	6,600	25,000	$12,650, MS-66, Jun-10
1923	35,715,000	796	63.4	93	13	35	65	160	185	570	1,000	$3,738, MS-67, Jun-10
1923S	6,142,000	939	53.0	67	300	400	550	1,000	1,300	8,000	27,500	$19,550, MS-66, Jun-10
1924	21,620,000	548	63.2	93	24	42	75	160	325	750	1,900	$4,313, MS-67, Jun-10
1924D	5,258,000	638	49.9	60	235	325	400	850	1,200	3,850	20,000	$3,450, MS-65, Jun-10
1924S	1,437,000	750	28.4	21	1,200	1,800	2,500	3,750	4,400	10,500	30,000	$20,125, MS-66 Star, Jun-10
1925	35,565,100	804	64.1	98	15	32	42	100	150	435	600	$7,475, MS-67, Jun-10
1925D	4,450,000	633	56.5	76	185	265	400	700	1,200	4,250	20,000	$9,200, MS-66, Jun-10
1925S	6,256,000	703	51.0	55	180	250	475	2,200	3,000	29,000		$40,250, MS-66, Jun-10
1926	44,693,000	1,248	64.3	98	10	20	32	75	100	190	375	$2,760, MS-67, Jun-10
1926D	5,638,000	654	56.7	78	185	300	350	500	1,500	4,100	9,200	$17,250, MS-67, Jun-10
1926S	970,000	1,291	28.0	14	900	2,800	4,800	9,500	14,500	95,000		$10,925, MS-64, Feb-10
1927	37,981,000	861	64.1	97	12	21	35	80	110	260	550	$2,990, MS-67, Jun-10
1927D	5,730,000	653	60.9	88	80	135	180	310	650	7,000	20,000	$16,100, MS-66, Jun-10
1927S	3,430,000	521	56.5	64	95	185	550	2,300	3,500	16,000	100,000	$2,990, MS-64, Feb-10
1928	23,411,000	728	63.9	95	13	23	32	80	110	275	650	$4,888, MS-67, Jun-10
1928D	6,436,000	1,378	63.5	98	45	50	60	110	125	600	3,500	$2,415, MS-66, Jun-10
1928S	6,936,000	610	61.4	85	26	110	260	600	750	4,000	19,000	$32,200, MS-67 Star, Jun-10
1929	36,446,000	985	63.7	97	12	20	40	75	95	285	675	$1,495, MS-66 CAC, Jun-10
1929D	8,370,000	650	63.1	96	32	45	60	130	285	1,275	2,200	$1,840, MS-66, Jun-10
1929S	7,754,000	778	63.6	96	12	25	55	80	145	400	700	$3,738, MS-67, Jun-10

* Included in number above. ** Included in number below. † Ranked in the *100 Greatest U.S. Coins* (third edition). **b.** The straight top bar of the underlying 3 is visible at the top of the 4. The start of the 3's diagonal is seen on the upper right, outside of the 4. On some coins, a hint of the curve of the lower portion of the 3 shows just above the crossbar of the 4. **c.** The date, chin, throat, feathers, and the tie on the braid are all doubled. "Beware of 1916 nickels with strike doubling on the date offered as this variety. . . . The true doubled die must look like the coin shown here" (*Cherrypickers' Guide to Rare Die Varieties*, fifth edition, volume I). **d.** Value in VF-20 is $11,000. **e.** The initial F, for Fraser—normally below the date—is clearly absent. Some dies exist with a partially missing or weak initial; these do not command the premium of the variety with a completely missing initial. **f.** Doubling is most obvious to the north on E PLURIBUS UNUM. Some coins show a die crack from the rim to the bison's rump, just below the tail. **g.** Value in VF-20 is $1,150. **h.** "Look for the small die crack immediately above the tie on the braid, leading slightly downward to the Indian's jaw. The beginning of this die break can usually be seen even on lower-grade coins" (*Cherrypickers' Guide to Rare Die Varieties*).

	Mintage	Cert	Avg	%MS	EF-40	AU-50	MS-60	MS-63	MS-64	MS-65	MS-66	Recent Auction Record
1930	22,849,000	1,150	63.6	95	$11	$20	$35	$75	$90	$210	$500	$3,335, MS-67, Jun-10
1930S	5,435,000	611	63.0	94	14	30	55	120	185	400	750	$805, MS-66, Jun-10
1931S	1,200,000	1,577	63.9	97	35	55	65	100	125	275	650	$8,625, MS-67, Jun-10
1934	20,213,003	914	63.8	94	10	18	50	65	110	300	500	$2,185, MS-67, Jun-10
1934D	7,480,000	1,042	63.5	97	20	45	80	125	240	550	1,850	$1,955, MS-66, Jun-10
1935	58,264,000	1,224	64.2	95	3	10	22	45	60	120	230	$1,725, MS-67, Jun-10
1935, DblDie Rev (i)	*	108	31.3	7	500	1,300	5,250	6,500	7,500	26,000		$25,300, MS-65, Jun-10
1935D	12,092,000	1,075	63.5	97	15	40	75	85	125	430	950	$2,760, MS-67, Jun-10
1935S	10,300,000	1,184	64.1	98	4	18	55	70	80	210	350	$3,450, MS-67 Star, Jun-10
1936	118,997,000	2,486	64.4	94	3	9	22	40	50	75	200	$1,610, MS-67 Secure CAC, Jun-10
1936D	24,814,000	1,887	64.6	98	4	12	38	45	55	95	300	$1,725, MS-67, Jun-10
1936D, 3-1/2 Legged (j)	*				4,900 (k)	8,000	12,000					$1,840, F-15, Jun-10
1936S	14,930,000	1,425	64.3	97	4	12	38	45	55	95	250	$1,955, MS-67, Jun-10
1937	79,480,000	6,450	65.5	99	3	9	22	40	45	60	100	$4,613, MS-68, Jun-10
1937D	17,826,000	3,426	65.1	98	4	10	32	42	50	60	85	$920, MS-67, Jun-10
1937D, 3-Legged (l)	*	4,749	50.9	31	1,200 (m)	1,400	2,500	5,250	9,000	35,000	57,500	$2,070, AU-58, Jun-10
1937S	5,635,000	2,714	65.1	99	3	9	32	42	50	65	150	$10,925, MS-68 Star, Jun-10
1938D	7,020,000	26,236	65.8	100	4	8	22	36	40	60	130	$4,888, MS-68 Star, Jun-10
1938D, D Over D	*	2,025	65.6	100	20	25	45	50	55	75	150	$805, MS-67, Jun-10
1938D, D Over S (n)	*	1,737	65.2	99	20	32	55	80	120	175	375	$13,800, MS-68, Feb-10

* Included in number above. **i.** Strong doubling is evident on FIVE CENTS, E PLURIBUS UNUM, and the eye, horn, and mane of the bison. This variety (FS-05-1935-801) is extremely rare above VF, and fewer than a dozen are known in MS. Do not mistake it for the more moderately doubled FS-05-1935-803, which commands much lower premiums. **j.** The right front leg has been partially polished off the die—similar to the 1937-D 3-Legged variety, but not as severe. (This variety is not from the same die as the 1937-D.) Fewer than 40 are known in all grades. Incorrectly listed by Breen as 1936-P. **k.** Value in VF-20 is $5,000. **l.** The reverse die was polished heavily, perhaps to remove clash marks, resulting in the shaft of the bison's right front leg missing. Beware altered specimens fraudulently passed as genuine. "Look for a line of raised dots from the middle of the bison's belly to the ground as one of the diagnostics on the genuine specimen" *(Cherrypickers' Guide to Rare Die Varieties)*. **m.** Value in VF-20 is $1,100. **n.** There are five different D Over S dies for this date. Varieties other than the one listed here (FS-05-1938D-511) command smaller premiums.

Proof Indian Head or Buffalo Nickels

PF-60 to 70 (Matte Proof). Matte Proofs were made from 1913 to 1916 and are rare. These have minutely granular or matte surfaces, are sharply struck with Full Details of the design on both sides, and have edges (as viewed edge-on) that are mirrored, a distinctive figure. These are easily confused with circulation strikes except for the features noted. Certified holders usually list these simply as "Proof," not "Matte Proof." Most Matte Proofs are in higher grades. *Obverse and Reverse:* Those Proofs with abrasion or contact marks can be graded PF-60 to 62; these are not widely desired. PF-64 can have some abrasion. Tiny flecks are not common, but are sometimes seen. At the Matte PF-65 level or higher there will no traces of abrasion or flecks. Differences between higher-grade Proofs are highly subjective, and one certified at PF-65 can be similar to another at PF-67, and vice-versa.

PF-60 to 70 (Mirror Proof). Some early Proofs of 1936 have satiny rather than mirrorlike fields. Later Proofs of 1936 and all of 1937 have a mirror surface in the fields. The motifs of the 1936 and 1937 mirror Proofs are lightly polished in the die (not frosty or matte). Most mirror (also called brilliant) Proofs are in higher grades. *Obverse and Reverse:* PF-60 to 62 coins can have abrasion or minor handling marks, but usually are assigned such grades because of staining or blotches resulting from poor cleaning. PF-63 and 64 can have minor abrasion and staining. Tiny flecks are sometimes seen, as are dark stripe lines from the glued seams in the cellophane envelopes used by the Mint. PF-65 and higher coins should be free of stains, flecks, and abrasion of any kind. Differences between higher-grade Proofs are highly subjective, and one certified PF-65 can be similar to another at PF-67, and vice-versa.

Matte Proof Indian Head or Buffalo Nickel (1913–1916)

Satin Proof Indian Head or Buffalo Nickel (1936)

Mirror Proof Indian Head or Buffalo Nickel (1936–1937)

	Mintage	Cert	Finest	PF-63	PF-64	PF-65	PF-66	Recent Auction Record
1913, Variety 1	1,520	299	PF-68	$1,200	$1,800	$3,250	$4,300	$9,775, PF-67 CAC, Jun-10
1913, Variety 2	1,514	237	PF-68	1,000	1,600	2,250	3,000	$5,463, PF-67, Jun-10
1914	1,275	413	PF-68	975	1,500	2,000	2,500	$5,175, PF-67 CAC, Jun-10
1915	1,050	330	PF-69	1,000	1,600	2,250	2,750	$11,513, PF-68, Jun-10
1916	600	167	PF-68	1,500	2,500	3,200	4,200	$8,625, PF-67, Jun-10

Chart continued on next page.

	Mintage	Cert	Finest	PF-63	PF-64	PF-65	PF-66	Recent Auction Record
1927, Presentation Strike (a)	unknown	5	PF-64		$30,000	$48,000	$75,000	
1936, Both kinds	4,420							
1936, Satin Finish		600	PF-68	$1,150	1,300	1,500	1,700	$8,338, PF-68, Jun-10
1936, Brilliant Finish		529	PF-68	1,250	1,650	1,950	2,200	$8,625, PF-68, Jun-10
1937	5,769	1,457	PF-68	1,100	1,400	1,600	1,800	$4,600, PF-68, Jun-10

a. Some experts believe that certain 1927 nickels were carefully made circulation strikes; such pieces are sometimes certified as "Specimens" or "Presentation Strikes." Professional numismatic opinions vary.

JEFFERSON (1938 TO DATE)

1938–2003: Designer Felix Schlag; weight 5 grams; composition (1938–1942, 1946 to date), .750 copper, .250 nickel, (1942–1945), .560 copper, .350 silver, .090 manganese, with net weight .05626 oz. pure silver; diameter 21.2 mm; plain edge; mints: Philadelphia, Denver, San Francisco.

2004: Designers Felix Schlag (obverse), Norman E. Nemeth (Peace Medal reverse), and Al Maletsky (Keelboat reverse).

2005: Designers Joe Fitzgerald (obverse), Jamie Franki (American Bison reverse), and Joe Fitzgerald (Ocean in View reverse).

2006 to date: Designers Jamie Franki (obverse) and Felix Schlag (reverse).

Monticello Reverse (1938–2003)

Wartime Silver Alloy (1942–1945)
Mintmark is above Monticello.

Peace Medal Reverse (2004)

Keelboat Reverse (2004)

Obverse (2005)

American Bison Reverse (2005)

Ocean in View Reverse (2005)

Obverse (2006 to Date)

Reverse (2006 to Date)

History. The Jefferson nickel, designed by Felix Schlag in a public competition, made its debut in 1938, and has been a numismatic favorite since. The obverse for many years featured a portrait of Thomas Jefferson after the famous bust by Jean Antoine Houdon, and the reverse a front view of Jefferson's home, Monticello.

From partway through 1942 to 1945 a copper-silver-manganese alloy replaced the traditional 75% copper and 25% nickel composition. These silver-content coins bear a distinctive P, D, or S mintmark above the dome of Monticello.

Starting in 1966, Felix Schlag's initials, FS, were added below the presidential bust; this continued through 2004, when the obverse portrait changed. The coinage dies were remodeled to strengthen the design in 1971, 1972, 1977, and 1982. The mintmark position, originally on the reverse to the right of Monticello, was moved to the obverse starting in 1968.

In 2004 special designs commemorating the Westward Journey (Lewis and Clark expedition) were introduced; the program continued through 2005. In 2006 a new obverse portrait debuted, along with a return to Monticello on the reverse.

Striking and Sharpness. On the obverse, check for weakness on the portrait, especially in the lower jaw area. On the reverse, most circulation strikes have weak details on the six steps of Monticello, especially under the third pillar from the left, as this section on the reverse was opposite in the dies (in the press) from the high parts of the Jefferson portrait, and metal could not effectively flow in both directions at once. Planchet weight allowance was another cause, the dies being spaced slightly too far apart. Jefferson nickels can be classified as "Full Steps" (FS) if either five or six of Monticello's porch steps (with the top step counting as one) are clear. Notations of 5FS or 6FS can indicate the number of visible steps. It is easier to count the incuse lines than the raised steps. If there are four complete, unbroken lines, the coin qualifies as Full Steps (with five steps); five complete, unbroken lines indicate six full steps. There must be no nicks, cuts, or scratches interrupting the incuse lines. It is difficult to determine a full five-step count on the 1938 and some 1939 issues, as the steps are wavy and ill-defined; a great deal of subjectivity is common for these dates.

Even if the steps are mostly or fully defined, check other areas to determine if a coin has Full Details overall. Interestingly, nickels of the 1950s and 1960s are among the most weakly struck. The silver-content coins of the 1940s usually are well struck. Some nickels of the 1950s to 1970s discolored easily, perhaps due to some impurities in the alloy.

Availability. All basic dates and mintmarks were saved in roll quantities. Scarce issues in MS include 1939-D and 1942-D. The low-mintage 1950-D was a popular speculation, and most of the mintage went into numismatic hands, making MS coins common. Many different dates and mints are rare if with 5FS or 6FS; consult *A Guide Book of Buffalo and Jefferson Nickels* for details.

MS-60 to 70 (Mint State). *Obverse and Reverse:* Mint luster is complete in the obverse and reverse fields, except in areas not fully struck up, in which graininess or marks from the original planchet surface can be seen. This may include the jaw, the back of Jefferson's head, and the higher-relief central features of Monticello.

MS-60, 61, and 62 can show some evidence of abrasion, usually on the same areas that display weak striking. At MS-63, evidences of abrasion are few, and at MS-65 fewer yet. In grades above MS-65, a Jefferson nickel should be mark-free.

Note: For modern issues of 2003 to date, check the higher parts of the obverse and reverse for abrasion and contact marks. Otherwise the same instructions apply.

Five Steps

Six Steps

1939, Doubled-Die Reverse
FS-05-1939-801.

1942-D, D Over Horizontal D
FS-05-1942D-501.

	Mintage	Cert	Avg	%MS	MS-64FS	MS-65	MS-65FS	MS-66	MS-66FS	MS-67	MS-67FS	Recent Auction Record
1938	19,496,000	726	65.5	98		$12	$150	$50	$250	$200	$2,500	$150, MS-66FS, Feb-10
1938D	5,376,000	1,658	66.2	100		15	125	35	200	150	1,000	$1,380, MS-67FS, Feb-10
1938S	4,105,000	931	66.0	99	$50	15	250	45	750	500	7,500	$374, MS-66FS, Feb-10
1939	120,615,000	983	65.7	96	20	6	45	45	200	225	1,500	$633, MS-67FS, Feb-10
1939, DblDie Rev (a)	*	149	55.0	55	575 (b)	1,000	2,400	2,000	5,500	4,500		$546, MS-64, Mar-10
1939D	3,514,000	978	65.7	97	180	125	450	150	1,000	300		$360, MS-67FS, Mar-10
1939S	6,630,000	521	65.6	99	125	45	350	125	1,250	400		$1,265, MS-66FS, Feb-10
1940	176,485,000	518	65.9	98		6	50	25	125	250	750	$460, MS-67FS, Feb-10
1940D	43,540,000	1,071	66.1	99		8	40	35	60	100	175	$161, MS-67FS, Feb-10
1940S	39,690,000	296	65.8	99		8	50	35	200	400	1,500	$2,300, MS-67FS, Feb-10
1941	203,265,000	413	65.9	99		8	40	30	150	225	1,000	$1,150, MS-67FS, Feb-10
1941D	53,432,000	1,086	66.3	100		9	30	30	60	75	175	$196, MS-67FS, Feb-10
1941S (c)	43,445,000	260	65.2	96		7	75	40	750	500	5,000	$34, MS-66FS, Mar-10
1942	49,789,000	537	65.4	100		10	75	45	300	250	750	$489, MS-66FS, Feb-10
1942D	13,938,000	840	65.8	99		55	75	75	175	300	500	$431, MS-67FS, Feb-10
1942D, D Over Horizontal D (d)	*	55	47.2	24	17,500 (e)	10,000						$8,050, MS-65, Feb-10

* Included in number above. **a.** Very strong doubling is evident to the east of the primary letters, most noticeably on MONTICELLO and FIVE CENTS. Lesser doubling is also visible on UNITED STATES OF AMERICA and the right side of the building. **b.** Value in MS-63 is $400. **c.** Large and small mintmark varieties exist. **d.** The initial D mintmark was punched into the die horizontally, then corrected. "This is the rarest of the major Jefferson nickel varieties in Mint State" (*Cherrypickers' Guide to Rare Die Varieties,* fifth edition, volume I). **e.** Value in MS-63 is $2,100.

1943-P, 3 Over 2
FS-05-1943P-101.

1943-P, Doubled-Die Obverse
The "Doubled Eye" variety. FS-05-1943P-106.

1945-P, Doubled-Die Reverse
FS-05-1945P-803.

	Mintage	Cert	Avg	%MS	MS-64FS	MS-65	MS-65FS	MS-66	MS-66FS	MS-67	MS-67FS	Recent Auction Record
1942P, Silver	57,873,000	3,665	66.4	100		$20	$75	$30	$125	$50	$1,500	$633, MS-67FS, Feb-10
1942S	32,900,000	3,385	66.3	100		18	150	45	225	100	3,000	$2,990, MS-67FS, Feb-10
1943P, 3 Over 2 (a)	*	228	56.8	71	$400 (b)	650	1,000	1,250	2,500	2,750	15,000	$552, MS-65, Mar-10
1943P	271,165,000	3,905	66.2	99		16	35	35	100	50	1,000	$748, MS-67FS, Jun-10
1943P, DblDie Obv (c)	**	99	63.4	87	425 (d)	400	900	900	1,750	1,750	7,500	$1,495, MS-66FS, Feb-10
1943D	15,294,000	6,440	66.4	100		16	40	30	50	50	500	$161, MS-67FS, Feb-10
1943S	104,060,000	3,885	66.4	100		16	40	30	100	65	1,000	$489, MS-67FS, Feb-10
1944P (e)	119,150,000	2,645	66.2	100		24	75	50	175	125	1,500	$35, MS-65FS, Mar-10
1944D	32,309,000	4,443	66.4	100		22	35	30	60	70	500	$89, MS-67FS, Feb-10
1944S	21,640,000	3,900	66.3	100		20	50	30	300	75	1,250	$1,610, MS-67FS, Feb-10
1945P	119,408,100	2,860	65.9	100		20	100	35	250	1,000	7,500	$3,738, MS-67FS, Mar-10
1945P, DblDie Rev (f)	**	182	64.5	97	350	425		3,750				$805, MS-66, Jun-10
1945D	37,158,000	4,545	66.4	100		20	35	30	50	100	450	$403, MS-67FS, Feb-10
1945S	58,939,000	4,242	66.3	100		20	200	30	750	100	1,500	$748, MS-66FS, Feb-10

Note: Genuine specimens of some wartime dates were struck in nickel, in error. * Included in number below. ** Included in number above. **a.** "This popular variety was created when the die was first hubbed with a 1942-dated hub, then subsequently hubbed with a 1943-dated hub. The diagonal of the 2 is visible within the lower opening of the 3. Doubling is also visible on LIBERTY and IN GOD WE TRUST. . . . There is at least one 1943-P five-cent piece that has a faint, short die gouge extending upward from the lower ball of the 3; this is often mistaken for the overdate" (*Cherrypickers' Guide to Rare Die Varieties*, fifth edition, volume I). **b.** Value in MS-63 is $290. **c.** This variety is nicknamed the "Doubled Eye." Doubling is visible on the date, LIBERTY, the motto, and, most noticeably, Jefferson's eye. **d.** Value in MS-63 is $195. **e.** 1944 nickels without mintmarks are counterfeit. **f.** There are several collectible doubled-die reverses for this date. Values are for the variety pictured (FS-05-1945P-801), with a strongly doubled reverse. The doubling spread increases from left to right.

	Mintage	Cert	Avg	%MS	MS-64FS	MS-65	MS-65FS	MS-66	MS-66FS	MS-67	MS-67FS	Recent Auction Record
1946	161,116,000	150	65.0	99	$50	$6	$175	$85	$1,000			$1,035, MS-66FS, Feb-10
1946D	45,292,200	525	65.5	99	10	6	30	30	75	$500	$2,500	$2,990, MS-67FS, Apr-09
1946S	13,560,000	495	65.6	99	30	4	125	30	500	100	1,250	$345, MS-66FS, Feb-10
1947	95,000,000	241	65.5	100	12	4	45	55	500	125		$253, MS-66FS, Feb-10
1947D	37,822,000	385	66.0	100	9	4	25	25	100	100	1,500	$460, MS-66FS, Feb-10
1947S	24,720,000	190	65.3	98	15	4	50	25	450	1,000	5,000	$276, MS-66FS, Feb-10

1949-D, D Over S
FS-05-1949D-501.

1954-S, S Over D
FS-05-1954S-501.

1955-D, D Over S
FS-05-1955D-501.

	Mintage	Cert	Avg	%MS	MS-64FS	MS-65	MS-65FS	MS-66	MS-66FS	MS-67	MS-67FS	Recent Auction Record
1948	89,348,000	102	65.3	98	$125	$4	$125	$50	$1,500			$1,495, MS-66FS, Feb-10
1948D	44,734,000	352	65.9	100		5	25	30	75			$17, MS-65, Aug-09
1948S	11,300,000	466	66.1	100		5	35	35	200	$175		$299, MS-66FS, Jan-10
1949	60,652,000	159	65.6	99	525	8	1,500	35				$1,553, MS-65FS, Feb-10
1949D	36,498,000	398	65.6	98		6	35	25	150	200		$161, MS-66FS, Feb-10
1949D, D Over S (a)	*	52	62.0	94	1,500	450	1,750	1,000				$334, MS-65, Mar-10
1949S	9,716,000	213	65.5	99		6	200	60	1,250			$978, MS-66FS, Feb-10
1950	9,796,000	377	65.8	100	45	7	175	45	500			$253, MS-66FS, Feb-10

* Included in number above. **a.** The top serif of the S is visible to the north of the D, with the upper left loop of the S visible to the west of the D. "This variety is quite rare in Mint State and highly sought after. Some may still be found in circulated grades. Some specimens have been located in original Mint sets" (*Cherrypickers' Guide to Rare Die Varieties*, fifth edition, volume I).

	Mintage	Cert	Avg	%MS	MS-64FS	MS-65	MS-65FS	MS-66	MS-66FS	MS-67	MS-67FS	Recent Auction Record
1950D	2,630,030	2,292	65.7	100		$20	$50	$55	$125	$250	$3,000	$59, MS-66, Mar-10
1951	28,552,000	190	65.5	99	$55	9	300	75	2,000			$1,150, MS-66FS, Feb-10
1951D	20,460,000	383	65.8	100		10	80	25	300	575		$276, MS-66FS, Feb-10
1951S	7,776,000	294	65.9	100	55	5	175	45	1,000			$633, MS-66FS, Feb-10
1952	63,988,000	135	65.5	100	375	4	750	150	2,000	350		$805, MS-65FS, Feb-10
1952D	30,638,000	279	65.8	100	90	10	175	25	500			$403, MS-66FS, Feb-10
1952S	20,572,000	323	65.9	100	50	4	300	30	2,500			$231, MS-65FS, Feb-10
1953	46,644,000	125	65.5	99	1,500	2	2,000	100	3,500			$2,760, MS-65RS, Feb-10
1953D	59,878,600	337	65.6	100	50	2	200	30	1,000	750		$868, MS-67, Feb-10
1953S	19,210,900	291	65.3	100	2,000	3		100				$1,265, MS-64FS, Feb-10
1954	47,684,050	131	65.0	100	60	4	300	25		250		$207, MS-65FS, Feb-10
1954D	117,183,060	141	64.5	99	125	3	700	75		250		$575, MS-65FS, Feb-10
1954S	29,384,000	299	64.8	99	2,000	4	3,500	150				$253, MS-66, Feb-10
1954S, S Over D (b)	*	149	63.0	95	90	100	500	1,500				$299, MS-65, Mar-10
1955	7,888,000	226	65.2	100	145	3	750	200				$575, MS-65FS, Feb-10
1955D	74,464,100	240	65.1	99	440	2	4,000	150				$375, MS-64FS, Feb-10
1955D, D Over S (c)	*	83	64.4	99	125			1,500				$162, MS-65, Jun-10
1956	35,216,000	388	65.5	99		2	50	35	275		5,000	$173, MS-66FS, Feb-10
1956D	67,222,940	272	65.6	100	185	2	675	30	3,000			$2,760, MS-66FS, Feb-10
1957	38,408,000	158	65.1	100		2	75	125	2,600			$1,725, MS-66FS, Feb-10
1957D	136,828,900	343	65.5	100	30	2	140	35	2,500			$2,530, MS-66FS, Feb-10
1958	17,088,000	94	64.8	99	50	2	650					$489, MS-65FS, Feb-10
1958D	168,249,120	274	65.4	99		2	25	35	90		3,500	$2,875, MS-67FS, Feb-10
1959	27,248,000	367	65.4	100		2	50	125	1,000			$753, MS-66FS, Feb-10
1959D	160,738,240	260	65.6	100	55	2	200	35	2,250			$1,610, MS-66FS, Feb-10
1960	55,416,000	230	65.3	100	500	2	1,500	50				$1,495, MS-65FS, Feb-10
1960D	192,582,180	190	65.6	99		2		100				$253, MS-66, Feb-10
1961	73,640,100	188	65.6	100	525	2	2,000	50	3,500			$2,530, MS-65FS, Feb-10
1961D	229,342,760	222	65.0	100		2						$1,610, MS-67, May-08
1962	97,384,000	224	65.2	100		2	45	25	500	425		$518, MS-66FS, Mar-10
1962D	280,195,720	118	64.5	97	275	2						$253, MS-64FS, Feb-10
1963	175,776,000	351	65.4	100		2	125		1,750			$116, MS-65FS, Jun-10
1963D	276,829,460	85	63.5	95	1,000	2	3,500					$7,475, MS-65FS, Feb-10
1964	1,024,672,000	215	65.2	100	100	2	325	60	2,000			$1,955, MS-66FS, Feb-10
1964D	1,787,297,160	264	65.4	100	110	2	750	55	6,300			$748, MS-65FS, Feb-10
1965 (d)	136,131,380	153	66.0	99	10	2	50	25	250	200		$15, MS-66, Aug-09
1966 (d)	156,208,283	37	65.2	97	10	2	50	25	250	200		$322, MS-65DCam, Feb-10
1967 (d)	107,325,800	158	65.7	99	10	2	50	25	250	200		$805, MS-67DCam, Feb-10
1968D	91,227,880	296	65.7	100		2		25				$16, MS-64, Aug-09
1968S	100,396,004	190	65.6	99	475	2	1,350	35	3,750	275		$3,738, MS-66FS, Feb-10
1969D	202,807,500	166	65.8	99		2		115				$115, MS-66, Feb-10
1969S	120,165,000	79	65.0	100		2		300				$345, MS-66, Feb-10
1970D	515,485,380	143	65.4	100		2		180				$99, MS-66, Mar-10
1970S	238,832,004	129	65.1	99	225	2	600	225				$546, MS-65FS, Feb-10
1971	106,884,000	137	64.9	99		2	30	50	125			$127, MS-66FS, Feb-10
1971D	316,144,800	400	66.0	100		2	20	30	60		875	$863, MS-67FS, Feb-10
1972	202,036,000	62	65.1	98		2	40	60	275			$299, MS-66FS, Feb-10
1972D	351,694,600	80	65.0	99		2	40	50	290			$345, MS-66FS, Feb-10
1973	384,396,000	100	65.0	100		2	30	45	150			$173, MS-66FS, Feb-10
1973D	261,405,000	170	65.5	99		2	25	30	80			$23, MS-65FS, Aug-09
1974	601,752,000	68	64.6	100	40	2	135	30	900			$150, MS-65FS, Mar-10
1974D	277,373,000	85	65.3	100		2	35	40	135		700	$1,495, MS-67FS, Feb-10
1975	181,772,000	138	65.5	100	25	2	35	25	250			$299, MS-66FS, Jun-10
1975D	401,875,300	103	65.3	100		2	35	25	300			$299, MS-66FS, Feb-10

* Included in number above. **b.** The overall strength of the strike is the important factor in this overmintmark's value. **c.** There are 10 or more different D Over S varieties for 1955. Values shown are for the strongest (FS-05-1955D-501); others command smaller premiums. **d.** Values and auction records for Special Mint Set coins are listed with the Proofs for this type.

Chart continued on next page.

	Mintage	Cert	Avg	%MS	MS-64FS	MS-65	MS-65FS	MS-66	MS-66FS	MS-67	MS-67FS	Recent Auction Record
1976	367,124,000	29	64.8	100	$28	$2	$175	$37	$675		$3,600	$4,035, MS-67FS, Feb-10
1976D	563,964,147	64	65.1	100		2	30	40	250			$374, MS-66FS, Jun-10
1977	585,376,000	53	65.4	100	45	2	125	48	850			$920, MS-66FS, Feb-10
1977D	297,313,422	60	65.1	100		2	30	40	250			$253, MS-66FS, Feb-10
1978	391,308,000	85	65.7	100	30	2	160	55	900			$1,150, MS-67FS, Mar-10
1978D	313,092,780	80	65.3	100		2	25	55	100			$104, MS-66FS, Feb-10
1979	463,188,000	63	65.3	98	40	2	220	40	850			$920, MS-66FS, Feb-10
1979D	325,867,672	69	64.2	97		2	30	37	150			$127, MS-66FS, Feb-10
1980P	593,004,000	68	65.5	100		2	40	30	200			$196, MS-66FS, Feb-10
1980D	502,323,448	109	65.2	100		2	20	60	250			$253, MS-66FS, Feb-10
1981P	657,504,000	161	65.8	99		2	475	30	3,500			$3,738, MS-66FS, Feb-10
1981D	364,801,843	122	65.0	100		2	25	35	175			$161, MS-66FS, Feb-10
1982P	292,355,000	23	64.5	91		2	40	35	250			$546, MS-66FS, Jun-10
1982D	373,726,544	19	64.5	95		2	50	25	350			$374, MS-66FS, Feb-10
1983P	561,615,000	24	63.6	88		2	300	55				$345, MS-65FS, Feb-10
1983D	536,726,276	22	64.1	91	90	2	175	35	850			$863, MS-66FS, Jun-10
1984P	746,769,000	103	65.6	100		2	25	60	70			$16, MS-65FS, Feb-08
1984D	517,675,146	96	65.2	100		2	28	65	250			$253, MS-66FS, Feb-10
1985P	647,114,962	106	65.6	100	23	2	35	60	375			$374, MS-66FS, Feb-10
1985D	459,747,446	87	65.5	100		2	30	40	200			$196, MS-66FS, Jun-10
1986P	536,883,483	106	65.8	100		2	30	35	150			$127, MS-66FS, Feb-10
1986D	361,819,140	78	65.3	100		2	35	50	250			$253, MS-66FS, Feb-10
1987P	371,499,481	291	66.0	100		2	15	60	20		250	$253, MS-67FS, Feb-10
1987D	410,590,604	216	65.5	100		2	19	30	45			$173, MS-67FS, Apr-08
1988P	771,360,000	71	66.0	100		2	25	35	70			$115, MS-67FS, Apr-08
1988D	663,771,652	112	65.0	99		2	20	32	125			$127, MS-66FS, Feb-10
1989P	898,812,000	174	65.9	100		2	18	28	27		400	$748, MS-67FS, Feb-10
1989D	570,842,474	96	65.1	100		2	40	50	175			$161, MS-66FS, Feb-10
1990P	661,636,000	118	65.9	99		2	20	30	30			$24, MS-66FS, Oct-09
1990D	663,938,503	86	65.0	100		2	28	40	170			$150, MS-66FS, Feb-10
1991P	614,104,000	45	65.6	100		2	40	60	185			$184, MS-66FS, Feb-10
1991D	436,496,678	48	65.1	100		2	22	50	110			$127, MS-66FS, Feb-10
1992P	399,552,000	74	65.8	100		3	18	28	47		1,550	$1,725, MS-67FS, Feb-10
1992D	450,565,113	72	64.9	100		2	15	30	150			$207, MS-66FS, Feb-10
1993P	412,076,000	86	65.7	100		2	25	35	50			$50, MS-66FS, Feb-10
1993D	406,084,135	116	65.2	100		2	13	25	20			$374, MS-67FS, Feb-10
1994P	722,160,000	105	65.7	100		2	35	45	70			$1,725, MS-70FS, Feb-10
1994P, Special Unc. (e)	167,703				40	45	45	50		50		$74, SP-69, Jan-10
1994D	715,762,110	75	64.6	99		2	25	35	85			$89, MS-66FS, Feb-10
1995P	774,156,000	116	66.2	100		2	18	28	65		250	$150, MS-67FS, Feb-10
1995D	888,112,000	41	65.0	100		2	15	25	190		1,200	$253, MS-66FS, Feb-10
1996P	829,332,000	143	65.6	100		2	10	45	20		200	$253, MS-67FS, Feb-10
1996D	817,736,000	164	65.1	100		2	10	50	20		175	$161, MS-67FS, Feb-10
1997P	470,972,000	49	65.7	100		2	40	60	75		325	$345, MS-67FS, Feb-10
1997P, Special Unc. (e)	25,000					115	125	130	135		145	$489, MS-67, Feb-10
1997D	466,640,000	64	64.9	98		2	35	45	75			$48, MS-66FS, Sep-08
1998P	688,272,000	55	65.1	100		2	35	45	140			$219, MS-66FS, Feb-10
1998D	635,360,000	73	64.1	96		2	50	60	360			$403, MS-66FS, Feb-10
1999P	1,212,000,000	146	65.4	97		2	10	22	25		220	$219, MS-67FS, Feb-10
1999D	1,066,720,000	139	65.6	99		2	15	25	45		300	$322, MS-66FS, Feb-10
2000P	846,240,000	103	65.7	100		2	10	18	20		500	$575, MS-67FS, Feb-10
2000D	1,509,520,000	161	66.0	99		2	10	18	20		400	$431, MS-67FS, Feb-10
2001P	675,704,000	73	65.9	99		2	10	12	15		40	$36, MS-67FS, Aug-09
2001D	627,680,000	53	65.7	100		2	10	12	15		130	$138, MS-67FS, Feb-10
2002P	539,280,000	62	65.6	100		2	10	12	15		75	$56, MS-67FS, Feb-10
2002D	691,200,000	47	65.5	98		2	10	12	75			$59, MS-66FS, Feb-10
2003P	441,840,000	171	65.8	99		2	10	12	16		50	$13, MS-65FS, Feb-08
2003D	383,040,000	116	65.2	100		2	10	12	70			$10, MS-63FS, Feb-08

e. Special "frosted" Uncirculated nickels were included in the 1993 Thomas Jefferson commemorative dollar packaging (sold in 1994) and in the 1997 Botanic Garden sets. They resemble Matte Proof coins.

	Mintage	Cert	Avg	%MS	MS-65FS	MS-66	MS-66FS	MS-67	MS-67FS	MS-68FS	MS-69FS	Recent Auction Record
2004P, Peace Medal	361,440,000	1,888	63.6	97	$7			$30				$109, MS-67, Feb-10
2004D, Peace Medal	372,000,000	466	65.6	100	5			30				$374, MS-68, Feb-10
2004P, Keelboat	366,720,000	225	65.6	100	5			20				$299, MS-68, Feb-10
2004D, Keelboat	344,880,000	260	65.9	100	5			20				
2005P, American Bison	448,320,000	4,130	66.7	100	6			25				$28, MS-69, Jan-10
2005D, American Bison	487,680,000	3,926	66.3	100	5			20				$489, MS-69, Feb-10
2005P, Ocean in View	394,080,000	3,184	66.5	100	5			20				$19, MS-66, Feb-10
2005D, Ocean in View	411,120,000	3,378	66.5	100	5			20				$15, MS-65, Aug-09
2006P, Monticello	693,120,000	1,444	66.5	100	$4	3	$5	8	$10	$20	$30	$40, MS-69FS, Feb-10
2006D, Monticello	809,280,000	1,576	66.7	100	4	3	5	8	10	20	30	$11, MS-67, Jul-08
2007P	571,680,000	248	66.2	100	4	3	5	8	10	20	30	$11, MS-68FS, Jul-08
2007D	626,160,000	216	66.1	100	4	3	5	8	10	20	30	$14, MS-68FS, Jul-08
2008P	279,840,000	72	66.0	100	4	3	5	8	10	20	30	
2008D	345,600,000	74	66.2	100	4	3	5	8	10	20	30	
2009P		258	65.9	100	4	3	5	8	10	20	30	
2009D		85	66.8	100	4	3	5	8	10	20	30	
2010P					4	3	5	8	10	20	30	
2010D					4	3	5	8	10	20	30	

Proof Jefferson Nickels

PF-60 to 70 (Proof). All Proof Jefferson nickels have mirror fields. Striking is usually with Full Details, although there are scattered exceptions. Most survivors are PF-64 and finer. Most since the 1970s have frosted or cameo contrast on the higher features. Special Mint Set (SMS) coins were struck in lieu of Proofs from 1965 to 1967; these in some instances closely resemble Proofs. *Obverse and Reverse:* Those Proofs with abrasion or contact marks can be graded PF-60 to 62 or even 63; these are not widely desired by collectors. PF-64 can have some abrasion. Tiny flecks are sometimes seen on coins of 1938 to 1942, as are discolorations (even to the extent of black streaks); these flaws are from cellophane holders. Collectors should avoid such coins. Undipped Proofs of the early era often have a slight bluish or yellowish tint. At PF-65 or higher there are no traces of abrasion or flecks. Evaluation of differences between higher-grade Jefferson Proofs is highly subjective; one certified at PF-65 might be similar to another at PF-67, and vice-versa.

Proof Jefferson Nickel

Proof Jefferson Nickel, Silver

	Mintage	Cert	Avg	PF-65	PF-66	PF-67	Recent Auction Record
1938	19,365	1,051	65.5	$125	$150	$225	$150, PF-67, Feb-10
1939	12,535	819	65.4	125	150	325	$299, PF-67, Feb-10
1940	14,158	816	65.4	120	140	260	$633, PF-66, Feb-10
1941	18,720	865	65.4	80	135	340	$322, PF-67, Feb-10
1942	29,600	1,497	65.7	75	80	125	$40, PF-65, Mar-10
1942P, Silver	27,600	2,406	65.5	200	225	250	$197, PF-67, Feb-10

	Mintage	Cert	Avg	PF-65	PF-66	PF-67	PF-68	Recent Auction Record
1950	51,386	882	66.1	$65	$75	$95	$290	$633, PF-67Cam, Feb-10
1951	57,500	1,065	66.7	60	65	80	165	$863, PF-68Cam, Feb-10
1952	81,980	1,013	66.9	40	45	50	100	$7,475, PF-67DCam, Feb-10
1953	128,800	1,202	67.1	45	50	55	110	$523, PF-68Cam, Feb-10
1954	233,300	1,318	67.2	22	25	35	45	$5,480, PF-68DCam, Feb-10
1955	378,200	2,130	67.5	15	20	25	40	$920, PF-68DCam, Feb-10
1956	669,384	1,245	67.4	4	15	25	40	$1,150, PF-67DCam, Feb-10

Chart continued on next page.

	Mintage	Cert	Avg	PF-65	PF-66	PF-67	PF-68	Recent Auction Record
1957	1,247,952	1,119	67.1	$4	$12	$20	$40	$633, PF-68Cam, Feb-10
1958	875,652	1,022	67.0	5	12	20	30	$207, PF-68Cam, Feb-10
1959	1,149,291	1,074	67.2	3	8	20	25	$1,610, PF-68DCam, Feb-10
1960	1,691,602	1,374	67.1	3	7	12	25	$374, PF-68DCam, Feb-10
1961	3,028,144	1,557	67.0	3	7	10	15	$2,760, PF-69DCam, Feb-10
1962	3,218,019	2,086	67.1	3	7	10	15	$748, PF-69DCam, Feb-10
1963	3,075,645	2,783	67.3	3	7	10	15	$357, PF-69DCam, Feb-10
1964	3,950,762	3,396	68.0	3	7	10	15	$253, PF-69DCam, Feb-10
1965, SMS	2,360,000	1,163	66.4	3 (a)	18	40		
1966, SMS	2,261,583	981	66.7	3 (b)	19	35		
1967, SMS	1,863,344	1,173	66.7	3 (c)	18	30		

a. Value in PF-64FS is $10; in PF-65FS, $55. **b.** Value in PF-64FS is $10; in PF-65FS, $65. **c.** Value in PF-64FS is $10; in PF-65FS, $60.

1979-S, Type 1
("Filled" S)

1979-S, Type 2
("Clear" S)

1981-S, Type 2
("Clear" S)

	Mintage	Cert	Avg	PF-66	PF-67Cam	PF-68DC	PF-69DC	Recent Auction Record
1968S	3,041,506	613	67.7	$2	$15	$22	$115	$127, PF-69DCam, Feb-10
1969S	2,934,631	546	67.7	2	10	35	400	$460, PF-69DCam, Feb-10
1970S	2,632,810	610	67.5	2	15	22	300	$276, PF-69DCam, Feb-10
1971, No S (a)	1,655	47	67.6	1,000	1,250	2,750		$3,450, PF-69Cam, Feb-10
1971S	3,220,733	586	67.6	3	15	22	490	$489, PF-69DCam, Feb-10
1972S	3,260,996	520	67.5	3	15	22	120	$121, PF-69DCam, Feb-10
1973S	2,760,339	182	67.8	2	10	15	20	$44, PF-69DCam, Sep-09
1974S	2,612,568	286	66.9	3	7	8	15	$25, PF-69DCam, Mar-08
1975S	2,845,450	385	67.8	3	7	8	15	$8,180, PF-69DCam, Aug-09
1976S	4,149,730	670	67.8	3	7	8	15	$36, PF-70DCam, Jan-10
1977S	3,251,152	501	68.0	2	7	8	15	$374, PF-70DCam, Jan-10
1978S	3,127,781	526	68.5	2	7	8	15	$374, PF-70DCam, Feb-10
1979S, All kinds	3,677,175							
1979S, Type 1 ("Filled" S)		569	68.5	2	7	8	15	$518, PF-70DCam, Feb-10
1979S, Type 2 ("Clear" S)		395	68.7	3	8	9	20	$863, PF-70DCam, Feb-10
1980S	3,554,806	713	68.5	2	7	8	15	$403, PF-70DCam, Feb-10
1981S, Type 1 ("Filled" S)	4,063,083	861	68.5	2	7	8	15	$489, PF7, Jan-10
1981S, Type 2 ("Clear" S)	*	341	68.6	4	8	10	20	$1,725, PF-70DCam, Feb-10
1982S	3,857,479	526	68.6	3	7	8	15	$84, PF-70DCam, Sep-09
1983S	3,279,126	508	68.7	3	7	8	15	$74, PF-70DCam, Sep-09
1984S	3,065,110	443	68.5	4	7	8	15	$138, PF-70DCam, Oct-09
1985S	3,362,821	457	68.8	3	7	8	15	$518, PF-70DCam, Feb-10
1986S	3,010,497	311	68.8	7	8	9	15	$50, PF-70DCam, Dec-09
1987S	4,227,728	474	68.8	3	7	8	15	$79, PF-70DCam, Dec-09
1988S	3,262,948	397	68.6	5	8	9	20	$389, PF-70DCam, Feb-10
1989S	3,220,194	393	68.9	4	7	8	15	$150, PF-70DCam, Feb-10
1990S	3,299,559	674	69.0	4	7	8	15	$40, PF-70DCam, Jan-10
1991S	2,867,787	568	69.1	5	7	8	15	$99, PF-70DCam, Feb-10
1992S	4,176,560	1,218	69.1	4	7	8	15	$62, PF-70DCam, Dec-09
1993S	3,394,792	1,266	69.0	4	7	8	15	$47, PF-70DCam, Oct-09
1994S	3,269,923	1,078	69.1	4	7	8	15	$32, PF-70DCam, Oct-09
1995S	2,797,481	1,095	69.1	5	8	9	15	$79, PF-70DCam, Feb-10

* Included in the number above. **a.** 1971 Proof nickels without the S mintmark were made in error after an assistant engraver forgot to punch a mintmark into a die. The U.S. Mint estimates that 1,655 such error coins were struck.

	Mintage	Cert	Avg	PF-66	PF-67Cam	PF-68DC	PF-69DC	Recent Auction Record
1996S	2,525,265	1,079	69.1	$3	$7	$8	$15	$56, PF-70DCam, Feb-10
1997S	2,796,678	1,088	69.2	3	7	8	15	$36, PF-70DCam, Dec-09
1998S	2,086,507	1,300	69.3	3	7	8	15	$47, PF-70DCam, Nov-09
1999S	3,347,966	4,908	69.1	4	7	8	15	$42, PF-70DCam, Sep-09
2000S	4,047,993	4,186	69.1	2	7	8	15	$65, PF-70DCam, Oct-09
2001S	3,184,606	3,296	69.2	2	7	8	15	$21, PF-70DCam, Dec-09
2002S	3,211,995	3,533	69.0	2	7	8	15	$32, PF-69DCam, Aug-09
2003S	3,298,439	7,203	69.2	2	7	8	15	$47, PF-70DCam, Dec-09

	Mintage	Cert	Avg	PF-67	PF-69DC	Recent Auction Record
2004S, Peace Medal	2,992,069	10,825	69.2	$5	$10	$127, PF-70DCam, Feb-10
2004S, Keelboat	2,965,422	10,840	69.2	5	10	$26, PF-70DCam, Oct-09
2005S, American Bison	3,344,679	17,950	69.2	5	10	$104, PF-70DCam, Feb-10
2005S, Ocean in View	3,344,679	17,690	69.2	5	10	$26, PF-70UCam, Jan-10
2006S, Monticello	3,054,436	6,262	69.4	5	10	$34, PF-70UCam, Jan-10
2007S	2,259,847	4,666	69.3	5	15	$50, PF-70DCam, Dec-09
2008S	1,998,108	2,912	69.6	5	15	$56, PF-70DCam, Jun-09
2009S		3,481	69.5	5	15	$79, PF-70UCam, Nov-09
2010S				5	15	

AN OVERVIEW OF HALF DISMES

Half dimes or five-cent silver coins were provided for in the Mint Act of April 2, 1792. The spelling was stated as *half disme*. The latter word (likely pronounced "deem," in the French mode) was used intermittently in government correspondence for years afterward, but on coins dated 1794 and beyond it appeared only as *dime*.

President George Washington, in his fourth annual message to the House of Representatives, November 6, 1792, referred to the half disme:

> In execution of the authority given by the Legislature, measures have been taken for engaging some artists from abroad to aid in the establishment of our Mint; others have been employed at home. Provision has been made of the requisite buildings, and these are now putting into proper condition for the purposes of the establishment.
>
> There has also been a small beginning in the coinage of half-dismes; the want of small coins in circulation calling the first attention to them. The regulation of foreign coins, in correspondence with the principles of our national Coinage, as being essential to their due operation, and to order in our money-concerns, will, I doubt not, be resumed and completed.

The 1792 half dismes are studied in *United States Pattern Coins* (the hobby's standard reference on pattern coins and experimental and trial pieces), and some numismatists have traditionally referred to them as patterns. It is true that they were struck at a private shop in Philadelphia while the official Mint buildings were still in planning. However, several factors point to their status as regular circulating coins. The half disme was authorized as a federal issue by congressional legislation. Its mintage was considerable—some 1,500 or so pieces—and, as noted by President Washington, the coins were meant to alleviate the national need for small change. Furthermore, nearly all surviving examples show signs of extensive wear.

The 1792 half dismes are not commonly collected, simply because they are not common coins; only 200 to 300 are estimated to still exist. However, their rarity, the romance of their connection to the nation's founding, and the mysteries and legends surrounding their creation (see next page) make them a perennial favorite among numismatists.

RECOMMENDED READING

Judd, J. Hewitt. *United States Pattern Coins* (10th ed., edited by Q. David Bowers), Atlanta, GA, 2009.
Logan, Russell, and McClosky, John. *Federal Half Dimes, 1792–1837,* Manchester, MI, 1998.
Newlin, H.P. *The Early Half-Dimes of the United States,* Philadelphia, 1883 (reprinted 1933).
Valentine, D.W. *The United States Half Dimes,* New York, 1931 (reprinted 1975).

HALF DISME
(1792)

Designer unknown (possibly Robert Birch); weight 1.35 grams; composition .8924 silver, .1076 copper; diameter 16.5 mm; reeded edge; minted at John Harper's shop, Philadelphia.

Shown 2x actual size.
Judd-7, Pollock-7, Logan-McCloskey-1.

History. Rumors and legends are par for the course with the 1792 half disme. Martha Washington is said to have posed for the portrait of Miss Liberty, despite the profile's dissimilarity to life images of the first lady. Longstanding numismatic tradition says that President George Washington had his own silver tableware taken to the mint factory to be melted down, with these little coins being the result. Whether these Washingtonian connections are true or not, other facts are certain: While the Philadelphia Mint was in the planning stage (its cornerstone would be laid on July 31, 1792), dies were being cut for the first federal coinage of that year. The designer may have been Robert Birch, a Mint engraver who created (or helped create) the dies for the half disme, the disme, and other coins. The half dismes were struck in a private facility owned by saw-maker John Harper, in mid-July. It is believed, from Thomas Jefferson's records, that 1,500 were made. Most were placed into circulation. The coin's designs, with a unique head of Miss Liberty and an outstretched eagle, would not be revived when normal production of the half dime denomination started at the Mint's official facilities in 1795.

Striking and Sharpness. These coins usually are fairly well struck, but with some lightness on Miss Liberty's hair above her ear, and on the eagle's breast. Some examples have adjustment marks from the planchet being filed to adjust the weight prior to striking.

Availability. Most of the estimated 200 to 300 surviving coins show extensive wear. Some AU and MS coins exist, several in choice and gem state, perhaps from among the four examples that Mint Director David Rittenhouse is said to have reserved for himself.

AG-3 (About Good). *Obverse:* Extreme wear has reduced the portrait to a very shallow state. Around the border some letters are worn away completely, some partially. 1792 can be seen but is weak and may be partly missing. *Reverse:* Traces of the eagle remain and there are scattered letters and fragments of letters. Most of the coin is worn flat.

G-4, 6 (Good). *Obverse:* There is hardly any detail on the portrait, except that the eye can be seen, as well as some thick hair tips. The date is clear. Around the border the edges of the letters are worn away, and some are weak overall. *Reverse:* The eagle is only in outline form. The letters are very worn, with some missing.

VG-8, 10 (Very Good). *Obverse:* The head has less detail than in Fine and is essentially flat except at the neck. Some hair, in thick strands, can be seen. The letters show extensive wear, but are readable. *Reverse:* The eagle is mostly flat, and the letters are well worn, some of them incomplete at the borders. Detail overall is weaker than on the obverse.

F-12, 15 (Fine). *Obverse:* The portrait, above the neck, is essentially flat, but details of the eye, the nose, and, to a lesser extent, the lips can be seen. The bust end and neck truncation are flat. Some hair detail can be seen to the right of the neck and behind the head, with individual strands blended into heavy groups. Both obverse and reverse at this grade and lower are apt to show marks, minor digs, and other evidence of handling. *Reverse:* Wear is more advanced than at VF, with significant reduction of the height of the lettering, and with some letters weak in areas, especially if the rim nearby is flat.

VF-20, 30 (Very Fine). *Obverse:* More wear is seen on the hair, including to the right of the forehead and face, where only a few strands may be seen. The hair tips at the right are well detailed. The bust end is flat on its high area. Letters all show light wear. *Reverse:* The eagle displays significant wear, with its central part flat and most of the detail missing from the right wing. The letters all show light wear.

EF-40, 45 (Extremely Fine). *Obverse:* The hair shows medium wear to the right of the face and on the bust end. The fields have no luster. Some luster may be seen among the hair strands and letters. *Reverse:* The eagle shows medium wear on its breast and the right wing, less so on the left wing. HALF DISME shows wear. The fields have no luster. Some luster may be seen among the design elements and letters.

AU-50, 53, 55, 58 (About Uncirculated). *Obverse:* Light wear is seen on the cheek and on the hair (not as easily observable, as certain areas of the hair may be lightly struck). Luster ranges from light and mostly in protected areas at AU-50, to extensive at 58. Friction is evident in the field, less so in the higher ranges. *Reverse:* Light wear is seen on the eagle, but is less noticeable on the letters. Luster ranges from light and mostly in protected areas at AU-50, to extensive at 58. Friction is evident in the field, less in the higher ranges.

MS-60 to 70 (Mint State). *Obverse:* No wear is visible. Luster ranges from nearly full at MS-60 to frosty at 65 or higher. Toning often masks the surface, so careful inspection is required. *Reverse:* No wear is visible. The field around the eagle is lustrous, ranging from not completely full at MS-60 to deep and frosty at 65 and higher.

	Mintage	Cert	Avg	%MS	VG-8	F-12	VF-20	EF-40	AU-50	MS-60	MS-62	Recent Auction Record
1792 †	1,500	39	49.1	46	$45,000	$55,000	$62,500	$95,000	$125,000	$225,000	$275,000	$34,500, G-6, Jun-10

† Ranked in the *100 Greatest U.S. Coins* (third edition).

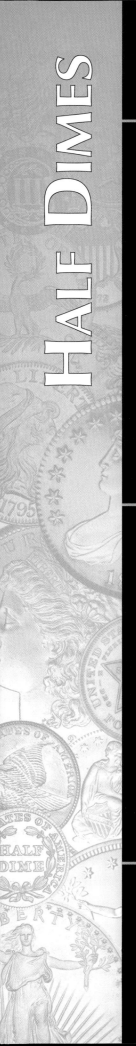

The first half dimes, dated 1794 and of the Flowing Hair type, were not actually struck until 1795. In that year additional half dimes with the 1795 date were made. In 1796 and 1797 the short-lived Draped Bust obverse combined with Small Eagle reverse was used, after which none were struck until 1801. From that year through 1805, excepting 1804, the Draped Bust obverse was used in combination with the Heraldic Eagle reverse. Then followed a long span of years without any coinage. In 1829 the laying of the cornerstone for the second Philadelphia Mint precipitated a new issue, the Capped Bust design, some examples of which were produced for the ceremony. Production was resumed for circulation, and half dimes of this motif were made through 1837. In that year the Liberty Seated motif, by Christian Gobrecht, was introduced, to be continued without interruption through 1873, although there were a number of design modifications and changes during that span.

Assembling a set of the different half-dime types is a challenge for the collector. The 1794 and 1795 Flowing Hair half dimes are fairly scarce at all levels and are quite rare in choice Mint State. Then come the Draped Bust obverse, Small Eagle reverse half dimes of 1796 and 1797. In the late 1960s, researcher Jim Ruddy found that of the various silver types (including the more famous 1796–1797 half dollars), half dimes of this type were the hardest to complete a photographic set of, from the lowest grades to the highest.

Draped Bust obverse, Heraldic Eagle reverse half dimes of the 1800–1805 years are scarce in all grades, more so than generally realized. In Mint State they are very rare, although on occasion some dated 1800 turn up (not often for the others). Finding a *sharply struck* example is next to impossible, and a collector may have to give up on this aspect and settle for one that has some weakness in areas.

Capped Bust half dimes and the several variations of Liberty Seated half dimes will pose no problem at all, and with some small amount of patience a collector will be able to find a sharply struck example in nearly any grade desired.

FOR THE COLLECTOR AND INVESTOR: HALF DIMES AS A SPECIALTY

Collecting half dimes early die varieties of 1794–1837, and/or by dates and mintmarks (beginning with the 1838-O), has captured the fancy of many numismatists over the years. As these coins are so small it is necessary to have a magnifying glass when studying the series—something the collector of silver dollars and double eagles does not need.

One of the earlier enthusiasts in the field was Philadelphia attorney and numismatist Harold P. Newlin, who in 1883 issued *A Classification of the Early Half Dimes of the United States.* Newlin's two favorite varieties were the 1792 half disme and the rare 1802, and after reading his enticing prose about the desirability of each, no doubt some collectors in 1883 put both coins on their "must have" lists.

Among early half dimes the rarest and most expensive is the 1802. In 1883, Newlin listed just 16 examples known to him. Although no one has compiled an up-to-date registry, it is likely that fewer than 30 exist. Most are well worn. Other early half dimes range from rare to very rare.

Capped Bust half dimes of the 1829–1837 years are all easily available as dates, but some of the die varieties are very rare. Today, most half dimes on the market are not attributed by varieties, making the search for such things rewarding when a rarity is found for the price of a regular coin.

In 1978 the numismatic world was startled to learn that Chicago dealer Edward Milas had located an 1870-S half dime, a variety not earlier known to exist and not listed in the annual Mint reports. Other than this coin, still unique today, the dates and mints in the Liberty Seated series 1837 to 1873-S are readily collectible by date and mint, with no great rarities. There are several very curious varieties within that span, the most interesting of which may be the 1858 Over Inverted Date. The date was first punched into the die upside down, the error noted, and then corrected.

RECOMMENDED READING

Blythe, Al. *The Complete Guide to Liberty Seated Half Dimes,* Virginia Beach, VA, 1992.
Breen, Walter. *United States Half Dimes: A Supplement,* New York, 1958.
Fivaz, Bill, and Stanton, J.T. *The Cherrypickers' Guide to Rare Die Varieties* (4th ed., vol. II), Atlanta, GA, 2006.
Logan, Russell, and McClosky, John. *Federal Half Dimes, 1792–1837,* Manchester, MI, 1998.
Newlin, Harold P. *The Early Half-Dimes of the United States,* Philadelphia, 1883 (reprinted 1933).
Valentine, D.W. *The United States Half Dimes,* New York, 1931 (reprinted 1975).

FLOWING HAIR
(1794–1795)

Designer Robert Scot; weight 1.35 grams; composition .8924 silver, .1076 copper; approx. diameter 16.5 mm; reeded edge. All coined at Philadelphia Mint.

Shown 2x actual size.
Logan-McCloskey-3.

History. Half dimes dated 1794 and 1795, of the Flowing Hair type, were all struck in the calendar year 1795, although dies were ready by the end of 1794. The Flowing Hair motif was also used on half dollars and silver dollars of the same years, but not on other denominations.

Striking and Sharpness. Many Flowing Hair half dimes have problems of one sort or another, including adjustment marks from the planchet being filed, and/or light striking in some areas. On the obverse, check the hair and stars, and on the reverse the breast of the eagle. It may not be possible to find a *needle-sharp* example, but with some extensive searching a fairly decent strike can be obtained. Sharp striking and excellent eye appeal add dramatically to the value.

Availability. Examples appear on the market with frequency, typically in lower circulated grades. Probably 250 to 500 could be classified as MS, most of these dated 1795. Some searching is needed to locate choice specimens in any grade. As a rule, half dimes are more readily available than are half dollars and dollars of the same design, and when found are usually more attractive and have fewer problems.

EF-40, 45 (Extremely Fine). *Obverse:* More wear is evident on the portrait, especially on the hair to the left of the face and neck; the cheek; and the tip of the neck truncation. Excellent detail remains in low-relief areas of the hair. The stars show wear, as do the date and letters. Luster, if present at all, is minimal and in protected areas. *Reverse:* The eagle, this being the focal point to check, shows more wear than at AU. Observe the coin in combination with knowledge of the die variety to determine its sharpness when it was first struck. Some were flat at the center at the time they were made. Additional wear is on the wreath and letters, but many details are present. Some luster may be seen in protected areas, and if present is slightly more abundant than on the obverse.

AU-50, 53, 55, 58 (About Uncirculated). *Obverse:* Light wear is seen on the hair area immediately to the left of the face and neck, on the cheek, and on the top of the neck truncation, more so at AU-50 than at 53 or 55. An AU-58 coin has minimal traces of wear. An AU-50 has luster in protected areas among the stars and letters, with little in the open fields or on the portrait. At AU-58, most luster is present in the fields, but is worn away on the highest parts of the motifs. *Reverse:* Light wear is seen on the eagle's body and right wing. At AU-50, detail is lost in most feathers in this area. However, striking can play a part, and some coins are weak to begin with. Light wear is seen on the wreath and lettering. Luster is the best key to actual wear. This ranges from perhaps 20% remaining in protected areas at AU-50 to nearly full mint bloom at 58.

MS-60 to 70 (Mint State). *Obverse:* At MS-60 some abrasion and contact marks are evident, most noticeably on the cheek and in the fields. Luster is present, but may be dull or lifeless, and interrupted in patches. At MS-63, contact marks are very few, and abrasion is hard to detect except under magnification. At MS-65 there is no abrasion, and contact marks are so minute as to require magnification. Luster should be full and rich. Coins graded above MS-65 are more theoretical than actual for this type—but they do exist, and are defined by having fewer marks as perfection is approached. *Reverse:* Comments apply as for the obverse, except that abrasion and contact marks are most noticeable on the eagle at the center. The field area is small and is protected by lettering and the wreath, and in any given grade shows fewer marks than on the obverse.

	Mintage	Cert	Avg	%MS	EF-40	AU-50	MS-60	MS-62	MS-63	MS-64	MS-65	Recent Auction Record
1794	*	114	51.2	38	$6,800	$11,000	$18,000	$23,500	$30,000	$37,000	$80,000	$5,463, VF-30, Apr-10
1795	86,416	338	50.5	36	5,000	7,500	13,500	16,500	19,500	23,000	37,500	$7,475, AU-58 CAC, Jun-10

* Included in number below.

DRAPED BUST, SMALL EAGLE REVERSE
(1796–1797)

Designer Robert Scot; weight 1.35 grams; composition .8924 silver, .1076 copper; approx. diameter 16.5 mm; reeded edge. All coined at Philadelphia Mint.

Shown 2x actual size.
Logan-McCloskey-2.

History. Although the Draped Bust obverse was used on various copper and silver coins circa 1795 to 1808, it was employed in combination with the *Small Eagle* reverse only on silver coins of 1795 to 1798—for the half dime series, only in 1796 and 1797.

Striking and Sharpness. Most 1796–1797 half dimes are weak in at least one area. Points to check for sharpness include the hair of Miss Liberty, the centers of the stars, the bust line, and, on the reverse, the center of the eagle. Check for planchet adjustment marks (these are infrequent). Dentils around the border are usually decent, but may vary in strength from one part of the border to another. Sharp striking and excellent eye appeal add to the value dramatically.

Availability. This type is fairly scarce in *any* grade; in MS-63 and finer, no more than a few dozen examples have been traced. As is true of other early silver types, beware of deeply toned or vividly iridescent-toned pieces whose true surface characters are flawed, but which are offered as MS; in truth some of these are barely better than EF.

EF-40, 45 (Extremely Fine). *Obverse:* More wear than at AU is evident on the upper hair area and the ribbon and on the drapery and bosom. Excellent detail remains in low-relief areas of the hair. The stars show wear, as do the date and letters. Luster, if present at all, is minimal and in protected areas. *Reverse:* The eagle (the focal point to check) shows more wear than at AU. On most examples, many feathers remain on the interior areas of the wings. Check the eagle, in combination with knowledge of the die variety, to determine the sharpness of the coin when it was first struck. Additional wear is evident on the wreath and letters, but many details are present. Some luster may be seen in protected areas and, if present, is slightly more abundant than on the obverse.

AU-50, 53, 55, 58 (About Uncirculated). *Obverse:* Light wear is seen on the hair area above the ear and extending to the left of the forehead, on the ribbon, and on the bosom—more so at AU-50 than at 53 or 55. An AU-58 coin has minimal traces of wear. An AU-50 coin has luster in protected areas among the stars and letters, with little in the open fields or on the portrait. At AU-58, most luster is present in the fields, but is worn away on the highest parts of the motifs. *Reverse:* Light wear is seen on the eagle's body (this area might be lightly struck) and the edges of the wings. Light wear is seen on the wreath and lettering. Luster is the best key to judging actual wear. This ranges from perhaps 20% remaining in protected areas at AU-50 to nearly full mint bloom at AU-58.

MS-60 to 70 (Mint State). *Obverse:* At MS-60 some abrasion and contact marks are evident, most noticeably on the cheek, on the drapery, and in the right field. Luster is present, but may be dull or lifeless, and interrupted in patches. At MS-63, contact marks are very few, and abrasion is hard to detect except under magnification, although this type is sometimes graded liberally due to its rarity. An MS-65 coin has no abrasion, and contact marks are so minute as to require magnification. Luster should be full and rich. Coins graded above MS-65 are more theoretical than actual for this type—but they do exist, and are defined by having fewer marks as perfection is approached. *Reverse:* Comments apply as for the obverse, except that abrasion and marks are most noticeable on the eagle at the center, a situation complicated by the fact that this area was often flatly struck. Grading is best done by the obverse, then verified by the reverse. The field area is small and is protected by lettering and the wreath, and in any given grade shows fewer marks than on the obverse.

1796, 6 Over 5

1796, LIKERTY

1797, 15 Stars
Shown 2x actual size.

1797, 16 Stars
Shown 2x actual size.

1797, 13 Stars
Shown 2x actual size.

	Mintage	Cert	Avg	%MS	EF-40	AU-50	MS-60	MS-62	MS-63	MS-64	MS-65	Recent Auction Record
1796, 6 Over 5	10,230	11	55.4	73	$8,000	$14,500	$25,000	$35,000	$42,000	$65,000	$90,000	$20,700, AU-55, Jan-10
1796	*	19	50.2	32	7,750	11,500	15,250	18,500	27,500	50,000	85,000	$34,500, MS-64, Jan-10
1796, LIKERTY (a)	*	39	48.8	33	7,750	12,500	16,500	21,500	35,000	55,000	88,000	$5,463, EF-40, Jun-10
1797, 15 Stars	44,527	23	48.7	17	7,750	11,500	15,250	18,500	25,000	40,000	80,000	$9,775, AU-55, Jun-10
1797, 16 Stars	*	17	44.2	41	7,500	11,500	15,250	18,500	25,000	37,500	75,000	$4,025, VF-25, Apr-10
1797, 13 Stars	*	4	45.8	0	12,500	22,500	45,000	55,000	65,000			$6,900, VF-25, Apr-10

* Included in number above. **a.** A die imperfection makes the B in LIBERTY somewhat resemble a K.

DRAPED BUST, HERALDIC EAGLE REVERSE (1800–1805)

Designer Robert Scot; weight 1.35 grams; composition .8924 silver, .1076 copper; approx. diameter 16.5 mm; reeded edge. All coined at Philadelphia Mint.

Shown 2x actual size.
Logan-McCloskey-1.

History. The combination of Draped Bust obverse / Heraldic Eagle reverse was used in the silver half dime series from 1800 to 1805. The obverse style, standardized with 13 stars, is the same as used in 1796 and 1797. During this span the rare 1802 was produced, and none were minted with the date 1804.

Striking and Sharpness. Most 1800–1805 half dimes are lightly struck in one area or another. The obverse stars usually show some weakness. On many coins the central details of Miss Liberty are not sharp. On the reverse the upper right of the shield and the adjacent part of the eagle's wing are often soft, and several or even most stars may be lightly defined (sharp stars show sharply peaked centers); high parts of the clouds are often weak. The area on the reverse opposite the bosom of Miss Liberty may be flat or weak, due to the metal having to flow in both directions when the coins were struck. (The area curving obliquely up and to the right of the eagle's head—exactly mirroring the curvature of the bust on the obverse—is especially prone to weakness of strike.) Dentils are likely to be weak or missing in areas. Many have Mint-caused planchet adjustment marks. In summary, *a sharply struck coin is a goal, not necessarily a reality.* Sharp striking and excellent eye appeal will add to the coin's value dramatically, this being particularly true for all issues from 1801 to 1805.

Availability. This is a challenging type to find with nice eye appeal. Many toned pieces are recolored. Some are porous or have other problems. The majority of pieces surviving today are dated 1800, and nearly all of the AU or finer coins are of this date.

VF-20, 30 (Very Fine). *Obverse:* The higher-relief areas of hair are well worn at VF-20, less so at 30. The drapery and bosom show extensive wear. The stars, being worn, appear larger than normal. *Reverse:* Wear is greater than at EF, including on the shield and wing feathers. Star centers are flat. Other areas have lost detail as well.

EF-40, 45 (Extremely Fine). *Obverse:* More wear than at AU is evident on the upper hair area and the ribbon, and on the drapery and bosom. Excellent detail remains in low-relief areas of the hair. The stars show wear, as do the date and letters. Luster, if present at all, is minimal and only in protected areas. *Reverse:* Wear is greater than at AU, overall. The neck lacks feather detail on its highest points. Feathers lose some detail near the edges of the wings, and some areas of the horizontal lines in the shield may be blended together. Some traces of luster may be seen, less so at EF-40 than at 45.

AU-50, 53, 55, 58 (About Uncirculated). *Obverse:* Light wear is seen on the hair area above the ear and extending to the left of the forehead, on the ribbon, and on the bosom, more so at AU-50 than at 53 or 55. An AU-58 coin has minimal traces of wear. Regarding luster: an AU-50 coin has luster in protected areas among the stars and letters, with little in the open fields or on the portrait. At AU-58, most luster is present in the fields, but is worn away on the highest parts of the motifs. *Reverse:* Comments as for MS coins, except that the eagle's neck, the tips and top of the wings, the clouds, and the tail show noticeable wear, as do other features. Luster ranges from perhaps 20% remaining in protected areas at AU-50 to nearly full mint bloom at 58. Often the reverse of this type retains much more luster than the obverse.

MS-60 to 70 (Mint State). *Obverse:* At MS-60 some abrasion and contact marks are evident, most notice- ably on the cheek, on the drapery, and in the right field. Luster is present, but may be dull or lifeless, and interrupted in patches. At MS-63, contact marks are very few, and abrasion is hard to detect except under magnification, although this type is sometimes graded liberally due to its rarity. An MS-65 coin has no abrasion, and contact marks are so minute as to require magnification. Luster should be full and rich. Coins graded above MS-65 are more theoretical than actual for this type—but they do exist, and are defined by having fewer marks as perfection is approached. *Reverse:* Comments apply as for the obverse, except that abrasion and contact marks are most noticeable on the eagle's neck, the tips of the wing, and the tail. The field area is complex—with stars above the eagle, the arrows and olive branch, and other features, there is not much open space. Accordingly, marks will not be as noticeable as on the obverse.

1800, LIBEKTY

1803, Large 8

1803, Small 8

	Mintage	Cert	Avg	%MS	EF-40	AU-50	MS-60	MS-62	MS-63	MS-64	MS-65	Recent Auction Record
1800	24,000	142	46.5	26	$5,750	$7,750	$12,000	$14,500	$20,000	$25,000	$47,500	$2,530, VF-25, Jul-10
1800, LIBEKTY (a)	16,000	39	42.9	31	5,750	7,750	12,000	14,500	20,000	25,000	50,000	$5,463, EF-40, Jun-10
1801	27,760	25	32.8	16	6,200	8,200	15,500	19,500	25,500	37,500	65,000	$4,313, VF-35 CAC, Apr-10
1802 †	3,060	3	50.0	0	160,000	300,000						$195,500, EF-45, Apr-09
1803, Large 8	37,850	6	45.5	50	6,000	8,000	14,000	18,000	22,500	35,000	48,500	$12,075, MS-62, Apr-10
1803, Small 8	*	2	58.0	50	6,750	9,000	25,000	30,000	35,000	50,000		$5,175, EF-40 Clipped Plan., Apr-10
1805	15,600	21	31.4	5	7,600	15,500	40,000					$3,738, VF-20, Apr-10

* Included in number above. † Ranked in the *100 Greatest U.S. Coins* (third edition). **a.** A defective die punch gives the R in LIBERTY the appearance of a K.

CAPPED BUST
(1829–1837)

Designer William Kneass; weight 1.35 grams; composition .8924 silver, .1076 copper; approx. diameter 15.5 mm; reeded edge. All coined at Philadelphia Mint.

Shown 2x actual size.
Logan-McCloskey-7.

History. Half dimes of the Capped Bust design were first struck the morning of July 4, 1829, to include in the cornerstone time capsule of the new (second) Philadelphia Mint building and, presumably, to have some inexpensive coins on hand for distribution as souvenirs. Engraver John Reich's design was not new; it had been used on half dollars as early as 1807. It was logical to employ it on the new half dime, a coin that had not been made since 1805. The new half dimes proved popular and remained in circulation for many years.

Striking and Sharpness. Striking varies among Capped Bust half dimes, and most show lightness in one area or another. On the obverse, check the hair details to the left of the eye and the star centers. On the reverse, check the eagle's feathers and neck. The motto, which can be a problem on certain other coins of this design (notably half dollars), is usually bold on the half dimes. Dentils range from well defined to somewhat indistinct, and, in general, are sharper on the obverse than on the reverse.

Availability. Finding an example in any desired grade should not be a challenge. Finding one with Full Details will take more time. Connoisseurship is required at the MS level, due to overgraded and recolored coins.

AU-50, 53, 55, 58 (About Uncirculated). *Obverse:* Light wear is seen on the cap, the hair below LIBERTY, the hair near the clasp, and the drapery at the bosom. At AU-50 and 53, luster remains only in protected areas. At AU-58, the luster is extensive except in the open area of the field, especially to the right. *Reverse:* Wear is visible on the eagle's neck, the top of the wings, the claws, and the flat band above the eagle. At AU-50 and 53, there will still be significant luster, more than on the obverse. An AU-58 coin has nearly full luster.

MS-60 to 70 (Mint State). *Obverse:* At MS-60 some abrasion and contact marks are evident, most noticeably on the cheek, on the hair below the left part of LIBERTY, and on the area near the drapery clasp. Luster is present, but may be dull or lifeless, and interrupted in patches. At MS-63, contact marks are very few, and abrasion is hard to detect except under magnification. An MS-65 coin has no abrasion, and has contact marks so minute as to require magnification. Luster should be full and rich, usually more so on half dimes than larger coins of the Capped Bust type. Grades above MS-65 are seen now and again, and have fewer marks as perfection is approached. *Reverse:* Comments apply as for the obverse, except that abrasion and contact marks are most noticeable on the eagle's neck, the top of the wings, the claws, and the flat band that surrounds the incuse motto. The field is mainly protected by design elements and does not show abrasion as much as does the obverse.

1834, 3 Over Inverted 3   1835, Small Date   1835, Large Date
FS-H10-1834-301.

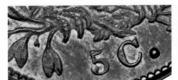

Small 5c   Large 5c

	Mintage	Cert	Avg	%MS	AU-50	MS-60	MS-62	MS-63	MS-64	MS-65	MS-66	Recent Auction Record
1829	1,230,000	579	60.1	73	$250	$375	$525	$750	$1,250	$2,850	$4,150	$8,625, MS-67 Star, Jul-10
1830	1,240,000	501	60.5	76	250	375	525	750	1,250	2,850	4,150	$978, MS-64, Jun-10
1831	1,242,700	634	61.7	79	250	375	525	750	1,250	2,850	4,150	$2,300, MS-65, Jul-10
1832	965,000	763	61.0	76	250	375	525	750	1,250	2,850	4,150	$5,175, MS-66, Apr-10
1833	1,370,000	507	60.7	74	250	375	525	750	1,250	2,850	4,150	$403, MS-62, Jun-10
1834	1,480,000	505	61.0	74	250	375	525	750	1,250	2,850	4,150	$1,093, MS-64, Apr-10
1834, 3 Over Inverted 3	*	9	47.4	33	500	600	800	1,200	2,250	3,500	5,000	$253, VF-35, Jun-10
1835, All kinds	2,760,000											
1835, Large Date and 5c		41	53.8	63	250	375	525	750	1,250	2,850	4,150	$2,070, MS-65, Feb-10
1835, Large Date, Small 5c		15	59.5	60	250	375	525	750	1,250	2,850	4,150	$127, EF-10, May-10
1835, Small Date, Large 5c		17	54.9	65	250	375	525	750	1,250	2,850	4,150	$2,070, MS-65, Jun-10
1835, Small Date and 5c		32	57.5	63	250	375	525	750	1,250	2,850	4,150	$431, AU-585, May-10
1836, Small 5c	1,900,000	29	51.8	45	250	375	525	750	1,250	2,850	4,150	$1,035, MS-63, Jul-10
1836, Large 5c	*	19	58.6	79	250	375	525	750	1,250	2,850	4,150	$322, AU-55, May-10
1836, 3 Over Inverted 3	*	27	53.0	48	475	600	800	1,100	1,750	3,400		$1,380, MS-64, Mar-09
1837, Small 5c	871,000	30	59.7	70	400	950	1,400	2,100	4,250	8,250		$3,594, MS-64, Apr-10
1837, Large 5c	*	22	52.0	55	250	400	650	875	1,550	4,750	7,000	$7,475, MS-66 CAC, Apr-10

* Included in number above.

Proof Capped Bust Half Dimes

PF-60 to 70 (Proof). True Proofs have fully mirrored fields. Scrutinize deeply toned pieces (deep toning often masks the true nature of a coin, e.g., if it is not a true Proof, or if it has been cleaned or repaired). Some pieces attributed as "Proofs" are not. This advice applies across the entire Capped Bust silver series. *Obverse and Reverse:* Proofs that are extensively cleaned and have many hairlines, or that are dull and grainy, are lower level, such as PF-60 to 62. These are not of great interest to specialists unless they are of rare die varieties (such as 1829, LM-1 to 3). With medium hairlines, PF-64 may be assigned, and with relatively few hairlines, PF-65. PF-66 should have hairlines so delicate that magnification is needed to see them. Above that, a Proof should be free of such lines. Grading is highly subjective with early Proofs, and eye appeal also is a factor.

Proof Capped Bust Half Dime
Shown 2x actual size.
Logan-McCloskey-4.

	Est Mintage	Cert	Finest	PF-60	PF-63	PF-64	PF-65	Recent Auction Record
1829	20–30	11	PF-67	$4,500	$10,000	$21,000	$31,000	$20,070, PF-64, Feb-09
1830	10–15	3	PF-66	4,500	12,500	23,500	37,000	$50,025, PF-65 CAC, Dec-08
1831	20–30	1	PF-67	4,500	12,500	24,000	38,000	$86,250, PF-67, Nov-07
1832	5–10	1	PF-64	4,500	12,500	25,000	40,000	$19,550, PF-64, Mar-04
1834	25–35	9	PF-66	4,500	10,000	20,000	30,000	$46,000, PF-66Cam, Apr-09
1836	5–10	2	PF-66	4,500	10,000	20,000	35,000	$57,500, PF-66, Jan-07
1837 (untraced)	5–10							

LIBERTY SEATED, NO STARS ON OBVERSE (1837–1838)

Variety 1, No Stars on Obverse (1837–1838): Designer Christian Gobrecht; weight 1.34 grams; composition .900 silver, .100 copper; diameter 15.5 mm; reeded edge; mints: Philadelphia, New Orleans.

Variety 1 (1837–1838)
Shown 2x actual size.

History. The Liberty Seated design without obverse stars, known as Variety 1, was used in the half dime and dime series only at the Philadelphia Mint in 1837 and the New Orleans Mint in 1838 (1838-O). The motif, by Christian Gobrecht, follows the obverse inaugurated on the 1836 silver dollar. Miss Liberty has no drapery at her elbow.

Striking and Sharpness. Check the highest parts of the Liberty Seated figure (especially the head and horizontal shield stripes) and, on the reverse, the leaves. Check the dentils on both sides. These coins are very attractive, and the starless obverse gives them a cameo-like appearance.

Availability. The Philadelphia coins are easily available in all grades. The 1838-O is a rarity in true Mint State, often is overgraded, and typically has low eye appeal. Grades above MS-65 are seen with regularity, more often than the related No Stars dimes.

AU-50, 53, 55, 58 (About Uncirculated). *Obverse:* Light wear is seen on the thighs and knees, bosom, and head. At AU-50 and 53, luster is less than at 58, where the luster is extensive but incomplete. Friction is seen in the large open field. *Reverse:* Wear is noticeable on the leaves and ribbon. At AU-50 and 53, there still is significant luster, more than on the obverse, as the design elements protect the small field areas. An AU-58 coin has nearly full luster—more so than on the obverse.

MS-60 to 70 (Mint State). *Obverse:* At MS-60 some abrasion and contact marks are evident, most noticeably on the bosom, thighs, and knees. Luster is present, but may be dull or lifeless, and interrupted in patches in the large open field. At MS-63, contact marks are very few, and abrasion is hard to detect except under magnification. An MS-65 coin has no abrasion, and contact marks are so minute as to require magnification. Luster should be full and rich.

Reverse: Comments apply as for the obverse, except that abrasion and contact marks are most noticeable on the highest parts of the leaves and the ribbon. The field is mainly protected by design elements and does not show abrasion as much as does the open-field obverse on a given coin.

1837, Small Date
Note the flat-topped 1.

1837, Large Date
Note the pointed-top 1.

	Mintage	Cert	Avg	%MS	AU-50	MS-60	MS-62	MS-63	MS-64	MS-65	MS-66	Recent Auction Record
1837, Small Date	1,405,000	37	61.1	70	$450	$800	$900	$1,200	$1,500	$3,400	$5,000	$1,610, MS-64, Jul-10
1837, Large Date	*	17	63.1	88	425	675	875	1,100	1,300	2,850	4,300	$3,220, MS-66, Jun-10
18380, No Stars	70,000	31	49.7	35	1,250	2,100	5,000	8,000	17,500	32,000		$1,105, EF-40, Mar-10

* Included in number above.

Proof Liberty Seated Half Dimes, Variety 1

PF-60 to 70 (Proof). It is likely that at least several dozen Proofs were made of the 1837 half dime. Today, attractive examples exist and are rare. Nearly all designated as Proofs are, indeed, Proofs. Seek an example with deep mirror surfaces. *Obverse and Reverse:* Proofs that are extensively cleaned and have many hairlines, or that are dull and grainy, are lower level, such as PF-60 to 62. These command little attention in the market. The 1837 half dime Proofs were often cleaned, resulting in coins that have lost much of their mirror surface. With medium hairlines and good reflectivity, PF-64 is assigned, and with relatively few hairlines, PF-65. In various grades hairlines are most easily seen in the obverse field. PF-66 should have hairlines so delicate that magnification is needed to see them. Above that, a Proof should be free of such lines.

Proof Liberty Seated Half Dime, Variety 1
Shown 2x actual size.

	Est Mintage	Cert	Finest	PF-60	PF-63	PF-64	PF-65	Recent Auction Record
1837	15–20	10	PF-67	$6,500	$14,000	$18,500	$37,500	$74,750, PF-67, Aug-07

LIBERTY SEATED, STARS ON OBVERSE (1838–1859)

Variety 2, Stars on Obverse (1838–1853): Designer Christian Gobrecht; weight 1.34 grams; composition .900 silver, .100 copper; diameter 15.5 mm; reeded edge; mints: Philadelphia, New Orleans.

Variety 2 (1838–1853)
Shown 2x actual size.

Variety 3, Arrows at Date, Reduced Weight (1853–1855): Designer Christian Gobrecht; weight 1.24 grams; composition .900 silver, .100 copper; diameter 15.5 mm; reeded edge; mints: Philadelphia, New Orleans.

Variety 3 (1853–1855)
Shown 2x actual size.

Variety 2 Resumed, With Weight Standard of Variety 3 (1856–1859): Designer Christian Gobrecht; weight 1.24 grams; composition .900 silver, .100 copper; diameter 15.5 mm; reeded edge; mints: Philadelphia, New Orleans.

Variety 2 Resumed, Weight Standard of Variety 3 (1856–1859)
Shown 2x actual size.

History. The Liberty Seated motif is essentially the same as before, but with 13 obverse stars added in 1838, and in 1839 a restyling (drapery added to the elbow) by Robert Ball Hughes. Arrows were added to the sides of the date starting in 1853, through 1855; these denoted the reduction of weight under the terms of the Act of February 21, 1853. The earlier weight standard resumed in 1856. The reverse design stayed the same during these changes.

Striking and Sharpness. Strike quality varies widely among these half dimes. Most from 1838 to 1852 are sharper than later ones, but there are exceptions. (Coins with "mushy" details are especially common among the high-mintage dates of the mid- to late 1850s.) On the obverse, check the star centers, the head and center of Miss Liberty, and the dentils. On the reverse, check the wreath leaves and dentils.

Availability. These are easily available as a type, but with many scarce varieties. Such issues as 1849-O and 1846 are extreme rarities at the true MS level. Quality varies widely, and many MS coins are artificially toned.

EF-40, 45 (Extremely Fine). *Obverse:* Wear is seen on all areas, more so than at AU, especially on the knees, bosom, and head. Little or no luster is seen. *Reverse:* Wear is seen on all areas, more so than at AU, most noticeably at the leaves to each side of the wreath apex, and on the ribbon. Leaves retain details except on the higher areas.

AU-50, 53, 55, 58 (About Uncirculated). *Obverse:* Light wear is seen on the knees, bosom, and head. At AU-50 and 53, luster is less than at 58, where the luster is extensive but incomplete. *Reverse:* Wear is evident on the leaves (especially at the top of the wreath) and ribbon. At AU-50 and 53, there still is significant luster. An AU-58 coin has nearly full luster, more so than on the obverse, as the design elements protect the small field areas.

MS-60 to 70 (Mint State). *Obverse:* At MS-60 some abrasion and contact marks are evident, most noticeably on the bosom and knees. Luster is present, but may be dull or lifeless. At MS-63, contact marks are very few, and abrasion is hard to detect except under magnification. An MS-65 coin has no abrasion, and contact marks are so minute as to require magnification. Luster should be full and rich. *Reverse:* Comments apply as for the obverse, except that in lower MS grades abrasion and contact marks are most noticeable on the highest parts of the leaves and the ribbon. At MS-65 or higher there are no marks visible to the unaided eye. The field is mainly protected by design elements and does not show abrasion as much as does the obverse on a given coin.

No Drapery From Elbow (1837–1840)

Drapery From Elbow (Starting 1840)

1838, Normal Stars
Shown 2x actual size.

1838, Small Stars
Shown 2x actual size.

1840-O, No Drapery,
Normal Reverse
Note four-leaf cluster next to DIME.

1840-O, No Drapery,
Transitional Reverse
Note three-leaf cluster next to DIME.

1848, Medium Date

1848, Large Date

1849, 9 Over 6
FS-H10-1849-302.

1849, 9 Over 8
FS-H10-1849-301.

1858, Repunched High Date
FS-H10-1858-301.

1858, Over Inverted Date
FS-H10-1858-302.

1860, Obverse of 1859, Reverse of 1860
Transitional pattern, with stars (Judd-247).

	Mintage	Cert	Avg	%MS	EF-40	AU-50	MS-60	MS-62	MS-63	MS-64	MS-65	Recent Auction Record
1838, No Drapery	2,225,000	595	62.0	82	$75	$160	$250	$310	$375	$750	$1,675	$374, MS-62, Jul-10
1838, No Drapery, Small Stars	*	31	62.8	90	185	360	560	700	1,000	1,650	3,500	$2,530, MS-66, Dec-09
1839, No Drapery	1,069,150	249	61.5	80	75	160	250	310	375	750	1,800	$1,840, MS-66, Jun-10
18390, No Drapery	1,060,000	62	56.3	53	80	170	500	875	1,850	3,000	4,500	$219, AU-50, Mar-10
1840, No Drapery	1,034,000	231	61.5	82	75	160	250	310	375	750	1,800	$546, MS-64, Jun-10
18400, No Drapery	695,000	39	57.8	36	85	285	725	1,100	2,250	4,400	12,500	$2,283, MS-62, Oct-09
18400, No Drapery, Transitional Rev (a)	100	2	26.0	0	800	1,250	1,600	2,500				
1840, Drapery	310,085	53	60.8	83	210	360	460	600	800	1,150	2,700	$978, MS-62 CAC, Jun-10
18400, Drapery	240,000	30	48.5	17	410	1,250	3,100	4,500	8,200			$1,035, EF-45, Jun-10
1841	1,150,000	154	62.0	86	75	145	210	265	320	560	1,250	$1,265, MS-66, Mar-10
18410	815,000	42	53.3	33	110	300	665	1,250	1,525	2,250	5,000	$2,185, MS-63, Feb-10
1842	815,000	145	61.7	77	75	145	210	265	325	560	1,250	$978, MS-65, Apr-10
18420	350,000	35	47.4	26	525	825	1,275	1,700	2,250	6,000	12,500	$345, VF-35, Mar-10
1843	1,165,000	186	61.0	76	75	145	210	265	325	560	1,250	$1,495, MS-66, Jun-10
1844	430,000	150	62.4	89	75	145	210	265	325	560	1,250	$1,265, MS-66, Jan-10
18440	220,000	25	46.7	20	1,100	2,500	5,500	8,000	12,000	19,000		$431, VF-20, Mar-10
1845	1,564,000	183	60.8	72	75	145	210	265	325	560	1,250	$127, AU-53, Jun-10
1846	27,000	40	34.4	3	2,400	4,600	11,000	13,000	18,500			$863, VG-8, Jul-10
1847	1,274,000	159	61.2	80	75	145	210	265	325	560	1,250	$196, MS-61, Jun-10
1848, Medium Date	668,000	80	60.1	65	75	145	250	385	500	1,100	2,750	$127, AU-50, Jul-10
1848, Large Date	*	32	59.2	56	130	285	500	1,000	1,400	2,000	3,500	$3,508, MS-66, Nov-08
18480	600,000	68	63.7	90	120	250	410	575	720	1,250	2,200	$2,530, MS-66, Feb-10
1849, All kinds	1,309,000											
1849, 9 Over 6 (b)					125	225	500	700	1,200	1,450	2,250	$1,840, MS-64 CAC, Jan-10
1849, 9 Over 8 (c)		13	57.0	62	175	260	620	800	1,400	2,000	2,750	$920, MS-63, Oct-09
1849, Normal Date					75	135	200	275	400	850	1,600	$748, MS-64, Jul-10
18490	140,000	49	51.2	39	475	1,000	2,200	3,000	4,000	7,250	10,500	$2,185, MS-62, Mar-10
1850	955,000	196	63.0	89	75	145	210	265	325	560	1,200	$518, MS-64, Jul-10
18500	690,000	58	58.1	60	120	310	700	950	1,650	2,600	3,800	$161, EF-40, Mar-10
1851	781,000	129	61.8	84	75	145	210	265	325	560	1,200	$460, MS-64, Jun-10
18510	860,000	96	59.5	69	110	235	500	600	800	1,200	3,800	$518, MS-62, Mar-10
1852	1,000,500	152	62.7	89	75	145	210	265	325	560	1,200	$431, MS-64, Jul-10
18520	260,000	44	53.5	45	260	525	865	1,300	2,000	4,700	7,250	$6,900, MS-65, Dec-09
1853, No Arrows	135,000	119	61.3	84	250	475	700	800	1,100	1,400	2,500	$1,725, MS-65, Jan-10
18530, No Arrows	160,000	21	38.7	10	1,700	2,900	6,000	8,750	12,000	19,000		$14,950, MS-63, Jan-10
1853, With Arrows	13,210,020	995	60.2	71	65	130	210	260	310	550	1,450	$489, MS-64 CAC, Jul-10
18530, With Arrows	2,200,000	74	57.5	57	75	150	275	500	750	1,500	3,250	$5,463, MS-66, Jun-10

* Included in number above. **a.** "This rare transitional variety exhibits large letters and open or split buds on the reverse die, along with a small O mintmark. The key diagnostic of the variety is three-leaf clusters on either side of the word DIME, while the common reverse has four-leaf clusters" (*Cherrypickers' Guide to Rare Die Varieties*, fourth edition, volume II). **b.** Fivaz and Stanton contend that this is actually a 9 Over 8 overdate (*Cherrypickers' Guide to Rare Die Varieties*). **c.** The 4 of the date is at least triple punched, with one secondary 4 south and one east of the primary 4. There is also a secondary numeral east of the lower portion of the 9.

Chart continued on next page.

	Mintage	Cert	Avg	%MS	EF-40	AU-50	MS-60	MS-62	MS-63	MS-64	MS-65	Recent Auction Record
1854	5,740,000	507	61.2	79	$65	$130	$210	$260	$310	$550	$1,500	$276, MS-63, Jul-10
18540	1,560,000	78	60.6	69	75	155	285	525	775	1,750	3,600	$1,610, MS-64, Dec-09
1855	1,750,000	203	62.0	82	65	130	210	260	310	550	1,875	$1,208, MS-65, Apr-10
18550	600,000	65	60.0	66	175	200	560	750	1,100	1,900	4,200	$1,380, MS-64, Apr-10
1856	4,880,000	391	61.4	81	65	130	180	200	300	550	1,100	$483, MS-64, May-10
18560	1,100,000	77	58.0	38	110	235	450	575	1,000	1,450	2,350	$374, AU-58, Dec-09
1857	7,280,000	651	62.0	86	65	130	180	200	300	550	1,100	$230, MS-63, Jun-10
18570	1,380,000	173	60.9	72	70	180	300	350	450	725	1,600	$2,070, MS-66, Apr-10
1858	3,500,000	608	62.5	87	65	130	180	200	300	550	1,100	$546, MS-64, Jun-10
1858, Repunched High Date (d)	*	4	48.5	25	235	350	650	850	1,200	1,900	3,000	$2,185, MS-65, Oct-08
1858, Over Inverted Date (e)	*	23	53.8	43	210	325	625	750	1,000	1,650	2,750	$161, VF-25, Dec-09
18580	1,660,000	181	61.9	82	80	150	250	350	450	600	1,450	$460, MS-63, May-10
1859	340,000	201	63.2	90	80	130	220	225	325	575	1,250	$489, MS-63 CAC, Jun-10
18590	560,000	93	61.9	84	130	200	250	275	350	800	1,950	$460, AU-58 CAC, May-10
1860, Obv of 1859, Rev of 1860 (With Stars) (f)	100	53	64.4	100	2,500	3,000	3,750	4,500	5,600			$2,588, MS-62, Mar-10

* Included in number above. **d.** The date was first punched into the die very high, then corrected and punched into its normal location. The original high-date punch is clearly visible within the upper portions of the primary date. **e.** The date was first punched into the die in an inverted orientation, and then corrected. The bases of the secondary digits are evident above the primary digits. **f.** This transitional issue, made surreptitiously at the Mint for a private collector, has the new Liberty Seated die made in the old style of 1859, but with the date of 1860. The reverse is the regular die of 1860, with a cereal wreath. Classified as Judd-267 (*United States Pattern Coins,* tenth edition).

Proof Liberty Seated Half Dimes, Varieties 2 and 3

PF-60 to 70 (Proof). Proofs were first widely sold to collectors in 1858, in which year an estimated 210 silver sets were distributed. It is believed that 800 Proofs were struck of 1859, of which slightly more than 400 found buyers. Proofs were made of earlier dates, but in much smaller numbers. Excellent strike and deeply mirrored fields characterized nearly all. The quality of Proofs on the market varies widely, mainly due to cleaning and dipping. Patience and care are needed to find a choice example. *Obverse and Reverse:* Proofs that are extensively cleaned and have many hairlines, or that are dull and grainy, are lower level, such as PF-60 to 62. These are not widely desired, save for the rare (in any grade) date of 1846. With medium hairlines and good reflectivity, a grade of PF-64 is justified, and with relatively few hairlines, PF-65. In various grades hairlines are most easily seen in the obverse field. PF-66 should have hairlines so delicate that magnification is needed to see them. Above that, a Proof should be free of such lines.

Proof Liberty Seated Half Dime, Variety 2
Shown 2x actual size.

Proof Liberty Seated Half Dime, Variety 3
Shown 2x actual size.

	Est Mintage	Cert	Finest	PF-60	PF-63	PF-64	PF-65	Recent Auction Record
1838	4–5	2	PF-66	$10,000	$12,500	$30,000	$50,000	$97,750, PF-66 Star, Jan-08
1839	5–10	4	PF-65	10,000	12,500	22,000	37,500	$27,600, PF-65Cam, Apr-08
1840, No Drapery	5–10	4	PF-66	10,000	12,500	22,000	37,500	$48,875, PF-66, Aug-07
1840, Drapery (untraced)	unknown							
1841	10–20	5	PF-65	10,000	15,000	25,000	45,000	$46,000, PF-65, Jan-08
1842	10–20	11	PF-68	8,000	12,000	15,000	26,000	$12,075, PF-64, Jan-10

	Est Mintage	Cert	Finest	PF-60	PF-63	PF-64	PF-65	Recent Auction Record
1843, Over 1843	10–20	1	PF-67	$8,000	$12,000	$15,000	$26,000	$69,000, PF-67, Jul-08
1844	15–25	8	PF-67	8,000	12,000	15,000	26,000	$21,850, PF-65 CAC, Jul-09
1845	10–15	6	PF-68	9,000	14,000	18,000	30,000	$92,000, PF-68, Jan-08
1846	10–20	7	PF-67	8,000	12,000	15,000	26,000	$63,250, PF-67, Apr-08
1847	8–12	3	PF-66	8,000	12,000	15,000	26,000	$43,125, PF-65, Jul-08
1848	6–8	2	PF-66	9,000	14,000	20,000	45,000	$63,250, PF-66, Jul-08
1849	8–12	3	PF-66	8,000	12,000	15,000	26,000	$48,875, PF-66, Apr-08
1850	8–12	3	PF-65	12,000	20,000	30,000	50,000	$57,500, PF-65, Jan-09
1852	10–15	6	PF-65	8,000	12,000	21,000	30,000	$16,100, PF-64Cam, Dec-09
1853, Arrows (extremely rare)	3–5	1	PF-64	20,000	25,000	32,000		
1854, Arrows	15–25	10	PF-66	4,750	8,500	11,000	14,000	$10,925, PF-65, May-09
1855, Arrows	15–25	17	PF-66	4,750	8,500	11,000	14,000	$18,400, PF-66 CAC, Jul-09
1856	40–60	20	PF-66	2,500	4,500	6,000	9,000	$6,900, PF-65, Dec-09
1857	40–60	26	PF-67	2,200	3,000	3,400	5,500	$2,760, PF-64, Apr-10
1858	300	81	PF-67	850	1,400	2,250	4,500	$1,840, PF-64, Mar-10
1859	800	214	PF-68	550	1,250	2,000	4,000	$2,530, PF-65, Jul-10
1859, Transitional (a)	20	7	PF-66	19,000	35,000	45,000	55,000	$40,250, PF-63, Feb-07

a. Classified as Judd-232 (*United States Pattern Coins,* tenth edition), this features the obverse design of 1859 and the reverse of 1860.

LIBERTY SEATED, LEGEND ON OBVERSE (1860–1873)

Variety 4, Legend on Obverse (1860–1873): Designer Christian Gobrecht; weight 1.24 grams; composition .900 silver, .100 copper; diameter 15.5 mm; reeded edge; mints: Philadelphia, New Orleans, San Francisco.

Variety 4 (1860–1873)
Shown 2x actual size.

History. In 1860 on the half dime the legend UNITED STATES OF AMERICA was moved to the obverse, in place of the stars. The reverse displayed a "cereal wreath" (as it was called in Mint records) enclosing the words HALF DIME.

Striking and Sharpness. Points to check include the head of Miss Liberty on the obverse, the wreath details on the reverse (particularly at the inside upper left, above H of HALF) and the dentils on both sides. Generally, MS coins have excellent luster, although some struck from relapped dies tend to be prooflike and with many striae. The word LIBERTY is not an infallible guide to grading at lower levels, as on some dies the shield was in lower relief, and the letters wore away less quickly. This guideline should be used in combination with other features.

Availability. These are easily available as a type, although some dates and varieties are rare. San Francisco coins, first made in 1863, are rare in MS for the first several years.

EF-40, 45 (Extremely Fine). *Obverse:* More wear than at AU is seen on all areas, especially the knees, bosom, and head. Little or no luster is seen. *Reverse:* More wear than at AU is seen on all areas, most noticeably at the high areas of the wreath and on the ribbon. Leaves retain excellent details except on the higher areas.

AU-50, 53, 55, 58 (About Uncirculated). *Obverse:* Light wear is seen on the knees, bosom, and head. At AU-50 and 53, luster is less evident than at 58, where the luster is extensive but incomplete. *Reverse:* Wear is observable on the leaves and ribbon. At AU-50 and 53 there still is significant luster, more so than on the obverse, as the design elements protect the small field areas. An AU-58 coin has nearly full luster.

MS-60 to 70 (Mint State). *Obverse:* At MS-60 some abrasion and contact marks are evident, most noticeably on the bosom and knees. Luster is present, but may be dull or lifeless. At MS-63, contact marks are very few, and abrasion is hard to detect except under magnification. An MS-65 coin has no abrasion, and contact marks are so minute as to require magnification. Luster should be full and rich, except for Philadelphia (but not San Francisco) half dimes of the early and mid-1860s. Most MS coins of 1861 to 1865, Philadelphia issues, have extensive die striae (from the dies being incompletely finished). Some low-mintage Philadelphia issues may be prooflike (and some may even be mislabeled as Proofs). Clashmarks are common in this era. *Reverse:* Comments apply as for the obverse, except that in lower MS grades abrasion and contact marks are most noticeable on the highest parts of the leaves and the ribbon, less so on HALF DIME. At MS-65 or higher there are no marks visible to the unaided eye. The field, mainly protected by design elements, does not show abrasion as much as does the obverse on a given coin.

1861, So-Called 1 Over 0
FS-H10-1861-301.

1872, Doubled-Die Obverse
FS-H10-1872-101.

Mintmark Below Bow
1860–1869, 1872–1873.

Mintmark Above Bow
1870–1872.

	Mintage	Cert	Avg	%MS	EF-40	AU-50	MS-60	MS-62	MS-63	MS-64	MS-65	Recent Auction Record
1860, Legend	798,000	448	63.4	92	$50	$80	$160	$180	$250	$350	$750	$748, MS-65, Mar-10
1860O	1,060,000	189	62.3	86	50	100	180	225	300	475	950	$403, MS-62, Jul-10
1861	3,360,000	476	61.7	83	50	80	160	180	250	350	800	$345, MS-64, Jun-10
1861, So-called 1 over 0	*				250	375	600	725	875	1,375	3,000	$2,875, MS-65 CAC, Jul-10
1862	1,492,000	555	63.3	92	65	110	180	200	260	350	750	$1,208, MS-66 CAC, Jul-10
1863	18,000	109	62.5	91	450	600	650	725	800	1,000	1,600	$1,265, MS-64 CAC, Jul-10
1863S	100,000	84	61.4	81	160	320	750	825	975	1,600	3,000	$891, MS-63, Dec-09
1864	48,000	43	62.0	86	875	1,000	1,200	1,275	1,350	1,650	2,450	$6,613, MS-67, Feb-10
1864S	90,000	46	57.9	65	275	425	675	950	1,300	1,850	3,600	$375, EF-45, May-10
1865	13,000	46	62.5	87	625	725	850	1,000	1,250	1,575	2,000	$863, EF-45, Jul-10
1865S	120,000	43	56.3	51	175	500	950	1,275	2,100	3,300	4,750	$403, AU-50, Sep-09
1866	10,000	53	62.7	91	625	650	775	900	1,100	1,300	2,300	$805, MS-62, Apr-10
1866S	120,000	61	61.0	77	160	325	475	650	900	1,450	3,400	$403, MS-62, Mar-10
1867	8,000	80	62.8	89	800	875	1,000	1,100	1,300	1,500	2,000	$1,093, MS-62, Apr-10
1867S	120,000	49	59.2	67	160	325	575	700	1,200	1,900	3,200	$518, MS-62, May-10
1868	88,600	69	62.8	91	300	450	675	700	850	1,100	1,700	$1,955, MS-66, Mar-10
1868S	280,000	130	62.1	77	45	130	300	400	600	1,000	2,750	$863, MS-64, May-10
1869	208,000	89	63.1	90	45	130	235	300	400	875	1,100	$2,530, MS-67, Sep-09
1869S	230,000	63	62.3	83	45	130	300	400	800	1,300	3,500	$299, MS-62, May-10
1870	535,000	229	62.6	88	45	80	150	200	275	400	900	$232, MS-62, Jul-10
1870S (unique) †		1	63.0	100				1,000,000				$661,250, MS-63, Jul-04
1871	1,873,000	386	62.2	84	45	80	150	200	275	375	850	$1,380, MS-66 CAC, Jul-10
1871S	161,000	99	61.8	76	80	180	275	300	450	700	2,000	$1,861, MS-65, Jan-10
1872	2,947,000	312	61.6	82	45	80	150	200	275	375	800	$920, MS-65, Mar-10
1872, DblDie Obv (a)	*	8	48.0	0	200	300	550	650	800			$60, VG-8, Jan-06
1872S, All kinds	837,000											
1872S, Mintmk above bow		120	62.7	86	45	80	150	200	275	375	750	$1,035, MS-66, Apr-10
1872S, Mintmk below bow		102	62.9	84	45	80	150	200	275	375	750	$345, MS-64, Jul-10
1873 (Close 3 only)	712,000	98	62.7	88	45	80	150	200	275	375	750	$374, MS-64 CAC, Jul-09
1873S (Close 3 only)	324,000	245	62.8	89	45	80	150	200	275	375	750	$920, MS-66, Mar-10

* Included in number above. † Ranked in the *100 Greatest U.S. Coins* (third edition). **a.** "Doubling is evident on UNITED STATES OF AMERICA and on most elements of Miss Liberty. AMERICA is the strongest point" (*Cherrypickers' Guide to Rare Die Varieties*, fourth edition, volume II).

Proof Liberty Seated Half Dimes, Variety 4

PF-60 to 70 (Proof). Proof coins were made in fair quantities each year and are readily available today. Generally, they are well made, with deeply mirrored fields, although some of the late 1860s and early 1870s can have weak areas. Average quality in the marketplace is higher than for larger Liberty Seated denominations. *Obverse and Reverse:* Proofs that are extensively cleaned and have many hairlines, or that are dull and grainy, are lower level, such as PF-60 to 62. These are not widely desired in the marketplace. With medium hairlines and good reflectivity, PF-64 is appropriate, and with relatively few hairlines, PF-65. In various grades hairlines are most easily seen in the obverse field. PF-66 should have hairlines so delicate that magnification is needed to see them. Above that, a Proof should be free of such lines.

Proof Liberty Seated Half Dime, Variety 4
Shown 2x actual size.

	Mintage	Cert	Finest	PF-60	PF-63	PF-64	PF-65	Recent Auction Record
1860	1,000	101	PF-68	$350	$575	$800	$1,750	$322, PF-62, Feb-10
1861	1,000	85	PF-67	350	575	800	1,750	$1,380, PF-65, Jul-10
1862	550	172	PF-67	350	575	800	1,750	$661, PF-64 CAC, May-10
1863	460	170	PF-67	350	575	800	1,850	$3,578, PF-67Cam, Jul-10
1864	470	133	PF-68	350	575	800	1,850	$1,323, PF-65, Jun-10
1865	500	158	PF-68	350	575	800	1,750	$1,093, PF-64, Apr-10
1866	725	157	PF-68	350	575	800	1,750	$920, PF-64, Apr-10
1867	625	212	PF-68	350	575	800	1,750	$1,610, PF-66Cam, Jul-10
1868	600	157	PF-67	350	575	800	1,750	$1,208, PF-65, Apr-10
1869	600	199	PF-68	350	575	800	1,750	$1,438, PF-65Cam, Jul-10
1870	1,000	162	PF-68	350	575	800	1,750	$1,610, PF-66Cam, Apr-10
1871	960	174	PF-69	350	575	800	1,750	$3,450, PF-67 Star, Apr-10
1872	950	163	PF-68	350	575	800	1,750	$805, PF-64, Jun-10
1873	600	211	PF-67	350	575	800	1,750	$2,760, PF-66Cam, Jun-10

AN OVERVIEW OF DIMES

A collection of dimes ranging from 1796 to date includes many interesting issues. As a type, none are super-rare, but earlier types, combining low mintages with commonly weak striking, can be a challenge for the collector.

The 1796–1797 dime with Draped Bust obverse, Small Eagle reverse is the rarest of the dime types by far, with fewer than 50,000 pieces minted. These hail from an era in which there was no numismatic interest in saving such coins. Finding a choice example in whatever grade desired will require time and effort.

Then comes the Draped Bust obverse, Heraldic Eagle reverse type, made from 1798 through 1807 (except for 1799). Today these are available easily enough in circulated grades, but are elusive in Mint State. Nearly all are lightly struck—another challenge. Capped Bust dimes of the 1809–1828 years also require connoisseurship to locate a sharply struck specimen. For all of these early types some compromise with perfection is required.

Later Capped Bust dimes of 1828 to 1837 can be found well struck, as can be the later variations within the Liberty Seated type. Barber, Mercury, and Roosevelt dimes are easy to find in just about any grade desired.

Proofs are most readily available from the Liberty Seated era to the present and are sometimes included in type sets, usually answering the call for sharply struck pieces, as most (but not all) were made with care.

FOR THE COLLECTOR AND INVESTOR: DIMES AS A SPECIALTY

Dimes have been a very popular denomination to collect on a systematic basis. Generally, interest is separated into different eras. Those of the early years, the Draped Bust and Capped Bust issues, 1796 to 1837, are enthusiastically sought not only for dates and major varieties (as, for example, those listed in the charts to follow), but also by die varieties. Aficionados use the book *Early United States Dimes, 1796–1837,* whose listings are by JR numbers, for John Reich, the designer of the Capped Bust silver issues. The John Reich Collectors Society, publisher of the *John Reich Journal,* serves as a forum for the exchange of ideas and new information.

Among early varieties, the 1796, 1797 16 stars, and 1797 13 stars are each rare in all grades. Dimes with the Heraldic Eagle reverse, 1798–1807, are generally scarce, but not prohibitively rare, although Mint State coins are elusive. Among the reverse dies some were shared with contemporary quarter eagles of like design and diameter—feasible as there is no indication of denomination on them. Indeed, there was no mark of value on any dime until 1809.

Among Classic Head dimes of the 1809–1828 years, the 1822 is the key date and is especially rare in high grades. Among the modified Classic Head dimes of 1829–1837, all varieties listed in this book are available without difficulty. An example of how a newly discovered variety can be considered unique or exceedingly rare, and later be recognized as plentiful, is provided by the 1830, 30 Over 29 overdate, first publicized by Don Taxay in 1970 in *Scott's Comprehensive Catalogue of United States Coinage* (cover-dated 1971). The overdate was then considered one of a kind, but since then dozens more have been identified.

Liberty Seated dimes of the various types have been a popular specialty over a long period of time. There are no impossible rarities except for the unique 1873-CC Without Arrows, but certain other varieties are very hard to find, including the Carson City issues of the early 1870s.

Barber dimes can be collected by date and mint from 1892 to 1916, except for the 1894-S, of which only 24 are believed to have been struck, with only about 10 accounted for today. The other varieties range from common to scarce. Mercury dimes, 1916–1945, have an enthusiastic following. The key issues are 1916-D (in particular); 1921; 1921-D; 1942, 2 Over 1; and 1942-D, 2 Over 1. Roosevelt dimes from 1946 to date can easily be collected by date and mint and are very popular.

RECOMMENDED READING

Ahwash, Kamal M. *Encyclopedia of United States Liberty Seated Dimes, 1837–1891,* Kamal Press, 1977.

Davis, David; Logan, Russell; Lovejoy, Allen; McCloskey, John; and Subjack, William. *Early United States Dimes, 1796–1837,* Ypsilanti, MI, 1984.

Fivaz, Bill, and Stanton, J.T. *The Cherrypickers' Guide to Rare Die Varieties* (4th ed., vol. II), Atlanta, GA, 2006.

Flynn, Kevin. *The 1894-S Dime: A Mystery Unraveled,* Rancocas, NJ, 2005.

Flynn, Kevin. *The Authoritative Reference on Roosevelt Dimes,* Brooklyn, NY, 2001.

Greer, Brian. *The Complete Guide to Liberty Seated Dimes,* Virginia Beach, VA, 2005.

Lange, David W. *The Complete Guide to Mercury Dimes* (2nd ed.), Virginia Beach, VA, 2005.

Lawrence, David. *The Complete Guide to Barber Dimes,* Virginia Beach, VA, 1991.

DRAPED BUST, SMALL EAGLE REVERSE (1796–1797)

Designer Robert Scot; weight 2.70 grams; composition .8924 silver, .1076 copper; approx. diameter 19 mm; reeded edge. All coined at Philadelphia Mint.

Shown 1.5x actual size.
John Reich–2.

History. Dimes were first minted for circulation in 1796. There are no records of publicity surrounding their debut. The coins featured the Draped Bust obverse, as used on cents and other silver coins, combined with the Small Eagle reverse. Some 1796 dimes exhibit prooflike surfaces, suggesting that they may have been "presentation pieces," but no records exist to confirm this possibility.

Striking and Sharpness. Most dimes of this type have weakness or problems in one area or another, usually more so on those dated 1797. Points to check for sharpness include the hair of Miss Liberty, the drapery lines on the bust, the centers of the stars, and, on the reverse, the breast and wing feathers of the eagle. Also check for adjustment marks. A sharply struck coin is a goal, not necessarily a reality. Sharp striking and excellent eye appeal add dramatically to the value.

Availability. This is the rarest and most expensive type in the dime series. Within any desired grade, examples should be selected with great care, as many have problems of one sort or another. MS coins are especially rare; when seen they are usually dated 1796. Dimes of 1797 are much rarer in all grades, and nearly impossible to find in MS-63 or finer.

F-12, 15 (Fine). *Obverse:* Wear is more extensive than at VF, particularly noticeable on the hair, face, and bosom, and the stars appear larger. About half the hair detail remains, most noticeably behind the neck and shoulder. The rim may be partially worn away and blend into the field. *Reverse:* Wear is more extensive than at VF. Feather details are diminished, with fewer than half remaining on the wings. The wreath and lettering are worn further, and the rim is usually weak in areas, although some dentils can be seen.

VF-20, 30 (Very Fine). *Obverse:* The higher-relief areas of hair are well worn at VF-20, less so at 30. The drapery and bosom show extensive wear. The stars are worn, making them appear larger than normal. *Reverse:* The body of the eagle shows few if any feathers, while the wings have about half of the feathers visible, depending on the strike. At VF-30 more than half of the feathers may show. The leaves lack most detail and are in outline form. Scattered, non-disfiguring marks are normal for this and lower grades. Any major defects should be noted separately.

EF-40, 45 (Extremely Fine). *Obverse:* More wear than at AU is evident on the upper hair area and the ribbon, and on the drapery and bosom. Excellent detail remains in low-relief areas of the hair. The stars show wear, as do the date and letters. Luster, if present at all, is minimal and in protected areas. *Reverse:* The eagle (the focal point to check) shows more wear than at AU. Many feathers remain on the interior areas of the wings. Additional wear is on the wreath and letters, but many details are present. Some luster may be seen in protected areas, and if present is slightly more abundant than on the obverse.

AU-50, 53, 55, 58 (About Uncirculated). *Obverse:* Light wear is seen on the hair area above the ear and extending to the left of the forehead, on the ribbon, and on the bosom, more so at AU-50 than at 53 or 55. An AU-58 coin has minimal traces of wear. Regarding luster: an AU-50 coin has luster in protected areas among the stars and letters, with little in the open fields or on the portrait. At AU-58, most luster is present in the fields, but is worn away on the highest parts of the motifs. *Reverse:* Light wear is seen on the eagle's body (note: the higher parts of this area might be lightly struck) and the edges of the wings. Light wear is seen on the wreath and lettering. Luster is the best key to actual wear. This ranges from perhaps 20% remaining in protected areas (at AU-50) to nearly full mint bloom (at AU-58).

MS-60 to 70 (Mint State). *Obverse:* At MS-60, some abrasion and contact marks are evident, most noticeably on the cheek, the drapery, and the right field. Luster is present, but may be dull or lifeless, and interrupted in patches. At MS-63, contact marks are very few, and abrasion is hard to detect except under magnification, although this type is sometimes graded liberally due to its rarity. An MS-65 coin has no abrasion, and contact marks are so minute as to require magnification. Luster should be full and rich. Coins graded above MS-65 are more theoretical than actual for this type—but they do exist, and are defined by having fewer marks as perfection is approached. *Reverse:* Comments apply as for the obverse, except that abrasion and marks are most noticeable on the eagle at the center, a situation complicated by the fact that this area was sometimes lightly struck. The field area is small and is protected by lettering and the wreath, and in any given grade shows fewer marks than on the obverse.

1797, 16 Stars   1797, 13 Stars

Shown 2x actual size.

	Mintage	Cert	Avg	%MS	VF-20	EF-40	AU-50	MS-60	MS-62	MS-63	MS-64	Recent Auction Record
1796	22,135	202	50.5	43	$6,250	$11,000	$16,500	$26,000	$32,500	$38,000	$55,000 **(a)**	$34,500, MS-63, May-10
1797, All kinds	25,261											
1797, 16 Stars		15	43.9	33	7,000	11,750	18,000	35,000	40,000	47,500		$8,625, AU-53, Jul-09
1797, 13 Stars		18	29.8	6	7,250	13,500	19,000	45,000	65,000	75,000		$4,313, VG-10, Jun-10

a. Value in MS-65 is $85,000.

DRAPED BUST, HERALDIC EAGLE REVERSE (1798–1807)

Designer Robert Scot; weight 2.70 grams; composition .8924 silver, .1076 copper; approx. diameter 19 mm; reeded edge. All coined at Philadelphia Mint.

Shown 1.5x actual size.
John Reich–3.

History. Dimes of this style were minted each year from 1798 to 1807 (with the exception of 1799 and 1805). The designs follow those of other silver coins of the era.

Striking and Sharpness. Nearly all have one area or another of light striking. On the obverse, check the hair details and drapery lines, and the star centers. On the reverse, the upper right of the shield and the adjacent part of the eagle's wing often are soft, and several or even most stars may be lightly defined (sharp stars show sharply peaked centers); high parts of the clouds are often weak. Dentils are likely to be weak or missing in areas on either side. Expect to compromise on the strike; a sharply struck coin is a goal, not necessarily a reality. Certain reverse dies of this type were also used to coin quarter eagles. Sharp striking and excellent eye appeal dramatically add to a Draped Bust dime's value, this being particularly true for 1805 and 1807 (which are usually weakly struck, especially 1807), the dates most often seen in MS.

Availability. Although certain die varieties are rare, the basic years are available, with 1805 and 1807 being the most often seen. As a class, MS coins are rare. Again, when seen they are usually dated 1805 or 1807, and have areas of striking weakness. Coins of 1801 through 1804 are scarce in VF and higher grades, very scarce in AU and better.

F-12, 15 (Fine). *Obverse:* Wear is more extensive than at VF, particularly noticeable on the hair, face, and bosom. The stars are worn and appear larger than normal. About half the hair detail remains, most noticeably behind the neck and shoulder. The rim may be partially worn away and blend into the field. *Reverse:* Wear is more extensive than at VF, with the shield and wing feathers being points to observe. About half of the feathers are visible (depending on striking). E PLURIBUS UNUM may have a few letters worn away. The clouds all seem to be connected. The stars are weak. Parts of the border and lettering may be weak.

VF-20, 30 (Very Fine). *Obverse:* The higher-relief areas of hair are well worn at VF-20, less so at VF-30. The drapery and bosom show extensive wear. The stars are worn, making them appear larger than normal. *Reverse:* Wear is greater than at EF, including on the shield and wing feathers. The star centers are flat. Other areas have lost detail, as well. E PLURIBUS UNUM is complete (this incuse feature tended to wear away slowly).

EF-40, 45 (Extremely Fine). *Obverse:* More wear than at AU is evident on the upper hair area and the ribbon and on the drapery and bosom. Excellent detail remains in low-relief areas of the hair. The stars show wear, as do the date and letters. Luster, if present at all, is minimal and in protected areas. *Reverse:* The neck lacks feather detail on its highest points. Feathers have lost some detail near the edges of the wings, and some areas of the horizontal lines in the shield may be blended together, particularly at the right (an area that is also susceptible to weak striking). Some traces of luster may be seen, less so at EF-40 than at EF-45.

AU-50, 53, 55, 58 (About Uncirculated). *Obverse:* Light wear is seen on the hair area above the ear and extending to the left of the forehead, on the ribbon, and on the drapery at the shoulder, more so at AU-50 than at 53 or 55. An AU-58 coin has minimal traces of wear. Regarding luster: an AU-50 coin has luster in protected areas among the stars and letters, with little in the open fields or on the portrait. At AU-58, most luster is present in the fields, but is worn away on the highest parts of the motifs. *Reverse:* Comments apply as for the obverse, except that the eagle's neck, the tips and top of the wings, the clouds, and the tail now show noticeable wear, as do other features. As always, a familiarity with a given die variety will help differentiate striking weakness from actual wear. Luster ranges from perhaps 20% remaining in protected areas (at AU-50) to nearly full mint bloom (at AU-58). Often the reverse of this type will retain much more luster than the obverse.

MS-60 to 70 (Mint State). *Obverse:* At MS-60 some abrasion and contact marks are evident, most noticeably on the cheek, the drapery at the shoulder, and the right field. Luster is present, but may be dull or lifeless, and interrupted in patches. At MS-63, contact marks are very few, and abrasion is hard to detect except under magnification. An MS-65 coin has no abrasion, and contact marks are so minute as to require magnification. Luster should be full and rich. Coins graded above MS-65 are more theoretical than actual for this type—but they do exist, and are defined by having fewer marks as perfection is approached. *Reverse:* Comments apply as for the obverse, except that abrasion and marks are most noticeable on the eagle's neck, the tips of the wing, and the tail. The field area is complex, without much open space, given the stars above the eagle, the arrows and olive branch, and other features. Accordingly, marks are not as noticeable as on the obverse.

1798, 8 Over 7

1798, 8 Over 7,
16 Stars on Reverse

Shown 2x actual size.

1798, 8 Over 7,
13 Stars on Reverse

1798, Normal 8

1798, Small 8

Shown 2x actual size.

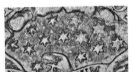

1804, 13 Stars on Reverse

1804, 14 Stars on Reverse

1805, 4 Berries

1805, 5 Berries

	Mintage	Cert	Avg	%MS	VF-20	EF-40	AU-50	MS-60	MS-62	MS-63	MS-64	Recent Auction Record
1798, All kinds	27,550											
1798, 8 Over 7, 16 Stars on Reverse		44	52.8	61	$2,300	$3,500	$5,000	$9,000	$15,000	$20,000		$1,668, F-12, Apr-10
1798, 8 Over 7, 13 Stars on Reverse		8	45.3	38	7,000	10,000	15,000					$4,720, AU-58, Jan-10
1798		14	49.9	36	2,500	3,750	4,600	8,000	15,000	20,000	$35,000 (a)	$5,750, AU-55, Jun-10
1798, Small 8		3	28.7	33	3,500	6,500	10,000	20,000				$2,530, VG-8, Jan-10
1800	21,760	42	42.0	12	3,250	5,000	9,000	20,000	35,000			$6,325, AU-53, Apr-10
1801	34,640	31	35.2	19	3,750	5,750	9,500	20,000	25,000	30,000		$920, G-6, Jan-10
1802	10,975	34	33.5	15	5,000	9,000	17,000	35,000	65,000			$13,800, AU-55, Feb-10
1803	33,040	32	32.3	9	3,000	5,500	9,000	45,000				$1,265, G-6, Dec-09
1804, All kinds	8,265											
1804, 13 Stars on Rev		2	55.0	0	15,000	25,000	53,000					$63,250, AU-55, Apr-09
1804, 14 Stars on Rev		6	30.5	0	20,000	40,000	85,000					$29,900, EF-40, Sep-08
1805, All kinds	120,780											
1805, 4 Berries		211	46.3	43	1,800	2,500	3,500	7,500	10,000	14,000	22,500 (b)	$1,035, F-12, Jun-10
1805, 5 Berries		33	39.6	30	2,000	3,000	4,000	9,000	12,500	20,000	30,000	$1,783, VF-20, Apr-09
1807	165,000	220	46.3	40	1,800	2,500	3,500	7,000	9,500	12,500	20,000 (c)	$4,600, AU-58, Jul-10

a. Value in MS-65 is $50,000. **b.** Value in MS-65 is $35,000. **c.** Value in MS-65 is $35,000.

CAPPED BUST,
VARIETY 1, WIDE BORDER
(1809–1828)

Designer John Reich; weight 2.70 grams; composition .8924 silver, .1076 copper; approx. diameter 18.8 mm; reeded edge. All coined at Philadelphia Mint.

Shown 1.5x actual size.
John Reich–1.

History. Dimes of this design were struck intermittently from 1809 to 1828. The design, by John Reich, closely follows that inaugurated with the Capped Bust half dollars of 1809 (themselves a modification of the earlier Capped Bust design).

Striking and Sharpness. Many if not most have areas of light striking. On the obverse, check the star centers, the hair details, and the drapery at the bosom. On the reverse, check the eagle, especially the area in and around the upper right of the shield. Dentils are sometimes weak, but are usually better defined on the reverse than on the obverse. The height of the rims on both sides can vary, and coins with a low rim or rims tend to show wear more quickly.

Availability. There are no extremely rare dates in this series, so all are available to collectors. In MS, most are scarce and some rare. Those exhibiting a strong strike, with Full Details, command a premium, especially the earlier dates.

EF-40, 45 (Extremely Fine). *Obverse:* Wear is more extensive than at AU, most noticeable on the higher areas of the hair. The cap shows more wear, as does the cheek. Stars still show their centers (unless lightly struck, and many are). Luster, if present, is in protected areas among the star points and close to the portrait. *Reverse:* The wings show wear on the higher areas of the feathers (particularly on the right wing), and some details are lost. Feathers in the neck are light. The eagle's claws show wear. Luster may be present in protected areas, even if there is little or none on the obverse.

AU-50, 53, 55, 58 (About Uncirculated). *Obverse:* Light wear is seen on the cap, the hair below LIB-ERTY, the hair near the clasp, and the drapery at the bosom. At AU-58, the luster is extensive except in the open area of the field, especially to the right. At AU-50 and 53, luster remains only in protected areas. As is true of all high grades, sharpness of strike can affect the perception of wear. *Reverse:* Wear is evident on the eagle's neck, the top of the wings, and the claws. At AU-50 and 53, there is significant luster, more than on the obverse. An AU-58 has nearly full luster.

MS-60 to 70 (Mint State). *Obverse:* At MS-60 some abrasion and contact marks are evident, most noticeably on the cheek and on the area near the drapery clasp. Luster is present, but may be dull or lifeless, and interrupted in patches. At MS-63, contact marks are very few, and abrasion is hard to detect except under magnification. An MS-65 coin has no abrasion, and contact marks are so minute as to require magnification. Luster should be full and rich. Grades above MS-65 have fewer marks as perfection is approached. *Reverse:* Comments apply as for the obverse, except that abrasion and contact marks are most noticeable on the eagle's neck, the top of the wings, the claws, and the flat band that surrounds the incuse motto. The field is mainly protected by design elements and does not show abrasion as much as does the obverse.

1811, 11 Over 09

1814, Small Date
Shown 2x actual size.

1814, Large Date

1814, STATESOFAMERICA
Shown 2x actual size.

1820, Large 0
Shown 2x actual size.

1820, Small 0

1820, STATESOFAMERICA
Shown 2x actual size.

1821, Large Date

1821, Small Date
Shown 2x actual size.

1823, 3 Over 2
Shown 2x actual size.

1823, 3 Over 2, Small E's

1823, 3 Over 2, Large E's

1824, 4 Over 2

1824 and 1827, Flat Top 1

1824 and 1827, Pointed Top 1

1828, Large Date, Curl Base 2

1828, Small Date, Square Base 2

The Small Date is of Variety 2 (see next section); for comparison purposes, both are illustrated here.

	Mintage	Cert	Avg	%MS	EF-40	AU-50	MS-60	MS-62	MS-63	MS-64	MS-65	Recent Auction Record
1809	51,065	38	43.5	45	$1,800	$2,100	$4,500	$5,500	$7,000	$12,500	$22,500	$1,265, F-12, May-10
1811, 11 Over 09	65,180	50	44.4	30	1,700	2,000	3,500	4,500	6,500	10,000	32,500	$1,725, EF-40, Jul-10
1814, All kinds	421,500											
1814, Small Date		31	57.3	65	600	1,200	2,500	3,500	5,000	7,500	15,000	$2,530, MS-60, Mar-10
1814, Large Date		23	57.5	61	500	1,000	2,000	3,000	4,000	6,500	12,500	$431, EF-40, May-10
1814, STATESOFAMERICA		11	50.4	55	650	1,250	2,500	3,500	4,500	6,000	12,000	$10,350, MS-65, Jul-09
1820, All kinds	942,587											
1820, Large 0		7	45.1	43	500	850	1,500	2,000	2,750	5,000	12,500	$1,236, MS-62, Apr-10
1820, Small 0		27	40.7	26	600	700	1,500	2,500	3,500	5,500	13,000	$2,065, AU-58, Jan-10
1820, STATESOFAMERICA		11	53.3	55	500	1,100	2,000	2,750	4,500	6,500	15,000	$9,200, MS-65, Jan-10
1821, All kinds	1,186,512											
1821, Small Date		38	57.6	66	520	850	1,750	2,200	3,500	5,000	13,500	$4,888, MS-64, Apr-10

Chart continued on next page.

	Mintage	Cert	Avg	%MS	EF-40	AU-50	MS-60	MS-62	MS-63	MS-64	MS-65	Recent Auction Record
1821, Large Date		36	45.0	28	$500	$800	$1,700	$2,000	$3,250	$5,000	$13,500	$10,638, MS-66, Apr-10
1822	100,000	35	30.6	31	3,800	7,000	12,000	20,000	30,000	40,000		$11,500, EF-45, Apr-10
1823, 3 Over 2, All kinds	440,000											
1823, 3 Over 2, Small E's		5	49.6	40	450	700	1,500	2,000	3,000	5,000	12,000	$185, VF-30, May-10
1823, 3 Over 2, Large E's		9	40.9	56	450	700	1,500	2,000	3,000	5,000	12,000	$173, F-12, May-10
1824, 4 Over 2, Flat Top 1	510,000	4	46.5	0	800	1,400	2,000	2,500	5,000	8,500	17,500	$7,475, MS-64 CAC, Jul-10
1824, 4 Over 2, Pointed Top 1	*	2	12.0	0	4,000							
1825	*	90	54.6	52	500	850	2,000	2,500	3,500	4,500	12,000	$546, EF-45, May-10
1827, Flat Top 1	1,215,000	2	38.5	50	1,000	2,500						
1827, Pointed Top 1	*	46	43.7	37	450	700	1,500	2,000	3,000	4,500	13,500	$10,800, MS-65, Feb-10
1828, Var 1, Lg Date, Curl Base 2	**	22	50.9	36	625	1,000	2,250	3,500	6,000	10,000	20,000	$431, VF-25, Mar-07

* Included in number above. **1828, Variety 1 and Variety 2, have a combined mintage of 125,000.

Proof Capped Bust Dimes, Variety 1, Wide Border

PF-60 to 70 (Proof). Proof Capped Bust dimes of 1809 to 1828 were struck in small numbers, likely mostly as part of presentation sets. As is the case with any and all early Proofs, a collector should insist on a coin with deeply and fully (not partially) mirrored surfaces, well struck, and with good contrast. Carefully examine deeply toned pieces (deep toning can mask the true nature of a coin, e.g., if it is not a true Proof, or if it has been cleaned or repaired). More than a few pieces attributed as "Proofs" are not Proofs at all. *Obverse and Reverse:* Proofs of this type can have areas of light striking, such as at the star centers. Proofs that are extensively cleaned and have many hairlines, or that are dull and grainy, are lower level, such as PF-60 to 62. These are not of great interest to specialists unless they are of rare die varieties. A PF-64 has fewer hairlines, but they are obvious, perhaps slightly distracting. A PF-65 should have fewer still and full mirrored surfaces (no trace of cloudiness or dullness). PF-66 should have hairlines so delicate that magnification is needed to see them. Above that, a Proof should be free of such lines. Grading is highly subjective with early Proofs, and eye appeal also is a major factor.

Proof Capped Bust Dime:
Variety 1, Wide Border
Shown 1.5x actual size.
John Reich–12.

	Est Mintage	Cert	Finest	PF-60	PF-63	PF-64	PF-65	Recent Auction Record
1820	2–5	1	PF-66	$12,000	$20,000	$40,000	$65,000	$80,500, PF-66, Feb-08
1821	5–8	4	PF-66	10,000	18,000	30,000	40,000	$55,200, PF-65, Apr-05
1822 (extremely rare)	2–5	n/a	n/a	15,000	25,000	50,000	70,000	
1824, 4 Over 2	4–6	4	PF-67	10,000	18,000	30,000	40,000	$42,550, PF-65, Jul-05
1825	4–6	3	PF-67	10,000	18,000	30,000	40,000	$11,500, PF-63, Apr-09
1827	10–15	7	PF-67	10,000	18,000	30,000	40,000	$120,750, PF-67, Feb-08

CAPPED BUST, VARIETY 2, MODIFIED DESIGN (1828–1837)

Designer John Reich; weight 2.70 grams; composition .8924 silver, .1076 copper; approx. diameter 18.5 mm; reeded edge. All coined at Philadelphia Mint.

Shown 1.5x actual size.
John Reich–7.

History. New equipment at the U.S. Mint was used to make the Small Date 1828 dimes, and those subsequent. The slightly modified design includes smaller dentils or beads in the border and other minor differences, and they are of uniform diameter. The 2 in the Small Date 1828 dime has a square (not curled) base.

Striking and Sharpness. Most dimes of this variety are fairly well struck, with fewer irregularities of strike than those of 1809 to 1828. On the obverse, check the hair and the brooch. The stars usually are sharp, but don't overlook them. On the reverse, check the details of the eagle. The dentils usually are sharp.

Availability. All dates are readily available, but certain die varieties range from rare to extremely rare. In MS the dates of the early 1830s to 1835 are the most readily available. Most have nice eye appeal.

EF-40, 45 (Extremely Fine). *Obverse:* The rims are more uniform than for the 1809–1828 type, striking is usually very sharp, and the wear occurs evenly on both sides. Wear is most noticeable on the higher areas of the hair. The cap shows wear, as does the cheek. Stars still show their centers. Luster, if present, is in protected areas among the star points and close to the portrait. *Reverse:* The wings show wear on the higher areas of the feathers (particularly on the right wing), and some details are lost. Feathers in the neck are light. The eagle's claws show wear. Luster may be present in protected areas.

AU-50, 53, 55, 58 (About Uncirculated). *Obverse:* The rims are more uniform than for the 1809–1828 type, striking is usually very sharp, and any abrasion occurs evenly on both sides. Light wear is seen on the cap, the hair below LIBERTY, the hair near the clasp, and the drapery at the bosom. At AU-50 and 53, luster remains only in protected areas. At AU-58, the luster is extensive except in the open area of the field, especially to the right. As is true of all high grades, sharpness of strike can affect the perception of wear. *Reverse:* Wear is evident on the eagle's neck, the top of the wings, and the claws. At AU-50 and 53, there still is significant luster. At AU-58, luster is nearly full.

MS-60 to 70 (Mint State). *Obverse:* The rims are more uniform than for the 1809–1828 type, striking is usually very sharp, and any abrasion occurs evenly on both sides. At MS-60, some abrasion and contact marks are evident, most noticeably on the cheek and on the area near the drapery clasp. Luster is present, but may be dull or lifeless, and interrupted in patches. At MS-63, contact marks are very few, and abrasion is hard to detect except under magnification. An MS-65 coin has no abrasion, and contact marks are so minute as to require magnification. Luster should be full and rich. Grades above MS-65 are seen now and again and are defined by having fewer marks as perfection is approached. *Reverse:* Abrasion and contact marks are most noticeable on the eagle's neck, the top of the wings, the claws, and the flat band that surrounds the incuse motto.

1828, Large Date, Curl Base 2

1828, Small Date, Square Base 2

1829, Curl Base 2

The Large Date is of Variety 1 (see previous section); for comparison purposes, both are illustrated here.

1829, Small 10c

1829, Medium 10c

Shown 2x actual size.

1829, Large 10c

1830, 30 Over 29

1830, Large 10c

1830, Small 10c

1833, Last 3 Normal

1833, Last 3 High

1834, Small 4

1834, Large 4

	Mintage	Cert	Avg	%MS	EF-40	AU-50	MS-60	MS-62	MS-63	MS-64	MS-65	Recent Auction Record
1828, Var 2, Sm Date, Sq Base 2	*	32	55.5	56	$400	$750	$1,300	$1,650	$2,500	$4,000	$10,000	$335, EF-45, Mar-10
1829, All kinds	770,000											
1829, Curl Base 2 (a)		8	7.0	0	(b)							$5,175, G-4, Apr-10
1829, Small 10c		40	48.2	43	350	450	1,000	1,500	2,000	3,750	8,000	$345, EF-45, Jun-10
1829, Medium 10c		4	43.0	50	375	500	1,500	2,000	2,500	4,000	8,500	$1,380, MS-62, Sep-09
1829, Large 10c		9	42.3	11	400	650	1,750	2,500	3,500	6,000	12,000	$21,240, MS-67, Jan-10
1830, All kinds	510,000											
1830, 30 Over 29 (c)		34	54.8	50	450	650	1,300	1,700	4,000	6,500	10,000	$489, AU-50, May-10
1830, Large 10c		24	36.3	29	300	500	1,200	2,000	2,500	4,000	9,000	$2,530, MS-64, Jun-10
1830, Small 10c		4	62.3	75	400	650	1,200	2,000	2,500	4,000	9,000	$2,530, MS-64, Sep-08
1831	771,350	273	57.0	62	300	450	1,000	1,300	1,800	3,500	7,500	$9,200, MS-65 CAC, Jul-10
1832	522,500	250	56.9	61	300	450	1,000	1,300	1,800	3,500	7,500	$7,475, MS-65, Jul-10
1833, All kinds	485,000											
1833		248	56.1	58	300	450	1,000	1,300	1,800	3,500	7,500	$1,380, MS-63, Apr-10
1833, Last 3 High		18	51.9	44	450	650	1,000	1,300	1,800	3,500	7,500	$374, AU-55, May-10
1834, All kinds	635,000											
1834, Small 4		8	42.1	50	300	450	1,500	1,850	2,250	4,500	9,000	$6,325, MS-66, Feb-10
1834, Large 4		42	46.2	38	300	450	1,000	1,300	1,800	3,500	7,500	$322, AU-50, May-10
1835	1,410,000	432	55.7	56	300	450	1,000	1,300	1,800	3,500	7,500	$3,738, MS-64, Jul-10
1836	1,190,000	186	56.8	53	300	450	1,000	1,300	1,800	3,500	7,500	$863, MS-62, May-10
1837	359,500	126	56.4	66	300	450	1,000	1,300	1,800	3,500	7,500	$14,950, MS-66 CAC, Apr-10

* 1828, Variety 1 and Variety 2, have a combined mintage of 125,000. **a.** Only one working die for the 1829 dime coinage featured a curled 2, rather than the normal square-based 2. Nearly all known specimens are in low grades. **b.** Value in F-12 is $15,000; in VF-20, $25,000. **c.** The tail of the 2 is evident to the right of the lower curve of the 3. The very top of the 9 is evident below the 0. Surface doubling from the initial 1829 punch is also evident on the 8. There are three of four known dies of this overdate; all are similar and command similar values. Today the variety is known to be more common than thought in the early 1970s, when it was first publicized.

Proof Capped Bust Dimes, Variety 2, Modified Design

PF-60 to 70 (Proof). Proofs were made of each year from 1828 to 1837, and are rare. Beware of so-called Proofs that have deeply toned surfaces or fields that show patches of mint frost. Use caution and take your time as you inspect coins for your collection. *Obverse and Reverse:* Generally, Proof dimes of this type are of better quality than the 1809–1828 type and have Full Details in almost all areas. Proofs that are extensively cleaned and have many hairlines, or that are dull and grainy, are lower level, such as PF-60 to 62. While every Capped Bust Proof deserves attention, those of lower levels are not of great interest to specialists unless they are of rare die varieties. With medium hairlines, an assigned grade of PF-64 may be in order, and with relatively few hairlines, PF-65. PF-66 should have hairlines so delicate that magnification is needed to see them. Above that, a Proof should be free of such lines.

Proof Capped Bust Dime:
Variety 2, Modified Design
Shown 1.5x actual size.
John Reich–4.

	Est Mintage	Cert	Finest	PF-60	PF-63	PF-64	PF-65	Recent Auction Record
1828	4–6	2	PF-65	$8,500	$15,000	$20,000	$30,000	$29,900, PF-65, Feb-08
1829	6–10	4	PF-65	8,000	13,500	20,000	30,000	$37,375, PF-66, Jun-02
1830	5–8	3	PF-65	8,000	13,500	20,000	30,000	$80,500, PF-65 CAC, Jan-09
1831	15–25	13	PF-67	8,000	13,500	20,000	30,000	$80,500, PF-66, Feb-08
1832 (extremely rare)	2–5	n/a	n/a					
1833	5–10	4	PF-66	8,500	15,000	25,000	40,000	$13,800, PF-64, Jan-09
1834	5–10	5	PF-67	8,000	13,500	20,000	30,000	$40,250, PF-65, Jul-09
1835	5–10	8	PF-66	8,000	13,500	20,000	30,000	$37,375, PF-65, Apr-09
1836	2–5	3	PF-64	8,500	15,000	25,000	35,000	$6,900, PF-66, Sep-98
1837	2–5	n/a	n/a	8,500	15,000	25,000	40,000	$23,000, MS-64 Specimen, Apr-10

LIBERTY SEATED, VARIETY 1, NO STARS ON OBVERSE (1837–1838)

Designer Christian Gobrecht; weight 2.67 grams; composition .900 silver, .100 copper; diameter 17.9 mm; reeded edge; mints: Philadelphia, New Orleans.

Shown 1.5x actual size.

History. The first of the Liberty Seated designs, with no stars on the obverse, was inspired by Christian Gobrecht's silver dollar of 1836. The reverse features a different motif, with a wreath and inscription. This type was made only at the Philadelphia Mint in 1837 and at the New Orleans Mint in 1838.

Striking and Sharpness. Check the highest parts of the Liberty Seated figure (especially the head and horizontal shield stripes) and, on the reverse, the leaves. Check the dentils on both sides.

Availability. The 1837 is readily available in all grades, including MS-65 and higher. The 1838-O is usually seen with wear and is a rarity if truly MS-63 or above. Beware coins with deep or vivid iridescent toning, which often masks friction or evidence of wear. Coins with uniformly grainy etching on both sides have been processed and should be avoided.

AU-50, 53, 55, 58 (About Uncirculated). *Obverse:* Light wear is seen on the thighs and knees, bosom, and head. At AU-50 and 53, luster is less than at 58, where the luster is extensive but incomplete. Friction is seen in the large open field. *Reverse:* Wear is evident on the leaves and ribbon. At AU-50 and 53, there still is significant luster, more than on the obverse, as the design elements protect the small field areas. An AU-58 coin has nearly full luster, more so than on the obverse.

MS-60 to 70 (Mint State). *Obverse:* At MS-60, some abrasion and contact marks are evident, most noticeably on the bosom, thighs, and knees. Luster is present, but may be dull or lifeless, and interrupted in patches in the large open field. At MS-63, contact marks are very few, and abrasion is hard to detect except under magnification. An MS-65 coin has no abrasion, and contact marks are so minute as to require magnification. Luster should be full and rich.

Reverse: Comments apply as for the obverse, except that abrasion and contact marks are most noticeable on the highest parts of the leaves and the ribbon. The field is mainly protected by design elements and does not show abrasion as much as does the open-field obverse on a given coin.

1837, Large Date   1837, Small Date

Shown 2x actual size.

	Mintage	Cert	Avg	%MS	AU-50	MS-60	MS-62	MS-63	MS-64	MS-65	MS-66	Recent Auction Record
1837, All kinds	682,500											
1837, Large Date		18	58.0	44	$700	$1,100	$1,400	$1,800	$4,000	$7,500	$10,000	$8,625, MS-66, Apr-10
1837, Small Date		28	53.6	43	725	1,200	1,500	2,000	4,500	8,000	15,000	$604, AU-50, May-10
18380	406,034	132	46.3	23	1,200	2,800	4,000	6,000	10,000	17,500	25,000	$776, EF-45, Jun-10

Proof Liberty Seated Dimes, Variety 1, No Stars on Obverse

PF-60 to 70 (Proof). Proofs of 1837 were struck in an unknown small quantity. The mintage appears to have been greater than that of the half dime of the same year. Examples have deep-mirror surfaces and are mostly quite attractive. Carefully examine deeply toned pieces to ensure the toning does not hide flaws. *Obverse and Reverse:*

Proofs that are extensively cleaned and have many hairlines, or that are dull and grainy, are lower level, such as PF-60 to 62. These command less attention in the marketplace than more visually appealing pieces. The dime Proofs of this year often were cleaned, resulting in coins that have lost much of their mirror surface. With medium hairlines

and good reflectivity, PF-64 is an appropriate designation, and with relatively few hairlines, PF-65. In various grades hairlines are most easily seen in the obverse field. PF-66 should have hairlines so delicate that magnification is needed to see them. Above that, a Proof should be free of such lines.

Proof Liberty Seated Dime:
Variety 1, No Stars on Obverse
Shown 1.5x actual size.

	Est Mintage	Cert	Finest	PF-60	PF-63	PF-64	PF-65	Recent Auction Record
1837	25–35	24	PF-67	$7,500	$11,000	$17,500	$30,000	$12,650, PF-64, Jul-09

LIBERTY SEATED, VARIETIES 2 AND 3, STARS ON OBVERSE (1838–1860)

Designer Christian Gobrecht; weight 2.67 grams (reduced to 2.49 grams 1853–1860); composition .900 silver, .100 copper; diameter 17.9 mm; reeded edge; mints: Philadelphia, New Orleans, San Francisco.

Variety 2, Stars on Obverse (1838–1853, 1856–1860)
Shown 1.5x actual size.

Variety 3, Stars on Obverse, Arrows at Date (1853–1855)
Shown 1.5x actual size.

No Drapery From Elbow, Tilted Shield (1838–1840)   **Drapery From Elbow, Upright Shield (1840–1891)**
Shown 2x actual size.

History. Liberty Seated dimes of the Stars on Obverse varieties were first made without drapery at Miss Liberty's elbow. These early issues have the shield tilted sharply to the left. Drapery was added in 1840, and the shield reoriented, this being the style of the 1840s onward. Variety 3 coins (minted in part of 1853, and all of 1854 and 1855) have arrows at the date, signifying the reduction in weight brought on by the Coinage Act of February 21, 1853. Liberty Seated dimes were made in large quantities, and circulated widely.

Striking and Sharpness. On the obverse, check the head of Miss Liberty, and the star centers. On the reverse, check the leaves. Check the dentils on both sides. Avoid coins struck from "tired" or overused dies, as evidenced by grainy rather than lustrous fields (on higher-grade coins).

Availability. These dimes are plentiful as a rule, although certain dates and varieties are rare. Most MS coins on the market are dated in the 1850s and are often found MS-63 to MS-65.

EF-40, 45 (Extremely Fine). *Obverse:* More wear than at AU is seen on all areas, especially the thighs and knees, bosom, and head. Little or no luster is seen. *Reverse:* Further wear than at AU is seen on all areas, most noticeably at the leaves to each side of the wreath apex and on the ribbon bow knot. Leaves retain details except on the higher areas.

AU-50, 53, 55, 58 (About Uncirculated). *Obverse:* Light wear is seen on the thighs and knees, bosom, and head. At AU-50 and 53, luster is less than at 58, where the luster is extensive but incomplete. *Reverse:* Wear is evident on the leaves (especially at the top of the wreath) and ribbon. At AU-50 and 53 there is significant luster. An AU-58 coin has nearly full luster, more so than on the obverse, as the design elements protect the small field areas.

MS-60 to 70 (Mint State). *Obverse:* At MS-60 some abrasion and contact marks are evident, most noticeably on the bosom and thighs and knees. Luster is present, but may be dull or lifeless. At MS-63, contact marks are very few, and abrasion is hard to detect except under magnification. An MS-65 coin has no abrasions, and contact marks are so minute as to require magnification. Luster should be full and rich. *Reverse:* Comments apply as for the obverse, except that abrasion and contact marks are most noticeable on the highest parts of the leaves and the ribbon. The field is mainly protected by design elements and does not show abrasion as much as does the open-field obverse on a given coin.

1838, Small Stars

1838, Large Stars

1838, So-Called Partial Drapery

1839-O, Repunched Mintmark

1841-O, Transitional Reverse, Small O

1841-O, Transitional Reverse, Large O

Regular Reverse Style of 1841-O

	Mintage	Cert	Avg	%MS	EF-40	AU-50	MS-60	MS-62	MS-63	MS-64	MS-65	Recent Auction Record
1838, All kinds	1,992,500											
1838, Small Stars		62	59.9	74	$175	$400	$700	$1,000	$1,350	$2,000	$4,000	$518, AU-58, Mar-10
1838, Large Stars		300	61.7	78	120	250	350	650	850	1,100	3,000	$661, MS-63, May-10
1838, Partial Drapery (a)		18	62.6	83	200	500	850	1,400	2,000			$4,888, MS-66, Apr-10
1839	1,053,115	185	62.4	78	110	250	400	600	850	1,100	3,000	$690, MS-62, May-10
18390	1,291,600	67	57.0	54	135	275	450	750	1,300	2,000	3,500	$863, AU-58, Feb-10
18390, Repunched Mintmark	*	n/a	n/a	n/a	150	325	750	1,000	1,500			$138, EF-45, Jan-05
1840, No Drapery	981,500	112	59.3	69	110	250	400	600	850	1,200	3,250	$276, AU-58, Jul-10
18400, No Drapery	1,175,000	20	48.8	30	150	350	1,200	2,000	2,500	5,000		$46,000, MS-65, Apr-09
1840, Drapery	377,500	16	49.4	38	300	450	900	3,000	5,200	10,000		$748, AU-50, Jul-10
1841 (b)	1,622,500	64	62.6	80	60	140	350	450	650	1,200	3,250	$1,840, MS-64, Apr-10
18410	2,007,500	55	55.8	38	85	225	900	1,200	1,800	2,750	4,750	$920, MS-62, Jun-10
18410, TransRev, Sm O (c)	*	1	4.0	0								
18410, TransRev, Lg O (c)	*	1	3.0	0								
1842	1,887,500	70	60.7	77	50	125	400	500	650	1,100	3,500	$834, MS-64, Dec-09
18420	2,020,000	51	49.5	31	225	1,300	2,500	4,000	5,500	7,500		$805, AU-50, Apr-10
1843	1,370,000	58	59.1	69	50	125	400	600	800	1,250	3,500	$1,265, MS-64, Nov-09
18430	150,000	21	28.1	0	600	2,100	5,000					$14,950, AU-53, Jun-10
1844	72,500	57	27.7	16	1,200	1,800	4,000	6,000	10,000	20,000	32,500	$431, VF-25, Jul-10
1845	1,755,000	119	60.4	76	50	125	400	600	800	1,250	3,500	$460, MS-62 CAC, May-10
18450	230,000	29	37.1	7	550	1,200	3,500	5,500				$518, EF-40, Jul-10
1846	31,300	30	28.4	3	1,000	2,500	5,500	10,000	17,500			$1,495, VF-30, Jul-10
1847	245,000	31	54.1	39	125	350	950	1,500	2,500	4,500	9,500	$2,990, MS-63, Feb-09
1848	451,500	45	58.8	69	85	150	550	600	850	1,500	6,500	$1,955, MS-64, Jul-10
1849	839,000	53	60.4	72	60	125	300	450	900	1,750	4,500	$374, MS-62, Jun-10
18490	300,000	56	50.8	36	300	750	2,500	3,500	6,000			$776, AU-55, May-10
1850	1,931,500	109	60.4	74	60	125	300	500	700	1,200	5,000	$1,840, MS-64, Apr-10
18500	510,000	16	51.4	44	175	375	1,200	2,000	2,600	4,500	6,500	$1,093, AU-58, Sep-08
1851	1,026,500	54	60.5	70	60	125	350	500	800	1,200	5,000	$4,025, MS-65, Mar-10
18510	400,000	22	54.5	27	175	450	2,250	3,000	3,750	6,500		$2,300, MS-62, Mar-10
1852	1,535,500	79	61.0	73	60	125	300	500	700	1,200	3,250	$2,875, MS-66, Apr-10
18520	430,000	43	58.4	63	250	350	1,600	2,000	2,750	4,000		$1,035, AU-58 CAC, Mar-10
1853, No Arrows	95,000	90	57.7	80	300	450	800	900	1,250	2,500	3,500	$3,738, MS-65, Jun-10

* Included in number above. **a.** The so-called "partial drapery" is not a design variation; rather, it is evidence of die clashing from the E in DIME on the reverse. **b.** Two examples are known of 1841, No Drapery, Small Stars, Upright Shield. One is a Proof (see next section) and the other is a circulation strike in VF. **c.** The 1841-O Transitional Reverse varieties were struck with a reverse die that was supposed to have been discontinued in 1840, but saw limited use into 1841. Note the closed buds (not open, as in the regular reverse die of 1841); also note that the second leaf from the left (in the group of four leaves to the left of the bow knot) reaches only halfway across the bottom of the U in UNITED.

	Mintage	Cert	Avg	%MS	AU-50	MS-60	MS-62	MS-63	MS-64	MS-65	MS-66	Recent Auction Record
1853, With Arrows	12,078,010	691	60.8	75	$175	$300	$450	$675	$1,100	$2,500	$4,000	$1,035, MS-64, Jul-10
18530	1,100,000	25	51.2	20	350	1,100	2,250	3,250	5,000	8,500		$2,013, AU-58 CAC, Jan-10
1854	4,470,000	173	60.9	71	175	300	450	675	1,100	2,500	4,000	$1,610, MS-65, Mar-10
18540	1,770,000	67	63.1	88	200	400	650	1,100	1,500	3,500	5,000	$253, AU-58, Dec-09
1855	2,075,000	83	62.1	83	185	325	500	1,000	1,400	3,200	4,500	$403, MS-62, Mar-10

	Mintage	Cert	Avg	%MS	EF-40	AU-50	MS-60	MS-62	MS-63	MS-64	MS-65	Recent Auction Record
1856, All kinds	5,780,000											
1856, Large Date		10	53.8	30	$60	$160	$400	$550	$850	$2,000		$2,530, MS-64, Dec-09
1856, Small Date		49	57.1	67	50	130	300	400	700	1,250	$2,750	$776, MS-64, Jun-10
18560	1,180,000	45	59.4	60	65	250	800	1,100	1,500	2,750	6,000	$2,300, MS-64, Aug-09
1856S	70,000	21	42.4	10	1,000	1,600	3,750	6,500	15,000	20,000	45,000	$690, VF-20, Apr-10
1857	5,580,000	266	61.9	82	50	130	300	450	700	1,000	2,500	$978, MS-64, Jul-10
18570	1,540,000	146	61.2	73	70	200	425	500	750	1,100	2,750	$805, MS-64, Mar-10
1858	1,540,000	117	61.8	81	50	130	300	450	700	1,000	2,500	$805, MS-64, May-10
18580	290,000	37	57.9	49	135	300	600	800	1,000	2,500	6,000	$7,763, MS-66, Apr-09
1858S	60,000	17	41.1	12	900	1,600	3,800	7,500	15,000	20,000		$805, VF-20, Mar-10
1859	429,200	133	63.5	91	60	140	300	450	700	1,000	2,500	$891, MS-64, May-10
18590	480,000	108	60.8	75	95	275	400	600	900	1,200	2,750	$518, MS-62, May-10
1859S	60,000	15	33.1	13	1,000	2,000	10,000	15,000	25,000			$1,323, VF-35 CAC, Dec-09
1860S	140,000	31	49.8	23	350	800	2,500	3,500	4,500	8,500	15,000	$431, EF-45, Jul-10

Proof Liberty Seated Dimes, Varieties 2 and 3

PF-60 to 70 (Proof). Proofs were made of most years and are mostly available from 1854 onward, with 1858 and especially 1859 being those often seen. Most are well struck. *Obverse and Reverse:* Proofs that are extensively cleaned and have many hairlines, or that are dull and grainy, are lower level, such as PF-60 to 62. Generally, these are not widely desired, save for the scarce (in any grade) dates of 1844 and 1846. With medium hairlines and good reflectivity, an assigned grade of PF-64 is appropriate, and with relatively few hairlines, PF-65. In various grades hairlines are most easily seen in the obverse field. PF-66 should have hairlines so delicate that magnification is needed to see them. Above that, a Proof should be free of such lines.

Proof Liberty Seated Dime:
Variety 2, Stars on Obverse

Proof Liberty Seated Dime: Variety 3,
Stars on Obverse, Arrows at Date

Proof 1859 Pattern Dime:
Obverse of 1859, Reverse of 1860

	Est Mintage	Cert	Finest	PF-60	PF-63	PF-64	PF-65	Recent Auction Record
1838 (a)	2–3	1	PF-67					$161,000, PF-67Cam, Jan-08
1839	4–5	3	PF-66	$7,500	$10,000	$25,000	$45,000	$60,375, PF-64, Jul-09
18390	2–3	1	PF-65		25,000	45,000	75,000	$74,750, PF-65, Oct-08
1840, No Drapery	4–5	4	PF-65	10,000	15,000	20,000	30,000	$27,600, PF-65Cam, Aug-07
1841 (a)	2–3	1	PF-63		65,000			$63,250, PF-63Cam, Jan-08
1841, No Drapery	2–3	1	PF-53		75,000			
1842	6–10	5	PF-65	10,000	15,000	25,000	40,000	$37,375, PF-65Cam, Apr-08
1843	10–15	10	PF-66	5,000	10,000	15,000	25,000	$16,110, PF-65, Dec-09
1844	4–8	3	PF-66	20,000	35,000	50,000	75,000	$103,500, PF-66, Jan-08
1845	6–10	5	PF-67	7,500	12,500	25,000	35,000	$14,950, PF-65Cam, Jul-09
1846	8–12	7	PF-65	10,000	15,000	25,000	40,000	$74,750, PF-65, Apr-08
1847	3–5	1	PF-66	8,000	13,000	25,000	40,000	$51,750, PF-66Cam, Jul-08
1848	10–15	10	PF-66	5,000	10,000	15,000	25,000	$23,000, PF-66, Jul-08
1849	4–6	3	PF-66	10,000	15,000	25,000	40,000	$63,250, PF-66, Apr-08
1850	4–6	3	PF-67	10,000	15,000	25,000	40,000	$80,500, PF-67 Star, Jan-08
1852	5–10	8	PF-67	5,000	10,000	15,000	25,000	$12,980, PF-65, Jan-10
1853	5–10	6	PF-66	12,500	30,000	50,000	75,000	$97,750, PF-66, Aug-07
1854	8–12	9	PF-66	10,000	15,000	25,000	40,000	$40,250, PF-66Cam, Jul-09
1855	8–12	10	PF-67	10,000	15,000	25,000	40,000	$14,950, PF-64, Jun-10
1856	40–50	26	PF-67	2,500	4,500	8,500	15,000	$3,738, PF-63, Jun-10
1857	45–60	34	PF-67	2,000	3,550	4,500	6,500	$6,490, PF-66Cam, Jan-10
1858	unknown	69	PF-67	1,000	1,750	2,500	4,500	$2,990, PF-65, Jul-10
1859	unknown	190	PF-68	950	1,500	2,500	4,000	$1,783, PF-64Cam, Jul-10
1859, Obv of 1859, Rev of 1860 (b)	unknown	13	PF-67	10,000	16,000	20,000	25,000	$27,600, PF-67, Jan-09

a. The 1838 and 1841 Proof dimes may be unique. **b.** In 1859 the Mint made a dime pattern, of which some 13 to 20 examples are known. These "coins without a country" do not bear the nation's identity (UNITED STATES OF AMERICA). They are transitional pieces, not made for circulation, but struck at the time that the dime's legend was being transferred from the reverse to the obverse (see Variety 4). For more information, consult *United States Pattern Coins,* 10th edition (Judd).

**Variety 4, Legend on Obverse
(1860–1873, 1875–1891)**
Shown 1.5x actual size.

LIBERTY SEATED, VARIETIES 4 AND 5, LEGEND ON OBVERSE (1860–1891)

Designer Christian Gobrecht; weight 2.49 grams (increased to 2.50 grams 1873–1891); composition .900 silver, .100 copper; diameter 17.9 mm; reeded edge; mints: Philadelphia, New Orleans, San Francisco, Carson City.

**Variety 5, Legend on Obverse,
Arrows at Date (1873–1874)**
Shown 1.5x actual size.

History. In 1860 the Liberty Seated design continued with UNITED STATES OF AMERICA replacing the stars on the obverse. A new reverse featured what the Mint called a "cereal wreath," encircling ONE DIME in two lines. In 1873 the dime was increased in weight to 2.50 grams (from 2.49); arrows at the date in 1873 and 1874 indicate this change, making Variety 5. Variety 4 (without the arrows) resumed from 1875 and continued to the end of the series in 1891.

Striking and Sharpness. Coins of these varieties usually are fairly well struck for the earlier years, somewhat erratic in the 1870s, and better from the 1880s to 1891. Many Civil War dimes of Philadelphia, 1861 to 1865, have parallel die striae from the dies not being finished (this being so for virtually all silver and gold issues of that period). Some dimes, especially dates from 1879 to 1881, are found prooflike. Points to check include the head of Miss Liberty on the obverse, the wreath details on the reverse, and the dentils on both sides. Issues of the Carson City Mint in the early 1870s, particularly 1873-CC With Arrows, are often seen with porous surfaces (a post-striking effect). Note: The word LIBERTY on the shield is not an infallible key to attributing lower grades. On some dies such as those of the early 1870s the shield was in low relief on the coins and wore away slowly, with the result that part or all of the word can be readable in grades below F-12.

Availability. While certain issues of the 1860s through 1881 range from scarce to very rare, those from 1882 to 1891 are for the most part very common, even in MS-63 and finer.

EF-40, 45 (Extremely Fine). *Obverse:* More wear than at AU is seen on all areas, especially the thighs and knees, bosom, and head. Little or no luster is seen. *Reverse:* Further wear than at AU is seen on all areas, most noticeably at on the high areas of the wreath and on the ribbon. The leaves retain excellent details except on the higher areas.

AU-50, 53, 55, 58 (About Uncirculated). *Obverse:* Light wear is seen on the thighs and knees, bosom, and head. At AU-50 and 53, luster is less than at AU-58, where the luster is extensive but incomplete. *Reverse:* Wear is evident on the leaves and ribbon. At AU-50 and 53, there still is significant luster. An AU-58 coin has nearly full luster, more so than on the obverse, as the design elements protect the small field areas.

MS-60 to 70 (Mint State). *Obverse:* At MS-60, some abrasion and contact marks are evident, most noticeably on the bosom and thighs and knees. Luster is present, but may be dull or lifeless. At MS-63, contact marks are very few, and abrasion is hard to detect except under magnification. An MS-65 coin has no abrasion, and contact marks are so minute as to require magnification. Luster should be full and rich, except for Philadelphia (but not San Francisco) dimes of the early and mid-1860s. Some low-mintage Philadelphia issues may be prooflike. Clashmarks are common. *Reverse:* Comments apply as for the obverse, except that in lower MS grades abrasion and contact marks are most noticeable on the highest parts of the leaves and the ribbon, less so on ONE DIME. At MS-65 or higher there are no marks visible to the unaided eye. The field is mainly protected by design elements and does not show abrasion as much as does the obverse on a given coin.

1861, Six Vertical Shield Lines

1872, Doubled-Die Reverse
FS-10-1872-801.

1873, Close 3

1873, Open 3

1873, With Arrows, Doubled-Die Obverse
FS-10-1873-2101.

1875-CC, Mintmark Above Bow

1875-CC, Mintmark Below Bow

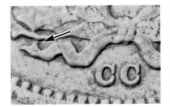

1876-CC, Variety I Reverse

1876-CC, Variety II Reverse
FS-10-1876CC-301.

1891-O, O Over Horizontal O
FS-10-1891o-501.

1891-S, Repunched Mintmark
FS-10-1891S-501.

	Mintage	Cert	Avg	%MS	EF-40	AU-50	MS-60	MS-62	MS-63	MS-64	MS-65	Recent Auction Record
1860	606,000	107	63.2	92	$40	$100	$200	$225	$300	$400	$1,350	$748, MS-64 Star, Apr-10
1860O	40,000	33	29.7	9	4,000	6,000	12,000					$7,763, AU-55, Apr-10
1861 (a)	1,883,000	118	61.7	84	40	100	185	225	300	400	1,350	$891, MS-65, Jul-10
1861S	172,500	20	45.3	35	400	600	2,000	3,500	5,500			
1862	847,000	157	63.5	94	40	80	185	225	350	500	1,500	$2,185, MS-66, Jun-10
1862S	180,750	15	51.5	40	275	400	1,500	2,500	4,000	6,000		$920, AU-50, Feb-09
1863	14,000	38	60.6	89	825	950	1,200	1,500	1,750	2,750	3,750	$978, VF-25, Sep-09
1863S	157,500	26	54.5	38	200	375	1,200	1,500	3,500	7,500	25,000	$3,450, MS-62, Mar-10
1864	11,000	37	59.2	81	875	1,100	1,200	1,500	1,750	2,250	4,000	$2,185, MS-64, Aug-09
1864S	230,000	28	57.0	61	140	325	950	1,150	1,500	2,750	5,500	$1,035, MS-62, Jul-10
1865	10,000	50	57.7	76	800	900	1,200	1,500	2,000	2,500	3,500	$1,150, VF-25, Mar-10
1865S	175,000	16	45.0	19	225	750	2,500	3,500	6,000			$834, EF-40 CAC, Mar-10
1866	8,000	38	58.4	82	850	1,200	1,500	1,750	2,000	2,500	3,500	$1,610, MS-63, Feb-10
1866S	135,000	25	45.0	40	225	325	1,000	2,000	3,500	5,000	17,500	$29,900, MS-65, Apr-08
1867	6,000	43	62.1	88	1,100	1,300	1,500	2,000	2,500	3,250	4,000	$4,888, MS-66, Jun-10
1867S	140,000	15	53.0	53	225	550	1,250	1,650	2,500	4,000	7,500	$374, EF-45, Dec-08
1868	464,000	33	62.1	91	65	150	300	500	850	1,250	3,500	$299, AU-53, Jan-09
1868S	260,000	14	61.9	79	125	225	400	600	1,000	2,000	5,000	$3,738, MS-65, Jun-07
1869	256,000	19	58.6	74	100	200	400	600	900	1,850	3,500	$4,600, MS-67, Apr-09
1869S	450,000	42	61.7	86	65	150	375	550	800	1,500	4,000	$299, AU-55, Mar-09
1870	470,500	60	61.4	85	50	100	200	300	450	950	1,850	$1,438, MS-65, Apr-10
1870S	50,000	28	44.1	46	600	850	1,700	2,000	2,500	3,000	6,000	$518, F-12, Oct-09
1871	906,750	55	61.2	76	50	150	250	300	425	900	2,000	$776, MS-64, May-10
1871CC	20,100	23	39.6	26	11,000	20,000	50,000					$2,875, VG-8, Apr-10
1871S	320,000	24	60.0	54	125	240	425	650	1,000	2,500	6,500	$127, F-15, Oct-09

a. The dime's dies were modified slightly in 1861. The first (scarcer) variety has only five vertical lines in the top part of the shield.

Chart continued on next page.

	Mintage	Cert	Avg	%MS	EF-40	AU-50	MS-60	MS-62	MS-63	MS-64	MS-65	Recent Auction Record
1872	2,395,500	62	61.1	81	$40	$90	$175	$225	$300	$750	$1,350	$633, MS-64 CAC, Jun-10
1872, DblDie Rev (rare) (b)	*	1	20.0	0	250	350	750	1,000				$2,300, MS-63, May-05
1872CC	35,480	32	22.6	0	8,500	18,500	50,000					$1,610, VG-8 CAC, Jun-10
1872S	190,000	15	56.4	47	225	400	1,200	1,650	2,500	4,000	9,500	$920, AU-58 CAC, Mar-10
1873, Close 3	1,506,900	36	58.8	64	40	90	150	200	250	650	1,500	$2,760, MS-66, Jun-10
1873, Open 3	60,000	26	52.4	54	130	200	600	850	1,500	2,500	7,500	$2,185, MS-64, Apr-10
1873CC (unique) † (c)	12,400	n/a	n/a	n/a					1,250,000			$891,250, MS-65, Jul-04
1873, With Arrows	2,377,700	136	60.0	71	140	300	550	600	900	1,650	4,000	$805, MS-63, Jul-10
1873, With Arrows, DblDie Obv (d)	*	3	27.0	33	1,000	1,500						$2,875, VF-35, Jul-10
1873CC	18,791	33	17.5	6	17,000	32,000						$4,313, VF-25, Apr-10
1873S	455,000	45	62.6	89	175	450	1,000	1,450	2,100	3,750	6,500	$805, MS-61, Apr-10
1874	2,939,300	211	59.9	72	140	310	600	750	1,000	1,750	4,000	$690, MS-63, Jun-10
1874CC	10,817	8	30.8	13	20,000	34,000	45,000					$8,625, G-6, Apr-10
1874S	240,000	30	59.1	67	225	500	900	1,200	2,000	4,000	8,500	$3,105, MS-64 CAC, Apr-10
1875	10,350,000	341	63.2	94	30	80	150	200	250	450	1,000	$242, MS-63, Jul-10
1875CC, All kinds	4,645,000											
1875CC, Above Bow		82	58.4	77	65	110	325	425	500	1,250	2,750	$805, MS-64, Apr-10
1875CC, Below Bow		46	59.0	76	70	125	350	400	550	1,150	2,500	$4,888, MS-66, Jul-10
1875S, All kinds	9,070,000											
1875S, Below Bow		41	62.7	88	30	85	160	200	250	450	1,200	$252, MS-62, Jul-10
1875S, Above Bow		23	63.3	87	30	80	150	200	250	450	1,200	$276, MS-62, Sep-09
1876	11,450,000	267	62.6	91	35	80	150	200	250	450	1,000	$2,300, MS-67, Jul-10
1876CC	8,270,000	271	60.8	85	65	100	230	300	450	550	1,500	$805, MS-64, Jun-10
1876CC, Variety II Rev (e)	*	1	45.0	0	250	350	600	850	1,250			$575, MS-63, May-05
1876S	10,420,000	75	61.8	83	35	80	150	200	250	450	1,750	$431, MS-64, Jan-09
1877	7,310,000	129	62.6	93	35	80	150	200	250	450	1,000	$1,150, MS-66, Jul-10
1877CC	7,700,000	322	62.7	92	65	100	230	300	400	600	1,350	$633, MS-64 CAC, Dec-09
1877S	2,340,000	80	63.2	94	35	80	150	200	250	450	1,250	$690, MS-64, Mar-10
1878	1,677,200	76	62.6	95	35	80	150	200	250	450	1,000	$719, MS-65, May-10
1878CC	200,000	56	57.9	80	400	575	1,100	1,500	1,750	3,000	4,000	$1,380, AU-55, Jul-10
1879	14,000	168	63.7	95	500	550	625	700	750	950	1,250	$1,380, MS-65, Jul-10
1880	36,000	131	63.1	93	400	500	650	700	750	950	1,250	$2,300, MS-67Star, Jun-10
1881	24,000	65	59.5	82	425	525	675	725	775	975	1,350	$518, MS-61 CAC, Jul-10
1882	3,910,000	332	63.8	96	35	80	150	200	250	450	1,000	$201, MS-63, Apr-10
1883	7,674,673	374	63.2	94	35	80	150	200	250	450	1,000	$489, MS-64 CAC, Jun-10
1884	3,365,505	322	64.0	96	35	80	150	200	250	450	1,000	$863, MS-66, Jun-10
1884S	564,969	49	61.1	80	100	300	750	950	1,200	1,850	5,000	$1,035, MS-63, Mar-10
1885	2,532,497	277	63.9	95	35	80	150	200	250	450	1,000	$604, MS-65, Feb-10
1885S	43,690	53	35.9	28	2,200	4,000	5,500	6,500	9,000	12,000	27,500	$3,450, AU-50, Jun-10
1886	6,376,684	489	63.2	93	35	80	150	200	250	450	1,000	$920, MS-66 CAC, Jun-10
1886S	206,524	40	63.8	90	135	200	600	850	1,200	2,000	4,500	$863, MS-63 CAC, Apr-10
1887	11,283,229	438	63.1	94	35	80	150	200	250	450	1,000	$9,200, MS-67 CAC, Jun-10
1887S	4,454,450	187	62.6	91	35	80	150	200	250	450	1,200	$805, MS-65 CAC, Mar-10
1888	5,495,655	263	62.7	92	35	80	150	200	250	450	1,000	$276, MS-64, Jun-10
1888S	1,720,000	52	62.1	81	35	100	250	450	650	1,000	2,750	$776, MS-64, Oct-09
1889	7,380,000	287	62.9	93	35	80	150	200	250	450	1,000	$920, MS-65, Jun-10
1889S	972,678	65	61.2	77	80	150	450	650	900	1,200	4,500	$403, MS-62, Jul-10
1890	9,910,951	431	63.4	94	35	80	150	200	250	450	1,000	$575, MS-65, Jul-10
1890S, Large S	1,423,076	92	61.9	84	85	150	350	550	700	1,000	1,750	$1,035, MS-64, May-10
1890S, Small S (rare)	*	n/a	n/a	n/a	—	—	—					$1,208, MS-65, Feb-06
1891	15,310,000	799	62.9	91	35	80	150	200	250	450	1,000	$776, MS-65, May-10
1891O	4,540,000	166	62.3	92	60	110	200	300	400	600	1,350	$431, MS-64, Jul-10
1891O, O Over Horizontal O (f)	*	2	51.5	0	225	—	—					$253, AU-58, May-10
1891S	3,196,116	150	63.1	92	35	80	175	225	300	500	1,100	$1,150, MS-65, Mar-10
1891S, Repunched Mintmark (g)	*	4	61.5	75	200	225	500					

* Included in number above. † Ranked in the *100 Greatest U.S. Coins* (third edition). **b.** The first die hubbing was almost completely obliterated by the second, which was rotated about 170 degrees from the first. The key indicators of this variety are inside the opening of the D, and near the center arm of the E in ONE. **c.** Most of the mintage of 1873-CC was melted after the law of 1873, affecting the statuses and physical properties of U.S. coinage, was passed. **d.** Doubling is evident on the shield and on the banner across the shield. Although well known for decades, very few specimens of this variety have been reported. **e.** The scarce Variety II reverse exhibits a single point to the end of the left ribbon; the common Variety I reverse has a split at the ribbon's end. **f.** The primary O mintmark was punched over a previously punched horizontal O. **g.** The larger primary S mintmark (known as the medium S) was punched squarely over the smaller S, which is evident within both loops.

Proof Liberty Seated Dimes, Varieties 4 and 5

PF-60 to 70 (Proof). Proof Liberty Seated dimes of these varieties were made continuously from 1860 to 1891. They exist today in proportion to their mintages. Some of the 1860s and early 1870s can be carelessly struck, with areas of lightness and sometimes with lint marks. Those of the mid-1870s onward usually are sharply struck and without problems. *Obverse and Reverse:* Proofs that are extensively cleaned and have many hairlines, or that are dull and grainy, are lower level, such as PF-60 to 62. These are not widely sought in the marketplace, save for the rare (in any grade) dates of 1863 through 1867. With medium hairlines and good reflectivity, PF-64 is appropriate, and with relatively few hairlines, PF-65. At various levels, hairlines are most easily seen in the obverse field. PF-66 should have hairlines so delicate that magnification is needed to see them. Above that, a Proof should be free of such lines.

**Proof Liberty Seated Dime:
Variety 4, Legend on Obverse**
Shown 1.5x actual size.

**Proof Liberty Seated Dime: Variety 5,
Legend on Obverse, Arrows at Date**
Shown 1.5x actual size.

	Mintage	Cert	Finest	PF-60	PF-63	PF-64	PF-65	Recent Auction Record
1860	1,000	147	PF-68	$350	$750	$1,250	$2,000	$6,325, PF-66, Jun-10
1861	1,000	89	PF-68	350	750	1,250	2,000	$1,898, PF-64, Jun-10
1862	550	94	PF-66	350	750	1,250	2,000	$374, PF-61, Jul-10
1863	460	146	PF-68	325	700	1,100	1,850	$1,035, PF-63, Jun-10
1864	470	147	PF-68	325	700	1,100	1,850	$863, PF-64Cam, Jul-10
1865	500	106	PF-67	350	750	1,250	2,000	$633, PF-62, Jun-10
1866	725	153	PF-68	325	700	1,100	1,850	$2,990, PF-64, Jun-10
1867	625	121	PF-68	325	700	1,100	1,850	$1,265, PF-64Cam, Jul-10
1868	600	138	PF-68	325	700	1,100	1,850	$3,450, PF-65Cam, Jul-10
1869	600	158	PF-67	325	700	1,100	1,850	$4,313, PF-66Cam, Jun-10
1870	1,000	136	PF-67	325	700	1,100	1,850	$1,093, PF-63, Jun-10
1871	960	129	PF-68	325	700	1,100	1,850	$1,610, PF-65, Jun-10
1872	950	123	PF-67	325	700	1,100	1,850	$690, PF-64, Jul-10
1873, Close 3	1,100	149	PF-68	325	700	1,100	1,850	$1,035, PF-64, Jun-10
1873, With Arrows	800	100	PF-67	750	1,500	2,500	5,500	$863, PF-62, Jun-10
1874	700	157	PF-67	750	1,500	2,500	5,500	$1,610, PF-64Cam, Jul-10
1875	700	151	PF-68	300	650	1,000	1,750	$1,495, PF-66Cam, Jul-10
1876	1,150	141	PF-68	300	650	1,000	1,750	$1,840, PF-66Cam, Jul-10
1876CC	3–4	5	PF-65					$178,200, PF-65, Jan-09
1877	510	110	PF-68	300	650	1,000	1,750	$1,380, PF-65Cam, Jul-10
1878	800	144	PF-67	300	650	1,000	1,750	$1,380, PF-64, Jun-10
1879	1,100	276	PF-68	300	650	1,000	1,750	$519, PF-63 CAC, Jul-10
1880	1,355	285	PF-68	300	650	1,000	1,750	$2,530, PF-67Cam, Jul-10
1881	975	232	PF-68	300	650	1,000	1,750	$374, PF-61, Jul-10
1882	1,100	315	PF-69	300	650	1,000	1,750	$1,150, PF-65, Jul-10
1883	1,039	269	PF-68	300	650	1,000	1,750	$5,750, PF-66, Jun-10
1884	875	284	PF-68	300	650	1,000	1,750	$1,553, PF-66Cam, Jul-10
1885	930	270	PF-69	300	650	1,000	1,750	$2,530, PF-67Cam, Jul-10
1886	886	275	PF-68	300	650	1,000	1,750	$1,495, PF-64, Jun-10
1887	710	184	PF-67	300	650	1,000	1,750	$1,926, PF-66 CAC, Jul-10
1888	832	202	PF-67	300	650	1,000	1,750	$1,093, PF-65, Jul-10
1889	711	163	PF-68	300	650	1,000	1,750	$3,738, PF-67Cam, Jun-10
1890	590	193	PF-68	300	650	1,000	1,750	$920, PF-63, Jun-10
1891	600	209	PF-68	300	650	1,000	1,750	$546, PF-63Cam, Jul-10
1891O *(extremely rare)*	2–3	1	PF-66					

BARBER OR LIBERTY HEAD
(1892–1916)

Designer Charles E. Barber; weight 2.50 grams; composition .900 silver, .100 copper (net weight: .07234 oz. pure silver); diameter 17.9 mm; reeded edge; mints: Philadelphia, Denver, New Orleans, San Francisco.

Shown 2x actual size.

History. This dime belongs to a suite of silver coins (including the quarter and half dollar) designed by U.S. Mint chief engraver Charles E. Barber. It features a large Liberty Head styled similarly to contemporary French coinage. The reverse of the dime continues the "cereal wreath" motif of the late Liberty Seated era.

Striking and Sharpness. Check the details of the hair on the obverse. The reverse usually is sharp. If weakness is seen, it is typically in the wreath details. The dentils usually are sharp on the obverse and reverse.

Availability. With the exception of the rare 1894-S, of which fewer than a dozen are known, all dates and mintmarks are collectible. Probably 90% or more of the survivors are in lower grades such as AG-3 and G-4. The word LIBERTY in the headband, a key to grading, tended to wear away quickly. Relatively few are in grades from Fine upward. MS coins are somewhat scarce, this being especially true of the branch-mint issues. MS-63 and finer Barber dimes usually are from the Philadelphia Mint or, if from a branch mint, are dated after 1905.

EF-40, 45 (Extremely Fine). *Obverse:* More wear than at AU is seen on the head. The hair above the forehead lacks most detail. LIBERTY shows wear but is strong. *Reverse:* More wear than at AU is seen on all areas, most noticeably at the wreath and ribbon. The leaves retain excellent details except on the higher areas.

AU-50, 53, 55, 58 (About Uncirculated). *Obverse:* Light wear is seen on the head, especially on the forward hair under LIBERTY. At AU-50 and 53, luster is less than at 58, where the luster is extensive but incomplete (especially on the higher parts and in the right

field). *Reverse:* Wear is seen on the leaves and ribbon. At AU-50 and 53, there still is significant luster. An AU-58 coin will have nearly full luster, more so than on the obverse, as the design elements protect the small field areas.

MS-60 to 70 (Mint State). *Obverse:* At MS-60, some abrasion and contact marks are evident, most noticeably on the cheek and the obverse field to the right. Luster is present, but may be dull or lifeless. Many Barber coins, especially of the earlier dates, have been cleaned. At MS-63, contact marks are very few;

abrasion still is evident, but less than at lower levels. An MS-65 coin may have minor abrasion on the cheek, but contact marks are so minute as to require magnification. Luster should be full and rich. *Reverse:* Comments apply as for the obverse, except that in lower MS grades abrasion and contact marks are most noticeable on the highest parts of the leaves and the ribbon, less so on ONE DIME. At MS-65 or higher, there are no marks visible to the unaided eye. The field is mainly protected by design elements and does not show abrasion as much as does the obverse on a given coin.

1893, 3 Over 2

1897, Repunched Date
FS-10-1897-301.

1905-O, Normal O

1905-O, Micro O

1912-S, Doubled-Die Obverse
FS-10-1912S-101.

	Mintage	Cert	Avg	%MS	EF-40	AU-50	MS-60	MS-62	MS-63	MS-64	MS-65	Recent Auction Record
1892	12,120,000	1,066	63.0	91	$30	$75	$125	$150	$200	$300	$650	$242, MS-64, Jul-10
1892O	3,841,700	183	61.4	83	75	95	175	225	300	500	1,250	$276, MS-63, Jul-10
1892S	990,710	94	56.9	70	280	330	425	600	775	1,500	3,500	$1,208, MS-64, Apr-10
1893, 3 Over 2	*	n/a	n/a	n/a	200	300	700	1,200	1,800	3,000	4,500	$1,495, AU-58, Oct-09
1893	3,339,940	239	61.9	89	45	75	150	200	225	300	950	$196, MS-62, May-10
1893O	1,760,000	118	60.3	84	190	230	325	450	650	1,250	2,500	$978, MS-64, Jun-10
1893S	2,491,401	103	59.7	76	85	150	290	425	700	1,500	3,250	$2,185, MS-65, Jan-10
1894	1,330,000	139	60.3	81	180	220	325	400	500	700	1,200	$1,323, MS-66, Mar-10
1894O	720,000	65	46.2	40	425	600	1,450	2,000	2,500	5,500	13,500	$16,100, MS-66, Jan-10
1895	690,000	106	54.8	68	550	625	725	1,100	1,500	1,850	2,500	$748, MS-63, Jul-10
1895O	440,000	146	27.4	16	2,400	3,400	6,000	7,000	8,500	15,000	20,000	$357, G-4, Mar-10
1895S	1,120,000	119	57.5	69	240	310	500	750	1,200	2,200	7,500	$1,610, MS-64, Mar-10
1896	2,000,000	102	62.1	90	100	120	175	300	500	650	1,150	$460, MS-63, Mar-10
1896O	610,000	59	42.7	42	450	650	1,000	1,600	2,400	4,500	8,500	$10,350, MS-66, Jan-10
1896S	575,056	75	53.5	67	400	550	850	1,100	1,500	3,000	4,500	$1,980, MS-64, Feb-10
1897	10,868,533	342	62.8	91	30	70	135	150	200	300	600	$3,220, MS-67, Jun-10
1897, Repunched Date (a)	**	n/a	n/a	n/a	80	120	200					
1897O	666,000	76	50.4	62	475	600	900	1,300	1,700	2,500	4,500	$2,070, MS-64, Jun-10
1897S	1,342,844	70	56.4	64	175	260	450	650	1,000	2,000	3,750	$863, MS-63, Sep-09
1898	16,320,000	402	62.7	89	26	75	115	150	170	250	675	$417, MS-64, Jun-10
1898O	2,130,000	54	59.6	78	190	280	450	650	1,200	1,750	3,250	$1,680, MS-64, Mar-10
1898S	1,702,507	43	61.3	77	80	150	375	600	1,200	2,000	3,500	$489, MS-62, May-10
1899	19,580,000	274	61.8	88	25	70	125	150	170	300	650	$150, MS-63, Jul-10
1899O	2,650,000	67	57.0	73	140	225	400	600	1,150	2,500	4,000	$5,175, MS-66, Jan-10
1899S	1,867,493	80	61.6	85	45	110	300	550	750	1,750	2,750	$4,313, MS-66, Jan-10
1900	17,600,000	214	61.9	86	25	70	110	135	170	250	850	$633, MS-65 CAC, May-10
1900O	2,010,000	68	57.3	68	220	350	600	750	1,000	2,500	5,000	$4,600, MS-65, Mar-10
1900S	5,168,270	112	60.5	71	30	70	175	300	400	650	1,750	$253, MS-62, Feb-10
1901	18,859,665	242	62.7	87	26	70	110	135	170	250	600	$431, MS-65, Jun-10
1901O	5,620,000	78	56.2	63	65	180	450	650	950	2,500	3,750	$345, MS-62, Jul-10
1901S	593,022	84	46.0	42	550	625	1,000	1,200	1,650	2,000	5,500	$1,738, MS-64, Mar-10
1902	21,380,000	178	60.7	80	25	70	110	135	170	250	600	$805, MS-66, Jul-10
1902O	4,500,000	67	59.2	70	65	150	400	650	1,000	1,500	4,000	$2,760, MS-65, Jul-10
1902S	2,070,000	58	60.0	78	140	200	400	650	1,000	1,500	4,000	$1,725, MS-64, Feb-10
1903	19,500,000	113	62.2	85	25	70	110	135	170	350	1,000	$575, MS-65, Jan-10
1903O	8,180,000	125	59.5	58	50	110	275	400	550	1,000	4,500	$8,050, MS-66 CAC, Feb-10
1903S	613,300	68	43.3	38	700	850	1,200	1,400	1,800	2,250	3,500	$863, AU-55, Mar-10
1904	14,600,357	158	62.3	91	25	70	110	135	200	375	1,500	$1,150, MS-65, May-10
1904S	800,000	83	52.1	58	325	475	800	1,000	1,500	3,000	4,500	$1,265, MS-63, Dec-10
1905	14,551,623	142	62.1	87	25	70	110	135	170	275	650	$2,185, MS-66, Jan-10
1905O	3,400,000	128	60.6	87	90	150	300	400	500	700	1,350	$5,750, MS-67, Mar-10
1905O, Micro O	**	28	31.8	21	100	150	350	1,500	3,000			$2,990, MS-62, Mar-10
1905S	6,855,199	141	59.5	76	40	95	250	285	325	600	850	$374, MS-64, Jul-10
1906	19,957,731	275	62.5	90	22	70	110	135	170	275	600	$2,185, MS-67, May-10
1906D	4,060,000	77	60.7	87	35	80	175	300	400	850	1,500	$2,300, MS-66, Jan-10
1906O	2,610,000	119	62.2	92	95	130	200	250	325	650	1,100	$368, MS-64, Jun-10
1906S	3,136,640	104	60.2	83	45	110	275	325	550	850	1,250	$276, MS-62, May-10
1907	22,220,000	315	62.3	90	22	70	110	135	170	275	600	$403, MS-65, Jun-10
1907D	4,080,000	68	61.6	85	45	110	300	450	900	1,500	2,250	$2,990, MS-66, Apr-10
1907O	5,058,000	125	61.4	86	70	110	200	250	375	450	1,200	$403, MS-64, Dec-09
1907S	3,178,470	72	58.6	68	65	150	400	500	750	1,500	2,500	$633, MS-63, Jun-10
1908	10,600,000	264	61.8	91	22	75	110	135	170	275	600	$311, MS-64, Jul-10
1908D	7,490,000	143	61.1	82	28	75	130	175	300	750	1,000	$161, MS-62, May-10
1908O	1,789,000	77	63.1	92	95	150	300	450	600	850	1,250	$804, MS-61, Mar-10
1908S	3,220,000	62	62.5	82	45	170	350	500	800	1,250	1,500	$276, AU-58, Jun-10
1909	10,240,000	223	62.6	93	22	75	110	135	170	275	600	$219, MS-64, Apr-10
1909D	954,000	67	60.1	81	140	225	500	650	1,000	1,400	2,500	$575, MS-62, Mar-10

* Included in number below. ** Included in number above. **a.** More than one repunched date exists for 1897. This listing is for FS-10-1897-301 (see the *Cherrypickers' Guide to Rare Die Varieties*), one of the most dramatic RPDs of the series. The secondary digits of the date are evident west of the primary digits.

Chart continued on next page.

	Mintage	Cert	Avg	%MS	EF-40	AU-50	MS-60	MS-62	MS-63	MS-64	MS-65	Recent Auction Record
1909O	2,287,000	88	59.4	81	$50	$90	$200	$350	$500	$1,100	$1,500	$2,990, MS-66, Jan-10
1909S	1,000,000	65	58.5	82	180	310	550	650	1,200	1,600	2,200	$1,955, MS-65, Jun-10
1910	11,520,000	379	63.3	93	22	75	110	135	170	275	600	$230, MS-64, Apr-10
1910D	3,490,000	72	61.8	88	45	95	220	300	450	650	1,500	$1,610, MS-66 CAC, Apr-10
1910S	1,240,000	46	59.5	74	100	180	425	550	700	1,100	2,250	$3,738, MS-66, Jan-10
1911	18,870,000	731	62.5	91	22	75	110	135	170	275	600	$805, MS-66, Aug-10
1911D	11,209,000	197	62.7	90	24	75	110	135	170	275	600	$265, MS-64, Jul-10
1911S	3,520,000	172	62.8	88	40	100	200	275	400	750	1,100	$431, MS-63, Jul-10
1912	19,349,300	765	62.7	92	22	75	110	135	170	275	600	$184, MS-63, Jul-10
1912D	11,760,000	236	60.1	82	22	75	110	135	170	275	600	$446, MS-65 CAC, Jun-10
1912S	3,420,000	146	61.7	79	32	90	170	225	300	500	850	$489, MS-64, Jan-10
1912S, DblDie Obv (b)	*	n/a	n/a	n/a	100	180	425					
1913	19,760,000	627	62.4	89	22	75	110	135	170	300	600	$253, MS-64, Jul-10
1913S	510,000	116	53.1	68	250	320	500	600	750	1,000	1,350	$374, AU-55, May-10
1914	17,360,230	673	62.5	92	22	75	110	135	170	275	600	$817, MS-66, Jul-10
1914D	11,908,000	369	61.6	86	22	75	110	135	170	275	600	$140, MS-63, Jul-10
1914S	2,100,000	136	61.8	89	40	80	175	225	350	650	1,100	$1,323, MS-65, Jun-10
1915	5,620,000	265	62.0	88	22	75	110	135	170	275	600	$446, MS-65, Jun-10
1915S	960,000	105	61.8	85	65	140	275	325	475	650	1,350	$2,990, MS-66, May-09
1916	18,490,000	952	62.1	88	22	75	110	135	170	275	600	$253, MS-64, Jul-10
1916S	5,820,000	245	62.4	87	22	75	110	135	170	275	650	$489, MS-65, Jan-10

* Included in number above. **b.** The doubling is most evident on UNITED.

Proof Barber Dimes

PF-60 to 70 (Proof). Proof Barber dimes survive in proportion to their mintages. PF-63 and 65 specimens are more easily found among dimes than among quarters and half dollars of this type. All were originally sold in silver-coin sets. The Proofs of 1892 to 1901 usually have cameo contrast between the designs and the mirror fields. Later Proofs vary in contrast. *Obverse and Reverse:* Proofs that are extensively cleaned and have many hairlines, or that are dull and grainy, are lower level, such as PF-60 to 62. These are not widely desired, save for the rare (in any grade) year of 1895, and even so most collectors would rather have a lustrous MS-60 than a dull PF-60. With medium hairlines and good reflectivity, PF-64 is assigned. Tiny horizontal lines on Miss Liberty's cheek, known as slide marks, from National and other album slides scuffing the relief of the cheek, are endemic among Barber silver coins. With noticeable marks of this type, the highest grade assignable is PF-64. With relatively few hairlines, a rating of PF-65 can be given. PF-66 should have hairlines so delicate that magnification is needed to see them. Above that, a Proof should be free of any hairlines or other problems.

Proof Barber Dime
Shown 1.5x actual size.

	Mintage	Cert	Finest	PF-60	PF-63	PF-64	PF-65	Recent Auction Record
1892	1,245	261	PF-67	$300	$600	$1,000	$1,750	$518, PF-63, Jun-10
1893	792	256	PF-69	300	600	1,000	1,750	$460, PF-63, Jul-10
1894	972	297	PF-68	300	600	1,000	1,750	$1,898, PF-66Cam, Jul-10
1894S † (a)	24	5	PF-66		1,500,000			$1,552,500, PF-64, Oct-07
1895	880	295	PF-68	300	600	1,000	1,750	$1,380, PF-65 CAC, Jul-10
1896	762	231	PF-68	300	600	1,000	1,750	$8,625, PF-66, Jun-10
1897	731	227	PF-68	300	600	1,000	1,750	$690, PF-64, Jun-10
1898	735	276	PF-68	300	600	1,000	1,750	$3,105, PF-67, Jul-10
1899	846	222	PF-68	300	600	1,000	1,750	$604, PF-63, Jun-10
1900	912	213	PF-68	300	600	1,000	1,750	$805, PF-64 CAC, Jul-10
1901	813	230	PF-68	300	600	1,000	1,750	$460, PF-62, Jun-10

† Ranked in the *100 Greatest U.S. Coins* (third edition). **a.** The reason for the low mintage of the Proof 1894-S dime is unknown. Popular theories, among others, include a rounding out of the Mint's record books, or a special presentation to bankers visiting the San Francisco Mint. Fewer than a dozen examples are known to exist.

	Mintage	Cert	Finest	PF-60	PF-63	PF-64	PF-65	Recent Auction Record
1902	777	176	PF-68	$300	$600	$1,000	$1,750	$978, PF-64 CAC, Jul-10
1903	755	200	PF-68	300	600	1,000	1,750	$633, PF-64, Jun-10
1904	670	203	PF-68	300	600	1,000	1,750	$863, PF-64, Jul-10
1905	727	192	PF-68	300	600	1,000	1,750	$805, PF-64Cam, Jul-10
1906	675	170	PF-68	300	600	1,000	1,750	$690, PF-64, Jul-10
1907	575	168	PF-67	300	600	1,000	1,750	$1,725, PF-64, Jun-10
1908	545	180	PF-68	300	600	1,000	1,750	$2,070, PF-66Cam, Jul-10
1909	650	231	PF-68	300	600	1,000	1,750	$3,738, PF-67Cam, Jul-10
1910	551	194	PF-68	300	600	1,000	1,750	$4,600, PF-67Cam, Jun-10
1911	543	223	PF-69	300	600	1,000	1,750	$1,265, PF-65Cam, Jul-10
1912	700	170	PF-68	300	600	1,000	1,750	$1,380, PF-65Cam, Jun-10
1913	622	181	PF-69	300	600	1,000	1,750	$863, PF-64, Jun-10
1914	425	152	PF-68	300	600	1,000	1,750	$576, PF-64, Jul-10
1915	450	132	PF-68	300	600	1,000	1,750	$805, PF-63, Jun-10

WINGED LIBERTY HEAD OR "MERCURY" (1916–1945)

Designer Adolph A. Weinman; weight 2.50 grams; composition .900 silver, .100 copper (net weight: .07234 oz. pure silver); diameter 17.9 mm; reeded edge; mints: Philadelphia, Denver, San Francisco.

Shown 2x actual size.

History. In 1916 a new dime, designed by sculptor Adolph A. Weinman (who also created the half dollar that debuted that year), replaced Charles Barber's Liberty Head type. Officially Weinman's design was known as the Winged Liberty Head, but numismatists commonly call the coin the *Mercury* dime, from Miss Liberty's wing-capped resemblance to the Roman god. The reverse depicts a fasces (symbolic of unity) and an olive branch. Production was continuous from 1916 to 1945, except for 1922, 1932, and 1933.

Striking and Sharpness. Many Mercury dimes exhibit areas of light striking, most notably in the center horizontal band across the fasces, less so in the lower horizontal band. The bands are composed of two parallel lines with a separation or "split" between. The term Full Bands, abbreviated FB, describes coins with both parallel lines in the center band distinctly separated. *In addition,* some dimes may display weak striking in other areas (not noted by certification services or others), including at areas of the obverse hair, rim, and date. Dimes of 1921 in particular can have FB but poorly struck dates.

Availability. Certain coins, such as 1916-D; 1921-P; 1921-D; 1942, 2 Over 1; and 1942-D, 2 Over 1, are elusive in any grade. Others are generally available in lower circulated grades, although some are scarce. In MS many of the issues before 1931 range from scarce to rare. If with FB and also sharply struck in other areas, some are rare. MS coins usually are very lustrous. In the marketplace certain scarce early issues such as 1916-D, 1921, and 1921-D are often graded slightly more liberally than are later varieties.

MS-60 to 70 (Mint State). *Obverse:* At MS-60, some abrasion and contact marks are evident on the highest part of the portrait, including the hair immediately to the right of the face and the upper left part of the wing. At MS-63, abrasion is slight at best, and slighter at 64. Album slide marks on the cheek, if present, should not exist at any grade above MS-64. An MS-65 coin should display no abrasion or contact marks except under magnification, and MS-66 and higher coins should have none at all. Luster should be full and rich.

Reverse: Comments apply as for the obverse, except that the highest parts of the fasces, these being the horizontal bands, are the places to check. The field is mainly protected by design elements and does not show contact marks readily.

Full Bands

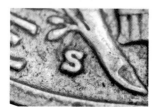

1928-S, Small Mintmark

1928-S, Large Mintmark
FS-10-1928S-501.

1929-S, Doubled-Die Obverse
FS-10-1929S-101.

	Mintage	Cert	Avg	%MS	MS-63	MS-64	MS-64FB	MS-65	MS-65FB	MS-66	MS-66FB	Recent Auction Record
1916	22,180,080	2,160	63.5	96	$45	$60	$70	$120	$175	$190	$425	$2,990, MS-68FB, Jun-10
1916D † (a)	264,000	2,194	14.1	9	18,000	20,000	25,000	30,000	45,000	35,000	60,000	$48,875, MS-65FB, Jun-10
1916S	10,450,000	757	61.1	92	65	90	170	255	750	550	1,500	$518, MS-65FB, Jul-10
1917	55,230,000	631	63.5	94	60	80	100	170	460	360	950	$345, MS-65FB, Jun-10
1917D	9,402,000	479	62.2	87	350	400	1,250	1,225	5,500	2,500	12,500	$978, MS-64FB, Jun-10
1917S	27,330,000	489	62.6	89	180	275	475	575	1,400	750	2,400	$949, MS-65FB Star, Jun-10
1918	26,680,000	340	63.2	93	125	160	350	460	1,500	1,250	2,500	$1,668, MS-66FB, Jun-10
1918D	22,674,800	394	62.5	91	250	310	3,500	675	30,000	1,450	80,000	$2,128, MS-64FB, Jun-10
1918S	19,300,000	326	62.7	91	275	450	2,200	725	8,750	2,200	12,500	$10,350, MS-66FB, Jun-10
1919	35,740,000	414	62.8	90	120	140	250	375	725	1,350	1,850	$360, MS-65FB, Jun-10
1919D	9,939,000	299	62.4	91	450	725	6,000	2,100	37,500	3,600	140,000	$9,200, MS-65FB, Jun-10
1919S	8,850,000	201	61.8	79	450	700	5,750	1,250	14,000	1,575	100,000	$6,900, MS-64FB, Jun-10
1920	59,030,000	632	63.8	98	75	100	150	260	525	585	1,200	$546, MS-66FB, Jul-10
1920D	19,171,000	344	62.8	89	350	400	1,500	825	4,750	2,450	5,750	$920, MS-64FB, Jul-10
1920S	13,820,000	227	62.7	87	325	465	2,500	1,450	8,250	2,850	16,500	$3,738, MS-65FB, Jun-10
1921	1,230,000	560	39.4	38	1,800	2,000	2,800	3,600	4,400	4,500	8,200	$2,185, MS-64FB, Jun-10
1921D	1,080,000	621	36.1	35	1,850	2,250	3,200	3,600	5,250	4,600	9,000	$7,935, MS-66FB, Jun-10
1923 (b)	50,130,000	759	64.0	97	45	55	65	130	350	450	625	$300, MS-65FB, Jun-10
1923S	6,440,000	245	61.7	85	400	575	2,000	1,250	7,250	2,800	18,500	$5,463, MS-66FB, Jun-10
1924	24,010,000	417	64.2	97	100	125	160	210	500	450	975	$345, MS-65FB, Jun-10
1924D	6,810,000	362	63.1	93	500	600	775	1,200	1,650	2,100	2,850	$863, MS-65FB, Jun-10
1924S	7,120,000	263	62.2	87	500	600	3,500	1,250	17,500	3,200	100,000	$2,185, MS-64FB, Apr-10
1925	25,610,000	283	63.4	93	85	130	225	225	1,000	550	3,250	$2,128, MS-65FB, Jul-10
1925D	5,117,000	247	61.1	77	800	1,000	1,500	1,800	3,600	2,400	4,800	$3,738, MS-65FB, Jul-10
1925S	5,850,000	209	62.6	87	500	700	1,400	1,500	4,500	2,800	12,750	$1,840, MS-65FB, Jun-10
1926	32,160,000	580	63.6	95	65	100	145	250	550	475	1,100	$690, MS-66FB, Jun-10
1926D	6,828,000	347	62.9	91	275	380	750	600	2,600	1,450	5,200	$1,610, MS-65FB, Jun-10
1926S	1,520,000	255	52.6	48	1,500	1,950	3,500	3,000	7,450	4,850	14,500	$3,565, MS-64FB, Jun-10
1927	28,080,000	445	63.4	95	60	100	140	150	385	310	965	$276, MS-65FB, Jul-10
1927D	4,812,000	211	61.0	79	400	500	2,000	1,300	8,400	2,800	15,250	$1,725, MS-64FB, Jun-10
1927S	4,770,000	174	62.4	87	550	700	2,650	1,500	7,500	2,350	14,500	$1,840, MS-64FB, Jun-10
1928	19,480,000	369	64.0	96	55	70	100	130	380	410	725	$299, MS-65FB, Jun-10
1928D	4,161,000	214	62.2	87	350	450	925	900	3,000	1,600	5,250	$6,900, MS-66FB CAC, Apr-10
1928S (c)	7,400,000	306	63.7	95	300	410	800	500	2,450	625	3,750	$1,610, MS-65FB, Jun-10
1929	25,970,000	697	64.6	98	35	40	55	75	190	115	335	$489, MS-66FB, May-10
1929D	5,034,000	1,007	64.4	100	40	42	70	75	240	130	535	$207, MS-65FB, Jul-10
1929S	4,730,000	318	64.0	95	45	70	140	125	585	480	875	$863, MS-66FB, Jun-10
1929S, DblDie Obv (d)	*	4	57.8	50	150	175		200				
1930 (b)	6,770,000	342	63.9	95	50	55	145	125	600	240	860	$748, MS-66FB, Jun-10
1930S	1,843,000	241	64.2	96	120	150	250	210	725	425	1,850	$1,725, MS-66FB, Jun-10
1931	3,150,000	367	63.8	95	70	85	235	150	840	260	1,175	$690, MS-65FB, Jun-10
1931D	1,260,000	461	64.3	97	140	165	190	280	440	380	675	$633, MS-66FB, Jun-10
1931S	1,800,000	303	62.7	92	150	180	800	300	2,600	475	4,000	$2,185, MS-65FB, Jun-10

* Included in number above. † Ranked in the *100 Greatest U.S. Coins* (third edition). **a.** Beware of altered or otherwise spurious mintmarks. **b.** Dimes dated 1923-D or 1930-D are counterfeit. **c.** Two mintmark styles exist: Large S (scarce) and Small S (common). About 80% of 1928-S dimes are of the Small S style. The scarcer Large S is worth about two to three times the values listed (which are for the Small S). **d.** Moderate doubling is evident on the date and IN GOD WE TRUST.

1936-S, Possible Overdate
FS-10-1936S-110.

1941-S, Small S

1941-S, Large S
FS-10-1941S-511.

1942, 2 Over 1
FS-10-1942-101.

1942-D, 2 Over 1
FS-10-1942D-101.

1943-S, Trumpet Tail Mintmark
FS-10-1943S-511.

1945-D, D Over Horizontal D
FS-10-1945D-506.

1945-S, S Over Horizontal S
FS-10-1945S-503.

1945-S, Normal S

1945-S, Micro S
FS-10-1945S-512.

	Mintage	Cert	Avg	%MS	MS-64FB	MS-65	MS-65FB	MS-66	MS-66FB	MS-67	MS-67FB	Recent Auction Record
1934	24,080,000	743	64.9	98	$40	$50	$140	$65	$220	$260	$370	$546, MS-67FB, Jun-10
1934D	6,772,000	571	64.5	97	120	85	325	230	950	465	2,750	$2,760, MS-67FB Star, Jun-10
1935	58,830,000	1,151	65.5	98	30	35	75	60	120	110	275	$345, MS-67FB, Jul-10
1935D	10,477,000	397	64.3	97	180	90	580	325	950	500	3,200	$2,760, MS-67FB, Feb-10
1935S	15,840,000	500	65.2	99	140	40	410	80	620	240	925	$633, MS-66FB, Jan-10
1936	87,500,000	1,257	65.3	98	30	30	90	48	120	140	275	$1,610, MS-68FB, Aug-09
1936D	16,132,000	466	64.8	97	120	55	375	80	420	325	600	$690, MS-67FB Star, Jun-10
1936S	9,210,000	891	65.5	100	40	35	95	55	165	190	440	$403, MS-67FB, Jun-10
1936S, Possible Overdate (a)	*	n/a	n/a	n/a	450	600						
1937	56,860,000	3,438	65.8	99	30	30	60	40	85	50	150	$104, MS-67FB, Jun-10
1937D	14,146,000	843	65.6	99	38	45	100	85	180	100	260	$690, MS-68FB, Jan-10
1937S	9,740,000	738	65.7	99	70	40	185	80	230	210	925	$219, MS-67, Feb-10
1938	22,190,000	1,249	65.6	99	30	30	85	55	110	65	285	$322, MS-67FB, Jul-10
1938D	5,537,000	1,395	65.6	100	32	35	65	75	120	235	265	$127, MS-66FB, Feb-10
1938S	8,090,000	781	65.4	99	42	40	160	80	230	275	400	$9,775, MS-68FB, Apr-09
1939	67,740,000	2,618	66.0	99	45	25	180	40	225	50	360	$89, MS-67, Feb-10

* Included in number above. **a.** "The secondary image of a 2 is evident beneath the 3 of the date. Most evident is the flat portion of the base of the underlying 2. Remains of what is likely a secondary 9 are evident to the left of the primary 9. Many die polish marks are also evident throughout the surface of the obverse. No doubling is evident on other elements. . . . The length of time between the striking of the last 1929-dated coins and this 1936 coin would seem to eliminate the possibility of a 2 underlying the 3. However, examination has matched the shapes on the image under the 3 to that of the 2 on 1929-dated dimes. Stranger things have happened. Keep in mind that 1936 was during the Great Depression, when Mint personnel wanted to save money whenever possible." (*Cherrypickers' Guide to Rare Die Varieties,* fourth edition, volume II)

Chart continued on next page.

	Mintage	Cert	Avg	%MS	MS-64FB	MS-65	MS-65FB	MS-66	MS-66FB	MS-67	MS-67FB	Recent Auction Record
1939D	24,394,000	2,486	65.9	100	$30	$28	$55	$60	$85	$110	$160	$8,338, MS-67FB, Apr-10
1939S	10,540,000	645	65.4	99	200	42	825	110	1,075	210	3,000	$3,105, MS-67FB, Oct-09
1940	65,350,000	2,613	65.9	99	25	30	50	45	70	65	220	$150, MS-67FB, Jun-10
1940D	21,198,000	1,799	65.7	99	26	35	50	50	65	80	180	$690, MS-68FB, Apr-10
1940S	21,560,000	1,786	65.7	99	30	35	100	40	140	55	480	$1,840, MS-68FB, Mar-10
1941	175,090,000	3,377	65.5	98	25	30	50	45	55	60	150	$161, MS-67FB, May-10
1941D	45,634,000	2,507	65.5	99	25	25	50	32	55	60	140	$161, MS-67FB, Jun-10
1941S	43,090,000	3,732	65.7	99	24	30	50	38	60	65	160	$1,035, MS-68FB, Jul-10
1941S, Large S (b)	*	19	49.2	53		325						
1942, 2 Over 1 (c)	**	1,084	40.0	9	12,500 (d)	15,000	35,000	18,000	40,000	—	—	$9,775, MS-63FB, Jan-10
1942	205,410,000	3,932	65.4	97	25	30	50	45	60	55	475	$633, MS-67FB, Jun-10
1942D, 2 Over 1 (e)	**	657	37.1	12	12,000 (f)	9,000	26,500	12,000	45,000	—	—	$8,625, MS64FB, Jun-10
1942D	60,740,000	3,338	65.2	97	25	30	50	45	55	75	180	$5,750, MS-68FB, Jul-10
1942S	49,300,000	1,329	65.5	98	30	35	150	50	225	125	650	$489, MS-67FB, Jun-10
1943	191,710,000	3,682	65.6	98	24	25	55	35	60	45	185	$374, MS-67FB, Jan-10
1943D	71,949,000	4,224	65.7	100	28	30	50	45	55	65	125	$127, MS-67FB, Jun-10
1943S	60,400,000	2,607	65.9	99	30	30	70	40	80	55	175	$1,955, MS-68FB, Aug-09
1943S, Trumpet Tail Mintmark (g)	*	3	65.3	100	500	450	750	500				
1944	231,410,000	4,395	65.6	99	24	25	80	45	165	50	425	$1,035, MS-67FB, Jan-10
1944D	62,224,000	5,381	65.9	100	25	30	50	48	55	55	120	$299, MS-67FB, Jul-10
1944S	49,490,000	4,154	65.9	100	25	30	55	50	75	60	180	$161, MS-67FB, Aug-10
1945	159,130,000	4,305	65.6	99	6,250	28	10,000	45	15,000	50	25,000	$9,200, MS-66FB, Jun-10
1945D	40,245,000	4,870	65.8	100	25	30	50	50	65	75	190	$690, MS-67FB CAC, Jul-10
1945D, D Over Horizontal D (h)	*	2	45.0	0	900	950						
1945S	41,920,000	4,616	66.1	100	30	30	125	40	165	60	640	$25,300, MS-68FB, Apr-10
1945S, S Over Horizontal S (i)	*	n/a	n/a	n/a	900	950						
1945S, Micro S (j)	*	916	65.4	99	150	100	650	120	1,000	400	4,000	$2,185, MS-67FB, Jun-10

* Included in number above. ** Included in number below. **b.** This is the "Trumpet Tail" S mintmark, which is rare for this date. The upper serif points downward and the lower serif is rounded, like the bell of a trumpet. There are several dies known for the Large S dime, including one that is repunched. For more information, see the *Cherrypickers' Guide.* **c.** Doubling is evident in the 42 over 41 overdate, and slightly evident on IN GOD WE TRUST. Values for this variety fluctuate. **d.** Value in MS-64 is $7,000. **e.** Doubling is evident in the 42 over 41 overdate, slightly evident on IN GOD WE TRUST, and as a D over D repunched mintmark (slanted west). Values for this variety fluctuate. **f.** Value in MS-64 is $7,000. **g.** This variety is considerably rarer than the 1941-S, Large S, which also features a Trumpet S mintmark. It is extremely rare in MS, and specimens with FB command a significant premium. The top serif of the S points downward, with the lower serif rounded, much like the bell of a trumpet. **h.** The first D mintmark was punched into the die horizontally and then corrected. **i.** The first S mintmark was punched into the die horizontally and then corrected. **j.** The S mintmark is significantly smaller than that of the normal S punch. This variety has the only mintmark punch of this type and size known to have been used during the 1940s.

Proof Winged Liberty Head (Mercury) Dimes

PF-60 to 70 (Proof). Proofs were minted from 1936 to 1942, and are available in proportion to their mintages. The dies were completely polished, including the portrait. *Obverse and Reverse:* Proofs that are extensively cleaned and have many hairlines, or that are dull and grainy, are lower level, such as PF-60 to 62. These are not widely desired in the marketplace, and represent coins that have been mistreated. With medium hairlines and good reflectivity, PF-63 or 64 is appropriate. Tiny horizontal lines on Miss Liberty's cheek, known as slide marks, from National and other album slides scuffing the relief of the cheek, are common; such coins should not be graded higher than PF-64, but sometimes are. With relatively few hairlines and no noticeable slide marks, a rating of PF-65 can be given. PF-66 should have hairlines so delicate that magnification is needed to see them. Above that, a Proof should be free of any hairlines or other problems.

Proof Winged Liberty Head (Mercury) Dime
Shown 1.5x actual size.

	Mintage	Cert	Avg	PF-64	PF-65	PF-66	Recent Auction Record
1936	4,130	1,000	65.0	$1,200	$2,100	$2,500	$1,323, PF-66 CAC, Jul-10
1937	5,756	1,153	65.4	650	850	1,250	$417, PF-66, Jul-10
1938	8,728	1,654	65.5	350	550	775	$253, PF-66, Jul-10

	Mintage	Cert	Avg	PF-64	PF-65	PF-66	Recent Auction Record
1939	9,321	1,813	65.9	$325	$450	$625	$2,185, PF-68, Jul-10
1940	11,827	1,990	65.6	250	425	575	$518, PF-67 CAC, Jul-10
1941	16,557	2,501	65.5	225	400	550	$359, PF-67, Jul-10
1942	22,329	3,723	65.7	225	400	550	$2,185, PF-68, Jul-10

ROOSEVELT
(1946 TO DATE)

Silver (1946–1964, and some modern Proofs): Designer John R. Sinnock; weight 2.50 grams; composition .900 silver, .100 copper (net weight: .07234 oz. pure silver); diameter 17.9 mm; reeded edge; mints: Philadelphia, Denver, San Francisco.

Clad (1965 to date): Designer John R. Sinnock; weight 2.27 grams; composition, outer layers of copper-nickel (.750 copper, .250 nickel) bonded to inner core of pure copper; diameter 17.9 mm; reeded edge; mints: Philadelphia, Denver, San Francisco, West Point.

Shown 2x actual size.

Shown 2x actual size.

History. After President Franklin D. Roosevelt died in 1945, the Treasury rushed to create a coin in his honor. The ten-cent denomination was particularly appropriate, given the president's active support of the March of Dimes' fundraising efforts to cure polio. The obverse of the coin bears Roosevelt's profile portrait, while the reverse features a torch flanked by branches of olive and oak.

Striking and Sharpness. Little attention has been paid to the sharpness of these coins. The obverse portrait is such that lightness of strike on the higher points is difficult to detect. On the reverse, check the leaves and the details of the torch. Some with complete separation on the lower two bands have been called Full Torch (FT), but interest seems to be minimal in today's marketplace.

Availability. All are common, although some are more common than others. MS coins in higher grades are usually very lustrous.

MS-60 to 70 (Mint State). *Obverse:* At MS-60, some abrasion and contact marks are evident on the cheek, the hair above the ear, and the neck. At MS-63, abrasion is slight at best, less so for MS-64. An MS-65 coin should display no abrasion or contact marks except under magnification, and MS-66 and higher coins should have none at all. Luster should be full and rich. *Reverse:* Comments apply as for the obverse, except that the highest parts of the torch, flame, and leaves are the places to check. On both sides the fields are protected by design elements and do not readily show contact marks.

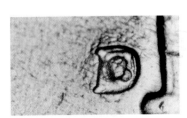

1950-D, D Over S
FS-10-1950D-501.

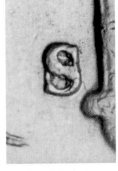

1950-S, S Over D
FS-10-1950S-501.

1963, Doubled-Die Reverse
FS-10-1963-805.

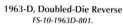

1963-D, Doubled-Die Reverse
FS-10-1963D-801.

1964-D, Doubled-Die Reverse
FS-10-1964D-801. Other varieties exist.

	Mintage	Cert	Avg	%MS	MS-63	MS-65	MS-66	MS-67	MS-68	Recent Auction Record
1946	255,250,000	1,325	66.0	100	$3.00	$12	$28	$110	$2,200	$633, MS-67FB, Mar-09
1946D	61,043,500	1,500	66.3	100	3.00	14	30	100	2,000	$15, MS-66, Aug-09
1946S	27,900,000	2,258	66.3	100	4.50	20	32	90	1,800	$161, MS-67FB, May-10
1947	121,520,000	805	66.2	100	6.00	12	24	55	1,600	$2,645, MS-67FB, Jan-09
1947D	46,835,000	994	66.2	100	6.50	12	24	30	1,200	$1,150, MS-68 Star, Sep-09
1947S	34,840,000	1,583	66.4	100	6.00	12	30	110	2,000	$224, MS-67FB, Jul-10
1948	74,950,000	864	66.1	100	4.00	12	30	85	1,800	$8,050, MS-68FB, Jan-09
1948D	52,841,000	971	66.3	100	6.00	12	32	85	1,850	$2,185, MS-68FB, Sep-09
1948S	35,520,000	1,232	66.4	100	5.50	12	32	100	2,200	$66, MS-67FB, May-10
1949	30,940,000	895	66.0	99	26.00	32	60	110	2,000	$1,955, MS-67FB, Jan-09
1949D	26,034,000	1,315	66.3	100	12.00	20	35	105	2,000	$161, MS-67FB, Jul-10
1949S	13,510,000	1,965	66.3	100	42.00	55	80	170	2,200	$79, MS-67, May-10
1950	50,130,114	1,160	66.1	99	13.00	16	40	135	2,600	$862, MS-67FB, Jan-09
1950D	46,803,000	1,166	66.3	100	6.00	12	28	90	1,950	$127, MS-67FB, May-10
1950D, D Over S (a)	*	n/a	n/a	n/a	400.00	650	850	1,100		
1950S	20,440,000	1,200	66.4	99	36.00	42	75	135	1,800	$1,380, MS-67FB, Jan-09
1950S, S Over D (b)	*	45	64.5	98	250.00	400	750	1,000		$230, MS-66, Apr-08
1951	103,880,102	1,190	66.1	100	2.50	10	30	90	1,850	$374, MS-67FB, May-10
1951D	56,529,000	734	66.2	100	2.50	10	28	130	2,500	$4,600, MS-68FB, Feb-10
1951S	31,630,000	1,302	66.4	100	12.50	22	48	110	4,000	$69, MS-67FB, May-10
1952	99,040,093	762	66.1	100	2.50	10	30	85	1,800	$59, MS-66FB, Nov-09
1952D	122,100,000	894	66.1	100	2.50	6	25	30	1,200	$207, MS-67FB, Jul-10
1952S	44,419,500	1,263	66.4	100	8.00	12	35	65	1,500	$74, MS-66FB, Jan-10
1953	53,490,120	638	66.1	100	3.00	8	15	70	1,600	$17, MS-66, Aug-09
1953D	136,433,000	846	66.2	100	3.00	8	20	45	1,400	$690, MS-67FB, Jan-09
1953S	39,180,000	1,898	66.3	100	2.50	8	25	65	1,500	$3,450, MS-68, Jan-09
1954	114,010,203	949	66.0	100	2.50	8	20	32	1,200	$2,875, MS-67FB, Jan-09
1954D	106,397,000	715	66.1	100	2.50	8	12	30	1,200	$748, MS-68, Sep-09
1954S	22,860,000	1,663	66.3	100	2.50	8	15	40	1,400	$374, MS-67FB, Jul-10
1955	12,450,181	1,529	66.1	100	2.50	8	16	25	1,000	$173, MS-66FB, Aug-09
1955D	13,959,000	1,007	65.9	100	2.50	8	15	24	1,000	$30, MS-67, Apr-10
1955S	18,510,000	2,046	66.1	100	2.50	8	15	60	1,500	$4,025, MS-67FB, Jan-09
1956	108,640,000	1,599	66.2	100	2.50	7	14	45	1,350	$3,450, MS-68, Jan-09
1956D	108,015,100	724	66.1	100	2.50	7	15	35	1,300	$2,990, MS-67FB, Jan-09
1957	160,160,000	1,724	66.3	100	2.50	7	14	60	1,500	$517, MS-67, Jan-09
1957D	113,354,330	995	66.2	100	2.50	7	14	20	1,000	$4,025, MS-67FB, Jan-09
1958	31,910,000	1,563	66.3	100	2.50	8	15	55	1,500	$16, MS-66, Aug-09
1958D	136,564,600	1,104	66.2	100	2.50	8	14	45	1,350	$2,530, MS-68FB, Sep-09
1959	85,780,000	1,159	66.0	100	2.50	7	15	35	1,250	$127, MS-67, Apr-10
1959D	164,919,790	883	66.1	99	2.50	7	14	25	1,000	$138, MS-67FB, Aug-09
1960	70,390,000	990	66.0	100	2.50	7	14	25	1,200	$1,553, MS-67FB, Aug-09

* Included in number above. **a.** The diagonal stroke of the initially punched S mintmark is visible within the opening of the primary D mintmark. The lower curve of the S is evident on the lower right curve of the D. **b.** The S mintmark is punched squarely over a previously punched D. CONECA lists this coin as an S Over Inverted S, indicating that the line enclosing the lower loop is that of the long upper serif on an inverted S. However, Fivaz and Stanton, in the *Cherrypickers' Guide to Rare Die Varieties,* fourth edition, volume II, "believe this to be an [overmintmark] (actually S/S/D) because the long upper serif of an S would not enclose the lower opening. In addition, the curve of the face of a D is clearly evident in the upper opening."

	Mintage	Cert	Avg	%MS	MS-63	MS-65	MS-66	MS-67	MS-68	Recent Auction Record
1960D	200,160,400	789	66.0	100	$2.25	$6	$15	$50	$1,400	$276, MS-67FB, Jun-10
1961	93,730,000	1,018	65.9	100	2.25	6	12	35	1,300	$28, MS-65, Oct-09
1961D	209,146,550	758	65.9	100	2.25	6	12	25	1,200	$1,610, MS-68 Star, Sep-09
1962	72,450,000	1,035	66.0	100	2.25	6	12	40	1,300	$1,495, MS-67FB, Jan-09
1962D	334,948,380	794	66.1	99	2.25	6	12	30	1,250	$575, MS-67FB, Jan-09
1963	123,650,000	922	66.0	100	2.25	6	12	30	1,250	$575, MS-66FB, Jan-09
1963, DblDie Rev (c)	*	7	64.9	100	35.00	55	80			
1963D	421,476,530	806	65.9	99	2.25	6	12	30	1,250	$5,175, MS-68, Sep-09
1963D, DblDie Rev (d)	*	13	63.5	92	120.00	200	275			
1964 (e)	929,360,000	1,035	65.8	99	2.25	6	12	30	1,250	$3,220, MS-67 SMS, Jan-10
1964D (e)	1,357,517,180	1,285	65.8	98	2.25	6	12	50	1,500	$74, MS-67, Aug-09
1964D, DblDie Rev (f)	*	18	58.6	33	100.00	150	225	450	—	

* Included in number above. ** Included in regular 1960 mintage. c. Doubling is evident on UNITED, E PLURIBUS, the olive branch, and the stem. Lesser doubling is also visible on ONE DIME. d. Doubling is evident on all reverse lettering, with the most obvious doubling on AMERICA and on the top of the flame. Most MS specimens are MS-63 and lower. e. The 9 in the date has either a pointed tail or a straight tail. f. There are several varieties of 1964-D with a doubled-die reverse. The variety pictured and valued here is FS-10-1964D-801. For more information, see the *Cherrypickers' Guide*.

1967, Doubled-Die Obverse
FS-10-1967-101.

1970, Doubled-Die Reverse
FS-10-1970-801.

1982, No Mintmark, Strong Strike
FS-10-1982-501.

1982, No Mintmark, Weak Strike
FS-10-1982-502.

	Mintage	Cert	Avg	%MS	MS-65	MS-66	MS-67	MS-68	Recent Auction Record
1965 (a)	1,652,140,570	48	65.8	98	$1.50	$6	$25		$69, MS-66Cam SMS, Aug-09
1966 (a)	1,382,734,540	42	65.4	95	1.25	6	30	$525	$51, MS-67Cam SMS, Apr-09
1967 (a)	2,244,007,320	76	65.5	95	1.00	5	25	275	$69, MS-68Cam SMS, Jul-09
1967, DblDie Obv (b)	*	n/a	n/a	n/a	400.00	600	850		
1968	424,470,400	103	65.8	100	1.00	5	25	800	$13, MS-66FB, Oct-08
1968D	480,748,280	297	66.4	100	1.00	5	20	600	$19, MS-66FB, Oct-08
1969	145,790,000	25	63.9	96	2.00	6	30		$98, MS-66FB, Sep-08
1969D	563,323,870	216	66.0	100	1.00	6	25	700	$10, MS-66, Mar-09
1970	345,570,000	82	64.0	96	1.00	6	30		$8, MS-66, Sep-04
1970, DblDie Rev (c)	*	n/a	n/a	n/a	300.00	650	—		$56, MS-65, Jun-09
1970D	754,942,100	183	65.4	98	1.00	5	25	1,000	$276, MS-66, Sep-08
1971	162,690,000	36	64.8	100	1.50	5	27		$11, MS-65, Aug-08
1971D	377,914,240	81	65.7	100	1.25	6	40		$64, MS-66FB, Oct-08

* Included in number above. a. Values and auction records for Special Mint Set coins are listed with the Proofs for this type. b. This is a very rare doubled die. Its doubling is evident on IN GOD WE TRUST, the date, and the designer's initials. c. Doubling on this extremely rare variety is evident on all reverse lettering, especially on UNITED STATES OF AMERICA, with slightly weaker doubling on ONE DIME.

Chart continued on next page.

	Mintage	Cert	Avg	%MS	MS-65	MS-66	MS-67	MS-68	Recent Auction Record
1972	431,540,000	58	65.1	98	$1.00	$6	$60		$99, MS-67, Mar-04
1972D	330,290,000	98	65.7	100	1.00	6	40		$69, MS-66FB, Sep-08
1973	315,670,000	40	65.3	100	1.00	5	25		$99, MS-67, Mar-04
1973D	455,032,426	71	65.4	100	1.00	6	50		$27, MS-66FB, Oct-08
1974	470,248,000	39	65.1	100	1.00	5	25		$52, MS-67, Mar-04
1974D	571,083,000	44	65.4	100	1.00	5	25	$700	$51, MS-67, Oct-07
1975	585,673,900	47	65.2	100	1.00	4	25		$14, MS-66FB, Sep-08
1975D	313,705,300	125	66.2	100	1.00	4	30		$11, MS-66, Mar-09
1976	568,760,000	77	66.0	100	1.00	4	25		$31, MS-66, Dec-07
1976D	695,222,774	48	66.1	100	1.00	4	45	400	$54, MS-67FB, Oct-08
1977	796,930,000	145	65.9	100	1.00	4	25		$64, MS-66FB, Oct-08
1977D	376,607,228	64	65.6	100	1.00	4	25	900	$64, MS-65FB, Dec-07
1978	663,980,000	54	65.8	100	1.00	4	30	850	$17, MS-65, Aug-08
1978D	282,847,540	47	65.9	100	1.00	4	25	925	$64, MS-66FB, Oct-08
1979	315,440,000	111	65.9	100	1.00	4	25		$21, MS-66, Dec-07
1979D	390,921,184	72	65.6	100	1.00	4	30	500	$28, MS-67, Dec-04
1980P	735,170,000	65	65.7	98	1.00	4	25	900	$26, MS-67, Mar-04
1980D	719,354,321	53	65.8	100	1.00	4	25	1,300	$13, MS-66, Feb-08
1981P	676,650,000	135	66.1	100	1.00	4	40	150	$19, MS-67FB, Oct-08
1981D	712,284,143	230	66.5	100	1.00	4	20	100	$38, MS-66FB, Aug-09
1982, No Mmk, Strong Strike (d)	*	337	61.1	94	225.00	300	650	2,150	$196, MS-65, Feb-10
1982, No Mmk, Weak Strike (d)	*	**	**	**	80.00	100	210		
1982P	519,475,000	39	65.1	95	5.00	12	30		$25, MS-66FB, Oct-08
1982D	542,713,584	23	65.1	91	1.50	5	20		$81, MS-66FB, Oct-08
1983P	647,025,000	40	65.4	95	5.00	12	25		$57, MS-66, Dec-07
1983D	730,129,224	33	65.6	94	1.50	5	20		$64, MS-67, Mar-04
1984P	856,669,000	95	66.6	100	1.00	4	20	120	$11, MS-67FB, Oct-08
1984D	704,803,976	48	65.3	100	1.25	4	20		$21, MS-67, Aug-09
1985P	705,200,962	67	66.5	100	1.25	4	25		$13, MS-67FB, Oct-08
1985D	587,979,970	122	66.8	100	1.25	4	30	170	$38, MS-66FB, Aug-09
1986P	682,649,693	64	66.1	100	1.50	4	20	390	$150, MS-66FB, Oct-08
1986D	473,326,970	66	66.1	100	1.50	4	20	120	$150, MS-66FB, Sep-08
1987P	762,709,481	57	65.9	98	0.75	4	25	290	$31, MS-67, Mar-08
1987D	653,203,402	71	66.0	99	0.75	4	20	80	$15, MS-65FB, Oct-08
1988P	1,030,550,000	62	65.7	97	0.75	4	35	200	$25, MS-66FB, Sep-08
1988D	962,385,489	68	66.1	100	0.75	4	40	295	$18, MS-67FB, Sep-08
1989P	1,298,400,000	77	66.1	100	0.75	5	20	145	$10, MS-66FB, Sep-08
1989D	896,535,597	98	66.4	100	0.75	6	30	120	$13, MS-67FB, Oct-08
1990P	1,034,340,000	34	66.0	97	1.50	5	20	170	$27, MS-67, Mar-04
1990D	839,995,824	48	66.2	100	0.75	4	25		$12, MS-67, Mar-04
1991P	927,220,000	24	65.9	96	0.75	4	20		$27, MS-67, Mar-04
1991D	601,241,114	24	65.0	100	0.75	4	20		$32, MS-67, Mar-04
1992P	593,500,000	39	66.7	100	0.75	4	35	100	$104, MS-67FB, Sep-08
1992D	616,273,932	23	65.9	100	0.75	4	30	150	$15, MS-66FB, Oct-08
1993P	766,180,000	62	66.0	95	0.75	4	30		$42, MS-67FB, Sep-08
1993D	750,110,166	37	66.0	100	0.75	4	25		$15, MS-66FB, Oct-08
1994P	1,189,000,000	25	65.8	96	0.75	4	25	490	$11, MS-66FB, Oct-08
1994D	1,303,268,110	19	64.7	100	0.75	4	25		$11, MS-66FB, Sep-08
1995P	1,125,500,000	32	66.7	100	0.75	4	30		$21, MS-66FB, Aug-09
1995D	1,274,890,000	47	65.7	96	1.00	5	35	395	$30, MS-67, Aug-09
1996P	1,421,163,000	74	66.5	97	0.75	4	25	45	$14, MS-68, Mar-09
1996D	1,400,300,000	105	65.7	99	0.75	4	20	40	$11, MS-67FB, Oct-08
1996W (e)	1,457,000	1,562	66.6	100	20.00	30	50	110	$61, MS-67FB, Sep-09
1997P	991,640,000	31	66.5	100	0.75	4	60	85	$21, MS-68, Oct-08
1997D	979,810,000	44	65.9	98	0.75	4	65	150	$11, MS-65FB, Oct-08
1998P	1,163,000,000	40	66.4	98	0.75	3	18	100	$11, MS-66FB, Sep-08
1998D	1,172,250,000	39	65.8	100	0.75	3	15	300	$11, MS-65FB, Nov-08

* Included in number below. ** Included in number above. **d.** The P mintmark was omitted from this working die. There are two versions of this variety: one with a strong strike, and one with a weak strike. The strong strike is far more valuable and in demand than the weak. **e.** The 1996-W dime was issued in Mint sets only.

	Mintage	Cert	Avg	%MS	MS-65	MS-66	MS-67	MS-68	Recent Auction Record
1999P	2,164,000,000	89	66.9	99	$0.75	$3	$15	$30	$21, MS-68FB, Jan-09
1999D	1,397,750,000	81	66.3	99	0.75	3	15	30	$25, MS-68FB, Oct-08
2000P	1,842,500,000	42	65.0	86	0.75	3	15	30	$11, MS-68FB, Oct-08
2000D	1,818,700,000	53	66.5	96	0.75	3	15	30	$11, MS-68FB, Sep-08
2001P	1,369,590,000	45	66.7	100	0.75	3	12	30	$21, MS-68, Mar-09
2001D	1,412,800,000	57	66.3	95	0.75	3	12	30	$14, MS-68FB, Oct-08
2002P	1,187,500,000	24	66.9	100	0.75	3	12	30	$11, MS-68FB, Sep-08
2002D	1,379,500,000	26	66.3	96	0.75	3	12	30	$14, MS-68FB, Oct-08
2003P	1,085,500,000	133	66.0	100	0.75	2	10	26	$11, MS-68FB, Oct-08
2003D	986,500,000	93	65.7	100	0.75	2	10	26	$11, MS-68FB, Sep-08
2004P	1,328,000,000	56	66.6	100	0.75	2	8	24	$104, MS-68FB, Sep-08
2004D	1,159,500,000	57	66.8	100	0.75	2	8	24	$21, MS-68FB, Oct-08
2005P	1,412,000,000	2,183	67.0	100	0.75	2	8	24	$17, MS-69 Satin, Oct-08
2005D	1,423,500,000	2,293	66.9	100	0.75	2	8	24	$16, MS-69 Satin, Sep-08
2006P	1,381,000,000	1,172	66.9	100	0.75	2	6	20	$16, MS-69FB Satin, Sep-08
2006D	1,447,000,000	1,146	66.8	100	0.75	2	6	20	$19, MS-68FB Satin, Dec-07
2007P	1,047,500,000	196	66.3	100	0.75	2	6	20	$19, MS-69FB Satin, Oct-08
2007D	1,042,000,000	209	66.5	100	0.75	2	6	20	$15, MS-69FB Satin, Oct-08
2008P	391,000,000	54	67.3	100	0.75	2	4	15	
2008D	624,500,000	66	67.5	100	0.75	2	4	15	
2009P		238	66.4	100	0.75	2	4	15	
2009D		125	68.2	100	0.75	2	4	15	
2010P		3	67.0	100	0.75	2	4	15	
2010D		2	66.5	100	0.75	2	4	15	

Proof Roosevelt Dimes

PF-60 to 70 (Proof). Proofs have been made of the 1950 to 1964 years, and again from 1968 to date. Those of the 1970s onward usually have frosted or cameo contrast. Special Mint Set (SMS) coins, struck in lieu of Proofs from 1965 to 1967, in some instances closely resemble Proofs. The majority of Proofs made in recent decades are at high levels, MS-66 to 68 or higher. *Obverse and Reverse:* Proofs that are extensively cleaned and have many hairlines, or that are dull and grainy, are lower level, such as PF-60 to 62. These are coins that have been mistreated, and they are not widely sought in the marketplace. Only a few Proof Roosevelt dimes are in this category. With medium hairlines and good reflectivity, assigned grades of PF-63 or 64 are appropriate. PF-65 may have hairlines so delicate that magnification is needed to see them. Above that, a Proof should be free of any hairlines or other problems.

Proof Roosevelt Dime

1960, Proof, Doubled-Die Obverse
FS-10-1960-102. Various die states exist.

1963, Proof, Doubled-Die Reverse
FS-10-1963-802. Other varieties exist

1968-S, Proof, Doubled-Die Obverse

1968-S, Proof, No Mintmark
FS-10-1968S-102.

1979-S, Type 1 ("Filled" S)   1979-S, Type 2 ("Clear" S)

	Mintage	Cert	Avg	PF-65	PF-66	PF-66Cam	PF-67	PF-67Cam	PF-67DC	Recent Auction Record
1950	51,386	830	66.3	$50.00	$65.00	$250.00	$120			$184, PF-66Cam, May-10
1951	57,500	1,062	66.7	50.00	65.00	225.00	100			$139, PF-67Cam, May-10
1952	81,980	795	66.6	35.00	50.00	175.00	85			$374, PF-67Cam, Jul-10
1953	128,800	993	66.8	38.00	55.00	160.00	80			$85, PF-67Cam, May-10
1954	233,300	1,135	67.0	18.00	25.00	75.00	30			$460, PF-69, May-10
1955	378,200	1,684	67.3	15.00	20.00	70.00	25			$253, PF-69, May-10
1956	669,384	1,102	67.2	8.00	10.00	50.00	18			$345, PF-68UCam, May-10
1957	1,247,952	1,452	67.3	4.00	8.00	70.00	25			$518, PF-69Cam Star, Jul-10
1958	875,652	1,034	67.0	4.00	8.00	25.00	10			$750, PF-69UCam, Mar-10
1959	1,149,291	1,119	67.1	3.00	6.00	25.00	10			$1,150, PF-69UCam, Jul-10
1960	1,691,602	2,010	67.2	3.00	10.00	50.00	18			$242, PF-69UCam, Mar-10
1960, DblDie Obv	*	41	66.6	350.00	400.00					$230, PF-69, Jul-10
1961	3,028,244	2,332	67.2	3.00	8.00	30.00	12			$207, PF-69UCam, Mar-10
1962	3,218,019	2,338	67.1	3.00	8.00	25.00	10			$99, PF-68DCam, May-10
1963	3,075,645	3,423	67.4	3.00	8.00	25.00	10			$127, PF-69DCam, Mar-10
1963, DblDie Rev (a)	*	432	67.0	350.00	400.00					$253, PF-67DCam, May-10
1964	3,950,762	4,296	67.7	3.00	8.00	25.00	10			$150, PF-69DCam, May-10
1965, SMS	2,360,000	934	66.8	11.00	13.00	75.00	15	$170	—	
1966, SMS	2,261,583	928	67.0	11.00	13.00	45.00	15	90	—	
1967, SMS	1,863,344	1,044	67.0	12.00	14.00	19.00	17	40	$1,500	
1968S	3,041,506	557	67.7	2.00	4.00	5.00	6	15	30	$13, PF-70Cam, Mar-09
1968S, DblDie Obv (b)	*	10	67.1	350.00	500.00		750	—	—	$184, PF-68, Jun-09
1968S, No Mintmark (c)	*	6	68.0	12,000.00	14,500.00		16,000	—	—	$18,400, PF-67, Jan-10
1969S	2,394,631	357	67.9	2.00	4.00	5.00	6	18	35	$206, PF-69DCam, Oct-09
1970S	2,632,810	505	67.3	2.00	4.00	5.00	6	18	35	$17, PF-70DCam, Aug-09
1970S, No Mintmark (c)	*	103	67.5	800.00	900.00	950.00	1,000	—	—	$805, PF-68Cam, Feb-10
1971S	3,220,733	422	67.8	2.00	4.00	5.00	6	15	30	$15, PF-68DCam, Aug-09
1972S	3,260,996	484	67.5	2.00	4.00	5.00	6	8	12	$127, PF-70DCam, Oct-09
1973S	2,760,339	302	67.4	2.00	4.00	5.00	6	9	14	$489, PF-70DCam, Oct-09
1974S	2,612,568	254	67.6	2.00	4.00	5.00	6	8	12	$69, PF-70DCam, Oct-09
1975S	2,845,450	401	67.9	2.50	4.00	5.00	6	8	10	$1,610, PF-70DCam, Jan-10
1975S, No Mintmark (c)	*	n/a	n/a	38,000.00	40,000.00	42,500.00	45,000	—	—	
1976S	4,149,730	667	67.9	2.50	4.00	5.00	6	8	10	$30, PF-70DCam, Dec-09
1977S	3,251,152	506	68.1	2.00	4.00	5.00	6	8	9	$69, PF-70DCam, Jan-10
1978S	3,127,781	477	68.6	2.00	4.00	5.00	6	8	9	$104, PF-70DCam, Feb-10
1979S, Type 1 ("Filled" S)	3,677,175	586	68.8	2.00	4.00	5.00	6	9	10	$74, PF-70DCam, Jan-10
1979S, Type 2 ("Clear" S)	*	456	69.0	3.25	6.00	7.00	8	10	15	$127, PF-70DCam, Dec-09
1980S	3,554,806	876	68.4	2.00	4.00	5.00	6	8	9	$40, PF-70DCam, Oct-09
1981S	4,063,083	1,209	68.8	2.00	4.00	5.00	6	8	10	$56, PF-70DCam, Dec-09

* Included in number above. **a.** Several less-valuable 1963 Proof DDRs exist. Values shown are for FS-10-1963-802. **b.** There are several 1968-S Proof doubled-die obverse varieties. The one listed here is FS-10-1968S-102 (see the *Cherrypickers' Guide to Rare Die Varieties*). **c.** The S mintmark was inadvertently left off the coinage die; this defect was probably discovered before the end of the die's life.

	Mintage	Cert	Avg	PF-65	PF-66	PF-66Cam	PF-67	PF-67Cam	PF-67DC	Recent Auction Record
1982S	3,857,479	528	68.9	$2.50	$4.00	$5.00	$6	$8	$10	$74, PF-70DCam, Dec-09
1983S	3,279,126	559	69.1	2.00	4.00	5.00	6	8	9	$150, PF-70DCam, Dec-09
1983S, No Mintmark (c)	*	74	68.6	750.00	850.00	925.00	1,000	—	—	$920, PF-69DCam, Mar-10
1984S	3,065,110	427	69.0	2.50	4.00	5.00	6	8	9	$138, PF-70DCam, Dec-08
1985S	3,362,821	482	69.0	2.00	4.00	5.00	6	8	9	$16, PF-69DCam, Aug-09
1986S	3,010,497	305	69.1	4.00	5.00	6.00	7	9	10	$15, PF-69DCam, Aug-09
1987S	4,227,728	480	69.1	3.00	4.00	5.00	6	8	9	$15, PF-69DCam, Aug-09
1988S	3,262,948	339	69.1	4.00	5.00	6.00	7	9	10	$15, PF-69DCam, Aug-09
1989S	3,220,194	345	69.0	4.00	4.50	5.00	6	8	9	$15, PF-69DCam, Aug-09
1990S	3,299,559	521	69.2	2.50	4.00	5.00	6	8	9	$56, PF-70DCam, Dec-09
1991S	2,867,787	538	69.4	4.00	5.00	6.00	7	8	9	$69, PF-70DCam, Dec-09
1992S	2,858,981	425	69.5	3.00	4.00	5.00	6	8	9	$53, PF-70DCam, Dec-09
1992S, Silver	1,317,579	989	69.2	5.00	6.00	7.00	8	10	12	$59, PF-70DCam, Feb-10
1993S	2,633,439	412	69.4	4.00	5.00	6.00	7	8	9	$62, PF-70DCam, Dec-09
1993S, Silver	761,353	783	69.1	6.50	7.00	8.00	9	10	12	$94, PF-70DCam, Feb-10
1994S	2,484,594	308	69.5	5.00	6.00	7.00	8	9	10	$59, PF-70DCam, Oct-09
1994S, Silver	785,329	767	69.1	7.50	8.00	9.00	10	12	14	$64, PF-70DCam, Dec-09
1995S	2,117,496	303	69.6	15.00	16.00	18.00	20	25	35	$84, PF-70DCam, Dec-09
1995S, Silver	679,985	902	69.1	20.00	23.00	25.00	30	35	40	$16, PF-69DCam, Aug-09
1996S	1,750,244	306	69.4	3.00	6.00	7.00	8	10	12	$42, PF-70DCam, Feb-10
1996S, Silver	775,021	784	69.1	8.00	10.00	13.00	15	20	25	$36, PF-70DCam, Jan-10
1997S	2,055,000	267	69.6	8.00	10.00	13.00	15	20	30	$69, PF-70DCam, Dec-09
1997S, Silver	741,678	839	69.2	18.00	20.00	26.00	18	25	40	$26, PF-70DCam, Dec-09
1998S	2,086,507	264	69.5	4.00	6.00	7.00	8	10	12	$17, PF-69DCam, Aug-09
1998S, Silver	878,792	934	69.3	6.00	8.00	9.00	10	12	15	$79, PF-70DCam, Feb-10
1999S	2,543,401	2,098	69.2	4.00	6.00	7.00	8	10	12	$67, PF-70DCam, Jan-10
1999S, Silver	804,565	2,938	69.1	7.00	8.00	10.00	12	13	16	$47, PF-70DCam, Sep-09
2000S	3,082,572	816	69.3	2.50	4.00	6.00	7	9	10	$59, PF-70DCam, Dec-09
2000S, Silver	965,421	3,320	69.3	5.00	6.00	7.00	8	10	12	$26, PF-70DCam, Mar-10
2001S	2,294,909	860	69.4	2.50	4.00	6.00	7	9	10	$50, PF-70DCam, Dec-09
2001S, Silver	889,697	2,744	69.3	5.00	6.00	7.00	8	10	12	$36, PF-70UCam, Feb-10
2002S	2,319,766	1,322	69.3	2.50	4.00	6.00	7	9	10	$44, PF-70DCam, Dec-09
2002S, Silver	892,229	2,386	69.3	5.00	6.00	7.00	8	10	12	$42, PF-70UCam, Mar-10
2003S	2,172,684	3,215	69.3	2.50	4.00	6.00	7	9	10	$52, PF-70DCam, Mar-10
2003S, Silver	1,125,755	3,448	69.3	4.50	5.00	6.50	8	10	12	$38, PF-70UCam, Mar-10
2004S	1,789,488	1,231	69.3	3.00	5.00	6.00	7	9	10	$69, PF-70DCam, Oct-09
2004S, Silver	1,175,934	3,311	69.4	5.00	6.00	7.00	8	10	12	$42, PF-70UCam, Feb-10
2005S	2,275,000	5,782	69.2	2.50	4.00	6.00	7	9	10	$40, PF-70DCam, Dec-09
2005S, Silver	1,069,679	4,264	69.4	5.00	6.00	7.00	8	10	12	$36, PF-70UCam, Mar-10
2006S	2,000,428	1,789	69.4	2.50	4.00	6.00	7	9	10	$69, PF-70DCam, Oct-09
2006S, Silver	1,054,008	1,952	69.5	5.00	6.00	7.00	8	10	12	$56, PF-70UCam, Feb-10
2007S	1,384,797	1,511	69.6	2.50	4.00	6.00	7	9	10	$40, PF-70DCam, Dec-09
2007S, Silver	875,050	2,371	69.6	5.00	6.00	7.00	8	10	12	$47, PF-70UCam, Mar-10
2008S	1,377,424	1,123	69.7	2.50	4.00	6.00	7	9	10	$56, PF-70DCam, Oct-09
2008S, Silver	620,664	2,508	69.8	5.00	6.00	7.00	8	10	12	$36, PF-70UCam, Mar-10
2009S		2,741	69.6	2.50	4.00	6.00	7	9	10	
2009S, Silver		2,026	69.9	5.00	6.00	7.00	8	10	12	$40, PF-70UCam, Mar-10
2010S		n/a	n/a	2.50	4.00	6.00	7	9	10	
2010S, Silver		n/a	n/a	5.00	6.00	7.00	8	10	12	

c. The S mintmark was inadvertently left off the coinage die; this defect was probably discovered before the end of the die's life.

AN OVERVIEW OF TWENTY-CENT PIECES

The twenty-cent piece, made in silver, proved to be the shortest-lived denomination in American coinage history. They were struck in quantity in their first year of issue, 1875, after which it was learned that the public confused them with quarter dollars. Mintages dropped sharply, and in 1877 and 1878 coinage was limited to just Proofs for collectors. Both sides of the twenty-cent piece were designed by Chief Engraver William Barber. The obverse is simply an adaptation of the Liberty Seated motif earlier used on other denominations. The reverse is new and depicts a perched eagle (of the same general appearance as introduced by Barber on the 1873 silver trade dollar).

Only one twenty-cent piece is needed for inclusion in a type set. By far the most readily available in Mint State is the 1875-S, followed by the 1875-CC. These are often somewhat lightly struck on the reverse, particularly near the top of the eagle's wings. The 1875 and 1876 Philadelphia coins are occasionally encountered in Mint State and are usually well struck.

Proofs are readily available for all years, 1875 through 1878.

FOR THE COLLECTOR AND INVESTOR: TWENTY-CENT PIECES AS A SPECIALTY

A full date-and-mintmark set of twenty-cent pieces consists of the 1875, 1875-CC, 1875-S, 1876, 1876-CC, 1877, and 1878, the last two years being available only in Proof format. The great challenge in forming a set is the 1876-CC, of which 10,000 were minted, but, seemingly, all but about two dozen were melted. Those that do survive are typically encountered in Mint State and are widely heralded when they are offered at auction.

LIBERTY SEATED
(1875–1878)

Designer William Barber; weight 5 grams; composition .900 silver, .100 copper; diameter 22 mm; plain edge; mints: Philadelphia, Carson City, San Francisco.

Shown 1.5x actual size.

History. The twenty-cent coin debuted in 1875 as a convenient denomination to make change in the West (at the time silver coins did not circulate in the East or Midwest). The coins sometimes were confused with quarter dollars, given their similar Liberty Seated design on the obverse, and their similar size. The quantity minted dropped considerably in 1876, and in 1877 and 1878 only Proofs were struck. Despite the brief time of their production, these coins were still seen in circulation through the early 1900s, by which time they were often casually used as quarters.

Striking and Sharpness. Areas of weakness are common. On the obverse, check the head of Miss Liberty and the stars. The word LIBERTY is *raised* on this coin, a curious departure from other Liberty

Seated coins of the era, on which it is recessed or incuse (the Gobrecht silver dollars of 1836 and 1839 being exceptions). On the reverse, check the eagle's feathers, especially the top of the wing on the left, but other areas can be weak as well. Some 1875-S coins are highly prooflike.

Availability. Most often seen is the high-mintage 1875-S, although the 1875 and 1875-CC are encountered with frequency. The 1876 is quite scarce and when seen is usually in high grades and well struck. The 1876-CC is a rarity, and only about two dozen are known, nearly all of which are MS. The eye appeal of MS coins can vary widely. The number of letters in LIBERTY on certain coins graded from VG through VF can vary widely in the marketplace.

AU-50, 53, 55, 58 (About Uncirculated). *Obverse:* Light wear is seen on the thighs and knees, bosom, and head. At AU-50 and 53, some luster is evident. At AU-58, the luster is extensive but incomplete, especially in the right field. *Reverse:* Wear is evident on the eagle's breast (the prime focal point) and the top of the wings. At AU-50 and 53, there are traces of luster. An AU-58 coin has nearly full luster, more so than on the obverse, as the design elements protect the small field areas.

MS-60 to 70 (Mint State). *Obverse:* At MS-60, some abrasion and contact marks are evident, most noticeably on the bosom and thighs and knees. Luster is present, but may be dull or lifeless. At MS-63, contact marks are very few, and abrasion is hard to detect except under magnification. An MS-65 coin has no abrasion, and contact marks are sufficiently minute as to require magnification. Check the knees of Liberty and the right field. Luster should be full

and rich. *Reverse:* Comments apply as for the obverse, except that in lower MS grades abrasion and contact marks are most noticeable on the eagle's breast and the top of the wing to the left. At MS-65 or higher, there are no marks visible to the unaided eye. The field is mainly protected by design elements and does not show abrasion as much as does the obverse on a given coin.

	Mintage	Cert	Avg	%MS	AU-50	MS-60	MS-62	MS-63	MS-64	MS-65	MS-66	Recent Auction Record
1875	36,910	313	57.2	60	$650	$900	$1,250	$1,500	$2,000	$6,000	$12,500	$1,300, MS-61 CAC, Jul-10
1875CC	133,290	499	49.5	50	1,250	2,000	3,000	4,250	5,750	12,500	40,000	$5,463, MS-63, Jun-10
1875S (a)	1,155,000	1,974	56.6	64	375	600	1,000	1,300	2,000	5,500	11,000	$4,600, MS-65, Jun-10
1876	14,640	350	60.3	73	625	900	1,100	1,500	2,500	6,000	15,000	$1,380, MS-62, Jul-10
1876CC †	10,000	7	64.6	100	150,000	225,000	275,000	300,000	350,000	400,000	500,000	$460,000, MS-66, Apr-09

† Ranked in the *100 Greatest U.S. Coins* (third edition). **a.** There are at least two misplaced-date die varieties of the 1875-S twenty-cent piece. These do not command a premium in the marketplace.

Proof Twenty-Cent Pieces

PF-20 to 70 (Proof). Proof coins were made of all years 1875 to 1878. Most often seen are those of 1875 and 1876. The 1877 and 1878 are Proof-only issues with no related circulation strikes. For some reason, high-quality Proofs of the last two years are very hard to find. Most have been cleaned or even lightly polished. Such coins are given "impaired Proof" designations such as PF-20 or PF-40. Many Proofs in the marketplace have been convincingly retoned to mask problems. Proofs are usually well struck, but more than just a few are somewhat flat on the hair details of Miss Liberty. *Obverse and Reverse:* Proofs that are extensively cleaned and have many hairlines, or that are dull and grainy, are lower level, such as PF-20 to 62. These are not widely desired. With medium hairlines and good reflectivity, an assigned grade of PF-64 is indicated, and with relatively few hairlines, PF-65. In various grades hairlines are most easily seen in the obverse field. PF-66 should have hairlines so delicate that magnification is needed to see them. Above that, a Proof should be free of such lines.

Proof Twenty-Cent Piece
Shown 2x actual size.

	Mintage	Cert	Finest	PF-20	PF-40	PF-60	PF-63	PF-64	PF-65	Recent Auction Record
1875	2,790	229	PF-67			$1,500	$3,000	$5,000	$10,000	$9,200, PF-66, Jun-10
1875S	*10–20*	2	PF-63			15,000	30,000	50,000	100,000	$103,500, PF-64, Jan-09
1876	1,260	270	PF-68			1,500	3,000	5,000	10,000	$14,663, PF-66 CAC, Jun-10
1877	350	230	PF-67	$3,300	$3,750	4,500	6,000	8,000	12,500	$6,900, PF-64Cam, Jun-10
1878	600	285	PF-67	2,550	2,800	4,500	6,000	8,000	12,500	$8,050, PF-65Cam, Jun-10

An Overview of Quarter Dollars

In 1796 the first silver quarters were struck at the Philadelphia Mint. The Draped Bust obverse in combination with the Small Eagle reverse was produced only in this year, after which no pieces of this denomination were produced until 1804. At that time the Draped Bust obverse was continued, but now with the Heraldic Eagle reverse. The coinage proved to be brief and lasted only through 1807, after which no quarters were struck until 1815. The new quarters dated 1815 were of the Capped Bust style, by John Reich. These were produced intermittently through 1838. In that year the Liberty Seated motif, by Christian Gobrecht, made its debut. Such pieces were produced continuously through 1891, with several modifications as to design and metallic content. The Liberty Head quarter, today called the Barber quarter after its designer, was introduced in 1892 and minted continuously through 1916. The obverse features the head of Miss Liberty, and the reverse a heraldic eagle. In late 1916 the Standing Liberty by Hermon A. MacNeil became the new design. This was produced through 1930, except for 1922. Some changes to both the obverse and reverse were made partway through 1917.

The Washington quarter dollar was struck in 1932 to observe the 200th anniversary of the birth of our first president. Pieces have been struck continuously since then, except for 1933, and with none dated 1975. In 1976 a special Bicentennial motif was introduced. Beginning in 1999 the statehood quarters were launched, issued at the rate of five per year, covering all 50 states, each coin having its own distinctive design. After this successful and popular program came quarter dollars with motifs celebrating the District of Columbia and U.S. territories. Others commemorating national parks have been slated for 2010 through 2021.

While there are no super-rarities among the different *types* of quarter dollars, the first one, the 1796 with Draped Bust obverse and Small Eagle reverse, is hard to find and expensive in all grades. The values are, of course, justified by the great demand for this single-year type.

The collector's greatest challenge in finding a decent strike is in the short-lived 1804–1807 type with Heraldic Eagle reverse. Sufficient quantities were made that examples from these years are not rarities, but nearly all are weakly struck. Quarters of the 1815–1828 Capped Bust type, large planchet, are available easily enough in worn grades but are scarce to rare in Mint State. Some cherrypicking is needed to find a sharp strike.

Respite from the sharp-strike difficulty is at last found with the 1831–1838 type, Capped Bust, small diameter, and without E PLURIBUS UNUM. Most are quite nice. Also, for the first time Mint State coins are generally available with frequency in the marketplace, although those with good eye appeal are in the distinct minority.

The Liberty Seated quarters of the several types made from 1838 to 1891 are generally available in proportion to their mintages, with an allowance for the earlier dates being scarcer than the later ones—as they had a longer time to become worn or lost. Many quarters of earlier dates were melted circa 1850–1853, when the price of silver rose on international markets, and such coins were worth slightly more in melt-down value than face value.

Barber quarters, 1892–1916, present no difficulty for the collector, except that there is a challenge to find an example with sharp striking overall, including in the telltale area on the reverse at and near the eagle's leg to the right. MS-65 and better Barber quarters are scarcer than generally known (the same can be said for Barber half dollars). Proofs were sold to collectors and saved, and thus they are available in proportion to their mintages, with probably 70% to 80% surviving.

The Variety 1 Standing Liberty quarter is a rarity if dated 1916, for only 52,000 were struck, and not many were saved. The feasible alternative is the 1917 Variety 1, which is often seen in Mint State, sharply struck, and very beautiful. Standing Liberty quarters of the Variety 2 design, minted from partway through 1917 to 1930, often are weakly struck on the head of Miss Liberty and on the shield rivets, and sometimes other places as well. Searching is needed to locate a nice example.

Washington quarters present no difficulty for collectors. The state, D.C./territorial, and national parks reverses are appealing in their diversity and make a fascinating study in themselves.

For the Collector and Investor: Quarter Dollars as a Specialty

The formation of a specialized collection of quarter dollars from 1796 to date, by dates, mints, and major varieties, is a considerable challenge. As a class, quarters are considerably more difficult to acquire than are either dimes or half dollars. Relatively few numismatists have ever concentrated on the series.

The 1796 is rare and popular both as a date and a type. The 1804, although elusive in worn grades, is of commanding importance if in AU or Mint State. The 1823, 3 Over 2 is a classic rarity and is nearly always encountered well worn. In the same decade the 1827 is famous. Although Mint records indicate that 4,000 circulation strikes were produced in calendar year 1827, they were probably struck from 1825-dated or earlier dies, as no unequivocal circulation strike has ever been located. There are, however, a dozen or so Proofs. Originals are distinguished by the 2 (in the 25 C. denomination) having a curved base, while restrikes, also very rare, have a square-base 2.

One of the unsolved mysteries in numismatics involves certain quarter dollars dated 1815 (the die variety known as Browning-1) and 1825, 5 Over 3 (Browning-2), which are often seen counter-stamped, above the cap, with either an E or an L. Hundreds exist. As other quarter-dollar die varieties were made during this period, but only these two bear counterstamps, it may be that this was done either at the Mint or elsewhere before they were generally distributed.

Ard W. Browning's 1925 text, *The Early Quarters of the United States, 1796–1838,* remains the standard reference on the series, together with new information added here and there, including in issues of the *John Reich Journal,* the magazine of the John Reich Collectors Society.

The panorama of Liberty Seated quarters from 1838 to 1891 is highlighted by several rarities, notably the 1842 Small Date (known only in Proof format) and the 1873-CC Without Arrows (of which only five are known, at least three being Mint State). The others are generally available, but some can be almost impossible to find in Mint State, the 1849-O, certain early San Francisco issues, and Carson City coins of the early 1870s being well known in this regard. From the mid-1870s onward Mint State coins are generally available, including choice and gem pieces. Proofs from 1858 onward can be found in proportion to their mintages, with later dates often being seen with higher numerical designations than are earlier ones.

Barber quarters are collectible by date and mint, although the "big three" rarities, the 1896-S, 1901-S, and 1913-S, are expensive and hard to find.

Standing Liberty quarters, 1916–1930, represent a short-lived series, one easy enough to collect in grades up to MS-63, except for the rare 1918-S, 8 Over 7 overdate. Finding higher-grade coins that are sharply struck is another matter entirely, and over the years few sets of this nature have been assembled.

Washington quarters are all collectible, with no great rarities. However, in relation to the demand for them, certain early issues are elusive, the 1932-D being best known in this regard. Modern issues, including the Bicentennial, statehood, D.C./territorial, and national parks coins, are at once plentiful, inexpensive, and interesting.

RECOMMENDED READING

Bowers, Q. David. *A Guide Book of Washington and State Quarters,* Atlanta, GA, 2006.
Bressett, Kenneth. *The Official Whitman Statehood Quarters Collector's Handbook,* New York, 2000.
Briggs, Larry. *The Comprehensive Encyclopedia of United States Seated Quarters,* Lima, Ohio, 1991.
Browning, Ard W. *The Early Quarter Dollars of the United States, 1796–1838,* New York, 1925 (reprinted 1992).
Cline, J.H. *Standing Liberty Quarters* (4th ed.), 2007.
Fivaz, Bill, and Stanton, J.T. *The Cherrypickers' Guide to Rare Die Varieties* (4th ed., vol. II), Atlanta, GA, 2006.
Haseltine, J.W. *Type Table of United States Dollars, Half Dollars and Quarter Dollars,* Philadelphia, 1881 (reprinted 1927, 1968).
Kelman, Keith N. *Standing Liberty Quarters,* 1976.
Lawrence, David. *The Complete Guide to Barber Quarters,* Virginia Beach, VA, 1989.
Tompkins, Steve M. *Early United States Quarters, 1796–1838,* Sequim, WA, 2010.

DRAPED BUST, SMALL EAGLE REVERSE (1796)

Designer Robert Scot; weight 6.74 grams; composition .8924 silver, .1076 copper; approx. diameter 27.5 mm; reeded edge. All coined at Philadelphia.

Browning-2.

History. The U.S. Mint coined its first quarter dollar in 1796. Its design followed that of other silver U.S. coins. Only 6,146 were made, followed by a production hiatus until 1804, by which time a new reverse was used. Thus the 1796 was isolated as a single-year type.

Striking and Sharpness. On the obverse, check the hair details and the star centers. Most are well struck. On the reverse, most are well struck except for the head of the eagle, which can be shallow or flat, especially on the B-2 variety (there are two known die varieties for this year, B-1 being the rarer). Rarely is a Full Details coin encountered. The dentils are unusually bold and serve to frame the motifs. Check for planchet adjustment marks. Sharp striking (as on B-2) will add to the value. Most MS specimens have excellent eye appeal.

Availability. Examples are available in all grades from well worn to superb MS. Nearly all of the latter are highly prooflike, but there are some exceptions.

AU-50, 53, 55, 58 (About Uncirculated). *Obverse:* Light wear is seen on the hair area above the ear and extending to left of the forehead, on the ribbon, on the drapery at the shoulder, and on the high points of the bust line, more so at AU-50 than at 53 or 55. An AU-58 coin has minimal traces of wear. Concerning luster: An AU-50 coin has luster in protected areas among the stars and letters, with little in the open fields or on the portrait. At AU-58, most luster remains in the fields, but is worn away on the highest parts of the motifs. *Reverse:* Light wear is seen on the eagle's body (note: this area is nearly always lightly struck) and the edges of the wings. Light wear is seen on the wreath and lettering. Luster is the best key to actual wear. This ranges from perhaps 20% remaining in protected areas (at AU-50) to nearly full mint bloom (at AU-58).

MS-60 to 70 (Mint State). *Obverse:* At MS-60, some abrasion and contact marks are evident, most noticeably on the cheek, the drapery, and the right field. Luster is present, but may be dull or lifeless, and interrupted in patches. On prooflike coins the contact marks are more prominent. At MS-63, contact marks are very few, and abrasion is hard to detect except under magnification, although this type is sometimes graded liberally due to its rarity. An MS-65 coin has no abrasion, and contact marks are so minute as to require magnification. Luster should be full and rich. Grades above MS-65 have fewer marks as perfection is approached. *Reverse:* Comments apply as for the obverse, except that abrasion and contact marks are most noticeable on the eagle at the center, a situation complicated by the fact that this area is typically flatly struck (except on the B-2 variety). Grading is best done by the obverse, then verified by the reverse. The field area is small and is protected by lettering and the wreath and in any given grade shows fewer marks than on the obverse.

	Mintage	Cert	Avg	%MS	AU-55	AU-58	MS-60	MS-62	MS-63	MS-64	MS-65	Recent Auction Record
1796 †	6,146	152	34.4	20	$52,500	$63,500	$70,000	$87,500	$105,000	$150,000	$270,000	$103,500, MS-64, Aug-08

† Ranked in the *100 Greatest U.S. Coins* (third edition).

DRAPED BUST, HERALDIC EAGLE REVERSE (1804–1807)

Designer Robert Scot; weight 6.74 grams; composition .8924 silver, .1076 copper; approx. diameter 27.5 mm; reeded edge. All coined at Philadelphia.

Browning-4.

History. Early on, the U.S. Mint's production of silver coins in any given year depended on requests made by depositors of silver; they were not made for the Mint's own account. After 1796 no quarters were struck until 1804. When production started up again, the Draped Bust obverse was used, but with the new Heraldic Eagle reverse—similar to that on other silver (and gold) denominations of the time.

Striking and Sharpness. Virtually all examples are lightly struck in one area or another. On the obverse, check the hair details and the star centers. On the reverse, check the shield, stars, feathers, and other design elements. The dentils and rims on both sides often have problems. Quarters of 1807 are usually the lightest struck. Also check for planchet adjustment marks. Sharp striking and excellent eye appeal add to a coin's value. This series often is misgraded due to lack of understanding of its strike anomalies.

Availability. All dates are collectible, with 1804 being scarcer than the others and a rarity in MS. Some die varieties are rare. High-grade coins with Full Details are very rare.

AU-50, 53, 55, 58 (About Uncirculated). *Obverse:* Light wear is seen on the hair area above the ear and extending to left of the forehead, on the ribbon, and on the drapery at the shoulder, more so at AU-50 than at 53 or 55. An AU-58 coin has minimal traces of wear. Concerning luster: An AU-50 coin has luster in protected areas among the stars and letters, with little in the open fields or on the portrait. At AU-58, most luster is present in the fields, but is worn away on the highest parts of the motifs. *Reverse:* The eagle's neck, the tips and top of the wings, the clouds, and the tail now show noticeable wear, as do other features. Luster ranges from perhaps 20% remaining in protected areas (at AU-50) to nearly full mint bloom (at AU-58). Often the reverse retains much more luster than the obverse, more so on quarter dollars than on other denominations of this design.

MS-60 to 70 (Mint State). *Obverse:* At MS-60, some abrasion and contact marks are evident, most noticeably on the cheek, the drapery, and the right field. Luster is present, but may be dull or lifeless, and interrupted in patches. At MS-63, contact marks are very few, and abrasion is hard to detect except under magnification. An MS-65 coin has no abrasion, and contact marks are so minute as to require magnification. Luster should be full and rich. Coins graded above MS-65 are more theoretical than actual for this type—but they do exist, and are defined by having fewer marks as perfection is approached. Expect weakness in some areas. *Reverse:* Comments apply as for the obverse, except that abrasion and contact marks are most noticeable on the eagle's neck, the tips of the wing, and the tail. The field area is complex, without much open space, given the stars above the eagle, the arrows and olive branch, and other features; accordingly, marks are not as noticeable as on the obverse.

1806, 6 Over 5

	Mintage	Cert	Avg	%MS	AU-50	AU-55	MS-60	MS-62	MS-63	MS-64	MS-65	Recent Auction Record
1804	6,738	99	17.2	5	$45,000	$65,000	$80,000	$115,000	$150,000	$285,000	$350,000	$40,250, EF-45, Feb-09
1805	121,394	214	27.4	6	5,250	6,500	9,000	15,000	20,000	36,000	87,500	$5,296, AU-50 CAC, Mar-10
1806, All kinds	206,124											
1806, 6 Over 5		95	30.1	9	5,900	7,250	10,500	17,000	24,000	38,000	95,000	$14,950, MS-62, Mar-10
1806		342	27.2	12	5,000	6,250	9,000	12,000	16,000	26,000	85,000	$23,000, MS-64, Jan-10
1807	220,643	165	30.4	18	5,000	6,250	10,000	12,500	17,500	32,000	80,000	$4,888, AU-58, Nov-09

CAPPED BUST, VARIETY 1, LARGE DIAMETER
(1815–1828)

Designer John Reich; weight 6.74 grams; composition .8924 silver, .1076 copper; approx. diameter 27 mm; reeded edge. All coined at Philadelphia.

Browning-1.

History. The Capped Bust design, by John Reich, was introduced on the half dollar of 1807 but was not used on the quarter until 1815.

Striking and Sharpness. Striking sharpness varies. On the obverse, check the hair of Miss Liberty, the broach clasp (a particular point of observation), and the star centers. On this type the stars are often well defined (in contrast with half dollars of the same design). On the reverse, check the neck of the eagle and its wings, and the letters. Examine dentils on both sides. When weakness occurs it is usually in the center.

Availability. Most quarters of this type range from slightly scarce to rare, with the 1823, 3 Over 2, and the 1827 being famous rarities. Typical coins range from well worn to Fine and VF. AU and MS coins are elusive (and are usually dated before the 1820s), and gems are particularly rare.

AU-50, 53, 55, 58 (About Uncirculated). *Obverse:* Light wear is seen on the cap, the hair below LIBERTY, the curl on the neck, the hair near the clasp, and the drapery. At AU-50 and 53, luster remains only in protected areas. At AU-58, the luster is extensive except in the open area of the field, especially to the right. *Reverse:* Wear is evident on the eagle's neck, the top of the wings, the claws, and the flat band above the eagle. At AU-50 and 53, there still is significant luster, more than on the obverse; an AU-58 coin has nearly full luster. Generally, light wear is most obvious on the obverse.

MS-60 to 70 (Mint State). *Obverse:* At MS-60, some abrasion and contact marks are evident, most noticeably on the cheek, the hair below LIBERTY, and the area near the drapery clasp. Luster is present, but may be dull or lifeless, and interrupted in patches. At MS-63, contact marks are very few, and abrasion is hard to detect except under magnification. An MS-65 coin has no abrasion, and contact marks are so minute as to require magnification. Luster should be full and rich. Grades above MS-65 are seen now and again; they have fewer marks as perfection is approached. *Reverse:* Comments apply as for the obverse, except that abrasion and contact marks are most noticeable on the eagle's neck, the top of the wings, the claws, and the flat band that surrounds the incuse motto. The field is mainly protected by design elements and does not show abrasion as much as does the obverse on a given coin.

1818, 8 Over 5

1818, Normal Date

1819, Small 9

1819, Large 9

1820, Small 0

1820, Large 0

1822, 25 Over 50c

1823, 3 Over 2

1824, 4 Over 2

1825, 5 Over 2

1825, 5 Over 4

1828, 25 Over 50c

	Mintage	Cert	Avg	%MS	AU-50	AU-55	MS-60	MS-62	MS-63	MS-64	MS-65	Recent Auction Record
1815	89,235	110	50.2	46	$1,900	$2,500	$3,200	$4,500	$7,000	$11,250	$35,000	$37,375, MS-66, Jan-10
1818, 8 Over 5	361,174	92	55.3	65	1,900	2,500	3,200	4,250	6,000	11,000	32,500	$16,100, MS-65, Jun-10
1818, Normal Date	*	375	45.4	37	1,700	2,400	3,000	4,000	5,750	10,750	27,000	$19,550, MS-66, Jan-10
1819, Small 9	144,000	28	23.5	11	1,900	2,500	3,200	4,500	7,500	14,000	32,500	$2,070, AU-50, Jan-10
1819, Large 9	*	17	40.2	12	1,900	2,700	3,500	6,250	11,000	20,000	40,000	$3,738, AU-55, Jan-10
1820, Small 0	127,444	13	39.4	15	1,900	2,400	3,000	4,500	6,000	16,000	45,000	$17,825, MS-64, Mar-10
1820, Large 0	*	20	41.7	15	2,200	3,000	3,500	5,750	10,000	18,000	37,500	$6,900, MS-64, Feb-10
1821	216,851	191	43.0	29	1,900	2,500	3,200	4,500	6,500	11,000	30,000	$6,325, MS-63, Jun-10
1822	64,080	84	43.8	19	2,600	3,350	3,850	5,750	8,500	25,000		$2,990, AU-50, Aug-09
1822, 25 Over 50c	*	12	38.1	25	24,000	28,000	40,000	55,000	70,000	100,000	150,000	$184,000, MS-66, Apr-09
1823, 3 Over 2	17,800	8	43.8	25	100,000	125,000	—					$74,750, VF-30, Apr-09
1824, 4 Over 2	168,000	52	28.5	6	5,000	8,000	20,000	30,000	50,000	100,000	150,000	$6,900, AU-50, Feb-09
1825, 5 Over 2	*	16	39.6	0	8,000	12,000	18,000	25,000	30,000	45,000	*	$8,050, AU-55, Sep-09
1825, 5 Over 4	*	116	45.8	23	1,900	2,500	3,200	4,500	6,000	11,000	30,000	$1,840, AU-55, Sep-09
1828	102,000	128	49.1	34	1,800	2,500	3,250	4,500	8,000	12,500	30,000	$3,577, MS-62, Nov-09
1828, 25 Over 50c	*	13	36.5	8	4,000	8,500	13,000	16,000	22,000	*	*	$11,500, AU-58, Jan-09

* Included in number above. *Note:* Although 4,000 1827 quarters were reported to have been made for circulation, their rarity today (only one worn piece is known, and it could be a circulated Proof) suggests that this quantity was for coins struck in calendar-year 1827 but bearing an earlier date, probably 1825.

Proof Capped Bust Quarters, Variety 1, Large Diameter

PF-60 to 70 (Proof). Proofs of some dates were struck for inclusion in sets and for numismatists. All authentic Proofs are rarities. Some deeply toned coins, and coins with patches of mint luster, have been described as Proofs, but most are not. *Obverse and Reverse:* Proofs that are exten- sively cleaned and have many hairlines, or that are dull and grainy, are lower level, such as PF-60 to 62. While any early Proof garners collector interest, lower levels are not of great interest to specialists unless they are of rare die varieties. With medium hairlines, an assigned grade of PF-64 may be in order, and with relatively few, PF-65. PF-66 should have hairlines so delicate that magnification is needed to see them. Above that, a Proof should be free of such lines. Grading is highly subjective with early Proofs, and eye appeal also is a factor.

Proof Capped Bust Quarter: Variety 1, Large Diameter
Shown 1.5x actual size.
Browning-4.

1827, Original
Curl-Base 2 in 25c.
(Shown 1.5x actual size.)

1827, Restrike
Square-Base 2 in 25c.
(Shown 1.5x actual size.)

	Est Mintage	Cert	Finest	PF-60	PF-63	PF-64	PF-65	Recent Auction Record
1820	6–10	2	PF-67		$45,000	$90,000	$130,000	$97,750, PF-64, May-08
1821	6–10	4	PF-67		40,000	65,000	100,000	$51,750, PF-64, Apr-09
1822	6–10	2	PF-68		40,000	60,000	100,000	$40,250, PF-63, Apr-09
1823, 3 Over 2	2–4	1	PF-64		100,000	150,000		$138,000, PF-64, Feb-99
1824, 4 Over 2	2–4	1	PF-63		50,000	75,000		
1825, 5 Over 4 Over 3	6–10	n/a	n/a		40,000	60,000		$4,313, PF-63, Jan-10
1827, 7 Over 3, Original †	20–30	4	PF-64		150,000	200,000	300,000	$126,500, PF-63, Jan-04
1827, 7 Over 3, Restrike	20–30	11	PF-66		50,000	80,000	115,000	$69,000, PF-66, Jul-09
1828	8–12	6	PF-66	$15,000	40,000	60,000	100,000	$14,950, PF-65, Jan-10

† Ranked in the *100 Greatest U.S. Coins* (third edition).

CAPPED BUST, VARIETY 2, REDUCED DIAMETER, MOTTO REMOVED (1831–1838)

Designer William Kneass; weight 6.74 grams; composition .8924 silver, .1076 copper; diameter 24.3 mm; reeded edge. All coined at Philadelphia.

Browning-1.

History. Capped Bust, Reduced Diameter quarter dollars are similar in overall appearance to the preceding type, but with important differences. The diameter is smaller, E PLURIBUS UNUM no longer appears on the reverse, and the dentils are smaller and restyled.

Striking and Sharpness. Nearly all coins of this type are very well struck. Check all areas for sharpness. Some quarters of 1833 and 1834 are struck from rusted or otherwise imperfect dies and can be less attractive than coins from undamaged dies.

Availability. Examples are readily available of all dates, including many of the first year of issue. Mint frost ranges from satiny (usual) to deeply frosty.

AU-50, 53, 55, 58 (About Uncirculated). *Obverse:* Grading guidelines are the same as for the 1815–1828 type, except the rims are more uniform, striking is usually very sharp, and the wear occurs evenly on both sides. Light wear is seen on the cap, the hair below LIBERTY, the curl on the neck, the hair near the clasp, and the drapery. At AU-50 and 53, luster remains only in protected areas. At AU-58, the luster is extensive except in the open area of the field, especially to the right. *Reverse:* Wear is evident on the eagle's neck, the top of the wings, and the claws. At AU-50 and 53, there still is significant luster, more than on the obverse. An AU-58 coin has nearly full luster.

MS-60 to 70 (Mint State). *Obverse:* Grading is similar to that of the 1815–1828 type, except the rims are more uniform, striking is usually very sharp, and the wear occurs evenly on both sides. At MS-60, some abrasion and contact marks are evident, most noticeably on the cheek, the hair below LIBERTY, and the area near the drapery clasp. Luster is present, but may be dull or lifeless, and interrupted in patches. At MS-63, contact marks are very few, and abrasion is hard to detect except under magnification. An MS-65 coin has no abrasion, and contact marks are so minute as to require magnification. Luster should be full and rich. Grades above MS-65 are seen now and again, and have fewer marks as perfection is approached. *Reverse:* Comments apply as for the obverse, except that abrasion and contact marks are most noticeable on the eagle's neck, the top of the wings, and the claws.

1831, Small Letters
Browning-2.

1831, Large Letters
Browning-6.

1834, O Over F in OF
FS-25-1834-901.

Shown 1.5x actual size.

	Mintage	Cert	Avg	%MS	AU-55	MS-60	MS-62	MS-63	MS-64	MS-65	MS-66	Recent Auction Record
1831, Small Letters	398,000	47	51.2	26	$950	$1,150	$2,400	$4,500	$10,000	$27,500	$40,000	$7,015, MS-64, Jan-10
1831, Large Letters	*	31	50.4	26	950	1,150	2,400	4,500	10,000	30,000	—	$1,380, AU-58, Mar-10
1832	320,000	111	51.2	39	950	1,150	2,400	5,000	12,000	32,500	50,000	$3,738, MS-63, Jun-10
1833	156,000	144	49.5	33	1,100	1,500	3,000	5,500	12,500	32,500	—	$868, AU-55, Oct-09
1834	286,000	352	50.0	35	950	1,150	2,400	4,300	8,500	24,000	40,000	$3,795, MS-63, Jun-10
1834, O Over F in OF (a)	*	36	46.8	17	1,000	1,300	2,800	5,000	12,000	27,500		$2,760, MS-62, Feb-06
1835	1,952,000	370	48.2	23	950	1,150	2,400	4,300	8,500	27,500	40,000	$1,150, AU-55, Nov-09
1836	472,000	129	42.4	24	950	1,150	2,600	4,700	13,000	30,000	—	$4,313, MS-62, Feb-10
1837	252,400	198	52.9	43	950	1,150	2,400	4,300	8,500	24,000	40,000	$6,334, AU-55, Jan-10
1838	366,000	178	51.8	39	950	1,150	2,400	4,300	8,500	27,500	40,000	$3,910, MS-63, Jun-10

* Included in number above. **a.** The OF is re-engraved with the letters connected at the top, and the first A in AMERICA is also re-engraved. Other identifying characteristics: there is no period after the C in the denomination; and the 5 and C are further apart than normal.

Proof Capped Bust Quarters, Variety 2, Reduced Diameter, Motto Removed

PF-60 to 70 (Proof). Proofs were struck for inclusion in sets and for sale or trade to numismatists. Most coins offered as Proofs are indeed of this format (as opposed to being high-grade circulation strikes mis-identified as Proofs). Avoid any that show patches of mint frost or that are darkly toned. *Obverse and Reverse:* Proofs that are extensively cleaned and have many hairlines, or that are dull and grainy, are lower level, such as PF-60 to 62. With medium hairlines, an assigned grade of PF-64 may be in order and with relatively few hairlines, PF-65. A PF-66 coin has hairlines so delicate that magnification is needed to see them. Above that, a Proof should be free of such lines. Grading is highly subjective with early Proofs, and eye appeal also is a factor.

**Proof Capped Bust Quarter: Variety 2,
Reduced Diameter, Motto Removed**
Shown 1.5x actual size.

	Est Mintage	Cert	Finest	PF-60	PF-63	PF-64	PF-65	Recent Auction Record
1831, Large Letters	20–25	9	PF-66	$10,000	$22,500	$40,000	$75,000	$51,750, PF-65Cam, Apr-09
1833	10–15	4	PF-65			85,000	175,000	$46,000, PF-65Cam, Apr-09
1834	20–25	9	PF-67	15,000	22,500	40,000	65,000	$58,650, PF-67, Sep-98
1835	10–15	5	PF-65	15,000	25,000	50,000	90,000	$20,700, PF-63, Dec-05
1836	8–12	2	PF-67	15,000	25,000	60,000	100,000	$97,950, PF-67, Jan-06
1837	8–12	2	PF-67	15,000	25,000	60,000	90,000	$132,250, PF-67, Aug-06
1838	8–12	2	PF-68	25,000	35,000	60,000	100,000	$46,000, PF-64, Apr-09

LIBERTY SEATED
(1838–1891)

Variety 1, No Motto Above Eagle (1838–1853): Designer Christian Gobrecht; weight 6.68 grams; composition .900 silver, .100 copper; diameter 24.3 mm; reeded edge; mints: Philadelphia, New Orleans.

Variety 2, Arrows at Date, Rays Around Eagle (1853): Designer Christian Gobrecht; weight 6.22 grams; composition .900 silver, .100 copper; diameter 24.3 mm; reeded edge; mints: Philadelphia, New Orleans.

Variety 3, Arrows at Date, No Rays (1854–1855): Designer Christian Gobrecht; weight 6.22 grams; composition .900 silver, .100 copper; diameter 24.3 mm; reeded edge; mints: Philadelphia, New Orleans, San Francisco.

Variety 1 Resumed, With Weight Standard of Variety 2 (1856–1865): Designer Christian Gobrecht; weight 6.22 grams; composition .900 silver, .100 copper; diameter 24.3 mm; reeded edge; mints: Philadelphia, New Orleans, San Francisco.

Variety 4, Motto Above Eagle (1866–1873): Designer Christian Gobrecht; weight 6.22 grams; composition .900 silver, .100 copper; diameter 24.3 mm; reeded edge; mints: Philadelphia, San Francisco, Carson City.

Variety 5, Arrows at Date (1873–1874): Designer Christian Gobrecht; weight 6.25 grams; composition .900 silver, .100 copper; diameter 24.3 mm; reeded edge; mints: Philadelphia, San Francisco, Carson City.

Variety 4 Resumed, With Weight Standard of Variety 5 (1875–1891): Designer Christian Gobrecht; weight 6.25 grams; composition .900 silver, .100 copper; diameter 24.3 mm; reeded edge; mints: Philadelphia, New Orleans, San Francisco.

History. The long-running Liberty Seated quarter-dollar design was introduced in 1838. Early issues lack drapery at the elbow and have small lettering on the reverse. Drapery was added in 1840 and continued afterward. In 1853 a reduction in weight was indicated with the addition of arrows at the date and rays on the reverse side (in the field around the eagle). The rays were omitted after 1853, but the arrows were retained through 1855. The motto IN GOD WE TRUST was added to the reverse in 1866. Arrows were placed at the date in the years 1873 and 1874 to denote the change of weight from 6.22 to 6.25 grams. The new weight, without the arrows, continued through 1891.

Striking and Sharpness. On the obverse, check the head of Miss Liberty and the star centers. If these are sharp, then check the central part of the seated figure. On the reverse, check the eagle, particularly the area to the lower left of the shield. Check the dentils on both sides. Generally, the earliest issues are well struck, as are those of the 1880s onward. The word LIBERTY is not an infallible guide to grading at lower levels, as on some dies the shield was in lower relief, and the letters wore away less quickly. This guideline should be used in combination with other features.

Availability. Coins of this type are available in proportion to their mintages. MS coins can range from rare to exceedingly rare, as they were mostly ignored by numismatists until the series ended. Quality can vary widely, especially among branch-mint coins.

EF-40, 45 (Extremely Fine). *Obverse:* Further wear than at AU is seen on all areas, especially the thighs and knees, bosom, and head. Little or no luster is seen on most coins. *Reverse:* Further wear than at AU is evident on the eagle's neck, claws, and wings. Some feathers in the right wing may be blended together.

AU-50, 53, 55, 58 (About Uncirculated). *Obverse:* Light wear is seen on the thighs and knees, bosom, and head. There is some luster at AU-50 and 53. At AU-58, the luster is extensive, but incomplete, especially in the right field. *Reverse:* Wear is evident on the eagle's neck, claws, and top of the wings. At AU-50 and 53, there still are traces of luster. An AU-58 coin has nearly full luster, more so than on the obverse, as the design elements protect the small field areas.

MS-60 to 70 (Mint State). *Obverse:* At MS-60, some abrasion and contact marks are evident, most noticeably on the bosom and thighs and knees. Luster is present, but may be dull or lifeless. At MS-63, contact marks are very few, and abrasion is hard to detect except under magnification. An MS-65 coin has no abrasion, and contact marks are sufficiently minute as to require magnification. Check the knees of Liberty and the right field. Luster should be full and rich. Most MS coins of the 1861 to 1865 years, Philadelphia issues, have extensive die striae (from the dies not being completely finished). *Reverse:* Comments apply as for the obverse, except that in lower MS grades abrasion and contact marks are most noticeable on the eagle's neck, the claws, and the top of the wings (harder to see there, however). At MS-65 or higher there are no marks visible to the unaided eye. The field is mainly protected by design elements and does not show abrasion as much as does the obverse on a given coin.

No Drapery   Drapery   1840-O, Drapery, Normal O   1840-O, Drapery, Large O

Shown 1.5x actual size.   *Shown 1.5x actual size.*

1842, Small Date   1842, Large Date

Philadelphia Small Date is Proof only.

1842-O, Small Date   1842-O, Large Date

1853, Repunched Date, No Arrows or Rays
FS-25-1853-301.

1853, 3 Over 4 (Arrows at Date, Rays Around Eagle)
FS-25-1853-1301.

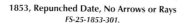

| 1854-O, Normal O | 1854-O, Huge O | 1854-O, Huge O (Detail) |

Shown 1.5x actual size.

	Mintage	Cert	Avg	%MS	AU-50	AU-55	MS-60	MS-62	MS-63	MS-64	MS-65	Recent Auction Record
1838, No Drapery	466,000	142	55.8	49	$750	$1,200	$2,000	$4,250	$6,750	$11,000	$35,000	$14,950, MS-65, Jan-10
1839, No Drapery	491,146	109	52.2	29	750	1,150	1,850	3,500	5,500	11,000	45,000	$9,200, MS-64, Sep-09
1840O, No Drapery	382,200	94	52.1	30	800	1,150	1,900	4,100	8,200	19,000	40,000	$805, AU-55, Feb-10
1840, Drapery	188,127	32	54.2	31	300	400	950	2,500	4,500	10,000	25,000	$14,950, MS-66, Apr-09
1840O, Drapery	43,000	54	55.6	43	500	900	1,300	2,500	3,900	7,500	25,000	$1,495, MS-62, Jan-09
1840O, Drapery, Large O (a)	*	n/a	n/a	n/a	4,750	6,000	9,000					$6,900, AU-53, Jan-06
1841	120,000	43	56.1	58	325	500	900	1,650	2,300	4,400	12,000	$4,313, MS-64, Mar-09
1841O	452,000	57	57.4	61	320	500	800	1,500	1,900	3,650	14,000	$805, AU-58, Nov-09
1842, Large Date (b)	88,000	37	53.5	41	650	1,000	1,750	2,200	4,500	9,000	15,000	$1,840, MS-62, Feb-10
1842O, All kinds	769,000											
1842O, Small Date		12	23.6	8	9,000	13,000	18,000	35,000	75,000	110,000	*	$74,750, MS-63, Aug-06
1842O, Large Date		23	46.8	39	600	850	1,750	2,800	4,800	9,000	*	$2,185, MS-61, Nov-05
1843	645,600	78	59.0	58	175	220	450	900	1,250	3,000	8,000	$4,888, MS-65, Dec-09
1843O	968,000	38	49.2	21	800	1,200	2,500	3,850	7,500	16,000	22,500	$10,350, MS-63, Mar-10
1844	421,200	66	58.5	50	175	250	525	1,250	1,500	3,500	9,500	$1,725, MS-63, Nov-09
1844O	740,000	42	52.1	33	360	550	1,400	2,500	3,700	5,500	12,000	$3,163, MS-64, Dec-09
1845	922,000	87	59.4	57	160	250	550	1,000	1,400	2,350	5,900	$4,888, MS-65, Feb-10
1846	510,000	60	57.6	47	180	280	600	950	1,500	4,000	12,000	$690, MS-61, Dec-08
1847	734,000	55	57.9	55	160	250	575	850	1,200	3,000	9,000	$7,475, MS-66, Apr-09
1847O	368,000	30	49.7	20	750	1,650	3,500	7,500	13,000	25,000	*	$1,265, EF-40 CAC, Jun-10
1848	146,000	28	50.9	39	300	450	1,150	1,850	3,750	6,500	15,000	$4,313, MS-63, Jan-10
1849	340,000	66	54.6	36	250	350	800	1,500	2,200	4,500	12,000	$3,738, MS-64, Feb-09
1849O	**	32	36.5	19	7,000	8,500	13,500	15,000	17,000	25,000	*	$4,560, AU-50, Feb-10
1850	190,800	31	57.5	55	240	400	1,000	1,750	2,800	5,250	11,000	$4,025, MS-64, Jun-09
1850O	412,000	50	53.8	44	475	800	1,600	2,700	3,400	8,000	20,000	$4,370, MS-64, Mar-10
1851	160,000	28	53.9	39	300	400	1,000	1,500	2,000	4,500	9,500	$863, AU-58, Jul-09
1851O	88,000	24	33.1	17	3,000	4,500	8,000	15,000	32,500	*	*	$2,760, AU-50, Jan-06
1852	177,060	40	57.3	63	300	375	675	1,200	2,000	4,000	7,500	$2,760, MS-64, Feb-10
1852O	96,000	22	35.2	9	5,000	7,000	9,000	27,500	42,500	*	*	$35,938, MS-63, Apr-09
1853, Repunched Dt, No Arrows or Rays (c)	44,200	34	51.6	56	3,000	3,500	4,000	5,000	7,800	8,900	10,000	$47,150, MS-65, Apr-09
1853, Var 2	15,210,020	807	54.3	45	300	450	900	1,200	2,000	4,200	15,000	$3,853, MS-64 CAC, Mar-10
1853, Var 2, 3 Over 4 (d)	*	39	43.3	26	650	1,200	2,000	3,500	5,500	17,500	*	$3,450, MS-63, May-09
1853O	1,332,000	65	49.4	22	1,100	1,600	3,250	6,000	11,000	22,500	30,000	$13,800, MS-64, Jan-10
1854	12,380,000	422	56.6	49	225	300	500	900	1,100	2,500	8,000	$288, AU-55, Mar-10
1854O	1,484,000	76	51.5	45	250	550	1,200	2,000	2,500	4,500	15,000	$1,380, MS-63, Jun-09
1854O, Huge O (e)	*	30	20.8	0	12,000	15,000	17,000	*	*	*	*	$1,610, VG-10 CAC, Jun-10
1855	2,857,000	112	56.5	44	225	300	575	1,025	1,450	4,000	12,000	$10,350, MS-66, Apr-09
1855O	176,000	28	44.1	39	2,000	2,250	5,000	10,000	15,000	35,000	*	$1,265, AU-53, Feb-06
1855S	396,400	19	49.4	26	1,100	2,000	3,000	5,500	8,500	18,500	40,000	$16,100, MS-64, May-09

* Included in number above. ** Included in 1850-O mintage. **a.** The O mintmark punch is about 25% larger than normal. There are two known reverse dies for this variety, with one showing doubled denticles. **b.** The Large Date was used on the Philadelphia Mint's 1842 coins struck for circulation. The 1842 Small Date was made in Proof format only (see Proof listings). **c.** The secondary 5 and 3 are evident south of the primary digits. In the past, this variety was erroneously attributed as a 53 Over 2 overdate. This is the only die known for 1853 that lacks the arrows and rays. **d.** In addition to the 3 punched over a 4, there is also evidence of the repunched 8 and 5 (weaker images slightly north and west of the primary digits). The right arrow shaft is also doubled, north of the primary. "On well-worn or late-die-state specimens, the doubling of the arrow shaft may be the only evidence of the overdate. This is the only quarter dollar date known to be punched over the *following year!*" (*Cherrypickers' Guide to Rare Die Varieties*, fourth edition, volume II). **e.** The Huge O mintmark is very large, extremely thick on the left side, and irregular, suggesting that it was carved into the die by hand.

1856-S, S Over Small S
FS-25-1856S-501.

1857, Clashed Reverse Die
FS-25-1857-901.

1873, Close 3

1873, Open 3

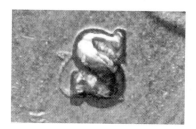

1877-S, S Over Horizontal S
FS-25-1877S-501.

	Mintage	Cert	Avg	%MS	EF-40	AU-50	MS-60	MS-62	MS-63	MS-64	MS-65	Recent Auction Record
1856	7,264,000	162	59.0	64	$75	$160	$325	$425	$575	$1,350	$4,100	$920, MS-64 CAC, Jan-10
1856O	968,000	50	54.2	38	80	250	1,100	1,800	2,500	5,000	12,000	$5,175, MS-64, Jun-09
1856S, All kinds	286,000											
1856S		17	43.2	18	500	1,200	6,500	10,000	15,000	20,000	45,000	$5,750, AU-58, Sep-09
1856S, S Over Small S (a)		4	19.5	0	750	1,400	6,750	*	*			$39,100, AU-58, Aug-07
1857	9,644,000	381	59.9	73	75	160	325	425	575	1,100	3,400	$6,038, MS-67, Jan-10
1857, Clashed Rev Die (b)	*	4	49.0	50	500	750						
1857O	1,180,000	51	55.8	31	150	400	1,200	2,200	4,000	8,000	*	$6,325, MS-64, Aug-09
1857S	82,000	35	51.9	31	600	1,200	4,000	6,000	8,750	14,500	*	$16,100, MS-64 CAC, Jan-10
1858	7,368,000	287	58.5	67	75	160	325	425	575	1,100	3,700	$920, MS-64 CAC, Jun-10
1858O	520,000	32	54.5	22	125	350	1,800	4,900	7,500	14,500	25,000	$4,888, MS-62, Mar-09
1858S	121,000	15	31.9	7	2,000	5,250	20,000	50,000	—			$5,175, EF-45, Jun-10
1859	1,343,200	92	58.9	61	80	160	400	800	1,100	2,000	5,750	$1,553, MS-64, Dec-09
1859O	260,000	31	56.5	35	135	400	1,250	2,500	4,000	6,000	12,000	$920, AU-53, Nov-09
1859S	80,000	10	40.4	0	4,200	17,500	55,000	*	*	*	*	$4,025, EF-40, Sep-08
1860	804,400	73	59.9	53	80	160	400	700	975	1,550	5,500	$15,525, MS-66 CAC, Jan-10
1860O	388,000	62	56.0	48	95	375	1,000	1,550	2,400	6,250	15,000	$5,463, MS-64, Oct-09
1860S	56,000	11	40.3	9	12,500	22,500	50,000	65,000	—			$9,200, VF-30, Nov-09
1861	4,853,600	446	60.5	67	80	160	325	450	750	1,300	4,000	$2,530, MS-65, Feb-10
1861S	96,000	19	29.8	0	2,000	10,000	40,000	*	*	*	*	$4,025, EF-40, May-10
1862	932,000	118	61.0	73	85	160	325	450	750	1,300	4,000	$5,808, MS-66 CAC, Jan-10
1862S	67,000	36	49.9	39	800	1,800	3,800	4,750	8,500	14,500	*	$2,530, AU-50, Nov-09
1863	191,600	46	60.2	70	240	375	625	850	1,100	1,550	4,400	$489, AU-50, Feb-10
1864	93,600	47	55.7	70	275	425	625	850	1,700	2,550	5,500	$5,980, MS-66, Aug-09
1864S	20,000	34	34.4	21	3,800	5,500	12,000	25,000	30,000	42,000	*	$4,025, EF-40, Mar-10
1865	58,800	36	50.4	39	275	500	800	1,050	1,400	3,000	8,000	$690, AU-55, Nov-09
1865S	41,000	35	50.6	46	1,000	1,500	3,000	5,000	6,000	8,000	15,000	$863, EF-40, Nov-09
1866, Var 4	16,800	37	56.3	76	1,600	1,850	2,200	2,400	2,600	3,750	6,250	$1,840, EF-40, Nov-09
1866S	28,000	17	32.8	24	2,500	3,000	4,500	7,500	10,000	15,000	40,000	$2,300, VF-35, Feb-09

* Included in number above. **a.** A larger S mintmark was punched over a much smaller S mintmark, the latter probably intended for half-dime production. **b.** The reverse clashed with the reverse die of an 1857 Flying Eagle cent. Images of the cent reverse die are easily visible on either side of the eagle's neck, within the shield, and below the eagle's left wing.

	Mintage	Cert	Avg	%MS	EF-40	AU-50	MS-60	MS-62	MS-63	MS-64	MS-65	Recent Auction Record
1867	20,000	17	51.5	59	$1,350	$1,650	$2,600	$4,000	$8,500	$17,000		$1,725, EF-45, Nov-09
1867S	48,000	10	37.1	20	4,500	8,400	18,000	25,000	35,000	50,000		$18,400, MS-62, Sep-09
1868	29,400	26	56.6	69	525	625	1,200	1,400	2,200	5,000	$9,000	$69,000, MS-66 CAC, Jan-10
1868S	96,000	31	47.9	35	900	1,500	3,500	6,100	7,750	15,500	25,000	$5,175, MS-62, Dec-09
1869	16,000	19	46.6	53	900	1,100	1,900	2,450	3,000	6,000	12,000	$80,500, MS-66, Jan-10
1869S	76,000	21	43.0	29	1,000	1,600	4,000	5,500	6,500	10,000	15,000	$978, EF-40, Aug-07
1870	86,400	26	53.6	42	275	450	800	1,100	2,200	4,500	8,750	$4,025, MS-65, Jan-10
1870CC	8,340	24	24.6	4	35,000	52,500	75,000					$40,250, AU-50, Sep-06
1871	118,200	33	57.3	70	225	350	600	900	1,500	4,400	8,000	$2,990, MS-64, Oct-09
1871CC	10,890	12	25.5	8	28,000	47,500						$6,900, VG-8, Aug-09
1871S	30,900	24	52.8	58	1,500	2,750	5,250	8,000	10,000	15,000	17,500	$5,750, AU-50, Nov-09
1872	182,000	41	53.0	49	190	300	650	1,200	2,100	3,900	7,900	$2,530, MS-63, Feb-10
1872CC	22,850	22	20.9	5	10,000	16,000	40,000	75,000				$12,075, EF-45, Apr-09
1872S	83,000	17	44.7	47	6,000	8,000	15,000	20,000	25,000	35,000	55,000	$86,250, MS-66, Sep-08
1873, Close 3	40,000	9	36.8	33	1,500	2,500	18,000	30,000	40,000			$34,500, MS-63, Apr-09
1873, Open 3	172,000	27	56.9	63	200	300	500	750	1,100	2,000	5,500	$9,200, MS-66 PL, Feb-09
1873CC, Var 4 † *(5 known)*	4,000	3	56.7	67			345,000	390,000	435,000	600,000		$431,250, MS-63, Jan-09
1873, Var 5	1,271,160	189	57.3	55	225	425	850	1,150	1,650	2,000	3,500	$630, AU-58, Feb-10
1873CC	12,462	17	20.8	6	25,000	30,000	50,000	70,000	80,000	110,000		$74,750, AU55, Jan-07
1873S	156,000	44	51.1	39	350	750	2,000	3,500	6,000	9,500	20,000	$1,092, AU-58, Jan-09
1874	471,200	70	58.7	61	200	450	900	1,200	1,550	2,200	4,700	$1,323, MS-63, Oct-09
1874S	392,000	132	60.8	81	265	485	950	1,200	1,450	1,850	3,750	$4,600, MS-66, Jan-10
1875	4,292,800	253	61.9	82	65	160	275	375	550	900	1,800	$1,553, MS-65, Apr-09
1875CC	140,000	39	52.3	36	600	1,000	2,500	3,500	6,500	10,000	40,000	$7,475, MS-64, Jun-10
1875S	680,000	78	58.5	68	200	300	600	1,100	1,400	2,000	4,000	$1,380, MS-64, Mar-10
1876	17,816,000	408	60.8	78	65	160	275	400	550	950	1,850	$518, MS-63, Mar-10
1876CC	4,944,000	220	57.4	64	120	250	600	1,000	1,300	2,000	4,500	$7,763, MS-63, May-09
1876S	8,596,000	240	61.2	78	65	160	275	400	550	1,000	2,000	$863, MS-64, Sep-09
1877	10,911,200	329	62.6	85	65	160	275	400	550	900	1,800	$7,708, MS-68, Feb-10
1877CC (c)	4,192,000	368	60.1	78	120	220	475	700	900	1,750	2,500	$703, MS-63, Dec-09
1877S	8,996,000	285	61.8	85	65	160	275	350	550	900	1,850	$252, MS-61, Feb-10
1877S, S Over Horiz S (d)	*	36	59.3	61	250	400	800	1,100	2,200	3,000	5,000	$1,725, MS-64, Aug-09
1878	2,260,000	83	61.7	80	65	150	250	350	550	1,300	2,900	$1,006, MS-64, May-10
1878CC	996,000	211	59.6	73	200	300	700	1,000	1,500	2,000	4,000	$3,220, MS-65, Jun-10
1878S	140,000	27	53.2	59	700	1,300	3,000	3,750	4,750	13,500	23,000	$3,220, AU-55, Nov-09
1879	13,600	194	63.8	93	325	400	575	700	800	1,150	2,400	$4,888, MS-67, Dec-09
1880	13,600	123	63.6	91	325	400	575	700	800	1,150	2,400	$1,898, MS-65, Mar-10
1881	12,000	92	62.4	89	375	425	625	750	850	1,300	2,500	$1,265, MS-64, Jan-10
1882	15,200	66	61.7	85	325	425	625	750	900	1,350	2,300	$2,789, MS-66, Mar-10
1883	14,400	72	63.1	93	325	425	625	750	900	1,450	2,200	$2,990, MS-66, Jan-10
1884	8,000	78	59.4	85	550	600	700	825	900	1,350	2,050	$2,070, MS-65, Feb-10
1885	13,600	80	61.4	83	325	400	675	950	1,100	1,700	2,750	$4,025, MS-66, Feb-09
1886	5,000	36	61.5	86	675	750	1,000	1,200	1,400	2,100	3,500	$3,220, MS-65, Jan-10
1887	10,000	96	62.2	85	475	525	750	1,000	1,100	1,350	2,050	$4,888, MS-66 CAC, Jun-10
1888	10,001	105	63.7	96	500	650	700	850	1,000	1,250	2,050	$575, MS-61, Mar-10
1888S	1,216,000	114	60.1	76	70	150	300	650	850	1,750	3,000	$253, AU-55, Mar-10
1889	12,000	167	64.4	94	325	450	600	675	750	1,000	1,800	$3,738, MS-65, Jan-10
1890	80,000	171	63.5	91	175	300	525	625	775	1,100	1,850	$920, MS-64, Mar-10
1891	3,920,000	534	62.3	84	65	160	260	350	550	1,000	1,800	$2,300, MS-66, Feb-10
1891O	68,000	25	45.6	40	1,200	2,000	4,000	5,500	8,000	20,000	50,000	$2,760, EF-45, Jul-09
1891S	2,216,000	154	61.3	81	70	160	260	350	550	1,000	2,300	$3,450, MS-66, Mar-10

* Included in number above. † Ranked in the *100 Greatest U.S. Coins* (third edition). **c.** The 1877-CC quarter with fine edge-reeding is scarcer than that with normally spaced reeding; in the marketplace, there is no price differential. **d.** This variety, known since the 1950s, was caused by an initial S mintmark being punched into the die horizontally, and then corrected with an upright S mintmark.

Proof Liberty Seated Quarters

PF-60 to 70 (Proof). Proofs of the earlier years are very rare. Beginning with 1856, they were made in larger numbers, and from 1859 onward the yearly production was in the multiple hundreds. Examples of the later era are readily available today. Some (1858 is an example) have lint marks, and others can have light striking (particularly in the 1870s and 1880s). Avoid "problem" coins and those with deep or artificial (and often colorful) toning. *Obverse and Reverse:* Proofs that are extensively cleaned and have many hairlines, or that are dull and grainy, are lower level, such as PF-60 to 62. With medium hairlines and good reflectivity, an assigned grade of PF-64 is appropriate and with relatively few hairlines, PF-65. In various grades hairlines are most easily seen in the obverse field. PF-66 should have hairlines so delicate that magnification is needed to see them. Above that, a Proof should be free of such lines.

Proof Liberty Seated Quarter: Variety 1,
No Motto Above Eagle (1838–1853)

1842, Small Date

1842, Large Date

Small Date is Proof only.

Proof Liberty Seated Quarter: Variety 2,
Arrows at Date, Rays Around Eagle (1853)

Proof Liberty Seated Quarter: Variety 3,
Arrows at Date, No Rays (1854–1855)

Proof Liberty Seated Quarter: Variety 1 Resumed,
Weight Standard of Variety 3 (1856–1865)

Proof Liberty Seated Quarter: Variety 4,
Motto Above Eagle (1866–1873)

Proof Liberty Seated Quarter: Variety 5,
Arrows at Date (1873–1874)

Proof Liberty Seated Quarter: Variety 4 Resumed,
Weight Standard of Variety 5 (1875–1891)

Coins designated Deep Cameo or Ultra Cameo bring a premium of 50% to 100% above listed values.

	Est Mintage	Cert	Finest	PF-60	PF-63	PF-64	PF-65	Recent Auction Record
1838	2–3			(extremely rare)				
1839	2–3	1	PF-65		(unique)		$500,000	$517,500, PF-65, Apr-08
1840, Drapery	5–8	3	PF-65			$75,000	125,000	$149,500, PF-65, Aug-07
1841	3–5	1	PF-66	$85,000	$125,000	150,000	200,000	$207,000, PF-66, Jul-09

	Mintage	Cert	Finest	PF-60	PF-63	PF-64	PF-65	Recent Auction Record
1842, Small Date † (a)	3–5	2	PF-66		$60,000	$85,000	$125,000	$126,500, PF-64, Apr-08
1843	10–15	7	PF-66	$12,500	20,000	35,000	50,000	$24,150, PF-64, Jul-09
1844 (2 known)	3–5	1	PF-66					$276,000, PF-66 CAC, Jul-09
1845	6–8	5	PF-66		35,000	50,000	85,000	$149,500, PF-66, Jan-09
1846	15–20	9	PF-65	5,000	10,000	20,000	35,000	$23,000, PF-65, Apr-08
1847	6–8	5	PF-66	5,000	10,000	20,000	35,000	$18,400, PF-65, Apr-09
1848	5–8	3	PF-66	5,000	10,000	20,000	35,000	$63,250, PF-66, Jul-08
1849	5–8	4	PF-66		8,500	15,000	30,000	$37,375, PF-66, Apr-08
1850	5–8	3	PF-68					$460,000, PF-68, Jan-08
1852	5–8	1	PF-65			75,000	125,000	$138,000, PF-65, Jul-08
1853	10–15	5	PF-67	30,000	50,000	100,000	150,000	$149,500, PF-65Cam, Apr-09
1854	20–30	8	PF-66	10,000	20,000	30,000	50,000	$21,850, PF-65, Sep-09
1855	20–30	9	PF-66	8,500	17,500	27,500	45,000	$16,100, PF-64Cam CAC, Jul-09
1855S	1–2	1	PF-64		(unique)			$86,250, PF-63, Mar-05
1856	40–50	26	PF-67	3,500	6,500	12,500	20,000	$17,250, PF-65 CAC, Jan-10
1857	40–50	36	PF-66	3,250	4,750	7,250	13,500	$5,463, PF-64 Cam, May-10
1858	300	59	PF-67	1,500	2,500	3,500	7,500	$2,990, PF-64 CAC, Jan-09
1859	800	141	PF-67	1,050	2,150	2,900	5,750	$8,625, PF-67, Jan-10
1860	1,000	100	PF-68	750	1,100	2,300	5,500	$820, PF-62, Nov-09
1861	1,000	89	PF-67	750	1,100	2,300	5,150	$1,264, PF-63, Nov-09
1862	550	127	PF-67	750	1,100	2,300	5,150	$3,220, PF-65, Jan-10
1863	460	139	PF-67	750	1,100	2,300	5,150	$1,955, PF-64, Jan-10
1864	470	171	PF-68	750	1,100	2,350	5,150	$5,463, PF-64 Cam, May-10
1865	500	161	PF-68	750	1,100	2,350	5,150	$1,955, PF-64, Mar-10
1866, No Motto † (b)	1	n/a	n/a		(unique)			
1866, Variety 4	725	137	PF-68	500	950	1,400	2,850	$1,495, PF-64Cam, Jan-10
1867	625	159	PF-68	500	950	1,400	2,850	$17,400, PF-66Cam CAC, Feb-10
1868	600	138	PF-66	500	950	1,400	2,850	$17,250, PF-65DCam, Oct-09
1869	600	151	PF-67	500	950	1,400	2,850	$2,875, PF-65DCam, May-09
1870	1,000	139	PF-67	500	950	1,350	2,600	$518, PF-60, Feb-10
1871	960	120	PF-68	500	950	1,350	2,600	$1,093, PF-64, Jan-10
1872	950	168	PF-68	500	950	1,350	2,100	$1,610, PF-64, Jan-10
1873	600	161	PF-68	500	950	1,350	2,100	$834, PF-63, Nov-09
1873, Variety 5	540	129	PF-68	900	1,450	3,500	7,050	$7,763, PF-65Cam, Mar-10
1874	700	226	PF-67	900	1,450	3,500	7,050	$6,325, PF-66, Jan-10
1875	700	163	PF-67	500	950	1,350	2,100	$1,265, PF-64 CAC, Feb-10
1876	1,150	207	PF-68	500	950	1,350	2,100	$1,380, PF-64Cam, Feb-10
1877	510	127	PF-67	500	950	1,350	2,100	$2,070, PF-65, Feb-10
1878	800	173	PF-67	500	950	1,350	2,100	$1,380, PF-64Cam, Feb-10
1879	1,100	285	PF-67	500	950	1,350	2,100	$1,323, PF-64Cam, Mar-10
1880	1,355	350	PF-68	500	950	1,350	2,100	$4,888, PF-66 CAC, Jan-10
1881	975	283	PF-68	500	950	1,350	2,100	$2,990, PF-66Cam, Mar-10
1882	1,100	286	PF-68	500	950	1,350	2,100	$1,035, PF-64, Mar-10
1883	1,039	320	PF-69	500	950	1,350	2,100	$2,301, PF-66, Feb-10
1884	875	272	PF-69	500	950	1,350	2,100	$1,449, PF-64Cam CAC, Mar-10
1885	930	260	PF-68	500	950	1,350	2,100	$4,313, PF-67, Feb-10
1886	886	280	PF-68	500	950	1,350	2,100	$12,075, PF-67 CAC, Jan-10
1887	710	219	PF-68	500	950	1,350	2,100	$1,668, PF-64, Feb-10
1888	832	207	PF-68	500	950	1,350	2,100	$2,530, PF-65, Jan-10
1889	711	176	PF-68	500	950	1,350	2,100	$2,700, PF-66Cam, Feb-10
1890	590	228	PF-69	500	950	1,350	2,100	$10,350, PF-68UC , Jun-10
1891	600	223	PF-68	500	950	1,350	2,100	$6,325, PF-67, Jan-10

† Ranked in the *100 Greatest U.S. Coins* (third edition). **a.** For the Philadelphia Mint's quarters of 1842, the Small Date was used on Proofs only. The 1842 Large Date was made in circulation-strike format (see regular listings). **b.** The unique 1866 Proof quarter dollar without motto (as well as the half dollar and dollar of the same design) is not mentioned in the Mint director's report. "Not a pattern, but a muling created at a later date as a numismatic rarity" (*United States Pattern Coins,* 10th edition). Saul Teichman dates its creation to the 1870s. It is classified as Judd-536.

BARBER OR LIBERTY HEAD
(1892–1916)

Designer Charles E. Barber; weight 6.25 grams; composition .900 silver, .100 copper (net weight: .18084 oz. pure silver); diameter 24.3 mm; reeded edge; mints: Philadelphia, Denver, New Orleans, San Francisco.

History. The Liberty Head design was by Charles E. Barber, chief engraver of the U.S. Mint. Barber quarters feature the same obverse motif used on dimes and half dollars of the era, with the designer's initial, B, found at the truncation of the neck of Miss Liberty. The reverse depicts a heraldic eagle.

Striking and Sharpness. On the obverse, check the hair details and other features. On the reverse, the eagle's leg at the lower right and the arrows can be weak. Also check the upper right of the shield and the nearby wing. Once these coins entered circulation and acquired wear, the word LIBERTY on the headband tended to disappear quickly.

Availability. Barber quarters in Fine or better grade are scarce. Today, among circulation strikes, 90% or more in existence are G-4 or below. MS coins are available of all dates and mints, but some are very elusive. The 1896-S, 1901-S, and 1913-S are the key dates in all grades.

EF-40, 45 (Extremely Fine). *Obverse:* Further wear than at AU is seen on the head. The hair above the forehead lacks most detail. LIBERTY shows wear, but is strong. *Reverse:* Further wear than at AU is seen on the head and tail of the eagle and on the tips of the wings, most evident at the left and right extremes of the wings. At this level and below, sharpness of strike on the reverse is not important.

AU-50, 53, 55, 58 (About Uncirculated). *Obverse:* Light wear is seen on the head, especially on the forward hair under LIBERTY. There is some luster at AU-50 and 53. At AU-58, the luster is extensive but incomplete, especially on the higher parts and in the right field. *Reverse:* Wear is evident on the head and tail of the eagle and on the tips of the wings. At AU-50 and 53, there still is significant luster. An AU-58 coin (as determined by the obverse) can have the reverse appear to be full MS.

MS-60 to 70 (Mint State). *Obverse:* At MS-60, some abrasion and contact marks are evident, most noticeably on the cheek and the obverse field to the right. Luster is present, but may be dull or lifeless. Many Barber coins have been cleaned, especially of the earlier dates. At MS-63, contact marks are very few. Abrasion still is evident, but less than at lower levels. The cheek of Miss Liberty virtually showcases abrasion. An MS-65 coin may have minor abrasion, but contact marks are so minute as to require magnification. Luster should be full and rich. *Reverse:* Comments apply as for the obverse, except that in lower MS grades abrasion and contact marks are most noticeable on the head and tail of the eagle and on the tips of the wings. At MS-65 or higher, there are no marks visible to the unaided eye. The field is mainly protected by design elements, and often appears to grade a point or two higher than the obverse.

1892, Variety 1 Reverse

1892, Variety 2 Reverse

Note position of wing tip relative to E in UNITED.

	Mintage	Cert	Avg	%MS	EF-40	AU-50	MS-60	MS-62	MS-63	MS-64	MS-65	Recent Auction Record
1892 (a)	8,236,000	1,355	62.1	80	$75	$125	$200	$275	$325	$525	$1,150	$3,335, MS-66, Mar-10
1892O	2,460,000	350	61.2	73	95	160	300	400	450	650	1,500	$4,370, MS-66, Mar-10
1892S	964,079	91	59.1	74	200	300	475	700	1,050	2,100	4,400	$2,070, MS-64 , Jan-10
1893	5,444,023	238	61.5	82	75	125	200	300	375	575	1,400	$489, MS-64 , Mar-10
1893O	3,396,000	153	61.6	80	100	170	275	400	500	800	1,800	$460, MS-63, Feb-10
1893S	1,454,535	68	57.3	75	170	300	450	700	1,100	2,400	5,500	$9,200, MS-66 CAC, Jan-10
1894	3,432,000	145	61.9	86	95	150	240	325	400	550	1,350	$1,955, MS-66, Feb-10
1894O	2,852,000	122	61.1	75	130	230	325	550	725	1,200	2,000	$978, MS-64 CAC, Jan-10
1894S	2,648,821	166	61.7	82	120	210	325	450	725	1,350	2,250	$7,475, MS-66, Aug-09

a. There are two varieties of the 1892 reverse. Variety 1: the eagle's wing covers only half of the E in UNITED; Variety 2: the eagle's wing covers most of the E. Coins of Variety 1 are somewhat scarcer.

	Mintage	Cert	Avg	%MS	EF-40	AU-50	MS-60	MS-62	MS-63	MS-64	MS-65	Recent Auction Record
1895	4,440,000	172	60.9	83	$80	$140	$225	$275	$450	$650	$1,600	$6,613, MS-67 CAC, Jan-10
1895O	2,816,000	86	62.4	80	140	230	400	600	875	1,400	2,550	$7,800, MS-66 CAC, Feb-10
1895S	1,764,681	75	59.6	72	170	275	420	700	1,050	2,200	3,600	$621, MS-62, Nov-09
1896	3,874,000	168	61.2	88	80	135	225	275	375	550	1,250	$4,169, MS-66, Feb-10
1896O	1,484,000	68	56.5	65	450	675	900	1,300	2,000	4,000	6,500	$322, EF-40, Feb-10
1896S	188,039	248	16.1	13	4,400	6,000	8,000	11,500	15,000	24,000	44,000	$13,225, MS-62, Nov-09
1897	8,140,000	205	61.1	81	70	105	200	275	325	550	1,250	$2,428, MS-66, Sep-09
1897O	1,414,800	67	54.1	61	385	600	850	1,300	1,800	2,350	3,300	$7,475, MS-66 CAC, Jan-10
1897S	542,229	64	53.6	63	400	600	900	1,200	1,700	3,000	7,500	$7,188, MS-65 CAC, Jan-10
1898	11,100,000	248	61.3	81	70	125	200	250	325	550	1,200	$1,955, MS-66, Feb-10
1898O	1,868,000	49	58.9	67	300	390	625	1,000	1,500	3,250	8,750	$2,416, MS-63, Jan-10
1898S	1,020,592	49	59.2	71	90	200	375	750	1,200	3,400	6,500	$1,495, MS-62, Sep-09
1899	12,624,000	251	60.5	80	75	125	200	275	325	525	1,200	$4,313, MS-66, Aug-09
1899O	2,644,000	81	60.6	77	120	250	375	600	800	1,250	2,500	$2,530, MS-65, Jan-10
1899S	708,000	41	61.0	63	140	260	400	700	1,200	1,800	3,750	$4,313, MS-65, Aug-09
1900	10,016,000	224	62.5	89	75	125	200	275	350	525	1,250	$414, MS-64 , Mar-10
1900O	3,416,000	77	59.1	77	140	300	500	700	850	1,300	3,100	$4,100, MS-66, Feb-10
1900S	1,858,585	83	56.9	42	80	130	350	600	1,000	1,750	4,200	$5,175, MS-67 , Sep-09
1901	8,892,000	189	59.3	80	80	135	200	275	325	550	1,350	$312, MS-63, Feb-10
1901O	1,612,000	44	48.2	48	450	625	850	1,300	1,850	3,150	4,400	$27,600, MS-67 , Jul-09
1901S	72,664	215	10.3	6	26,000	31,000	37,000	41,000	46,000	62,500	85,000	$327,750, MS-68, Mar-10
1902	12,196,967	196	60.9	81	65	115	200	275	325	525	1,200	$12,650, MS-67 , Jul-09
1902O	4,748,000	52	55.6	60	140	225	475	800	1,300	1,900	3,900	$14,950, MS-66 CAC, May-10
1902S	1,524,612	80	59.5	71	160	240	500	675	900	1,300	3,000	$920, MS-64 , Feb-10
1903	9,759,309	83	59.3	72	60	115	200	300	450	600	2,400	$1,610, MS-65, Sep-09
1903O	3,500,000	63	57.2	60	120	275	425	750	1,200	2,100	4,400	$7,475, MS-66, May-10
1903S	1,036,000	70	59.4	79	150	275	425	600	825	1,500	2,200	$1,783, MS-65, Sep-09
1904	9,588,143	133	61.2	75	70	120	220	275	350	525	1,200	$1,553, MS-66, Dec-09
1904O	2,456,000	83	58.7	64	240	450	800	1,050	1,250	1,600	2,450	$5,031, MS-66 CAC, Jan-10
1905	4,967,523	127	61.6	83	70	120	220	300	375	550	1,300	$2,070, MS-66, Sep-09
1905O	1,230,000	57	57.0	72	260	350	475	750	1,250	2,100	5,500	$1,495, MS-63, Mar-10
1905S	1,884,000	71	59.8	72	105	225	350	600	1,000	1,400	3,500	$4,600, MS-66, Sep-09
1906	3,655,760	154	62.4	88	70	115	200	275	325	525	1,200	$2,185, MS-66, Aug-09
1906D	3,280,000	100	62.0	84	70	145	225	325	450	700	1,850	$1,153, MS-65, Jan-10
1906O	2,056,000	110	62.8	88	100	200	300	400	550	800	1,400	$5,463, MS-66, Aug-09
1907	7,132,000	292	60.9	79	60	105	200	275	325	525	1,200	$960, MS-65 CAC, Feb-10
1907D	2,484,000	82	61.6	85	70	175	235	400	650	1,100	2,250	$546, MS-63, Mar-10
1907O	4,560,000	140	60.3	81	70	135	210	300	475	750	1,750	$1,380, MS-65, Mar-10
1907S	1,360,000	61	60.6	85	140	280	475	700	1,000	1,800	2,600	$7,475, MS-67 CAC, Jan-10
1908	4,232,000	184	61.6	83	70	115	200	275	325	525	1,200	$834, MS-65, Dec-09
1908D	5,788,000	173	60.1	75	70	115	225	300	350	550	1,275	$473, MS-64 , Jan-10
1908O	6,244,000	189	59.9	83	65	115	185	275	325	525	1,200	$805, MS-65, Mar-10
1908S	784,000	76	58.1	76	325	465	750	925	1,100	2,050	4,250	$4,620, MS-66, Mar-10
1909	9,268,000	376	61.0	82	65	110	200	275	325	525	1,200	$4,255, MS-67 , Mar-10
1909D	5,114,000	191	59.9	73	85	150	200	275	325	550	1,350	$978, MS-65, Mar-10
1909O	712,000	54	51.9	70	325	500	800	1,200	1,800	3,700	7,000	$13,800, MS-66, Jul-09
1909S	1,348,000	83	60.8	84	90	185	285	475	750	1,300	1,900	$18,400, MS-67 CAC, Jan-10
1910	2,244,000	151	61.8	87	80	140	200	275	325	550	1,200	$4,888, MS-67 CAC, Jan-10
1910D	1,500,000	92	60.9	80	125	240	350	600	825	1,150	1,600	$2,070, MS-66, Dec-09
1911	3,720,000	219	60.9	82	70	125	200	275	325	525	1,100	$460, MS-64 , Jan-10
1911D	933,600	66	58.5	71	325	500	700	1,000	1,300	2,100	4,900	$1,725, MS-64 , Sep-09
1911S	988,000	120	61.0	84	165	280	375	550	750	1,000	1,500	$2,040, MS-66 CAC, Feb-10
1912	4,400,000	341	61.2	85	70	115	200	275	325	525	1,100	$431, MS-64 CAC, Jan-10
1912S	708,000	75	60.7	80	115	220	350	600	925	1,400	1,900	$1,265, MS-64 CAC, Jan-10
1913	484,000	95	55.5	65	400	525	800	1,000	1,100	1,300	3,750	$4,140, MS-65, Mar-10
1913D	1,450,800	135	60.7	79	85	175	275	325	375	550	1,150	$1,840, MS-66, Sep-09
1913S	40,000	245	15.9	18	7,250	8,000	10,500	13,000	16,000	23,500	30,000	$14,950, MS-62 CAC, Mar-10
1914	6,244,230	485	61.3	84	65	115	200	275	325	525	1,100	$863, MS-65, Mar-10
1914D	3,046,000	258	61.6	83	65	115	200	275	325	525	1,150	$1,955, MS-66 CAC, Jan-10

Chart continued on next page.

	Mintage	Cert	Avg	%MS	EF-40	AU-50	MS-60	MS-62	MS-63	MS-64	MS-65	Recent Auction Record
1914S	264,000	110	36.5	40	$600	$750	$1,000	$1,300	$1,500	$2,250	$3,100	$1,150, AU-53, Dec-09
1915	3,480,000	369	61.3	85	65	115	200	275	325	550	1,200	$403, MS-64 , Jan-10
1915D	3,694,000	502	61.7	84	70	115	200	275	325	525	1,100	$2,530, MS-66, Feb-10
1915S	704,000	129	60.9	79	115	200	285	350	425	675	1,300	$3,220, MS-66, Aug-09
1916	1,788,000	336	61.7	83	70	115	200	275	325	525	1,100	$2,530, MS-66 CAC, Jan-10
1916D	6,540,800	1,194	61.7	86	70	115	200	275	325	525	1,100	$1,093, MS-65, Mar-10

Proof Barber Quarters

PF-60 to 70 (Proof). Proofs exist in proportion to their mintages. Choicer examples tend to be of later dates. Most are sharply struck, although more than just a few are weak on the eagle's leg at the lower right and on certain parts of the arrows. The Proofs of 1892 to 1901 usually have cameo contrast between the designs and the mirror fields. *Obverse and Reverse:*

Proofs that are extensively cleaned and have many hairlines, or that are dull and grainy, are lower level, such as PF-60 to 62. With medium hairlines and good reflectivity, an assigned grade of PF-64 is appropriate. Tiny horizontal lines on Miss Liberty's cheek, known as slide marks, from National and other album slides scuffing the relief of the cheek, are

endemic on all Barber silver coins. With noticeable marks of this type, the highest grade assignable is PF-64. With relatively few hairlines, a rating of PF-65 can be given. PF-66 should have hairlines so delicate that magnification is needed to see them. Above that, a Proof should be free of any hairlines or other problems.

Proof Barber Quarter

Coins designated Deep Cameo or Ultra Cameo bring a premium of 50% to 100% above listed values.

	Mintage	Cert	Finest	PF-60	PF-63	PF-64	PF-65	Recent Auction Record
1892	1,245	368	PF-68	$450	$775	$1,175	$1,850	$3,360, PF-66Cam, Feb-10
1893	792	271	PF-69	450	775	1,175	1,850	$2,013, PF-66, Jan-10
1894	972	319	PF-69	450	775	1,175	1,850	$810, PF-63Cam, Feb-10
1895	880	251	PF-68	450	775	1,175	1,850	$5,462, PF-67, Jan-10
1896	762	309	PF-69	450	775	1,175	1,850	$1,380, PF-65, Feb-10
1897	731	245	PF-68	450	775	1,175	1,850	$10,350, PF-67 CAC, Jan-10
1898	735	290	PF-69	450	775	1,175	1,850	$8,625, PF-68 CAC Star, Jan-10
1899	846	189	PF-68	450	775	1,175	1,850	$840, PF-63, Feb-10
1900	912	254	PF-68	450	775	1,175	1,850	$4,600, PF-67 CAC Star, Jun-10
1901	813	229	PF-68	450	775	1,175	1,850	$7,188, PF-68Cam, Feb-10
1902	777	206	PF-68	450	775	1,175	1,850	$8,050, PF-67 CAC, Apr-09
1903	755	271	PF-69	450	775	1,175	1,850	$1,553, PF-64Cam, Mar-10
1904	670	248	PF-69	450	775	1,175	1,850	$6,900, PF-67 Secure, Jun-10
1905	727	233	PF-68	450	775	1,175	1,850	$1,610, PF-65, Feb-10
1906	675	190	PF-68	450	775	1,175	1,850	$1,265, PF-64Cam, Jan-10
1907	575	249	PF-68	450	775	1,175	1,850	$3,594, PF-67Cam, Mar-10
1908	545	164	PF-69	450	775	1,175	1,850	$5,175, PF-67, Nov-09
1909	650	236	PF-68	450	775	1,175	1,850	$748, PF-63, Mar-10
1910	551	250	PF-68	450	775	1,175	1,850	$1,093, PF-64, Jan-10
1911	543	237	PF-69	450	775	1,175	1,850	$5,100, PF-66DCam, Feb-10
1912	700	197	PF-68	450	775	1,175	1,850	$1,610, PF-65Cam, Oct-09
1913	613	220	PF-69	450	775	1,175	1,850	$2,185, PF-66Cam, Dec-09
1914	380	194	PF-68	450	775	1,175	1,850	$7,475, PF-67, Jan-10
1915	450	156	PF-68	450	775	1,175	1,850	$1,080, PF-64, Feb-10

STANDING LIBERTY, VARIETY 1, NO STARS BELOW EAGLE (1916–1917)

Designer Hermon A. MacNeil; weight 6.25 grams; composition .900 silver, .100 copper (net weight: .18084 oz. pure silver); diameter 24.3 mm; reeded edge; mints: Philadelphia, Denver, San Francisco.

Full Head Details, Variety 1

History. The Standing Liberty quarter dollar, designed by sculptor Hermon A. MacNeil (whose initial, M, is located above and to the right of the date), was greeted with wide acclaimed from its first appearance. All of 1916 and many of 1917 are of the Variety 1 design, with the right breast of Miss Liberty exposed on the obverse and with no stars below the eagle on the reverse. Variety 2 (see next section) has modified designs.

Striking and Sharpness. Many if not most 1916 quarters are somewhat lightly struck on the head and body of Miss Liberty. The 1917 Variety 1 quarters usually are quite well struck. When light striking is found, it is usually on the higher-relief parts of the head, the right knee (not as obvious), and the rivets on the left side of the shield. The 1917 Philadelphia Mint coins are usually sharper than the other varieties of this type. A misleading term, Full Head (FH), is widely used to describe quarters that have only *partial* head details. See further comments regarding Variety 2 coins, wherein the problem is more serious.

Availability. The 1916 quarter is the key to the series. Examples tend to be liberally graded in the real-life marketplace, especially in EF and AU, this in contrast to more careful grading for the less valuable 1917 issues. Circulated coins of 1916 and 1917 often have the date worn partly away, due to the high position of this feature in the design. On MS coins the luster is usually rich and attractive. No Proof coins of this type were officially issued, but specimen strikings dated 1917 are known to exist.

MS-60 to 70 (Mint State). *Obverse:* At MS-60 some abrasion and contact marks are evident on the higher areas, which also are the areas most likely to be weakly struck. This includes the rivets on the shield to the left and the central escutcheon on the shield, the head, and the right leg of Miss Liberty. The luster may be incomplete in those areas on weakly struck coins, even those certified above MS-65—the original planchet surface may be revealed, as it was not smoothed out by striking. Accordingly, grading is best done by evaluating abrasion and mint luster as it is observed. Luster may be dull or lifeless at MS-60 to 62 but should have deep frost at MS-63 or better, particularly in the lower-relief areas. At MS-65 or better, it should be full and rich. *Reverse:* Striking is usually quite good. Check the eagle's breast and the surface of the right wing. Luster may be dull or lifeless at MS-60 to 62 but should have deep frost at MS-63 or better, particularly in the lower-relief areas. At MS-65 or better, it should be full and rich.

	Mintage	Cert	Avg	%MS	MS-60	MS-63	MS-63FH	MS-64	MS-64FH	MS-65	MS-65FH	Recent Auction Record
1916 †	52,000	709	46.3	51	$15,000	$16,500	$18,000	$19,500	$22,500	$24,000	$30,000	$10,925, AU-55 CAC, May-10
1917, Variety 1	8,740,000	4,875	62.5	89	250	350	400	400	600	750	1,100	$2,128, MS-67FH, Mar-10
1917D, Variety 1	1,509,200	1,418	62.2	84	300	425	550	500	900	900	2,000	$1,610, MS-65FH, Mar-10
1917S, Variety 1	1,952,000	821	61.0	82	340	475	700	600	1,350	1,100	2,750	$4,025, MS-66FH, Mar-10

† Ranked in the *100 Greatest U.S. Coins* (third edition).

STANDING LIBERTY, VARIETY 2, STARS BELOW EAGLE (1917–1930)

Designer Hermon A. MacNeil; weight 6.25 grams; composition .900 silver, .100 copper (net weight: .18084 oz. pure silver); diameter 24.3 mm; reeded edge; mints: Philadelphia, Denver, San Francisco.

History. Variety 2 of the Standing Liberty design was introduced in 1917 and continued to the end of the series. Miss Liberty is clothed in a jacket of chainmail armor, and the reverse is slightly redesigned, with stars below the eagle. These changes came at the suggestion of the designer, Hermon A. MacNeil.

Striking and Sharpness. Most coins of this design have areas of light striking. On the obverse these are most notable on the head of Miss Liberty and on the shield, the latter often with the two lower-left rivets weak or missing and with the center emblem on the shield weak. The center of the standing figure can be weak as well, as can the upper-left area at and near the date. After 1924 the date was slightly recessed, eliminating that problem. On the reverse, check the eagle's breast. A misleading term, Full Head (FH), is widely used to describe quarters that have only *partial* head details; such coins often actually have the two lower-left shield rivets poorly struck or not visible at all. Most third-party grading services define these criteria for "Full Head" designation (in order of importance): a full, unbroken hairline from Liberty's brow down to the jawline; all three leaves on the head showing; and a visible earhole.

Availability. The 1918-S, 8 Over 7, is recognized as the key issue, and the 1919-D, 1921, 1923-S, and 1927-S as quite scarce. MS coins are readily available for most issues, but Full Details coins can be *extreme* rarities. Circulated coins dated from 1917 through 1924 often have the date worn partly away, due to the high position of this feature in the design. On MS coins the luster usually is rich and attractive. No Proof coins of this type were officially issued, but specimen strikings of the first variety, dated 1917, are known to exist.

MS-60 to 70 (Mint State). *Obverse:* At MS-60, some abrasion and contact marks are evident on the higher areas, which are also the areas most likely to be weakly struck. This includes the lower left two rivets and the ornament at the center of the shield, the head, and the right leg of Miss Liberty. The luster may not be complete in those areas on weakly struck coins, even those certified above MS-65—the original planchet surface may be revealed as it was not smoothed out by striking. Accordingly, grading is best done by evaluating abrasion as it is observed, plus evaluation of the mint luster. This may be dull or lifeless at MS-60 to 62, but should have deep frost at MS-63 or better, particularly in the lower-relief areas.

At MS-65 or better, it should be full and rich. *Reverse:* Striking is usually better, permitting observation of luster in all areas. Check the eagle's breast and the surface of the right wing. Luster may be dull or lifeless at MS-60 to 62, but should have deep frost at MS-63 or better, particularly in the lower-relief areas. At MS-65 or better, it should be full and rich.

1918-S, 8 Over 7

Full Head (FH) Details, Variety 2
Note (1) the full unbroken hairline from brow to neck; (2) all three leaves clearly visible in Liberty's cap; and (3) a visible ear hole.

Pedestal Date (1917–1924)

Recessed Date (1925–1930)

	Mintage	Cert	Avg	%MS	MS-60	MS-63	MS-63FH	MS-64	MS-64FH	MS-65	MS-65FH	Recent Auction Record
1917, Variety 2	13,880,000	1,187	62.3	86	$200	$275	$350	$350	$600	$600	$900	$690, MS-65FH, Mar-10
1917D, Variety 2	6,224,400	630	61.2	77	260	350	600	500	1,000	1,300	3,000	$4,600, MS-67, Jan-10
1917S, Variety 2	5,552,000	606	61.3	78	260	350	900	500	1,600	1,100	3,250	$2,415, MS-65FH, Nov-09
1918	14,240,000	688	62.4	82	150	225	450	350	700	700	1,750	$3,960, MS-66FH, Feb-10
1918D	7,380,000	556	61.1	71	275	400	1,000	650	2,200	1,300	4,000	$1,898, MS-66, Mar-10
1918S	11,072,000	753	59.4	73	200	300	2,200	700	3,500	1,300	12,000	$2,645, MS-65, Mar-10
1918S, 8 Over 7 † (a)	*	279	40.1	19	19,000	32,500	100,000	40,000	120,000	75,000	*	$29,900, MS-64, Feb-10
1919	11,324,000	881	62.5	85	175	250	400	350	650	600	1,500	$1,955, MS-66FH, May-10
1919D	1,944,000	327	53.2	52	850	1,450	10,000	2,200	15,000	3,000	25,000	$2,530, MS-63, Feb-10
1919S	1,836,000	359	52.2	47	750	1,600	8,500	2,500	15,000	4,000	30,000	$5,750, MS-65, Jan-10
1920	27,860,000	1,344	62.4	84	150	225	400	350	750	600	1,500	$633, MS-64FH CAC, Feb-10
1920D	3,586,400	300	56.5	67	325	750	1,500	1,300	3,000	2,000	6,500	$5,750, MS-65FH, Mar-09
1920S	6,380,000	444	60.4	73	250	750	5,500	1,200	8,000	2,200	24,000	$8,625, MS-64FH , Feb-10
1921	1,916,000	682	51.8	59	1,600	2,100	3,000	3,000	4,000	4,000	5,500	$2,530, MS-64, Jun-10
1923	9,716,000	1,241	63.2	89	160	240	450	350	1,800	600	4,000	$259, MS-64, Mar-10
1923S	1,360,000	572	52.9	56	2,600	3,400	3,800	4,000	4,500	5,000	6,500	$3,163, MS-63FH, Mar-10

* Included in number above. † Ranked in the *100 Greatest U.S. Coins* (third edition). **a.** This clear overdate was caused by the use of two differently dated hubs when the die was made. "Because of the boldness of the 7, this variety can be confirmed easily in low grades. . . . This variety is extremely rare in high grades. We recommend authentication because alterations do exist. Genuine specimens have a small die chip above the pedestal, just to the left of the lowest star on the right" (*Cherrypickers' Guide to Rare Die Varieties*, fourth edition, volume II).

	Mintage	Cert	Avg	%MS	MS-60	MS-63	MS-63FH	MS-64	MS-64FH	MS-65	MS-65FH	Recent Auction Record
1924	10,920,000	871	62.8	88	$165	$275	$400	$350	$650	$600	$1,400	$1,955, MS-65FH, Oct-09
1924D	3,112,000	1,299	63.8	94	275	350	1,000	425	2,000	600	4,500	$690, MS-66 CAC, Feb-10
1924S	2,860,000	465	60.7	78	350	1,000	1,800	1,200	3,500	1,750	5,250	$1,610, MS-65, Feb-10
1925	12,280,000	961	62.7	88	150	250	350	350	500	600	1,000	$460, MS-64FH, Feb-10
1926	11,316,000	980	62.6	86	150	250	350	350	700	600	2,000	$4,025, MS-66FH, Mar-10
1926D	1,716,000	1,891	63.5	98	175	250	6,000	350	10,000	550	18,000	$7,475, MS-64FH CAC, Feb-10
1926S	2,700,000	331	59.2	70	350	775	5,750	1,200	11,000	2,000	25,000	$4,313, MS-66, Jun-10
1927	11,912,000	1,103	61.9	84	120	225	350	350	600	550	1,100	$748, MS-64FH CAC, Feb-10
1927D	976,000	783	62.9	94	250	310	650	400	1,100	600	3,000	$1,208, MS-66 CAC, Feb-10
1927S	396,000	700	33.6	20	4,500	7,000	30,000	8,000	60,000	10,000	150,000	$149,500, MS-66FH, Mar-09
1928	6,336,000	756	62.2	85	120	225	400	350	600	550	1,750	$805, MS-66 CAC, Jan-10
1928D	1,627,600	1,269	63.7	96	140	235	1,400	350	2,800	550	5,000	$374, MS-65, Mar-10
1928S (b)	2,644,000	1,165	63.8	94	140	235	350	350	575	550	900	$1,495, MS-66FH, Feb-10
1929	11,140,000	1,435	62.5	86	120	225	350	325	500	525	850	$1,265, MS-66FH, Feb-10
1929D	1,358,000	773	61.6	81	140	230	1,400	350	2,200	525	5,000	$4,888, MS-65FH, Feb-10
1929S	1,764,000	1,146	63.0	90	140	230	350	350	500	525	850	$604, MS-65FH, Mar-10
1930	5,632,000	2,757	62.7	86	135	225	325	325	475	525	750	$2,300, MS-67 CAC, Mar-10
1930S	1,556,000	873	63.4	90	135	225	350	325	500	525	850	$489, MS-64FH, Mar-10

b. Large and small mintmarks exist; their values are the same.

WASHINGTON, EAGLE REVERSE
(1932–1998)

Silver (1932–1964): Designer John Flanagan; weight 6.25 grams; composition .900 silver, .100 copper (net weight: .18084 oz. pure silver); diameter 24.3 mm; reeded edge; mints: Philadelphia, Denver, San Francisco.

Clad (1965–1998): Designer John Flanagan; weight 5.67 grams; composition outer layers of copper-nickel (.750 copper, .250 nickel) bonded to inner core of pure copper; diameter 24.3 mm; reeded edge.

Bicentennial variety: Designers John Flanagan and Jack L. Ahr; diameter 24.3 mm; reeded edge. Silver issue—Weight 5.75 grams; composition outer layers of .800 silver, .200 copper bonded to inner core of .209 silver, .791 copper (net weight.0739 oz. pure silver). Copper-nickel issue—Weight 5.67 grams; composition outer layers of .750 copper, .250 nickel bonded to inner core of pure copper.

Silver Proofs (1992–1998): Designer John Flanagan; weight 6.25 grams; composition .900 silver, .100 copper (net weight: .18084 oz. pure silver); diameter 24.3 mm; reeded edge; mint: San Francisco.

History. The Washington quarter, designed by New York sculptor John Flanagan, originally was intended to be a commemorative coin, but it ultimately was produced as a regular circulation issue. The obverse is from a bust by Jean Antoine Houdon. Flanagan's initials, JF, are at the base of Washington's neck. The reverse features a modernistic eagle. In October 1973, the Treasury announced an open contest for the selection of suitable designs for the Bicentennial reverses of the quarter, half dollar, and dollar, with $5,000 to be awarded to each winner. Twelve semifinalists were chosen, and from these the symbolic entry of Jack L. Ahr was selected for the quarter reverse. It features a colonial drummer facing left, with a victory torch encircled by 13 stars at the upper left. Except for the dual dating, "1776–1976," the obverse remained unchanged. Only pieces with this dual dating were coined during

1975 and 1976. They were struck for general circulation and included in all the Mint's offerings of Proof and Uncirculated coin sets. (The grading instructions below are for the regular Eagle Reverse variety.)

Striking and Sharpness. The relief of both sides of the Washington quarter issues from 1932 to 1998 is shallow. Accordingly, any lightness of strike is not easily seen. Nearly all are well struck. On all quarters of 1932 and some of 1934 the motto IN GOD WE TRUST is light, as per the design. It was strengthened in 1934.

Availability. The 1932-D and S are key issues but not rarities. All others are readily available in high grades, but some are scarcer than others.

MS-60 to 70 (Mint State). *Obverse:* At MS-60, some abrasion and contact marks are evident on the hair above the ear and at the top of the head below E (LIBERTY). At MS-63, abrasion is slight, and less is evident at MS-64. An MS-65 coin should display no abrasion or contact marks except under magnification, and MS-66 and higher coins should have none at all. Luster should be full and rich. *Reverse:* Comments apply as for the obverse, except that the eagle's breast and legs are the places to check. On both sides the fields are protected by design elements and do not show contact marks readily.

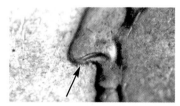 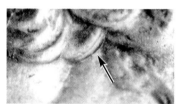

1932, Doubled-Die Obverse
FS-25-1932-101.

1934, Doubled-Die Obverse
FS-25-1934-101.

1934, Light Motto
FS-25-1934-401.

1934, Heavy Motto
FS-25-1934-403.

	Mintage	Cert	Avg	%MS	MS-60	MS-62	MS-63	MS-64	MS-65	MS-66	MS-67	Recent Auction Record
1932	5,404,000	1,484	63.0	90	$25	$40	$50	$90	$425	$1,000	$20,000	$1,265, MS-66 CAC, Jun-10
1932, DblDie Obv (a)	*	10	56.6	20	350	400	500	600	750			
1932D	436,800	2,151	48.5	41	1,050	1,850	2,500	3,250	12,500	150,000	*	$3,450, MS-64, Jun-10
1932S	408,000	2,878	54.4	56	500	1,100	1,300	1,500	5,000	20,000	*	$3,738, MS-65 Secure, Jun-10
1934, All kinds	31,912,052											
1934, DblDie Obv (b)		131	46.9	40	1,550	2,000	2,400	3,250	4,750	7,500	*	$891, MS-62, Dec-09
1934, Light Motto (c)		246	63.6	92	50	75	100	350	450	800	4,000	$156, MS-64, Feb-10
1934, Heavy Motto (d)		33	62.9	85	30	40	50	65	135	750	3,500	$805, MS-65, Apr-09
1934D	3,527,200	1,024	61.8	83	250	300	350	500	1,300	2,000	15,000	$1,260, MS-66, Feb-10
1935	32,484,000	1,586	64.8	96	22	30	35	50	150	200	750	$109, MS-66, Mar-10
1935D	5,780,000	968	62.5	86	250	275	300	350	750	1,000	5,000	$1,622, MS-67, Jun-10
1935S	5,660,000	1,024	63.5	90	100	120	135	160	350	650	3,500	$240, MS-65, Feb-10

* Included in number above. **a.** The doubling is evident on the earlobe, the nostril, and the braid of hair. **b.** Very strong doubling is visible on the motto, LIBERTY, and the date. **c.** "Notice the considerable weakness in the letters of the motto. In addition, the center point of the W is pointed" (*Cherrypickers' Guide to Rare Die Varieties,* fourth edition, volume II). **d.** The motto has very thick letters, and the central apex of the W is pointed, rising slightly above the other letters.

1937, Doubled-Die Obverse

1942-D, Doubled-Die Obverse
FS-25-1942D-101.

1942-D, Doubled-Die Reverse
FS-25-1942D-801.

1943, Doubled-Die Obverse
FS-25-1943-103. Other varieties exist.

1943-S, Doubled-Die Obverse
FS-25-1943S-101.

1950-D, D Over S
FS-25-1950D-601. Other varieties exist.

1950-S, S Over D
FS-25-1950S-601.

	Mintage	Cert	Avg	%MS	AU-50	MS-60	MS-63	MS-64	MS-65	MS-66	MS-67	Recent Auction Record
1936	41,300,000	1,480	64.8	97	$10	$25	$35	$50	$120	$200	$700	$5,175, MS-68 CAC, Jun-10
1936D	5,374,000	915	61.3	80	270	575	950	1,100	1,400	2,500	10,000	$1,035, MS-65, Jun-10
1936S	3,828,000	1,082	64.2	98	50	120	150	200	400	750	2,500	$2,185, MS-67, Mar-09
1937	19,696,000	874	64.7	98	18	25	35	50	90	200	1,100	$472, MS-67, Jan-10
1937, DblDie Obv (a)	*	23	31.1	13	1,250	2,500	4,500	8,000	12,000	18,000	*	$4,313, MS-63, Oct-09
1937D	7,189,600	879	64.3	96	30	70	90	110	150	400	3,000	$1,725, MS-67, Aug-09
1937S	1,652,000	889	63.8	96	95	150	220	250	400	900	3,000	$173, MS-63, Jan-10
1938	9,472,000	876	63.9	92	45	95	110	140	230	400	2,250	$219, MS-66, Feb-10
1938S	2,832,000	1,074	64.6	98	55	105	140	170	250	400	2,000	$720, MS-67, Feb-10
1939	33,540,000	1,521	65.3	98	12	15	25	40	60	100	400	$178, MS-67, Dec-09
1939D	7,092,000	981	64.9	98	20	40	50	65	125	200	1,000	$748, MS-67, Mar-09
1939S	2,628,000	917	64.3	95	60	95	135	200	340	600	3,000	$204, MS-65, Feb-10
1940	35,704,000	1,069	65.2	97	6	17	35	45	60	120	500	$69, MS-66, Oct-09
1940D	2,797,600	986	64.4	96	65	120	165	200	300	500	2,750	$240, MS-65, Feb-10
1940S	8,244,000	1,004	65.3	98	16	21	32	45	65	120	1,200	$2,875, MS-67, Sep-09
1941	79,032,000	1,268	65.3	98	6	8	14	25	45	80	700	$4,025, MS-68 Star, Feb-09
1941D	16,714,800	721	65.2	98	13	32	55	60	70	250	2,500	$2,070, MS-67, Jul-09
1941S	16,080,000	997	64.6	96	11	28	55	60	70	200	2,000	$5,060, MS-68 Star, Jan-09

* Included in number above. **a.** Very strong doubling is evident on the motto, LIBERTY, the date, and the end of the braid ribbons. "This variety is considered one of the most important in the series" (*Cherrypickers' Guide to Rare Die Varieties*, fourth edition, volume II).

Chart continued on next page.

	Mintage	Cert	Avg	%MS	AU-50	MS-60	MS-63	MS-64	MS-65	MS-66	MS-67	Recent Auction Record
1942	102,096,000	1,019	64.7	95	$4	$6	$9	$20	$35	$200	$2,500	$1,840, MS-67, Apr-09
1942D	17,487,200	953	65.4	99	10	17	20	30	40	200	1,100	$834, MS-67, Jun-09
1942D, DblDie Obv (b)	*	31	35.9	10	1,200	2,000	4,000	5,000	6,000	10,000	*	$1,725, MS-60, Jun-10
1942D, DblDie Rev (c)	*	18	45.6	44	500	900	1,800	2,500	3,200	5,500		$1,093, MS-65, Apr-09
1942S	19,384,000	1,021	64.2	94	20	70	115	140	175	400	1,500	$403, MS-66, Jan-10
1943	99,700,000	1,667	65.4	98	4	5	9	15	40	100	600	$44, MS-66, Sep-09
1943, DblDie Obv (d)	*	9	54.4	67	1,000	2,000	3,500	4,500	5,500	8,000	*	$104, AU-58, Oct-06
1943D	16,095,600	875	65.4	99	15	28	39	50	60	120	800	$259, MS-66, Jan-10
1943S	21,700,000	1,041	65.3	98	13	26	42	50	60	120	900	$39, MS-64, Jan-10
1943S, DblDie Obv (e)	*	95	47.1	53	350	500	1,300	1,500	3,500	6,500	8,000	$2,300, MS-65, Mar-10
1944	104,956,000	1,859	65.5	99	4	5	9	15	35	60	600	$661, MS-67, Nov-09
1944D	14,600,800	1,584	65.8	100	10	17	20	30	40	70	600	$54, MS-66, Oct-09
1944S	12,560,000	1,576	65.7	100	10	14	20	30	35	60	600	$489, MS-67, Feb-10
1945	74,372,000	1,173	65.2	99	4	5	10	15	38	150	1,500	$30, MS-65, Oct-09
1945D	12,341,600	920	65.5	100	12	18	25	30	42	70	1,300	$21, MS-65, Jan-09
1945S	17,004,001	1,228	65.4	99	7	9	13	20	35	60	1,000	$84, MS-66, Jan-10
1946	53,436,000	718	65.4	99	4	5	10	15	40	100	1,750	$138, MS-67, Mar-09
1946D	9,072,800	2,209	65.6	100	5	6	10	20	45	80	1,200	$1,725, MS-67, Aug-09
1946S	4,204,000	4,286	65.6	100	4	5	10	20	40	60	800	$115, MS-66, Dec-09
1947	22,556,000	1,262	65.6	100	5	11	19	25	45	80	800	$345, MS-67, Jan-10
1947D	15,338,400	2,107	65.8	100	5	11	17	20	40	60	350	$138, MS-67, Jan-10
1947S	5,532,000	3,928	65.8	100	4	9	15	20	35	55	325	$322, MS-67, Feb-10
1948	35,196,000	1,825	65.6	100	4	5	9	20	35	60	500	$109, MS-67, Jan-10
1948D	16,766,800	1,174	65.4	100	7	13	18	25	55	120	900	$150, MS-66, Jan-10
1948S	15,960,000	1,952	65.5	99	5	7	13	20	45	70	750	$21, MS-64, Nov-09
1949	9,312,000	937	65.3	98	14	35	47	55	65	120	900	$94, MS-66, Aug-09
1949D	10,068,400	1,034	65.4	99	9	16	38	45	50	140	900	$16,100, MS-68, Mar-09
1950	24,920,126	1,069	65.5	99	5	7	10	15	35	70	1,100	$690, MS-67, Sep-09
1950D	21,075,600	1,032	65.1	98	5	7	10	15	35	70	900	$42, MS-65, Feb-10
1950D, D Over S (f)	*	83	48.4	35	200	300	500	1,500	5,000	10,000	25,000	$15,525, MS-66, Nov-09
1950S	10,284,004	1,065	65.0	96	8	12	16	20	45	60	800	$1,898, MS-65, Feb-10
1950S, S Over D (g)	*	81	56.9	67	250	350	550	800	2,000	3,500	6,000	$2,990, MS-66 CAC, Jun-10
1951	43,448,102	1,121	65.6	99	5	6	9	15	25	50	500	$2,530, MS-68, Feb-09
1951D	35,354,800	1,171	65.5	100	5	6	9	15	35	60	1,500	$460, MS-67, Dec-09
1951S	9,048,000	1,128	65.9	100	7	10	15	20	40	80	1,100	$44, MS-65, Sep-09
1952	38,780,093	900	65.7	99	7	10	12	15	25	60	600	$253, MS-67, Dec-09
1952D	49,795,200	678	65.3	99	4	5	9	15	30	90	3,500	$460, MS-65, Feb-10
1952S	13,707,800	1,424	65.8	99	6	12	20	25	42	80	300	$253, MS-67, Feb-10
1953	18,536,120	729	65.5	99	5	6	10	15	40	80	600	$2,530, MS-68, Feb-09
1953D	56,112,400	726	65.2	99	4	5	9	15	35	100	1,500	$920, MS-67 Star, May-09
1953S	14,016,000	1,849	65.7	100	4	5	9	15	34	60	800	$748, MS-67, Jan-10
1954	54,412,203	1,608	65.5	99	4	5	12	20	32	60	750	$6,325, MS-68 Star, Feb-10
1954D	42,305,500	771	65.4	100	4	6	10	15	35	60	2,500	$24, MS-65, Oct-09
1954S	11,834,722	3,218	65.7	100	4	5	9	15	36	60	750	$36, MS-66, Aug-09
1955	18,180,181	1,787	65.5	99	4	5	9	15	27	60	1,000	$1,840, MS-67, Apr-09
1955D	3,182,400	1,726	64.7	100	5	7	10	15	60	400	2,000	$489, MS-66, Sep-09
1956	44,144,000	2,595	65.9	100	4	5	10	15	21	50	150	$38, MS-66, Aug-09
1956D	32,334,500	735	65.3	99	4	5	9	15	27	60	3,000	$196, MS-67, May-09
1957	46,532,000	1,620	65.8	99	4	5	9	15	27	50	200	$84, MS-67, Feb-10
1957D	77,924,160	1,318	65.7	99	4	5	8	15	25	60	300	$115, MS-67, Oct-09
1958	6,360,000	3,257	65.9	100	4	5	8	15	20	50	150	$21, MS-64, Aug-09
1958D	78,124,900	1,634	65.7	100	4	5	8	15	25	50	400	$863, MS-67, May-09
1959	24,384,000	1,425	65.6	100	4	5	7	15	25	50	1,000	$89, MS-66, Mar-10
1959D	62,054,232	1,135	65.2	99	4	5	7	15	25	60	1,500	$546, MS-67, Jan-09
1960	29,164,000	982	65.5	100	4	5	7	15	20	80	1,000	$5,750, MS-67, Sep-09
1960D	63,000,324	647	65.2	99	4	5	7	15	20	50	2,000	$1,438, MS-67, Jan-09

* Included in number above. **b.** Doubling is evident, with a very strong spread, on LIBERTY, the date, and the motto. **c.** Doubling on this popular variety is most prominent on the eagle's beak, the arrows, and the branch above the mintmark. **d.** Doubling is very strong on the motto, LIBERTY, and the date. **e.** Very strong doubling is visible on the motto, LIBERTY, the designer's initials, and the date. "Values for this variety are generally firm, but do change with market conditions and demand fluctuations" *(Cherrypickers' Guide)*. **f.** The upper left curve of the underlying S is visible west and north of the D mintmark. Most Mint State specimens have brilliant surfaces. **g.** Most Mint State specimens have a frosty luster, rather than the brilliant surface seen on most of this year's Mint State D Over S coins.

	Mintage	Cert	Avg	%MS	AU-50	MS-60	MS-63	MS-64	MS-65	MS-66	MS-67	Recent Auction Record
1961	37,036,000	941	65.3	100	$4	$5	$7	$15	$15	$60	2,500	$15, MS-65, Aug-09
1961D	83,656,928	598	65.0	99	4	5	7	15	15	150	4,000	$26, MS-65, Jul-09
1962	36,156,000	1,111	65.5	99	4	5	7	15	15	60	1,200	$431, MS-67, Aug-09
1962D	127,554,756	562	65.1	98	4	5	7	15	15	120	2,000	$17, MS-65, Mar-09
1963	74,316,000	1,634	65.5	99	4	5	7	10	15	60	1,500	$30, MS-64, Sep-09
1963D	135,288,184	562	65.2	99	4	5	7	10	12	60	1,750	$75, MS-66, Jan-09
1964	560,390,585	1,267	65.1	98	4	5	6	10	12	50	1,000	$6,325, MS-67 SMS, Jan-10
1964D	704,135,528	1,506	64.9	95	4	5	6	10	12	50	700	$1,725, MS-67, Jan-10

1966, Doubled-Die Reverse
FS-25-1966-801.

1970-D, Doubled-Die Obverse
FS-25-1970D-101.

1989-D, Repunched Mintmark
FS-25-1989D-501.

	Mintage	Cert	Avg	%MS	MS-63	MS-65	MS-66	MS-67	Recent Auction Record
1965 (a)	1,819,717,540	68	63.8	94	$1.00	$9	$25	$80	$475, MS-68Cam SMS, Dec-09
1966 (a)	821,101,500	38	64.1	92	1.00	7	25	60	$36, MS-67Cam SMS, Nov-09
1966, DblDie Rev (b)	*	2	58.0	50	900.00	1,400	2,250		
1967 (a)	1,524,031,848	31	65.7	100	1.00	6	35	90	$575, MS-67UC SMS, Feb-10
1968	220,731,500	141	66.0	99	1.25	8	25	45	$219, MS-67, Dec-07
1968D	101,534,000	294	66.1	100	1.10	6	15	40	$81, MS-67, Apr-08
1969	176,212,000	50	65.0	96	3.00	10	35	150	$196, MS-66, Aug-09
1969D	114,372,000	226	65.8	99	2.50	10	25	40	$30, MS-66, Aug-09
1970	136,420,000	199	65.4	100	1.00	10	40	50	$86, MS-66, Nov-07
1970D	417,341,364	649	65.9	99	1.00	6	10	25	$38, MS-67, Aug-09
1970D, DblDie Obv (c)	*	1	66.0	100	650.00	800	1,100		$29, MS-65, Dec-08
1971	109,284,000	62	64.6	97	1.00	5	25	*	$323, MS-66, Dec-09
1971D	258,634,428	136	65.5	99	1.00	5	20	50	$173, MS-67, Feb-09
1972	215,048,000	103	65.6	100	1.00	5	25	80	$50, MS-66, Nov-09
1972D	311,067,732	419	66.0	100	1.00	5	20	30	$51, MS-67, May-08
1973	346,924,000	87	65.6	100	1.00	5	25	80	$35, MS-66, Jun-08
1973D	232,977,400	101	65.2	100	1.00	5	15	80	$84, MS-66, Nov-07
1974	801,456,000	69	65.1	99	1.00	5	15	80	$352, MS-67, Dec-07
1974D	353,160,300	103	65.6	100	1.00	7	25	35	$299, MS-67, Dec-07
1776–1976, Copper-Nickel Clad	809,784,016	285	65.7	99	1.00	6	15	35	$92, MS-67, Feb-07
1776–1976D, Copper-Nickel Clad	860,118,839	468	65.6	97	1.00	6	15	60	$99, MS-67, Aug-09
1776–1976S, Silver Clad	11,000,000	490	66.2	100	4.00	7	15	40	$99, MS-67, Nov-09
1977	468,556,000	85	65.5	99	1.00	6	20	50	$121, MS-67, Apr-08
1977D	256,524,978	62	65.1	100	1.00	6	25	60	$431, MS-67, Feb-07
1978	521,452,000	101	65.5	100	1.00	6	20	50	$121, MS-67, Apr-08
1978D	287,373,152	58	65.1	98	1.00	6	20	80	$331, MS-67, Dec-07

* Included in number above. **a.** Values and auction records for Special Mint Set coins are included with the Proofs for this type. **b.** Very strong doubling is visible on all reverse lettering. Note that this is not the 1966 Special Mint Set issue. **c.** This extremely rare variety (fewer than a half dozen known) shows very strong doubling on the date, IN GOD WE TRUST, and the ERTY of LIBERTY.

Chart continued on next page.

	Mintage	Cert	Avg	%MS	MS-63	MS-65	MS-66	MS-67	Recent Auction Record
1979	515,708,000	79	65.4	100	$1.00	$6	$20	$65	$150, MS-67, Apr-08
1979D	489,789,780	75	65.2	100	1.00	6	20	65	$489, MS-66, Apr-08
1980P	635,832,000	272	65.8	100	1.00	6	15	40	$258, MS-67, Dec-07
1980D	518,327,487	81	65.5	100	1.00	6	15	80	$1,380, MS-67, Feb-07
1981P	601,716,000	123	65.8	100	1.00	6	15	45	$48, MS-66, Nov-07
1981D	575,722,833	147	65.5	100	1.00	6	15	70	$21, MS-66, Mar-09
1982P	500,931,000	44	65.5	100	7.00	30	60	120	$11, MS-65, Dec-07
1982D	480,042,788	67	65.6	100	3.50	18	60	100	$552, MS-67, Dec-07
1983P	673,535,000	161	64.8	97	21.00	55	125	250	$115, MS-66, May-08
1983D	617,806,446	92	64.5	95	10.00	42	150	300	$161, MS-66, Feb-08
1984P	676,545,000	81	65.4	98	1.00	9	20	60	$11, MS-66, Jul-08
1984D	546,483,064	42	63.9	98	1.00	9	50	150	$39, MS-66, Mar-09
1985P	775,818,962	123	65.6	98	1.00	9	20	40	$75, MS-66, Apr-08
1985D	519,962,888	116	65.8	100	1.00	9	20	40	$86, MS-66, Nov-07
1986P	551,199,333	111	64.9	98	2.50	12	20	65	$150, MS-66, Feb-07
1986D	504,298,660	140	65.6	99	5.00	15	20	40	$104, MS-66, Nov-07
1987P	582,499,481	70	64.9	100	0.50	9	40	90	$59, MS-66, Dec-07
1987D	655,594,696	78	65.6	100	0.50	6	20	70	$431, MS-67, Feb-07
1988P	562,052,000	64	65.0	98	1.25	14	25	80	$104, MS-66, Nov-07
1988D	596,810,688	78	65.4	100	0.50	10	20	60	$66, MS-66, Nov-07
1989P	512,868,000	67	65.3	99	0.75	8	25	70	$216, MS-66, Aug-09
1989D	896,535,597	54	64.9	96	0.75	4	20	60	$74, MS-66, Aug-09
1989D, RPM (c)	*								
1990P	613,792,000	72	66.0	100	0.75	10	20	40	$76, MS-66, Nov-07
1990D	927,638,181	84	65.5	100	0.75	10	20	60	$374, MS-67, Dec-07
1991P	570,968,000	57	65.9	100	0.75	12	25	40	$90, MS-66, Nov-07
1991D	630,966,693	46	65.1	100	0.75	12	25	100	$86, MS-66, Nov-07
1992P	384,764,000	43	65.6	100	1.50	16	30	100	$242, MS-66, Feb-08
1992D	389,777,107	50	65.1	98	1.00	16	30	100	$60, MS-66, Nov-07
1993P	639,276,000	99	65.8	96	1.00	7	20	40	$690, MS-67, Nov-07
1993D	645,476,128	86	65.9	100	1.00	7	20	40	$66, MS-66, Nov-07
1994P	825,600,000	59	65.7	100	1.00	10	25	40	$104, MS-66, Nov-07
1994D	880,034,110	68	64.9	96	1.00	10	25	70	$128, MS-66, Nov-07
1995P	1,004,336,000	78	66.5	100	1.25	12	20	40	$124, MS-67, Nov-07
1995D	1,103,216,000	92	66.0	100	1.00	12	20	40	$219, MS-67, Dec-07
1996P	925,040,000	105	66.4	100	0.50	10	20	40	$184, MS-68, Oct-07
1996D	906,868,000	134	66.2	99	0.50	10	20	40	$235, MS-68, Dec-07
1997P	595,740,000	64	66.2	100		10	20	40	$196, MS-67, Nov-07
1997D	599,680,000	80	66.0	99	0.75	12	20	40	$69, MS-67, Dec-07
1998P	896,268,000	93	66.5	99	0.50	7	20	40	$39, MS-67, Apr-08
1998D	821,000,000	87	65.4	97	0.50	7	20	70	$42, MS-66, Apr-08

* Included in number above. **c.** The secondary D mintmark is visible west of the primary D.

Proof Washington Quarters, Eagle Reverse

PF-60 to 70 (Proof). Dates available in Proof are 1936 to 1942 and 1950 to 1964 (from the Philadelphia Mint) and 1968 to 1998 (from San Francisco). Proof coins from 1937 through 1972 were made from special dies with high relief and minor detail differences. Certain later Proofs are available in clad metal as well as in silver.

Special Mint Set (SMS) coins were struck in lieu of Proofs from 1965 to 1967; these in some instances closely resemble Proofs. The majority of Proofs made in recent decades are in high levels, PF-66 to 68 or higher. *Obverse and Reverse:* Proofs that are extensively cleaned and have many hairlines, or that are dull and grainy, are

lower level, such as PF-60 to 62. Most low-level Proofs are of the 1936 to 1942 dates. With medium hairlines and good reflectivity, assigned grades of PF-63 or 64 are appropriate. PF-66 should have hairlines so delicate that magnification is needed to see them. Above that, a Proof should be free of any hairlines or other problems.

Proof Washington Quarter, Eagle Reverse

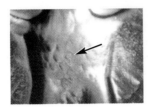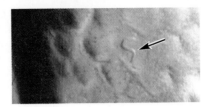

1952, Die Damage
"Superbird" variety. FS-25-1952-901.

	Mintage	Cert	Avg	PF-64	PF-65	PF-66	PF-67	Recent Auction Record
1936	3,837	860	64.4	$1,000	$1,600	$2,250	$8,500	$863, PF-64 CAC, Mar-10
1937	5,542	854	65.1	350	450	600	1,350	$863, PF-67, Oct-09
1938	8,045	1,104	65.1	200	275	500	1,200	$2,760, PF-68, Jul-09
1939	8,795	1,072	65.4	150	200	275	600	$2,070, PF-68, Jul-09
1940	11,246	1,314	65.4	100	140	225	400	$1,035, PF-68, Feb-09
1941	15,287	1,571	65.5	100	140	200	400	$518, PF-68, Sep-09
1942	21,123	1,942	65.3	100	140	200	350	$2,645, PF-68, Sep-09
1950	51,386	1,128	65.8	60	70	90	150	$121, PF-64 CAC, Feb-10
1951	57,500	1,130	66.1	55	65	80	125	$74, PF-66, Feb-10
1952	81,980	1,028	66.2	40	45	70	110	$1,955, PF-67UC, Dec-09
1952, Die Damage (a)	*			225	300	600		$253, PF-67, Feb-10
1953	128,800	1,746	66.7	40	45	60	80	$1,150, PF-68UCam, Jul-09
1954	233,300	2,035	67.0	15	25	35	60	$2,415, PF-68DCam, Mar-09
1955	378,200	2,210	67.2	15	25	35	50	$1,725, PF-69UCam, Sep-09
1956	669,384	2,176	67.3	10	15	25	50	$1,265, PR69DCam, Jan-09
1957	1,247,952	1,846	67.0	10	15	25	45	$150, PF-68Cam, Feb-10
1958	875,652	1,350	66.8	10	15	30	40	$661, PF-68UCam, Dec-09
1959	1,149,291	1,569	67.2	10	12	25	35	$348, PF-68UCam, Jan-10
1959, DblDie Obv (b)	*	26	66.5	150	175	275		$34, PF-66, Sep-09
1960	1,691,602	2,329	66.8	8	10	20	30	$127, PF-67DCam, Mar-10
1961	3,028,244	3,186	67.2	8	10	20	30	$253, PF-69UCam, Jan-10
1962	3,218,019	3,113	67.0	8	10	20	30	$403, PF-69UCam, Jan-10
1963	3,075,645	3,920	67.4	8	10	20	30	$115, PF-68DCam, Nov-09
1964	3,950,762	3,819	67.7	8	10	20	30	$47, PF-68UCam, Sep-09

* Included in number above. **a.** "There is an unusual S-shaped mark on the breast of the eagle. The cause of this mark is unknown. The nickname for this well-known variety is, suitably, 'Superbird'!" (*Cherrypickers' Guide to Rare Die Varieties,* fourth edition, volume II). **b.** Dramatic doubling is evident on all obverse lettering, especially IN GOD WE TRUST. There are at least five different doubled-die obverses for this date; the one featured here is FS-25-1959-101.

1968-S, Doubled-Die Reverse
FS-25-1968S-801.

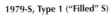

| 1979-S, Type 1 ("Filled" S) | 1979-S, Type 2 ("Clear" S) |

1981-S, Type 1 ("Filled" S)

1981-S, Type 2 ("Clear" S)

1990-S, Doubled-Die Obverse
FS-25-1990S-101.

	Mintage	Cert	Avg	PF-65	PF-67Cam	PF-68Cam	PF-68DC	Recent Auction Record
1965, SMS	2,360,000	1,067	66.6	$12	$375	$600	—	
1966, SMS	2,261,583	999	66.7	12	135	1,750	—	
1967, SMS	1,863,344	1,457	66.9	12	50	250	—	
1968S	3,041,506	518	67.3	5	15	30	$150	$161, PF-68DCam, Sep-09
1968S, DblDie Rev (a)	*	16	65.8	550				$45, PF-66, Dec-08
1969S	2,934,631	531	67.8	5	15	20	100	$920, PR69DCam, Aug-09
1970S	2,632,810	538	67.7	5	15	25	125	$978, PR69DCam, Aug-09
1971S	3,220,733	528	67.6	5	15	25	300	$1,725, PF-69UCam, Jan-10
1972S	3,260,996	435	67.9	5	10	20	30	$15, PF-67, Aug-09
1973S	2,760,339	293	68.0	5	7	10	20	$30, PR69DCam, Jul-09
1974S	2,612,568	268	68.0	5	7	10	20	$10,925, PF-70DCam, Jan-09
1776–1976S, Copper-Nickel Clad	7,059,099	1,273	67.9	4	10	14	20	$403, PF-70DCam, Jan-10
1776–1976S, Silver Clad	4,000,000	2,294	68.2	8	12	16	25	$1,438, PF-70DCam, Jul-09
1977S	3,251,152	527	68.6	4	8	14	16	$174, PF-70DCam, Jan-10
1978S	3,127,781	501	68.6	4	8	14	16	$150, PF-70DCam, Jan-10
1979S, All kinds (b)	3,677,175							
1979S, Type 1 ("Filled" S)		686	68.7	4	8	14	16	$115, PF-70DCam, Jan-10
1979S, Type 2 ("Clear" S)		460	68.9	6	10	16	25	$207, PF-70DCam, Jan-10
1980S	3,554,806	856	68.6	4	8	14	16	$89, PF-70DCam, Jan-10
1981S, All kinds (c)	4,063,083							
1981S, Type 1 ("Filled" S)		912	68.6	4	8	14	16	$127, PF-70DCam, Jan-10
1981S, Type 2 ("Clear" S)		368	68.8	6	10	16	25	$863, PF-70DCam, Dec-09
1982S	3,857,479	629	68.9	4	8	14	16	$127, PF-70DCam, Jan-10
1983S	3,279,126	596	68.8	4	8	14	16	$138, PF-70DCam, Jan-10
1984S	3,065,110	457	68.9	4	8	14	16	$230, PF-70DCam, Jan-10
1985S	3,362,821	556	68.9	4	8	14	16	$210, PF-70DCam, Jan-10
1986S	3,010,497	413	69.0	4	8	14	16	$115, PF-70DCam, Jan-10
1987S	4,227,728	554	69.0	4	8	14	16	$89, PF-70DCam, Jan-10
1988S	3,262,948	379	69.0	4	8	14	16	$109, PF-70DCam, Jan-10
1989S	3,220,194	457	68.9	4	8	14	16	$79, PF-70DCam, Jan-10
1990S	3,299,559	625	69.1	4	8	14	16	$50, PF-70DCam, Jan-10
1990S, DblDie Obv (d)	*	3	68.0	450	800			
1991S	2,867,787	586	69.3	4	8	14	16	$69, PF-70DCam, Jan-10
1992S	2,858,981	502	69.2	4	8	14	16	$50, PF-70DCam, Jan-10
1992S, Silver	1,317,579	1,051	69.1	5	10	18	22	$109, PF-70DCam, Jan-10
1993S	2,633,439	460	69.4	4	8	14	16	$62, PF-70DCam, Jan-10
1993S, Silver	761,353	787	69.0	6	10	18	22	$207, PF-70DCam, Jan-10

* Included in number above. **a.** Doubling is evident on all reverse lettering around the rim and the left tips. **b.** The mintmark style was changed during 1979 Proof production, creating two distinctly different types. "The Type II is the rare variety, and is easily distinguished from the common Type I. The Type I has a very indistinct blob, whereas the Type II shows a well-defined S" (*Cherrypickers' Guide to Rare Die Varieties*, fourth edition, volume II). **c.** The mintmark style was changed during the 1981 Proof production, creating two distinct types. "The Type II is the rare variety, and is not easily distinguished from the common Type I. For most collectors, the easiest difference to discern on the Type II is the flatness on the top curve of the S, which is rounded on the Type I. Additionally, the surface of the Type II mintmark is frosted, and the openings in the loops slightly larger" (*Cherrypickers' Guide*). **d.** Very strong doubling is visible on the date and the mintmark, with slightly less dramatic doubling on IN GOD WE TRUST.

	Mintage	Cert	Avg	PF-65	PF-67Cam	PF-68Cam	PF-68DC	Recent Auction Record
1994S	2,484,594	388	69.3	$4	$8	$14	$16	$69, PF-70DCam, Jan-10
1994S, Silver	785,329	771	69.1	8	12	20	25	$230, PF-70DCam, Jan-10
1995S	2,117,496	305	69.4	8	10	16	20	$69, PF-70DCam, Jan-10
1995S, Silver	679,985	883	69.0	8	12	20	25	$219, PF-70DCam, Jan-10
1996S	1,750,244	382	69.2	5	8	14	18	$84, PF-70DCam, Jan-10
1996S, Silver	775,021	791	69.0	8	12	20	25	$138, PF-70DCam, Jan-10
1997S	2,055,000	338	69.5	5	8	14	18	$69, PF-70DCam, Jan-10
1997S, Silver	741,678	847	69.2	8	12	20	25	$89, PF-70DCam, Jan-10
1998S	2,086,507	396	69.5	6	8	14	18	$115, PF-70DCam, Jan-10
1998S, Silver	878,792	995	69.2	7	10	18	22	$99, PF-70DCam, Jan-10

WASHINGTON, STATEHOOD, D.C., TERRITORIAL, AND NATIONAL PARKS (1999 TO DATE)

Clad : Designers John Flanagan and others; weight 5.67 grams; composition outer layers of copper-nickel (.750 copper, .250 nickel) bonded to inner core of pure copper; diameter 24.3 mm; reeded edge.

Silver Proofs: Designers John Flanagan and others; weight 6.25 grams; composition .900 silver, .100 copper (net weight: .18084 oz. pure silver); diameter 24.3 mm; reeded edge; mint: San Francisco.

History. In 1999 the U.S. Mint introduced a new program of statehood quarters. These were released at the rate of five new reverse designs each year, in combination with a restyled obverse, through 2008. The coins became very popular and are still widely collected with enthusiasm. In 2009 a similar program of quarter dollars was issued for Washington, D.C., and the five U.S. territories. A similar program for national parks and historic sites started in 2010 and will run through 2021. Circulation strikes are made at the Philadelphia and Denver mints, and special silver-content and Proof issues at San Francisco. Each coin combines a modified obverse depicting George Washington, without a date. The reverses are distinctive and bear the date of issue, the date of statehood (for the state quarters), and other design elements. Each state or district/territory selected its own design.

Some statehood quarters were accidentally made with "disoriented" dies and are valued higher than ordinary pieces. Normal United States coins have dies oriented in coin alignment, such that the reverse appears upside down when the coin is flipped from right to left. Values for the rotated-die quarters vary according to the amount of shifting. The most valuable are those that are shifted 180 degrees, so that both sides appear upright when the coin is turned over (called *medal alignment*).

Striking and Sharpness. These quarters can have light striking on the highest area of the obverse. On the reverse there can be weak areas, depending on the design, seemingly more often seen on Denver Mint coins. Some in the statehood quarter series were struck through grease, obliterating portions of both the obverse (usually) and reverse designs.

Availability. All modern quarters are readily available in high grades. Typical MS coins are MS-63 and 64 with light abrasion. MS-65 and higher coins are in the minority, but enough exist that finding them is no problem. Around MS-68 many issues are scarce, and higher grades are scarcer yet.

MS-60 to 70 (Mint State). *Obverse:* At MS-60, some abrasion and contact marks are evident on the highest-relief parts of the hair and the cheek. Abrasion is slight at MS-63, and slighter at MS-64. An MS-65 coin should display no abrasion or contact marks except under magnification, and MS-66 and higher coins should have none at all. Luster should be full. *Reverse:* Check the highest-relief areas of the design (these differ from coin to coin). Otherwise, comments are as for the obverse.

1999
Delaware

1999
Georgia

1999
Pennsylvania

1999
Connecticut

1999
New Jersey

2000
Massachusetts

2000
New Hampshire

2000
Maryland

2000
Virginia

2000
South Carolina

2001
New York

2001
Vermont

2001
North Carolina

2001
Kentucky

2001
Rhode Island

2002
Tennessee

2002
Indiana

2002
Ohio

2002
Mississippi

2002
Louisiana

2003
Illinois

2003
Missouri

2003
Alabama

2003
Arkansas

2003
Maine

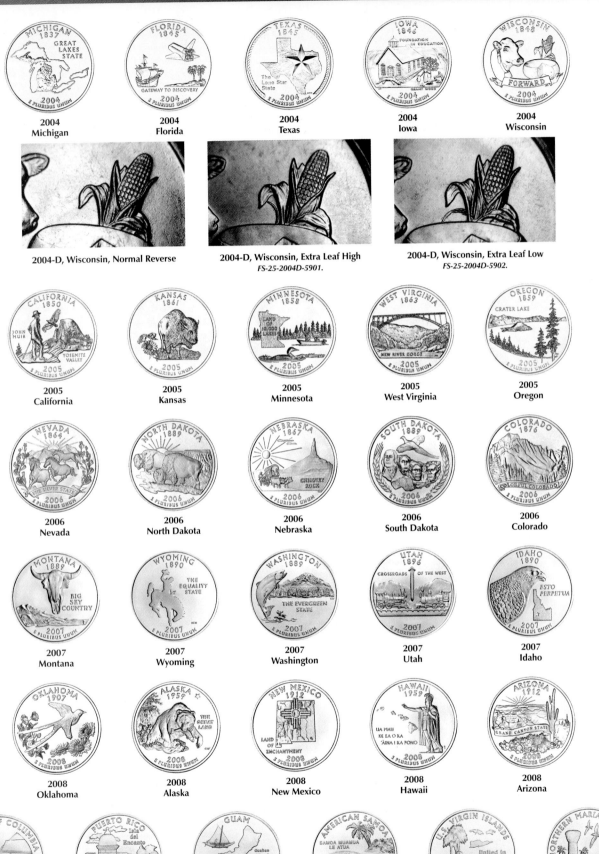

2004
Michigan

2004
Florida

2004
Texas

2004
Iowa

2004
Wisconsin

2004-D, Wisconsin, Normal Reverse

2004-D, Wisconsin, Extra Leaf High
FS-25-2004D-5901.

2004-D, Wisconsin, Extra Leaf Low
FS-25-2004D-5902.

2005
California

2005
Kansas

2005
Minnesota

2005
West Virginia

2005
Oregon

2006
Nevada

2006
North Dakota

2006
Nebraska

2006
South Dakota

2006
Colorado

2007
Montana

2007
Wyoming

2007
Washington

2007
Utah

2007
Idaho

2008
Oklahoma

2008
Alaska

2008
New Mexico

2008
Hawaii

2008
Arizona

2009
District of Columbia

2009
Puerto Rico

2009
Guam

2009
American Samoa

2009
U.S. Virgin Islands

2009
Northern Mariana
Islands

**2010
Hot Springs
National Park**

**2010
Yellowstone
National Park**

**2010
Yosemite
National Park**

**2010
Grand Canyon
National Park**

**2010
Mt. Hood
National Forest**

	Mintage	Cert	Avg	%MS	MS-63	MS-65	MS-66	MS-67	Recent Auction Record
1999P, Delaware	373,400,000	1,086	66.0	100	$1.25	$3.00	$25	$65	$32, MS-67, Aug-09
1999D, Delaware	401,424,000	1,253	66.0	100	1.25	3.00	25	65	$36, MS-67, Aug-09
1999P, Pennsylvania	349,000,000	990	66.1	100	1.25	3.00	25	65	$253, MS-68, Apr-08
1999D, Pennsylvania	358,332,000	878	65.9	100	1.25	3.00	25	65	$299, MS-68, Apr-08
1999P, New Jersey	363,200,000	963	66.1	100	1.25	3.00	25	65	$14, MS-67, Apr-08
1999D, New Jersey	299,028,000	1,064	66.0	100	1.25	3.00	25	65	$47, MS-67, Aug-09
1999P, Georgia	451,188,000	1,071	65.7	100	1.25	3.00	25	65	$19, MS-67, Apr-08
1999D, Georgia	488,744,000	1,080	65.8	99	1.25	3.00	25	65	$38, MS-67, Aug-09
1999P, Connecticut	688,744,000	1,170	65.6	99	1.25	3.00	25	65	$219, MS-68, Apr-08
1999D, Connecticut	657,880,000	2,161	65.3	100	1.25	3.00	25	65	$24, MS-67, Aug-09
2000P, Massachusetts	628,600,000	772	66.2	100	1.00	2.00	15	50	$30, MS-68, Aug-09
2000D, Massachusetts	535,184,000	606	66.1	100	1.00	2.00	15	50	$127, MS-68, Apr-08
2000P, Maryland	678,200,000	575	65.9	100	1.00	2.00	15	50	$39, MS-68, Apr-08
2000D, Maryland	556,532,000	604	66.0	100	1.00	2.00	15	50	$27, MS-67, Jul-08
2000P, South Carolina	742,576,000	569	66.0	100	1.00	2.00	15	50	$27, MS-68, Apr-08
2000D, South Carolina	566,208,000	708	66.3	100	1.00	2.00	15	50	$15, MS-67, Mar-09
2000P, New Hampshire	673,040,000	532	65.6	99	1.00	2.00	15	50	$207, MS-68, Apr-08
2000D, New Hampshire	495,976,000	542	66.0	100	1.00	2.00	15	50	$633, MS-68, Dec-07
2000P, Virginia	943,000,000	640	66.1	100	1.00	2.00	15	50	$92, MS-68, Apr-08
2000D, Virginia	651,616,000	551	66.1	99	1.00	2.00	15	50	$10, MS-66, Jun-08
2001P, New York	655,400,000	367	66.1	100	1.00	1.25	15	50	$25, MS-68, Jan-09
2001D, New York	619,640,000	440	66.2	100	1.00	1.25	15	50	$15, MS-66, Aug-09
2001P, North Carolina	627,600,000	357	66.3	100	1.00	1.25	15	50	$21, MS-68, Apr-08
2001D, North Carolina	427,876,000	388	66.3	100	1.00	1.25	15	50	$15, MS-66, Aug-09
2001P, Rhode Island	423,000,000	285	66.0	100	1.00	1.25	15	50	$86, MS-68, Apr-08
2001D, Rhode Island	447,100,000	337	66.0	100	1.00	1.25	15	50	$33, MS-67, Dec-07
2001P, Vermont	423,400,000	1,841	65.7	100	1.00	1.25	15	50	$45, MS-68, Apr-08
2001D, Vermont	459,404,000	347	66.3	100	1.00	1.25	15	50	$15, MS-66, Oct-09
2001P, Kentucky	353,000,000	362	66.3	100	1.00	1.25	15	50	$16, MS-65, Aug-09
2001D, Kentucky	370,564,000	275	66.1	100	1.00	1.25	15	50	$460, MS-68, Dec-07
2002P, Tennessee	361,600,000	272	66.5	100	1.50	3.00	10	40	$11, MS-66, Jan-09
2002D, Tennessee	286,468,000	272	66.4	100	1.50	3.00	10	40	$18, MS-68, Apr-08
2002P, Ohio	217,200,000	315	66.7	100	1.00	1.25	10	40	$15, MS-68, Apr-08
2002D, Ohio	414,832,000	250	66.3	100	1.00	1.25	10	40	$15, MS-68, Apr-08
2002P, Louisiana	362,000,000	241	66.7	100	1.00	1.25	10	40	$31, MS-68, Apr-08
2002D, Louisiana	402,204,000	196	66.3	100	1.00	1.25	10	40	$25, MS-68, Jan-09
2002P, Indiana	362,600,000	287	66.5	99	1.00	1.25	10	40	$15, MS-68, Apr-08
2002D, Indiana	327,200,000	223	66.4	100	1.00	1.25	10	40	$18, MS-68, Apr-08
2002P, Mississippi	290,000,000	258	66.3	100	1.00	1.25	10	40	$19, MS-68, Apr-08
2002D, Mississippi	289,600,000	202	66.4	100	1.00	1.25	10	40	$51, MS-68, Apr-08
2003P, Illinois	225,800,000	239	66.0	100	1.00	1.25	10	40	$11, MS-67, Apr-08
2003D, Illinois	237,400,000	2,042	65.2	100	1.00	1.25	10	40	
2003P, Alabama	225,000,000	248	65.7	100	1.00	1.25	10	40	$59, MS-67, Dec-07
2003D, Alabama	232,400,000	2,047	65.1	100	1.00	1.25	10	40	$13, MS-66, Apr-06
2003P, Maine	217,400,000	227	65.8	100	1.00	1.25	10	40	$17, MS-67, Apr-08
2003D, Maine	231,400,000	2,044	65.2	100	1.00	1.25	10	40	$1,093, MS-68, Dec-07
2003P, Missouri	225,000,000	240	65.9	99	1.00	1.25	10	40	$57, MS-68, Apr-08
2003D, Missouri	228,200,000	2,059	65.1	100	1.00	1.25	10	40	$4,313, MS-68, Dec-07
2003P, Arkansas	228,000,000	218	65.8	100	1.00	1.25	10	40	$60, MS-68, Apr-08
2003D, Arkansas	229,800,000	2,093	65.2	100	0.65	1.40	10	40	$460, MS-68, Dec-07

	Mintage	Cert	Avg	%MS	MS-63	MS-65	MS-66	MS-67	Recent Auction Record
2004P, Michigan	233,800,000	2,320	65.2	100	$0.75	$1.00	$10	$40	$21, MS-68, Apr-08
2004D, Michigan	225,800,000	326	67.2	100	0.75	1.00	10	40	$16, MS-68, Jan-09
2004P, Florida	240,200,000	2,298	65.1	100	0.75	1.00	10	40	$64, MS-68, Apr-08
2004D, Florida	241,600,000	259	66.9	100	0.75	1.00	10	40	$15, MS-68, Apr-08
2004P, Texas	278,800,000	2,344	65.1	100	0.75	1.00	10	40	$115, MS-68, Dec-07
2004D, Texas	263,000,000	255	66.9	100	0.75	1.00	10	40	$19, MS-68, Apr-08
2004P, Iowa	213,800,000	2,281	65.1	100	0.75	1.00	10	40	$25, MS-68, Jan-09
2004D, Iowa	251,400,000	232	66.8	100	0.75	1.00	10	40	$15, MS-68, Apr-08
2004P, Wisconsin	226,400,000	2,499	65.2	100	0.75	1.00	10	40	$31, MS-67, Apr-08
2004D, Wisconsin	226,800,000	2,687	65.7	100	0.75	1.00	10	40	$33, MS-68, Apr-08
2004D, Wisconsin, Extra Leaf High (a)	*	4,304	64.9	96	200.00	250.00	300	500	$219, MS-65, Feb-10
2004D, Wisconsin, Extra Leaf Low (a)	*	5,738	64.9	97	150.00	200.00	275	450	$150, MS-65, Feb-10
2005P, California	257,200,000	3,245	66.8	100	0.50	0.75	10	40	$2, MS-69 Satin, Aug-09
2005D, California	263,200,000	2,770	66.9	100	0.50	0.75	10	40	$351, MS-68, Dec-07
2005P, Minnesota	239,600,000	3,240	66.9	100	0.50	0.75	10	40	$56, MS-68 Satin, Aug-09
2005D, Minnesota	248,400,000	2,873	67.1	100	0.50	0.75	10	40	$21, MS-69 Satin, Dec-08
2005P, Oregon	316,200,000	3,204	67.0	100	0.50	0.75	10	40	$10, MS-67 Satin, Jul-08
2005D, Oregon	404,000,000	2,831	67.1	100	0.50	0.75	10	40	$17, MS-69 Satin, Sep-09
2005P, Kansas	263,400,000	2,837	66.6	100	0.50	0.75	10	40	$26, MS-69 Satin, Mar-10
2005D, Kansas	300,000,000	2,834	67.0	100	0.50	0.75	10	40	$25, MS-69 Satin, Jan-09
2005P, West Virginia	365,400,000	3,092	66.8	100	0.50	0.75	10	40	$10, MS-67 Satin, Jul-08
2005D, West Virginia	356,200,000	2,577	66.8	100	0.50	0.75	10	40	$184, MS-68, Apr-08
2006P, Nevada	277,000,000	1,292	66.5	100	0.50	0.75	10	40	$28, MS-68 Satin, Aug-09
2006D, Nevada	312,800,000	1,601	66.8	100	0.50	0.75	10	40	$18, MS-69 Satin, Aug-09
2006P, Nebraska	318,000,000	1,441	66.9	100	0.50	0.75	10	40	$40, MS-69 Satin, Jun-08
2006D, Nebraska	273,000,000	1,804	67.1	100	0.50	0.75	10	40	$23, MS-69 Satin, Dec-08
2006P, Colorado	274,800,000	1,377	66.7	100	0.50	0.75	10	40	$32, MS-69 Satin, Aug-09
2006D, Colorado	294,200,000	1,840	67.0	100	0.50	0.75	10	40	$11, MS-69 Satin, Jan-09
2006P, North Dakota	305,800,000	1,284	66.6	100	0.50	0.75	10	40	$148, MS-69 Satin, Nov-07
2006D, North Dakota	359,000,000	1,767	67.0	100	0.50	0.75	10	40	$25, MS-69 Satin, Aug-09
2006P, South Dakota	245,000,000	1,440	66.8	100	0.50	0.75	10	40	$42, MS-69 Satin, Jan-09
2006D, South Dakota	265,800,000	1,696	67.0	100	0.50	0.75	10	40	$104, MS-69 Satin, Nov-07
2007P, Montana	257,000,000	384	66.4	100	0.50	0.60	10	40	
2007D, Montana	256,240,000	420	66.3	100	0.50	0.60	10	40	
2007P, Washington	265,200,000	394	66.3	100	0.50	0.60	10	40	
2007D, Washington	280,000,000	425	66.4	100	0.50	0.60	10	40	$24, MS-69 Satin, Jan-09
2007P, Idaho	294,600,000	366	66.4	100	0.50	0.60	10	40	
2007D, Idaho	286,800,000	371	66.4	100	0.50	0.60	10	40	$368, MS-68, Dec-07
2007P, Wyoming	243,600,000	310	66.0	100	0.50	0.60	10	40	
2007D, Wyoming	320,800,000	396	66.3	100	0.50	0.60	10	40	
2007P, Utah	255,000,000	389	66.1	100	0.50	0.60	10	40	
2007D, Utah	253,200,000	470	66.4	100	0.50	0.60	10	40	
2008P, Oklahoma	222,000,000	117	66.5	99	0.50	0.60	10	40	
2008D, Oklahoma	194,600,000	124	66.4	100	0.50	0.60	10	40	
2008P, New Mexico	244,200,000	111	66.2	100	0.50	0.60	10	40	
2008D, New Mexico	244,400,000	101	66.5	100	0.50	0.60	10	40	
2008P, Arizona	244,600,000	136	66.3	100	0.50	0.60	10	40	
2008D, Arizona	265,000,000	74	66.5	99	0.50	0.60	10	40	
2008P, Alaska	251,800,000	93	66.4	100	0.50	0.60	10	40	
2008D, Alaska	254,000,000	74	66.1	100	0.50	0.60	10	40	
2008P, Hawaii	254,000,000	87	66.3	100	0.50	0.60	10	40	
2008D, Hawaii	263,600,000	87	66.2	100	0.50	0.60	10	40	
2009P, District of Columbia	83,600,000	244	67.2	100	0.50	0.60	10	40	
2009D, District of Columbia	88,800,000	271	67.4	100	0.50	0.60	10	40	
2009P, Puerto Rico	53,200,000	210	66.8	100	0.50	0.60	10	40	
2009D, Puerto Rico	86,000,000	251	67.5	100	0.50	0.60	10	40	

* Included in number above. **a.** Some 2004-D Wisconsin quarters show one of two different die flaws on the reverse, in the shape of an extra leaf on the corn.

Chart continued on next page.

	Mintage	Cert	Avg	%MS	MS-63	MS-65	MS-66	MS-67	Recent Auction Record
2009P, Guam	45,000,000	213	67.2	100	$0.50	$0.60	$10	$40	
2009D, Guam	42,600,000	199	67.4	100	0.50	0.60	10	40	
2009P, American Samoa	42,600,000	296	67.5	100	0.50	0.60	10	40	
2009D, American Samoa	39,600,000	361	67.9	100	0.50	0.60	10	40	
2009P, U.S. Virgin Islands	41,000,000	263	67.1	100	0.50	0.60	10	40	
2009D, U.S. Virgin Islands	41,000,000	300	67.7	100	0.50	0.60	10	40	
2009P, Northern Mariana Islands	35,200,000	245	67.8	100	0.50	0.60	10	40	
2009D, Northern Mariana Islands	37,600,000	279	67.6	100	0.50	0.60	10	40	
2010P, Hot Springs National Park		458	66.1	100	0.50	0.60	10	40	
2010D, Hot Springs National Park		1,339	65.6	100	0.50	0.60	10	40	
2010P, Yellowstone National Park					0.50	0.60	10	40	
2010D, Yellowstone National Park					0.50	0.60	10	40	
2010P, Yosemite National Park					0.50	0.60	10	40	
2010D, Yosemite National Park					0.50	0.60	10	40	
2010P, Grand Canyon National Park					0.50	0.60	10	40	
2010D, Grand Canyon National Park					0.50	0.60	10	40	
2010P, Mt. Hood National Forest					0.50	0.60	10	40	
2010D, Mt. Hood National Forest					0.50	0.60	10	40	

Proof Washington Statehood, D.C., Territorial, and National Parks Quarters

PF-60 to 70 (Proof). Statehood and D.C./territorial quarter Proofs were made in San Francisco. For certain later issues of Washington quarters as well as for all statehood and territorial issues, Proofs are available in clad metal as well as silver strikings. On some Proofs, over-polishing of dies has eliminated some details, as on part of the WC (for William Cousins) initials on certain 1999 Delaware pieces. *Obverse and Reverse:* Only a few have been cleaned, and most approach perfection and can be designated PF-68 to 70 (the latter only if no contact marks or other problems can be seen under magnification). A cleaned coin with extensive hairlines is not collectible for most numismatists and would be classified at a lower level such as PF-60 to 63. Those with lighter hairlines qualify for PF-64 or 65.

Proof Washington Quarter, Territorial

	Mintage	Cert	Avg	PF-66DC	PF-69DC	Recent Auction Record
1999S, Delaware	3,713,359	5,256	69.1	$8.00	$20	$150, PF-70DCam, Jan-10
1999S, Delaware, Silver	804,565	7,596	69.0	45.00	50	$31, PF-69UCam, Apr-09
1999S, Pennsylvania	3,713,359	5,147	69.1	8.00	20	$374, PF-70DCam, Dec-09
1999S, Pennsylvania, Silver	804,565	7,430	69.1	35.00	50	$1,725, PF-70DCam, Jul-09
1999S, New Jersey	3,713,359	5,171	69.1	8.00	20	$288, PF-70DCam, Oct-09
1999S, New Jersey, Silver	804,565	7,426	69.1	35.00	50	$42, PF-69UCam, May-09
1999S, Georgia	3,713,359	5,208	69.1	8.00	20	$184, PF-70DCam, Jan-09
1999S, Georgia, Silver	804,565	7,474	69.1	35.00	50	$150, PF-70UCam, Mar-10
1999S, Connecticut	3,713,359	5,208	69.2	8.00	20	$127, PF-70DCam, Feb-10
1999S, Connecticut, Silver	804,565	7,387	69.1	35.00	50	$575, PF-70DCam, Jan-10
2000S, Massachusetts	4,020,172	3,812	69.2	4.00	15	$127, PF-70DCam, May-09
2000S, Massachusetts, Silver	965,421	8,440	69.2	7.00	20	$150, PF-70DCam, Aug-09
2000S, Maryland	4,020,172	3,751	69.2	4.00	15	$138, PF-70DCam, Dec-09
2000S, Maryland, Silver	965,421	8,543	69.2	7.00	20	$144, PF-70DCam, Oct-09
2000S, South Carolina	4,020,172	3,802	69.2	4.00	15	$94, PF-70DCam, Aug-09
2000S, South Carolina, Silver	965,421	8,253	69.2	7.00	20	$69, PF-70UCam, Feb-10
2000S, New Hampshire	4,020,172	3,811	69.2	4.00	15	$130, PF-70DCam, Dec-09
2000S, New Hampshire, Silver	965,421	8,278	69.1	7.00	20	$144, PF-70DCam, Nov-09
2000S, Virginia	4,020,172	3,795	69.2	4.00	15	$30, PF-70UCam, Feb-10
2000S, Virginia, Silver	965,421	8,395	69.1	7.00	20	$144, PF-70DCam, Oct-09

QUARTER DOLLARS, 1796 TO DATE

	Mintage	Cert	Avg	PF-66DC	PF-69DC	Recent Auction Record
2001S, New York	3,094,140	3,149	69.2	$8.00	$15	$62, PF-70UCam, Jan-10
2001S, New York, Silver	889,697	5,831	69.2	15.00	20	$460, PF-70DCam, Dec-09
2001S, North Carolina	3,094,140	3,300	69.2	8.00	15	$55, PF-70DCam, Jun-09
2001S, North Carolina, Silver	889,697	5,787	69.2	15.00	20	$150, PF-70DCam, Dec-09
2001S, Rhode Island	3,094,140	2,907	69.2	8.00	15	$115, PF-70DCam, Oct-09
2001S, Rhode Island, Silver	889,697	5,849	69.2	15.00	20	$201, PF-70DCam, Oct-09
2001S, Vermont	3,094,140	3,042	69.3	8.00	15	$47, PF-70UCam, Jun-09
2001S, Vermont, Silver	889,697	5,868	69.2	15.00	20	$161, PF-70DCam, Jan-10
2001S, Kentucky	3,094,140	2,943	69.2	8.00	15	$130, PF-70DCam, Dec-09
2001S, Kentucky, Silver	889,697	5,806	69.2	15.00	20	$13, PF-70DCam, Oct-08
2002S, Tennessee	3,084,245	2,640	69.2	5.00	15	$89, PF-70DCam, Oct-09
2002S, Tennessee, Silver	892,229	6,239	69.2	10.00	20	$144, PF-70DCam, Oct-09
2002S, Ohio	3,084,245	2,650	69.3	5.00	15	$99, PF-70DCam, Oct-09
2002S, Ohio, Silver	892,229	6,300	69.2	10.00	20	$115, PF-70DCam, Dec-09
2002S, Louisiana	3,084,245	2,654	69.2	5.00	15	$56, PF-70UCam, Feb-10
2002S, Louisiana, Silver	892,229	6,061	69.2	10.00	20	$150, PF-70DCam, Dec-09
2002S, Indiana	3,084,245	2,665	69.2	5.00	15	$40, PF-70DCam, Oct-09
2002S, Indiana, Silver	892,229	6,199	69.2	10.00	20	$130, PF-70DCam, Dec-09
2002S, Mississippi	3,084,245	2,699	69.3	5.00	15	$34, PF-70UCam, Mar-10
2002S, Mississippi, Silver	892,229	6,428	69.2	10.00	20	$150, PF-70DCam, Dec-09
2003S, Illinois	3,408,516	5,097	69.2	5.00	15	$62, PF-70UCam, Mar-10
2003S, Illinois, Silver	1,125,755	7,067	69.2	8.00	20	$62, PF-70UCam, Feb-10
2003S, Alabama	3,408,516	5,172	69.3	5.00	15	$47, PF-70DCam, Oct-09
2003S, Alabama, Silver	1,125,755	7,065	69.2	8.00	20	$36, PF-70UCam, Mar-10
2003S, Maine	3,408,516	5,037	69.2	5.00	15	$36, PF-70UCam, Mar-10
2003S, Maine, Silver	1,125,755	6,986	69.2	8.00	20	$115, PF-70DCam, Nov-09
2003S, Missouri	3,408,516	5,233	69.3	5.00	15	$38, PF-70UCam, Feb-10
2003S, Missouri, Silver	1,125,755	7,085	69.2	8.00	20	$115, PF-70DCam, Oct-09
2003S, Arkansas	3,408,516	5,168	69.3	5.00	15	$44, PF-70UCam, Feb-10
2003S, Arkansas, Silver	1,125,755	7,104	69.3	8.00	20	$104, PF-70UCam, Mar-10
2004S, Michigan	2,740,684	3,474	69.3	5.00	15	$28, PF-70UCam, Jan-10
2004S, Michigan, Silver	1,769,786	8,418	69.3	9.00	20	$42, PF-70UCam, Jan-10
2004S, Florida	2,740,684	3,440	69.2	5.00	15	$36, PF-70UCam, Dec-09
2004S, Florida, Silver	1,769,786	8,298	69.2	9.00	20	$16, PF-70DCam, Dec-09
2004S, Texas	2,740,684	3,512	69.3	5.00	15	$28, PF-70UCam, Dec-09
2004S, Texas, Silver	1,769,786	8,587	69.3	9.00	20	$69, PF-70DCam, Oct-09
2004S, Iowa	2,740,684	3,526	69.3	5.00	15	$79, PF-70DCam, Jan-10
2004S, Iowa, Silver	1,769,786	8,490	69.3	9.00	20	$79, PF-70DCam, Jan-10
2004S, Wisconsin	2,740,684	3,550	69.3	5.00	15	$56, PF-70DCam, Oct-09
2004S, Wisconsin, Silver	1,769,786	8,631	69.3	9.00	20	$56, PF-70UCam, Jan-10
2005S, California	3,262,960	8,303	69.3	4.50	15	$24, PF-70UCam, Mar-10
2005S, California, Silver	1,678,649	9,456	69.4	9.00	20	$94, PF-70DCam, Dec-09
2005S, Minnesota	3,262,960	8,283	69.3	4.50	15	$40, PF-70UCam, Mar-10
2005S, Minnesota, Silver	1,678,649	9,259	69.4	9.00	20	$127, PF-70UCam, Mar-10
2005S, Oregon	3,262,960	8,244	69.3	4.50	15	$59, PF-70DCam, Oct-09
2005S, Oregon, Silver	1,678,649	9,292	69.4	9.00	20	$99, PF-70DCam, Oct-09
2005S, Kansas	3,262,960	8,303	69.3	4.50	15	$44, PF-70UCam, Feb-10
2005S, Kansas, Silver	1,678,649	9,442	69.3	9.00	20	$115, PF-70DCam, Nov-09
2005S, West Virginia	3,262,960	8,315	69.3	4.50	15	$26, PF-70UCam, Mar-10
2005S, West Virginia, Silver	1,678,649	9,323	69.5	9.00	20	$38, PF-70UCam, Feb-10
2006S, Nevada	2,882,428	5,756	69.5	4.50	15	$74, PF-70DCam, Dec-09
2006S, Nevada, Silver	1,585,008	8,205	69.5	8.00	20	$104, PF-70DCam, Mar-10
2006S, Nebraska	2,882,428	5,753	69.4	4.50	15	$89, PF-70UCam, Aug-09
2006S, Nebraska, Silver	1,585,008	8,075	69.5	8.00	20	$23, PF-70UCam, Dec-08
2006S, Colorado	2,882,428	5,751	69.4	4.50	15	$29, PF-70DCam, Nov-08
2006S, Colorado, Silver	1,585,008	8,153	69.6	8.00	20	$36, PF-70UCam, Jun-09
2006S, North Dakota	2,882,428	5,760	69.4	4.50	15	$29, PF-70UCam, Dec-08
2006S, North Dakota, Silver	1,585,008	8,157	69.5	8.00	20	$11, PF-70DCam, Oct-08
2006S, South Dakota	2,882,428	5,768	69.5	4.50	15	$69, PF-70DCam, Dec-09
2006S, South Dakota, Silver	1,585,008	8,183	69.6	8.00	20	$66, PF-70UCam, Jun-09

Chart continued on next page.

	Mintage	Cert	Avg	PF-66DC	PF-69DC	Recent Auction Record
2007S, Montana	2,002,812	3,217	69.5	$4.50	$15	$30, PF-70UCam, Feb-10
2007S, Montana, Silver	1,094,993	6,781	69.5	8.00	20	$56, PF-70UCam, Feb-10
2007S, Washington	2,002,812	3,158	69.5	4.50	15	$34, PF-70UCam, Feb-10
2007S, Washington, Silver	1,094,993	6,741	69.4	8.00	20	$47, PF-70UCam, Feb-10
2007S, Idaho	2,002,812	3,173	69.5	4.50	15	$53, PF-70DCam, Oct-09
2007S, Idaho, Silver	1,094,993	6,797	69.4	8.00	20	$104, PF-70UCam, Mar-10
2007S, Wyoming	2,002,812	3,100	69.4	4.50	15	$74, PF-70DCam, Oct-09
2007S, Wyoming, Silver	1,094,993	6,675	69.4	8.00	20	$84, PF-70UCam, Feb-10
2007S, Utah	2,002,812	3,117	69.5	4.50	15	$84, PF-70DCam, Nov-09
2007S, Utah, Silver	1,094,993	6,729	69.4	8.00	20	$40, PF-70UCam, Feb-10
2008S, Oklahoma	2,047,284	3,332	69.5	4.50	15	$30, PF-70UCam, Mar-10
2008S, Oklahoma, Silver	1,020,768	6,829	69.5	8.00	20	$45, PF-70UCam, Jul-08
2008S, New Mexico	2,047,284	3,399	69.4	4.50	15	$37, PF-70UCam, Jul-08
2008S, New Mexico, Silver	1,020,768	6,739	69.5	8.00	20	$60, PF-70UCam, Nov-08
2008S, Arizona	2,047,284	3,481	69.6	4.50	15	$53, PF-70UCam, Mar-10
2008S, Arizona, Silver	1,020,768	7,048	69.6	8.00	20	$28, PF-70UCam, Feb-10
2008S, Alaska	2,047,284	3,316	69.5	4.50	15	$40, PF-70UCam, Mar-10
2008S, Alaska, Silver	1,020,768	6,968	69.6	8.00	20	$104, PF-70UCam, Mar-10
2008S, Hawaii	2,047,284	3,338	69.4	4.50	15	$50, PF-70UCam, Mar-10
2008S, Hawaii, Silver	1,020,768	6,990	69.4	8.00	20	$127, PF-70DCam, Oct-09
2009S, District of Columbia		4,083	69.6	4.50	15	
2009S, District of Columbia, Silver		5,434	69.7	8.00	20	
2009S, Puerto Rico		4,066	69.6	4.50	15	$38, PF-70DCam, Feb-10
2009S, Puerto Rico, Silver		5,571	69.8	8.00	20	$104, PF-70UCam, Mar-10
2009S, Guam		3,969	69.6	4.50	15	$47, PF-70UCam, Mar-10
2009S, Guam, Silver		5,302	69.7	8.00	20	$53, PF-70UCam, Jan-10
2009S, American Samoa		4,137	69.6	4.50	15	$84, PF-70DCam, Mar-10
2009S, American Samoa, Silver		5,490	69.8	8.00	20	$62, PF-70UCam, Jan-10
2009S, U.S. Virgin Islands		4,104	69.6	4.50	15	$104, PF-70DCam, Mar-10
2009S, U.S. Virgin Islands, Silver		5,481	69.8	8.00	20	$60, PF-70UCam, Mar-10
2009S, Northern Mariana Islands		4,106	69.6	4.50	15	$50, PF-70DCam, Mar-10
2009S, Northern Mariana Islands, Silver		5,452	69.8	8.00	20	$47, PF-70UCam, Jan-10
2010S, Hot Springs National Park		1,964	69.5	4.50	15	
2010S, Hot Springs National Park, Silver		10	69.5	8.00	20	
2010S, Yellowstone National Park		1,962	69.5	4.50	15	
2010S, Yellowstone National Park, Silver		10	69.5	8.00	20	
2010S, Yosemite National Park		1,961	69.4	4.50	15	
2010S, Yosemite National Park, Silver		10	69.5	8.00	20	
2010S, Grand Canyon National Park		1,966	69.4	4.50	15	
2010S, Grand Canyon National Park, Silver		10	69.5	8.00	20	
2010S, Mt. Hood National Forest		1,956	69.4	4.50	15	
2010S, Mt. Hood National Forest, Silver		10	69.5	8.00	20	

AN OVERVIEW OF HALF DOLLARS

A collection of half dollars is one of the most satisfying in the American series. The panorama is extensive, and ranges from the early Flowing Hair issues of 1794 and 1795 down to the present day. The large size of such pieces makes them convenient to view and enjoy.

Among the types, the 1794–1795 Flowing Hair half dollar is readily available in circulated grades and rare in Mint State, but at any level is hard to find well struck and without adjustment marks. Most on the market are dated 1795. Careful selection is advised.

The next type, 1796–1797 with Draped Bust obverse and Small Eagle reverse, is the scarcest in the American silver series excepting the 1839 Gobrecht dollar. (However, the latter is available in Proof restrike form, yielding choice and gem examples, so it can be considered in a different category from the circulation-strike 1796–1797 half dollar type.) It might not be possible to be particular, but, finances permitting, a collector should take some time and endeavor to find a specimen sharply struck on both sides. Needle-sharp striking is more of a theory than a practicality, and some compromise may be necessary.

Half dollars of the 1801–1807 type, obverse as preceding but now with the Heraldic Eagle reverse, are plentiful enough in worn grades but somewhat scarce in Mint State. Striking is seldom needle sharp and ranges from average to very poor. However, there are enough coins in the marketplace that collectors can afford to take their time and select a sharp strike.

Capped Bust half dollars with lettered edge, 1807–1836, abound in just about any grade desired. Again, striking is a consideration, and some searching is needed. Generally, those in the late 1820s and the 1830s are better struck than are those of earlier dates, the earlier coins being scarcer and more expensive in any event.

The short-lived type of 1836–1837, Capped Bust with reeded edge, denomination spelled as 50 CENTS, is available easily enough through the high-mintage 1837, but most have problems with striking. Then comes the 1838–1839 type of the same obverse style, its reverse modified with a slightly different eagle and with the denomination as HALF DOL. Generally these are fairly well struck.

Liberty Seated half dollars of the several styles within the series, 1839–1891, admit of no great rarities for the type collector, save for the 1839 No Drapery in levels of MS-63 and finer. However, among the earlier types in particular, sharply struck pieces are in the minority. Curiously, the most readily available Mint State Liberty Seated half dollars also are the lowest mintage issues, the dates 1879 and later, as these were recognized as desirable at the time of issue, and were widely saved.

Barber half dollars were not popular in their time, and while Proofs exist in proportion to their production figures, Mint State coins are quite scarce. In fact, as a type, a Barber half dollar dated 1900 or later in Mint State is the scarcest of all silver issues of that century. Well-struck MS-63 and better Barber half dollars, with the upper-right corner of the shield and the leg at lower right showing full details, are significantly scarcer than generally realized.

Liberty Walking half dollars minted from 1916 to 1947 are plentiful in all grades. Again, some attention should be made to striking sharpness, at which time the search becomes more intense. Fortunately, there are countless thousands of MS-63 and finer coins of the 1940s on the market, giving collectors a wide choice. Then come Franklin half dollars, made only from 1948 to 1963, with representative coins easy enough to acquire in about any grade desired. Kennedy half dollars exist in several varieties, all of which are available without any problem. Among these and other modern coins care needs to be taken for value received versus price paid. Modern issues in, for example, MS-65 and 66, selected for quality, are for many collectors preferable to MS-69 or 70 coins offered at a much higher price.

FOR THE COLLECTOR AND INVESTOR: HALF DOLLARS AS A SPECIALTY

Many collectors over the years have pursued half dollars by date and variety. Except for the series of copper cents, half dollars are the most generally available coins over a nearly continuous span, making them possible to collect for reasonable cost. Also, enough die varieties exist that this can form another focus of interest and importance.

In general, the half dollars of the early era form a concentration in themselves. Die varieties can be attributed by Overton numbers, as listed by Al C. Overton in his immensely popular *Early Half Dollar Die Varieties 1794–1836.* To this, Glenn R. Peterson's book, *The Ultimate Guide to Attributing Bust Half Dollars,* is also useful. The John Reich Collectors Society publishes the *John Reich Journal* and serves as a forum for the exchange of information, updates and die varieties, and the like.

Among rarities in the early years, the 1796 and 1797 with Draped Bust obverse and Small Eagle reverse are perhaps the most famous, needed for variety collections as well as one example for a type set. Variety enthusiasts aspire to get two of 1796—one with 15 stars on the obverse and the other with 16 stars—plus the 1797.

Draped Bust half dollars from 1801 through 1807 have a number of rare die varieties (as listed by Overton), but the basic varieties are easy enough to find. The 1805, 5 Over 4 overdate is particularly popular, as there was no "perfect date" 1804, and this is the closest collectors can come to it.

A vast and interesting field in early American numismatics is that of the Capped Bust half dollar, 1807–1836, with a lettered edge. Several hundred different die combinations exist, and many collectors are active in their pursuit, using the Overton book as a road map. All the major varieties are readily collectible except the 1817, 7 Over 4 overdate, of which only about a half dozen exist. The 1815, 5 Over 2 is considered the key issue among the specific dates (rather than varieties of dates). The majority of these occur in VF grade, not often lower and not often higher either—an interesting situation. During the 1820s vast quantities of these were transferred among banks. While many if not most of the varieties listed herein can be obtained in Mint State, most collectors opt for VF or EF, these grades showing the necessary details but also permitting a budget to be stretched to include more varieties, rather than just a few high-grade pieces. Choice and gem examples can be found here and there, and are most plentiful among the later dates.

Among the Capped Bust half dollars of reduced size, 1836–1837, the 1836 is a key date, and fewer than 5,000 are believed to have been minted. The next type, 1838 and 1839, Capped Bust, reeded edge, with a modified eagle on the reverse, includes the famous 1838-O rarity, of which only 20 are said to have been struck (per a note published in 1894 in the catalog of the Friesner Collection). These have a prooflike surface. Interestingly, they were not struck until 1839. In the same year, 1839-O half dollars were also struck, to the extensive quantity of 178,976 pieces; they are unusual as the mintmark is on the obverse, an odd placement for the era.

The series of Liberty Seated half dollars is generally collected by varieties listed herein, although certain dedicated specialists will consult the *Complete Guide to Liberty Seated Half Dollars,* by Randy Wiley and Bill Bugert—a volume that delineates many interesting features, including the number of different reeds on the edges of certain coins.

Among Liberty Seated half dollars there is just one "impossible" rarity, that being the 1853-O without arrows at the date. Only three exist, and each shows extensive wear. Half dollars were first struck at the San Francisco Mint in 1855 and at the Carson City Mint in 1870. Generally, large quantities were minted of most dates and mintmark varieties of Liberty Seated half dollars, making them readily obtainable today. Except for the later dates, 1879–1891, Mint State pieces are generally scarce, gems especially so. Many specialists in half dollars belong to the Liberty Seated Collectors Club (LSCC) and receive its magazine, *The Gobrecht Journal.*

Proof Liberty Seated halves can be collected by date sequence from 1858 onward. Survivors exist in proportion to the mintage quantities. Generally, those before the mid-1870s often come cleaned or hairlined, and more care is needed in selecting choice specimens than is necessary for the later dates.

Barber half dollars were made continuously from 1892 through 1915, in such quantities that today there are no great rarities. However, a number of issues are quite scarce, even in well-worn grades, and in MS-63 and better many are difficult to find. These coins had little honor in the era in which they were issued, and few numismatists saved them. Proofs were made each year from 1892 to 1915 and can be obtained in proportion to their mintages. However, those of 1914 and 1915 are hard to find with choice, original surfaces— decades ago a collector hoarded these two dates and polished those in his possession.

Liberty Walking half dollars are popular to collect by date and mint. Scarce varieties include the 1917-S with obverse mintmark, the three issues of 1921, and the low mintage 1938-D, although the latter is not inordinately expensive. Uncirculated or Mint State pieces are most readily available for 1916 and 1917, and then especially so in the 1930s and 1940s. Striking can be a problem, particularly for issues of the mid-1920s and also the later varieties. For example, with a needle-sharp strike the 1923-S is an extreme rarity. Among later coins the 1940-S and 1941-S often are weakly struck.

Franklin half dollars minted from 1948 through 1963 have been very popular in recent decades. The complete series of dates and mintmarks is short and contains no scarce or rare pieces in grades such as MS-63 and MS-64. However, consider the element of sharp striking, usually defined as Full Bell Lines (FBL) on the reverse, and certain otherwise common dates become elusive. Proofs of most years can also be readily collected.

Kennedy half dollars are easily enough collected, and so many have been made by this time that nearly 200 dates and mintmarks extend from 1964 to present. The wise collector will select coins that have a meeting point between a high grade such as MS-65 or MS-66 (or equivalent Proofs) and a reasonable price.

RECOMMENDED READING

Fivaz, Bill, and Stanton, J.T. *The Cherrypickers' Guide to Rare Die Varieties* (4th ed., vol. II), Atlanta, GA, 2006.

Flynn, Kevin. *The Authoritative Reference on Barber Half Dollars,* Brooklyn, NY, 2005.

Fox, Bruce. *The Complete Guide to Walking Liberty Half Dollars,* Virginia Beach, VA, 1993.

Haseltine, J.W. *Type Table of United States Dollars, Half Dollars and Quarter Dollars,* Philadelphia, 1881 (reprinted 1927, 1968).

Lawrence, David. *The Complete Guide to Barber Halves,* Virginia Beach, VA, 1991.

Overton, Al C. *Early Half Dollar Die Varieties, 1794–1836,* Colorado Springs, CO, 1967 (3rd ed., 1990, edited by Donald Parsley).

Peterson, Glenn R. *The Ultimate Guide to Attributing Bust Half Dollars,* Rocky River, OH, 2000.

Tomaska, Rick. *A Guide Book of Franklin and Kennedy Half Dollars,* Atlanta, GA, 2011.

Wiley, Randy, and Bugert, Bill. *The Complete Guide to Liberty Seated Half Dollars,* Virginia Beach, VA, 1993.

FLOWING HAIR
(1794–1795)

Designer Robert Scot; weight 13.48 grams; composition .8924 silver, .1076 copper; approx. diameter 32.5 mm; edge: FIFTY CENTS OR HALF A DOLLAR with decorations between the words.

Overton-105.

History. The Flowing Hair design inaugurated the half-dollar denomination. The same motif was used on half dimes and silver dollars of the same years. Early half dollars have been extensively collected by die varieties, of which many exist for most dates. Valuations given below are in each case for the most common variety; scarcer ones, as listed by Overton, generally command higher prices.

Striking and Sharpness. Many have problems of one sort or another, including adjustment marks from the planchet being filed and mushy dentils. On the obverse, check the hair details and the stars. On the reverse, check the breast of the eagle in particular. As with other silver coins of this design, it may not be possible to find a *needle-sharp* example, but with some extensive searching a fairly decent strike can be obtained. Sharp striking and excellent eye appeal add to the value dramatically. However, very few 1794 and 1795 halves are uniformly sharp on both sides.

Availability. Probably 3,500 to 6,000 exist. Most are dated 1795, the 1794 being considered a rare date. Typical grades are Good to Fine. EF and AU grades are elusive in regard to the total population. Probably 100 or so could be graded MS (nearly all of them 1795). Unlike half dollars of the 1796–1797 type, none of these are known to have been made with prooflike surfaces.

AU-50, 53, 55, 58 (About Uncirculated). *Obverse:* Light wear is seen on the hair area immediately to the left of the face and above the forehead, on the cheek, and, to a lesser extent, on the top of the neck truncation. An AU-58 coin has minimal traces of wear. Regarding luster: an AU-50 coin has luster in protected areas among the stars and letters, with little in the open fields or on the portrait. At AU-58, much luster is present in the fields but is worn away on the highest parts of the motifs. *Reverse:* Light wear is seen on the eagle's body and the upper part of both wings. On well-struck pieces the details of the wing features are excellent. At AU-50, detail is lost in some feathers in this area. However, strik-ing can play a part, as some coins were weakly struck to begin with. Light wear is seen on the wreath and letter-ing, but is harder to discern. Luster is the best key to actual wear. This will range from perhaps 20% remain-ing in protected areas (at AU-50) to nearly full mint bloom (at AU-58).

MS-60 to 70 (Mint State). *Obverse:* At MS-60, some abrasion and contact marks are evident, most noticeably on the cheek and in the fields. Luster is present, but may be dull or lifeless, and interrupted in patches, perhaps as much from old cleaning as from contact the coin may have received. At MS-63, contact marks are very few, and abrasion is present, but not as noticeable. An MS-65 coin has no abrasion, and contact marks are very few. Luster should be full and rich. Higher grades are seldom seen in this type, but are defined in theory by having fewer marks as perfection is approached. *Reverse:* Com-ments apply as for the obverse, except that abrasion and contact marks are most noticeable on the eagle at the center. This area is often lightly struck, so in all grades do not mistake weak striking for actual wear. Knowl-edge of specific die varieties is helpful in this regard. The field area is small and is protected by lettering and the wreath, and in any given grade shows fewer marks than on the obverse.

1795, Normal Date

1795, Recut Date

1795, 2 Leaves Under Each Wing

1795, 3 Leaves Under Each Wing

	Mintage	Cert	Avg	%MS	AU-50	AU-55	AU-58	MS-60	MS-62	MS-63	MS-64	Recent Auction Record
1794	23,464	285	19.2	2	$77,500	$95,000	$110,000	$140,000	$250,000	$350,000	$450,000	$18,400, VF-20, Jun-10
1795, All kinds (a)	299,680											
1795, Normal Date		272	21.1	3	18,000	25,000	32,500	43,000	65,000	100,000	250,000	$1,650, AU-55, Mar-10
1795, Recut Date		18	22.2	0	20,000	26,000	33,500	45,000	65,000	100,000	250,000	$17,250, AU-58, Feb-09
1795, 3 Leaves Under Each Wing		10	23.8	0	32,000	38,000	45,000	60,000				$16,100, EF-40, Jan-07

a. Varieties of 1795 are known with the final S in STATES over a D; with the A in STATES over an E; and with the Y in LIBERTY over a star. All are scarce. Some 1795 half dollars were weight-adjusted by insertion of a silver plug in the center of the blank planchet before the coin was struck.

DRAPED BUST, SMALL EAGLE REVERSE (1796–1797)

Designer Robert Scot; weight 13.48 grams; composition .8924 silver, .1076 copper; approx. diameter 32.5 mm; edge: FIFTY CENTS OR HALF A DOLLAR with decorations between words.

Overton-101.

History. Robert Scot's Draped Bust design is similar to that used on the half dime, dime, quarter, and silver dollar of this era.

Striking and Sharpness. On the obverse, check the hair details and the stars. On the reverse, first check the breast of the eagle, but examine other areas as well. Also check the dentils on both sides. Look especially for coins that do not have significant adjustment marks.

Coins of this denomination are on average better struck than are half dimes, dimes, quarters (which have reverse problems), and dollars.

Availability. Examples are rare in any grade. MS coins are particularly rare, and when seen are nearly always dated 1796. Some of these have partially prooflike surfaces. Any half dollar of this type has strong market demand.

AU-50, 53, 55, 58 (About Uncirculated). *Obverse:* Light wear is seen on the hair area above the ear and extending to the left of the forehead, on the ribbon, and on the drapery at the shoulder, more so at AU-50 than at 53 or 55. An AU-58 coin has minimal traces of wear. Regarding luster: an AU-50 coin has luster in protected areas among the stars and letters, with little in the open fields or on the portrait. At AU-58, most luster is present in the fields, but is worn away on the highest parts of the motifs. *Reverse:* Light wear is seen on the eagle's body and the edges of the wings. Light wear is seen on the wreath and lettering. Luster is the best key to actual wear; it ranges from perhaps 20% remaining in protected areas (at AU-50) to nearly full mint bloom (at AU-58).

MS-60 to 70 (Mint State). *Obverse:* At MS-60, some abrasion and contact marks are evident, most noticeably on the cheek, the drapery at the shoulder, and the right field. Also check the hair to the left of the forehead. Luster is present, but may be dull or lifeless, and interrupted in patches. At MS-63, contact marks are few, and abrasion is hard to detect, although this type is sometimes graded liberally due to its rarity. An MS-65 coin has no abrasion, and contact marks are so minute as to require magnification. Luster should be full and rich. Coins graded above MS-65 are more theoretical than actual for this type, although some notable pieces have crossed the auction block. These are defined by having fewer marks as perfection is approached. *Reverse:* Comments apply as for the obverse, except that abrasion and contact marks are most noticeable on the eagle at the center, a situation that should be evaluated by considering the original striking (which can be quite sharp, but with many exceptions). The field area is small and is protected by lettering and the wreath, and in any given grade shows fewer marks than on the obverse.

1796, 15 Stars   1796, 16 Stars

Shown 1.25x actual size.

	Mintage	Cert	Avg	%MS	AU-50	AU-55	AU-58	MS-60	MS-62	MS-63	MS-64	Recent Auction Record
1796, 15 Stars †	3,918	12	39.3	33	$145,000	$170,000	$210,000	$290,000	$335,000	$385,000	$500,000	$207,000, AU-58, Jul-08
1796, 16 Stars †	*	11	30.7	18	165,000	190,000	240,000	315,000	365,000	420,000	525,000	$83,375, VF-30, Jul-08
1797, 15 Stars †	*	50	27.2	10	180,000	225,000	275,000	330,000	450,000	550,000	700,000	$1,380,000, MS-66, Jul-08

* Included in number above. † Ranked in the *100 Greatest U.S. Coins* (third edition).

DRAPED BUST, HERALDIC EAGLE REVERSE (1801–1807)

Designer Robert Scot; weight 13.48 grams; composition .8924 silver, .1076 copper; approx. diameter 32.5 mm; edge: FIFTY CENTS OR HALF A DOLLAR with decorations between words.

Overton-101.

History. The half dollar's Draped Bust, Heraldic Eagle design is similar to that of other silver coins of the era.

Striking and Sharpness. Most have light striking in one area or another; on the obverse, check the hair details and, in particular, the star centers. On the reverse, check the stars above the eagle, the clouds, the details of the shield, and the eagle's wings. Check the dentils on both sides. Adjustment marks are sometimes seen, but not as often as on earlier half dollar types. Typically, the earlier years are better struck; many of 1806 and nearly all of 1807 are poorly struck. Sharp striking and excellent eye appeal add to the value dramatically, this being particularly true for 1805 to 1807, which are often weak (particularly 1807).

Availability. Earlier years are scarce in the marketplace, beginning with the elusive 1801 and including the 1802, after which they are more readily available. Some die varieties are scarce. Most MS coins are dated 1806 and 1807, but all are scarce. Finding sharply struck high-grade coins is almost impossible, a goal more than a reality.

EF-40, 45 (Extremely Fine). *Obverse:* More wear is evident on the upper hair area and the ribbon, and on the drapery and bosom than at AU. Excellent detail remains in low-relief areas of the hair. The stars show wear, as do the date and letters. Luster, if present at all, is minimal and in protected areas. *Reverse:* Wear is greater than at AU, overall. The neck lacks feather detail on its highest points. Feathers have lost some detail near the edges of the wings, and some areas of the horizontal lines in the shield may be blended together. Some traces of luster may be seen, less at EF-40 than at EF-45.

AU-50, 53, 55, 58 (About Uncirculated). *Obverse:* Light wear is seen on the hair area above the ear and extending to left of the forehead, on the ribbon, and on the bosom, more so at AU-50 than at 53 or 55. An AU-58 coin has minimal traces of wear. Regarding luster: an AU-50 coin has luster in protected areas among the stars and letters, with little in the open fields or on the portrait. At AU-58, most luster is present in the fields, but is worn away on the highest parts of the motifs. *Reverse:* Comments as preceding, except that the eagle's neck, the tips and top of the wings, the clouds, and the tail now show noticeable wear, as do other features. Luster ranges from perhaps 20% remaining in protected areas (at AU-50) to nearly full mint bloom (at AU-58). Often the reverse of this type retains much more luster than the obverse.

MS-60 to 70 (Mint State). *Obverse:* At MS-60, some abrasion and contact marks are evident, most noticeably on the cheek, the drapery at the shoulder, and the right field. Luster is present, but may be dull or lifeless, and interrupted in patches. At MS-63, contact marks are very few, and abrasion is hard to detect except under magnification. An MS-65 coin has no abrasion, and contact marks are so minute as to require magnification. Luster should be full and rich. Coins grading above MS-65 are more theoretical than actual for this type—but they do exist, and are defined by having fewer marks as perfection is approached. Later years usually have areas of flat striking. *Reverse:* Comments apply as for the obverse, except that abrasion and contact marks are most noticeable on the eagle's neck, the tips of the wing, and the tail. The field area is complex, without much open space, given the stars above the eagle, the arrows and olive branch, and other features. Accordingly, marks are not as noticeable as on the obverse.

1803, Small 3

1803, Large 3

1805, 5 Over 4

1805, Normal Date

1806, 6 Over 5

1806, 6 Over Inverted 6

1806, Knobbed-Top 6, Large Stars
With traces of overdate.

1806, Knobbed-Top 6, Small Stars

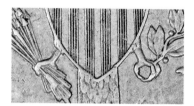

1806, Stem Not Through Claw

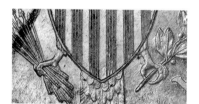

1806, Stem Through Claw

	Mintage	Cert	Avg	%MS	EF-40	AU-50	AU-55	MS-60	MS-62	MS-63	MS-64	Recent Auction Record
1801	30,289	112	26.8	3	$7,400	$17,500	$23,000	$47,500	$75,000	$100,000		$4,888, EF-40, Jun-10
1802	29,890	82	30.8	1	7,400	17,500	23,000	45,000	67,500			$9,775, EF-45, Aug-09
1803, All kinds	188,234											
1803, Small 3		28	37.9	4	2,750	6,000	9,000	22,500	32,500	50,000	$195,000	$4,025, AU-50, Jun-10
1803, Large 3		72	30.3	3	2,050	5,400	7,500	15,000	27,000	35,000	85,000	$1,380, EF-40, Feb-10
1805, All kinds	211,722											
1805, 5 Over 4		89	31.0	1	3,000	7,000	11,500	29,000	65,000	90,000		$10,350, AU-58, Feb-10
1805, Normal Date		88	29.3	0	2,000	5,250	7,500	13,000	22,500			$1,955, EF-45, Feb-10
1806, All kinds	839,576											
1806, 6 Over 5		150	32.2	3	1,800	4,750	6,400	10,000	19,000	27,000	37,500	$1,783, EF-45, Feb-10
1806, 6 Over Inverted 6		57	26.0	2	3,600	7,500	9,500	17,500	27,500	34,000	60,000	$1,495, VF-20 CAC, May-10
1806, Knbd 6, Lg Stars												
(Traces of Overdate)		26	28.6	0	1,525	4,550	6,250	8,750	17,500	22,500	32,500	$1,725, EF-40, Jan-10
1806, Knbd 6, Sm Stars		22	27.4	0	1,525	4,550	6,250	8,750	17,500	22,500	32,500	$1,553, EF-40, Feb-10
1806, Knbd 6, Stem Not												
Through Claw					125,000							$126,500, EF-40, Jan-09
1806, Pointed 6, Stem												
Through Claw		193	33.2	6	1,475	4,200	5,500	7,800	12,000	16,000	28,500	$1,725, EF-45, Feb-10
1806, Pointed 6, Stem Through												
Claw, E Over A in STATES		4	16.0	0								
1806, Pointed 6, Stem Not												
Through Claw		78	37.1	8	1,475	4,200	5,500	7,800	12,000	16,000	28,500	$4,888, AU-55, Jun-10
1807	301,076	800	35.5	9	1,500	4,200	5,500	7,800	11,500	15,500	27,500	$9,200, MS-62, Jun-10

CAPPED BUST, LETTERED EDGE (1807–1836)

Designer John Reich; weight 13.48 grams; composition .8924 silver, .1076 copper; approx. diameter 32.5 mm. 1807–1814—Edge: FIFTY CENTS OR HALF A DOLLAR. 1814–1831—Edge: Star added between DOLLAR and FIFTY. 1832–1836—Edge: Vertical lines added between words.

First Style (1807–1808)
Overton-104.

Remodeled Portrait and Eagle (1809–1836)
Overton-109.

History. The Capped Bust design was created by Mint assistant engraver John Reich; the motif was widely used, in several variations, on much of the era's coinage. Reich was the first artist to consistently include the denomination in his designs for U.S. gold and silver coins. The half dollar, minted continuously from 1807 to 1836, except 1816, was the largest silver coin of the realm at the time (silver dollars had not been struck since 1804).

Striking and Sharpness. On the obverse, check the hair and broach details. Stars are often flatly struck on Capped Bust half dollars, much more so than on other denominations. On the reverse, check the motto band and the eagle's head, and the wing to the left, as well as other areas (neck feathers, often lightly struck on other denominations of Capped Bust silver, are usually fairly sharp on half dollars). The E PLURIBUS UNUM band is often weak in the area left of its center; this does not normally occur on other Capped Bust silver coins. Inspect the dentils on both sides. Generally, later dates are better struck than are earlier ones. Many half dollars have semi-prooflike surfaces, or patches of mirrorlike character interspersed with luster. Others can have nearly full prooflike surfaces, with patches of luster being in the minority (and often in the left obverse field); some of these have been mischaracterized as "Proofs." Some issues from the early 1830s have little digs or "bite marks" on the portrait, possibly from some sort of a gadget used to eject them from the press. Unlike the Capped Bust half dime, dime, and quarter dollar, the half dollar is particularly subject to very wide variations in striking quality.

Availability. Examples of most dates and overdates are easily found in just about any grade desired, from Fine and VF to MS. (As the largest silver coin struck between 1803 and 1836, these half dollars spent much of their time in bags, transferred from bank to bank, rather than wearing down in circulation.) The later years are the most readily available and are also seen in higher average grades. Many die varieties range from scarce to rare.

AU-50, 53, 55, 58 (About Uncirculated). *Obverse:* Light wear is seen on the cheek, the hair below the left part of LIBERTY, the cap, and the front part of the bosom and drapery. Some of this apparent "wear" may be related to the original planchet surface (as noted under MS, below), but at the AU level the distinction is less important. At AU-50 and 53, luster remains only in protected areas. On a well-struck coin, at AU-58 the luster is extensive except in the open area of the field, especially to the right. *Reverse:* Wear is evident on the eagle's head, the top of the wings, the claws, and the flat band above the eagle. At AU-50 and 53, there still is significant luster, more than on the obverse. An AU-58 coin has nearly full luster.

MS-60 to 70 (Mint State). *Obverse:* At MS-60, some abrasion and contact marks are evident, most noticeably on the cheek, the hair below the left part of LIBERTY, the cap, and the front part of the bosom and drapery. These areas also coincide with the highest parts of the coin and are thus susceptible to lightness of strike. Complicating matters is that when an area is lightly struck, and the planchet is not forced into the deepest parts of the die, the original planchet surface (which may exhibit scuffing and nicks) is visible. A lightly struck coin can have virtually perfect luster in the fields, and yet appear to be "worn" on the higher parts, due to the lightness of strike. In practice, the original planchet surface will usually be considered as wear on the finished coin, which of course is not true. Such grades as high AU and low MS levels are often assigned to pieces that, if well struck, would be MS-64 and MS-65. If a coin has original planchet abrasions, but otherwise is a gem, those abrasions must be taken into consideration. Apart from this, on well-struck coins in lower MS grades, luster is present, but may be dull or lifeless, and interrupted in patches. At MS-63, on a well-struck coin, contact marks are very few, and abrasion is hard to detect except under magnification. A well-struck MS-65 coin has no abrasion, and contact marks are so minute as to require magnification. Luster should be full and rich. Grades above MS-65 are seen now and again and are defined by having fewer marks as perfection is approached. *Reverse:* Comments apply as for the obverse, except that nearly all coins with weak striking on the obverse (so as to reveal original planchet surface) do not show such original surface on the reverse, except perhaps on the motto ribbon. Accordingly, market grading is usually by the obverse only, even if the reverse seems to be in much better preservation. On well-struck coins, abrasion and contact marks are most noticeable on the eagle's head, the top of the wings, the claws, and the flat band that surrounds the incuse motto. The field is mainly protected by design elements and on a given coin does not show abrasion as much as does the obverse.

1807, Small Stars

1807, Large Stars

1807, Large Stars, 50 Over 20

1807, "Bearded" Liberty

1808, 8 Over 7

1809, xxxx Edge
Experimental edge has "xxxx" between the words.

1809, ||||| Edge
Experimental edge has "|||||" between the words.

1811, (18.11), 11 Over 10
The date is "punctuated" with a period.

1811, Small 8

1811, Large 8

1812, 2 Over 1, Small 8

1812, 2 Over 1, Large 8

1812, Two Leaves Below Wing

1812, Single Leaf Below Wing

1813, 50 C. Over UNI.

1814, 4 Over 3

1814, E Over A in STATES

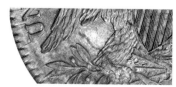

1814, Two Leaves Below Wing

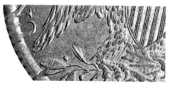

1814, Single Leaf Below Wing

1815, 5 Over 2

1817, 7 Over 3

1817, 7 Over 4

1817, Dated 181.7
The date is "punctuated" with a period between the second 1 and the 7.

1817, Two Leaves Below Wing

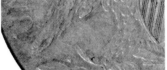

1817, Single Leaf Below Wing

1818, First 8 Small, Second 8 Over 7

1818, First 8 Large, Second 8 Over 7

1819, Small 9 Over 8

1819, Large 9 Over 8

1820, 20 Over 19, Square Base 2

1820, 20 Over 19, Curl Base 2

1820, Curl Base, No Knob 2, Small Date

1820, Square Base, Knob 2, Large Date

1820, Square Base, No Knob 2, Large Date

1820, Broken Serifs on E's

1822, 2 Over 1

1823, Normal Date

1823, Broken 3

1823, Patched 3

1823, Ugly 3

1824, Normal Date

1824, 4 Over 1

1824, 4 Over Various Dates
Probably 4 Over 2 Over 0.

1824, 4 Over 4
4 Over 4 varieties are easily mistaken for the scarcer 4 Over 1. Note the distance between the 2's and 4's in each.

1827, 7 Over 6

1827, Square Base 2

1827, Curl Base 2

1828, Curl Base, No Knob 2

1828, Curl Base, Knob 2

1828, Square Base 2, Large 8's

1828, Square Base 2, Small 8's

1828, Large Letters

1828, Small Letters

1829, 9 Over 7

1830, Small 0

1830, Large 0

1830, Large Letters

Experimental Edge of 1830
Raised segment lines angled to the right.

Experimental Edge of 1830–1831
Raised segment lines angled to the left.

Edge Adopted for Coinage, 1830–1836
Straight vertical lines.

1832, Large Letters Reverse
Note the prominent die crack.
Shown 1.5x actual size.

| 1834, Large Date | 1834, Small Date | 1834, Large Letters | 1834, Small Letters |

1836, Over 1336

	Mintage	Cert	Avg	%MS	AU-50	AU-55	MS-60	MS-62	MS-63	MS-64	MS-65	Recent Auction Record
1807, All kinds	750,500											
1807, Small Stars		20	36.9	0	$4,000	$5,150	$6,850	$10,000	$14,000	$25,000	$55,000	$10,350, AU-58, Nov-09
1807, Large Stars		17	43.4	6	3,400	4,750	6,100	8,500	12,500	21,000		$5,750, AU-58, Dec-09
1807, Large Stars, 50 Over 20					2,400	3,450	5,500	7,750	10,000	19,000	32,500	$5,031, EF-40 CAC, Jun-10
1807, "Bearded" Liberty (a)					8,000	11,000	18,500	30,000	—			$8,625, AU-55, May-08
1808, All kinds	1,368,600											
1808, 8 Over 7		137	45.4	12	1,250	1,850	3,400	6,000	8,500	15,500		$1,265, AU-50, Sep-09
1808		408	46.2	19	600	975	1,800	3,300	4,150	8,500	20,000	$2,990, AU-55, Mar-10
1809, All kinds	1,405,810											
1809, Normal Edge		127	42.4	13	750	1,000	2,000	3,250	4,250	8,500	20,000	$2,070, MS-62, Feb-10
1809, xxxx Edge		36	41.3	6	900	1,650	3,250	4,600	6,300	10,750		$863, AU-50, Dec-08
1809, IIIII Edge		86	40.2	12	925	1,750	3,500	5,000	8,000	14,000	22,000	$1,006, AU-53, Aug-09
1810	1,276,276	450	46.6	19	550	975	1,850	3,350	4,250	9,000	20,000	$12,650, MS-65 , Dec-09
1811, All kinds	1,203,644											
1811, (18.11), 11 Over 10		91	45.6	16	900	1,250	2,250	6,000	8,500	13,000		$1,208, AU-55, Nov-09
1811, Small 8		151	46.3	21	635	850	1,825	3,250	4,000	6,500	19,000	$2,703, MS-63, Mar-10
1811, Large 8		49	46.1	2	635	850	1,825	3,250	4,000	6,500	19,000	$805, AU-55, Sep-09
1812, All kinds	1,628,059											
1812, 2 Over 1, Small 8		95	45.9	20	650	1,250	2,900	4,250	5,000	8,750	18,500	$1,025, AU-50, Mar-10
1812, 2 Over 1, Large 8		20	33.3	0	21,000	28,500	35,000	60,000	—			$17,250, AU-50, Feb-07
1812		213	44.2	13	500	775	1,750	2,500	3,150	5,500	14,000	$3,163, MS-63, Nov-09
1812, Single Leaf Below Wing					6,250	8,500	11,500	20,000	—			
1813, All kinds	1,241,903											
1813		150	45.5	12	500	775	1,750	2,500	3,500	7,000	17,000	$4,600, MS-64, Sep-09
1813, 50 C. Over UNI		56	50.2	23	950	1,350	2,000	4,000	5,500	15,000		$7,475, MS-64, Sep-09
1814, All kinds	1,039,075											
1814, 4 Over 3		83	43.1	16	1,350	1,775	2,400	4,250	5,750	11,000	19,500	$1,898, AU-53, Dec-09

a. Also called the Bearded Goddess variety; a die crack gives the illusion of long whiskers growing from Miss Liberty's chin.

Chart continued on next page.

	Mintage	Cert	Avg	%MS	AU-50	AU-55	MS-60	MS-62	MS-63	MS-64	MS-65	Recent Auction Record
1814, E Over A in STATES		18	43.9	11	$775	$1,000	$1,900	$2,850	$3,850	$8,750		$1,725, AU-55, Feb-10
1814		143	46.1	14	500	800	1,750	2,500	3,250	6,500	$14,000	$1,093, AU-58, Mar-10
1814, Single Leaf Below Wing		18	34.2	0	1,375	1,750	2,750	3,750	5,000	10,000		$1,380, AU-50, May-09
1815, 5 Over 2	47,150	201	43.1	12	7,500	9,500	15,500	23,000	37,000	60,000		$7,188, AU-50, Aug-09
1817, All kinds	1,215,567											
1817, 7 Over 3		133	41.0	15	2,100	2,800	5,500	10,000	13,000	23,500	42,500	$3,220, AU-55 CAC, Jun-10
1817, 7 Over 4 (8 known) †		2	20.0	0	355,000							$356,500, AU-50, Jul-09
1817, Dated 181.7		16	47.2	13	575	1,000	1,800	2,450	3,400	7,700	17,500	$1,955, AU-50, Jan-10
1817		149	40.1	9	500	775	1,500	2,350	3,300	7,000	16,500	$776, AU-55, Jan-10
1817, Single Leaf Below Wing		6	52.7	17	900	1,450	2,500	3,500	4,250	10,000		$1,783, AU-50, Jan-08
1818, All kinds	1,960,322											
1818, 8 Over 7, Small 8		38	50.1	13	825	1,375	1,700	3,750	5,650	9,000	18,000	$1,380, AU-58, Aug-09
1818, 8 Over 7, Large 8		49	44.2	10	850	1,400	2,000	4,000	5,900	10,000	19,000	$6,325, MS-64, Apr-09
1818		156	48.1	9	400	700	1,400	2,350	3,050	4,500	14,000	$863, AU-50, Feb-10
1819, All kinds	2,208,000											
1819, Small 9 Over 8		35	39.5	3	550	775	1,600	2,400	3,250	6,750	17,500	$21,850, MS-65 , Nov-09
1819, Large 9 Over 8		93	47.6	10	600	875	1,675	2,400	3,250	6,750	17,500	$460, AU-50, Mar-10
1819		113	46.3	19	375	650	1,450	2,300	3,000	5,700	15,500	$5,463, MS-64, Jan-10
1820, All kinds	751,122											
1820, 20 Over 19, Square 2		28	46.3	18	1,350	1,750	2,850	4,700	7,000	11,000	25,000	$2,185, AU-58, Feb-10
1820, 20 Over 19, Curl Base 2		41	46.5	2	1,125	1,650	2,350	4,250	5,500	9,000	18,000	$6,900, MS-63, Mar-10
1820, Curl Base 2, Small Date		26	49.8	12	825	1,150	1,700	3,000	4,250	6,500	15,500	$1,840, AU-55, Dec-08
1820, Sq Base Knob 2, Lg Dt		43	49.4	14	825	1,150	1,500	2,500	3,500	6,500	15,500	$1,725, AU-58, Apr-09
1820, Sq Base No Knob 2, Lg Dt		42	47.4	10	825	1,150	1,500	2,500	3,500	6,500	15,500	$2,760, MS-62, Aug-09
1820, Broken Serifs on E's		8	38.4	25	2,250	2,750	5,000	7,000	9,000	18,000	37,500	$46,000, MS-66, Apr-09
1821	1,305,797	468	51.1	22	500	800	1,200	1,700	2,700	4,200	15,000	$546, AU-53, Jan-10
1822, All kinds	1,559,573											
1822		151	48.4	17	375	525	1,150	1,700	2,800	4,100	15,000	$489, AU-55, Mar-10
1822, 2 Over 1		87	50.9	30	750	950	1,450	2,550	3,800	7,500	17,500	$12,650, MS-64, Jan-10
1823, All kinds	1,694,200											
1823, Broken 3		38	42.0	16	1,050	1,600	2,100	3,000	4,250	5,500	*	$1,725, AU-50, Jan-10
1823, Patched 3		40	52.1	38	650	1,000	1,400	2,350	3,100	6,000	20,000	$3,068, AU-58, Nov-09
1823, Ugly 3		20	48.6	15	650	950	1,350	2,300	3,050	4,000	15,000	$920, AU-53, Mar-09
1823, Normal		176	48.3	16	375	550	1,200	1,900	2,300	3,850	14,000	$4,140, MS-61, Nov-09
1824, All kinds	3,504,954											
1824, 4 Over Various Dates		44	49.8	11	550	875	1,450	2,300	3,100	6,000	15,000	$1,150, AU-53, Sep-09
1824, 4 Over 1		76	50.4	38	550	875	1,550	2,350	3,100	6,000	15,000	$3,594, MS-64, Jun-10
1824, 4 Over 4 (2 varieties)		107	49.7	24	525	850	1,400	2,300	2,900	6,000	15,000	$5,175, MS-64, Jun-10
1824, Normal		196	47.2	16	400	525	1,100	1,475	1,850	3,700	14,000	$3,220, MS-64, Mar-10
1825	2,943,166	890	53.7	33	375	525	1,100	1,475	1,900	3,700	13,000	$1,150, MS-62, Mar-10
1826	4,004,180	1,255	54.5	34	375	525	1,100	1,475	1,900	3,700	9,500	$2,818, MS-64, Mar-10
1827, All kinds	5,493,400											
1827, 7 Over 6		130	51.6	26	500	700	1,400	1,700	2,400	4,100	14,000	$1,093, AU-58, Sep-09
1827, Square Base 2		475	49.8	18	400	575	1,075	1,550	2,050	3,850	10,000	$21,103, MS-67, Jan-10
1827, Curl Base 2		36	50.4	17	350	525	1,050	1,475	1,850	3,600	10,000	$1,093, AU-58, Sep-09
1828, All kinds	3,075,200											
1828, Curl Base No Knob 2		52	54.5	29	350	525	1,050	1,475	1,850	3,600	10,000	$1,840, MS-62, Mar-09
1828, Curl Base Knob 2		29	50.7	14	350	525	1,050	1,475	1,850	3,600	10,000	$4,600, MS-63, Jan-10
1828, Square Base 2, Large 8's		33	50.1	12	350	525	1,050	1,475	1,850	3,600	10,000	$955, AU-58, Mar-09
1828, Square Base 2, Small 8's, Large Letters		191	51.6	20	350	525	1,050	1,475	1,850	3,600	10,000	$546, AU-55, Mar-10
1828, Square Base 2, Small 8's and Letters		18	49.6	0	450	675	1,400	1,700	2,550	3,800	11,000	$1,150, AU-58, Mar-10
1829, All kinds	3,712,156											
1829, 9 Over 7		176	53.8	30	425	700	1,400	2,300	3,500	6,500	15,000	$2,070, MS-62, Dec-09
1829		253	50.4	17	325	525	1,000	1,375	1,800	3,350	10,000	$328, AU-53, Mar-10
1829, Large Letters		21	54.0	24	350	525	1,150	1,475	2,400	3,750	10,500	$403, AU-55, Jan-09

† Ranked in the *100 Greatest U.S. Coins* (third edition).

	Mintage	Cert	Avg	%MS	AU-50	AU-55	MS-60	MS-62	MS-63	MS-64	MS-65	Recent Auction Record
1830, All kinds	4,764,800											
1830, Small 0		341	49.2	15	$350	$525	$1,050	$1,475	$1,850	$3,650	$10,000	$9,488, MS-65, May-10
1830, Large 0		91	53.2	20	350	525	1,050	1,475	1,850	3,650	10,000	$2,185, MS-63, Oct-09
1830, Large Letters		9	31.8	11	9,000	14,000	—					$18,400, MS-63, Jan-06
1831	5,873,660	1,299	54.9	34	325	450	1,050	1,375	1,800	3,300	9,000	$8,913, MS-65, Jun-10
1832, All kinds	4,797,000											
1832		431	50.9	15	325	450	1,000	1,375	1,800	3,300	9,000	$518, AU-55, Mar-10
1832, Large Letters		44	52.4	9	325	450	1,000	1,375	1,800	3,300	9,000	$1,210, MS-62, Jan-09
1833	5,206,000	1,086	54.3	28	325	450	1,000	1,375	1,800	3,300	9,000	$2,542, MS-64, Mar-10
1834, All kinds	6,412,004											
1834, Large Dt and Letters		96	52.6	20	325	450	1,000	1,375	1,850	3,400	9,000	$1,553, MS-63, Mar-10
1834, Large Dt, Small Letters		117	51.9	21	325	450	1,000	1,375	1,850	3,400	9,000	$518, AU-55, Mar-10
1834, Small Dt, Stars, Letters		269	51.2	14	325	450	1,000	1,375	1,850	3,400	9,000	$5,750, MS-65, Jan-10
1835	5,352,006	671	53.0	27	325	450	1,000	1,375	1,850	3,400	9,000	$3,220, MS-65 , Sep-09
1836, All kinds	6,545,000											
1836		247	50.7	16	325	450	1,000	1,375	1,850	3,400	9,000	$2,875, MS-64, Feb-10
1836 Over 1336					375	550	1,200	1,550	2,200	4,000	10,000	$903, AU-55, Mar-10
1836, 50 Over 00		42	50.8	19	800	1,250	2,100	3,000	4,000	6,500		$3,220, AU-58, Feb-09
1836, Beaded Border on Reverse (b)		23	46.7	26	450	600	1,250	1,450	1,850	3,450	9,000	$1,035, MS-62, Mar-10

b. The same beaded-border reverse die was used for Proofs of 1833, 1834, and 1835 with the crushed edge lettering; all are very rare.

Proof Capped Bust, Lettered Edge, Half Dollars

PF-60 to 70 (Proof). Proofs were made in limited numbers, in most years from 1818 to 1836, for presentation purposes and for distribution to numismatists. True Proofs have deeply mirrored surfaces. Impostors are often seen, with deeply toned surfaces or with patches of mint luster. This situation is more prevalent with half dollars than with any other Capped Bust denomination. There are some crushed-lettered-edge ("CLE") Proofs of the 1833 to 1835 era that are especially beautiful

and are more deeply mirrorlike than original issues. Some of these are restrikes (not necessarily an important consideration, but worth noting), believed to have been made at the Mint beginning in the spring of 1859. *Obverse and Reverse:* Proofs of this type have confused experts for a long time (as have large copper cents of the same era). Proofs that were extensively cleaned and therefore have many hairlines, or that are dull and grainy, are lower level, such as PF-60 to 62.

While any early Proof half dollar will generate interest among collectors, lower levels are not of great interest to specialists unless they are of rare die varieties. With medium hairlines, an assigned grade of PF-64 may be in order and with relatively few, PF-65. PF-66 should have hairlines so delicate that magnification is needed to see them. Above that, a Proof should be free of such lines. Grading is highly subjective with early Proofs, with eye appeal being a major factor.

Proof Capped Bust, Lettered Edge, Half Dollar
Overton-103.

	Est Mintage	Cert	Finest	PF-63	PF-64	PF-65	Recent Auction Record
1818	3–5	4	PF-66	$50,000	$75,000	$100,000	$126,500, PF-66, Jan-08
1820	3–5	1	PF-63	50,000	75,000	100,000	
1821	3–5	3	PF-65	50,000	75,000	100,000	
1822	3–5	1	PF-64	50,000	75,000	100,000	$27,600, PF-64, Aug-99
1823	3–5	1	PF-63	50,000	75,000	100,000	
1825	3–5	1	PF-66	50,000	75,000	100,000	$32,200, PF-62, May-08
1826	3–5	1	PF-65	50,000	75,000	100,000	$80,500, PF-65, Jan-06
1827	5–8	3	PF-67	50,000	75,000	100,000	$80,500, PF-64, Aug-07
1829	6–9	6	PF-66	40,000	70,000	90,000	$25,300, PF-63, Jul-08
1830	3–5	1	PF-64	40,000	70,000	90,000	$36,800, PF-64, Jul-04
1831	3–5	1	PF-65	40,000	70,000	90,000	$69,000, PF-65, Jan-06
1832	6–9	5	PF-68	40,000	70,000	90,000	$29,900, PF-63, Jan-08
1833	unverified	2	PF-65				

Chart continued on next page.

	Est Mintage	Cert	Finest	PF-63	PF-64	PF-65	Recent Auction Record
1833, Crushed Lettered Edge	3–5	n/a	n/a	$40,000	$70,000	$90,000	
1834	8–12	6	PF-67	40,000	70,000	90,000	$25,300, PF-63, Aug-07
1834, Crushed Lettered Edge	3–5	n/a	n/a	40,000	70,000	90,000	
1835	5–8	3	PF-65	40,000	70,000	90,000	$43,125, PF-64, Aug-07
1835, Crushed Lettered Edge	3–5	n/a	n/a	40,000	70,000	90,000	
1836, Lettered Edge	8–12	6	PF-67	40,000	70,000	90,000	$23,000, PF-63, Apr-09
1836, 50 Over 00	3–5	2	PF-67	50,000	80,000	110,000	$81,937, PF-65, Oct-06

CAPPED BUST, REEDED EDGE (1836–1839)

Designer Christian Gobrecht; weight 13.36 grams; composition .900 silver, .100 copper; diameter 30 mm; reeded edge. All coined at Philadelphia.

Reverse 50 CENTS
(1836–1837)

Reverse HALF DOL.
(1838–1839)

History. This half dollar type features a slight restyling of John Reich's Capped Bust design. It is of smaller diameter than the preceding type, and made with a reeded edge. The reverse is of two variations: the 1836–1837, with 50 CENTS; and the 1838–1839, with HALF DOL.

Striking and Sharpness. The key points for observation are the stars on the obverse. On the reverse, check the border letters and the details of the eagle. The 1839-O nearly always shows die cracks, often extensive (these have no effect on desirability or market value).

Availability. The 1836 is rare. The 1838-O is a famous rarity, and the 1839-O is scarce. The others are easily available in nearly any grade desired, with 1837 being the most common.

AU-50, 53, 55, 58 (About Uncirculated). *Obverse and Reverse:* Grading guidelines are the same as for the 1807–1836 type, except on this type the rims are more uniform. On the 1836–1837 dates the reverse rim is generally lower than the obverse, causing the reverse to wear slightly more quickly. On the 1838–1839 type (with slightly different lettering) the wear occurs evenly on both sides.

MS-60 to 70 (Mint State). *Obverse and Reverse:* Grading guidelines are the same as for the 1807–1836 type, except on this type the rims are more uniform. On the 1836–1837 dates the reverse rim is generally lower than the obverse, causing the reverse to wear slightly more quickly. On the 1838–1839 type (with slightly different lettering) the wear occurs evenly on both sides, and light striking showing areas of the original planchet on the obverse does not occur here.

1839, Regular Letters Reverse   1839, Small Letters Reverse

Shown 1.25x actual size.

	Mintage	Cert	Avg	%MS	AU-50	AU-55	MS-60	MS-62	MS-63	MS-64	MS-65	Recent Auction Record
1836	1,200+	172	48.8	17	$4,050	$5,500	$9,250	$12,500	$19,500	$35,000	$65,000	$2,530, VF-35, Jun-10
1837	3,629,820	1,015	56.2	44	400	625	1,200	1,600	2,250	4,750	17,000	$14,950, MS-66, Jun-10
1838	3,546,000	780	55.2	34	375	600	1,200	1,600	2,500	5,000	22,000	$4,485, MS-64, Feb-10
1839	1,392,976	315	54.0	33	475	725	1,400	1,600	3,000	5,500	35,000	$3,758, MS-64, Feb-10
1839, Small Letters Reverse (ex. rare)		2	52.5	0	60,000							$50,025, AU-50, Jan-10
18390	116,000	212	49.8	24	1,275	1,750	3,500	5,000	6,500	14,000	45,000	$1,725, AU-55, Jan-10

Proof Capped Bust, Reeded Edge, Half Dollars

PF-60 to 70 (Proof). Proofs of 1836 are occasionally encountered and are quite rare. Authentic Proofs of 1837 exist but for all practical purposes are unobtainable. Most 1838-O (a rarity) and a few 1839-O have been called branch-mint Proofs. *Obverse and Reverse:* Proofs in grades of PF-60 to 62 show extensive hairlines and cloudiness. At PF-63, hairlines are obvious, but the mirrored fields are attractive. PF-64 and 65 coins have fewer hairlines, but they still are obvious when the coin is slowly turned while held at an angle to the light. PF-66 coins require a magnifier to discern hairlines, and higher grades should have no hairlines.

Proof Capped Bust, Reeded Edge, Half Dollar

	Est Mintage	Cert	Finest	PF-60	PF-63	PF-64	PF-65	Recent Auction Record
1836, Reeded Edge	10–15	11	PF-65	$30,000	$45,000	$65,000	$90,000	$51,750, PF-64, Apr-09
1837	4–6	2	PF-65	30,000	50,000	75,000	100,000	$32,200, PF-62, Jul-08
1838	3–5	n/a	n/a	30,000	50,000	75,000	100,000	$161,000, PF-66, Jan-07
18380 † (a)	20	4	PF-64	375,000	600,000	750,000		$632,500, PF-63 CAC, Feb-08
1839, Reeded Edge (unverified)	n/a	n/a	n/a					
18390	5–10	5	PF-65	100,000	150,000	200,000	250,000	$80,500, PF-63, Jul-09

† Ranked in the *100 Greatest U.S. Coins* (third edition). **a.** The 1838-O was the first branch-mint half dollar, though it was not mentioned in the Mint director's report. The New Orleans chief coiner stated that only 20 were struck.

LIBERTY SEATED
(1839–1891)

Variety 1, No Motto Above Eagle (1839–1853): Designer Christian Gobrecht; weight 13.36 grams; composition .900 silver, .100 copper; diameter 30.6 mm; reeded edge; mints: Philadelphia, New Orleans.

Variety 1
(1839–1853)

Variety 2, Arrows at Date, Rays Around Eagle (1853): Designer Christian Gobrecht; weight 12.44 grams; composition .900 silver, .100 copper; diameter 30.6 mm; reeded edge; mints: Philadelphia, New Orleans, San Francisco, Carson City.

Variety 2
(1853)

Continued on next page.

Variety 3, Arrows at Date, No Rays (1854–1855): Designer Christian Gobrecht; weight 12.44 grams; composition .900 silver, .100 copper; diameter 30.6 mm; reeded edge; mints: Philadelphia, New Orleans, San Francisco.

Variety 3
(1854–1855)

Variety 1 Resumed, With Weight Standard of Variety 2 (1856–1866): Designer Christian Gobrecht; weight 12.44 grams; composition .900 silver, .100 copper; diameter 30.6 mm; reeded edge; mints: Philadelphia, New Orleans, San Francisco.

Variety 1, Weight Standard of Variety 2
(1856–1866)

Variety 4, Motto Above Eagle (1866–1873): Designer Christian Gobrecht; weight 12.44 grams; composition .900 silver, .100 copper; diameter 30.6 mm; reeded edge; mints: Philadelphia, San Francisco, Carson City.

Variety 4
(1866–1873)

Variety 5, Arrows at Date (1873–1874): Designer Christian Gobrecht; weight 12.50 grams; composition .900 silver, .100 copper; diameter 30.6 mm; reeded edge; mints: Philadelphia, San Francisco, Carson City.

Variety 5
(1873–1874)

Variety 4 Resumed, With Weight Standard of Variety 5 (1875–1891): Designer Christian Gobrecht; weight 12.50 grams; composition .900 silver, .100 copper; diameter 30.6 mm; reeded edge; mints: Philadelphia, San Francisco, Carson City.

Variety 4 Resumed,
Weight Standard of Variety 5
(1875–1891)

History. Half dollars of the Liberty Seated type were struck every year from 1839 to 1891. The designs varied slightly over the years, but with the basic obverse and reverse motifs remaining the same (e.g., from 1842 to 1853 the coins bore a modified reverse with large letters in the legend, and in 1846 the date size was enlarged).

Large quantities were made until 1879, at which time there was a glut of silver coins in commerce. After that mintages were reduced.

Striking and Sharpness. On the obverse, first check the head of Miss Liberty and the star centers. On coins of the Arrows at Date subtype, especially 1855, the word LIBERTY tends to wear more quickly compared to earlier and later varieties. On the reverse, check the eagle at the lower left. Afterward, check all other features. Generally, the higher-mintage issues are the least well struck, and many New Orleans Mint coins can be lightly struck as well, particularly those in the 1850s. The luster on MS coins usually is very attractive. Resurfaced dies often are prooflike, some with the drapery polished away (as with 1877-S, in particular).

Above and beyond issues of strike, the Small Letters coins of 1839 to 1842 have narrower, lower rims that afforded less protection to the central devices of the reverse. In contrast, the No Motto, Large

Letters coins have wider, higher rims that tended to better protect the central devices.

Many pre–Civil War dates, particularly of the 1840s, show evidence of extensive die polishing in the fields (especially evident in the open expanses of the obverse).

From grades of EF downward, sharpness of strike of stars and the head does not matter to connoisseurs.

Availability. Collecting these coins is a popular pursuit with many enthusiasts. Examples of the higher-mintage dates are readily available, with earlier years being much scarcer than later ones. Most often seen among MS coins are issues from the mid-1870s onward. Circulated coins from well worn through AU can be found of most dates and mintmarks; these are avidly sought.

AU-50, 53, 55, 58 (About Uncirculated). *Obverse:* Light wear is seen on the thighs and knees, bosom, and head. There is some luster at AU-50 and 53. At AU-58, the luster is extensive, but incomplete, especially in the right field. *Reverse:* Wear is evident on the eagle's neck, the claws, and the top of the wings. At AU-50 and 53, there are traces of luster. An AU-58 coin has nearly full luster, more so than on the obverse, as the design elements protect the small field areas.

MS-60 to 70 (Mint State). *Obverse:* At MS-60, some abrasion and contact marks are evident, most noticeably on the bosom and thighs and knees. Luster is present, but may be dull or lifeless. At MS-63, contact marks are very few, and abrasion is hard to detect except under magnification. An MS-65 coin has no abrasion, and contact marks are sufficiently minute as to require magnification. Check the knees of Liberty and the right field. Luster should be full and rich. Most MS coins of the 1861 to 1865 years, Philadelphia issues, have extensive

die striae (from dies not being completely finished); note that these are raised (whereas cleaning hairlines are incuse). *Reverse:* Comments as preceding, except that in lower MS grades abrasion and contact marks are most noticeable on the eagle's head, neck, and claws, and the top of the wings (harder to see there, however). At MS-65 or higher there are no marks visible to the unaided eye. The field mainly is protected by design elements and on a given coin does not show abrasion as much as does the obverse.

No Drapery From Elbow (1839)   Drapery From Elbow (Starting 1839)

Small Letters in Legend (1839–1841)   1840 (Only), Medium Letters, Large Eagle   Large Letters in Legend (1842–1853)

Shown 1.25x actual size.

1842, Small Date   1842, Medium Date   1844-O, Doubled Date
FS-50-1844o-301.

1846, Medium Date

1846, Tall Date

1846-O, Medium Date

1846-O, Tall Date

1847, 7 Over 6
FS-50-1847-301.

1855, 1855 Over 854
FS-50-1855-301.

1861- DieO, Cracked Obverse
FS-50-1861o-401.

1873, Close 3

1873, Open 3

1877, 7 Over 6
FS-50-1877-301.

	Mintage	Cert	Avg	%MS	AU-50	AU-55	MS-60	MS-62	MS-63	MS-64	MS-65	Recent Auction Record
1839, No Drapery From Elbow	*	137	47.1	14	$2,500	$4,000	$6,500	$18,000	$27,500	$75,000	$150,000	$1,495, EF-45, Jun-10
1839, Drapery From Elbow	1,972,400	122	53.4	40	275	375	550	1,750	2,250	3,700	24,000	$3,393, MS-64, Feb-10
1840, Small Letters	1,435,008	167	55.3	38	275	375	550	900	1,400	2,500	7,000	$1,380, MS-63, Jul-09
1840, Medium Letters (a)	*	32	45.0	22	1,500	2,250	3,750	5,500	7,500	13,500	21,000	$10,638, MS-63, Jan-10
18400	855,100	60	53.2	30	275	350	650	1,700	2,400	12,500		$6,900, MS-65 , Jan-10
1841	310,000	52	57.0	40	400	600	1,400	2,000	2,500	4,500	10,000	$3,450, MS-63, Jan-10
18410	401,000	75	54.3	35	300	550	850	1,800	2,500	5,200	30,000	$4,025, MS-64, May-10
1842, Sm Date, Sm Letters	**				7,500	10,000	17,500					
18420, Sm Date, Sm Letters	203,000	29	36.5	3	7,500	10,000	18,000	27,500	38,000			$43,125, MS-62, Jan-09
1842, Medium Date	2,012,764	70	53.8	24	325	525	850	1,500	2,000	2,800	8,000	$2,743, MS-64, Apr-09
1842, Sm Date, Lg Letters	***	40	53.4	33	350	625	1,150	2,250	3,400	12,000	23,000	$2,185, MS-63, May-09
18420, Medium Date, Large Letters	754,000	35	54.9	43	300	550	1,000	3,000	4,000	8,000	16,000	$776, AU-55, Nov-09
1843	3,844,000	150	55.9	49	225	325	500	800	1,100	2,300	9,000	$748, MS-62, Mar-09
18430	2,268,000	69	56.2	58	225	350	600	1,250	2,050	4,500	15,000	$2,300, MS-63, Jan-10
1844	1,766,000	90	57.5	50	225	325	500	800	1,650	3,700	13,500	$1,093, MS-63, Oct-09
18440	2,005,000	67	51.8	45	250	475	775	1,600	2,450	4,500	13,500	$3,450, MS-63, Jul-09
18440, Doubled Date (b)	***	13	42.2	0	6,600	8,500	12,000	19,000	—			$6,613, AU-55, Sep-08
1845	589,000	43	51.5	35	325	525	900	2,200	3,300	7,500	15,000	$805, AU-58, Apr-08
18450	2,094,000	89	48.3	30	225	350	700	1,400	2,150	4,000	12,000	$518, AU-55, Mar-09
18450, No Drapery (c)	***	15	53.2	27	325	575	1,300	3,000	4,500	10,000		$16,100, MS-64, Jan-10
1846, All kinds	2,210,000											
1846, Medium Date		31	56.8	35	250	350	600	1,100	1,500	3,700	12,000	$3,450, MS-64, Oct-09
1846, Tall Date		52	56.5	40	275	400	800	2,000	3,100	12,000		$436, AU-58, Mar-10
1846, 6 Over Horizontal 6 (d)		33	52.3	27	1,350	1,650	3,500	8,000	11,000	15,000	25,000	$2,990, AU-58, Sep-07
18460, Medium Date	2,304,000	51	44.1	24	300	425	1,000	1,600	2,400	4,500	12,000	$1,725, MS-61, Jan-10
18460, Tall Date	***	21	43.4	14	1,850	2,750	6,500	8,000	13,500			$5,175, AU-55, Jul-09
1847, 7 Over 6 (e)	*	3	50.7	33	17,500	27,500	35,000	50,000				$27,600, AU-55, Apr-08
1847	1,156,000	74	54.5	35	225	325	475	800	1,300	2,500	7,000	$20,700, MS-67, Apr-09
18470	2,584,000	56	54.4	41	250	400	750	1,700	2,600	8,000	20,000	$4,025, MS-63, Oct-09
1848	580,000	51	58.5	63	500	750	1,000	1,400	1,750	3,000	8,000	$546, AU-53, Nov-09

* Included in number below. ** Included in "1842, Medium Date" mintage. *** Included in number above. **a.** The 1840, Medium Letters, half dollars were struck at the New Orleans Mint from a reverse die of the previous style, without mintmark. **b.** This rare variety shows all four numerals protruding from the rock above the primary date. **c.** The drapery is missing because of excessive polishing of the die. **d.** This variety can be detected in low grades. **e.** Remains of an underlying 6 are visible below and between the primary 4 and 7. "The overdate might not be evident on later die states" *(Cherrypickers' Guide to Rare Die Varieties, fourth edition, volume II).*

	Mintage	Cert	Avg	%MS	AU-50	AU-55	MS-60	MS-62	MS-63	MS-64	MS-65	Recent Auction Record
18480	3,180,000	67	55.5	37	$275	$375	$850	$1,600	$2,400	$4,500	$14,000	$1,725, MS-63, Aug-09
1849	1,252,000	83	57.0	46	350	450	950	1,600	2,400	4,750	20,000	$1,006, MS-62, Jan-10
18490	2,310,000	49	57.8	39	300	425	800	1,700	2,500	5,500	15,000	$3,450, MS-64, Jul-09
1850	227,000	71	55.9	38	900	1,250	1,900	3,500	4,500	7,500	25,000	$1,323, AU-55, Feb-10
18500	2,456,000	81	58.0	58	275	350	600	900	1,300	3,750	10,000	$2,990, MS-64, Jul-09
1851	200,750	39	57.7	59	1,100	1,400	2,250	3,000	3,950	6,300	13,500	$6,325, MS-64, May-09
18510	402,000	33	57.7	61	325	425	675	900	1,300	3,300	9,000	$6,613, MS-65, Feb-09
1852	77,130	60	57.1	58	1,250	1,500	1,850	2,200	2,500	4,500	9,000	$3,335, MS-64, Aug-09
18520	144,000	33	47.7	18	1,400	1,900	3,500	7,000	10,500	21,500	31,500	$2,530, AU-58, Sep-08
18530, Variety 1 *(3 known)* † (f)												$368,000, VF-35, Oct-06
1853, Variety 2	3,532,708	812	54.4	38	500	850	1,500	2,700	3,600	5,500	24,000	$2,875, MS-63, May-10
18530, Variety 2	1,328,000	137	48.6	22	875	1,300	2,750	4,250	6,000	15,000	40,000	$575, AU-55, Dec-09
1854	2,982,000	311	56.1	39	325	500	725	1,300	1,850	2,850	9,000	$1,093, MS-62, Mar-10
18540	5,240,000	474	55.6	43	325	500	725	1,300	1,850	2,850	9,000	$19,550, MS-67, Jan-10
1855, All kinds	759,500											
1855, 1855 Over 854		34	47.2	26	625	1,000	2,250	3,300	4,600	8,250	20,000	$4,600, MS-62, Jan-09
1855, Normal Date		114	56.2	46	325	500	750	1,300	1,850	3,000	12,500	$1,840, MS-64, Oct-09
18550	3,688,000	389	55.9	42	325	500	750	1,300	1,850	3,000	11,000	$4,744, MS-65, Oct-09
1855S	129,950	53	35.0	9	7,000	12,500	27,000	42,000	—			$7,763, AU-53, Sep-09
1856	938,000	80	57.7	58	225	300	500	850	1,100	2,350	6,800	$7,188, MS-66, Jan-10
18560	2,658,000	193	55.9	53	225	325	500	850	1,100	2,450	7,000	$6,038, MS-65, Apr-09
1856S	211,000	23	45.6	13	1,100	2,000	4,000	10,000	15,000			$1,495, AU-53, May-07
1857	1,988,000	151	56.8	47	220	300	500	850	1,100	2,400	5,500	$3,278, MS-65, Jun-09
18570	818,000	46	52.0	20	250	375	950	2,250	3,400	7,250	13,500	$12,650, MS-64, May-10
1857S	158,000	28	48.1	11	1,150	2,300	4,750	14,000	22,500	35,000		$16,675, MS-62, Jan-08
1858	4,225,700	372	56.5	44	225	300	450	800	1,100	2,050	6,100	$1,840, MS-64, Jan-10
18580	7,294,000	256	54.0	37	225	325	450	800	1,100	2,250	7,500	$7,475, MS-65, Sep-09
1858S	476,000	49	53.0	27	425	625	1,000	2,750	4,000	7,900	13,500	$9,200, MS-65, Sep-09
1859	747,200	114	58.1	50	250	300	450	800	1,100	2,050	5,500	$1,840, MS-64, Dec-09
18590	2,834,000	129	53.3	36	225	325	450	800	1,150	2,500	7,500	$1,840, MS-63, Dec-09
1859S	566,000	48	55.9	52	300	450	950	2,150	3,000	6,750	15,500	$4,600, MS-64, Dec-08
1860	302,700	59	57.6	49	275	350	600	850	1,100	2,050	5,600	$2,070, MS-64, Jan-10
18600	1,290,000	181	57.0	56	225	325	450	850	1,150	2,200	5,600	$8,625, MS-66, Dec-09
1860S	472,000	53	54.7	43	240	375	700	2,050	2,900	5,900		$5,750, MS-64, Feb-09
1861	2,887,400	326	59.3	62	225	300	500	800	1,100	2,150	5,500	$4,025, MS-64, Mar-10
18610 (g)	2,532,633	198	57.6	59	240	325	500	800	1,100	2,700	6,500	$5,175, AU-58, Jun-10
18610, Cracked Obv (h)	***	18	39.7	11	700	900	1,500	2,000	2,500			$3,738, AU-50, Jul-09
1861S	939,500	66	55.5	44	275	400	725	1,700	2,300	4,750	14,000	$1,725, MS-63, Aug-09
1862	253,000	66	57.4	67	325	450	675	800	1,100	2,250	5,750	$6,325, MS-65, Aug-09
1862S	1,352,000	73	48.3	26	275	400	750	1,500	2,300	5,750	15,000	$431, AU-55, Jan-10
1863	503,200	70	60.4	73	300	375	600	900	1,150	2,250	5,750	$5,405, MS-65 CAC, Mar-10
1863S	916,000	80	56.8	46	275	400	650	1,350	1,950	4,600	15,000	$374, AU-55, Feb-10
1864	379,100	78	59.8	73	325	400	575	975	1,275	2,600	7,500	$1,265, MS-63, Mar-09
1864S	658,000	39	51.3	33	275	500	875	2,300	3,000	6,000	16,500	$978, AU-58, Jul-09
1865	511,400	53	58.0	62	325	525	850	1,000	1,250	2,375	6,750	$10,925, MS-66, Apr-09
1865S	675,000	45	54.1	51	250	375	650	1,350	1,750	5,500	10,000	$9,200, MS-64, Sep-08
1866S, Variety 1	60,000	37	30.2	16	3,400	4,700	6,000	15,000	20,000	33,500	65,000	$4,600, AU-53, Jan-09
1866, Variety 5	744,900	69	56.1	61	225	300	475	975	1,300	2,500	6,300	$920, MS-62, Jan-09
1866S, Variety 4	994,000	46	52.9	41	250	400	625	1,700	2,200	5,000	13,500	$3,565, MS-64, May-10
1867	449,300	40	54.5	48	280	325	525	1,100	1,550	3,450	6,900	$13,800, MS-66, Jan-10
1867S	1,196,000	57	57.0	47	250	375	625	1,750	2,300	5,500	13,000	$1,725, MS-62, Feb-09
1868	417,600	32	54.3	50	300	450	625	950	1,200	2,750	6,250	$460, AU-55, Jul-09
1868S	1,160,000	46	51.5	26	250	375	625	1,400	1,800	4,000	10,000	$2,530, MS-62, Oct-09
1869	795,300	90	57.3	47	250	350	525	850	1,200	2,300	6,000	$1,150, MS-62, Oct-09
1869S	656,000	42	55.8	55	250	400	825	1,800	2,450	4,250	7,000	$5,031, MS-65, Oct-09

*** Included in number above. † Ranked in the *100 Greatest U.S. Coins* (third edition). **f.** Value in F-12 is $290,000; in VF-20, $400,000. **g.** The 1861-O mintage includes 330,000 half dollars struck by the United States government; 1,240,000 struck for the State of Louisiana after it seceded from the Union; and 962,633 struck after Louisiana joined the Confederate States of America. All of these coins were made from federal dies, rendering it impossible to distinguish one from another. **h.** In 1861, the New Orleans Mint used a federal obverse die and a Confederate reverse die to strike a handful of Confederate half dollars. That particular obverse die was also paired with a regular federal reverse die to strike some 1861-O half dollars, which today are popular among collectors, especially in higher grades. Their identifying feature is a die crack running from the denticles to the right of the sixth star down to Miss Liberty's nose (and to her shoulder below her jaw).

Chart continued on next page.

	Mintage	Cert	Avg	%MS	AU-50	AU-55	MS-60	MS-62	MS-63	MS-64	MS-65	Recent Auction Record
1870	633,900	49	55.1	49	$200	$300	$475	$750	$1,100	$2,800	$6,000	$475, AU-58, Sep-09
1870CC	54,617	39	23.6	3	27,500	37,500	85,000	140,000	—			$21,850, AU-50, Dec-09
1870S	1,004,000	29	47.3	24	275	400	850	1,850	2,850	6,000	14,000	$920, AU-55, Dec-09
1871	1,203,600	112	57.4	57	220	300	500	750	1,100	2,300	6,000	$207, AU-50, Sep-09
1871CC	153,950	33	28.2	6	4,300	6,000	15,000	35,000	50,000	80,000		$4,744, AU-50, Mar-09
1871S	2,178,000	75	51.9	33	220	300	600	950	1,450	2,750	8,500	$1,438, MS-63, Aug-09
1872	880,600	46	56.5	41	250	300	500	900	1,400	2,750	5,500	$863, MS-62, Jul-09
1872CC	257,000	49	33.3	0	4,000	6,250	19,000	50,000	100,000			$5,463, AU-55, Mar-09
1872S	580,000	33	52.7	42	350	550	1,200	2,000	2,750	5,250	12,000	$7,475, MS-65, Jun-10
1873, Close 3, Variety 4	587,000	54	53.5	35	250	325	600	850	1,100	1,900	5,000	
1873, Open 3, Variety 4	214,200	11	34.1	9	11,000	14,500	19,000					$16,100, AU-55, Jan-09
1873CC, Variety 4	122,500	32	41.7	19	3,750	5,500	10,000	33,000	50,000	65,000	85,000	$25,875, MS-63, Mar-10
1873S, Variety 4 (i)	5,000											
1873, Variety 5	1,815,150	216	55.7	50	400	525	925	1,450	1,950	3,650	19,000	$17,250, MS-65 , Jan-10
1873CC, Variety 5	214,560	73	42.1	18	3,350	4,250	7,500	15,000	20,000	30,000	60,000	$2,875, AU-50, Sep-09
1873S, Variety 5	228,000	38	48.4	26	775	1,100	2,500	3,800	6,000	18,000	45,000	$920, AU-55, Oct-09
1874	2,359,600	284	56.3	54	400	500	925	1,350	1,800	3,500	17,000	$2,415, MS-64, Aug-09
1874CC	59,000	44	38.5	25	6,000	8,000	11,500	22,500	28,500	45,000	80,000	$9,258, AU-55, Nov-09
1874S	394,000	45	50.8	47	700	950	1,800	2,500	3,500	4,750	30,000	$3,738, MS-64, Dec-08
1875	6,026,800	255	58.7	65	185	250	475	625	750	1,350	3,900	$2,128, MS-64, Jun-09
1875CC	1,008,000	97	56.5	64	280	425	775	1,650	2,250	3,900	9,000	$6,325, MS-65 , Jan-10
1875S	3,200,000	225	61.6	83	185	250	475	625	750	1,350	3,900	$1,380, MS-64, Aug-09
1876	8,418,000	258	58.9	66	185	250	475	625	750	1,350	3,900	$3,335, MS-65 , Aug-09
1876CC	1,956,000	127	54.8	58	250	400	675	1,200	1,600	2,700	4,400	$1,610, MS-60, Sep-09
1876S	4,528,000	149	59.0	68	185	250	475	625	750	1,350	3,900	$2,760, MS-65 , May-09
1877	8,304,000	252	59.3	72	185	250	475	625	750	1,350	3,900	$978, MS-64, May-09
1877, 7 Over 6 (j)	***				1,300	2,750	4,500	7,000	12,000	25,000		$3,335, MS-62, Aug-09
1877CC	1,420,000	175	58.9	77	275	400	700	850	1,175	2,050	4,900	$1,610, MS-62, Feb-10
1877S	5,356,000	385	59.6	71	185	250	475	625	750	1,350	3,750	$6,325, MS-65 , Feb-10
1878	1,377,600	77	57.7	64	200	300	475	625	800	1,500	4,000	$207, AU-55, Oct-09
1878CC	62,000	28	28.5	14	4,500	6,000	8,000	18,000	22,500	32,500	50,000	$21,275, MS-63, Jan-10
1878S	12,000	12	37.4	50	70,000	80,000	90,000	105,000	130,000	165,000	230,000	$184,000, MS-64, Apr-09
1879	4,800	240	63.3	91	675	750	850	1,050	1,150	1,400	3,900	$14,950, MS-67, Jan-10
1880	8,400	84	62.4	88	675	750	850	1,050	1,150	1,400	3,900	$3,260, MS-65 , Mar-10
1881	10,000	90	60.1	86	675	750	850	1,050	1,150	1,650	4,000	$1,725, MS-64, Jul-09
1882	4,400	62	61.9	85	675	750	850	1,050	1,150	1,650	4,000	$1,898, MS-64, Feb-10
1883	8,000	70	60.1	80	675	750	850	1,100	1,250	1,400	3,900	$3,220, MS-65PL, Jan-10
1884	4,400	85	63.9	94	825	900	950	1,100	1,250	1,400	3,900	$25,300, MS-67, Jul-08
1885	5,200	61	60.7	82	825	900	950	1,100	1,300	1,600	4,000	$1,265, MS-63, Jan-10
1886	5,000	83	58.9	82	825	900	950	1,100	1,300	1,600	4,000	$1,495, MS-64, Jul-09
1887	5,000	107	58.0	76	825	925	1,050	1,250	1,350	1,700	4,000	$863, MS-62, Nov-09
1888	12,001	102	60.5	83	650	725	825	1,050	1,150	1,600	4,000	$4,830, MS-66, Feb-10
1889	12,000	99	59.6	80	650	725	825	1,050	1,150	1,400	3,900	$8,050, MS-66, Oct-08
1890	12,000	77	63.7	88	650	725	825	1,050	1,150	1,400	3,900	$9,200, MS-67, Jun-10
1891	200,000	138	61.7	83	225	300	450	625	775	1,350	3,800	$1,840, MS-64, Mar-10

*** Included in number above. **i.** The 1873-S, No Arrows, half dollar is unknown in any collection. **j.** The top portion of a 6 is visible on the upper surface of the last 7.

Proof Liberty Seated Half Dollars

PF-60 to 70 (Proof). Proofs were made in most years, with production beginning in a particularly significant way in 1858, when an estimated 210 silver sets were sold. Today, Proofs are readily available from 1858 through 1891. Quality often is lacking, with lint marks seen on some issues of the late 1850s and early 1860s. Light striking is occasionally seen on the star centers and the head of Miss Liberty; connoisseurs avoid these, but most buyers will not be aware. Slide marks (usually seen on the right knee) from coin albums can be a problem, more so on Liberty Seated half dollars than on smaller denominations of this design. *Obverse and Reverse:* Proofs that are extensively cleaned and have many hairlines, or that are dull and grainy, are lower level, such as PF-60 to 62. These are not widely desired, save for the low-mintage (in circulation-strike format) years from 1879 to 1891. With medium hairlines and good reflectivity, an assigned grade of PF-64 is appropriate, and with relatively few hairlines, PF-65. In various grades hairlines are most easily seen in the obverse field. PF-66 should have hairlines so delicate that magnification is needed to see them. Above that, a Proof should be free of such lines.

Proof Liberty Seated Half Dollar, Variety 1, No Motto Above Eagle
(1839–1852, 1856–1866)

Proof Liberty Seated Half Dollar, Variety 2, Arrows at Date, Rays Around Eagle
(1853)

Proof Liberty Seated Half Dollar, Variety 3, Arrows at Date, No Rays
(1854–1855)

Proof Liberty Seated Half Dollar, Variety 4, Motto Above Eagle
(1866–1873, 1875–1891)

Proof Liberty Seated Half Dollar, Variety 5, Arrows at Date
(1873–1874)

1866, No Motto, Irregular Issue
Judd-538.

	Est Mintage	Cert	Finest	PF-60	PF-63	PF-64	PF-65	Recent Auction Record
1839, No Drapery From Elbow	4–6	6	PF-65	$100,000	$145,000	$175,000	$250,000	$74,750, PF-62, Jan-10
1839, With Drap From Elbow	unverified	1	PF-64		125,000	175,000	250,000	$184,000, PF-64, Apr-08
1840, Small Letters	4–8	6	PF-65			75,000	100,000	$109,250, PF-65, Aug-07
1841	4–8	5	PF-65	20,000	45,000	65,000	85,000	$69,000, PF-64, May-08
1842, Small Date, Large Letters	4–8	6	PF-66	15,000	27,500	37,500	60,000	$69,000, PF-66, Apr-08
1843	4–8	4	PF-66	15,000	27,500	37,500	60,000	$40,250, PF-64, Jul-09
1844	3–6	2	PF-66					$149,500, PF-66Cam, Jan-08
1845	3–6	2	PF-66	15,000	27,500	37,500	60,000	$57,500, PF-64, May-08
1846, Medium Letters	15–20	10	PF-65	11,000	21,000	32,500	52,500	$51,750, PF-65, Jul-09
1847	15–20	14	PF-66	11,000	21,000	32,500	52,500	$16,100, PF-64, Apr-09
1848	4–8	3	PF-66	13,000	27,500	37,500	60,000	$28,750, PF-64, Jul-09
1849	4–8	4	PF-66	13,000	27,500	37,500	60,000	$41,688, PF-65, Jan-10
1850	4–8	4	PF-66	13,000	27,500	37,500	60,000	$34,500, PF-64, Jul-09
1852	3–6	3	PF-65		30,000	45,000	85,000	$74,750, PF-65, Jul-08
1852O	2–3	1	PF-62		35,000	50,000		$24,150, PF-62, May-01
1853, Arrows and Rays	5–10	5	PF-66		50,000	85,000	150,000	$149,500, PF-66, Aug-07
1854, Arrows	15–20	13	PF-66	8,500	13,500	19,500	29,000	$27,600, PF-65, Apr-09
1855, Arrows	15–20	7	PF-66	7,500	12,500	25,000	35,000	$20,700, PF-64 CAC, Dec-09
1855S (unique)	1–2	1	PF-65		150,000			$112,125, PF-63, May-10
1855, 55 Over 54	1–2			10,000	15,000	30,000	55,000	$12,075, PF-63, Apr-09
1856	20–30	19	PF-67	4,000	6,750	13,000	25,000	$19,550, PF-65, Mar-09
1857	30–50	36	PF-67	3,000	4,900	9,500	25,000	$6,613, PF-64, Feb-10

	Mintage	Cert	Finest	PF-60	PF-63	PF-64	PF-65	Recent Auction Record
1858	300+	48	PF-68	$1,400	$2,250	$3,800	$8,000	$1,725, PF-63, Mar-09
1859	800	129	PF-67	1,150	2,000	3,650	7,250	$978, PF-61, Aug-09
1860	1,000	116	PF-67	800	1,550	3,000	6,300	$7,475, PF-65, Oct-09
1861	1,000	96	PF-67	800	1,550	3,000	6,300	$2,990, PF-63 CAC, Jan-10
1862	550	174	PF-67	800	1,550	3,000	6,300	$3,220, PF-64, Feb-10
1863	460	107	PF-68	800	1,550	3,000	6,300	$2,070, PF-64, Feb-10
1864	470	139	PF-68	800	1,550	3,000	6,300	$3,479, PF-64, Feb-10
1865	500	180	PF-67	800	1,550	3,000	6,300	$8,050, PF-66Cam, Jan-10
1866, No Motto † (a)	1	1	PF-62		(unique)			
1866, With Motto	725	110	PF-68	750	1,400	2,100	4,000	$1,035, PF-63, Feb-10
1867	625	154	PF-67	750	1,400	2,100	4,000	$3,450, PF-65Cam, Jan-10
1868	600	148	PF-68	750	1,400	2,100	4,000	$4,888, PF-65 CAC, Jan-10
1869	600	137	PF-68	750	1,400	2,100	4,000	$978, PF-61, Feb-10
1870	1,000	117	PF-67	750	1,400	2,100	3,900	$4,025, PF-65, Jan-10
1871	960	133	PF-68	750	1,400	2,100	3,900	$2,760, PF-64 CAC, Feb-10
1872	950	138	PF-67	750	1,400	2,100	3,900	$2,760, PF-64 CAC, Dec-09
1873	600	155	PF-68	750	1,400	2,100	3,900	$1,351, PF-63 CAC, Nov-09
1873, Arrows	550	131	PF-66	1,000	2,650	4,500	12,500	$978, PF-62, Dec-09
1874	700	177	PF-68	1,000	2,650	4,500	12,500	$2,990, PF-64, Mar-10
1875	700	123	PF-68	750	1,400	2,100	3,900	$3,680, PF-65, Mar-10
1876	1,150	193	PF-67	750	1,400	2,100	3,900	$2,300, PF-64, Oct-09
1877	510	149	PF-66	750	1,400	2,100	3,900	$1,323, PF-63, Feb-10
1878	800	199	PF-68	750	1,400	2,100	3,900	$4,313, PF-66Cam, Feb-10
1879	1,100	281	PF-68	750	1,400	2,100	3,900	$1,955, PF-64, Feb-10
1880	1,355	340	PF-67	750	1,400	2,100	3,900	$5,750, PF-65, Jan-10
1881	975	305	PF-68	750	1,400	2,100	3,900	$4,600, PF-66Cam, Jan-10
1882	1,100	289	PF-68	750	1,400	2,100	3,900	$10,638, PF-67, Feb-10
1883	1,039	293	PF-68	750	1,400	2,100	3,900	$3,220, PF-65, Jun-10
1884	875	206	PF-67	750	1,400	2,100	3,900	$3,601, PF-65 CAC, Feb-10
1885	930	275	PF-68	750	1,400	2,100	3,900	$2,990, PF-65, Dec-09
1886	886	225	PF-68	750	1,400	2,100	3,900	$1,524, PF-64, Nov-09
1887	710	163	PF-68	750	1,400	2,100	3,900	$4,888, PF-66Cam, Dec-09

† Ranked in the *100 Greatest U.S. Coins* (third edition). **a.** Classified as Judd-538 (*United States Pattern Coins,* 10th edition). This fantasy piece was deliberately struck for pharmacist and coin collector Robert Coulton Davis, likely around 1869 or in the early 1870s, along with the No Motto Proof quarter and dollar of the same date.

	Mintage	Cert	Finest	PF-60	PF-63	PF-64	PF-65	Recent Auction Record
1888	832	210	PF-68	$750	$1,400	$2,100	$3,900	$2,875, PF-65Cam, Feb-10
1889	711	173	PF-67	750	1,400	2,100	3,900	$2,185, PF-64, Jan-10
1890	590	191	PF-68	750	1,400	2,100	3,900	$7,475, PF-67Cam, Feb-10
1891	600	175	PF-68	750	1,400	2,100	3,900	$2,768, PF-65, Mar-10

BARBER OR LIBERTY HEAD
(1892–1915)

Designer Charles E. Barber; weight 12.50 grams; composition .900 silver, .100 copper; diameter 30.6 mm; reeded edge; mints: Philadelphia, Denver, New Orleans, San Francisco.

History. Charles E. Barber, chief engraver of the U.S. Mint, crafted the eponymous "Barber" or Liberty Head half dollars along with similarly designed dimes and quarters of the same era. Barber's initial, B, is at the truncation of Miss Liberty's neck. Production of the coins was continuous from 1892 to 1915, stopping a year before the Barber dime and quarter.

Striking and Sharpness. On the obverse, check the hair details and other features. On the reverse, the eagle's leg at the lower right and the arrows often are weak, and there can be weakness at the upper right of the shield and the nearby wing area. At EF and below, sharpness of strike on the reverse is not important.

Availability. Most examples seen in the marketplace are well worn. There are no rarities, although some are scarcer than others. Coins that are Fine or better are much scarcer—in particular the San Francisco Mint issues of 1901, 1904, and 1907. MS coins are available of all dates and mints, but some are very elusive.

AU-50, 53, 55, 58 (About Uncirculated). *Obverse:* Light wear is seen on the head, especially on the forward hair under LIBERTY. There is some luster at AU-50 and 53. At AU-58, the luster is extensive but incomplete, especially on the higher parts and in the right field. *Reverse:* Wear is seen on the head and tail of the eagle and on the tips of the wings. At AU-50 and 53, there is significant luster. An AU-58 coin (as determined by the obverse) can have the reverse appear to be full MS.

MS-60 to 70 (Mint State). *Obverse:* At MS-60, some abrasion and contact marks are evident, most noticeably on the cheek and the obverse field to the right. Luster is present, but may be dull or lifeless. Many Barber coins have been cleaned, especially of the earlier dates. At MS-63, contact marks are very few; abrasion still is evident but less than at lower levels. An MS-65 coin may have minor abrasion, but contact marks are so minute as to require magnification. Luster should be full and rich. *Reverse:* Comments apply as for the obverse, except that in lower MS grades abrasion and contact marks are most noticeable on the head and tail of the eagle and on the tips of the wings. At MS-65 or higher there are no marks visible to the unaided eye. The field is mainly protected by design elements, so the reverse often appears to grade a point or two higher than the obverse.

1892-O, Normal O

1892-O, Micro O
FS-50-1892o-501.

1909-S, Inverted Mintmark
FS-50-1909S-501.

1911-S, Repunched Mintmark
FS-50-1911S-501.

	Mintage	Cert	Avg	%MS	AU-50	AU-55	MS-60	MS-62	MS-63	MS-64	MS-65	Recent Auction Record
1892	934,000	783	61.3	81	$300	$375	$500	$675	$825	$1,150	$2,900	$13,800, MS-67, Jan-10
1892O	390,000	235	50.5	56	675	725	900	1,200	1,800	2,350	3,800	$920, AU-58, Nov-09
1892O, Micro O (a)	*	11	36.5	45	18,000	21,000	25,000	30,000	45,000	70,000	100,000	$20,700, AU-55, Jan-10
1892S	1,029,028	153	43.8	42	675	750	950	1,700	2,150	2,900	4,750	$3,450, MS-65 , Jan-10
1893	1,826,000	220	58.2	65	300	400	550	850	1,050	1,900	4,600	$1,035, MS-63, Mar-10
1893O	1,389,000	157	58.7	76	425	500	650	1,100	1,350	2,750	8,500	$1,610, MS-64, Dec-09
1893S	740,000	92	41.2	43	650	800	1,200	3,000	4,100	8,800	21,500	$9,488, MS-64, Aug-09
1894	1,148,000	152	58.5	74	375	425	525	800	1,000	1,850	3,750	$1,553, MS-64, Mar-10

* Included in number above. **a.** This variety "was created when an O mintmark punch for quarters was used in place of the regular, larger mintmark intended for use on half dollar dies. . . . Many examples show strong strike doubling on reverse" (*Cherrypickers' Guide to Rare Die Varieties*, fourth edition, volume II).

Chart continued on next page.

	Mintage	Cert	Avg	%MS	AU-50	AU-55	MS-60	MS-62	MS-63	MS-64	MS-65	Recent Auction Record
1894O	2,138,000	135	55.8	70	$350	$400	$500	$700	$950	$1,850	$5,500	$3,795, MS-65, Feb-10
1894S	4,048,690	151	55.8	66	330	475	575	1,050	1,400	2,900	9,000	$2,300, MS-64, Feb-10
1895	1,834,338	140	58.3	72	325	425	525	700	900	1,600	3,700	$2,990, MS-65, Oct-09
1895O	1,766,000	86	55.5	60	375	475	600	1,150	1,500	2,500	6,500	$2,300, MS-64, Aug-09
1895S	1,108,086	110	59.2	77	380	475	575	1,100	1,400	2,450	6,600	$2,185, MS-63, Mar-10
1896	950,000	90	58.1	74	325	425	525	675	850	1,950	4,500	$2,428, MS-64, Aug-09
1896O	924,000	51	37.7	35	750	975	1,550	3,500	5,350	14,500	22,500	$9,491, MS-63, Aug-09
1896S	1,140,948	78	44.4	53	750	975	1,450	2,700	3,500	5,250	9,000	$3,565, MS-64, Nov-09
1897	2,480,000	174	58.4	70	300	350	475	650	800	1,150	3,000	$1,121, MS-64, Mar-10
1897O	632,000	112	30.6	28	1,250	1,400	1,700	3,200	4,000	6,250	9,750	$7,188, MS-66, Dec-09
1897S	933,900	95	38.1	41	975	1,100	1,500	2,700	3,600	4,600	6,500	$1,955, MS-62, Jan-10
1898	2,956,000	146	58.9	70	340	380	475	600	800	1,150	3,500	$7,188, MS-66, Nov-09
1898O	874,000	67	49.7	52	600	800	1,200	2,400	3,200	4,100	9,500	$7,590, MS-65, Aug-09
1898S	2,358,550	79	52.2	38	400	575	900	2,500	3,600	6,250	9,850	$5,175, MS-64, Aug-09
1899	5,538,000	229	56.0	60	300	350	475	650	800	1,050	3,250	$978, MS-64, Nov-09
1899O	1,724,000	89	52.0	61	375	425	675	1,150	1,500	3,600	8,900	$3,738, MS-64, Sep-09
1899S	1,686,411	79	53.9	53	325	425	675	1,500	2,100	3,200	6,100	$10,350, MS-67, Jan-10
1900	4,762,000	227	59.6	73	300	350	500	650	800	1,150	3,250	$2,875, MS-65, Jan-10
1900O	2,744,000	54	50.6	50	400	550	850	2,550	3,250	6,000	13,000	$12,075, MS-65, Aug-09
1900S	2,560,322	74	52.3	42	325	450	650	1,600	2,250	4,000	9,500	$3,450, MS-64, Jan-10
1901	4,268,000	205	57.2	58	300	350	500	650	800	1,150	3,500	$535, MS-62, Mar-10
1901O	1,124,000	52	54.4	63	450	600	1,300	2,900	4,600	8,000	13,000	$7,783, MS-64, Aug-09
1901S	847,044	50	41.2	36	1,200	1,500	2,200	6,000	7,250	9,500	16,500	$1,064, AU-50, Nov-09
1902	4,922,000	178	58.2	63	300	350	475	650	800	1,200	3,750	$2,760, MS-65, Jul-09
1902O	2,526,000	95	56.3	59	350	475	750	2,150	3,600	5,750	8,850	$5,175, MS-64, Nov-09
1902S	1,460,670	52	53.7	65	400	500	750	1,500	2,700	5,400	8,600	$5,463, MS-63, Aug-09
1903	2,278,000	79	54.0	62	325	400	550	1,100	1,500	3,350	8,600	$6,038, MS-65, Aug-09
1903O	2,100,000	124	57.0	69	350	475	675	1,150	1,600	2,350	8,100	$1,840, MS-64, Dec-09
1903S	1,920,772	78	53.9	67	375	475	600	1,250	1,650	2,750	5,500	$11,500, MS-66, Jan-09
1904	2,992,000	123	56.3	59	300	350	500	900	1,100	1,400	4,450	$4,025, MS-65, Mar-10
1904O	1,117,600	61	47.0	38	600	850	1,200	2,750	3,300	6,100	10,500	$21,850, MS-66, Jan-10
1904S	553,038	77	32.7	19	1,750	3,000	9,000	15,500	19,000	22,500	38,000	$18,400, MS-64, Nov-09
1905	662,000	76	55.6	63	325	400	550	1,125	1,650	3,000	5,350	$604, AU-58, Jan-10
1905O	505,000	104	56.1	77	450	550	750	1,200	1,550	2,200	4,050	$2,070, MS-64, May-10
1905S	2,494,000	80	52.3	58	375	450	650	1,400	1,800	3,600	8,350	$8,338, MS-66, Jun-10
1906	2,638,000	239	58.4	69	300	350	475	575	800	1,150	2,900	$920, MS-64, Dec-09
1906D	4,028,000	177	53.9	58	300	350	475	575	800	1,250	3,500	$1,093, MS-64, Jun-09
1906O	2,446,000	77	55.5	61	300	400	600	1,100	1,300	2,700	5,500	$4,456, MS-65, Jan-10
1906S	1,740,154	90	58.1	64	300	400	600	1,000	1,250	3,200	5,200	$2,530, MS-64, Mar-10
1907	2,598,000	220	60.0	77	300	350	475	575	800	1,150	2,900	$2,415, MS-65, Feb-10
1907D	3,856,000	211	57.2	67	310	375	475	575	800	1,050	2,900	$17,250, MS-67, Jan-10
1907O	3,946,600	210	57.6	70	325	425	550	625	850	1,150	2,900	$1,006, MS-64, Feb-10
1907S	1,250,000	58	50.7	55	600	800	1,250	2,500	5,250	8,600	11,500	$17,250, MS-66, Jan-09
1908	1,354,000	129	59.7	78	300	350	475	575	800	1,050	2,900	$7,475, MS-67, Jun-10
1908D	3,280,000	224	56.9	65	300	350	475	575	800	1,050	2,900	$978, MS-64, Aug-09
1908O	5,360,000	200	56.7	71	300	390	525	625	850	1,100	2,900	$2,530, MS-65, Dec-09
1908S	1,644,828	51	54.6	71	380	500	850	1,675	2,400	3,750	5,000	$3,048, MS-64, Jan-10
1909	2,368,000	300	57.2	71	300	375	475	575	800	1,050	2,900	$2,990, MS-65, Aug-09
1909O	925,400	79	51.3	62	500	650	800	1,200	1,750	2,650	4,300	$3,450, MS-65, Aug-09
1909S	1,764,000	80	52.9	60	315	390	600	850	1,250	2,650	4,300	$6,325, MS-66 Star, Jun-10
1909S, Inv Mintmark (b)	*				425	475	675	1,200	1,400			$12,650, MS-67, Jan-09
1910	418,000	117	54.2	65	400	475	600	850	1,100	1,500	3,700	$863, MS-63, Mar-10
1910S	1,948,000	71	51.8	61	325	420	700	1,650	2,000	2,800	5,900	$2,415, MS-64, Aug-09
1911	1,406,000	264	59.1	72	300	350	475	575	800	1,050	2,900	$920, MS-64, Jan-10
1911D	695,080	93	59.9	75	325	375	525	575	800	1,300	2,900	$1,035, MS-64, Mar-10
1911S	1,272,000	57	50.9	58	300	400	600	1,050	1,450	2,750	5,100	$4,888, MS-66, Sep-09
1911S, RPM (c)	*				450	550	750	1,200	1,700	3,250	5,500	$4,888, MS-65, Dec-09

* Included in number above. **b.** The S mintmark was punched into the die upside-down (with the top slightly wider than the base). **c.** The lower serif of the underlying mintmark is visible protruding from the primary serif.

	Mintage	Cert	Avg	%MS	AU-50	AU-55	MS-60	MS-62	MS-63	MS-64	MS-65	Recent Auction Record
1912	1,550,000	263	59.1	75	$300	$350	$475	$575	$800	$1,050	$2,900	$920, MS-63, Feb-10
1912D	2,300,800	384	59.1	72	300	350	475	575	800	1,050	2,900	$4,025, MS-66, Jun-10
1912S	1,370,000	135	54.7	72	300	400	525	750	1,100	2,500	4,400	$633, MS-62, Mar-10
1913	188,000	137	35.2	35	850	950	1,150	1,400	1,900	2,900	4,600	$2,760, MS-64, Jul-09
1913D	534,000	204	57.8	63	300	350	485	625	975	1,400	5,000	$1,610, MS-64, Feb-10
1913S	604,000	107	56.3	73	325	425	600	850	1,250	2,350	4,000	$1,955, MS-64, Feb-10
1914	124,230	210	34.4	40	950	1,100	1,300	1,600	1,900	3,450	9,500	$1,495, AU-50, Nov-09
1914S	992,000	108	53.5	64	300	350	550	800	1,150	2,300	4,750	$1,553, MS-64, Aug-09
1915	138,000	170	26.6	19	850	1,050	1,350	2,000	2,500	4,350	6,000	$1,495, MS-62, Feb-10
1915D	1,170,400	462	59.6	74	300	350	475	575	800	1,050	2,900	$863, MS-64, Aug-09
1915S	1,604,000	322	57.4	72	300	350	475	575	800	1,050	2,900	$12,075, MS-67 Star, Oct-09

Proof Barber Half Dollars

PF-60 to 70 (Proof). Proof Barber half dollars exist in proportion to their mintages. Choicer examples tend to be of later dates, similar to other Barber coins. Most are sharply struck, although many are weak on the eagle's leg at the lower right and on certain parts of the arrows and/or the upper right of the shield and the nearby wing. The Proofs of 1892 to 1901 usually have cameo contrast between the designs and the mirror fields. Those of 1914 and 1915 often have extensive hairlines or other problems. *Obverse and Reverse:* Proofs that are extensively cleaned and have many hairlines, or that are dull and grainy, are lower level, such as PF-60 to 62; these are not widely desired. With medium hairlines and good reflectivity, an assigned grade of PF-64 is appropriate. Tiny horizontal lines on Miss Liberty's cheek, known as slide marks, from National and other album slides scuffing the relief of the cheek, are endemic on all Barber silver coins. With noticeable marks of this type, the highest grade assignable is PF-64. With relatively few hairlines, a rating of PF-65 can be given. PF-66 should have hairlines so delicate that magnification is needed to see them. Above that, a Proof should be free of any hairlines or other problems.

Proof Barber Half Dollar

	Mintage	Cert	Finest	PF-60	PF-63	PF-64	PF-65	Recent Auction Record
1892	1,245	335	PF-68	$800	$1,100	$1,850	$3,600	$15,525, PF-68, Feb-10
1893	792	260	PF-68	800	1,100	1,850	3,600	$6,038, PF-67Cam, Jun-10
1894	972	305	PF-68	800	1,100	1,850	3,600	$1,214, PF-64, Mar-10
1895	880	324	PF-69	800	1,100	1,850	3,600	$1,677, PF-64, Mar-10
1896	762	246	PF-68	800	1,100	1,850	3,600	$3,119, PF-64, Mar-10
1897	731	305	PF-69	800	1,100	1,850	3,600	$8,050, PF-67 CAC, Feb-10
1898	735	246	PF-68	800	1,100	1,850	3,600	$2,703, PF-65Cam, Mar-10
1899	846	188	PF-69	800	1,100	1,850	3,600	$16,675, PF-68, Feb-10
1900	912	267	PF-68	800	1,100	1,850	3,600	$9,200, PF-67Cam, Jun-10
1901	813	253	PF-69	800	1,100	1,850	3,600	$7,475, PF-67 , Feb-10
1902	777	206	PF-68	800	1,100	1,850	3,600	$6,900, PF-67 , Feb-10
1903	755	226	PF-68	800	1,100	1,850	3,600	$2,415, PF-65, Jan-10
1904	670	236	PF-68	800	1,100	1,850	3,600	$6,900, PF-67 , Feb-10
1905	727	197	PF-68	800	1,100	1,850	3,600	$1,380, PF-64, Feb-10
1906	675	227	PF-68	800	1,100	1,850	3,600	$7,763, PF-67 , Feb-10
1907	575	171	PF-68	800	1,100	1,850	3,600	$6,900, PF-67 , Feb-10
1908	545	152	PF-68	800	1,100	1,850	3,600	$7,188, PF-67 , Feb-10
1909	650	267	PF-68	800	1,100	1,850	3,600	$19,550, PF-68 CAC, Feb-10
1910	551	225	PF-68	800	1,100	1,850	3,600	$12,650, PF-68, Feb-10
1911	543	226	PF-68	800	1,100	1,850	3,600	$587, PF-61, Mar-10
1912	700	171	PF-68	800	1,100	1,850	3,600	$920, PF-63, Jul-09

Chart continued on next page.

	Mintage	Cert	Finest	PF-60	PF-63	PF-64	PF-65	Recent Auction Record
1913	627	180	PF-68	$800	$1,100	$1,850	$3,600	$8,625, PF-67, Feb-10
1914	380	160	PF-68	800	1,100	1,850	3,600	$8,338, PF-67, Feb-10
1915	450	162	PF-68	800	1,100	1,850	3,600	$1,504, PF-64, Mar-10

LIBERTY WALKING
(1916–1947)

Designer Adolph A. Weinman; weight 12.50 grams; composition .900 silver, .100 copper (net weight: .36169 oz. pure silver); diameter 30.6 mm; reeded edge; mints: Philadelphia, Denver, San Francisco.

History. The Liberty Walking half dollar was designed by Adolph A. Weinman, the sculptor who also created the Mercury or Winged Liberty Head dime. His monogram appears under the tips of the eagle's wing feathers. Mintage was intermittent, with none struck in 1922, 1924, 1925, 1926, 1930, 1931, and 1932. On the 1916 coins and some of the 1917 coins, the mintmark is located on the obverse, below IN GOD WE TRUST. Other coins of 1917, and those through 1947, have the mintmark on the reverse, under the pine branch.

Striking and Sharpness. Most circulation-strike Liberty Walking half dollars are lightly struck. In this respect they are similar to Standing Liberty quarters of the same era. On the obverse, the key points to check are Miss Liberty's left hand, the higher parts and lines in the skirt, and her head; after that, check all other areas. *Very few* coins are sharply struck in these areas, and for some issues sharp strikes might not exist at all. On the reverse, check the breast of the eagle.

Availability. All dates and mintmarks are readily collectible, although some, such as 1917-S (obverse mintmark), 1919-D, the three issues of 1921, and 1938-D, are scarce. Earlier years are often seen with extensive wear. MS coins are most often seen of the three issues of 1916, the 1917, and from 1933 to 1947. Issues in the 1940s were saved in large quantities and are common. As noted, coins with Full Details can range from scarce to extremely rare for certain dates. Half dollars dated 1928-D are counterfeit.

AU-50, 53, 55, 58 (About Uncirculated). *Obverse:* Light wear is seen on the higher-relief areas of Miss Liberty, the vertical area from her head down to the date. There is some luster at AU-50 and 53. At AU-58, the luster in the field is extensive, but is interrupted by friction and light wear. *Reverse:* Wear is most evident on the eagle's breast immediately under the neck feathers, the left leg, and the top of the left wing. At AU-50 half or more of the luster is gone. Luster is nearly complete at AU-58.

MS-60 to 70 (Mint State). *Obverse:* At MS-60, some abrasion and contact marks are evident on the higher areas, which also are the areas most likely to be weakly struck. This includes Miss Liberty's left arm, her hand, and the areas of the skirt covering her left leg. The luster may not be complete in those areas on weakly struck coins (even those certified above MS-65)—the original planchet surface may be revealed, as it was not smoothed out by striking. Accordingly, grading is best done by evaluating abrasion as it is observed in the right field, plus evaluating the mint luster. Luster may be dull or lifeless at MS-60 to 62, but should have deep frost at MS-63 or better, particularly in the lower-relief areas. At MS-65 or better, it should be full and rich. Sometimes, to compensate for flat striking, certified coins with virtually flawless luster in the fields, evocative of an MS-65 or 66 grade, are called MS-63 or a lower grade. *Reverse:* Striking usually is better, permitting observation of luster in all areas except the eagle's body, which may be lightly struck. Luster may be dull or lifeless at MS-60 to 62, but should have deep frost at MS-63 or better, particularly in the lower-relief areas. At MS-65 or better, it should be full and rich.

Mintmark Location, 1916–1917

Mintmark Location, 1917–1947

	Mintage	Cert	Avg	%MS	AU-55	MS-60	MS-62	MS-63	MS-64	MS-65	MS-66	Recent Auction Record
1916	608,000	1,080	59.7	82	$300	$350	$400	$450	$700	$2,000	$3,250	$1,610, MS-65, Mar-10
1916D, Obv Mintmark	1,014,400	1,217	60.2	80	280	360	475	600	900	2,300	4,000	$460, MS-63, Mar-10
1916S, Obv Mintmark	508,000	561	51.3	65	900	1,200	1,600	1,900	3,000	6,250	14,000	$6,900, MS-65 CAC, Jun-10

	Mintage	Cert	Avg	%MS	AU-55	MS-60	MS-62	MS-63	MS-64	MS-65	MS-66	Recent Auction Record
1917	12,292,000	1,757	62.5	87	$90	$150	$175	$200	$325	$1,100	$2,000	$253, MS-64, Mar-10
1917D, Obv Mintmark	765,400	698	59.1	73	400	600	1,000	1,350	2,000	6,500	18,500	$2,530, MS-64, May-10
1917D, Rev Mintmark	1,940,000	415	57.5	60	650	900	1,600	2,000	4,000	15,500	30,000	$3,738, MS-64 CAC, Jun-10
1917S, Obv Mintmark	952,000	342	51.4	52	1,550	2,400	4,000	5,000	7,750	21,000	36,000	$4,313, AU-58, Jun-10
1917S, Rev Mintmark	5,554,000	622	59.8	72	200	350	1,500	2,050	3,100	12,750	31,000	$1,495, MS-63, Mar-10
1918	6,634,000	613	60.1	75	325	650	800	950	1,300	3,300	9,000	$3,220, MS-65 , Dec-09
1918D	3,853,040	545	57.8	68	700	1,300	2,200	3,150	6,500	23,000	45,000	$1,265, MS-61, Mar-10
1918S	10,282,000	693	59.1	71	300	500	1,500	2,250	4,900	14,500	45,000	$2,128, MS-63 CAC, Mar-10
1919	962,000	353	52.4	59	1,000	1,300	2,700	3,450	4,000	6,500	10,000	$6,325, MS-65 , Jun-10
1919D	1,165,000	346	47.5	47	3,000	5,750	9,500	17,500	28,000	125,000	265,000	$8,338, MS-62, Mar-10
1919S	1,552,000	292	46.2	36	2,250	3,250	6,000	8,500	12,000	18,500	29,000	$9,200, MS-63, Jun-10
1920	6,372,000	687	61.2	81	220	325	500	700	1,200	4,000	13,000	$575, MS-63, Mar-10
1920D	1,551,000	239	51.0	60	1,050	1,400	2,750	3,750	6,250	18,500	40,000	$21,850, MS-66, Feb-10
1920S	4,624,000	377	56.2	62	650	850	2,250	2,900	4,000	12,750	28,500	$4,600, MS-64, Feb-10
1921	246,000	541	31.8	32	3,300	4,250	6,250	7,500	9,500	16,500	35,000	$3,450, EF-45 CAC, Jun-10
1921D	208,000	613	26.9	27	4,250	5,500	10,000	13,250	16,000	26,000	50,000	$11,500, MS-63, Jan-10
1921S	548,000	587	24.7	15	11,250	14,500	22,000	28,000	43,000	85,000	200,000	$10,925, AU-55, Nov-09
1923S	2,178,000	338	54.9	62	900	1,500	2,800	3,600	5,000	14,000	30,000	$2,530, MS-63, Jan-10
1927S	2,392,000	506	59.2	77	550	950	1,600	1,950	3,100	8,000	24,000	$4,888, MS-64 CAC, Jun-10
1928S (a,b)	1,940,000	376	57.8	70	550	950	2,000	2,700	3,800	9,750	23,000	$3,450, MS-64 Secure, Jun-10
1929D	1,001,200	652	60.0	71	280	385	550	700	1,200	2,750	4,500	$1,265, MS-64, Mar-10
1929S	1,902,000	615	60.2	77	280	385	750	1,000	1,200	3,400	5,000	$2,445, MS-65 , Dec-09

a. Large and small mintmark varieties exist. b. Half dollars dated 1928-D are counterfeit.

1936, Doubled-Die Obverse
FS-50-1936-101.

1945, Missing Designer's Initials
FS-50-1945-901.

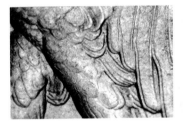

1946, Doubled-Die Reverse
FS-50-1946-801.

	Mintage	Cert	Avg	%MS	AU-50	MS-60	MS-62	MS-63	MS-64	MS-65	MS-66	Recent Auction Record
1933S	1,786,000	739	59.5	64	$250	$600	$1,000	$1,250	$1,600	$3,250	$5,000	$2,760, MS-65 , Jun-10
1934	6,964,000	2,096	63.9	92	26	85	100	110	120	525	700	$5,463, MS-68, Feb-10
1934D (a)	2,361,000	1,175	63.2	92	90	150	190	225	325	1,350	2,700	$2,300, MS-66, Mar-10
1934S	3,652,000	693	61.4	76	100	150	600	800	1,150	4,100	5,500	$4,140, MS-65 , Mar-10
1935	9,162,000	1,974	63.9	95	25	45	60	75	80	350	500	$495, MS-66, Mar-10
1935D	3,003,800	844	63.0	91	70	140	220	260	400	1,850	4,250	$3,220, MS-66, Jan-10
1935S	3,854,000	753	62.7	89	100	140	375	440	600	2,400	4,250	$4,600, MS-66, Jun-10
1936	12,614,000	2,833	64.3	96	25	45	60	75	80	260	400	$748, MS-66, Mar-10
1936, DblDie Obv (b)	*				750	1,500						
1936D	4,252,400	1,458	64.1	96	55	80	100	115	125	625	900	$690, MS-66, Dec-09
1936S	3,884,000	1,162	64.0	97	60	130	170	200	220	750	1,200	$1,150, MS-66, Dec-09
1937	9,522,000	2,643	64.2	95	25	40	60	70	80	275	400	$1,495, MS-67, Jan-10
1937D	1,676,000	1,014	63.7	93	110	225	270	300	330	675	1,050	$1,380, MS-67, Feb-10

* Included in number above. a. Large and small mintmark varieties exist. b. Valuations are theoretical, as no examples have yet been discovered grading better than Fine. Value in VG-8 is $325; in F-12, $450. "Extremely strong doubling is evident on the date. Less doubling is evident on IN GOD WE TRUST, the skirt, and some other elements" (*Cherrypickers' Guide to Rare Die Varieties*, fourth edition, volume II). Several varieties exist; this one is FS-50-1936-101.

Chart continued on next page.

	Mintage	Cert	Avg	%MS	AU-50	MS-60	MS-62	MS-63	MS-64	MS-65	MS-66	Recent Auction Record
1937S	2,090,000	1,109	63.9	96	$60	$175	$195	$210	$225	$700	$1,100	$920, MS-65, Mar-10
1938	4,110,000	1,884	64.1	95	45	70	150	170	190	425	500	$2,197, MS-67, Jan-10
1938D	491,600	1,495	53.7	68	250	525	600	650	750	1,400	1,950	$1,150, MS-65, Mar-10
1939	6,812,000	3,153	64.6	96	25	45	55	70	75	200	300	$66, MS-64, Mar-10
1939D	4,267,800	2,577	64.5	97	28	45	65	80	90	210	400	$1,208, MS-65, Feb-10
1939S	2,552,000	1,669	64.7	97	80	150	170	190	210	350	700	$1,955, MS-67, Jan-10
1940	9,156,000	3,428	64.5	96	15	30	45	55	65	170	275	$633, MS-67, Sep-09
1940S	4,550,000	2,643	64.0	98	22	50	65	75	100	300	900	$817, MS-66, Nov-09
1941	24,192,000	8,874	64.5	96	13	35	45	50	55	150	275	$920, MS-67, Mar-10
1941D	11,248,400	4,832	64.6	97	18	40	55	60	65	170	290	$207, MS-66, Feb-10
1941S	8,098,000	4,998	63.5	93	30	75	95	110	220	900	1,900	$1,208, MS-66, Feb-10
1942	47,818,000	12,833	64.2	94	13	40	45	50	55	155	275	$345, MS-65, Mar-10
1942D	10,973,800	3,679	64.6	97	18	40	60	75	90	300	400	$863, MS-67, Dec-09
1942S (a)	12,708,000	3,824	63.9	97	18	40	50	60	100	550	975	$174, MS-64, Mar-10
1943	53,190,000	12,930	64.2	95	13	35	40	45	55	150	275	$546, MS-67, Feb-10
1943D	11,346,000	4,534	64.9	98	25	50	65	75	85	275	400	$806, MS-67, Mar-10
1943S	13,450,000	4,501	64.1	98	25	45	50	55	70	425	650	$2,530, MS-67, Dec-09
1944	28,206,000	7,359	64.1	96	13	35	40	45	55	170	275	$1,380, MS-67, Jan-10
1944D	9,769,000	5,232	64.8	98	20	40	50	55	60	165	275	$920, MS-67, Feb-10
1944S	8,904,000	5,235	64.0	99	17	40	55	65	70	525	1,150	$1,265, MS-66, Jan-10
1945	31,502,000	10,359	64.2	96	13	35	40	45	55	165	275	$92, MS-65, Mar-10
1945, Missing Initials	*				200	300	400	500				
1945D	9,966,800	7,778	64.9	99	18	35	50	55	60	150	275	$93, MS-65, Mar-10
1945S	10,156,000	6,302	64.4	99	18	40	45	50	60	160	600	$431, MS-66, Mar-10
1946	12,118,000	5,289	64.1	97	13	40	45	50	55	200	400	$1,611, MS-67, Jan-10
1946, DblDie Rev (c)	*	109	52.9	50	100	250	325	400	750	3,000	5,500	$1,150, MS-64, Feb-10
1946D	2,151,000	10,920	64.8	100	35	45	55	60	65	150	275	$863, MS-67, Jan-10
1946S	3,724,000	7,547	64.8	100	20	42	50	55	60	175	300	$5,175, MS-67, Jan-10
1947	4,094,000	6,156	64.4	98	25	45	50	55	65	220	400	$4,313, MS-67, Feb-10
1947D	3,900,600	7,054	64.7	99	30	45	55	60	65	170	400	$92, MS-65, Mar-10

* Included in number above. **a.** Large and small mintmark varieties exist. **c.** Very strong doubling is visible on E PLURIBUS UNUM, the eagle's wing feathers and left wing, and the branch.

Proof Liberty Walking Half Dollars

PF-60 to 70 (Proof). Proofs were made beginning in 1936 and continuing through 1942. The entire die was polished (including the figure of Miss Liberty and the eagle), generating coins of low contrast. Proofs usually are fairly well struck. Most Proofs of 1941 are from over-polished dies, with the AW monogram of the designer no longer present. Striking sharpness can vary. A full head and complete left-hand details are points to check for. *Obverse and Reverse:* Proofs that are extensively cleaned and have many hairlines, or that are dull and grainy, are lower level, such as PF-60 to 62. With medium hairlines and good reflectivity, assigned grades of PF-63 or 64 are appropriate. Tiny horizontal lines on Miss Liberty's leg, known as slide marks, from National and other album slides scuffing the relief of the cheek, are common; coins with such marks should not be graded higher than PF-64, but sometimes are. With relatively few hairlines and no noticeable slide marks, a rating of PF-65 can be given. PF-66 should have hairlines so delicate that magnification is needed to see them. Above that, a Proof should be free of any hairlines or other problems.

Proof Liberty Walking Half Dollar

	Mintage	Cert	Avg	PF-64	PF-65	PF-66	PF-67	Recent Auction Record
1936	3,901	1,254	64.8	$3,300	$4,250	$6,000	$13,000	$5,175, PF-66 CAC, Jun-10
1937	5,728	1,399	65.2	750	1,000	1,500	1,900	$978, PF-66, Mar-10
1938	8,152	1,672	65.4	650	750	1,000	1,500	$638, PF-65, Mar-10
1939	8,808	1,794	65.6	550	650	850	1,200	$610, PF-65, Mar-10
1940	11,279	2,101	65.5	500	600	750	1,100	$727, PF-67, Mar-10
1941 (a)	15,412	2,843	65.4	500	600	700	1,000	$691, PF-67, Mar-10
1942	21,120	3,937	65.6	500	600	700	1,000	$920, PF-67, Mar-10

a. The variety without the designer's initials was created by the over-polishng of dies.

FRANKLIN
(1948–1963)

Designer John R. Sinnock; weight 12.50 grams; composition .900 silver, .100 copper (net weight: .36169 oz. pure silver); diameter 30.6 mm; reeded edge; mints: Philadelphia, Denver, San Francisco.

History. U.S. Mint chief engraver John R. Sinnock developed a motif for a silver half dime in 1942; it was proposed but never adopted for regular coinage. In 1948 Sinnock's Franklin half dollar was introduced, its design an adaptation of his earlier half-dime motif. The Liberty Bell is similar to that used by Sinnock on the 1926 Sesquicentennial commemorative half dollar modeled from a sketch by John Frederick Lewis. The coin-collecting community paid little attention to the Franklin half dollar at the time, but today the coins are widely collected.

Striking and Sharpness. Given the indistinct details of the obverse, sharpness of strike usually is ignored. On the reverse, if the bottom lines of the Liberty Bell are complete the coin may be designated as Full Bell Lines (FBL).

Availability. All dates and mintmarks are easily available in grades from VF upward. Lower-level MS coins can be unattractive due to contact marks and abrasion, particularly noticeable on the obverse. High-quality gems are generally inexpensive, although varieties that are rare with FBL can be costly amid much competition in the marketplace. Most numismatists collect MS coins. Grades below EF are not widely desired.

MS-60 to 70 (Mint State). *Obverse:* At MS-60, some abrasion and contact marks are evident on the cheek, on the hair left of the ear, and the neck. At MS-63, abrasion is slight at best, less so for MS-64. An MS-65 coin should display no abrasion or contact marks except under magnification, and MS-66 and higher coins should have none at all. Luster should be full and rich. As details are shallow on this design, the amount and "depth" of luster is important to grading. *Reverse:* General comments apply as for the obverse. The points to check are the bell harness, the words PASS AND STOW on the upper area of the Liberty Bell, and the bottom of the bell.

1948, Doubled-Die Reverse
FS-50-1948-801.

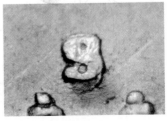

1949-S, Repunched Mintmark
FS-50-1949S-501.

1951-S, Doubled-Die Reverse
FS-50-1951S-801.

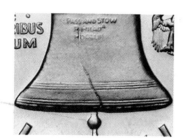

Full Bell Lines

1955, Clashed Obverse Die
"Bugs Bunny" variety.
FS-50-1955-401.

1959, Doubled-Die Reverse
FS-50-1959-801.

	Mintage	Cert	Avg	%MS	MS-63	MS-64	MS-64FBL	MS-65	MS-65FBL	MS-66	MS-66FBL	Recent Auction Record
1948	3,006,814	2,611	64.2	97	$25	$35	$55	$80	$175	$400	$600	$7,475, MS-67FBL, Jan-10
1948, DblDie Rev (a)	*				125	175	200	240	325	600		
1948D	4,028,600	2,419	64.2	98	20	30	55	125	250	900	1,200	$63, MS-66FBL, Mar-09
1949	5,614,000	1,756	63.3	89	65	80	90	140	230	400	800	$322, MS-66FBL, Mar-10
1949D	4,120,600	1,879	63.6	96	70	90	180	650	750	2,500	7,500	$10,350, MS-66FBL, Jan-10
1949S	3,744,000	2,153	64.2	96	100	130	300	150	750	225	1,000	$299, MS-65FBL, Mar-10
1949S, DblMintmark (b)	*				140	190	225	270	350	630		
1950	7,742,123	1,527	63.8	94	40	55	90	110	300	400	650	$12,650, MS-67FBL, Feb-09
1950D	8,031,600	1,510	63.6	95	50	80	110	270	450	900	1,300	$2,530, MS-66FBL, Jan-10
1951	16,802,102	1,740	64.2	97	20	35	90	75	325	200	650	$2,070, MS-66FBL, Feb-09
1951D	9,475,200	1,310	63.9	97	40	55	100	160	450	850	1,200	$1,955, MS-66FBL, Jan-10
1951S	13,696,000	1,827	64.3	98	35	55	250	75	650	800	1,200	$748, MS-66FBL, Sep-09
1951S, DblDie Rev (c)	*	5	64.4	100	70	95	325	165	750	850		$322, MS-65, Sep-09
1952	21,192,093	1,841	64.2	97	20	30	80	75	200	250	650	$2,415, MS-67 Star, Dec-09
1952D	25,395,600	1,526	64.0	98	20	30	85	130	425	600	1,200	$2,530, MS-66FBL, Jan-10
1952S	5,526,000	1,672	64.7	99	70	85	400	110	650	300	3,500	$431, MS-66, Mar-10
1953	2,668,120	1,504	64.1	98	40	45	200	130	500	800	1,600	$7,475, MS-66FBL, Jan-10
1953D	20,900,400	1,892	64.1	98	18	25	50	120	375	600	850	$161, MS-65FBL, Mar-10
1953S	4,148,000	3,610	64.9	100	35	60	10,000	80	25,000	700		$11,788, MS-65FBL, Nov-09
1954	13,188,202	2,691	64.4	99	16	25	40	70	200	350	850	$99, MS-65FBL, Mar-10
1954D	25,445,580	3,451	64.3	99	20	30	35	110	200	400	850	$834, MS-66FBL, Jun-09
1954S	4,993,400	6,023	64.9	100	25	40	75	55	350	500	900	$863, MS-66FBL, Jun-09
1955	2,498,181	4,054	64.3	99	40	45	60	65	160	200	550	$115, MS-65FBL, Mar-10
1955, Clashed Obv Die (d)	*				60	65	75	80	200	250	650	$47, MS-63, Jan-10
1956	4,032,000	3,775	64.7	99	20	25	40	50	200	90	650	$3,680, MS-67FBL, Jun-10
1957	5,114,000	3,169	64.8	100	15	20	60	55	250	100	750	$2,645, MS-67FBL, Jun-09
1957D	19,966,850	3,036	64.5	99	14	20	30	60	150	90	1,000	$2,760, MS-67FBL, Sep-09
1958	4,042,000	4,351	64.8	100	15	20	40	55	150	90	1,200	$2,645, MS-67FBL, Jun-09
1958D	23,962,412	4,022	64.6	100	13	15	30	50	80	80	750	$4,025, MS-67FBL Star, Dec-09
1959	6,200,000	3,126	64.4	99	13	15	40	75	250	1,000	1,700	$2,530, MS-67, Mar-10
1959, DblDie Rev (e)	*				85	90	180	120	375	1,125		$115, MS-65, Aug-09
1959D	13,053,750	2,905	64.3	100	13	20	35	110	160	800	1,200	$863, MS-66FBL, Sep-09
1960	6,024,000	2,855	64.3	100	13	15	35	110	250	500	2,000	$3,220, MS-66FBL, Feb-10
1960D	18,215,812	2,453	64.0	99	13	30	50	300	1,000	600	3,000	$109, MS-65 , Mar-10
1961	8,290,000	2,934	64.4	99	13	25	150	90	1,000	600	4,000	$748, MS-65FBL, Jun-09
1961D	20,276,442	2,226	64.2	99	13	25	75	110	800	1,000	2,000	$34, MS-64, Mar-10
1962	9,714,000	2,136	64.3	99	13	20	150	100	1,600	750	10,000	$1,840, MS-65FBL, Jan-10
1962D	35,473,281	2,882	64.2	99	13	25	75	110	500	1,000	3,500	$920, MS-65, Sep-09
1963	22,164,000	7,679	64.5	100	13	15	125	50	800	800	2,500	$431, MS-65FBL, Mar-10
1963D	67,069,292	5,775	64.3	99	13	15	30	50	250	350	1,000	$805, MS-66FBL, Mar-10

* Included in number above. **a.** Doubling is visible on E PLURIBUS UNUM, UNITED, HALF DOLLAR, the dots, and the Liberty Bell's clapper. "There are several similar, yet lesser, DDRs for this date" (*Cherrypickers' Guide to Rare Die Varieties,* fourth edition, volume II). The variety listed and pictured is FS-50-1948-801. **b.** The secondary mintmark is visible south of the primary. CONECA lists two other repunched mintmarks for this date; the one illustrated and listed here is FS-50-1949S-501. **c.** Doubling is evident on the eagle's tail feathers and left wing, as well as on E PLURIBUS UNUM. This variety is FS-50-1951S-801. **d.** This variety, popularly known as the "Bugs Bunny," has evidence of clash marks that appear as two buckteeth on Benjamin Franklin. **e.** Strong doubling is evident on the eagle; doubling is also visible on E PLURIBUS UNUM, UNITED, and portions of the Liberty Bell.

Proof Franklin Half Dollars

PF-60 to 70 (Proof). Proofs were made from 1950 to 1963 and are available today in proportion to their mintages. Those with cameo-frosted devices are in the minority and often sell for strong premiums. Virtually all Proofs are well struck.

Only a few Proof Franklin half dollars are in the lower PF-60 to 62 range. *Obverse and Reverse:* Proofs that are extensively cleaned and have many hairlines, or that are dull and grainy, are lower level, such as PF-60 to 62. With medium hairlines and good reflectivity, assigned grades of PF-63 or 64 are appropriate. PF-66 should have hairlines so delicate that magnification is needed to see them. Above that, a Proof should be free of any hairlines or other problems.

Proof Franklin Half Dollar

1957, Proof, Tripled-Die Reverse
FS-50-1957-801.

1961, Proof, Doubled-Die Reverse
FS-50-1961-801.

	Mintage	Cert	Avg	PF-64	PF-65	PF-65Cam	PF-65DC	PF-66	Recent Auction Record
1950	51,386	2,181	64.8	$450	$500	$1,500	$10,000	$650	$1,380, PF-67, Jan-10
1951	57,500	2,162	65.0	350	425	700	3,500	550	$1,725, PF-65DCam, Feb-10
1952	81,980	2,471	65.3	200	250	400	4,500	300	$546, PF-67Cam, Mar-10
1953	128,800	2,951	65.5	150	225	300	2,000	300	$1,035, PF-67Cam, Mar-10
1954	233,300	3,942	66.2	80	110	125	400	130	$690, PF-68 CAC, Feb-10
1955	378,200	5,076	66.7	70	90	110	400	110	$805, PF-67DCam, Feb-10
1956	669,384	7,889	67.1	35	45	55	100	60	$3,220, PF-69DCam, Jan-10
1957	1,247,952	6,110	66.8	25	30	60	300	35	$1,610, PF-68DCam, Jan-10
1957, TripDie Rev (a)	*			75	90	175	800	150	
1958	875,652	4,275	66.5	35	50	75	800	60	$1,265, PF-69Cam, Mar-10
1959	1,149,291	4,616	66.6	20	25	60	2,000	45	$2,300, PF-68 CAC, Feb-10
1960	1,691,602	6,329	66.6	16	20	45	100	30	$633, PF-68DCam, Feb-10
1960, DblDie Obv (b)	*	61	66.2	75	85	175	400	150	$81, PF-65, Nov-08
1961	3,028,244	9,655	66.7	20	25	40	125	35	$776, PF-68DCam, Feb-10
1961, DblDie Rev (c)	*	68	65.6	1,500	2,000	3,500		4,000	$3,320, PF-66, Feb-10
1962	3,218,019	14,154	66.6	13	15	25	70	25	$5,750, PF-69DCam, Jan-10
1962, DblDie Obv (d)	*			25	30	50	150	60	
1963	3,075,645	13,339	66.8	13	20	25	70	25	$2,990, PF-69DCam, Jan-10

* Included in number above. **a.** A closely tripled image is evident on E PLURIBUS UNUM, portions of UNITED STATES OF AMERICA, and HALF DOLLAR. **b.** Doubling is visible on LIBERTY, TRUST, and the date. **c.** Other reverse doubled dies exist for this date. The variety pictured and listed here (FS-50-1961-801) is by far the most dramatic. Very strong doubling is evident on the reverse lettering. **d.** Doubling is visible on the 62 of the date and on WE TRUST.

KENNEDY
(1964 TO DATE)

Designers Gilroy Roberts and Frank Gasparro. 1964—Weight 12.50 grams; composition .900 silver, .100 copper (net weight: .36169 oz. pure silver); diameter 30.6 mm; reeded edge; mints: Philadelphia, Denver, San Francisco. 1965–1970—Weight 11.50 grams; composition, outer layers of .800 silver and .200 copper bonded to inner core of .209 silver, .791 copper (net weight .1479 oz. pure silver). 1971 to date—Weight 11.34 grams; composition, outer layers of copper-nickel (.750 copper, .250 nickel) bonded to inner core of pure copper; diameter 30.6 mm; reeded edge; mints: Philadelphia, Denver, San Francisco. Modern silver Proofs—Weight 12.50 grams; composition .900 silver, .100 copper (net weight: .36169 oz. pure silver); diameter 30.6 mm; reeded edge; mint: San Francisco.

Bicentennial variety: Designers Gilroy Roberts and Seth Huntington; diameter 30.6 mm; reeded edge. Silver clad—Weight 11.50 grams; composition outer layers of .800 silver, .200 copper bonded to inner core of .209 silver, .791 copper (net weight .14792 oz. pure silver). Copper-nickel clad—Weight 11.34 grams; composition outer layers of copper-nickel (.750 copper, .250 nickel) bonded to inner core of pure copper.

History. Kennedy half dollars, minted from 1964 to date, were struck in 90% silver the first year, then with reduced silver content through 1970, and in later years in copper-nickel (except for special silver issues made for collectors). The obverse, by Chief Engraver Gilroy Roberts, features a portrait of President John F. Kennedy, while the reverse, by Frank Gasparro, displays a modern version of a heraldic eagle. The 1976 Bicentennial coin shows Philadelphia's Independence Hall, a design by Seth G. Huntington, similar to that of the 1926 Sesquicentennial commemorative quarter eagle. The obverse was unchanged except for the dual dating 1776–1976.

They were the only coins struck during 1975 and 1976 and were used for general circulation as well as being included in Proof and Uncirculated sets for 1975 and 1976.

Striking and Sharpness. Nearly all are well struck. Check the highest points of the hair on the obverse and the highest details on the reverse.

Availability. All issues are common in high circulated grades as well as MS.

MS-60 to 70 (Mint State). *Obverse:* At MS-60, some abrasion and contact marks are evident on the cheek, and on the hair to the right of the forehead and temple. Abrasion is slight at MS-63, and even slighter at MS-64. An MS-65 coin should display no abrasion or contact marks except under magnification, and MS-66 and higher coins should have none at all. Luster should be full and rich. *Reverse:* Comments apply as for the obverse, except that the highest parts of the eagle at the center are the key places to check.

1964, Doubled-Die Obverse
FS-50-1964-102.

1964-D, Doubled-Die Obverse
FS-50-1964D-101.

1964-D, Repunched Mintmark
FS-50-1964D-502.

1972, Doubled-Die Obverse
FS-50-1972-101.

1972-D, Missing Designer's Initials
FS-50-1972D-901.

1974-D, Doubled-Die Obverse
FS-50-1974D-101.

	Mintage	Cert	Avg	%MS	MS-63	MS-65	MS-66	MS-67	Recent Auction Record
1964	273,304,004	1,599	64.2	95	$7	$15	$40	$250	$69, MS-66, Nov-09
1964, DblDie Obv (a)	*	3	64.0	100	35	65	250		$21, MS-65, Jul-06
1964D	156,205,446	774	63.9	94	7	15	40	400	$84, MS-66, Aug-09
1964D, DblDie Obv (b)	*	27	61.7	67	50	65	160		$1,150, MS-66, Feb-08
1964D, RPM (c)	*	4	64.0	100	40	55	110		$15, MS-63, Dec-06
1965	65,879,366	217	64.4	95	4	15	35	200	$150, MS-65, Oct-08
1966	108,984,932	206	63.7	91	4	10	35	120	$44, MS-65, Sep-09
1967	295,046,978	302	63.9	88	4	20	40	90	$21, MS-65, Oct-08
1968D	246,951,930	493	64.6	97	4	20	60	200	$36, MS-66, Sep-09
1969D	129,881,800	572	64.5	97	4	25	100	300	$15, MS-64, Feb-09
1970D	2,150,000	1,146	64.5	100	14	30	100	400	$28, MS-64, Oct-09
1971	155,164,000	104	64.0	96	3	10	30	60	$42, MS-66, Sep-08
1971D	302,097,424	523	65.3	96	3	10	18	50	$11, MS-66, Oct-08
1972	153,180,000	165	64.8	96	3	15	25	100	$75, MS-66, Jun-07
1972, DblDie Obv (d)	*				55	100	130	275	
1972D	141,890,000	237	65.1	97	3	8	12	50	$57, MS-67, Oct-08
1972D, Missing Initials	*	1	58.0	0	50	75	150	250	
1973	64,964,000	107	64.7	96	3	10	50	90	$22, MS-65, Sep-08
1973D	83,171,400	228	65.3	99	3	10	15	120	$15, MS-66, Jun-08
1974	201,596,000	109	64.6	96	3	15	20	60	$37, MS-66, Mar-08
1974D	79,066,300	163	64.9	98	3	15	40	75	$13, MS-66, Dec-08
1974D, DblDie Obv (e)	*	257	63.8	94	60	110	225	450	$219, MS-65, Oct-09
1976	234,308,000	217	64.7	97	3	15	30	80	$14, MS-64, Aug-06
1976D	287,565,248	490	65.2	99	3	8	20	35	$16, MS-66, Aug-09
1976S, Silver Clad	11,000,000	508	65.9	100	6	10	15	30	$99, MS-68, Aug-09
1977	43,598,000	209	65.5	99	2	15	25	70	$11, MS-65, Oct-08
1977D	31,449,106	79	65.0	97	2	10	20	60	$21, MS-66, Aug-07
1978	14,350,000	147	65.2	99	2	12	18	75	$19, MS-66, Jul-08
1978D	13,765,799	112	65.2	100	2	8	15	200	$18, MS-66, Sep-08
1979	68,312,000	178	65.3	98	2	10	25	150	$11, MS-66, Oct-08
1979D	15,815,422	153	65.2	100	2	10	20	150	$11, MS-66, Sep-08
1980P	44,134,000	161	65.6	100	2	10	15	30	$15, MS-67, Oct-08
1980D	33,456,449	92	64.7	97	2	8	30	150	$138, MS-66, Sep-08
1981P	29,544,000	165	65.4	99	2	10	25	150	$11, MS-66, Oct-08
1981D	27,839,533	71	64.3	97	2	10	50	70	$403, MS-67, Oct-06
1982P	10,819,000	203	64.9	98	5	15	25	50	$10, MS-65, Oct-08
1982D	13,140,102	116	65.5	98	5	15	50	70	$21, MS-66, Sep-08
1983P	34,139,000	82	64.9	95	6	20	40	100	$35, MS-66, Oct-08
1983D	32,472,244	58	64.9	97	6	20	50	200	$13, MS-66, Oct-08
1984P	26,029,000	135	65.6	99	2	10	30	60	$98, MS-66, Sep-08
1984D	26,262,158	119	65.2	100	2	8	35	90	$11, MS-66, Sep-08
1985P	18,706,962	165	66.0	100	4	10	35	50	$150, MS-67, Oct-08
1985D	19,814,034	220	66.1	100	4	10	15	30	$25, MS-67, Oct-08
1986P	13,107,633	156	66.1	99	4	10	35	50	$11, MS-66, Oct-08
1986D	15,336,145	246	66.2	100	4	10	20	30	$20, MS-67, Apr-09
1987P (f)	2,890,758	160	65.7	100	4	10	35	50	$22, MS-65, Oct-09
1987D (f)	2,890,758	263	66.1	100	4	10	20	50	$21, MS-67, Oct-08
1988P	13,626,000	107	65.9	100	4	10	25	40	$35, MS-67, Oct-08
1988D	12,000,096	203	66.2	100	4	10	20	50	$11, MS-67, Sep-08
1989P	24,542,000	166	65.8	99	3	15	35	60	$99, MS-67, Aug-09
1989D	23,000,216	180	66.1	100	3	10	25	75	$53, MS-67, Aug-09
1990P	22,278,000	98	66.0	100	3	10	15	200	$11, MS-66, Sep-08
1990D	20,096,242	124	65.8	100	3	10	15	50	$31, MS-66, Oct-08
1991P	14,874,000	109	66.1	100	3	10	20	35	$229, MS-67, Oct-08
1991D	15,054,678	129	65.8	99	3	10	15	250	$920, MS-67, Sep-08

* Included in number above. **a.** There are several doubled-die obverses for the 1964 Kennedy half dollar. The one pictured and listed is FS-50-1964-102. **b.** Doubling on this variety is evident on the date, IN GOD WE TRUST, the designer's initials, and LI and TY of LIBERTY. "This is a very popular variety. It is extremely rare above MS-65" (*Cherrypickers' Guide to Rare Die Varieties,* fourth edition, volume II). There are other doubled-die obverses for 1964-D; the one pictured and listed is FS-50-1964D-101. **c.** There are several repunched mintmarks for 1964-D. The one listed is FS-50-1964D-502. **d.** Doubling is strongly evident on IN GOD WE TRUST and on the date. This variety is very rare above MS-65. **e.** Strong doubling is visible on IN GOD WE TRUST, the date, and LIBERTY. **f.** Not issued for circulation; included with Mint and Souvenir sets.

Chart continued on next page.

	Mintage	Cert	Avg	%MS	MS-63	MS-65	MS-66	MS-67	Recent Auction Record
1992P	17,628,000	125	66.0	100	$3	$10	$30	$60	$11, MS-67, Oct-08
1992D	17,000,106	84	66.0	100	3	10	15	45	$22, MS-67, Sep-08
1993P	15,510,000	241	66.5	99	3	10	25	50	$19, MS-67, Sep-08
1993D	15,000,006	509	66.1	100	3	10	15	60	$11, MS-66, Oct-08
1994P	23,718,000	293	65.8	100	3	10	25	50	$10, MS-66, Oct-08
1994D	23,828,110	109	65.8	100	3	10	25	50	$92, MS-67, Oct-08
1995P	26,496,000	154	66.1	99	2	10	15	50	$11, MS-67, Sep-08
1995D	26,288,000	230	66.2	100	2	10	20	60	$13, MS-67, Oct-08
1996P	24,442,000	183	66.1	99	2	10	15	35	$29, MS-67, Jun-08
1996D	24,744,000	202	66.2	100	2	10	15	35	$11, MS-67, Oct-08
1997P	20,882,000	92	66.2	100	2	10	20	40	$16, MS-67, Oct-08
1997D	19,876,000	207	65.9	100	2	10	15	30	$27, MS-67, Sep-08
1998P	15,646,000	106	66.3	99	2	10	20	50	$23, MS-67, Sep-08
1998D	15,064,000	118	65.7	99	2	10	35	45	$13, MS-67, Oct-08
1999P	8,900,000	156	66.4	100	2	8	30	40	$10, MS-66, Oct-08
1999D	10,682,000	155	66.3	100	2	8	15	40	$10, MS-66, Oct-08
2000P	22,600,000	87	66.2	100	2	8	15	50	$48, MS-67, Oct-08
2000D	19,466,000	193	66.1	100	2	8	20	40	$27, MS-67, Oct-08
2001P	21,200,000	206	65.9	100	2	8	20	60	$19, MS-67, Apr-09
2001D	19,504,000	232	65.9	100	2	8	20	100	$21, MS-67, Sep-09
2002P (g)	3,100,000	105	65.9	100	2	8	15	30	$42, MS-68, Sep-08
2002D (g)	2,500,000	139	66.1	100	2	8	20	50	$13, MS-67, Oct-08
2003P (g)	2,500,000	229	65.8	100	2	8	15	25	$37, MS-67, Oct-08
2003D (g)	2,500,000	203	65.7	100	2	8	15	25	$14, MS-67, Oct-08
2004P (g)	2,900,000	211	66.3	100	2	8	15	25	$11, MS-67, Sep-08
2004D (g)	2,900,000	271	66.4	100	2	8	15	25	$196, MS-68, Oct-08
2005P (g)	3,800,000	2,645	66.9	100	2	6	12	25	$23, MS-69 Satin, Mar-09
2005D (g)	3,500,000	2,381	66.6	100	2	6	12	25	$11, MS-66, Oct-08
2006P (g)	2,400,000	1,452	66.8	100	2	6	12	25	$42, MS-69 Satin, Jan-09
2006D (g)	2,000,000	1,447	66.8	100	2	6	12	25	$12, MS-67, Oct-08
2007P (g)	2,400,000	445	66.6	100	2	6	12	25	$21, MS-69 Satin, Jan-09
2007D (g)	2,400,000	405	66.6	100	2	6	12	25	$15, MS-69, Jan-09
2008P (g)	1,700,000	176	66.5	100	2	6	12	25	$45, MS-67, Oct-08
2008D (g)	1,700,000	93	66.1	100	2	6	12	25	
2009P (g)		214	66.8	100	2	6	12	25	
2009D (g)		208	66.8	100	2	6	12	25	
2010P (g)		100	66.9	100	2	6	12	25	
2010D (g)		75	66.3	100	2	6	12	25	

g. Not issued for circulation.

Proof Kennedy Half Dollars

PF-60 to 70 (Proof). Proofs of 1964 were struck at the Philadelphia Mint. Those from 1968 to date have been made in San Francisco. All are easily obtained; most are PF-63 or finer. Most from the 1970s to date have cameo contrast. Special Mint Set (SMS) coins were struck in lieu of Proofs from 1965 to 1967; in some instances, these closely resemble Proofs.

Silver Proofs have been struck in recent years for Silver Proof sets. In 1998, a special Matte Proof silver Kennedy half dollar was struck for inclusion in the Robert F. Kennedy commemorative coin set. *Obverse and Reverse:* Proofs that are extensively cleaned and have many hairlines, or that are dull and grainy, are lower level, such as PF-60 to 62. With medium hairlines and good reflectivity, assigned grades of PF-63 or 64 are appropriate. With relatively few hairlines a rating of PF-65 can be given. PF-66 should have hairlines so delicate that magnification is needed to see them. Above that, a Proof should be free of any hairlines or other problems.

Proof Kennedy Half Dollar

1964, Proof, Heavily Accented Hair
FS-50-1964-401.

1966, Special Mint Set, Doubled-Die Obverse
FS-50-1966-103.

1967, Special Mint Set, Quintupled-Die Obverse
FS-50-1967-101.

1979-S, Type 1 ("Filled" S)

1979-S, Type 2 ("Clear" S)

1981-S, Type 1 ("Filled" S)

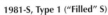

1981-S, Type 2 ("Clear" S)

1988-S, Doubled-Die Obverse
FS-50-1988S-101.

	Mintage	Cert	Avg	PF-65	PF-67Cam	PF-68DC	PF-69DC	Recent Auction Record
1964	3,950,762	9,664	67.5	$10	$70	$120	$150	$42, PF-67Cam, Feb-10
1964, Heavily Accented Hair (a)	*	4,352	66.7	30	150	4,000		$104, PF-67, Mar-10
1965, Special Mint Set	2,360,000	2,336	66.2	8	60	300		$99, PF-66Cam, Feb-10
1966, Special Mint Set	2,261,583	2,285	66.5	8	60	300		$24, PF-66, Oct-09
1966, SMS, DblDie Obv (b)	*	205	66.4	110	275			$56, SP-67, Mar-10
1967, Special Mint Set	1,863,344	2,794	66.4	9	60	300		$99, PF-65DCam, Feb-10
1967, SMS, QuintDie Obv (c)	*	4	66.3	135	500			$63, PF-66, Aug-07
1968S	3,041,506	1,683	67.6	6	15	60	175	$173, PF-69DCam, Feb-10
1969S	2,934,631	2,671	67.9	6	12	50	175	$128, PF-69DCam, Feb-10
1970S	2,632,810	2,298	67.9	20	30	80	300	$518, PF-69DCam, Feb-10
1971S	3,220,733	1,184	67.7	6	15	120	1,200	$1,840, PF-69UCam, May-09
1972S	3,260,996	808	67.9	6	16	30	60	$15, PF-68, Aug-09
1973S	2,760,339	535	68.2	6	16	25	30	$17, PF-68, Feb-10
1974S	2,612,568	604	68.1	5	8	20	25	$14, PF-68DCam, Feb-10
1976S	7,059,099	1,498	67.7	5	15	25	40	$17, PF-69DCam, May-09
1976S, Silver Clad (d)	4,000,000	2,561	68.2	6	15	25	45	$2,530, PF-70DCam, Dec-09
1977S	3,251,152	826	68.6	6	12	20	25	$431, PF-70DCam, Dec-09
1978S	3,127,781	1,043	68.7	5	12	20	25	$360, PF-70DCam, Dec-09
1979S, All kinds (e)	3,677,175							
1979S, Type 1 ("Filled" S)		1,390	68.8	5	15	25	35	$230, PF-70DCam, Jan-10
1979S, Type 2 ("Clear" S)		532	68.8	12	35	45	55	$25, PF-69, Jan-09

* Included in number above. **a.** This variety "is identifiable by the enhanced hairline in the central area of the hair, just below the part. However, the easiest way to identify the variety is the weak or broken lower left serif of the I (in LIBERTY)" (*Cherrypickers' Guide to Rare Die Varieties,* fourth edition, volume II). **b.** There are several doubled-die obverse varieties of the 1966 Special Mint Set half dollar. The one listed is FS-50-1966-103, with strong doubling evident on the profile, IN GOD WE TRUST, the eye, the hair, and the designer's initials. **c.** "A prominent quintupled (at least) spread is evident on RTY of LIBERTY, with strong multiple images on all obverse lettering and portions of the hair" (*Cherrypickers' Guide).* **d.** Mintage figures for 1976-S silver coins are approximate. Many were melted in 1982. **e.** The mintmark style of 1979-S Proof coins was changed during production, resulting in two distinct types. The scarcer, well-defined Clear S is easily distinguished from the more common blob-like Filled S.

Chart continued on next page.

	Mintage	Cert	Avg	PF-65	PF-67Cam	PF-68DC	PF-69DC	Recent Auction Record
1980S	3,554,806	1,465	68.7	$5	$12	$20	$25	$161, PF-70DCam, May-09
1981S, All kinds (f)	4,063,083							
1981S, Type 1 ("Filled" S)		1,638	68.7	18	35	45	55	$489, PF-70DCam, Dec-09
1981S, Type 2 ("Clear" S)		464	68.7	5	12	20	25	$37, PF-69DCam, Mar-09
1982S	3,857,479	817	68.9	7	12	20	25	$489, PF-70DCam, Jan-09
1983S	3,279,126	836	68.9	6	12	20	25	$253, PF-70DCam, Dec-09
1984S	3,065,110	648	68.9	7	12	20	25	$431, PF-70DCam, Jan-09
1985S	3,362,821	818	68.9	5	12	20	25	$345, PF-70DCam, Jan-10
1986S	3,010,497	598	69.0	8	12	20	25	$299, PF-70DCam, Dec-09
1987S	4,227,728	986	68.9	6	12	20	25	$173, PF-70DCam, Dec-09
1988S	3,262,948	682	69.0	6	12	20	25	$518, PF-70DCam, Feb-10
1988S, DblDie Obv (g)	*	7	68.9	110	160			
1989S	3,220,194	715	69.0	8	12	20	25	$150, PF-70DCam, Dec-09
1990S	3,299,559	850	69.0	7	12	20	25	$138, PF-70DCam, Dec-09
1991S	2,867,787	759	69.3	12	15	25	30	$104, PF-70DCam, Dec-09
1992S	2,858,981	565	69.2	8	15	20	25	$94, PF-70DCam, Dec-09
1992S, Silver	1,317,579	1,264	69.0	13	18	30	35	$84, PF-70DCam, Dec-09
1993S	2,633,439	571	69.3	12	20	30	40	$79, PF-70DCam, Mar-10
1993S, Silver	761,353	1,001	69.0	30	35	40	50	$109, PF-70UCam, Dec-09
1994S	2,484,594	455	69.3	10	20	25	35	$56, PF-70UCam, Mar-10
1994S, Silver	785,329	976	69.1	35	40	45	50	$138, PF-70DCam, Mar-10
1995S	2,117,496	404	69.3	25	30	35	50	$69, PF-70UCam, Jan-10
1995S, Silver	679,985	1,077	69.0	40	50	60	70	$184, PF-70DCam, Jan-10
1996S	1,750,244	431	69.2	12	18	25	30	$109, PF-70DCam, Dec-09
1996S, Silver	775,021	952	69.0	30	35	40	50	$207, PF-70DCam, Dec-09
1997S	2,055,000	408	69.3	20	30	40	50	$65, PF-70UCam, Dec-09
1997S, Silver	741,678	1,015	69.2	35	60	70	80	$259, PF-70DCam, Dec-09
1998S	2,086,507	428	69.3	12	20	30	35	$65, PF-70UCam, Dec-09
1998S, Silver	878,792	1,152	69.2	20	35	50	60	$138, PF-70DCam, Jan-10
1998S, Silver, Matte Finish (h)		1,219	69.2	300				$150, SP-69, Jan-10
1999S	2,543,401	2,216	69.1	15	20	25	30	$104, PF-70UCam, Feb-10
1999S, Silver	804,565	3,908	69.1	40	45	50	60	$575, PF-70DCam, Jan-10
2000S	3,082,483	1,587	69.2	6	12	16	20	$110, PF-70DCam, Mar-10
2000S, Silver	965,421	5,252	69.2	13	20	25	30	$95, PF-70UCam, Feb-10
2001S	2,294,909	982	69.1	9	13	16	25	$150, PF-70UCam, Dec-09
2001S, Silver	889,697	3,586	69.2	20	25	30	35	$144, PF-70DCam, Oct-09
2002S	2,319,766	1,587	69.2	7	13	16	25	$74, PF-70UCam, Dec-09
2002S, Silver	892,229	3,718	69.3	18	25	30	35	$150, PF-70DCam, Jun-09
2003S	2,172,684	3,286	69.1	7	12	18	20	$196, PF-70DCam, Dec-09
2003S, Silver	1,125,755	4,927	69.2	12	18	20	25	$104, PF-70DCam, Nov-09
2004S	1,789,488	1,425	69.1	15	18	25	30	$44, PF-70UCam, Jun-09
2004S, Silver	1,175,934	4,719	69.2	12	18	25	30	$44, PF-70UCam, Dec-09
2005S	2,275,000	6,579	69.1	7	12	18	20	$42, PF-70UCam, Mar-10
2005S, Silver	1,069,679	6,069	69.3	12	18	20	25	$115, PF-70DCam, Oct-09
2006S	2,000,428	2,423	69.3	7	12	18	20	$144, PF-70DCam, Oct-09
2006S, Silver	1,054,008	3,055	69.4	12	18	20	25	$104, PF-70UCam, Feb-10
2007S	1,384,797	2,699	69.3	7	12	18	20	$150, PF-70DCam, Mar-10
2007S, Silver	875,050	2,772	69.4	12	18	20	25	$84, PF-70UCam, Feb-10
2008S	1,377,424	1,470	69.3	7	12	18	20	$38, PF-70UCam, Sep-09
2008S, Silver	620,684	2,482	69.5	12	18	20	25	$40, PF-70UCam, Sep-09
2009S		3,189	69.3	7	12	18	20	$44, PF-70UCam, Mar-10
2009S, Silver		2,709	69.3	12	18	20	25	$62, PF-70DCam, Dec-09
2010S				7	12	18	20	
2010S, Silver				12	18	20	25	

* Included in number above. **f.** The mintmark style of 1981-S Proof coins was changed during production, creating two different types. The scarcer Clear S is not easily distinguished from the common Filled S. The Clear S is flat on the top curve of the S, compared to the Clear S, which has a more rounded top. The surface of the Clear S is frosted, and the openings in the loops are slightly larger. **g.** Clear doubling is visible on IN GOD WE TRUST, the date, and the mintmark. Some doubling is also evident on LIBERTY and the mintmark. **h.** Minted for inclusion in the Robert F. Kennedy commemorative set (along with an RFK commemorative dollar).

AN OVERVIEW OF SILVER AND RELATED DOLLARS

The silver dollar was authorized by Congress on April 2, 1792, and first coined in 1794. This denomination includes some of the most popular series in American numismatics. Starting in 1971, the U.S. Mint has released copper-nickel, clad, and other non-silver dollar coins, which are also included in this section.

The first silver dollar type, with Flowing Hair, is easy enough to obtain in grades from VF through low Mint State. Striking usually ranges from poor to barely acceptable, and adjustment marks (from an overweight planchet being filed down to correct weight) are often seen. Accordingly, careful examination is needed to find a good example.

The silver dollar with the Draped Bust obverse in combination with the Small Eagle reverse was made from 1795 through 1798, with most examples being dated 1796 or 1797. Today both the 1796 and 1797 exist in about the same numbers. Although mintage figures refer to the quantities produced in the given calendar year, these do not necessarily refer to the dates on the coins themselves. Silver dollars of this type are fairly scarce. Sharpness of strike presents a challenge to the collector, and usually there are weaknesses in details, particularly on the reverse eagle.

Next follows the 1798–1804 type with Draped Bust obverse and Heraldic Eagle reverse. Many such coins exist, again mostly in grades from VF through lower Mint State levels. Striking can be indifferent, but the population is such that collectors have more to choose from.

The Gobrecht silver dollars of 1836 (starless obverse, stars on reverse, plain edge) and 1839 (stars on obverse, starless reverse, reeded edge) present a special challenge in the formation of a type set. For quite a few years these were considered to be *patterns,* and thus anyone forming a type set of regular-issue U.S. coins did not have to notice them. However, in recent decades research by R.W. Julian (in particular), Walter Breen, and others, has revealed that the vast majority of 1836 and 1839 silver dollars originally produced went into circulation at face value. Accordingly, they were coins of the realm at the time, were freely spent, and are deserving of a place among regular coinage types.

The 1836 Gobrecht dollar is easy enough to find, although expensive. The original coinage amounted to 1,600, to which an unknown number of restrikes can be added. The main problem arises with the 1839, made only to the extent of 300 pieces. Those that exist nearly always have abundant signs of circulation. This is the rarest of all major United States design types, even outclassing the 1796–1797 half dollar and the 1808 quarter eagle.

In 1840 the regular Liberty Seated dollar made its appearance, with the reverse depicting a perched eagle holding an olive branch and arrows. This style was continued through 1865; however, in 1866 the motto IN GOD WE TRUST was added to the reverse. Generally, both of these types can be easily enough found in circulated grades from VF up, as well as low Mint State levels. MS-63 and higher pieces are in the minority, particularly of the 1840–1865 type.

Morgan silver dollars, made by the hundreds of millions from 1878 through 1921, are easily found, with the 1881-S being at once the most common of all varieties existing today in gem condition and also usually seen with sharp strike and nice appearance.

Peace silver dollars of 1921 through 1935 exist in large quantities. Some collectors select the first year of issue, 1921, as a separate type, as the design is in high relief. The 1921 is plentiful in Mint State, but rarely comes sharply struck at the obverse and reverse center. Later Peace dollars with shallow relief abound in MS-63 and finer grades, although strike quality can be a problem.

Among later silver dollars of the Eisenhower, Susan B. Anthony, Sacagawea, Native American, and Presidential types, large supplies are in the hands of dealers and collectors, and finding an excellent example is easy.

FOR THE COLLECTOR AND INVESTOR: SILVER AND RELATED DOLLARS AS A SPECIALTY

Generally, silver dollars of the 1794–1803 years are collected by dates and major types.

Although the 1794, of which an estimated 135 or so exist today, is famous and expensive, other varieties are eminently affordable in such decent grades as VF and EF. Beyond the listings herein, there is a rich panorama of die varieties, most extensively delineated in the 1993 two-volume study, *Silver Dollars and Trade Dollars of the United States: A Complete Encyclopedia.* This built upon earlier works, including J.W. Haseltine's *Type Table of United States Dollars, Half Dollars and Quarter Dollars,* and, especially, the long-term standard work by M.H. Bolender, *The United States Early Silver Dollars from 1794 to 1803.* In many instances among early dollars the number of aficionados desiring a particularly rare die combination may be even smaller than the population of specimens—with the result that not much premium has to be paid.

The 1804 silver dollar is a study in itself. These were first struck in 1834 from 1804-dated dies prepared at that time, as no originals were ever made. Later, probably circa 1859, a new reverse die was made up, and combined with the earlier 1804 obverse (made in 1834). Those made in 1834 and around that time are today known as Class I dollars, whereas those made with a different reverse, beginning in 1859 and continuing perhaps through the 1870s, are known as Class III. An intermediate variety, from the Class III die combination but with a plain instead of lettered edge, is in the Smithsonian Institution's National Numismatic Collection and is known as Class II. All varieties combined comprise 15 different specimens. This has been called the "King of American Coins" for well over a century and has achieved great fame. Interested numismatists are directed to *The Fantastic 1804 Dollar, Tribute Edition* (2009).

After 1803 it is a long jump to 1836, when silver dollars (of the Gobrecht design) were again struck for circulation. In 1839 more Gobrecht dollars were struck, with the design modified. In addition to the listings in this book are a number of other die combinations, edge and metal varieties, etc., including pieces of the year 1838, most of which are pattern restrikes (studied in *United States Pattern Coins*). These are avidly desired and collected.

Forming a specialized collection of Liberty Seated dollars from 1840 through 1873 has been a pursuit of many collectors over the years. Generally, the Philadelphia Mint dates are available without difficulty, although the 1851 and 1852 are typically acquired as Proof restrikes—originals of both years being prohibitively rare. Most difficult to find in higher grades are coins of the branch mints, including the famous 1870-S, of which only 10 are known to exist and for which no mintage quantity figure was ever listed in official reports. Branch-mint pieces, beginning with the 1846-O, were placed into circulation and used extensively. Beginning in 1870, dollars of this type were struck at Carson City; these also are seen with evidence of circulation. The only exceptions to this are certain dollars of 1859-O and 1860-O which turned up in very "baggy" preservation among Treasury hoards, to the extent of several thousand pieces of both dates combined.

Morgan silver dollars from 1878 through 1921 are one of the most active and popular areas in American numismatics. Approximately 100 different major varieties can be collected, although certain unusual varieties (not basic dates and mintmarks) can be dropped or added as desired. The vast majority of Morgan dollars can be found in Mint State. When these coins were first minted there was little need for them in circulation, and hundreds of millions of coins piled up in Treasury and other vaults. Although many were melted in 1918, enough remained that untold millions exist today in the hands of the public.

Although varieties such as the 1881-S are common and are normally seen in high grades with sharp strike, others with high mintages, the 1886-O and 1896-O being examples, are quite rare in MS-63 and finer, and when seen usually have rather poor eye appeal. Accordingly, quite a bit of discernment is recommended for the savvy collector.

Peace silver dollars, minted from 1921 to 1935, include the High Relief style of 1921, and the shallow-relief motif of 1922 to 1935. A basic set of 24 different dates and mintmarks is easily enough obtained, including in Mint State. The most elusive is the 1934-S.

Eisenhower dollars from 1971 through 1978 are easily obtained in choice and gem Mint State, although some of the circulation strikes, especially the early years, tend to be bagmarked. There are many different varieties made especially for collectors, including Proofs and some in silver clad metals.

In 1979 the Susan B. Anthony dollar was introduced; it had an unpopular reception by the American public. The series was thus short lived, beginning in 1979 and ending in 1981, and comprising strikings from the Philadelphia, Denver, and San Francisco mints. Then, in 1999, the Mint struck more than 40 million additional Anthony dollars, expanding the series to include 1999-P and 1999-D coins.

Like the Anthony dollar, more recent issues of Sacagawea dollars, the related Native American dollars, and the ongoing Presidential dollar series are all readily collectible in high-end Mint State and Proof.

RECOMMENDED READING

Bolender, M.H. *The United States Early Silver Dollars From 1794 to 1803* (5th ed.), Iola, WI, 1987.

Bowers, Q. David. *The Rare Silver Dollars Dated 1804,* Wolfeboro, NH, 1999.

Bowers, Q. David. *Silver Dollars and Trade Dollars of the United States: A Complete Encyclopedia,* Wolfeboro, NH, 1993.

Bowers, Q. David. *A Guide Book of Morgan Silver Dollars* (3rd ed.), Atlanta, GA, 2007.

Burdette, Roger W. *A Guide Book of Peace Dollars,* Atlanta, GA, 2008.

Fey, Michael S., and Oxman, Jeff. *The Top 100 Morgan Dollar Varieties,* Morris Planes, NJ, 1997.

Fivaz, Bill, and Stanton, J.T. *The Cherrypickers' Guide to Rare Die Varieties* (4th ed., vol. II), Atlanta, GA, 2006.

Haseltine, J.W. *Type Table of United States Dollars, Half Dollars and Quarter Dollars,* Philadelphia, 1881 (reprinted 1927, 1968).

Judd, J. Hewitt. *United States Pattern Coins* (10th ed., Q. David Bowers, editor), Atlanta, GA, 2009.

Logies, Martin A. *The Flowing Hair Silver Dollars of 1794,* 2004.

Newman, Eric P., and Bressett, Kenneth E. *The Fantastic 1804 Dollar, Tribute Edition,* Atlanta, GA, 2009.

Van Allen, Leroy C., and Mallis, A. George. *Comprehensive Catalogue and Encyclopedia of U.S. Morgan and Peace Silver Dollars,* New York, 1997.

FLOWING HAIR
(1794–1795)

Designer Robert Scot; weight 26.96 grams; composition .8924 silver, .1076 copper; approx. diameter 39–40 mm; edge: HUNDRED CENTS ONE DOLLAR OR UNIT with decorations between words.

Bowers-Borckardt-27, Bolender-5.

History. The first U.S. silver dollars were of the Flowing Hair design. In 1794 only 1,758 were released (slightly more were struck), and the next year nearly 100 times that amount. These coins were popular in their time and circulated for decades afterward. Many were used in international trade, particularly in the Caribbean.

Striking and Sharpness. On the obverse, check the hair details. It is essential to check the die variety, as certain varieties were struck with very little detail at the center. Accordingly, high-grade examples can appear to be well worn on the hair. Check the star centers, as well. On the reverse, check the breast and wings of the eagle. All 1794 dollars are lightly struck at the lower left of the obverse (often at portions of the date) and to a lesser extent the corresponding part of the reverse. Many coins of both dates have planchet adjustment marks, often heavy and sometimes even disfiguring; these are not noted by the certification services. Expect weakness in some areas on dollars of this type; a coin with Full Details on both sides is virtually unheard of. Sharp striking and excellent eye appeal add to the value dramatically. These coins are very difficult to find problem-free, even in MS.

Availability. The 1794 is rare in all grades, with an estimated 125 to 135 known, including a handful in MS. The 1795 is easily available, although some die varieties range from scarce to rare. Many if not most have been dipped at one time or another, and many have been retoned, often satisfactorily. The existence of *any* luster is an exception between EF-40 and AU-58. MS coins are quite scarce, especially at MS-63 or above.

Varieties listed are those most significant to collectors, but numerous minor variations may be found because each of the early dies was made individually. (Values of variations not listed in this guide depend on collector interest and demand.) Blanks were weighed before the dollars were struck and overweight pieces were filed to remove excess silver. Coins with old adjustment marks from this filing process may be worth less than values shown here. Some Flowing Hair dollars were weight-adjusted through insertion of a small (8 mm) silver plug in the center of the blank planchet before the coin was struck.

EF-40, 45 (Extremely Fine). *Obverse:* More wear than at AU is evident on the portrait, especially on the hair to the left of the face and neck (again, remember that some varieties were struck with flatness in this area), the cheek, and the tip of the neck truncation. Excellent detail remains in low-relief areas of the hair. The stars show wear, as do the date and letters. Luster, if present at all, is minimal and in protected areas. *Reverse:* The eagle (the focal point to check) shows more wear than at AU. Most or nearly all detail is well defined. These aspects should be reviewed in combination with knowledge of the die variety, to determine the sharpness of the coin when it was first struck. Most silver dollars of this type were flat at the highest area of the center at the time they were made, as this was opposite the highest point of the hair in the press when the coins were struck. Additional wear is on the wreath and letters, but many details are present. Some luster may be seen in protected areas, and if present is slightly more abundant than on the obverse.

AU-50, 53, 55, 58 (About Uncirculated). *Obverse:* Light wear is seen on the hair area immediately to the left of the face and neck (except that some varieties were flatly struck in this area to begin with), on the cheek, and on the top of the neck truncation, more so at AU-50 than at 53 or 55. An AU-58 coin has minimal traces of wear. An AU-50 coin has luster in protected areas among the stars and letters, with little luster in the open fields or on the portrait. Some certified coins have virtually no luster, but are considered to be of high quality in other aspects. At AU-58, most luster is partially present in the fields. On any high-grade dollar, luster is often a better key to grading than is the appearance of wear. *Reverse:* Light wear is seen on the eagle's body and the upper edges of the wings. At AU-50, detail is lost for some of the feathers in this area. However, striking can play a part, and some coins are weak to begin with. Light wear is seen on the wreath and lettering. Again, luster is the best key to actual wear. This ranges from perhaps 20% remaining in protected areas (at AU-50) to two-thirds or more (at

AU-58). As a general rule, the reverse will have more luster than the obverse.

MS-60 to 70 (Mint State). *Obverse:* At MS-60, some abrasion and contact marks are evident, most noticeably on the cheek and in the fields. Luster is present, but may be dull or lifeless, and interrupted in patches. At MS-63, contact marks are very few, and abrasion is light and not obvious. An MS-65 coin has little or no abrasion, and contact marks are minute. Luster should be full and rich. Coins graded above MS-65 are more theoretical than actual for this type—but they do exist, and are defined by having fewer marks as perfection is approached. *Reverse:* Comments apply as for the obverse, except that abrasion and contact marks are most noticeable on the eagle, at the center, although most dollars of this type are lightly struck in the higher points of that area. The field area is small and is protected by lettering and the wreath, and in any given grade shows fewer marks than the obverse.

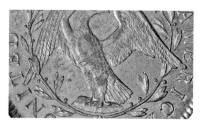

1795, Two Leaves Beneath
Each Wing

1795, Three Leaves Beneath
Each Wing

1795, Silver Plug
Bowers-Borckardt-15, Bolender-7.

	Mintage	Cert	Avg	%MS	AU-55	AU-58	MS-60	MS-62	MS-63	MS-64	MS-65	Recent Auction Record
1794 † (a)	1,758	32	34.2	16	$375,000	$475,000	$625,000	$800,000	$1,000,000	$1,250,000	$2,000,000	$97,750, F-15, Jun-10
1794, Silver Plug (b)	*	1	66.0	100								
1795, All kinds	160,295											
1795, Two Leaves		169	30.9	8	25,000	35,000	55,000	95,000	150,000	245,000	350,000	$172,500, MS-64, Jun-10
1795, Three Leaves		134	34.4	4	23,500	32,500	50,000	85,000	135,000	225,000	300,000	$9,200, EF-40, Jun-10
1795, Silver Plug					50,000	75,000	85,000	150,000				$54,625, AU-50, Apr-09

* Included in number above. † Ranked in the *100 Greatest U.S. Coins* (third edition). **a.** Value in EF-40 is $250,000; in AU-50, $325,000. **b.** This unique piece, graded SP-66, shows evidence of adjustment marks, as well as traces of a silver plug that was added to bring the coin's weight up to specification. It reportedly sold for $7.85 million in 2010.

DRAPED BUST, SMALL EAGLE REVERSE
(1795–1798)

Designer Robert Scot; weight 26.96 grams; composition .8924 silver, .1076 copper; approx. diameter 39–40 mm; edge: HUNDRED CENTS ONE DOLLAR OR UNIT with decorations between words.

Bowers-Borckardt-51, Bolender-14.

History. The Draped Bust silver dollar with the Small Eagle reverse, inaugurated in 1795, brought the first appearance of this popular obverse portrait—a depiction of Miss Liberty that later was used on other silver denominations as well as copper half cents and cents. The motif was continued into 1798.

Striking and Sharpness. On the obverse, check the highest areas of the hair, the bust line, and the centers of the stars. On the reverse, check the feathers on the eagle's breast and wings. Examine the dentils. Planchet adjustment marks are common and should be avoided. Studying die varieties can be helpful. For example, the Small Letters reverse, a long-lived die design used from 1795 to 1798, has shallow relief and is usually seen with a low rim, with the result that its grade is lower than that of the obverse. On some reverse dies the eagle has very little detail. Fairly sharp striking (not necessarily Full Details) and excellent eye appeal add to the value dramatically.

Availability. These silver dollars are readily available as a type, although certain varieties range from scarce to very rare. MS coins are elusive and when seen are usually of the 1795 date, sometimes with prooflike surfaces. Most coins have been dipped and/or retoned, some successfully. These coins acquired marks more readily than did lower denominations, and such are to be expected (but should be noted along with the grade, if distracting). Careful buying is needed to obtain coins with good eye appeal. Many AU examples are deeply toned and recolored.

The Smithsonian's National Numismatic Collection includes a unique Specimen 1794 dollar, plugged, and a unique Specimen 1797 10 Stars Left, 6 Stars Right dollar.

AU-50, 53, 55, 58 (About Uncirculated). *Obverse:* Light wear is seen on the hair area above the ear and extending to the left of the forehead, on the ribbon, and on the drapery at the shoulder, more so at AU-50 than at 53 or 55. An AU-58 coin has minimal traces of wear. Concerning luster: An AU-50 coin has luster in protected areas among the stars and letters, with little in the open fields or on the portrait. At AU-58, most luster is present in the fields, but is worn away on the highest parts of the motifs. *Reverse:* Light wear is seen on the eagle's body (note: this area might be lightly struck) and the edges of the wings. Light wear is seen on the wreath and lettering. Luster is the best key to actual wear; this ranges from perhaps 20% remaining in protected areas (at AU-50) to nearly full mint bloom (at AU-58).

MS-60 to 70 (Mint State). *Obverse:* At MS-60, some abrasion and contact marks are evident, most noticeably on the cheek, the drapery at the shoulder, and the right field. Luster is present, but may be dull or lifeless, and interrupted in patches. At MS-63, contact marks are few, and abrasion is harder to detect. Many coins listed as MS are deeply toned, making it impossible to evaluate abrasion and even light wear; these are best avoided completely. An MS-65 coin has no abrasion, and contact marks are so minute as to require magnification. Luster should be full and rich.

Coins grading above MS-65 are more theoretical than actual for this type—but they do exist, and are defined by having fewer marks as perfection is approached. *Reverse:* Comments apply as for the obverse, except that abrasion and contact marks are most noticeable on the eagle at the center, a situation complicated by the fact that this area was often flatly struck, not only on the famous Small Letters dies used from 1795 to 1798, but on some others as well. Grading is best done by the obverse, then verified by the reverse. In MS the amount of luster is usually a good key to grading. The field area is small and is protected by lettering and the wreath, and in any given grade shows fewer marks than on the obverse.

1795, Off-Center Bust

1795, Centered Bust

Small Date

Large Date

Small Letters

Large Letters

1797, 10 Stars Left,
6 Right

1797, 9 Stars Left,
7 Right

1798, 15 Stars
on Obverse

1798, 13 Stars
on Obverse

	Mintage	Cert	Avg	%MS	AU-50	AU-55	AU-58	MS-60	MS-62	MS-63	MS-64	Recent Auction Record
1795, All kinds	42,738											
1795, Off-Center Bust (a)		73	37.4	4	$17,500	$21,000	$32,500	$55,000	$85,000	$110,000	$160,000	$12,650, AU-50, Feb-10
1795, Centered Bust (b)		28	36.8	14	17,000	20,000	30,000	45,000	78,000	105,000	150,000	$109,250, MS-64, Jul-09
1796, All kinds	79,920											
1796, Small Date, Small Letters (3 varieties)		21	41.0	0	18,000	23,500	32,500	65,000	90,000	145,000		$21,850, AU-55, Jan-10
1796, Small Date, Large Letters		38	35.5	0	15,500	32,500	48,500	55,000	90,000	145,000		$13,340, AU-50, Mar-10
1796, Large Date, Small Letters		37	34.7	8	15,500	28,500	42,500	55,000	90,000	145,000		$23,000, AU-55, May-09
1797, All kinds	7,776											
1797, 10 Stars Left, 6 Right (c)		83	36.6	4	16,000	23,500	32,500	60,000	90,000	115,000	150,000	$13,800, AU-53, Jun-10
1797, 9 Stars Left, 7 Right, Large Letters		60	35.4	5	16,000	28,500	48,000	60,000	90,000	115,000	150,000	$13,808, AU-55, Jun-10
1797, 9 Stars Left, 7 Right, Small Letters		27	28.4	0	37,500	55,000	75,000	95,000				$48,875, AU-55, Jan-06
1798, All kinds (d)	327,536											
1798, 15 Stars on Obverse		26	36.5	8	25,000	35,000	50,000	90,000	115,000	140,000		$74,750, MS-60, Apr-08
1798, 13 Stars on Obverse		22	41.9	5	18,500	27,500	42,500	80,000	110,000			$23,000, AU-58, Apr-09

a. Value in MS-65 is $500,000. b. Value in MS-65 is $450,000. c. Value in MS-65 is $250,000. d. The Mint struck 327,536 silver dollars in 1798, but did not record how many of each type (Small Eagle reverse and Heraldic Eagle reverse).

DRAPED BUST, HERALDIC EAGLE REVERSE (1798–1804)

Designer Robert Scot; weight 26.96 grams; composition .8924 silver, .1076 copper; approx. diameter 39–40 mm; edge: HUNDRED CENTS ONE DOLLAR OR UNIT with decorations between words.

Bowers-Borckardt-241, Bolender-6.

History. The design of the silver dollar closely follows that of other silver coins of the era. The two earliest reverse dies of 1798 have five vertical lines in the stripes in the shield. All dollar dies thereafter have four vertical lines. Production of the Draped Bust dollar continued through early 1804, but the last were from earlier-dated dies. Later, in 1834, new dies were made with the 1804 date, and still later, in 1859, additional 1804-dated dollars were struck. As a class these can be called *novodels,* rather than *restrikes,* as no originals were ever made. The 1804 dollars were produced in Proof format.

Striking and Sharpness. Very few coins have Full Details. On the obverse, check the highest points of the hair, the details of the drapery, and the centers of the stars. On the reverse, check the shield, the eagle, the stars above the eagle, and the clouds. Examine the dentils on both sides. Planchet adjustment marks are often seen, but they usually are lighter than on the earlier types. The relief of the dies and the height of the rims can vary, affecting sharpness. Sharp striking and excellent eye appeal add to the value dramatically. Top-grade MS coins, when found, usually are dated 1800.

Availability. This is the most readily available type among the early silver dollars. Most often seen are the dates 1798 and 1799. Many varieties are available in any grade desired, although MS-63 and 65 coins are elusive. Other die varieties are rare at any level. As with other early dollars, connoisseurship is needed to acquire quality coins. These coins usually have problems. To evaluate them for the market it is necessary to grade them, determine the quality of striking, and examine the characteristics of the surface. Nearly all have been dipped or cleaned.

AU-50, 53, 55, 58 (About Uncirculated). *Obverse:* Light wear is seen on the hair area above the ear and extending to the left of the forehead, on the ribbon, and on the drapery and bosom, more so at AU-50 than at 53 or 55. An AU-58 coin has minimal traces of wear. Concerning luster: An AU-50 coin has luster in protected areas among the stars and letters, with little in the open fields or on the portrait. At AU-58, much luster is present in the fields, but is worn away on the highest parts of the motifs. *Reverse:* Comments apply as for the obverse, except that the eagle's neck, the tips and top of the wings, the clouds, and the tail show noticeable wear, as do other features. Luster ranges from perhaps 20% remaining in protected areas (at AU-50) to nearly full mint bloom (at AU-58). Sometimes the reverse of this type retains much more luster than the obverse, depending on the height of the rim and the depth of the strike (particularly at the center).

MS-60 to 70 (Mint State). *Obverse:* At MS-60, some abrasion and contact marks are evident, most noticeably on the cheek, the drapery, and the right field. Luster is present, but may be dull or lifeless, and interrupted in patches. At MS-63, contact marks are very few, and abrasion is hard to detect except under magnification. Knowledge of the die variety is desirable, but on balance the portraits on this type are usually quite well struck. An MS-65 coin has no abrasion, and contact marks are so minute as to require magnification. Luster should be full and rich. Coins grading above MS-65 are more theoretical than actual for this type—but they do exist and are defined by having fewer marks as perfection is approached. *Reverse:* Comments apply as for the obverse, except that abrasion and contact marks are most noticeable on the eagle's neck, the tips of the wing, and the tail. The field area is complex, without much open space, given the stars above the eagle, the arrows and olive branch, and other features. Accordingly, marks will not be as noticeable as on the obverse.

1798, Knob 9

1798, Pointed 9

Four Vertical Lines
in Shield's Stripes

Five Vertical Lines
in Shield's Stripes

1798, Pointed 9,
Close Date

1798, Pointed 9,
Wide Date

1798, Pointed 9,
10 Arrows

1798, Pointed 9,
4 Berries

1799, 99 Over 98,
15-Star Reverse

1799, 99 Over 98,
13-Star Reverse

1799, Irregular Date

1799, Normal Date

1799, Irregular Date,
15-Star Reverse

1799, Irregular Date,
13-Star Reverse

1799, 8 Stars Left,
5 Stars Right

1800, Very Wide Date,
Low 8

1800, "Dotted Date"

1800, Only 12 Arrows

1800, AMERICAI

1802, 2 Over 1, Narrow Date

1802, 2 Over 1, Wide Date

1802, Narrow Normal Date

1802, Wide Normal Date

1803, Small 3

1803, Large 3

	Mintage	Cert	Avg	%MS	AU-55	AU-58	MS-60	MS-62	MS-63	MS-64	MS-65	Recent Auction Record
1798, Knob 9, 5 Vertical Lines	*	43	36.5	2	$10,000	$15,000	$21,000	$36,000	$65,000	—	—	$86,250, MS-63, Apr-09
1798, Knob 9, 4 Vertical Lines	*	17	43.9	12	13,000	18,000	—					$3,738, EF-40, Jan-07
1798, Knob 9, 10 Arrows	*				13,000	18,000	—					$6,325, AU-55, Feb-10
1798, Pointed 9, Close Date	*	119	36.5	3	12,000	15,000	21,000	36,000	65,000	$100,000	$155,000	$8,625, AU-55, Jun-10
1798, Pointed 9, Wide Date	*	131	37.1	8	12,000	15,000	21,000	36,000	65,000	100,000	155,000	$6,325, AU-53, Jun-10
1798, Pointed 9, 5 Vertical Lines	*				18,000	22,000	25,000	—	—	—	—	$6,325, AU-50, Feb-10
1798, Pointed 9, 10 Arrows	*	34	35.3	6	12,000	15,000	21,000	36,000	75,000	—	—	$16,215, MS-61, Jan-10
1798, Pointed 9, 4 Berries	*	23	29.9	0	11,000	14,000	21,000	35,000	60,000	100,000	155,000	$6,325, AU-50, Feb-10

Note: The two earliest reverse dies of 1798 have five vertical lines in the stripes in the shield. All dollar dies thereafter have four vertical lines. * The Mint struck 327,536 silver dollars in 1798, but did not record how many of each type (Small Eagle reverse and Heraldic Eagle reverse).

	Mintage	Cert	Avg	%MS	AU-50	AU-58	MS-60	MS-62	MS-63	MS-64	MS-65	Recent Auction Record
1799, All kinds	423,515											
1799, 99 Over 98, 15-Star Reverse (a)		33	42.4	12	$9,000	$15,000	$23,500	$37,500	$57,500	$115,000	—	$9,775, AU-58, Jun-10
1799, 99 Over 98, 13-Star Reverse		23	39.7	9	9,000	14,500	24,000	36,000	57,500	110,000	—	$16,100, MS-61, Jan-10
1799, Irregular Date, 15-Star Reverse		9	31.8	0	9,500	16,500	24,000	—	—	—	—	$9,200, AU-53, Apr-08
1799, Irregular Date, 13-Star Reverse		18	39.1	11	9,000	15,000	24,000	36,000	57,500	105,000	$175,000	$48,875, MS-63, Jan-10
1799, Normal Date		308	35.5	5	9,000	15,000	24,000	36,000	57,500	105,000	175,000	$10,925, AU-55, Jun-10
1799, 8 Stars Left, 5 Right		27	35.9	4	11,500	18,500	30,000	55,000	90,000	155,000	—	$13,800, AU-55, Jun-10
1800, All kinds	220,920											
1800, Very Wide Date, Low 8		17	36.1	0	8,500	16,000	24,000	38,000	60,000	115,000	—	$6,210, AU-50, Mar-10
1800, "Dotted Date" (b)		29	38.3	10	8,500	15,000	24,000	38,000	60,000	115,000	175,000	$9,200, AU-55, Oct-09
1800, Only 12 Arrows		21	42.2	19	8,500	16,000	24,000	38,000	60,000	115,000	—	$7,188, AU-50, Jun-10
1800, Normal Dies		116	37.8	3	8,500	15,000	24,000	36,000	57,500	105,000	175,000	$6,325, AU-50, May-10
1800, AMERICAI (c)		31	38.3	10	8,500	16,500	26,500	47,500	—	—	—	$20,125, AU-58, Apr-09
1801	54,454	234	37.6	4	9,500	20,000	32,500	47,500	80,000	155,000	250,000	$6,900, AU-53, Jun-10
1802, All kinds	41,650											
1802, 2 Over 1, Narrow Date		14	40.9	14	9,500	18,000	30,000	45,000	67,500	115,000	—	$7,575, AU-50, Jan-10
1802, 2 Over 1, Wide Date		22	33.6	5	12,500	19,500	31,000	47,500	70,000	120,000	—	$8,050, AU-53, Feb-10
1802, Narrow Normal Date		46	41.3	17	8,750	13,500	22,500	40,000	67,500	105,000	240,000	$5,750, AU-50, Feb-10
1802, Wide Normal Date		6	42.2	0	11,500	18,500	37,500	48,500	75,000	125,000	300,000	$12,650, AU-55, Jan-09
1803, All kinds	85,634											
1803, Small 3		48	38.0	8	9,500	15,000	25,000	42,500	70,000	115,000	—	$46,000, MS-63, Jul-07
1803, Large 3		46	35.3	4	9,000	15,000	25,000	42,500	70,000	115,000	—	$6,038, EF-45, Jun-10

a. The engraver of the reverse die accidentally engraved 15 stars, instead of the 13 needed to represent the original Colonies. He attempted to cover the two extra stars under the leftmost and rightmost clouds, but their points stick out slightly. **b.** The "dotted" date is the result of die breaks. **c.** A reverse die flaw resulted in what appears to be a sans-serif letter I after AMERICA. "Perhaps from a punch or from a stray piece of metal during the die making process" (Bowers, *Silver Dollars & Trade Dollars of the United States*).

Proof Draped Bust Dollars

PF-60 to 70 (Proof). There were no Proofs coined in the era this type was issued. Years afterward, in 1834, the U.S. Mint fabricated new dies with the 1804 date and struck an unknown number of Proofs, perhaps a dozen or so, for inclusion in presentation Proof sets for foreign dignitaries. Today these are called Class I 1804 dollars. Eight examples are known, one of which shows circulation. Circa 1858 the Mint prepared a new reverse die dated 1804 and struck an unknown number of examples for private sale to collectors and dealers—the Class III dollars. No records were kept. These were artificially worn to give them the appearance of original dollars struck in 1804.

Sometime between circa 1858 and the 1870s, the Mint prepared new obverse dies dated 1801, 1802, and 1803, and struck Proof dollars for secret sale to the numismatic market. Many if not most were distributed through J.W. Haseltine, a Philadelphia dealer who had close connections with Mint officials. Today these are known as "Proof restrikes." All are rare, the 1801 being particularly so.

Class I 1804 dollars typically show hairlines and light abrasion. Grading is usually very liberal, in view of the fame of this rarity (not that this is logical). Circulated examples of Class I and Class III 1804 dollars have been graded using prefixes such as

EF and AU. Proof restrikes of 1801 to 1803 generally survive in much higher grades, PF-64 or finer.

Detailed historical and technical information may be found in *The Fantastic 1804 Dollar, Tribute Edition* (Newman/Bressett, 2009).

Obverse and Reverse: For lower Proof levels, extensive abrasion is seen in the fields, or even evidence of circulation. Numbers assigned by grading services have been erratic. No rules are standardized, and grading has not been consistent.

Proof Draped Bust Dollar (Restrike)
Bowers-Borckardt-302.

1804 Dollar

1804, First Reverse   **1804, Second Reverse**
Note the position of the words STATES OF in relation to the clouds.

	Est Mintage	Cert	Finest	PF-63	PF-64	PF-65	Recent Auction Record
1801, Restrike † (a)	2 known				$1,000,000	$1,350,000	
1802, Restrike † (a)	4 known	4	PF-65		800,000	1,000,000	$920,000, PF-65Cam, Apr-08
1803, Restrike † (a)	3 known	6	PF-66		800,000	1,000,000	$672,750, PF-66, Feb-07
1804, First Reverse, Original, Class I	8 known	6	PF-67				$4,140,000, PF-68, Aug-99
1804, Second Reverse, Restrike, Class III	6 known	4	PF-65				$2,300,000, PF-58, Apr-09
1804, Second Reverse, Restrike, Plain Edge, Class II (b)	1						
1804, Electrotype of Unique Plain-Edge Specimen (c)	4						

Note: The 1804 dollars as a group are ranked among the *100 Greatest U.S. Coins*. † Ranked in the *100 Greatest U.S. Coins* (third edition). **a.** "The Proof silver dollars of 1801, 1802, and 1803 are all extremely rare, valuable, and desirable, although none of them were made anywhere near the dates on the coins, nor do they share any die characteristics with any real silver dollars made from 1801 to 1803" (*100 Greatest U.S. Coins,* third edition). **b.** The plain-edge restrike is in the Smithsonian's National Numismatic Collection. **c.** These electrotypes were made by the U.S. Mint.

GOBRECHT
(1836–1839)

1836, No Stars on Obverse, Stars on Reverse: Designer Christian Gobrecht; weight 26.96 grams; composition .8924 silver, .1076 copper; diameter 39–40 mm; plain edge.

No Stars on Obverse, Stars on Reverse

1838–1839, Stars on Obverse, No Stars on Reverse: Designer Christian Gobrecht; weight 26.73 grams; composition .900 silver, .1000 copper; diameter 39–40 mm; reeded edge.

Stars on Obverse, No Stars on Reverse

History. Suspension of silver-dollar coinage was lifted in 1831, but it was not until 1835 that the Mint took steps to resume coinage. Late in that year Director R.M. Patterson ordered engraver Christian Gobrecht to prepare a pair of dies based on designs by Thomas Sully and Titian Peale. The first obverse die, dated 1836, bore the seated figure of Liberty on the obverse with the inscription C. GOBRECHT F. (the last letter for *Fecit,* Latin for "made it") in the field above the date. On the reverse was a large eagle flying left, surrounded by 26 stars and the legend UNITED STATES OF AMERICA • ONE DOLLAR •. It is unknown whether coins from these dies were struck at that time. A new obverse die was prepared with Gobrecht's name on the base of Miss Liberty, and in December 1836, 1,000 coins were struck for circulation. These coins weighed 416 grains, which was the standard enacted in 1792.

In January 1837 the standard weight of the dollar was lowered to 412-1/2 grains, and pieces were struck in March 1837 using the dies of 1836. The dies were oriented in medal fashion (top to top when the coin is rotated on its y axis) to distinguish them from those struck in December 1836. Dollars issued for circulation in 1836, 1837, and 1839 are found with different die alignments. The "original" issue of December 1836 has the normal coin orientation (reverse upright when coin is turned on the x axis), with the eagle flying upward.

From the late 1850s to the 1870s the Mint continued to strike Gobrecht dollars to satisfy collector demand. Mules, which had mismatched designs or edge devices, were made in that period and are very rare. Restrikes and mules are seldom seen in worn condition.

As a group, the Gobrecht dollars are ranked among the *100 Greatest U.S. Coins.*

Original 1836 die orientation using either "coin" or "medal" turn.

Die alignment of original issues dated 1838 and 1839.

Gobrecht dollars, both original issues and restrikes, were made in either coin-turn orientation ↑↓ (I and III), or medal-turn orientation ↑↑ (II and IV), and were struck in four basic die alignments.

- Die alignment I: ↑↓, head of Liberty opposite DO of DOLLAR, eagle flying upward.
- Die alignment II: ↑↑, head of Liberty opposite ES of STATES, eagle flying upward.

- Die alignment III: ↑↓, head of Liberty opposite N of ONE, eagle flying level.
- Die alignment IV: ↑↑, head of Liberty opposite F of OF, eagle flying level.

Rotated dies are common for original issue and restrike Gobrecht dollars. The 600 coins produced for circulation in March 1837 had dies that rotated from die alignment II to die alignment IV during the striking.

Striking and Sharpness. Striking is usually very good. Check the details on Miss Liberty's head and the higher parts of the eagle. Note that the word LIBERTY is raised.

Availability. 1836 Gobrecht dollars are available in grades from so-called Very Fine upward (the coins were struck as Proofs, and worn examples are properly designated as PF-30, PF-40, and so on; however, sometimes they are found graded as Fine, VF, and EF for levels below PF-50). Most in the marketplace range from PF-50 to 62. Most have contact marks. Truly pristine PF-65 and better examples are very elusive. The demand for these coins is intense. For the 1839, circulated grades typically are PF-50 or higher, often with damage. Pristine Proofs are available, but virtually all are restrikes.

Proof Gobrecht Dollars

PF-20, 25, 30, 35 (Impaired Proof, sometimes designated VF). *Obverse:* Many details of the gown are worn away, but the lower-relief areas above and to the right of the shield remain well defined. Hair detail is mostly or completely gone. LIBERTY is weak at the center. *Reverse:* Considerable wear is evident on the eagle, with only about 60% of the feathers visible.

PF-40 to 45 (Impaired Proof, sometimes designated EF). *Obverse:* Wear is seen on all areas, especially the thighs and knees, bosom, and head. The center of LIBERTY, which is in relief, is weak. *Reverse:* Wear

is evident on the eagle, including the back edge of the closest wing, the top of the farthest wing, and the tail.

PF-50, 53, 55, 58 (Impaired Proof, sometimes designated AU). *Obverse:* Light wear is seen on the thighs and knees, bosom, and head. At PF-50 and 53, most if not all mirror surface is gone and there are scattered marks. At PF-58, the Proof surface is extensive, but the open fields show abrasion. *Reverse:* Wear is most evident on the eagle's breast and the top of the wings. Mirror surface ranges from none (at PF-50) to perhaps 60% complete (at PF-58).

PF-60 to 70 (Proof). *Obverse and Reverse:* Many Proofs have been extensively cleaned and have many hairlines and dull fields. This is more applicable to 1836 than to 1839. Grades are PF-60 to 61 or 62. With medium hairlines and good reflectivity, an assigned grade of PF-64 is appropriate, and with relatively few hairlines, PF-65. In various grades hairlines are most easily seen in the obverse field. PF-66 should have hairlines so delicate that magnification is needed to see them. Above that, a Proof should be free of such lines.

	Cert	PF-40	PF-50	PF-60	PF-62	PF-63	PF-64	PF-65	Recent Auction Record
1836. C. GOBRECHT F. on base. Judd-60. Plain edge, no stars on obverse, stars in field on reverse. Die alignment I, ↑↓. Circulation issue. 1,000 struck **(a)**	111	$13,500 **(b)**	$18,500	$21,500	$25,000	$30,000	$42,500	$75,000	$18,400, AU-55, May-10
1836. As above. Plain edge. Judd-60. Die alignment II and die alignment IV, ↑↑. Circulation issue struck in 1837. 600 struck **(a)**	*	13,500 **(c)**	18,500	21,500	25,000	30,000	42,500	75,000	$10,350, PF-40, Jan-10

* Included in number above. **a.** Originals. Although these are listed in Judd as patterns, they are considered circulation strikes. **b.** Value in PF-20 is $11,000. **c.** Value in PF-20 is $11,000.

	Cert	PF-40	PF-50	PF-60	PF-62	PF-63	PF-64	PF-65	Recent Auction Record
1838. Obverse stars added around border, reeded edge. Judd-84. Designer's name removed. Reverse eagle flying in plain field. Die alignment IV, ↑↑. (a)	17	$22,500	$25,000	$30,000	$40,000	$55,000	$75,000	$100,000	$83,375, PF-64, Jul-08
1839. As above. Reeded edge. Judd-104. Die alignment IV, ↑↑. Circulation issue. 300 struck (a)	41	20,000 (b)	25,000	30,000	35,000	40,000	50,000	80,000	$25,300, PF-58, Apr-09

a. Originals. Although these are listed in Judd as patterns, they are considered circulation strikes. b. Value in PF-20 is $15,000.

Restrike Gobrecht Dollar

	Cert	PF-40	PF-50	PF-60	PF-62	PF-63	PF-64	PF-65	Recent Auction Record
1836. Name below base; eagle in starry field; plain edge. Judd-58. Die alignment III, ↑↓, and die alignment IV, ↑↑. (a)	10 (b)	$17,500	$20,000	$35,000	$45,000	$55,000	$65,000	$85,000	$63,250, PF-64, May-10
1836. Name on base; plain edge. Judd 60. Die alignment III, ↑↓. (30–40 known) (a)	**	15,000 (c)	20,000	22,500	25,000	35,000	45,000	75,000	$21,850, PF-62, Sep-07
1836. C. GOBRECHT F. on base. Judd-61. Reeded edge. No stars on obverse, stars in field on reverse. Die alignment IV, ↑↑. (a)					*(extremely rare)*				$195,000, PF-63, May-03
1838. Designer's name removed; reeded edge. Judd-84. Die alignment III, ↑↓, and die alignment IV, ↑↑. (a)	17	25,000	30,000	35,000	45,000	60,000	80,000	125,000	$37,375, PF-64, Apr-09
1839. Designer's name removed; eagle in plain field; reeded edge. Judd-104. Die alignment III, ↑↓, and die alignment IV, ↑↑. (a)	41	20,000 (d)	25,000	27,500	32,500	37,500	45,000	65,000	$37,375, PF-64, Jan-10

Note: Restrikes were produced from the late 1850s to the 1870s, and are not official Mint issues. They were all oriented in either die alignment III (coin turn) or die alignment IV (medal turn), with the eagle flying level. Almost all were struck from a cracked reverse die. For detailed analysis of these pieces, consult *United States Pattern Coins,* 10th edition. a. Restrikes. Listed in Judd as patterns. b. Many originals were certified as restrikes in years past. This figure includes some of these originals. c. Value in PF-20 is $12,500. d. Value in PF-20 is $17,500.

LIBERTY SEATED
(1840–1873)

No Motto (1840–1865): Designer Christian Gobrecht; weight 26.73 grams; composition .900 silver, .100 copper (net weight .77344 oz. pure silver); diameter 38.1 mm; reeded edge; mints: Philadelphia, New Orleans.

No Motto
(1840–1865)

With Motto IN GOD WE TRUST (1866–1873): Designer Christian Gobrecht; weight 26.73 grams; composition .900 silver, .100 copper (net weight .77344 oz. pure silver); diameter 38.1 mm; reeded edge; mints: Philadelphia, New Orleans, Carson City, San Francisco.

With Motto IN GOD WE TRUST
(1866–1873)

History. The Liberty Seated dollar was minted every year from 1840 to 1873, with an obverse design modified from that of the 1839 Gobrecht dollar. The flying eagle of the Gobrecht dollar was replaced with a perched eagle similar to that of contemporary quarter and half dollars. The dollars, minted in modest numbers, circulated in the United States through 1850. In that year the rising value of silver on the international markets brought the cost of minting each coin to more than $1. Production continued for the international, rather than domestic, market, through 1873, when the trade dollar took the Liberty Seated dollar's place.

Striking and Sharpness. On the obverse, check the head of Miss Liberty and the centers of the stars. On the reverse, check the feathers of the eagle. The dentils usually are sharp. Dollars of 1857 usually are weakly struck, but have semi-prooflike surfaces. The word LIBERTY is in a high-relief area on the coin, with the result that it wore away quickly. Therefore this feature cannot be used as the only guide to grading an obverse. From EF downward, strike sharpness in the stars and the head does not matter to connoisseurs.

Availability. All issues from 1840 to 1850 are available in proportion to their mintages. Those of 1851 to the late 1860s are either scarce or rare in circulated grades, and in MS they range from rare to extremely rare, despite generous mintages in some instances. The later-date coins were shipped to China and later melted. Coins of the 1870s are more readily available, although some are scarce to rare.

AU-50, 53, 55, 58 (About Uncirculated). *Obverse:* Light wear is seen on the thighs and knees, bosom, and head. There is some luster at AU-50 and 53. At AU-58, the luster is extensive but incomplete, especially in the right field. *Reverse:* Wear is visible on the eagle's neck, the claws, and the top of the wings. At AU-50 and 53, there are traces of luster. An AU-58 coin has nearly full luster.

MS-60 to 70 (Mint State). *Obverse:* At MS-60, some abrasion and contact marks are evident, most noticeably on the bosom and thighs and knees. Luster is present, but may be dull or lifeless. At MS-63, contact marks are very few, and abrasion is minimal. An MS-65 coin has no abrasion in the fields (but may have a hint on the knees), and contact marks are trivial. Check the knees of Liberty and the right field. Luster should be full and rich on later issues, not necessarily so for dates in the 1840s. Most MS coins of 1861 to 1865, Philadelphia issues, have extensive die striae (from the die being incompletely finished). *Reverse:* Comments apply as for the obverse, except that in lower MS grades, abrasion and marks are most noticeable on the eagle's head, the neck, the claws, and the top of the wings (harder to see there, however). At MS-65 or higher, there are no marks visible to the unaided eye. The field is mainly protected by design elements and does not show abrasion as much as does the obverse on a given coin.

1851, Original, High Date   1852, Original

1869, Repunched Date
FS-S1-1869-302. Other varieties exist.

	Mintage	Cert	Avg	%MS	AU-50	AU-55	MS-60	MS-62	MS-63	MS-64	MS-65	Recent Auction Record
1840	61,005	188	51.6	24	$1,250	$1,750	$3,750	$12,000	$22,500	$40,000	$110,000	$2,703, AU-58, Nov-09
1841	173,000	175	52.6	26	1,250	1,500	3,000	5,000	7,500	16,000	90,000	$3,881, MS-62, Dec-09
1842	184,618	394	50.9	19	1,250	1,500	2,500	4,000	6,000	17,500	90,000	$1,035, AU-55, Dec-09
1843	165,100	314	49.8	16	1,250	1,500	3,000	5,500	12,000	20,000	100,000	$1,093, AU-58, Oct-09
1844	20,000	121	53.3	16	1,600	2,500	6,500	9,500	16,000	25,000	100,000	$7,188, MS-62, Jun-10
1845	24,500	129	50.5	14	1,600	3,250	9,500	15,000	24,500	28,500	100,000	$1,791, AU-58, Mar-10
1846	110,600	355	52.2	20	1,000	1,500	2,500	4,500	6,500	14,000	90,000	$863, AU-55, Dec-09
1846O	59,000	137	49.0	15	1,600	3,500	7,500	13,500	18,000	30,000	100,000	$6,613, MS-61, Jun-10
1847	140,750	330	52.5	20	1,000	1,600	2,750	5,000	7,500	15,000	90,000	$1,380, AU-58 CAC, Mar-10
1848	15,000	78	49.5	13	1,600	2,750	4,750	9,000	14,000	50,000	115,000	$11,500, MS-63, Nov-09
1849	62,600	220	55.2	30	1,000	1,500	2,800	4,500	7,500	14,000	90,000	$4,888, MS-63, Oct-09
1850	7,500	96	54.6	29	2,750	4,250	7,500	10,000	16,000	25,000	90,000	$2,990, AU-58, Oct-09
1850O	40,000	110	45.7	13	3,750	8,500	13,500	18,000	25,000	35,000	120,000	$2,070, AU-50, Mar-10
1851, Original, High Date † (a,b)	1,300	21	61.8	76	27,500	32,000	45,000	57,500	65,000	80,000	140,000	$54,625, MS-63, Sep-09
1852, Original † (a)	1,100	16	60.3	75	27,500	30,000	40,000	50,000	60,000	75,000	140,000	$34,730, MS-62, Sep-09
1853	46,110	131	58.8	60	1,400	2,750	4,000	6,000	8,000	15,000	85,000	$5,006, MS-63, Nov-09
1854	33,140	39	57.8	51	5,500	7,000	8,500	11,000	13,000	20,000	95,000	$4,428, AU-50, Nov-09
1855	26,000	51	55.5	39	5,000	6,750	8,000	13,500	18,000	25,000	90,000	$4,485, AU-55, Mar-09
1856	63,500	46	51.9	30	2,500	3,000	6,000	10,000	12,500	20,000	85,000	$3,450, AU-60, Oct-09
1857	94,000	76	58.4	71	2,000	2,500	3,500	7,000	10,000	20,000	85,000	$8,625, MS-64, Dec-09
1859	255,700	72	57.3	49	1,250	1,800	3,000	4,500	7,500	15,000	85,000	$1,381, AU-55, Aug-09
1859O	360,000	437	55.8	57	800	1,300	2,250	3,500	6,000	12,000	65,000	$6,325, MS-64, Nov-09
1859S	20,000	116	47.6	17	3,500	5,500	16,500	22,000	35,000	50,000	130,000	$9,488, MS-61, Sep-09
1860	217,600	102	57.5	55	950	1,300	2,500	3,500	6,000	12,000	65,000	$1,411, MS-61, Mar-10
1860O	515,000	635	56.8	62	800	1,200	2,000	3,000	5,000	10,000	52,500	$1,266, MS-61, Mar-10
1861	77,500	70	58.2	67	2,500	3,500	4,500	5,500	6,500	15,000	65,000	$3,105, AU-53, Nov-09
1862	11,540	74	58.1	73	2,000	3,000	3,750	5,000	7,000	15,000	65,000	$6,900, MS-64, Jun-10
1863	27,200	70	55.7	64	1,500	2,500	3,750	5,500	7,500	17,500	65,000	$4,888, MS-63, May-10
1864	30,700	65	51.5	32	2,000	3,000	3,750	5,500	8,000	20,000	57,500	$18,400, MS-65, May-09
1865 (c)	46,500	62	52.5	40	1,500	2,400	3,000	6,000	8,000	20,000	80,000	$3,105, AU-55, Mar-09
1866	48,900	77	53.9	43	1,500	1,850	2,250	4,500	8,000	20,000	65,000	$2,645, AU-58, Nov-09
1867	46,900	57	54.2	47	1,500	1,850	2,250	4,200	6,500	15,000	70,000	$1,955, MS-61, Mar-10
1868	162,100	75	52.1	23	1,500	1,850	2,500	5,000	8,000	20,000	65,000	$4,025, MS-62, Aug-09

* Included in number above. ** The Mint shows no record of 1870-S dollars being struck, but about a dozen are known to exist. † Ranked in the *100 Greatest U.S. Coins* (third edition). **a.** Silver dollars of 1851 and 1852 are found in three formats: originals struck for circulation, original Proofs, and Proof restrikes made years later. See the next section for a discussion of the Proofs. **b.** See the Proof chart for a discussion of the 1851 Philadelphia dollar struck over a New Orleans dollar. **c.** There is a common doubled-die reverse variety for 1865, which does not command a premium in today's market. "Doubling is evident only on the U of UNITED. . . . This is probably the most common variety for this date" (*Cherrypickers' Guide to Rare Die Varieties*, fourth edition, volume II).

	Mintage	Cert	Avg	%MS	AU-50	AU-55	MS-60	MS-62	MS-63	MS-64	MS-65	Recent Auction Record
1869	423,700	86	52.6	40	$1,000	$1,600	$2,250	$4,500	$6,000	$14,000	$65,000	$978, AU-50, Mar-09
1869, RPD (d)	*				1,100	1,750	2,500	4,800	6,500			$920, MS-60, Jul-04
1870	415,000	148	53.0	37	1,000	1,350	2,500	3,500	5,000	10,000	55,000	$1,093, AU-53, Nov-09
1870CC	11,758	163	41.5	11	9,500	15,000	27,500	35,000	50,000	100,000	—	$8,338, AU-55, Nov-09
1870S † (e)	**	4	47.0	0	1,250,000	1,500,000	2,200,000	2,500,000	—	—	—	$503,125, EF-40, Apr-09
1871	1,073,800	457	50.1	31	950	1,300	1,850	4,000	5,500	8,000	50,000	$2,530, MS-62, Mar-10
1871CC	1,376	42	41.0	10	25,000	50,000	75,000	150,000	200,000	300,000	—	$20,700, AU-50, Sep-09
1872	1,105,500	311	49.3	27	950	1,300	1,850	3,500	5,000	8,000	50,000	$840, AU-53, Nov-09
1872CC	3,150	68	44.5	22	12,500	17,500	28,000	50,000	75,000	160,000	250,000	$12,075, AU-55, Apr-09
1872S	9,000	89	45.3	12	3,750	7,500	12,000	20,000	35,000	100,000		$9,775, AU-58, Oct-09
1873	293,000	133	55.3	50	950	1,500	2,200	4,000	5,500	10,000	60,000	$4,025, MS-64, Mar-10
1873CC	2,300	26	41.9	15	38,500	60,000	100,000	160,000	200,000	300,000	500,000	$37,375, AU-58, Apr-09
1873S (f)	700											

* Included in number above. ** The Mint shows no record of 1870-S dollars being struck, but about a dozen are known to exist. † Ranked in the *100 Greatest U.S. Coins* (third edition). **d.** There are several repunched dates known for 1869. The one listed is FS-S1-1869-302. The top flag of a secondary 1 is evident midway between the primary 1 and the 8. **e.** The 1870-S silver dollars may have been struck as mementos of the laying of the cornerstone of the San Francisco Mint (May 25, 1870). **f.** The 1873-S is unknown in any collection, public or private, despite Mint records indicating that 700 were struck. None has ever been seen.

Proof Liberty Seated Dollars

PF-60 to 70 (Proof). Proof Liberty Seated dollars were made for all dates. All of 1851 and 1853 are restrikes, as are most of 1852. In 1858 only Proofs were struck, to the extent of an estimated 210 pieces, with no related circulation strikes. Most early dates were restruck at the Mint, augmenting the supply of originals. Today, Proofs from 1858 to 1873 are readily available, but high-quality examples with superb eye appeal are in the minority. Most Proofs prior to 1860 survive only in grades below PF-65 if strict grading is applied. Nearly all Proofs are very well struck. *Obverse and Reverse:* Proofs that are extensively cleaned and have many hairlines, or that are dull and grainy, are lower level, such as PF-60 to 62. These are not widely desired, except for use as fillers for the dates (most circulation-strike dollars are rare after 1849 and before 1870). The rarities of 1851, 1852, and 1858 are in demand no matter what the grade. With medium hairlines and good reflectivity, an assigned grade of PF-64 is appropriate, and with relatively few hairlines, PF-65. In various grades hairlines are most easily seen in the obverse field. PF-66 should have hairlines so delicate that magnification is needed to see them. Above that, a Proof should be free of such lines.

1866, Proof, No Motto
Judd-540.

1851, Restrike
Date is centered.

1852, Restrike

Proof Liberty Seated Dollar

	Est Mintage	Cert	Finest	PF-60	PF-63	PF-64	PF-65	Recent Auction Record
1840	40–60	25	PF-65	$17,500	$27,500	$40,000	$75,000	$20,700, PF-63, Jan-10
1841	10–15	4	PF-63		85,000	175,000	250,000	$74,750, PF-63, Apr-08
1842	10–15	8	PF-65	17,500	35,000	50,000	100,000	$20,700, PF-62, Jul-09
1843	10–15	7	PF-64	17,500	35,000	50,000	100,000	$37,375, PF-64, Dec-09
1844	10–15	8	PF-66	17,500	35,000	50,000	100,000	$37,375, PF-64, Jan-10
1845	10–15	11	PF-67	16,000	25,000	35,000	65,000	$46,000, PF-65, Apr-09
1846	10–15	13	PF-66	16,000	25,000	35,000	65,000	$25,300, PF-64, Jul-09
1847	10–15	16	PF-65	16,000	25,000	35,000	65,000	$17,825, PF-63, Apr-09
1848	10–15	10	PF-67	16,000	25,000	35,000	65,000	$29,900, PF-64, Feb-10
1849	10–15	9	PF-67	20,000	45,000	60,000	85,000	$37,375, PF-65 Star, Sep-09
1850	20–30	19	PF-66	16,000	25,000	35,000	65,000	$25,300, PF-64, Dec-09
1851, Restrike (a)	35–50	18	PF-66	25,000	35,000	40,000	70,000	$29,900, PF-63, Apr-09
1852, Original (a)	20–30	3	PF-65	30,000	40,000	50,000	75,000	$57,500, PF-65Cam, Jan-09
1852, Restrike (a)	20–30	12	PF-65	16,000	25,000	35,000	75,000	$31,050, PF-63, Sep-09
1853	15–20	6	PF-66	17,500	30,000	50,000	85,000	$24,150, PF-61, Jan-09
1854	40–60	17	PF-66	10,000	15,000	25,000	35,000	$20,700, PF-64, May-09
1855	40–60	15	PF-66	12,500	16,500	27,500	40,000	$12,650, PF-63, Apr-09
1856	40–60	36	PF-66	8,500	12,500	17,500	30,000	$14,950, PF-64, Feb-10
1857	50–70	29	PF-66	8,500	12,500	17,500	30,000	$13,225, PF-64, Apr-09

a. Silver dollars of 1851 and 1852 are found in three formats: originals struck for circulation, original Proofs, and Proof restrikes made years later. "As part of [Mint Director] James Ross Snowden's restriking activities in 1859, Proof examples of certain rare silver dollars of earlier dates were made, including the 1851 and 1852. For the 1851 dollar, the original die (with four-date digit logotype slanting slightly upward and the date close to the base of Liberty) probably could not be located in 1859. In any event, a different die, not originally used in 1851, with the date horizontal and centered, was employed. Whether this die was created new in 1859 and given an 1851 date, or whether it was made in 1851 and not used at that time, is not known" (*United States Pattern Coins*, 10th edition).

	Mintage	Cert	Finest	PF-60	PF-63	PF-64	PF-65	Recent Auction Record
1858 (a)	300	68	PF-66	$12,500	$15,000	$25,000	$40,000	$8,913, PF-62, Jun-10
1859	800	137	PF-67	2,500	5,000	7,500	15,000	$3,220, PF-63, Feb-10
1860	1,330	143	PF-67	2,500	5,000	7,500	15,000	$4,888, PF-64, Mar-10
1861	1,000	90	PF-67	2,500	5,000	7,500	15,000	$26,450, PF-66, Jun-10
1862	550	155	PF-67	2,500	5,000	7,500	15,000	$4,313, PF-63, Dec-09
1863	460	137	PF-69	2,500	5,000	7,500	15,000	$4,600, PF-63, Jan-10
1864	470	135	PF-68	2,500	5,000	7,500	15,000	$6,613, PF-64 CAC, Mar-10
1865	500	170	PF-68	2,500	5,000	7,500	15,000	$3,091, PF-61 CAC, Nov-09
1866, No Motto † (b)	2 known	1	PF-65					
1866, With Motto	725	214	PF-69	2,500	5,000	7,500	15,000	$69,000, PF-67Cam Star CAC, Jun-10
1867	625	201	PF-68	2,500	5,000	7,500	15,000	$10,925, PF-65Cam, Feb-10
1868	600	189	PF-68	2,500	5,000	7,500	15,000	$2,703, PF-62, Mar-10
1869	600	202	PF-67	2,500	5,000	7,500	15,000	$2,300, PF-61, Feb-10
1870	1,000	195	PF-66	2,500	5,000	7,500	15,000	$3,220, PF-63, Mar-10
1871	960	178	PF-67	2,500	5,000	7,500	15,000	$3,105, PF-63, Mar-10
1872	950	162	PF-67	2,500	5,000	7,500	15,000	$8,338, PF-64DCam, Feb-10
1873	600	174	PF-68	2,500	5,000	7,500	15,000	$9,775, PF-65Cam, Mar-10

† Ranked in the *100 Greatest U.S. Coins* (third edition). **a.** In 1858 only Proofs, not circulation strikes, were made. **b.** The 1866, No Motto, dollar is classified as Judd-540 (*United States Pattern Coins*). Two examples of this fantasy piece are known; at least one was deliberately struck for pharmacist and coin collector Robert Coulton Davis, likely around 1869 or in the early 1870s, along with the No Motto Proof quarter and half dollar of the same date. The three-coin set is on display at the American Numismatic Association's Edward C. Rochette Money Museum in Colorado Springs. "A second 1866 'No Motto' silver dollar resurfaced in the 1970s before entering a private Midwestern collection in the early 1980s. After not meeting its auction reserve price in September 2003, the coin was sold privately for nearly a million dollars some time later" (*100 Greatest U.S. Coins*, third edition).

TRADE DOLLARS (1873–1885)

The trade dollar was authorized and minted under the Coinage Act of 1873. It was intended not as a regular-circulation coin for domestic business, but as an international trade unit for commerce with Asia. Trade dollars are presented separately from other dollar coins, starting on page 258.

MORGAN
(1878–1921)

Designer George T. Morgan; weight 26.73 grams; composition .900 silver, .100 copper (net weight .77344 oz. pure silver); diameter 38.1 mm; reeded edge; mints: Philadelphia, New Orleans, Carson City, Denver, San Francisco.

History. The Morgan dollar, named for designer George T. Morgan, was struck every year from 1878 to 1904, and again in 1921. The coin's production benefited Western silver interests by creating an artificial federal demand for the metal, whose market value had dropped sharply by 1878. Hundreds of millions of the coins, stored in cloth bags of 1,000 each, piled up in government vaults. In the 1900s some were melted, but immense quantities were bought by collectors and investors; today they are the most widely collected of all coins of their era.

Striking and Sharpness. On coins of 1878 to 1900, check the hair above Miss Liberty's ear and, on the reverse, the breast feathers of the eagle. These are weak on many issues, particularly those of the New Orleans Mint. From 1900 to 1904 a new reverse hub was used, and breast feathers, while discernible, are not as sharp. In 1921 new dies were made in lower relief, with certain areas indistinct. Many Morgan dollars have partially or fully prooflike surfaces. These are designated as Prooflike (PL), Deep Prooflike

(DPL), or Deep Mirror Prooflike (DMPL). Certification practices can be erratic, and some DMPL coins are not fully mirrored. All prooflike coins tend to emphasize contact marks, with the result that lower MS levels can be unattractive. *A Guide Book of Morgan Silver Dollars* (Bowers) and other references furnish information as to which dates and mintmarks are easily found with Full Details and which usually are weak, as well as the availability of the various levels of prooflike surface.

Availability. All dates and mints of Morgan dollars are available in grades from well worn to MS. Some issues such as certain Carson City coins are rare if worn and common in MS. Other issues such as the 1901 Philadelphia coins are common if worn and are rarities at MS-65. The 1889-CC and 1893-S, and the Proof 1895, are considered to be the key issues. Varieties listed herein are those most significant to collectors. Numerous other variations exist. Values are shown for the most common pieces. Values of varieties not listed in this guide depend on collector interest and demand.

MS-60 to 70 (Mint State). *Obverse:* At MS-60, some abrasion and contact marks are evident, most noticeably on the cheek and on the hair above the ear. The left field also shows such marks. Luster is present, but may be dull or lifeless. At MS-63, contact marks are extensive but not distracting. Abrasion still is evident, but less than at lower levels (the cheek of Miss Liberty showcases abrasion). An MS-65 coin may have minor abrasion, but contact marks are so minute as to require magnification. Luster should be full and rich. Coins with prooflike surfaces such as PL, DPL, and DMPL display abrasion and contact marks much more noticeably than coins with frosty surfaces; in grades below MS-64 many are unattractive. *Reverse:* Comments apply as for the obverse, except that in lower MS grades abrasion and contact marks are most noticeable on the eagle's breast. At MS-65 or higher there are no marks visible to the unaided eye. The field is mainly protected by design elements, so the reverse often appears to grade a point or two higher than the obverse.

First Reverse
Eight tail feathers.

Second Reverse
Parallel top arrow feather, concave breast.

Third Reverse
Slanted top arrow feather, convex breast.

1878, Doubled Tail Feathers
FS-S1-1878-032.

1878, 8 Feathers, Obverse Die Gouge
The "Wild Eye" variety. VAM 14-11. FS-S1-1878-014.

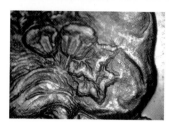

1878, 7 Over 8 Tail Feathers, Tripled Leaves
VAM 44. FS-S1-1878-044.

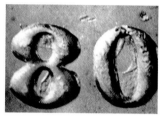

1880, 80 Over 79
VAM 6. FS-S1-1880-006.

1880-CC, 80 Over 79
VAM 4. FS-S1-1880CC-004.

1880-CC, 8 Over High 7
VAM 5. FS-S1-1880CC-005.

1880-CC, 8 Over Low 7
VAM 6. FS-S1-1880CC-006.

1880-O, 80 Over 79
VAM 4. FS-S1-1880o-004.

1880-O, Die Gouge
The "Hangnail" variety. VAM 49. FS-S1-1880o-048.

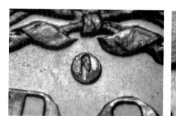

1881-O, Repunched Mintmark
VAM 5. FS-S1-1881o-005.

1882-O, O Over S
VAM 4. FS-S1-1882o-004.

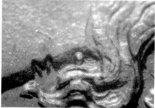
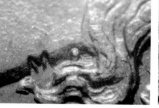

1884, Large Dot
VAM 3. FS-S1-1884-003.

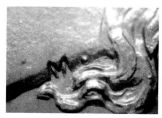

1884, Small Dot
VAM 4. FS-S1-1884-004.

1885, Die Chip
VAM 8. FS-S1-1885-008.

1886, Repunched Date
VAM 20. FS-S1-1886-020.

1887, 7 Over 6
VAM 2. FS-S1-1887-002.

1887-O, 7 Over 6
VAM 3. FS-S1-1887o-003.

1888-O, Obverse Die Break
The "Scarface" variety.
VAM 1b. FS-S1-1888o-001b.

1888-O, Doubled-Die Obverse
The "Hot Lips" variety.
VAM 4. FS-S1-1888o-002.

1889, Die Break
The "Bar Wing" variety.
VAM 22. FS-S1-1889-022.

1889-O, Clashed Die
VAM 1A. FS-S1-1889o-001a.

1890-CC, Die Gouge
The "Tailbar" variety.
VAM 4. FS-S1-1890CC-004.

1890-O, Die Gouges
The "Comet" variety.
VAM 10. FS-S1-1890o-010.

1891-O, Clashed Die
VAM 1A. FS-S1-1891o-001a.

1891-O, Pitted Reverse Die
VAM 1B. FS-S1-1891o-001b.

1899-O, Micro O
VAM 4, 6, 31, and 32. FS-S1-1899o-501.

1900-O, Obverse Die Crack
VAM 29A. FS-S1-1900o-029a.

1900-O, O Over CC
Various VAMs. FS-S1-1900o-501.

1901, Doubled-Die Reverse
The "Shifted Eagle" variety.
VAM 3. FS-S1-1901-003.

1903-S, Small S Mintmark
VAM 3. FS-S1-1903S-002.

	Mintage	Cert	Avg	%MS	MS-63	MS-64	MS-65	MS-66	MS-63 DMPL	MS-64 DMPL	MS-65 DMPL	Recent Auction Record
1878, 8 Feathers	749,500	8,565	62.4	96	$200	$450	$1,475	$10,000	$850	$5,000	$22,000	$10,063, MS-64PL, Jun-10
1878, 8 Feathers, Obverse Die Gouge (a) *		5	63.0	80	10,000							$368, MS-64, Mar-10
1878, 7 Feathers	9,759,300											$2,013, MS-64DM, Feb-10
1878, 7 Over 8, Clear Doubled Feathers *		4,917	62.5	96	400	550	2,750	15,000	1,250	5,500	16,000	$2,300, MS-65, Feb-10
1878, 7 Over 8, Tripled Leaves (b) *					22,000							$17,250, MS-62, Jan-09
1878, 7 Feathers, 2nd Reverse *		11,013	62.4	95	150	330	1,350	6,000	400	2,250	10,000	$1,840, MS-64DPL, Mar-10
1878, 7 Feathers, 3rd Reverse *		3,942	62.0	93	185	550	2,750	14,000	1,000	5,500	23,000	$437, MS-64 CAC, Mar-10
1878CC	2,212,000	16,301	62.3	95	400	650	1,500	6,000	1,700	2,800	10,000	$5,290, MS-66, Mar-10
1878S	9,774,000	30,194	63.4	99	75	115	300	1,000	150	2,200	10,000	$1,150, MS-64DPL, Mar-10
1879	14,806,000	8,150	63.1	96	65	150	1,050	3,500	350	2,100	15,000	$576, MS-65, Mar-10
1879CC, CC Over CC	756,000	1,273	54.0	65	7,250	11,000	40,000	60,000	14,000	25,000	40,000	$63,250, MS-64DM, Jul-08
1879CC, Clear CC *		2,342	54.3	72	7,500	10,000	32,500	50,000	13,000	42,000	60,000	$8,625, MS-64, Jun-10
1879O	2,887,000	5,791	61.9	87	200	500	3,500	20,000	2,000	4,000	22,000	$6,325, MS-65 CAC, Jun-10
1879S, 2nd Reverse	9,110,000	1,497	61.0	88	400	1,375	8,000	45,000	3,000	8,000	21,000	$1,150, MS-64, Jan-10
1879S, 3rd Reverse *		76,376	64.3	100	65	75	175	325	125	450	1,400	$196, MS-65, Mar-10
1880	12,600,000	9,964	63.0	97	65	165	825	4,000	250	1,000	6,500	$8,050, MS-65DMPL, Jun-10
1880, 80 Over 79 (c) *		33	50.5	12	350	650	3,000					$12,650, MS-64, Apr-08
1880CC, All kinds	591,000											
1880CC, 80 Over 79, 2nd Rev (d)		491	63.0	99	650	1,700	3,300	6,000	2,500	5,000	20,000	$1,754, MS-65, Mar-10
1880CC, 8 Over 7, 2nd Rev					600	1,100	2,900	6,000	2,500	5,000	20,000	$1,671, MS-65, Mar-10
1880CC, 8 Over High 7, 3rd Rev (e)		336	63.5	100	550	825	1,800	3,000	1,500	3,250	6,500	$1,495, MS-65PL, Feb-10
1880CC, 8 Over Low 7, 3rd Rev (f)		252	63.4	100	690	825	2,000	5,000	2,000	3,500	7,000	$1,208, MS-65, Mar-10
1880CC, 3rd Reverse					550	825	1,750	3,000	1,500	3,250	6,500	$1,898, MS-66, Mar-10
1880O, All kinds	5,305,000											
1880O, 80 Over 79 (g)		189	59.5	67	500	2,500	*	*	3,000	8,000	*	$2,990, MS-63DM, Feb-10
1880O		6,401	61.3	83	400	1,650	25,000	60,000	1,400	7,500	75,000	$1,380, MS-64, May-10
1880O, Die Gouge (h)		142	55.3	33	—							$489, MS-63, Dec-08
1880S, All kinds	8,900,000											
1880S, 80 Over 79		481	64.1	99	70	120	350	750	140	400	1,500	$863, MS-67, Jun-09
1880S, 0 Over 9		442	64.2	99	70	120	350	750	140	400	1,500	$2,070, MS-67, Feb-10
1880S		112,609	64.4	100	55	70	175	325	120	320	725	$805, MS-67, Mar-10
1881	9,163,000	7,333	63.3	98	70	175	850	3,500	500	1,400	20,000	$589, MS-65, Mar-10
1881CC	296,000	14,136	63.7	99	700	775	1,150	1,750	850	1,250	3,000	$5,060, MS-67, Mar-10
1881O	5,708,000	11,954	62.9	96	55	200	1,800	15,000	200	2,000	35,000	$18,400, MS-65DMPL, Jun-10
1881O, RPM (i)	*				300	—						$460, MS-64, Mar-10
1881O, DblDie Obv (j)	*	13	57.4	31	300	—						$253, MS-64, Nov-04
1881S	12,760,000	182,522	64.2	100	50	65	175	325	120	320	725	$5,175, MS-68 CAC, Jun-10
1882	11,100,000	12,088	63.4	99	55	80	550	2,500	240	1,050	6,500	$1,209, MS-66, Mar-10
1882CC	1,133,000	23,697	63.5	100	275	350	550	1,500	450	600	2,000	$1,208, MS-65DMPL, Mar-10
1882O	6,090,000	12,500	63.1	97	55	150	1,150	12,000	140	1,250	6,200	$12,265, MS-65PL, Mar-10
1882O, O Over S (k)	*	2,562	57.4	48	1,300	3,850	33,000	70,000	3,100	8,000	62,500	$1,840, MS-64, May-10
1882S	9,250,000	60,345	64.4	100	50	60	175	325	140	850	3,750	$10,925, MS-68 CAC, Jun-10
1883	12,290,000	16,685	63.9	99	55	80	200	600	120	500	1,600	$1,093, MS-65DPL, Mar-10
1883CC	1,204,000	32,390	63.8	100	265	300	500	900	400	550	1,550	$1,035, MS-65DMPL, Mar-10
1883O	8,725,000	86,361	63.6	100	50	60	175	325	120	400	1,350	$284, MS-65, Mar-10
1883S	6,250,000	3,770	56.6	41	2,750	5,500	30,000	90,000	13,000	55,000	90,000	$1,955, MS-63, Mar-10
1884, All kinds	14,070,000				50	60	225	1,000	180	800	4,500	$1,495, MS-66PL, Feb-10
1884, Large Dot (l)		56	54.3	39	150	—						$47, AU-50, Aug-09
1884, Small Dot (l)		197	61.9	91	175	—						$55, MS-61, May-09
1884CC	1,136,000	36,841	63.7	100	275	300	500	1,000	450	550	1,400	$863, MS-66, Mar-10

* Included in number above. † Ranked among the *100 Greatest U.S. Coins* (third edition). **a.** Two spikes protrude from the front of Liberty's eye. "Fewer than a dozen specimens are known of this Top 100 variety and any sale is a landmark event" (*Cherrypickers' Guide to Rare Die Varieties*, fourth edition, volume II). **b.** Called the "King of VAMs" (Van Allen / Mallis varieties), this variety shows three to five weak tail feathers under the seven primary feathers. On the obverse, tripling is evident on the cotton bolls and the leaves, and doubling on LIBERTY. Values are fluid for this popular variety. **c.** Several die varieties exist; values shown are for the most common. **d.** The top crossbar and diagonal stem of an underlying 79 are clearly seen within the 8. Extensive polishing marks are visible within the 0. **e.** An almost complete 7 is visible inside the last 8 of the date. The top edge of the 7 touches the top inside of the 8. **f.** A complete 7 is visible inside the last 8 of the date. The crossbar of the underlying 7 can be seen in the top loop and the diagonal of the 7 is visible in the lower loop. **g.** The crossbar of the underlying 7 is visible within the upper loop of the second 8. The 1 and the first 8 are slightly doubled to the right. **h.** On the reverse of the "Hangnail" variety, a die gouge runs from the bottom of the arrow feather, across the feathers, and out the eagle's rightmost tail feather. On the obverse, the top-left part of the second 8 has a spike. Value in MS-60 is $500. **i.** A diagonal image, the remains of one or two additional O mintmark punches, is visible within the primary O. **j.** Clear doubling is evident on the back outside of Liberty's ear. **k.** Several varieties exist. **l.** A raised dot, either Large or Small, is visible after the designer's initial and on the reverse ribbon. "These dots varieties are thought to have been used as some sort of identifier" (*Cherrypickers' Guide to Rare Die Varieties*, fourth edition, volume II).

	Mintage	Cert	Avg	%MS	MS-63	MS-64	MS-65	MS-66	MS-63 DMPL	MS-64 DMPL	MS-65 DMPL	Recent Auction Record
18840	9,730,000	139,923	63.7	100	$50	$60	$175	$325	$120	$325	$1,350	$1,495, MS-67, Mar-10
1884S	3,200,000	5,301	53.0	7	30,000	100,000	250,000	350,000	60,000	135,000	275,000	$80,500, MS-64, Jun-10
1885	17,787,000	55,534	63.8	100	50	60	175	325	120	325	800	$1,553, MS-67PL, Mar-10
1885, Die Chip (m)	*				165	—						$9,488, MS-66DMPL, Jun-10
1885CC	228,000	13,909	63.7	100	700	800	1,750	2,400	1,100	1,400	2,300	$1,150, MS-67, Feb-10
18850	9,185,000	145,344	63.8	100	50	60	175	325	120	325	900	$1,323, MS-65, Mar-10
1885S	1,497,000	4,705	61.8	89	350	650	1,750	7,000	2,000	5,250	45,000	$1,380, MS-67, Mar-10
1886	19,963,000	94,449	64.0	100	50	60	175	325	120	400	1,200	$1,093, MS-67, Apr-07
1886, RPD (n)	*	1	61.0	100	725	—						$42,550, MS-64DPL, Jun-10
18860	10,710,000	3,734	57.1	36	3,500	10,000	165,000	500,000	20,000	70,000	250,000	$1,495, MS-62, Jan-06
18860, Clashed Die (o)	*	154	48.0	8	5,000	—						$805, MS-64, Mar-10
1886S	750,000	3,120	61.7	86	475	750	3,000	10,000	2,400	8,250	27,000	$2,070, MS-65 CAC, May-10
1887, 7 Over 6	**	924	62.6	95	800	1,350	5,250	15,000	2,400	5,000	30,000	$863, MS-67, Dec-09
1887	20,290,000	139,148	63.8	100	50	60	175	325	120	325	1,050	$5,463, MS-64, Feb-10
18870, 7 Over 6	*	453	60.9	85	3,000	12,000	32,500	50,000				$27,600, MS-65DMPL, Jun-10
18870	11,550,000	7,612	62.5	96	125	400	2,500	50,000	360	1,800	12,000	$690, MS-64 CAC, Mar-10
1887S	1,771,000	4,666	61.9	87	325	700	3,250	10,000	3,100	7,000	27,500	$2,185, MS-65DM, Feb-10
1888	19,183,000	34,541	63.8	100	50	60	200	2,500	180	450	2,650	$1,840, MS-66, Mar-10
18880	12,150,000	17,046	63.4	99	55	75	450	15,000	125	500	2,650	$8,050, MS-62, Jan-09
18880, Obv Die Break (p)	*	31	61.6	100	12,000							$5,750, AU-58, Aug-09
18880, DblDie Obv (q)	*	395	31.4	1	30,000	—						$7,763, MS-66, Jun-10
1888S	657,000	3,304	61.7	87	500	900	3,250	13,000	1,100	3,200	15,500	$103, MS-66, Mar-10
1889	21,726,000	26,639	63.3	98	55	70	185	1,600	160	600	3,700	$92, MS-63, Nov-04
1889, Die Break (r)	*	140	59.1	63	700		2,500					$25,300, MS-62, Jun-10
1889CC	350,000	2,875	37.5	16	40,000	60,000	350,000	500,000	45,000	65,000	350,000	$48,875, MS-65DMPL, Jun-10
18890	11,875,000	3,415	61.3	89	450	900	7,000	20,000	1,000	6,250	14,000	$374, EF-45, Feb-09
18890, Clashed Die (s)	*	22	40.0	5	—	—						$1,124, MS-65, Mar-10
1889S	700,000	4,493	62.1	87	450	650	2,200	5,500	1,800	5,500	37,500	$2,300, MS-65PL, Jan-10
1890	16,802,000	10,732	63.0	97	65	165	2,000	14,000	260	2,500	19,000	$1,162, MS-64, Mar-10
1890CC	2,309,041	5,342	59.7	87	1,100	2,500	6,500	25,000	1,500	3,200	13,750	$6,325, MS-64DMPL, Jul-09
1890CC, Die Gouge (t)	*	261	52.4	59	3,100	—						$1,438, MS-65, Mar-10
18900	10,701,000	7,091	62.8	98	140	350	1,750	10,000	180	1,350	10,000	$1,639, MS-65, Oct-09
18900, Die Gouges (u)	*	41	61.4	88	220	—						$3,450, MS-66, Jan-10
1890S	8,230,373	6,957	62.6	94	125	275	1,000	4,500	650	3,750	9,500	$7,188, MS-65 CAC, Jun-10
1891	8,693,556	4,851	62.0	93	200	600	6,500	16,000	2,100	7,000	23,000	$4,313, MS-65, Mar-10
1891CC	1,618,000	7,462	61.4	91	800	1,450	5,000	15,000	2,500	5,250	33,000	$57,500, MS-65DMPL, Jun-10
18910	7,954,529	3,578	62.1	94	350	900	8,100	20,000	2,900	7,500	34,000	$322, AU-55, Jun-08
18910, Clashed Die (v)	*	94	35.9	1	1,750	—						
18910, Pitted Rev Die (w)	*	4	54.0	0	—	—						$5,750, MS-66PL, Jun-10
1891S	5,296,000	4,531	62.7	94	160	300	1,500	5,000	380	3,500	19,500	$1,553, MS-64PL, Feb-10
1892	1,036,000	3,186	61.1	82	450	1,000	4,200	45,000	1,000	3,250	19,500	$6,613, MS-65, Jun-10
1892CC	1,352,000	4,187	59.7	86	2,350	3,500	9,000	30,000	5,000	9,750	36,500	$57,500, MS-65DMPL, Jun-10
18920	2,744,000	3,863	61.6	88	325	800	5,500	50,000	7,500	20,000	47,500	$115,000, MS-65, Jan-10
1892S	1,200,000	2,376	43.2	2	55,000	100,000	150,000	250,000	75,000	130,000	225,000	$26,450, MS-66, Jun-10
1893	378,000	3,006	56.9	63	1,500	2,850	8,250	55,000	15,000	30,000	60,000	$10,350, MS-64, Jun-10
1893CC	677,000	2,650	47.3	58	6,500	15,950	62,700	90,000	24,000	46,000	85,000	$5,290, MS-63, Jun-10
18930	300,000	1,904	49.2	31	8,000	17,500	220,000	400,000	25,000	80,000	250,000	$17,250, AU-50, Jun-10
1893S † (x)	100,000	1,996	21.9	1	150,000	300,000	600,000	900,000	200,000	400,000	700,000	$43,125, MS-65 CAC, Jun-10
1894	110,000	2,345	49.8	34	5,750	10,000	45,000	65,000	32,000	52,500	80,000	$9,660, MS-64, Mar-10
18940	1,723,000	3,093	53.1	28	4,100	10,000	60,000	90,000	8,500	23,500	62,500	

* Included in number above. **Included in number below. † Ranked among the *100 Greatest U.S. Coins* (third edition). **m.** A large, raised die chip is evident below the second 8. **n.** Repunching is especially evident in the base of the 1, and the lower loop of the 6. **o.** Clashing of the E of LIBERTY is evident between the eagle's tail feathers and the bow on the wreath. **p.** A major die break runs from the rim between E and P, through the field, and all the way across Liberty's face and neck. This variety is nicknamed "Scarface." **q.** Doubling is visible on the lips (especially), nose, eye, chin, entire profile, and part of the hair. This variety is nicknamed "Hot Lips." Value in MS-60 is $25,000. **r.** A die break is visible on the top of the eagle's right wing. This variety is nicknamed the "Bar Wing." Different obverse die pairings exist. **s.** The E of LIBERTY is visible in the field below the eagle's tail feathers and slightly left of the bow. This variety is extremely rare in Mint State, and unknown above MS-61. Value in MS-60 is $2,250. **t.** A heavy die gouge extends from between the eagle's first tail feather and the lowest arrow feather to the leaves in the wreath below. "This is an extremely popular and highly marketable variety, especially in Mint State" (*Cherrypickers' Guide to Rare Die Varieties*). This variety is nicknamed the "Comet." **u.** Die gouges are evident to the right of the date. This variety is nicknamed the "Comet." **v.** The evidence of a clashed die is visible below the eagle's tail feathers and slightly left of the bow, where the E in LIBERTY has been transferred from the obverse die. **w.** Pitting on the reverse is visible around the ONE and on the bottom of the wreath above and between ONE and DOLLAR. This variety is rare in circulated grades, and unknown in Mint State. **x.** "All 1893-S Morgan dollars were struck from a single die pairing. Genuine 1893-S silver dollars display a diagonal die scratch in the top of the T in LIBERTY. This diagnostic can be seen even on very low-grade examples" (*100 Greatest U.S. Coins,* third edition). Beware of altered or otherwise fraudulent mintmarks.

Chart continued on next page.

	Mintage	Cert	Avg	%MS	MS-63	MS-64	MS-65	MS-66	MS-63 DMPL	MS-64 DMPL	MS-65 DMPL	Recent Auction Record
1894S	1,260,000	2,257	59.5	77	$1,200	$2,100	$6,000	$17,000	$6,000	$21,000	$30,000	$1,524, MS-64, Feb-10
1895O	450,000	3,327	44.7	4	50,000	85,000	165,000	350,000	60,000	150,000	250,000	$18,400, MS-62, Jun-10
1895S	400,000	1,576	47.1	44	6,000	8,500	30,000	100,000	12,500	20,000	37,500	$5,060, MS-63, Feb-10
1896	9,976,000	28,078	63.6	99	50	60	175	400	120	360	1,500	$937, MS-65DMPL, Mar-10
1896O	4,900,000	4,225	55.6	26	8,000	47,500	150,000	400,000	20,000	60,000	200,000	$6,038, MS-63, Jun-10
1896S	5,000,000	1,120	52.8	56	4,000	5,000	19,000	85,000	21,000	50,000	100,000	$3,220, MS-63, Feb-10
1897	2,822,000	11,239	63.6	98	50	60	250	1,200	120	380	4,000	$949, MS-66, Mar-10
1897O	4,004,000	4,346	56.2	29	5,000	17,000	50,000	125,000	16,500	35,000	70,000	$2,300, MS-62, Feb-10
1897S	5,825,000	6,119	63.2	96	120	185	650	1,500	240	1,100	3,100	$1,121, MS-66, Mar-10
1898	5,884,000	14,222	63.7	99	50	65	275	750	160	360	1,300	$6,325, MS-66DMPL, Jun-10
1898O	4,440,000	51,463	64.0	100	50	60	175	325	120	340	1,000	$139, MS-65, Mar-10
1898S	4,102,000	2,198	60.9	78	550	950	2,000	5,500	1,000	3,800	16,500	$3,450, MS-64DM, Feb-10
1899	330,000	6,999	62.8	95	350	500	950	2,000	600	1,100	2,650	$628, MS-65, Mar-10
1899O	12,290,000	38,383	63.8	100	50	60	175	325	120	450	1,650	$1,610, MS-67, Feb-10
1899O, Micro O (y)	*	265	36.9	5	800	—						$1,380, MS-61, Sep-08
1899S	2,562,000	2,168	61.8	85	450	750	1,750	3,000	1,100	5,750	25,000	$5,175, MS-66, Feb-10
1900	8,830,000	22,426	63.8	99	50	60	175	600	2,800	9,000	42,500	$432, MS-66, Mar-10
1900O	12,590,000	30,298	63.9	100	50	60	185	550	420	900	6,000	$219, MS-65, Mar-10
1900O, Obv Die Crack (z)	*	29	28.6	10	—	—						$75, VF-35, Feb-09
1900O, O Over CC (aa)	*	2,333	60.8	88	1,000	1,750	3,500	6,250	6,000	8,500	19,000	$1,553, MS-65, Mar-10
1900S	3,540,000	2,773	61.9	85	400	550	1,500	3,500	7,000	20,000	36,000	$979, MS-65, Mar-10
1901 (bb)	6,962,000	3,350	54.8	18	17,500	50,000	250,000	450,000	30,000	70,000		$40,250, MS-64, Jan-10
1901, DblDie Rev (cc)	*	71	44.7	4								$9,200, MS-61, Dec-09
1901O	13,320,000	26,418	63.8	100	50	60	175	750	360	1,250	10,000	$460, MS-66, Mar-10
1901S	2,284,000	1,836	60.9	81	750	900	3,000	12,500	11,000	21,000	30,000	$5,750, MS-65PL, Jun-10
1902	7,994,000	4,358	63.6	97	125	200	500	1,100	7,500	13,000	20,000	$313, MS-65, Mar-10
1902O	8,636,000	44,082	63.7	100	50	60	175	550	300	3,000	15,500	$2,760, MS-64DM, Jan-10
1902S	1,530,000	2,308	61.5	85	700	1,000	2,750	9,000	3,600	8,500	15,000	$6,325, MS-66, Jun-10
1903	4,652,000	8,994	63.8	98	110	150	300	550	2,400	7,500	35,000	$4,025, MS-67, Jun-10
1903O	4,450,000	5,816	63.6	99	550	600	820	1,200	450	1,550	6,500	$634, MS-66, Mar-10
1903S	1,241,000	1,213	41.8	22	6,500	8,200	12,000	20,000	10,000	15,000	38,000	$5,290, MS-63, Jun-10
1903S, Small S (dd)	*	66	26.3	2	—	—						$23,000, AU-55, Jun-06
1904	2,788,000	3,087	62.4	92	350	600	4,000	11,000	6,500	52,500	70,000	$3,738, MS-65, Mar-10
1904O	3,720,000	93,648	63.9	100	50	60	175	325	125	360	1,100	$1,955, MS-67, Jan-10
1904S	2,304,000	1,403	49.5	41	4,500	6,000	10,000	25,000	5,000	6,000	19,000	$7,475, MS-65 Secure, Jun-10
1921	44,690,000	53,747	63.6	99	35	40	160	750	1,800	8,500	12,000	$1,610, MS-64DMPL, Jan-10
1921D	20,345,000	10,938	63.3	96	60	150	350	1,100	2,200	7,000	11,000	$4,313, MS-67, Jan-10
1921S	21,695,000	8,925	63.2	97	60	175	1,250	11,000	3,100	12,000	30,000	$1,610, MS-63DMPL, Mar-10

* Included in number above. **y.** The O mintmark is smaller than normal; its punch was probably intended for a Barber half dollar. Five different dies are known, all scarce. **z.** A die break is visible from the rim through the date to just below the lower point of the bust. This variety is unknown in Mint State. Value in AU-50 is $550. **aa.** An O mintmark was punched into the die over a previously punched CC mintmark. There are at least seven different dies involved; the one pictured is VAM 9. **bb.** Beware of a fraudulently removed mintmark intended to make a less valuable 1901-O or 1901-S appear to be a 1901 dollar. **cc.** Doubling is visible on the eagle's tail feathers, and also on IN GOD WE TRUST, as well as on the arrows, wreath, and bow. This variety is nicknamed the "Shifted Eagle." It is very rare in Mint State. Value in MS-60 is $5,000. **dd.** The S mintmark is smaller than normal, possibly intended to be punched into a Barber half dollar die.

Proof Morgan Dollars

PF-60 to 70 (Proof). Morgan dollar Proofs were struck in all years from 1878 to 1904. Those from 1878 to 1901 generally have cameo contrast, while those of 1902 to 1904 have the portrait lightly polished in the die. Some Proofs are lightly struck. Check the hair above Miss Liberty's ear (in particular), and the eagle's breast feathers on the reverse. In 1921 quite a few so-called Zerbe Proofs were made with fields that are slightly reflective but have many microscopic die-finish lines. A very small number of deeply mirrored 1921 coins were made, called Chapman Proofs. Some Zerbe Proofs have been miscertified as Chapman Proofs. *Obverse and Reverse:* Proofs that are extensively cleaned and have many hairlines, or that are dull and grainy, are lower level, such as PF-60 to 62. These are not widely desired, except for the solitary date of 1895. With medium hairlines and good reflectivity, an assigned grade of PF-64 is appropriate, and with relatively few hairlines, PF-65. In various grades hairlines are most easily seen in the obverse field. Horizontal slide marks on the cheek of Miss Liberty are common and are from abrasion from the clear slides on National and related coin albums. PF-66 may have hairlines so delicate that magnification is needed to see them. Above that, a Proof should be free of such lines, including slide marks.

Proof Morgan Dollar

	Mintage	Cert	Finest	PF-60	PF-63	PF-64	PF-65	Recent Auction Record
1878, 8 Tail Feathers	500	130	PF-67	$2,500	$3,500	$6,000	$10,000	$12,650, PF-65Cam, Aug-09
1878, 7 Tail Feathers	250	97	PF-67	2,250	4,000	7,500	12,500	$13,513, PF-65Cam, Jun-10
1878, Round Breast					75,000	150,000	200,000	$155,250, PF-64, Nov-04
1879	1,100	301	PF-68	1,500	2,750	3,750	6,000	$5,463, PF-64Cam, Jun-10
1879O (a)	4–8	5	PF-66			100,000	150,000	$184,000, PF-64, Mar-10
1880	1,355	395	PF-69	1,500	2,750	3,750	6,000	$23,000, PF-68Cam, Jun-10
1881	984	250	PF-69	1,500	2,750	3,750	6,000	$5,175, PF-65Cam, Feb-10
1882	1,100	335	PF-68	1,500	2,750	3,750	6,000	$24,150, PF-68, Feb-10
1883	1,039	280	PF-68	1,500	2,750	3,750	6,000	$9,200, PF-67, Jun-10
1883O (b)	4–8	2	PF-64			100,000	150,000	$121,000, PF-66, Apr-97
1884	875	188	PF-68	1,500	2,750	3,750	6,000	$3,738, PF-63Cam, Mar-10
1885	930	240	PF-69	1,500	2,750	3,750	6,000	$1,840, PF-62 CAC, Feb-10
1886	886	221	PF-68	1,500	2,750	3,750	6,000	$1,610, PF-62, Mar-10
1887	710	196	PF-68	1,500	2,750	3,750	6,000	$1,495, PF-61, Jan-10
1888	833	182	PF-67	1,500	2,750	3,750	6,000	$8,050, PF-66Cam, Mar-10
1889	811	174	PF-68	1,500	2,750	3,750	6,000	$2,990, PF-63Cam, Jan-10
1890	590	223	PF-69	1,500	2,750	3,750	6,000	$4,313, PF-64Cam, Jan-10
1891	650	215	PF-68	1,500	2,750	3,750	6,000	$3,450, PF-64, Feb-10
1892	1,245	340	PF-68	1,500	2,750	3,750	6,000	$4,025, PF-64, Feb-10
1893	792	222	PF-68	1,500	2,750	3,750	6,000	$3,220, PF-64, Mar-10
1893CC (c)	4–8	9	PF-67			100,000	150,000	$54,625, PF-62, Jun-08
1894	972	321	PF-69	1,750	3,000	4,500	7,500	$6,900, PF-66Cam, Jun-10
1895 † (d)	880	342	PF-69	37,500	47,500	52,500	70,000	$92,000, PF-68, Jun-10
1895O (e)	2–3	5	PF-66		(extremely rare)			
1896	762	268	PF-69	1,500	2,750	3,750	6,000	$4,313, PF-64Cam, Mar-10
1897	731	187	PF-68	1,500	2,750	3,750	6,000	$1,438, PF-62, Mar-10
1898	735	253	PF-69	1,500	2,750	3,750	6,000	$19,550, PF-68 Star, Jan-10
1899	846	212	PF-69	1,500	2,750	3,750	6,000	$7,475, PF-66, Feb-10
1900	912	247	PF-68	1,500	2,750	3,750	6,000	$32,200, PF-68Cam CAC Star, Jun-10
1901	813	263	PF-68	1,500	2,750	3,750	6,000	$6,613, PF-65, Jun-10
1902	777	215	PF-68	1,500	2,750	3,750	6,000	$6,613, PF-66, Jun-10
1903	755	252	PF-68	1,500	2,750	3,750	6,000	$2,415, PF-63, Mar-10
1904	650	266	PF-68	1,500	2,750	3,750	6,000	$1,955, PF-62, Jan-10
1921, Zerbe (f)	150–250	40	PF-67	3,000	5,000	7,500	12,500	$6,900, PF-65, May-08
1921S, Zerbe (f)	1–2					75,000	125,000	$92,000, PF-64, Jan-06
1921, Chapman (g)	25–40	20	PF-67		25,000	35,000	50,000	$34,500, PF-64, Apr-09

* Included in number above. † Ranked among the *100 Greatest U.S. Coins* (third edition). **a.** Some numismatists classify these as Deep Mirror Prooflike circulation strikes, rather than as Proofs. **b.** "A numismatic tradition exists, dating back well over a century, that 12 full Proofs were struck of the 1883-O Morgan dollar. And, they may have been, although the differentiation between a cameo DMPL and a 'branch mint Proof' would be difficult to explain" (*A Guide Book of Morgan Silver Dollars*, third edition). **c.** Some numismatists classify these as Deep Mirror Prooflike circulation strikes, rather than as Proofs. **d.** Mint records indicate that 12,000 1895 Morgan dollars were struck for circulation; however, none have ever been seen. In order to complete their collections, date-by-date collectors are forced to acquire one of the 880 Proofs struck that year, causing much competition for this, "The King of the Morgan Dollars." **e.** Some numismatists classify these as Deep Mirror Prooflike circulation strikes, rather than as Proofs. **f.** "Pieces called Zerbe Proofs are simply circulation strikes with a semi-prooflike character, not as nice as on the earlier-noted [mirrorlike] prooflike pieces, struck from dies that were slightly polished, but that retained countless minute striae and preparation lines. In the view of the writer [Bowers], Zerbe Proofs have no basis in numismatic fact or history, although opinions differ on the subject. It seems highly unlikely that these were produced as Proofs for collectors. If indeed they were furnished to Farran Zerbe, a leading numismatic entrepreneur of the era, it is likely that they were simply regular production pieces. Zerbe had a fine collection and certainly knew what a brilliant Proof should look like, and he never would have accepted such pieces as mirror Proofs" (*A Guide Book of Morgan Silver Dollars*, third edition). **g.** Breen stated that 12 Chapman Proofs were minted (*Walter Breen's Encyclopedia of U.S. and Colonial Proof Coins, 1792–1977*); Bowers estimates fewer than 30 (*A Guide Book of Morgan Silver Dollars*, third edition). These are sometimes called *Chapman Proofs* because Philadelphia coin dealer Henry Chapman advertised them for sale within a few months of their production.

PEACE
(1921–1935)

Designer Anthony de Francisci; weight 26.73 grams; composition .900 silver, .100 copper (net weight .77344 oz. pure silver); diameter 38.1 mm; reeded edge; mints: Philadelphia, Denver, San Francisco.

History. In 1921, following the Pittman Act of 1918, the U.S. Treasury struck millions more silver dollars of the Morgan type while a new Peace dollar was in development. Sculptor and medalist Anthony de Francisci created the Peace design, originally intended as a commemorative of the end of the hostilities of the Great War. The obverse features Miss Liberty, and the reverse an eagle perched before the rising sun. The designer's monogram is located in the field of the coin under the neck of Miss Liberty. Coins of 1921 were struck in high relief; this caused weakness at the centers, so the design was changed to low relief in 1922. The dollars were struck until 1928, then again in 1934 and 1935. Legislation dated August 3, 1964, authorized the coinage of 45 million silver dollars, and 316,076 dollars of the Peace design dated 1964 were struck at the Denver Mint in 1965. Plans for completing this coinage were subsequently abandoned and all of these coins were melted. None were preserved or released for circulation; details are found in *A Guide Book of Peace Dollars* (Burdette).

Striking and Sharpness. Peace dollars of 1921 are always lightly struck at the center of the obverse, with hair detail not showing in an area. The size of this flat spot can vary. For this and other Peace dollars, check the hair detail at the center and, on the reverse, the feathers on the eagle. Many coins are struck from overly used dies, giving a grainy appearance to the fields, particularly the obverse. On many Peace dollars tiny white "milk spots" are seen, left over from when they were struck; these are not as desirable in the marketplace as unspotted coins.

Availability. All dates and mintmarks are readily available. Although some are well worn, they are generally collected in EF and finer grades. MS coins are available for each, with the 1934-S considered to be the key date. San Francisco issues of the 1920s, except for 1926-S, are often heavily bagmarked. The appearance of luster varies from issue to issue and can be deeply frosty, or—in the instance of Philadelphia Mint coins of 1928, 1934, and 1935—satiny or "creamy."

AU-50, 53, 55, 58 (About Uncirculated). *Obverse:* Light wear is seen on the cheek and the highest-relief areas of the hair. The neck truncation edge also shows wear. Some luster exists at AU-50 to 55. At AU-58, the luster is extensive, but incomplete. *Reverse:* Wear is evident on the eagle's shoulder and back. Otherwise, comments apply as for the obverse.

MS-60 to 70 (Mint State). *Obverse:* At MS-60, some abrasion and contact marks are evident, most notice-ably on the cheek and on the hair to the right of the face and forehead. Luster is present, but may be dull or lifeless. At MS-63, contact marks are extensive but not distracting. Abrasion still is evident, but less than at lower levels. MS-64 coins are slightly finer. Some Peace dollars have whitish "milk spots" in the field; while these are not caused by handling, but seem to have been from liquid at the mint or in storage, coins with these spots are rarely graded higher than MS-63 or 64. An MS-65 coin may have minor abrasion, but contact marks are so minute as to require magnification. Luster should be full and rich on earlier issues, and either frosty or satiny on later issues, depending on the date and mint. *Reverse:* At MS-60 some abrasion and contact marks are evident, most noticeably on the eagle's shoulder and nearby. Otherwise, comments apply as for the obverse.

1921, Line Through L
VAM 3. FS-S1-1921-1003.

1922, Die Break in Field
VAM 1F. FS-S1-1922-001f.

1922, Die Break at Ear
The "Ear Ring" variety.
VAM 2A. FS-S1-1922-002a.

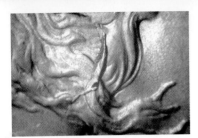

1922, Die Break in Hair
The 1922 "Extra Hair" variety.
VAM 2C. FS-S1-1922-002c.

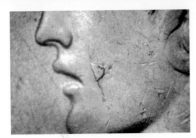

1922, Die Break on Cheek
The "Scar Cheek" variety.
VAM 5A. FS-S1-1922-005a.

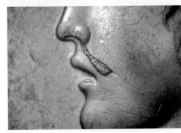

1922, Die Break at Nose
The "Moustache" variety.
VAM 12A. FS-S1-1922-012a.

1923, Die Break at Jaw
The "Whisker Jaw" variety.
VAM 1A. FS-S1-1923-001a.

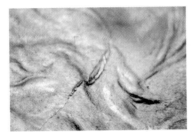

1923, Die Break in Hair
The 1923 "Extra Hair" variety.
VAM 1B. FS-S1-1923-001b.

1923, Die Break on O in DOLLAR
The "Tail on O" variety.
VAM 1C. FS-S1-1923-001c.

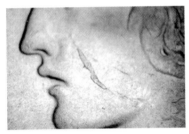

1923, Die Break on Cheek
The "Whisker Cheek" variety.
VAM 1D. FS-S1-1923-001d.

1923, Doubled-Die Obverse
The "Double Tiara" variety.
VAM 2. FS-S1-1923-002.

1923-S, Pitted Reverse
VAM 1C. FS-S1-1923S-001c.

1924, Die Break on Wing
The "Broken Wing" variety.
VAM 5A. FS-S1-1924-005a.

1925, Missing Ray
VAM 5. FS-S1-1925-005.

1926-S, Reverse Dot
The "Extra Berry" variety.
VAM 4. FS-S1-1926S-004.

1934-D, Doubled-Die Obverse, Small D
VAM 4. FS-S1-1934D-004.

	Mintage	Cert	Avg	%MS	AU-50	MS-60	MS-62	MS-63	MS-64	MS-65	MS-66	Recent Auction Record
1921, High Relief	1,006,473	10,240	60.3	82	$180	$285	$400	$500	$900	$2,750	$6,500	$1,840, MS-64, Mar-10
1921, High Relief, Line Through L (a)	*	35	60.7	80	275	400	575	700	1,250	3,750		$1,380, MS-64, Mar-08
1922, High Relief (1 known)	35,401				—							$805, MS-64, Feb-07
1922, Normal Relief	51,737,000	133,294	63.7	100	21	22	27	35	55	175	800	$575, MS-66, Mar-10
1922, Die Break in Field (b)	*	11	56.7	27	600	1,000	2,000	3,000				$933, MS-62, Dec-08
1922, Die Break at Ear (c)	*	22	59.4	59	500	750	1,500	2,500				$1,035, MS-63, Jun-05
1922, Die Break in Hair (d)	*	105	54.9	50	175	250	350	425				$518, MS-64, Jun-05
1922, Die Break on Cheek (e)	*	13	57.3	46	200	350	500	650				$403, MS-61, Jun-05
1922, Die Break at Nose (f)	*	68	59.2	56	200	350	450	600				$276, MS-63, Jan-07
1922D	15,063,000	5,228	63.4	96	19	30	45	55	100	450	2,500	$434, MS-65, Mar-10
1922S	17,475,000	4,151	62.8	94	19	30	60	75	225	2,500	20,000	$2,530, MS-65, Dec-09
1923	30,800,000	202,067	63.8	100	19	22	27	35	55	175	800	$2,415, MS-67, Mar-10
1923, Die Break at Jaw (g)	*	91	62.3	86	100	175	225	300	425	550		$403, MS-64, Feb-07
1923, Die Break in Hair (h)	*	48	61.6	85	150	250	325	400				
1923, Die Break on O (i)	*	29	58.7	79	550	1,100						
1923, Die Break on Cheek (j)	*	37	60.4	68	150	350	525	650				$575, MS-64, Feb-07
1923, DblDie Obv (k)	*	39	62.3	85	50	60	110	150	250	350		$51, MS-64, May-09
1923D	6,811,000	2,592	62.7	92	20	55	100	125	350	1,500	5,250	$691, MS-65, Mar-10
1923S	19,020,000	4,458	62.6	94	21	32	75	85	350	8,000	24,000	$2,070, MS-65, Feb-10
1923S, Pitted Rev (l)	*	20	58.1	50	60	85	140	175				$98, MS-62, Feb-09
1924	11,811,000	32,047	63.7	98	19	22	27	35	55	175	800	$542, MS-66, Mar-10
1924, Die Break on Wing (m)	*	21	61.7	81	450	525	575	800				$633, MS-65, Jun-05
1924S	1,728,000	5	56.2	40	70	275	400	550	1,750	12,500	30,000	$4,888, MS-65, Jun-10
1925	10,198,000	32,854	64.0	99	19	22	27	35	55	175	800	$311, MS-66, Mar-10
1925, Missing Ray (n)	*	38	62.9	89	60	95	125	150	300	400		$633, MS-65, Jul-07
1925S	1,610,000	4,189	62.1	89	42	78	140	180	1,000	2,750	—	$8,051, MS-65, Mar-10
1926	1,939,000	6,102	63.3	97	20	40	70	85	125	375	2,000	$290, MS-65, Mar-10
1926D	2,348,700	2,819	62.6	89	35	70	125	150	330	650	2,250	$560, MS-65, Mar-10
1926S	6,980,000	4,262	62.8	92	24	45	80	100	300	1,000	5,000	$1,265, MS-65, Feb-10
1926S, Rev Dot (o)	*	25	54.6	48	50	75	120	150				$115, MS-62, Jun-05
1927	848,000	3,642	62.3	91	55	75	135	165	385	2,500	20,000	$473, MS-64, Mar-10
1927D	1,268,900	2,443	61.4	82	85	165	275	350	1,000	5,500	22,000	$664, MS-64, Mar-10
1927S	866,000	2,984	61.9	88	75	170	325	375	900	11,500	40,000	$5,175, MS-65, Jun-10
1928	360,649	4,512	60.9	79	550	580	800	900	1,500	6,000	20,000	$3,220, MS-65, Jun-10
1928S	1,632,000	3,908	61.4	83	65	200	550	650	2,200	25,000	—	$25,300, MS-65, Mar-10
1934	954,057	4,005	62.7	91	52	120	200	275	450	900	3,250	$2,540, MS-66, Mar-10
1934D (p)	1,569,500	3,538	61.6	83	55	120	350	450	800	2,200	4,500	$1,064, MS-65, May-10
1934D, DblDie Obv, Small D (q)	*	26	55.8	35	600	1,000	1,500	2,500				$374, AU-58, Mar-09
1934S	1,011,000	2,502	51.8	42	650	2,000	3,750	4,500	5,800	8,500	29,000	$3,450, MS-64, Jun-10
1935	1,576,000	4,947	63.0	93	40	90	110	150	235	700	2,500	$1,726, MS-65, Mar-10
1935S (r)	1,964,000	2,588	62.0	86	100	265	350	425	600	1,700	2,750	$897, MS-65 CAC, Mar-10
1964D (s)	316,076				*(none known to exist)*							

* Included in number above. **a.** A ray runs through the first L in DOLLAR, instead of behind it. **b.** A die break is visible in the field above DOLLAR. "This variety has turned out to be much rarer than previously thought, and is very scarce in grades above EF" (*Cherrypickers' Guide to Rare Die Varieties,* fourth edition, volume II). **c.** A major die break near Liberty's ear, dangling down to her neck, gives this variety its nickname, the "Ear Ring." Several die states are known. **d.** An irregular line of raised metal runs along the back of Liberty's hair. This is called the "Extra Hair" variety. Several die states are known. **e.** Liberty's cheek has a raised, almost triangular chunk of metal along a vertical die break. Also, the reverse is lightly tripled. This variety, called the "Scarface," is very scarce in Mint State. **f.** A die break is visible running from Liberty's nose along the top of her mouth. This is known as the "Moustache" variety. **g.** A die break bridges Liberty's cheek and jaw. This is the "Whisker Jaw" variety. **h.** A significant die break runs diagonally across the strands of Liberty's hair; die breaks may also be visible toward the back of her hair. This variety is nicknamed the 1923 "Extra Hair." **i.** A die break trails from the O of DOLLAR. This variety, called the "Tail on O," is very rare in any grade. **j.** A die break runs down Liberty's cheek toward the junction of the chin and neck. This is the "Whisker Cheek" variety. **k.** Doubling is most evident in the wide spread on the rays of Liberty's tiara, especially those under the BER of LIBERTY. This is the "Double Tiara" variety. **l.** "Pitting runs from the eagle's back tail-feathers, just to the right of the mintmark, upward to the N in ONE. . . . This is the most important Pitted Reverse variety in the Peace dollar series" (*Cherrypickers' Guide to Rare Die Varieties*). **m.** A dramatic die break runs down and across the entire width of the eagle's back. This is the "Broken Wing" variety. **n.** This variety is the result of a reverse die polished with too much gusto. The partially effaced remains of bold clash marks are evident, but the topmost internal ray is missing. **o.** A raised circular dot of metal is visible to the left of the bottom olive leaf. This is nicknamed the "Extra Berry" variety. **p.** Varieties exist with small and large mintmarks. **q.** The obverse shows strong doubling on most letters of IN GOD WE TRUST, the rays on the right, and especially on Liberty's profile. The mintmark is a small D, shaped much like that of the 1920s-era D punches. **r.** Varieties exist with either three or four rays below ONE. They are valued equally in the marketplace. **s.** The entire mintage of 1964-D Peace dollars was melted by government order. Deceptive reproductions exist.

Proof Peace Dollars

PF-60 to 70 (Proof). Some Sandblast Proofs were made in 1921 and a limited issue in 1922 in high relief. These are rare today. Seemingly, a few Satin Proofs were also made in 1921. Sandblast Proofs of 1922 have a peculiar whitish surface in most instances, sometimes interrupted by small dark flecks or spots. There are a number of impostors among certified "Proofs." *Obverse and Reverse:* Proofs of both types usually display very few handling marks or defects. To qualify as Satin PF-65 or Sandblast PF-65 or finer, contact marks must be microscopic.

Proof Peace Dollar

	Est Mintage	Cert	Avg	PF-60	PF-63	PF-64	PF-65	Recent Auction Record
1921, Satin Finish Proof	10–20	17	63.6	$10,000	$25,000	$50,000	$75,000	$32,200, PF-64, Jul-09
1921, Matte Finish Proof	5–8	3	64.0			50,000	75,000	$161,000, PF-66, Apr-09
1922, High Relief, Matte Proof	10–15	10	65.4			100,000	125,000	$172,500, PF-67, Jul-03
1922, Low Relief, Matte Proof	3–6	3	65.3			50,000	75,000	$35,200, PF-65, Nov-88
1922, Low Relief, Satin Proof	3–6	2	64.0			50,000	75,000	$44,850, PF-60, Nov-09

EISENHOWER
(1971–1978)

Designer Frank Gasparro; diameter 38.1 mm; reeded edge; mints: Philadelphia, Denver, San Francisco. Silver issue: weight 24.59 grams; composition, outer layers of .800 silver, .200 copper bonded to inner core of .209 silver, .791 copper (net weight .3161 oz. pure silver). Copper-nickel issue: weight 22.68 grams; composition, outer layers of .750 copper, .250 nickel bonded to inner core of pure copper.

Bicentennial variety: Designers Frank Gasparro and Dennis R. Williams; diameter 38.1 mm; reeded edge; mints: Philadelphia, Denver, San Francisco. Silver issue—Weight 24.59 grams; composition, outer layers of .800 silver, .200 copper bonded to inner core of .209 silver, .791 copper (net weight .3161 oz. pure silver). Copper-nickel issue—Weight 22.68 grams; composition, outer layers of .750 copper, .250 nickel bonded to inner core of pure copper.

History. Honoring both President Dwight D. Eisenhower and the first landing of man on the moon, this design is the work of Chief Engraver Frank Gasparro, whose initials are on the truncation and below the eagle. The reverse is an adaptation of the official Apollo 11 insignia. Collectors' coins were struck in 40% silver composition, and the circulation issue (for some time a staple of the casino trade) in copper-nickel.

The dies for the Eisenhower dollar were modified several times by changing the relief, strengthening the design, and making Earth (above the eagle) more clearly defined.

Low-relief (Variety 1) dies, with flattened Earth and three islands off Florida, were used for all copper-nickel issues of 1971, Uncirculated silver coins of 1971, and most copper-nickel coins of 1972.

High-relief (Variety 2) dies, with round Earth and weak or indistinct islands, were used for all Proofs of 1971, all silver issues of 1972, and the reverse of some exceptional and scarce Philadelphia copper-nickel coins of 1972.

Improved high-relief reverse dies (Variety 3) were used for late 1972 Philadelphia copper-nickel coins and for all subsequent issues. Modified high-relief dies were also used on all issues beginning in 1973.

A few 1974-D and 1977-D dollars were made, in error, in silver clad composition.

A special reverse design was selected for the nation's Bicentennial. Nearly a thousand entries were submitted after the Treasury announced an open competition in October 1973. After the field was narrowed down to 12 semifinalists, the judges chose the rendition of the Liberty Bell superimposed on the moon to appear on the dollar coins. The obverse remained unchanged except for the dual date 1776–1976, which appeared on all dollars made during 1975 and 1976. These dual-dated coins were included in the various offerings of Proof and Uncirculated coins made by the Mint. They were also struck for general circulation. The lettering was modified early in 1975 to produce a more attractive design.

Striking and Sharpness. Striking generally is very good. On the obverse, check the high parts of the portrait, and on the reverse, the details of the eagle.

Availability. MS coins are common in the marketplace, although several early varieties are elusive at MS-65 or better. Lower grades are not widely collected.

MS-60 to 70 (Mint State). *Obverse:* At MS-60, some abrasion and contact marks are evident, most noticeably on the cheek, jaw, and temple. Luster is present, but may be dull or lifeless. At MS-63, contact marks are extensive but not distracting. Abrasion still is evident, but less than at lower levels. MS-64 coins are slightly finer. An MS-65 coin may have minor abrasion, but contact marks are so minute as to require magnification. Luster should be full and rich. *Reverse:* At MS-60, some abrasion and contact marks are evident, most noticeably on the eagle's breast, head, and talons. Otherwise, the same comments apply as for the obverse.

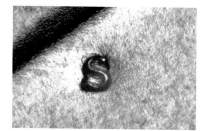

1971-S, Silver Clad, Repunched Mintmark

1971-S, Silver Clad, Polished Die
The "Peg Leg R" variety.

	Mintage	Cert	Avg	%MS	MS-63	MS-65	MS-66	Recent Auction Record
1971, Copper-Nickel Clad	47,799,000	1,133	64.0	96	$6	$120	$400	$94, MS-65, Jan-10
1971D, Copper-Nickel Clad	68,587,424	2,072	65.0	99	5	50	150	$20, MS-64, Jan-10
1971S, Silver Clad	6,868,530	1,607	65.2	100	9	20	40	$299, MS-67, Mar-09
1971S, Silver Clad, RPM (a)	*					225	375	$79, MS-64, Jan-10
1971S, Silver Clad, Polished Die (b)	*					225	375	$56, MS-64, Jan-10
1972, Copper-Nickel Clad, All kinds	75,890,000							
1972, Copper-Nickel Clad, Variety I		977	64.2	98	5	100	500	$44, MS-65, Jul-09
1972, Copper-Nickel Clad, Variety II		285	62.4	86	65	200	1,000	$104, MS-63, Jan-10
1972, Copper-Nickel Clad, Variety III		812	64.3	99	5			$150, MS-65, Jan-09
1972D, Copper-Nickel Clad	92,548,511	1,256	64.9	98	5	30	250	$127, MS-66, Jan-09
1972S, Silver Clad	2,193,056	2,283	66.4	100	9	15	20	$33, MS-67, Sep-09
1973, Copper-Nickel Clad	2,000,056	691	64.5	100	13	75	800	$62, MS-65, Aug-09
1973D, Copper-Nickel Clad	2,000,000	673	64.5	100	13	50	200	$180, MS-66, Feb-10
1973S, Silver Clad	1,883,140	1,566	66.1	100	12	20	40	$109, MS-68, Jan-10

* Included in number above. **a.** A secondary S is visible protruding northwest of the primary S. "This is one of fewer than a half dozen RPMs known for the entire series" (*Cherrypickers' Guide to Rare Die Varieties,* fourth edition, volume II). **b.** The left leg of the R in LIBERTY was overpolished. This is popularly known as the "Peg Leg R" variety.

	Mintage	Cert	Avg	%MS	MS-63	MS-65	MS-66	Recent Auction Record
1974, Copper-Nickel Clad	27,366,000	929	64.6	99	$6	$100	$900	$489, MS-66, Jan-09
1974D, Copper-Nickel Clad	45,517,000	1,603	65.0	100	6	50	200	$127, MS-66, Jan-09
1974S, Silver Clad	1,900,156	1,912	66.2	100	9	20	25	$127, MS-68, Dec-09
1776–1976, Copper-Nickel Clad, Var 1	4,019,000	586	64.2	100	8	150		$150, MS-65, Jan-09
1776–1976, Copper-Nickel Clad, Var 2	113,318,000	1,887	64.9	99	5	40	150	$69, MS-66, Jan-10
1776–1976D, Copper-Nickel Clad, Var 1	21,048,710	1,199	64.9	100	5	100	250	$104, MS-66, Jan-09
1776–1976D, Copper-Nickel Clad, Var 2	82,179,564	1,410	64.9	99	5	30	60	$59, MS-66, Aug-09
1776–1976, Silver Clad, Variety 2								
1776–1976S, Silver Clad, Variety 1	11,000,000	1,153	66.1	100	10	20	30	$328, MS-68, Aug-09
1977, Copper-Nickel Clad	12,596,000	2,239	65.0	100	6	50	200	$150, MS-66, Jan-09
1977D, Copper-Nickel Clad	32,983,006	1,890	64.9	100	6	45	150	$108, MS-66, Feb-10
1978, Copper-Nickel Clad	25,702,000	693	64.9	100	6	45	200	$219, MS-66, May-09
1978D, Copper-Nickel Clad	33,012,890	2,619	64.9	100	6	55	225	$24, MS-68, Sep-09

Proof Eisenhower Dollars

PF-60 to 70 (Proof). Proofs were made of the various issues (both copper-nickel clad and silver clad from 1971 to 1976; copper-nickel only in 1977 and 1978). All are readily available in today's marketplace. Nearly all are well struck and of high quality.

Obverse and Reverse: Proofs that are extensively cleaned and have many hairlines, or that are dull and grainy, are lower level, such as PF-60 to 62. There are not many of these in the marketplace. With medium hairlines and good reflectivity, assigned grades of PF-63 or 64 are appropriate. With relatively few hairlines a rating of PF-65 can be given. PF-66 may have hairlines so delicate that magnification is needed to see them. Above that, a Proof should be free of any hairlines or other problems.

Proof Eisenhower Dollar

Proof Eisenhower Dollar, Bicentennial

1971-S, Proof, Doubled-Die Obverse

1972-S, Proof, Silver Clad, Doubled-Die Obverse

1973-S, Proof, Silver Clad, Doubled-Die Obverse

	Mintage	Cert	Avg	PF-65	PR-67Cam	PF-67DC	PF-68DC	Recent Auction Record
1971S, Silver Clad	4,265,234	4,151	68.2	$10	$15	$20	$25	$30, PF-68Cam, Dec-09
1971S, Silver Clad, DblDie Obv (a)	*	18	67.6	275	500			$36, PF-66DCam, Aug-09
1972S, Silver Clad	1,811,631	3,277	68.2	10	15	20	25	$1,725, PF-70DC, Jan-10
1972S, Silver Clad, DblDie Obv (b)	*			125	275			$25, PF-67, Mar-08
1973S, Copper-Nickel Clad	2,760,339	850	68.2	12	16	20	30	$30, PF-69DCam, Aug-09
1973S, Silver Clad	1,013,646	2,767	68.2	35	36	38	40	$30, PF-67Cam, Dec-09

* Included in number above. **a.** Strong doubling is visible on IN GOD WE TRUST, the date, and LIBER of LIBERTY. There are at least two doubled-die obverses for this date (valued similarly); the one listed is FS-S1-1971S-103. "This obverse is also paired with a minor doubled-die reverse" (*Cherrypickers' Guide to Rare Die Varieties,* fourth edition, volume II). **b.** A medium spread of doubling is evident on IN GOD WE TRUST, LIBERTY, and slightly on the date.

Chart continued on next page.

	Mintage	Cert	Avg	PF-65	PR-67Cam	PF-67DC	PF-68DC	Recent Auction Record
1973S, Silver Clad, DblDie Obv (b)	*			$175	$350			
1974S, Copper-Nickel Clad	2,612,568	784	68.1	10	15	$25	$30	$26, PF-69DCam, Jan-09
1974S, Silver Clad	1,306,579	3,153	68.3	12	20	30	35	$79, PF-68Cam, Feb-10
1776–1976S, Copper-Nickel Clad, Variety 1	2,845,450	918	67.8	10	15	20	30	$16, PF-68Cam, Jun-09
1776–1976S, Copper-Nickel Clad, Variety 2	4,149,730	1,413	68.1	8	12	15	30	$24, PF-69DCam, Aug-09
1776–1976S, Silver Clad, Variety 1	4,000,000	3,104	68.1	15	20	25	35	$4,600, PF-70DC, Jan-10
1977S, Copper-Nickel Clad	3,251,152	1,400	68.4	10	15	20	25	$450, PF-68Cam, Feb-10
1978S, Copper-Nickel Clad	3,127,781	1,412	68.5					$3,450, PF-70DC, Sep-09

* Included in number above. **b.** A medium spread of doubling is evident on IN GOD WE TRUST, LIBERTY, and slightly on the date.

SUSAN B. ANTHONY
(1979–1999)

Designer Frank Gasparro; weight 8.1 grams; composition outer layers of copper-nickel (.750 copper, .250 nickel) bonded to inner core of pure copper; diameter 26.5 mm; reeded edge; mints: Philadelphia, Denver, San Francisco.

History. The Susan B. Anthony dollar was designed by Frank Gasparro, chief engraver of the U.S. Mint, following a congressional mandate. It features a portrait of the famous suffragette, along with an eagle-and-Moon motif reduced from the coin's larger predecessor, the Eisenhower dollar. Legislators hoped that these so-called mini-dollars would be an efficient substitute for paper dollars, which wear much more quickly in circulation. A large mintage in 1979 was followed by smaller quantities in 1980 and 1981, and then a hiatus of almost 20 years. A final coinage was struck in 1999.

Striking and Sharpness. Most are well struck, but check the highest areas of both sides.

Availability. Susan B. Anthony dollars are readily available in MS, although those of 1981 are scarcer. Circulated coins are not widely sought by collectors.

MS-60 to 70 (Mint State). *Obverse:* At MS-60, some abrasion and contact marks are evident, most noticeably on the cheek and upper center of the hair. Luster is present, but may be dull or lifeless. At MS-63, contact marks are extensive but not distracting. Abrasion still is evident, but less than at lower levels. MS-64 coins are slightly finer. An MS-65 coin may have minor abrasion, but contact marks are so minute as to require magnification. Luster should be full and rich. *Reverse:* At MS-60, some abrasion and contact marks are evident, most noticeably on the eagle's breast, head, and talons. Otherwise, the same comments apply as for the obverse.

1979-P, Narrow Rim
The "Far Date" variety.

1979-P, Wide Rim
The "Near Date" variety.

	Mintage	Cert	Avg	%MS	MS-64	MS-65	MS-66	Recent Auction Record
1979P, Narrow Rim (a)	360,222,000	425	65.2	98	$6	$10	$20	$14, MS-66, Jul-08
1979P, Wide Rim (a)	*	879	64.6	95	50	80	150	$104, MS-66, Aug-09
1979D	288,015,744	566	65.4	98	7	12	25	$299, MS-67, Jul-09
1979S	109,576,000	472	65.4	99	6	10	20	$276, MS-67, Aug-09
1980P	27,610,000	912	65.9	100	5	10	15	$54, MS-67, Dec-08

* Included in number above. **a.** The obverse design was modified in 1979 to widen the border rim. Late issues of 1979-P and subsequent issues have the wide rim. The 1979-P Wide Rim dollar is nicknamed the "Near Date" because the numerals are closer to the rim.

	Mintage	Cert	Avg	%MS	MS-64	MS-65	MS-66	Recent Auction Record
1980D	41,628,708	759	65.8	100	$5	$10	$15	$57, MS-67, Dec-08
1980S	20,422,000	654	65.5	100	10	15	25	$37, MS-66, Jul-08
1981P (b)	3,000,000	593	65.6	100	12	25	70	$42, MS-66, Jul-08
1981D (b)	3,250,000	731	65.7	100	10	14	25	$374, MS-67, Jul-08
1981S (b)	3,492,000	399	64.5	100	20	35	150	$40, MS-64, Oct-09
1999P (c)	29,592,000	541	66.3	100	5	10	15	$28, MS-67, Sep-09
1999D (c)	11,776,000	670	66.6	100	5	10	15	$345, MS-68, Aug-09

b. 1981-P, -D, and -S dollars were issued only in Mint Sets. **c.** Dies for the 1999 dollars were further modified to strengthen details on the reverse.

Proof Anthony Dollars

PF-60 to 70 (Proof). Proofs were made of all issues and are readily available in today's market. *Obverse and Reverse:* Proofs that are extensively cleaned and have many hairlines, or that are dull and grainy, are lower level, such as PF-60 to 62.

This comment is more theoretical than practical, as nearly all Proofs have been well kept. With medium hairlines and good reflectivity, assigned grades of PF-63 or 64 are appropriate. With relatively few hairlines a rating of PF-65 can be given. PF-66

may have hairlines so delicate that magnification is needed to see them. Above that, all the way to PF-70, a Proof should be free of any hairlines or other problems under strong magnification.

Proof Anthony Dollar

1979-S, Filled S (Type I)

1979-S, Clear S (Type II, Rounded)
1981-S, First S (Type I, Rounded)

1981-S, Clear S
(Type II, Flat)

1980-S, Repunched Mintmark
FS-C1-1980S-501.

	Mintage	Cert	Avg	PF-65	PF-68DC	PF-69DC	Recent Auction Record
1979S, Filled S (a)	3,677,175	3,304	68.9	$6	$10	$15	$115, PF-70DCam, Dec-09
1979S, Clear S (a)	*	1,405	68.7	90	110	125	$79, PF-69DCam, Mar-10
1980S	3,554,806	3,194	68.8	6	10	15	$127, PF-70DCam, Jan-10
1980S, RPM (b)	*			350	600		
1981S, First S	4,063,083	3,665	68.8	6	10	15	$84, PF-70DCam, Dec-09
1981S, Clear S	*	1,252	68.6	200	275	300	$109, PF-66DCam, Mar-10
1999P		4,475	69.2	30	35	40	$104, PF-70DCam, Dec-09

* Included in number above. **a.** The S mintmark punch was changed in 1979 to create a clearer mintmark. **b.** "The remnants of a previously punched S appear left of the primary S. . . . Very few specimens of this variety have surfaced to date" (*Cherrypickers' Guide to Rare Die Varieties,* fourth edition, volume II).

SACAGAWEA
(2000–2008)

Designers: Glenna Goodacre (obverse), Thomas D. Rogers Sr. (reverse); weight 8.1 grams; composition, pure copper core with outer layers of manganese brass (.770 copper, .120 zinc, .070 manganese, and .040 nickel); diameter 26.5 mm; plain edge; mints: Philadelphia, Denver, San Francisco; 22-karat gold numismatic specimens dated 2000-W were struck at West Point in 1999.

History. The Sacagawea dollar was launched in 2000. The obverse shows a modern artist's conception of Sacagawea, the Shoshone Indian who assisted the Lewis and Clark expedition, and her infant son. (No known contemporary portraits of Sacagawea exist.) The reverse shows an eagle in flight.

Striking and Sharpness. Most are very well struck. Check the higher design points.

Availability. These coins are common in high grades, and are usually collected in MS and Proof.

MS-60 to 70 (Mint State). *Obverse:* At MS-60, some abrasion and contact marks are evident, most noticeably on the cheekbone and the drapery near the baby's head. Luster is present, but may be dull or lifeless. At MS-63, contact marks are extensive but not distracting. Abrasion still is evident, but less than at lower levels. MS-64 coins are slightly finer. An MS-65 coin may have minor abrasion, but contact marks are so minute as to require magnification. Luster should be full and rich. *Reverse:* At MS-60, some abrasion and contact marks are evident, most noticeably on the eagle's breast. Otherwise, the same comments apply as for the obverse.

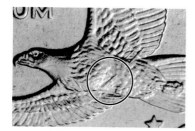

2000-P, Reverse Die Aberrations
The "Speared Eagle" variety.

2000-P, Normal Feathers

2000-P, Boldly Detailed Tail Feathers

	Mintage	Cert	Avg	%MS	MS-64	MS-65	MS-66	Recent Auction Record
2000P	767,140,000	5,746	66.7	100	$2.50	$8	$12	$65, MS-68PL, Aug-09
2000P, Rev Die Aberrations (a)	*	1	64.0	100		—		$16, MS-64, Aug-09
2000P, Goodacre Presentation Finish (b)	5,000	4,772	66.4	100		400		$575, MS-67, Feb-10
2000P, Boldly Detailed Tail Feathers (c)	5,500	643	67.2	100		—		$13,800, MS-68, Jan-10
2000D	518,916,000	346	66.0	100	4.00	10	15	$19, MS-64, Mar-09
2001P	62,468,000	364	67.1	100	2.00	4	6	$31, MS-68, Mar-09
2001D	70,939,500	335	66.3	100	2.00	4	6	$16, MS-66, Mar-09
2002P (d)	3,865,610	633	66.7	100	2.00	4	10	$15, MS-67, Aug-09
2002D (d)	3,732,000	579	66.1	100	2.00	4	8	$27, MS-67, Jul-08
2003P	3,080,000	508	66.8	100	3.00	5	8	$37, MS-68, Jul-08
2003D	3,080,000	643	66.6	100	3.00	5	8	$57, MS-67, Jul-08
2004P	2,660,000	4,308	66.9	100	2.00	4	8	$71, MS-68, Jul-08
2004D	2,660,000	4,264	66.6	100	2.00	4	8	$31, MS-67PL, Feb-09
2005P	2,520,000	1,897	66.7	100	7.00	10	20	$26, MS-69 Satin, Aug-09
2005D	2,520,000	2,019	66.6	100	7.00	10	20	$15, MS-69 Satin, Sep-08
2006P	4,900,000	1,066	66.9	100	2.00	4	8	$115, MS-69 Satin, Jul-08
2006D	2,800,000	1,079	66.4	100	2.00	4	8	$13, MS-65, Jul-08
2007P (d)	3,640,000	411	66.7	100	3.00	5	8	$39, MS-69 Satin, Dec-08
2007D (d)	3,920,000	611	66.5	100	3.00	5	8	$31, MS-69 Satin, May-09
2008P (d)	1,820,000				3.00	5	8	
2008D (d)	1,820,000				3.00	5	8	

* Included in number above. **a.** Two spike-like die aberrations appear through the breast of the eagle. This variety is nicknamed the "Speared Eagle." **b.** A group of 5,000 coins, dated 2000 and with a special finish, were presented to sculptor Glenna Goodacre in payment for the obverse design. **c.** The feathers of the eagle are finely enhanced. This is nicknamed the "Cheerios" variety, as the coins were included as a promotion in boxes of Cheerios cereal. **d.** Not issued for circulation.

Proof Sacagawea Dollars

PF-60 to 70 (Proof). Proofs have been made each year and are readily available. *Obverse and Reverse:* Proofs that are extensively cleaned and have many hairlines, or that are dull and grainy, are lower level, such as PF-60 to 62. This comment is more theoretical than practical, as nearly all Proofs have been well kept. With medium hairlines and good reflectivity, assigned grades of PF-63 or 64 are appropriate. With relatively few hairlines a rating of PF-65 can be given. PF-66 may have hairlines so delicate that magnification is needed to see them. Above that, all the way to PF-70, a Proof should be free of any hairlines or other problems under strong magnification.

Proof Sacagawea Dollar

	Mintage	Cert	Avg	PF-69DC	Recent Auction Record
2000S	4,047,904	11,135	69.1	$25	$489, PF-70DCam, Mar-10
2001S	3,183,740	7,573	69.1	100	$403, PF-70DCam, Jan-10
2002S	3,211,995	6,829	69.2	40	$26, PF-69Ucam, Jan-10
2003S	3,298,439	9,539	69.2	60	$84, PF-70DCam, Jan-10
2004S	2,965,422	9,452	69.1	30	$50, PF-70UCam, Dec-09
2005S	3,344,679	14,671	69.2	25	$74, PF-70DCam, Mar-10
2006S	3,054,436	6,461	69.3	20	$26, PF-69Ucam, Jan-10
2007S	2,259,847	7,210	69.2	20	$62, PF-70UCam, Sep-09
2008S	1,998,108	4,599	69.2	20	$79, PF-70DCam, Dec-09

NATIVE AMERICAN (2009 TO DATE)

Designers: Glenna Goodacre (obverse), Norm Nemeth (2009 reverse), Thomas Cleveland (2010 reverse); weight 8.1 grams; composition, pure copper core with outer layers of manganese brass (.770 copper, .120 zinc, .070 manganese, and .040 nickel); diameter 26.5 mm; lettered edge; mints: Philadelphia, Denver, San Francisco.

Agriculture (2009) Common Obverse Great Law of Peace (2010)

History. Since 2009, the reverse of the golden dollar has featured an annually changing design that memorializes Native Americans and, in the words of the authorizing legislation, "the important contributions made by Indian tribes and individual Native Americans to the development [and history] of the United States." The coins are marked (incuse) on their edges with the year of minting, the mintmark, and the legend E PLURIBUS UNUM. The Native American $1 Coin Act also specifies that at least 20% of the total mintage of dollar coins in any given year (including Presidential dollars) will be Native American dollars.

Striking and Sharpness. Most examples are very well struck. Check the higher points of the design.

Availability. Native American dollars are common in high grades, and are usually collected in MS and Proof. Distribution for public circulation has been slow despite Mint efforts such as the $1 Coin Direct Ship program (intended "to make $1 coins readily available to the public, at no additional cost [including shipping], so they can be easily introduced into circulation—particularly by using them for retail transactions, vending, and mass transit").

MS-60 to 70 (Mint State). *Obverse and reverse:* At MS-60, some abrasion and contact marks are evident, most noticeably on the high points of the design, including, on the obverse, Sacagawea's cheekbone and the drapery near the baby's head. Luster is present, but may be dull or lifeless. At MS-63, contact marks are extensive but not distracting. Abrasion is still evident, but less than at lower levels. MS-64 coins are slightly finer. An MS-65 coin may have minor abrasion, but contact marks are so minute as to require magnification. Luster should be full and rich.

	Est Mintage	Cert	Avg	%MS	MS-64	MS-65	MS-66	Recent Auction Record
2009P	767,140,000	766	66.8	100	$3	$5	$8	
2009D	518,916,000	643	66.5	100	3	5	8	
2010P	767,140,000	386	66.0	100	3	8	8	
2010D	1,820,000	245	65.8	100	3	5	8	

Proof Native American Dollars

PF-60 to 70 (Proof). Proofs have been made each year and are readily available. *Obverse and Reverse:* Proofs that are extensively cleaned and have many hairlines, or that are dull and grainy, are lower level, such as PF-60 to 62. This comment is more theoretical than practical, as nearly all Native American dollar Proofs have been well kept. With medium hairlines and good reflectivity, assigned grades of PF-63 or 64 are appropriate. With relatively few hairlines a rating of PF-65 can be given. PF-66 may have hairlines so delicate that magnification is needed to see them. Above thtat, all the way to PF-70, a Proof should be free of any hairlines or other problems under strong magnification.

Proof Native American Dollar

	Mintage	Cert	Avg	PF-69DC	Recent Auction Record
2009S	4,047,904	7,029	69.3	$20	$138, PF-70UCam, Feb-10
2010S	3,183,740				

PRESIDENTIAL
(2007–2016)

Various designers; weight 8.1 grams; composition, pure copper core with outer layers of manganese brass (.770 copper, .120 zinc, .070 manganese, and .040 nickel; diameter 26.5 mm; plain edge; mints: Philadelphia, Denver, San Francisco.

Obverse Style, 2007–2008
No motto on obverse.

Obverse Style, 2009–2016
Motto beneath portrait.

Common Reverse

Date, Mintmark, and Mottos Incused on Edge
IN GOD WE TRUST moved to obverse in 2009.

History. Presidential dollars debuted in 2007 and are being issued at the rate of four designs per year, starting with George Washington and continuing in order of office. Each coin has a common reverse showing the Statue of Liberty. The motto IN GOD WE TRUST was moved from the edge to the obverse in 2009.

Striking and Sharpness. These usually are well struck, but check the higher-relief parts of each side.

Availability. Presidential dollars are very common in MS. Most have from a few to many bagmarks, with true MS-65 and better coins in the minority.

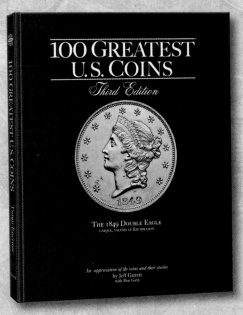
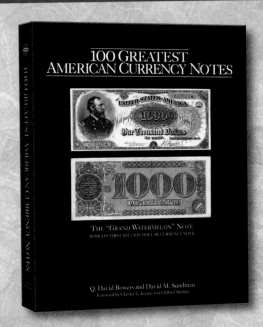

MS-60 to 70 (Mint State). *Obverse:* At MS-60, some abrasion and contact marks are evident, most noticeably on the highest-relief areas of the portrait, the exact location varying with the president depicted. Luster is present, but may be dull or lifeless. At MS-63, contact marks are extensive but not distracting. Abrasion still is evident, but less than at lower levels. MS-64 coins are slightly finer. An MS-65 coin may have minor abrasion, but contact marks are so minute as to require magnification. Luster should be full and rich. *Reverse:* At MS-60, some abrasion and contact marks are evident, most noticeably on the cheek and arm. Otherwise, the same comments apply as for the obverse.

2007, Washington	2007, J. Adams	2007, Jefferson	2007, Madison
2008, Monroe	2008, J.Q. Adams	2008, Jackson	2008, Van Buren
2009, Harrison	2009, Tyler	2009, Polk	2009, Taylor
2010, Fillmore	2010, Pierce	2010, Buchanan	2010, Lincoln

	Est Mintage	Cert	Avg	%MS	MS-64	MS-65	MS-66	Recent Auction Record
2007P, Washington	176,680,000	18,000	65.1	100	$1.50	$2	$6	$42, MS-68 Satin, Apr-09
2007, Washington, Plain Edge (a)	*	40,577	64.7	100	30.00	40	100	$109, MS-66, Apr-08
2007D, Washington	163,680,000	15,142	65.2	100	1.50	2	6	$17, MS-65, Aug-09
2007P, J. Adams	112,420,000	18,919	64.7	100	1.50	2	6	$29, MS-66, Aug-09
2007D, J. Adams	112,140,000	6,561	65.3	100	1.50	2	6	$25, MS-69 Satin, May-09
2007P, Jefferson	100,800,000	5,380	65.4	100	1.50	2	6	$65, MS-65, Oct-09
2007D, Jefferson	102,810,000	6,434	65.5	100	1.50	2	6	$16, MS-65, Aug-09
2007P, Madison	84,560,000	3,121	65.5	100	1.50	2	6	$16, MS-66, Aug-09
2007D, Madison	87,780,000	3,818	65.7	100	1.50	2	6	$15, MS-66, Aug-09
2008P, Monroe	64,260,000	2,270	65.5	100	1.50	2	6	$11, MS-67, Jul-08
2008D, Monroe	60,230,000	2,084	65.6	100	1.50	2	6	$11, MS-67, Jul-08
2008P, J.Q. Adams	57,540,000	2,601	65.9	100	1.50	2	6	
2008D, J.Q. Adams	57,720,000	2,342	65.9	100	1.50	2	6	
2008P, Jackson	61,180,000	2,986	65.7	100	1.50	2	6	
2008D, Jackson	61,070,000	2,231	65.5	100	1.50	2	6	

* Included in number above. **a.** Some circulation-strike Washington dollars are known without the normal edge lettering (date, mintmark, IN GOD WE TRUST, and E PLURIBUS UNUM).

	Est Mintage	Cert	Avg	%MS	MS-64	MS-65	MS-66	Recent Auction Record
2008P, Van Buren	51,520,000	1,455	65.8	100	$1.50	$2	$6	
2008D, Van Buren	50,960,000	1,200	65.6	100	1.50	2	6	
2009P, Harrison		1,485	66.0	100	1.50	2	6	
2009D, Harrison		1,514	65.8	100	1.50	2	6	
2009P, Tyler		1,194	65.7	100	1.50	2	6	
2009D, Tyler		1,173	65.6	100	1.50	2	6	
2009D, Tyler, 2010 Edge								
2009P, Polk		1,328	66.3	100	1.50	2	6	
2009D, Polk		1,077	66.0	100	1.50	2	6	
2009P, Taylor		1,144	66.4	100	1.50	2	6	
2009D, Taylor		1,113	66.2	100	1.50	2	6	
2010P, Fillmore		920	66.0	100				
2010D, Fillmore		786	66.1	100				
2010P, Pierce		833	66.0	100				
2010D, Pierce		858	66.1	100				
2010P, Buchanan		191	67.2	100				
2010D, Buchanan		265	67.3	100				
2010P, Lincoln		343	66.9	100				
2010D, Lincoln		508	67.4	100				

Proof Presidential Dollars

PF-60 to 70 (Proof). Proofs have been struck of each issue and are readily available. All have been well struck and are of exceptional quality. *Obverse and Reverse:* Proofs that are extensively cleaned and have many hairlines, or that are dull and grainy, are lower level, such as PF-60 to 62. (This comment is more theoretical than practical, as nearly all Proofs have been well kept.) With medium hairlines and good reflectivity, assigned grades of PF-63 or 64 are appropriate. With relatively few hairlines a rating of PF-65 can be given. PF-66 may have hairlines so delicate that magnification is needed to see them. Above that, all the way to PF-70, a Proof should be free of any hairlines or other problems under strong magnification.

Proof Presidential Dollar

	Est Mintage	Cert	Avg	PF-69DC	Recent Auction Record
2007S, Washington	3,362,237	42,839	69.2	$20	$36, PF-70Cam, Dec-09
2007S, J. Adams	3,362,237	42,593	69.2	20	$26, PF-70Cam, Dec-09
2007S, Jefferson	3,362,237	42,745	69.2	20	$75, PF-70DCam, Oct-09
2007S, Madison	3,362,237	43,026	69.2	20	$62, PF-70DCam, Jan-10
2008S, Monroe	2,824,791	21,987	69.2	15	$69, PF-70DCam, Mar-10
2008S, J.Q. Adams	2,824,791	21,982	69.3	15	$69, PF-70DCam, Mar-10
2008S, Jackson	2,824,791	21,946	69.2	15	$59, PF-70DCam, Mar-10
2008S, Van Buren	2,824,791	22,015	69.3	15	$47, PF-70UCam, Mar-10
2009S, Harrison		14,669	69.2	15	
2009S, Tyler		14,657	69.2	15	
2009S, Polk		14,644	69.2	15	$127, PF-70DCam, Feb-10
2009S, Taylor		14,711	69.3	15	$47, PF-70DCam, Mar-10
2010S, Fillmore		8,038	69.1		
2010S, Pierce		8,067	69.2		
2010S, Buchanan		8,073	69.1		
2010S, Lincoln		8,396	69.1		

An Overview of Trade Dollars

A new denomination, the silver trade dollar, was authorized by the Coinage Act of 1873. This provided that a coin weighing 420 grains, 90% silver, be struck for use in the export trade. By comparison, contemporary Liberty Seated silver dollars weighed 412.5 grains. Produced in quantity from 1873 through 1878, the trade dollars were a great success, particularly in China, where merchants preferred silver to gold and would not accept paper money of any kind. Coinage would have continued except for the Bland-Allison Act of February 28, 1878, which authorized the government to buy millions of ounces of silver each year and resume the production of standard silver dollars (which had not been minted since 1873). The trade dollar was discontinued forthwith; however, Proof impressions were made for numismatists through 1883, plus a small quantity of Proofs distributed privately in 1884 and 1885, these last two being great rarities today.

Choosing a trade dollar for a type set is easy enough to do, the choices being a circulation strike, which requires some connoisseurship, or a Proof, most of which are sharply struck and attractive. Enough exist in both formats that collectors will easily find a nice example, except that MS-65 and better pieces are elusive.

For the Collector and Investor: Trade Dollars as a Specialty

There are two great rarities among trade dollars: the Proof-only 1884, of which just 10 are known, and the Proof-only 1885, of which only five are known. Neither was produced openly, and examples were sold for the private profit of Mint officials, going to John W. Haseltine, a Philadelphia dealer who was a favored outlet for such things. The existence of these coins was not generally known to numismatists until 1907–1908, when examples began to appear on the market. As to the mintage figures, the numbers 5 and 10 have no official origin, but are said to represent the number once held by Haseltine. Relatively few numismatists have been able to afford examples of these two dates.

Beyond the above, a complete collection of trade dollars of the 1873 to 1883 years can be formed with some effort. Proofs were made of each year during this span, and after 1878 *only* Proofs were made, at the Philadelphia Mint, with no branch-mint issues. These had greater appeal to collectors of an earlier era, and more were saved, with the result that Proofs of the otherwise common dates 1873–1877 are much harder to find today, especially in choice condition.

Circulation strikes were regularly produced from 1873 through 1878, with emphasis on the San Francisco and Carson City mints, these being closest to the Orient, where the coins were used in commerce. Some trade dollars (but not many) went into domestic circulation (they were legal tender until that status was repealed on July 22, 1876). Later, after 1876, they traded widely in the United States but were valued by their silver content, not their face value. In 1878 the 412.5-grain Morgan dollar was worth $1.00 in circulation, while the heavier 420-grain trade dollar was worth only its melt-down value of about $0.90.

Very few of the circulating issues were saved by numismatists, with the result today that assembling a collection in choice or gem Mint State can be a great challenge. The key issue, by far, is the 1878-CC, with the lowest mintage in the series—scarce in any and all grades. As trade dollars became numismatically popular in the United States, thousands were repatriated from China, often bearing Chinese characters called *chopmarks,* which were applied by bankers and merchants. More often than not the imported coins had been harshly cleaned in China, as the owners thought shiny coins were more desirable. However, many choice and undamaged pieces were imported as well. The pieces with chopmarks are collectible in their own right in view of their historical significance.

Collectors are warned that many modern counterfeit trade dollars lurk in the marketplace.

Recommended Reading

Bowers, Q. David. *Silver Dollars and Trade Dollars of the United States: A Complete Encyclopedia,* Wolfeboro, NH, 1993.
Fivaz, Bill, and Stanton, J.T. *The Cherrypickers' Guide to Rare Die Varieties* (4th ed., vol. II), Atlanta, GA, 2006.
Willem, John M. *The United States Trade Dollar* (2nd ed.), Racine, WI, 1965.

LIBERTY SEATED
(1873–1885)

Designer William Barber; weight 27.22 grams; composition .900 silver, .100 copper (net weight .7874 oz. pure silver); diameter 38.1 mm; reeded edge; mints: Philadelphia, Carson City, San Francisco.

History. Trade dollars were minted under the Coinage Act of 1873. Containing 420 grains of .900 fine silver, they were heavier than the Liberty Seated dollar (of 412.5 grains). They were made for use in the China export trade and proved to be a great success. Some circulated in the United States, until they were demonetized by the Act of July 22, 1876. The Bland-Allison Act of 1878 provided for the new "Morgan" silver dollar, and trade dollars were discontinued, although Proofs continued to be made through 1885.

Modifications to the trade dollar design are distinguished as follows.

Reverse 1: Berry under eagle's left talon; arrowhead ends over 0. (Used on all coins from all mints in 1873 and 1874, and occasionally in 1875 and 1876.)

Reverse 2: Without extra berry under talon; arrowhead ends over 2. (Used occasionally at all mints from 1875 through 1876, and on all coins from all mints 1877 through 1885.)

Obverse 1: Ends of scroll point to left; extended hand has only three fingers. (Used on coins at all mints, 1873 through 1876.)

Obverse 2: Ends of scroll point downward; extended hand has four fingers. (Used in combination with Reverse 2 on one variety of 1876S, and on all coins at all mints from 1877 through 1885.)

Striking and Sharpness. Weakness is often seen. On the obverse, check Miss Liberty's head and the star centers first. On the reverse, check the feathers on the eagle, particularly on the legs. Luster can range from dull to deeply frosty. In EF and lower grades, strike sharpness on the stars and the head does not matter to connoisseurs.

Availability. Although the 1878-CC is a rarity, other dates and mintmarks are readily collected in grades from EF to MS. Lower grades are not often seen, for these coins did not circulate for a long time. Many used in China have counterstamps, called *chopmarks,* which are of interest to collectors. On an MS-63 or better coin a chopmark will decrease value, but on EF and AU coins they are eagerly sought. MS coins are mostly in the lower ranges, often with unsatisfactory surfaces. True gems are very scarce. *Note:* In recent years a flood of modern counterfeit trade dollars, many coming from China, has deluged the market.

EF-40, 45 (Extremely Fine). *Obverse:* More wear than at AU is seen on all areas, especially the head, the left breast, the left arm, the left leg, and the bale on which Miss Liberty is seated. Little or no luster is seen on most coins. *Reverse:* More wear than at AU is evident on the eagle's head, legs, claws, and wings, although on well-struck coins nearly all feather details on the wings are sharp.

AU-50, 53, 55, 58 (About Uncirculated). *Obverse:* Light wear is seen on the knees, bosom, and head. There is some luster at AU-50 to 55. At AU-58, the luster is extensive but incomplete. *Reverse:* Wear is visible on the eagle's head, the claws, and the top of the wings. There are traces of luster at AU-50 to 55. An AU-58 coin has nearly full luster.

MS-60 to 70 (Mint State). *Obverse:* At MS-60, some abrasion and contact marks are evident, most noticeably on the left breast, left arm, and left knee. Luster is present, but may be dull or lifeless. Many of these coins are light in color or even brilliant, having been repatriated from China, and have been cleaned to remove sediment and discoloration. At MS-63, con-tact marks are very few, and abrasion is minimal. An MS-65 coin has no abrasion in the fields (but may have a hint on the higher parts of the seated figure), and contact marks are trivial. Luster should be full and rich. *Reverse:* Comments apply as for the obverse, except that in lower MS grades abrasion and contact marks are most noticeable on the eagle's head, the claws, and the top of the wings. At MS-65 or higher there are no marks visible to the unaided eye. The field is mainly protected by design elements and does not show abrasion as much as does the obverse on a given coin.

Reverse 1
Arrowheads end over 0; berry under eagle's left talon.

Reverse 2
Arrowheads end over 2; no berry under talon.

Obverse 1
Hand has three fingers; scroll points left.

Obverse 2
Hand has four fingers; scroll points downward.

1875-S, S Over CC
FS-T1-1875S-501.

1876-CC, Doubled-Die Reverse
FS-T1-1876CC-801.

1876-S, Doubled-Die Obverse
FS-T1-1876S-101.

1877, Doubled-Die Obverse
FS-T1-1877-101.

1877-S, Repunched Date
FS-T1-1877S-301.

1877-S, Doubled-Die Reverse
FS-T1-1877S-801.

1877-S, Doubled-Die Reverse
FS-T1-1877S-802.

1878-S, Doubled-Die Reverse
FS-T1-1878S-801.

	Mintage	Cert	Avg	%MS	EF-40	AU-50	MS-60	MS-62	MS-63	MS-64	MS-65	Recent Auction Record
1873	396,635	126	60.6	79	$250	$350	$1,150	$2,800	$3,500	$6,500	$18,000	$1,438, MS-61, Jan-10
1873CC	124,500	107	54.3	31	650	1,500	10,000	18,000	22,500	50,000	110,000	$10,063, MS-62 CAC, Mar-10
1873S	703,000	92	59.8	74	250	375	1,450	3,800	4,950	6,750	18,000	$2,070, MS-62, Sep-09
1874	987,100	106	60.0	73	250	350	1,000	2,000	2,750	5,250	17,750	$2,990, MS-64, Jan-10
1874CC	1,373,200	189	59.5	70	475	675	3,200	5,500	7,500	10,000	32,000	$1,783, AU-55, Jun-10
1874S	2,549,000	259	60.2	74	225	325	1,200	2,200	3,000	5,250	17,500	$1,208, MS-62, Feb-10
1875	218,200	90	59.0	76	550	1,000	2,800	4,500	5,600	11,000	17,500	$6,325, MS-64 CAC, Mar-10
1875, Rev 2	*				550	1,000	2,800	4,500	5,600	11,000	17,500	$6,325, MS-64, Jan-07
1875CC, All kinds	1,573,700											
1875CC		228	57.8	61	450	750	2,600	4,750	5,850	12,000	35,000	$6,440, MS-63, Aug-09
1875CC, Rev 2		2	59.5	50	425	750	2,900	4,500	5,500	11,500	33,000	$1,035, AU-58, May-07
1875S, All kinds	4,487,000											
1875S		772	61.3	82	225	300	1,050	1,800	2,475	4,000	13,000	$1,038, MS-62 CAC, Mar-10
1875S, Rev 2		1	55.0	0	250	350	800	1,850	2,675	4,100	13,500	$2,760, MS-64, Mar-07
1875S, S Over CC (a)		47	59.1	53	950	1,500	4,675	9,000	13,750	25,000	52,500	$10,925, MS-63, Jun-10
1876	455,000	354	60.9	84	250	350	1,050	2,000	2,750	4,100	16,000	$8,338, MS-65, Jun-10
1876, Obv 2, Rev 2 (ex. rare)	*					—						
1876, Rev 2	*	1	55.0	0	225	300	1,050	1,850	2,475	4,000	16,000	$2,760, MS-63, Feb-07
1876CC, All kinds	509,000											
1876CC		100	57.5	47	500	1,000	4,750	18,000	24,500	35,000	80,000	$3,450, AU-58, Dec-09
1876CC, Rev 1					500	1,250	4,750	17,500	23,500	34,000	78,000	$3,220, MS-60, Feb-06
1876CC, DblDie Rev (b)		25	55.9	32	650	1,550	5,250			—		$10,925, MS-61, Jan-10
1876S, All kinds	5,227,000											
1876S		597	59.7	70	200	325	1,075	1,800	2,575	4,000	16,000	$979, MS-62, Mar-10
1876S, DblDie Obv (c)					1,400	1,750	2,200					
1876S, Rev 2					195	300	1,075	1,800	2,575	4,000	16,000	$2,530, MS-63, Apr-07
1876S, Obv 2, Rev 2					250	375	1,200	2,000	2,875	4,200	17,500	$23,000, MS-66, Mar-06
1877	3,039,200	377	57.2	65	190	300	1,075	1,800	2,575	4,800	20,000	$6,038, MS-64, Feb-10
1877, DblDie Obv (d)	*	1	62.0	100	300	400	1,250					
1877CC	534,000	107	56.6	60	625	750	2,575	10,000	14,950	22,000	60,000	$19,550, MS-64, Mar-10
1877S	9,519,000	971	58.4	66	190	300	1,075	1,800	2,575	4,000	13,000	$9,775, MS-65, Jun-10
1877S, Repunched Date (e)	*				300	425	1,300					$322, AU-58, Aug-05
1877S, DblDie Rev (f)	*	2	55.5	0	550	800	1,600					
1877S, DblDie Rev (g)	*	1	40.0	0	300	400	1,200					$8,625, MS-65, May-07
1878					1,500							
1878CC (h)	97,000	75	47.8	35	2,500	4,250	15,000	23,000	27,500	55,000	100,000	$11,227, AU-58, Feb-10
1878S	4,162,000	634	56.5	57	190	300	1,050	1,800	2,475	4,000	12,500	$6,900, MS-65, Jan-10
1878S, DblDie Rev (i)	*	6	57.5	50	450	550	1,300					$1,495, MS-61, Aug-08

* Included in number above. **a.** A weak C from the underlying CC mintmark is visible to the right of the S mintmark. **b.** Doubling is visible on the branches on the right, the eagle's talons, the right wing tip, and the eagle's beak; and is very strong on E PLURIBUS UNUM. Weaker doubling is seen on UNITED STATES OF AMERICA. "Considered by most to be the strongest reverse doubled die in the series, this variety is one of the highlights of the trade dollar varieties and is thought to be extremely rare in grades above AU" (*Cherrypickers' Guide to Rare Die Varieties*, fourth edition, volume II). **c.** Doubling is visible on Liberty's hand, chin, and left foot, and on the olive branch. "This DDO is easily the rarest doubled die in the series, and is considered extremely rare in grades above AU. Most known examples are cleaned. The variety is known as the king of the trade dollar varieties" (*Cherrypickers' Guide to Rare Die Varieties*). **d.** Doubling on this rare variety is evident on the wheat stalks, LIBERTY, IN GOD WE TRUST, and stars 11, 12, and 13. **e.** A secondary 7 protrudes prominently south from the last 7. **f.** Doubling is visible on E PLURIBUS UNUM, the ribbon, and UNITED STATES OF AMERICA. There are at least two different doubled-die reverses for 1877-S; this one is FS-T1-1877S-801. "Considered a highlight of the trade dollar varieties" (*Cherrypickers' Guide to Rare Die Varieties*). **g.** Minor doubling is visible on nearly all reverse lettering, especially on 420 GRAINS. This reverse doubled die is more common than the preceding; it is listed as FS-T1-1877S-802. **h.** On July 19, 1878, a quantity of 44,148 trade dollars was melted by the Mint. Many of these may have been 1878-CC. **i.** Strong doubling is visible on the entire lower left of the reverse, on the arrow points and shafts, and on 420 GRAINS; slight doubling is evident on the motto. Rare in AU and higher grades. There are at least two doubled-die reverses for this date; the one listed is FS-T1-1878S-801.

Proof Trade Dollars

PF-60 to 70 (Proof). Proofs were made for collectors from 1873 to 1883, in quantity to supply the demand. In addition, a few were secretly made in 1884 and 1885. Today most survivors are of high quality, although gems of the 1873 to 1877 years are much harder to find than are those of 1878 to 1883. Some Proofs are lightly struck on the head and the stars on the obverse and the leg feathers of the eagle on the reverse. *Obverse and Reverse:* Proofs that are extensively cleaned and have many hairlines, or that are dull and grainy, are lower level, such as PF-60 to 62. These are not widely desired. With medium hairlines and good reflectivity, an assigned grade of PF-64 is appropriate, and with relatively few hairlines, PF-65. In various grades hairlines are most easily seen in the obverse field. PF-66 may have hairlines so delicate that magnification is needed to see them. Above that, a Proof should be free of such lines.

Proof Trade Dollar

	Mintage	Cert	Finest	PF-60	PF-63	PF-64	PF-65	Recent Auction Record
1873	865	143	PF-67	$1,750	$3,000	$5,000	$10,000	$4,025, PF-63, Feb-10
1874	700	181	PF-67	1,750	3,000	5,000	10,000	$4,313, PF-64Cam, May-10
1875	700	210	PF-67	1,750	3,000	5,000	10,000	$21,850, PF-66 , Feb-10
1876	1,150	254	PF-67	1,750	3,000	5,000	10,000	$14,950, PF-66, Mar-09
1877	510	189	PF-67	1,750	3,000	5,000	10,000	$9,775, PF-65 Star, Jun-10
1878	900	301	PF-67	1,750	3,000	5,000	10,000	$7,475, PF-65Cam, Feb-10
1879	1,541	516	PF-68	1,750	3,000	5,000	10,000	$3,910, PF-64, Feb-10
1880	1,987	638	PF-68	1,750	3,000	5,000	10,000	$7,475, PF-65Cam, Jun-10
1881	960	387	PF-68	1,750	3,000	5,000	10,000	$3,738, PF-64, Dec-09
1882	1,097	474	PF-68	1,750	3,000	5,000	10,000	$6,325, PF-64 Dcam, Jun-10
1883	979	434	PF-69	1,750	3,000	5,000	10,000	$10,350, PF-66 Cam, Jun-10
1884 † (a)	10	6	PF-67			450,000	650,000	$603,750, PF-65, Nov-05
1885 † (a)	5	1	PF-61		1,200,000	*2,000,000*	*2,500,000*	$1,006,250, PF-62 , Nov-04

† Ranked in the *100 Greatest U.S. Coins* (third edition). **a.** Trade dollars of 1884 and 1885 were unknown to the numismatic community until 1907–1908. None are listed in the Mint director's report, and numismatists believe that they are not a part of the regular Mint issue.

AN OVERVIEW OF GOLD DOLLARS

Coinage of the gold dollar was authorized by the Act of March 3, 1849, after the start of the California Gold Rush.

Although a case could be made for designating the Small Head, Open Wreath gold dollar as a separate type, it is not generally collected as such. Instead, pieces dated from 1849 through 1854 are collectively designated as Type 1. Examples today are readily available in all grades, although truly choice and gem Mint State pieces are in the minority.

In contrast, the Type 2 design, produced at the Philadelphia Mint in part of 1854, and at the Philadelphia, Charlotte, Dahlonega, and New Orleans mints in 1855, and only at the San Francisco Mint in 1856, is a great challenge. Examples are scarcer in all grades than are those of Types 1 and 3. Choice and gem coins are especially rare. Striking is a great problem, and while some sharp pieces exist, probably 80% or more have areas of weakness, typically at the 85 (center two digits) of the date, but often on the headdress and elsewhere. Further, the borders are sometimes imperfect.

Type 3 gold dollars, made from 1856 through 1889, are easier to acquire in nearly any grade desired, including choice and gem Mint State, most of which are well struck and have excellent eye appeal. Among Type 3 gold dollars the dates from 1879 through 1889 inclusive are most often seen, as these were widely saved by coin dealers and collectors at the time and did not circulate to any appreciable extent. Some of these have very low mintage figures, making them very appealing to collectors.

FOR THE COLLECTOR AND INVESTOR: GOLD DOLLARS AS A SPECIALTY

Forming a specialized collection of gold dollars is a fascinating pursuit, one that has drawn the attention of many numismatists over the years. A complete run of date-and-mintmark issues from 1849 through 1889 includes no impossible rarities, although the 1875, with just 20 Proofs and 400 circulation strikes made, is the key date. While the dollars of 1879 through 1889 often have remarkably low mintages, they were saved in quantity, and certain of these dates are easily obtainable (although not necessarily inexpensive).

The branch-mint gold dollars of the early years present a special challenge. Among the Charlotte Mint varieties the 1849 comes with an Open Wreath (of which just five are presently known, with a rumor of a sixth) and with a Close Wreath, the latter being scarce but available. Later Charlotte gold dollars, extending through 1859, range from scarce to rare. The 1857-C is notorious for its poor striking.

Gold dollars were struck at the Dahlonega Mint from 1849 through 1861. In the latter year the facility was under the control of the Confederate States of America, and thus the 1861-D gold dollars, rare in any event, are even more desirable as true Confederate coins. The New Orleans Mint also produced gold dollars, which in general are better struck than those of the Charlotte and Dahlonega mints. From 1854 intermittently to 1860, and then in 1870, gold dollars were struck in San Francisco. These Western issues are usually sharply defined and range from scarce to rare. In particular, choice and gem Mint State pieces are elusive.

RECOMMENDED READING

Akers, David W. *Gold Dollars (and Other Gold Denominations),* Englewood, OH, 1975–1982.
Bowers, Q. David. *A Guide Book of Gold Dollars,* Atlanta, GA, 2008.
Bowers, Q. David. *United States Gold Coins: An Illustrated History,* Wolfeboro, NH, 1982.
Breen, Walter. *Major Varieties of U.S. Gold Dollars (and Other Gold Denominations),* Chicago, 1964.
Fivaz, Bill. *United States Gold Counterfeit Detection Guide,* Atlanta, GA, 2005.
Fivaz, Bill, and Stanton, J.T. *The Cherrypickers' Guide to Rare Die Varieties* (4th ed., vol. II), Atlanta, GA, 2006.
Garrett, Jeff, and Guth, Ron. *Encyclopedia of U.S. Gold Coins, 1795–1933* (2nd ed.), Atlanta, GA, 2008.

GOLD DOLLARS, 1849–1889

LIBERTY HEAD
(1849–1854)

Designer James B. Longacre; weight 1.672 grams; composition .900 gold, .100 copper (net weight .04837 oz. pure gold); diameter 13 mm; reeded edge; mints: Philadelphia, Charlotte, Dahlonega, New Orleans, San Francisco.

Open Wreath Reverse   *Close Wreath Reverse*

Mintmark is below wreath. Coins shown 2x actual size.

History. U.S. Mint chief engraver James Barton Longacre designed the nation's gold dollars. This first type measured 13 mm in diameter, which proved to be inconvenient, and the two later types were enlarged to 15 mm.

Striking and Sharpness. As a rule, Philadelphia coins are sharper than those of the Charlotte and Dahlonega mints. On the obverse, check the highest areas of the hair below the coronet. On the reverse, check the wreath and the central two figures in the date. On both sides check the dentils, which can be mushy or indistinct (par-ticularly on Charlotte and Dahlonega coins, which often have planchet roughness as well).

Availability. All dates and mintmarks are readily collectible, save for the 1849-C Open Wreath variety. MS coins often are found for the Philadelphia issues but can be elusive for the branch mints. Charlotte and Dahlonega coins often have striking problems. The few gold dollars of this type that are less than VF in grade usually are damaged or have problems.

AU-50, 53, 55, 58 (About Uncirculated). *Obverse:* Light wear on the hair below the coronet and the cheek is very noticeable at AU-50, and progressively less at higher levels to AU-58. Luster is minimal at AU-50 and scattered and incomplete at AU-58. Some tiny nicks and contact marks are to be expected and should be mentioned if they are distracting. *Reverse:* Light wear on the 1, the wreath, and the ribbon characterize an AU-50 coin, progressively less at higher levels to AU-58. Otherwise, the same comments apply as for the obverse.

MS-60 to 70 (Mint State). *Obverse:* At MS-60 to 62, there is abrasion on the hair below the coronet (an area that can be weakly struck, as well) and on the cheeks. Marks may be seen. At MS-63, there may be slight abrasion. Luster is irregular. At MS-64, abrasion is less. Luster is rich on most coins, less so on Charlotte and Dahlonega varieties. At MS-65 and above, luster is deep and frosty. At MS-66, and higher, no marks at all are visible without magnification. *Reverse:* On MS-60 to 62 coins, there is abrasion on the 1, the highest parts of the leaves, and the ribbon. Otherwise, the same comments apply as for the obverse.

1849, With L   1849, No L

	Mintage	Cert	Avg	%MS	AU-55	AU-58	MS-60	MS-62	MS-63	MS-64	MS-65	Recent Auction Record
1849, Open Wreath, So-Called Small Head, With L (a)	688,567	686	61.3	80	$300	$375	$650	$1,300	$1,850	$2,500	$5,750	$11,500, MS-66, Feb-10
1849, Open Wreath, So-Called Small Head, No L (a)	*	326	62.3	87	385	500	1,000	1,400	2,100	3,000	6,500	$345, AU-55, Apr-10
1849, Open Wreath, So-Called Large Head (a)	*				295	360	600	1,100	1,350	2,250	5,500	$1,006, MS-63, Jun-10
1849, Close Wreath	*	305	61.9	85	295	360	600	1,100	1,350	2,250		$460, MS-62, Jul-10
1849C, Open Wreath *(extremely rare)*	*	3	40.0	33	350,000	400,000			750,000			$218,500, EF-45, Feb-10
1849C, Close Wreath	11,634	89	55.1	33	4,000	5,000	9,000	12,500	18,500	35,000		$4,313, AU-58, Mar-10
1849D, Open Wreath	21,588	274	57.0	39	3,500	3,750	5,250	8,000	12,500	21,500	55,000	$5,750, MS-62, Mar-10
1849O, Open Wreath	215,000	581	58.3	49	560	600	1,200	2,250	4,000	7,500	12,500	$2,990, MS-63, Apr-10
1850	481,953	406	60.5	74	285	300	400	675	1,150	2,250	5,500	$1,610, MS-64, Jul-10
1850C	6,966	84	54.7	27	4,500	6,500	9,000	14,000	30,000			$25,300, MS-62, Feb-10
1850D	8,382	93	55.3	26	5,000	7,500	10,500	17,500	26,000	37,500		$8,625, MS-61, Mar-10
1850O	14,000	174	58.4	44	1,500	2,000	3,400	5,250	7,500	13,500		$2,530, MS-61, May-10

* Included in number above. **a.** It is now well known that the so-called Small Head and Large Head coins are from the same punch.

	Mintage	Cert	Avg	%MS	AU-55	AU-58	MS-60	MS-62	MS-63	MS-64	MS-65	Recent Auction Record
1851	3,317,671	3,497	61.4	85	$275	$290	$350	$575	$1,150	$1,675	$5,500	$1,725, MS-64 CAC, Jul-10
1851C	41,267	407	57.6	37	2,250	2,550	3,250	4,750	6,500	12,500	25,000	$2,070, AU-58 CAC, Jul-10
1851D	9,882	131	58.4	43	2,750	3,250	5,000	8,000	15,000	23,500	45,000	$12,075, MS-63, Jul-10
1851O	290,000	721	59.2	52	410	450	850	1,400	2,500	5,500	13,000	$978, MS-62, Jul-10
1852	2,045,351	3,133	61.5	85	275	290	350	575	1,150	1,675	5,500	$431, MS-62, Jun-10
1852C	9,434	140	57.2	43	2,750	3,000	4,500	6,500	12,000	21,500	32,500	$4,433, MS-62, Mar-10
1852D	6,360	103	56.8	30	3,600	4,750	8,500	15,000	26,500			$3,457, AU-55, Mar-10
1852O	140,000	423	57.3	36	700	850	1,400	2,250	6,000	10,500	20,000	$805, AU-58, Jul-10
1853	4,076,051	8,356	61.5	85	275	290	350	575	1,150	1,675	5,500	$5,750, MS-66+, Jul-10
1853C	11,515	118	57.1	37	2,600	3,500	5,000	8,000	13,500	26,500	40,000	$9,775, MS-63, Feb-10
1853D	6,583	102	57.9	31	4,250	5,500	9,000	14,500	27,500	37,500	55,000	$74,750, MS-66, Feb-10
1853O	290,000	1,077	59.9	62	385	425	800	1,300	2,600	5,500	11,000	$253, AU-58, Jul-10
1854	855,502	3,015	61.6	88	275	290	350	575	1,150	1,675	5,500	$345, AU-58, Jul-10
1854D	2,935	79	56.7	33	7,000	8,500	12,500	16,500	35,000			$9,200, MS-61, Mar-10
1854S	14,632	148	58.6	40	1,150	1,450	2,500	3,500	6,000	11,000	27,500	$1,495, AU-55, Mar-10

Proof Liberty Head Gold Dollars

PF-60 to 70 (Proof). A few Proofs were coined in the early years, and they are, for all practical purposes, unobtainable. Fewer than a dozen are known. *Obverse and*

Reverse: PF-60 to 62 coins have extensive hairlines and may have nicks and contact marks. At PF-63, hairlines are prominent, but the mirror surface is very reflective.

PF-64 coins have fewer hairlines. At PF-65, hairlines should be minimal and mostly seen only under magnification.

Proof Liberty Head Gold Dollar

Shown 2x actual size.

	Mintage	Cert	Avg	PF-60	PF-63	PF-64	PF-65	Recent Auction Record
1849, Open Wreath, Small Head, No L *(2–3 known)*	unknown	2	63.0	(extremely rare)				
1850 *(2 known)*	unknown			(extremely rare)				
1854	unknown			(unique, in the Bass Foundation Collection)				

INDIAN PRINCESS HEAD, SMALL HEAD (1854–1856)

Designer James B. Longacre; weight 1.672 grams; composition .900 gold, .100 copper (net weight .04837 oz. pure gold); diameter 15 mm; reeded edge; mints: Philadelphia, Charlotte, Dahlonega, New Orleans, San Francisco.

Mintmark is below wreath. Shown 2x actual size.

History. This style of gold dollar, with the diameter increased from 13 mm to 15 mm, was first made in 1854. The design proved difficult to strike, leading to its modification in 1856.

Striking and Sharpness. On the obverse, check the highest area of the hair below the coronet and the tips of the feathers. Check the let-

ters. On the reverse, check the ribbon bow knot and in particular the two central digits of the dates. Examine the digits on both sides. Nearly all have problems. This type is often softly struck in the centers, with weak hair detail and the numerals 85 in the date sometimes faint—this should not be confused with wear. The 1855-C and 1855-D coins are often poorly struck and on rough planchets.

Availability. All are collectible, but the Charlotte and Dahlonega coins are rare. With patience, Full Details coins are available of 1854, 1855, and 1856-S, but virtually impossible to find for the branch-mint issues of 1855. The few gold dollars of this type that are less than VF in grade usually are damaged or have problems.

AU-50, 53, 55, 58 (About Uncirculated). *Obverse:* Light wear on the hair below the coronet, the cheek, and the tips of the feather plumes is very noticeable at AU-50, progressively less at higher levels to AU-58. Luster is minimal at AU-50 and scattered and incomplete at AU-58. Some tiny nicks and contact marks are to be expected and should be mentioned if they are distracting. *Reverse:* Light wear on the 1, the wreath, and the ribbon knot characterize an AU-50 coin, progressively less at higher levels to AU-58. Otherwise, the same comments apply as for the obverse.

MS-60 to 70 (Mint State). *Obverse:* At MS-60 to 62, there is abrasion on the hair below the band lettered LIBERTY (an area that can be weakly struck, as well), on the tips of the feather plumes, and throughout the field. Contact marks may also be seen. At MS-63, there should be only slight abrasions. Luster is irregular. At MS-64, abrasions and marks are less. Luster is rich on most coins, less so on Charlotte and Dahlonega issues. At MS-65 and above, luster is deep and frosty, with no marks at all visible without magnification at MS-66 and higher. *Reverse:* At MS-60 to 62, there may be abrasions on the 1, on the highest parts of the leaves, on the ribbon knot, and in the field. Otherwise, the same comments apply as for the obverse.

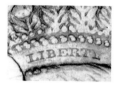 

1854, Doubled-Die Obverse
FS-G1-1854-1101.

	Mintage	Cert	Avg	%MS	AU-55	AU-58	MS-60	MS-62	MS-63	MS-64	MS-65	Recent Auction Record
1854	783,943	5,028	57.4	29	$950	$1,200	$1,950	$3,900	$9,000	$13,750	$30,000	$546, AU-55, Jul-10
1854, Doubled-Die Obverse (a)	*				1,100	1,350	2,350	4,150	10,000			$3,163, MS-62, Nov-06
1855	758,269	4,596	57.3	29	950	1,200	1,950	3,900	9,000	13,750	30,000	$370, EF-45, Jul-10
1855C	9,803	176	50.9	8	13,500	20,000	26,500	37,500				$11,500, AU-58, Mar-10
1855D	1,811	38	55.3	13	27,500	32,500	48,500	57,500	95,000	135,000		$27,600, AU-50, Apr-10
1855O	55,000	492	54.8	13	2,500	4,250	8,500	14,500	27,500	42,500		$1,380, AU-50, Jun-10
1856S	24,600	228	54.8	15	3,500	4,750	8,500	16,000	31,500	50,000		$1,669, EF-45 CAC, Jul-10

* Included in number above. **a.** Check for strong doubling on UNITED STATES OF AMERICA, the beads in the headdress, the feathers, and portions of LIBERTY.

Proof Indian Princess Head, Small Head, Gold Dollars

PF-60 to 70 (Proof). Proofs exist of the 1854 and 1855 issues, but were made in very small quantities. *Obverse and Reverse:* PF-60 to 62 coins have extensive hairlines and may have nicks and contact marks. At PF-63, hairlines are prominent, but the mirror surface is very reflective. PF-64 coins have fewer hairlines. At PF-65, hairlines should be minimal and mostly seen only under magnification. There should be no nicks or marks. PF-66 and higher coins have no marks or hairlines visible to the unaided eye.

Proof Indian Princess Head, Small Head, Gold Dollar
Shown 2x actual size.

	Est Mintage	Cert	Avg	PF-60	PF-63	PF-64	PF-65	Recent Auction Record
1854	4 known	5	64.6	$100,000	$200,000	$275,000	$350,000	$218,500, PF-64DCam, Mar-09
1855	unknown	8	65.0	75,000	150,000	200,000	300,000	$373,750, PF-66DCam, Jan-08

INDIAN PRINCESS HEAD, LARGE HEAD
(1856–1889)

Designer James B. Longacre; weight 1.672 grams; composition .900 gold, .100 copper (net weight .04837 oz. pure gold); diameter 15 mm; reeded edge; mints: Philadelphia, Charlotte, Dahlonega, San Francisco.

Mintmark is below wreath. Shown 2x actual size.

History. The design of the Indian Princess Head was modified in 1856. The new portrait is larger and in shallower relief. After this change, most (but not all) gold dollars were struck with strong detail. Gold dollars of this type did not circulate extensively after 1861, except in the West. As they did not see heavy use, today most pieces are EF or better. MS coins are readily available, particularly of the dates 1879 through 1889 (during those years the coins were popular among investors and speculators, and many were saved).

Striking and Sharpness. These dollars usually are well struck, but many exceptions exist. Charlotte and Dahlonega coins are usually weak in areas and can have planchet problems. On all coins, check the hair details on the obverse. The word LIBERTY can be only partially present or missing completely, as the dies were made this way for some issues, particularly in the 1870s; this does not affect their desirability. On the reverse, check the ribbon knot and the two central date numerals. Check the dentils on both sides. Copper stains are sometimes seen on issues of the 1880s due to incomplete mixing of the alloy. Many coins of the 1860s onward have highly prooflike surfaces.

Availability. All are collectible, but many issues are scarce. Most MS-65 or finer coins are dated from 1879 to 1889. The few gold dollars of this type that are less than VF usually are damaged or have problems.

AU-50, 53, 55, 58 (About Uncirculated). *Obverse:* Light wear on the hair below the coronet, the cheek, and the tips of the feather plumes is very noticeable at AU-50, progressively less at higher levels to AU-58. Luster is minimal at AU-50 and scattered and incomplete at AU-58. Some tiny nicks and contact marks are to be expected and should be mentioned if they are distracting. *Reverse:* Light wear on the 1, the wreath, and the ribbon knot characterize an AU-50 coin, progressively less at higher levels to AU-58. Otherwise, the same comments apply as for the obverse.

MS-60 to 70 (Mint State). *Obverse:* At MS-60 to 62, there is abrasion on the hair below the band lettered LIBERTY (an area that can be weakly struck, as well), on the tips of the feather plumes, and throughout the field. Contact marks may also be seen. At MS-63, there should be only slight abrasions. Luster is irregular. At MS-64, abrasions and marks are less. Luster is rich on most coins, less so on Charlotte and Dahlonega issues. At MS-65 and above, luster is deep and frosty, with no marks at all visible without magnification at MS-66 and higher. *Reverse:* At MS-60 to 62, there may be abrasions on the 1, on the highest parts of the leaves, on the ribbon knot, and in the field. Otherwise, the same comments apply as for the obverse.

1862, Doubled-Die Obverse
FS-G1-1862-101.

	Mintage	Cert	Avg	%MS	AU-55	AU-58	MS-60	MS-62	MS-63	MS-64	MS-65	Recent Auction Record
1856, All kinds	1,762,936											
1856, Upright 5		224	59.6	56	$425	$450	$550	$900	$1,500	$2,150	$7,500	$431, MS-61, Jul-10
1856, Slant 5		868	60.2	67	285	300	400	550	1,150	1,400	3,250	$1,064, MS-64, Jul-10
1856D	1,460	30	56.1	20	11,000	16,500	30,000	45,000	85,000			$10,350, AU-55, Mar-10
1857	774,789	895	60.6	73	285	300	400	550	1,150	1,400	3,000	$1,495, MS-64 CAC, Jul-10
1857C	13,280	128	53.1	6	5,250	7,000	12,500	22,000				$3,220, AU-55, Mar-10
1857D	3,533	83	54.7	16	5,000	6,500	10,000	16,500				$6,900, AU-58, Apr-10
1857S	10,000	114	54.3	14	2,000	2,750	6,000	8,500	20,000	40,000		$1,955, AU-55, Jul-10
1858	117,995	183	60.7	70	275	315	400	700	1,150	1,500	5,500	$10,925, MS-67, Feb-10
1858D	3,477	110	55.5	32	5,000	6,750	9,500	13,500	20,000	37,500	65,000	$1,380, VF-25, Mar-10
1858S	10,000	90	54.2	11	1,850	2,250	6,000	9,500	16,500	19,500	30,000	$1,955, AU-55, Jul-10

Chart continued on next page.

	Mintage	Cert	Avg	%MS	AU-55	AU-58	MS-60	MS-62	MS-63	MS-64	MS-65	Recent Auction Record
1859	168,244	324	61.2	77	$275	$315	$400	$650	$1,150	$1,400	$2,450	$460, MS-62, Jun-10
1859C	5,235	72	57.3	33	6,750	8,000	12,000	16,000	32,500			$5,188, AU-58, Jun-10
1859D	4,952	117	57.2	28	5,000	6,750	8,500	12,000	18,500	32,000	60,000	$4,600, AU-58, Apr-10
1859S	15,000	145	51.8	10	1,900	2,350	5,500	8,750	16,000	25,000		$403, EF-40, Jul-10
1860	36,514	147	61.3	82	295	315	425	650	1,300	2,500	6,750	$546, MS-62, Jun-10
1860D	1,566	64	54.8	19	10,000 (a)	12,500	18,500	27,500	45,000	75,000		$12,650, MS-61, Feb-10
1860S	13,000	143	56.0	24	1,100	1,250	2,750	4,000	6,500	12,500	27,500	$1,265, AU-58, Jun-10
1861	527,150	1,105	61.5	87	275	300	400	650	1,150	1,375	2,500	$1,065, MS-64 CAC, Mar-10
1861D	1,250	29	57.8	34	45,000 (b)	55,000	65,000	75,000	115,000	135,000	185,000	$38,813, AU-58 CAC, Jul-08
1862	1,361,355	2,396	61.9	90	285	300	400	650	1,150	1,375	2,500	$1,179, MS-64 CAC, Jul-10
1862, Doubled-Die Obverse (c)	*	11	61.3	73	400	500	650	900	1,350			$748, MS-63, Feb-07
1863	6,200	36	61.8	78	3,750	4,500	6,000	7,000	9,500	13,500	20,000	$3,738, AU-58, Apr-10
1864	5,900	72	61.6	81	1,300	1,500	1,850	2,500	4,000	5,500	8,000	$978, AU-58, Feb-09
1865	3,725	35	62.4	86	1,200	1,450	2,000	2,750	4,000	5,500	8,500	$1,265, MS-66, Feb-10
1866	7,100	69	62.8	88	900	1,000	1,150	1,350	2,150	3,000	5,000	$4,313, MS-65, Feb-10
1867	5,200	67	61.4	69	850	950	1,200	1,400	2,000	2,750	4,500	$9,200, MS-67 Star, Mar-10
1868	10,500	117	61.0	78	625	750	1,000	1,500	2,000	2,750	4,500	$446, AU-55, Jul-10
1869	5,900	87	61.8	82	800	900	1,150	1,600	2,250	2,750	5,500	$748, AU-58, Jun-10
1870	6,300	116	61.9	80	750	850	1,000	1,500	2,000	2,750	5,500	$5,750, MS-66, Jul-10
1870S	3,000	54	60.2	59	1,650	2,150	2,750	4,000	7,500	11,500	22,500	$1,610, AU-58, Dec-09
1871	3,900	105	62.3	88	675	750	900	1,250	1,900	2,250	4,000	$863, MS-61, Sep-09
1872	3,500	67	60.4	70	700	850	1,000	1,350	2,250	3,000	5,000	$1,610, MS-62, Jun-10
1873, Close 3	1,800	86	60.3	66	1,250	1,350	1,700	2,500	4,500	7,500	15,000	$2,300, MS-62, Jul-10
1873, Open 3	123,300	1,774	61.9	92	275	300	400	650	1,100	1,375	2,350	$3,450, MS-66, Jun-10
1874	198,800	3,178	62.3	94	275	300	400	650	1,100	1,375	2,350	$2,295, MS-66, Jul-10
1875	400	30	61.6	87	6,000 (d)	7,000	8,000	9,500	12,500	15,000	27,500	$6,038, AU-58, Jun-10
1876	3,200	126	61.5	79	600	650	750	1,000	1,300	1,500	3,500	$863, MS-63, Jun-10
1877	3,900	168	62.2	84	600	650	775	1,000	1,350	1,550	3,500	$2,185, MS-64, Feb-10
1878	3,000	132	61.9	89	600	650	775	1,000	1,350	1,550	3,500	$978, MS-63, Mar-10
1879	3,000	198	63.6	94	475	525	600	800	1,400	1,600	3,500	$1,955, MS-65, Jun-10
1880	1,600	310	65.6	99	400	450	575	700	1,300	1,500	2,750	$6,038, MS-67 CAC, Jun-10
1881	7,620	392	65.1	98	400	450	575	700	1,300	1,500	2,750	$4,313, MS-67 CAC, Jul-10
1882	5,000	208	64.5	97	400	450	575	700	1,300	1,500	2,750	$10,350, MS-68 CAC, Jun-10
1883	10,800	492	64.5	97	400	450	575	700	1,300	1,500	2,750	$9,775, MS-68, Jul-10
1884	5,230	197	63.5	97	400	450	575	700	1,300	1,500	2,750	$4,313, MS-65 CAC, Jun-10
1885	11,156	424	63.8	96	400	450	575	700	1,300	1,500	2,750	$375, MS-61, Jun-10
1886	5,000	272	63.3	97	400	450	575	700	1,300	1,500	2,750	$1,150, MS-64, Jul-10
1887	7,500	464	63.8	99	400	450	550	700	1,150	1,375	2,350	$1,725, MS-65, Mar-10
1888	15,501	685	63.9	98	400	450	500	650	1,150	1,375	2,350	$3,220, MS-67, Jun-10
1889	28,950	1,836	64.3	98	400	450	500	650	1,100	1,375	2,360	$4,313, MS-67, Jul-10

* Included in number above. **a.** Value in EF-40 is $4,250; in AU-50, $7,750. **b.** Value in EF-40 is $18,500; in AU-50, $29,500. **c.** Doubling, visible on the entire obverse, is most evident on the tops of the hair curls and the feathers. **d.** Value in EF-40 is $4,000; in AU-50, $5,500.

Proof Indian Princess Head, Large Head, Gold Dollars

PF-60 to 70 (Proof). Proofs were made of all years. Most range from rare to very rare, with some dates in the 1880s being exceptions. Some later dates have high Proof mintages, but likely many of these coins were sold to the jewelry trade (as the Mint was reluctant to release circula-tion strikes to this market sector). Such coins were incorporated into jewelry and no longer exist as collectible coins. *Obverse and Reverse:* PF-60 to 62 coins have extensive hairlines and may have nicks and contact marks. At PF-63, hairlines are prominent, but the mirror sur-face is very reflective. PF-64 coins have fewer hairlines. At PF-65, hairlines should be minimal and mostly seen only under magnification. There should be no nicks or marks. PF-66 and higher coins have no marks or hairlines visible to the unaided eye.

Proof Indian Princess Head, Large Head, Gold Dollar
Shown 2x actual size.

	Mintage	Cert	Avg	PF-60	PF-63	PF-64	PF-65	Recent Auction Record
1856, Slant 5	unknown	5	65.8	$15,000	$27,500	$35,000	$65,000	$86,250, PF-66UCam Star, Jan-10
1857	unknown	6	64.8	8,500	15,000	20,000	40,000	$16,100, PF-63Cam, Jun-08
1858	unknown	14	64.4	6,500	12,000	15,000	30,000	$92,000, PF-67UCam, Nov-09
1859	80	13	64.7	5,500	8,500	10,000	17,500	$6,325, PF-63Cam, Mar-10
1860	154	16	64.4	3,750	7,500	10,000	15,000	$5,463, PF-63Cam, Jul-10
1861	349	14	64.9	3,750	6,750	8,500	13,500	$23,000, PF-66 CAC, Jan-10
1862	35	16	64.8	3,750	6,750	8,500	15,000	$7,475, PF-63UCam, Apr-08
1863	50	19	64.7	4,250	7,500	9,000	17,500	$20,700, PF-65DCam, Mar-08
1864	50	15	64.3	4,250	8,000	10,000	15,000	$17,394, PF-65Cam Star, Apr-09
1865	25	14	65.2	4,750	8,500	11,500	16,500	$14,950, PF-65, Sep-05
1866	30	23	65.3	4,750	8,500	11,500	16,500	$19,550, PF-66Cam, Jan-07
1867	50	12	63.5	3,750	7,000	10,000	15,000	$14,950, PF-64DCam, Aug-07
1868	25	10	64.4	4,000	7,500	10,000	17,500	$7,475, PF-63Cam, Mar-09
1869	25	13	64.1	4,250	7,500	11,500	17,500	$10,350, PF-64Cam, Feb-09
1870	35	11	62.5	3,750	7,250	10,000	15,000	$6,325, PF-63, Mar-09
1871	30	5	65.6	3,750	7,250	10,000	15,000	
1872	30	17	64.6	4,250	7,500	11,500	17,500	$17,250, PF-66UCam, Apr-09
1873, Close 3	25	6	63.0	7,750	15,000	22,500	32,500	$16,100, PF-64, May-08
1874	20	7	64.3	5,250	10,000	15,000	20,000	$16,100, PF-65, Feb-09
1875	20	12	64.1	12,500	18,500	27,500	37,500	$40,250, PF-66 Star, Oct-08
1876	45	17	64.6	3,750	6,000	11,000	15,000	$4,312, PF-63, Sep-06
1877	20	17	64.6	4,250	7,000	11,000	15,000	$17,250, PF-65UCam, Jan-08
1878	20	15	64.3	3,750	6,500	11,000	15,000	$26,450, PF-66DCam, Jan-06
1879	30	9	64.3	3,750	5,750	10,500	15,000	$7,188, PF-64, Feb-09
1880	36	29	64.2	3,750	5,500	10,500	15,000	$7,763, PF-64DCam, Mar-08
1881	87	29	64.5	3,750	5,500	8,500	13,500	$9,200, PF-65Cam , Jun-10
1882	125	39	65.1	3,500	5,500	8,500	13,500	$27,600, PF-67UCam, Nov-09
1883	207	43	64.9	3,250	5,500	8,000	13,000	$17,250, PF-67Cam, Oct-09
1884	1,006	67	65.2	3,250	5,500	7,500	12,500	$4,025, PF-63, Mar-10
1885	1,105	124	64.8	3,250	5,500	7,500	12,500	$5,750, PF-64 CAC, Jun-09
1886	1,016	79	64.4	3,250	5,500	7,500	12,500	$4,313, PF-63, Mar-10
1887	1,043	61	64.6	3,250	5,500	7,500	12,500	$11,500, PF-66 CAC, Apr-10
1888	1,079	96	64.5	3,250	5,000	7,000	11,500	$7,763, PF-64DCam, Feb-10
1889	1,779	34	64.2	3,250	5,000	7,000	11,500	$9,775, PF-66, May-09

An Overview of
Gold Quarter Eagles

The quarter eagle, denominated at $2.50, was authorized by the Act of April 2, 1792.

Early types in the series range from rare to very rare. The first, the 1796 without stars on the obverse, Heraldic Eagle motif on the reverse, is a classic, one of the most desired of all pieces needed for a type set, and accordingly expensive. Most examples are in such grades as EF and AU.

Quarter eagles with stars on the obverse and with the Heraldic Eagle reverse were produced from 1796 intermittently through 1807. Today they exist in modest numbers, particularly in grades such as EF and AU, but on an absolute basis are fairly rare.

The stand-alone 1808 Capped Bust type, by John Reich, of which only 2,710 were minted, is the rarest single type coin in the entire American copper, nickel, silver, and gold series, possibly excepting the 1839 Gobrecht dollar (in a different category, as Proof restrikes were made). Examples of the 1808 can be found in various grades from VF through AU, and only rarely higher.

The next style of quarter eagle, from 1821 through 1827, is scarce, but when seen is usually in grades such as EF, AU, or even the low levels of Mint State. The same can be said for the modified quarter eagle of 1829 through early 1834.

Finally, with the advent of the Classic Head in late 1834, continuing through 1839, quarter eagles become more readily available. Specimens can be found in nearly any grade from VF into the lower levels of Mint State. Then come the Liberty Head quarter eagles, minted continuously from 1840 through 1907, in sufficient numbers and for such a long time that it is not difficult to obtain a specimen, with choice and gem Mint State coins being plentiful for the dates of the early 20th century.

The last quarter eagles are of the Indian Head type, minted from 1908 through 1929. These pieces are plentiful today, but grading can be difficult, as the highest part on the coin is the *field,* and this area was immediately subject to contact marks and wear. Although many opportunities exist in the marketplace, a collector should approach a purchase with care, seeking an example that has frosty, lustrous fields.

For the Collector and Investor: Gold Quarter Eagles as a Specialty

Collecting quarter eagles by dates, mintmarks, and major varieties is a very appealing pursuit. Although many are scarce and rare—this description applies to any variety from 1796 through early 1834—none are truly impossible to obtain. Among the Classic Head issues of 1834–1839, branch-mint coins are especially scarce in higher grades.

Liberty Head quarter eagles, produced continuously from 1840 through 1907, include a number of key issues, such as the famous 1854-S (usually seen in well-circulated grades), the Proof-only 1863 (of which only 30 were struck), and a number of elusive mintmarks. Of particular interest is the 1848 coin with CAL. counterstamped on the reverse, signifying that the coin was made from gold bullion brought in a special shipment from California.

Recommended Reading

Akers, David W. *Gold Dollars (and Other Gold Denominations),* Englewood, OH, 1975–1982.

Bowers, Q. David. *United States Gold Coins: An Illustrated History,* Wolfeboro, NH, 1982.

Breen, Walter. *Major Varieties of U.S. Gold Dollars (and Other Gold Denominations),* Chicago, 1964.

Dannreuther, John W., and Bass, Harry W. *Early U.S. Gold Coin Varieties,* Atlanta, GA, 2006.

Fivaz, Bill. *United States Gold Counterfeit Detection Guide,* Atlanta, GA, 2005.

Fivaz, Bill, and Stanton, J.T. *The Cherrypickers' Guide to Rare Die Varieties* (4th ed., vol. II), Atlanta, GA, 2006.

Garrett, Jeff, and Guth, Ron. *Encyclopedia of U.S. Gold Coins, 1795–1933* (2nd ed.), Atlanta, GA, 2008.

CAPPED BUST TO RIGHT
(1796–1807)

Designer Robert Scot; weight 4.37 grams; composition .9167 gold, .0833 silver and copper; approx. diameter 20 mm; reeded edge.

No Stars on Obverse (1796)

Stars on Obverse (1796–1807)
Bass-Dannreuther-1.

History. The first quarter eagles were struck intermittently during the late 1790s and early 1800s, with consistently small mintages. The earliest issues of 1796 lack obverse stars. They likely circulated domestically, rather than being exported in international trade.

Striking and Sharpness. Most have light striking in one area or another. On the obverse, check the hair details and the stars. On the reverse, check the shield, stars, and clouds. Examine the dentils on both sides. Planchet adjustment marks are seen on many coins and are not noted by the certification services. On high-grade coins the luster usually is very attractive. Certain reverse dies of this type were also used to make dimes.

Availability. Most in the marketplace are EF or AU. MS coins are elusive; when seen, they usually are of later dates.

VF-20, 30 (Very Fine). *Obverse:* The higher-relief areas of hair are well worn at VF-20, less so at VF-30. The stars are flat at their centers. *Reverse:* Wear is greater, including on the shield and wing feathers. The star centers are flat. Other areas have lost detail as well. E PLURIBUS UNUM is easy to read.

EF-40, 45 (Extremely Fine). *Obverse:* Wear is evident all over the portrait, with some loss of detail in the hair to the left of Miss Liberty's face. Excellent detail remains in low-relief areas of the hair, such as the front curl and the back of the head. The stars show wear, as do the date and letters. Luster, if present at all, is minimal and in protected areas. *Reverse:* Wear is greater than at AU. The neck lacks feather detail on its highest points. Feathers have lost some detail near the edges of the wings, and some areas of the horizontal lines in the shield may be blended together. Some traces of luster may be seen, less so at EF-40 than at EF-45. Overall, the reverse appears to be in a slightly higher grade than the obverse.

AU-50, 53, 55, 58 (About Uncirculated). *Obverse:* Light wear is seen on the cheek, the hair immediately to the left of the face, and the cap, more so at AU-50 than at 53 or 55. An AU-58 coin has minimal traces of wear. An AU-50 coin has luster in protected areas among the stars and letters, with little in the open fields or on the portrait. At AU-58 most luster is present in the fields, but is worn away on the highest parts of the motifs. The 1796 No Stars type has less luster in any given grade. *Reverse:* Abrasion and contact marks are most noticeable on the upper part of the eagle and the clouds. The eagle's neck, the tips and top of the wings, the clouds, and the tail show noticeable wear, as do other features. Luster ranges from perhaps 40% remaining in protected areas at AU-50 to nearly full mint bloom at AU-58. Often the reverse of this type retains much more luster than does the obverse.

MS-60 to 70 (Mint State). *Obverse:* At MS-60, some abrasion and contact marks are evident, most notice-ably on the hair to the left of Miss Liberty's forehead and on the higher-relief areas of the cap. On the No Stars on Obverse quarter eagles, there is some abrasion in the field—more so than the Stars on Obverse coins, on which the field is more protected. Luster is present, but may be dull or lifeless, and interrupted in patches. At MS-63, contact marks are few, and abrasion is very light. An MS-65 coin has hardly any abrasion, and contact marks are so minute as to require magnification. Luster should be full and rich. Coins grading above MS-65 exist more in theory than in reality for this type—but they do exist, and are defined by having fewer marks as perfection is approached. *Reverse:* Comments apply as for the obverse, except that abrasion and contact marks are most noticeable on the upper part of the eagle and the clouds. The field area is complex; there is not much open space, with stars above the eagle, the arrows and olive branch, and other features. Accordingly, marks are not as noticeable as on the obverse.

1798, Close Date   **1798, Wide Date**

	Mintage	Cert	Avg	%MS	AU-50	AU-55	AU-58	MS-60	MS-62	MS-63	MS-64	Recent Auction Record
1796, No Stars on Obverse (a)	963	38	57.4	32	$115,000	$135,000	$175,000	$245,000	$375,000	$500,000	$1,000,000	$97,750, AU-50, May-10
1796, Stars on Obverse (b)	432	22	59.2	55	95,000	130,000	175,000	225,000	275,000	375,000	600,000	$80,500, AU-53, May-10
1797	427	15	45.7	13	70,000	82,500	100,000	140,000	185,000	235,000	350,000	$103,500, AU-55, Jul-08
1798, All kinds	1,094											
1798, Close Date					30,000	42,500	57,500	70,000	90,000	135,000		$48,875, AU-55, Jul-08
1798, Wide Date					31,000	43,500	57,500	70,000	90,000	135,000		$71,875, MS-62, Jul-09

a. Value in MS-65 is $1,600,000. **b.** Value in in MS-65 is $1,600,000.

1804, 13-Star Reverse   1804, 14-Star Reverse

	Mintage	Cert	Avg	%MS	AU-50	AU-55	AU-58	MS-60	MS-62	MS-63	MS-64	Recent Auction Record
1802, 2 Over 1	3,035	81	57.1	38	$17,500	$19,500	$24,500	$35,000	$45,000	$60,000	$100,000	$19,550, AU-58, Feb-10
1804, 13-Star Reverse	*	3	51.7	0	225,000	325,000	375,000					$322,000, AU-58, Jul-09
1804, 14-Star Reverse	3,327	64	53.3	20	17,500	22,500	25,000	35,000	55,000	100,000		$17,250, AU-53, Apr-09
1805	1,781	53	55.3	32	17,500	22,500	25,000	35,000	55,000			$18,400, AU-50 CAC, Apr-10
1806, 6 Over 4, 8 Stars Left, 5 Right	1,136	25	52.4	32	17,500	22,500	25,000	35,000	55,000	100,000		$4,888, G-4, Jul-10
1806, 6 Over 5, 7 Stars Left, 6 Right	480	15	57.2	47	39,500	57,500	70,000	100,000	145,000	200,000		$37,375, AU-58, Jan-10
1807	6,812	127	55.8	44	16,500	21,500	24,500	35,000	52,500	85,000	145,000 (c)	$24,150, MS-61, Jan-10

* Included in number below. **c.** Value in MS-65 is $300,000.

CAPPED BUST TO LEFT, LARGE SIZE
(1808)

Designer John Reich; weight 4.37 grams; composition .9167 gold, .0833 silver and copper; approx. diameter 20 mm; reeded edge.

History. John Reich's Capped Bust was an adaptation of the design introduced in 1807 on the half dollar. On the quarter eagle it was used for a single year only, with fewer than 3,000 coins struck, making it the rarest of the major gold coin types.

Striking and Sharpness. All examples are lightly struck on one area or another, particularly the stars and rims. The rims are low and sometimes missing or nearly so (on the obverse), causing quar-ter eagles of this type to wear more quickly than otherwise might be the case.

Availability. Examples are rare in any grade. Typical grades are EF and AU. MS coins are rare. Lower grades are rarely seen, as the coins did not circulate to any great extent. Gold coins of this era were not seen in circulation after 1821, so they did not get a chance to acquire significant wear.

VF-20, 30 (Very Fine). *Obverse:* Wear on the portrait has reduced the hair detail, especially to the right of the face and the top of the head, but much can still be seen. *Reverse:* Wear on the eagle is greater than at EF, and details of feathers near the shield and near the top of the wings are weak or missing. All other features show wear, but most are fairly sharp. Generally, Capped Bust gold coins at this grade level lack eye appeal.

EF-40, 45 (Extremely Fine). *Obverse:* More wear than at AU is seen on the portrait, the hair, the cap, and the drapery near the clasp. Luster is likely to be absent on the obverse due to the low rim. *Reverse:* Wear is extensive on the eagle, including the top of the wings, the head, the top of the shield, and the claws. Some traces of luster may be seen in protected areas, less so at EF-40 than at EF-45.

AU-50, 53, 55, 58 (About Uncirculated). *Obverse:* Light wear is seen on the cheek and higher-relief areas of the hair and cap. Friction and scattered marks are in the field, ranging from extensive at AU-50 to minimal at AU-58. The low rim affords little protection to the field of this coin, but the stars in relief help. Luster may be seen in protected areas, minimal at AU-50, but less so at AU-58. At AU-58 the field retains some luster as well. *Reverse:* Abrasion is most noticeable on the eagle's neck and highest area of the wings. The eagle's neck, the top of the wings, the leaves, and the arrowheads show noticeable wear, as do other features. Luster ranges from perhaps 40% remaining in protected areas at AU-50 to nearly full mint bloom at AU-58. Often the reverse of this type retains much more luster than does the obverse, as on this type the motto, eagle, and lettering protect the surrounding flat areas.

MS-60 to 70 (Mint State). *Obverse:* At MS-60, some abrasion and contact marks are seen on the cheek, on the hair below the LIBERTY inscription, and on the highest-relief folds of the cap. Luster is present, but may be dull or lifeless, and interrupted in patches. At MS-63, contact marks are few, and abrasion is very light. Abrasion is even less at MS-64. Quarter eagles of this type are almost, but not quite, non-existent in a combination of high grade and nice eye appeal. *Reverse:* Comments apply as for the obverse, except that abrasion is most noticeable on the eagle's neck and highest area of the wings.

	Mintage	Cert	Avg	%MS	AU-50	AU-55	AU-58	MS-60	MS-62	MS-63	MS-64	Recent Auction Record
1808	2,710	44	54.1	36	$90,000	$105,000	$115,000	$150,000	$235,000	$375,000	$500,000	$83,375, AU-55, Feb-10

CAPPED HEAD TO LEFT
(1821–1834)

Designer John Reich; weight 4.37 grams; composition .9167 gold, .0833 silver and copper; approx. diameter 20 mm (1821–1827), approx. 18.2 mm (1829–1834); reeded edge.

Bass-Dannreuther-1.

History. Quarter eagles dated 1821 through 1827 have a larger diameter and larger letters, dates, and stars than those of 1829 to 1834. The same grading standards apply to both. Gold coins of this type did not circulate in commerce, because their face value was lower than their bullion value. Most wear was due to use as pocket pieces, or minor handling.

Striking and Sharpness. Most are well struck. On the obverse, check the hair details (which on the Large Diameter style can be light in areas) and the stars. On the reverse, check the eagle. On both sides inspect the dentils. Fields are often semi-prooflike on higher grades.

Availability. All are rare. Grades are from EF to MS, with choice examples in the latter category being scarce, and gems being very rare.

EF-40, 45 (Extremely Fine). *Obverse:* More wear than at AU is seen on the portrait, the hair, the cap, and the drapery near the clasp. Luster is likely to be absent on the obverse due to the low rim. *Reverse:* Wear is extensive on the eagle, including the top of the wings, the head, the top of the shield, and the claws. Some traces of luster may be seen in protected areas, less so at EF-40 than at EF-45.

AU-50, 53, 55, 58 (About Uncirculated). *Obverse:* Light wear is seen on the cheek and higher-relief areas of the hair and cap. Friction and scattered marks are in the field, ranging from extensive at AU-50 to minimal at AU-58. The low rim affords little protection to the field of this coin, but the stars in relief help. Luster may be seen in protected areas, minimal at AU-50, but less so at AU-58. At AU-58 the field retains some luster as well. *Reverse:* Abrasion is most noticeable on the eagle's neck and highest area of the wings. The eagle's neck, the top of the wings, the leaves, and the arrowheads show noticeable wear, as do other features. Luster ranges from perhaps 40% remaining in protected areas at AU-50 to nearly full mint bloom at AU-58. Often the reverse of this type retains much more luster than does the obverse, as on this type the motto, eagle, and lettering protect the surrounding flat areas.

MS-60 to 70 (Mint State). *Obverse:* At MS-60, some abrasion and contact marks are seen on the cheek, on the hair below the LIBERTY inscription, and on the highest-relief folds of the cap. Luster is present, but may be dull or lifeless, and interrupted in patches. At MS-63, contact marks are few, and abrasion is very light. Abrasion is even less at MS-64. Quarter eagles of this type are almost, but not quite, non-existent in a combination of high grade and nice eye appeal. *Reverse:* Comments apply as for the obverse, except that abrasion is most noticeable on the eagle's neck and highest area of the wings.

	Mintage	Cert	Avg	%MS	AU-55	AU-58	MS-60	MS-62	MS-63	MS-64	MS-65	Recent Auction Record
1821	6,448	20	57.6	45	$17,500	$23,500	$32,500	$45,000	$75,000	$125,000		$103,500, MS-63, Jan-09
1824, 4 Over 1	2,600	25	56.1	36	18,500	25,000	35,000	45,000	80,000	135,000		$24,150, MS-61, Feb-10
1825	4,434	51	59.0	57	17,500	23,500	32,500	42,500	60,000	85,000		$115,000, MS-66, Jan-10
1826, 6 Over 6	760	7	56.9	0	30,000	35,000	45,000					$40,250, AU-58PL, Jan-10
1827	2,800	28	59.2	71	25,000	32,500	37,500	42,500				$21,850, AU-53 Star, Jul-09
1829	3,403	47	59.7	57	15,000	17,500	22,500	26,500	35,000	45,000	$85,000	$51,750, MS-64, Jul-10
1830	4,540	48	60.2	50	15,000	17,500	22,500	26,500	35,000	45,000	85,000	$29,900, MS-63, Jan-10
1831	4,520	65	60.6	66	15,000	17,500	22,500	26,500	35,000	45,000	85,000	$32,200, MS-64, Jan-10
1832	4,400	41	57.6	46	15,000	17,500	22,500	26,500	35,000	45,000	95,000	$48,875, MS-64, Sep-08
1833	4,160	49	59.8	55	15,000	17,500	22,500	26,500	35,000	45,000	95,000	$14,950, AU-53, Mar-10
1834, With Motto	4,000	9	56.8	22	55,000	65,000	75,000	85,000	115,000			$20,125, AU-55, Sep-97

Proof Capped Head to Left Quarter Eagles

PF-60 to 70 (Proof). Proof Capped Head to Left quarter eagles were made on a limited basis for presentation and for distribution to numismatists. All examples are exceedingly rare today. They usually are encountered only when great collections are dispersed. In the past, some prooflike examples have been auctioned or sold as actual Proofs. *Obverse and Reverse:* PF-60 to 62 coins have extensive hairlines and may have nicks and contact marks. At PF-63, hairlines are prominent, but the mirror surface is very reflective. PF-64 coins have fewer hairlines. At PF-65, hairlines should be minimal and mostly seen only under magnification. There should be no nicks or marks. PF-66 and higher coins should have no marks or hairlines visible to the unaided eye.

Proof Capped Head to Left Quarter Eagle
Shown 1.5x actual size.
Bass-Dannreuther-1.

	Est Mintage	Cert	Avg	PF-60	PF-63	PF-64	PF-65	Recent Auction Record
1821	3–5	2	64.5		$200,000	$250,000		$241,500, PF-64Cam, Jan-07
1824, 4 Over 1	3–5				*(unique, in the Smithsonian's National Numismatic Collection)*			
1825 (a)	unknown							
1826, 6 Over 5 (b)	unknown							
1827 (c)	unknown							
1829	2–4				*(extremely rare; 2–3 known)*			
1830 (d)	unknown							
1831	6–10	3	64.3		100,000	135,000		$74,750, PF-63, Apr-09
1832	2–4				*(unique, in the Bass Foundation Collection)*			
1833	2–4	2	66.5		*(extremely rare; 3–4 known)*			
1834, With Motto	4–8				*(extremely rare; 3–5 known)*			

a. The 1825 quarter eagle might not exist in Proof; see the *Encyclopedia of U.S. Gold Coins, 1795–1933*. **b.** Proofs have been reported, but none have been authenticated. **c.** Proof 1827 quarter eagles almost certainly were made, but none are known to exist. **d.** Examples identified as Proofs are extremely rare, many are impaired, and none have been certified.

CLASSIC HEAD, NO MOTTO ON REVERSE (1834–1839)

Designer William Kneass; weight 4.18 grams; composition .8992 gold, .1008 silver and copper (changed to .900 gold in 1837); diameter 18.2 mm; reeded edge; mints: Philadelphia, Charlotte, Dahlonega, New Orleans.

Breen-6151.

Mintmark is above date.

History. Gold quarter eagles had not circulated at face value in the United States since 1821, as the price of bullion necessitated more than $2.50 worth of gold to produce a single coin. Accordingly, they traded at their bullion value. The Act of June 28, 1834, provided lower weights for gold coins, after which the issues (of new designs to differentiate them from the old) circulated effectively. The Classic Head design by William Kneass is an adaptation of the head created by John Reich for the cent of 1808. The reverse illustrates a perched eagle. The motto E PLURIBUS UNUM, seen on earlier gold coins, no longer is present. These coins circulated widely until mid-1861 (for this reason, many show extensive wear). After that, they were hoarded because of public uncertainty during the Civil War.

Striking and Sharpness. Weakness is often seen on the higher areas of the hair curls. Also check the star centers. On the reverse, check the rims. The dentils usually are well struck.

Availability. Most coins range from VF to AU or lower ranges of MS. Most MS coins are of the first three years. MS-63 to 65 examples are rare. Good eye appeal can be elusive.

VF-20, 30 (Very Fine). *Obverse:* Wear on the portrait has reduced the hair detail, especially to the right of the face and the top of the head, but much can still be seen. *Reverse:* Wear is greater than at EF, including on the shield and wing feathers. Generally, Classic Head gold at this grade level lacks eye appeal.

EF-40, 45 (Extremely Fine). *Obverse:* Wear is seen on the portrait overall, with reduction or elimination of some separation of hair strands, especially in the area close to the face. The cheek shows light wear. Luster is minimal or nonexistent at EF-40, and may survive in among the letters of LIBERTY at EF-45. *Reverse:* Wear is greater than at AU. On most (but not all) coins the eagle's neck lacks some feather detail on its highest points. Feathers have lost some detail near the edges and tips of the wings. Some areas of the horizontal lines in the shield may be blended together. Some traces of luster may be seen, less so at EF-40 than at EF-45.

AU-50, 53, 55, 58 (About Uncirculated). *Obverse:* Friction is seen on the higher parts, particularly the cheek and hair (under magnification) of Miss Liberty. Friction and scattered marks are in the field, ranging from extensive at AU-50 to minimal at AU-58. Luster may be seen in protected areas, minimal at AU-50 but more visible at AU-58. On an AU-58 coin the field retains some luster as well. *Reverse:* Abrasion is most noticeable on the eagle's neck and the highest area of the wings. The eagle's neck, the top of the wings, the leaves, and the arrowheads now show noticeable wear, as do other features. Luster ranges from perhaps 40% remaining in protected areas at AU-50 to nearly full mint bloom at AU-58. Often the reverse of this type retains much more luster than does the obverse.

MS-60 to 70 (Mint State). *Obverse:* At MS-60, some abrasion and contact marks are seen on the portrait, most noticeably on the cheek, as the hair details are complex. Luster is present, but may be dull or lifeless, and interrupted in patches. Many low-level MS coins have grainy surfaces. At MS-63, contact marks are few, and abrasion is very light. Abrasion is even less at MS-64. An MS-65 coin has hardly any abrasion, and contact marks are minute. Luster should be full and rich and is often more intense on the obverse. Grades above MS-65 are defined by having fewer marks as perfection is approached. *Reverse:* Comments apply as for the obverse, except that abrasion is most noticeable on the eagle's neck and the highest area of the wings.

1836, Script 8   **1836, Block 8**

	Mintage	Cert	Avg	%MS	AU-55	AU-58	MS-60	MS-62	MS-63	MS-64	MS-65	Recent Auction Record
1834, No Motto	112,234	913	56.6	34	$2,000	$2,750	$3,750	$5,500	$10,500	$14,500	$45,000	$1,898, AU-58, Jul-10
1835	131,402	283	54.4	32	2,000	2,750	3,750	5,500	12,000	15,000	50,000	$10,350, MS-63 CAC, Apr-10
1836, All kinds	547,986											
1836, Script 8 (a)		390	52.8	23	2,000	2,750	3,750	5,500	10,500	14,500	45,000	$9,200, MS-63, Jul-10
1836, Block 8		357	51.1	20	2,000	2,750	3,750	5,500	10,500	14,500	45,000	$13,800, MS-64, Jul-10
1837	45,080	226	52.6	20	2,750	3,500	5,750	8,500	16,500	25,000	55,000	$25,300, MS-64, Apr-10
1838	47,030	236	53.9	28	2,000	2,750	4,750	6,500	12,500	20,000	47,500	$6,555, MS-62 CAC, Mar-10
1838C	7,880	65	55.8	17	13,000 (b)	16,000	26,500	38,500	50,000	65,000		$7,475, AU-53, Jul-10
1839	27,021	70	51.5	10	3,500	5,500	7,500	13,000	22,500			$489, F-15, Jun-10
1839C	18,140	219	52.9	8	8,500	17,500	27,500	40,000	50,000			$2,645, VF-30, Jul-10
1839D	13,674	107	49.9	14	12,500 (c)	18,500	30,000	40,000	47,500	75,000		$17,825, MS-61, Sep-09
1839O	17,781	318	52.6	20	4,500	6,500	9,500	22,500	27,500	45,000		$3,738, AU-53, Jul-10

Note: So-called 9 Over 8 varieties for Philadelphia, Charlotte, and Denver mints were made from defective punches. **a.** Also known as the "Head of 1835." **b.** Value in EF-40 is $4,000; in AU-50, $10,000. **c.** Value in EF-40 is $4,500; in AU-50, $9,000.

Proof Classic Head, No Motto, Quarter Eagles

PF-60 to 70 (Proof). Proof Classic Head, No Motto, quarter eagles were made in small quantities. Today probably only a couple dozen or so survive, most bearing the 1834 date. *Obverse and Reverse:* PF-60 to 62 coins have extensive hairlines and may have nicks and contact marks. At PF-63, hairlines are prominent, but the mirror surface is very reflective. PF-64 coins have fewer hairlines. At PF-65, hairlines should be minimal and mostly seen only under magnification. There should be no nicks or marks. PF-66 and higher coins should have no marks or hairlines visible to the unaided eye.

Proof Classic Head, No Motto, Quarter Eagle
Shown 1.5x actual size.

	Est Mintage	Cert	Avg	PF-60	PF-63	PF-64	PF-65	Recent Auction Record
1834, No Motto	15–25	8	64.3	$35,000	$100,000	$135,000	$225,000	
1835	5–8	1	65.0	35,000	100,000	135,000	250,000	
1836	5–8	7	65.1	30,000	115,000	150,000	250,000	$253,000, PF-66UCam, Jan-07
1837	3–5 (a)			32,500	125,000	175,000	275,000	
1838	2–4			(unique, in the Bass Foundation Collection)				
1839	4–6 (b)	2	62.0	(extremely rare)				$136,679, PF-62, Aug-06

a. Two Proofs of 1837 are known; one is in the Smithsonian's National Numismatic Collection. A third example has been rumored, but its existence is not verified. **b.** Three 1839 Proofs are reported to exist; only two are presently accounted for.

LIBERTY HEAD
(1840–1907)

Designer Christian Gobrecht; weight 4.18 grams; composition .900 gold, .100 copper (net weight .12094 oz. pure gold); diameter 18 mm; reeded edge; mints: Philadelphia, Charlotte, Dahlonega, New Orleans, San Francisco.

Mintmark is above denomination.

History. The Liberty Head quarter eagle debuted in 1840 and was a workhorse of American commerce for decades, being minted until 1907. Christian Gobrecht's design closely follows those used on half eagles and eagles of the same era.

In 1848, about 230 ounces of gold were sent to Secretary of War Marcy by Colonel R.B. Mason, military governor of California. The gold was turned over to the Mint and made into quarter eagles. The distinguishing mark CAL. was punched above the eagle on the reverse of these coins, while they were in the die. Several specimens with prooflike surfaces are known.

A modified reverse design (with smaller letters and arrowheads) was used on Philadelphia quarter eagles from 1859 through 1907. A few Philadelphia Mint pieces were made in 1859, 1860, and 1861 with the old Large Letters reverse design.

Striking and Sharpness. On the obverse, check the highest points of the hair, and the star centers. On the reverse, check the eagle's neck, and the area to the lower left of the shield and the lower part of the eagle. Examine the dentils on both sides. Branch-mint coins struck before the Civil War often are lightly struck in areas and have weak dentils. Often, a certified EF coin from the Dahlonega or Charlotte mints will not appear any sharper than a VF coin from Philadelphia. There are exceptions, and some C and D coins are sharp. The careful study of photographs is useful in acquainting you with the peculiarities of a given date or mint. Most quarter eagles from the 1880s to 1907 are sharp in all areas. Tiny copper staining spots can be a problem.

Availability. Early dates and mintmarks are generally scarce to rare in MS and very rare in MS-63 to 65 or finer, with only a few exceptions. Coins of Charlotte and Dahlonega (all of which are especially avidly collected) are usually EF or AU, or overgraded low MS. Rarities for the type include 1841, 1854-S, and 1875. Coins of the 1860s onward generally are seen with sharper striking and in higher average grades. Typically, San Francisco quarter eagles are in lower average grades than are those from the Philadelphia Mint, as Philadelphia coins did not circulate at par in the East and Midwest from late December 1861 until December 1878, and thus did not acquire as much wear. MS coins are readily available for the early-1900s years, and usually have outstanding eye appeal.

VF-20, 30 (Very Fine). *Obverse:* The higher-relief areas of hair are worn flat at VF-20, less so at VF-30. The hair to the right of the coronet is merged into heavy strands. The stars are flat at their centers. *Reverse:* Much of the eagle is flat, with less than 50% of the feather detail remaining. The vertical shield stripes, being deeply recessed, remain bold.

EF-40, 45 (Extremely Fine). *Obverse:* Wear is evident on all high areas of the portrait, including the hair to the right of the forehead, the tip of the coronet, and the hair bun. The stars show light wear at their centers. Luster, if present at all, is minimal and in protected areas such as between the star points. *Reverse:* Wear is greater than at AU. The neck of the eagle is nearly smooth, much detail is lost on the right wing, and there is flatness at the lower left of the shield, on the leaves, and on the arrowheads. Some traces of luster may be seen, less so at EF-40 than at EF-45. Overall, the reverse appears to be in a slightly higher grade than the obverse.

AU-50, 53, 55, 58 (About Uncirculated). *Obverse:* Light wear is seen on the face, the hair to the right of the face, and the highest area of the hair bun, more so at AU-50 than at 53 or 55. An AU-58 coin has minimal traces of wear. An AU-50 coin has luster in protected areas among the stars and letters, with little in the open fields or on the portrait. At AU-58, most luster is present in the fields, but is worn away on the highest parts of the motifs. *Reverse:* Abrasion and contact marks are most noticeable on the eagle's neck and to the lower left of the shield. The eagle shows wear in all of the higher areas, as well as the leaves and arrowheads. Luster ranges from perhaps 40% remaining in protected areas at AU-50 to nearly full mint bloom at AU-58.

Often the reverse of this type retains more luster than the obverse.

MS-60 to 70 (Mint State). *Obverse:* At MS-60, some abrasion and contact marks are evident, most noticeably on the hair to the right of Miss Liberty's forehead, and on the jaw. Luster is present, but may be dull or lifeless, and interrupted in patches. At MS-63, contact marks are few, and abrasion is very light. An MS-65 coin has hardly any abrasion, and contact marks are so minute as to require magnification. Luster should be full and rich. Grades above MS-65 usually are found late in the series and are defined by having fewer marks as perfection is approached. *Reverse:* Comments apply as for the obverse, except that abrasion and contact marks are most noticeable on the eagle's neck and to the lower left of the shield.

| 1843-C, Small Date, Crosslet 4 | 1843-C, Large Date, Plain 4 | 1843-O, Small Date, Crosslet 4 | 1843-O, Large Date, Plain 4 |

	Mintage	Cert	Avg	%MS	EF-40	AU-50	AU-55	AU-58	MS-60	MS-62	MS-63	Recent Auction Record
1840	18,859	93	49.7	17	$900	$2,750	$3,750	$4,500	$6,750	$8,500	$12,500 (a)	$575, VF-35, Apr-10
1840C	12,822	133	51.2	11	2,200	4,750	6,750	8,000	11,500	23,000	32,500	$3,220, AU-55, Jun-10
1840D	3,532	39	47.7	5	8,500	12,500	20,000	25,000	35,000	75,000		$8,050, AU-50, Mar-10
1840O	33,580	108	52.8	15	950	2,000	2,750	5,000	10,000	20,000	27,500	$920, EF-45, Apr-10
1841	unknown				100,000	125,000	145,000	155,000				
1841C	10,281	103	51.3	6	2,200	3,500	6,000	10,000	16,000	25,000		$5,750, AU-58, Jun-10
1841D	4,164	56	46.4	5	4,500	9,000	12,500	15,000	27,500	45,000	55,000	$48,875, MS-63, Mar-10
1842	2,823	23	49.4	4	2,750	6,500	12,000	15,000	22,500	35,000		$2,760, VF-30, May-08
1842C	6,729	53	47.5	6	3,250	7,500	10,500	15,000	23,500	35,000		$6,038, AU-55, Mar-10
1842D	4,643	62	47.6	8	4,500	10,000	16,000	20,000	32,500	55,000		$32,775, MS-61, Mar-10
1842O	19,800	131	47.9	11	1,400	2,500	4,500	7,500	13,000	15,000	27,500	$1,840, AU-53, Jun-10
1843	100,546	177	54.6	11	485	850	1,200	1,550	2,750	5,000	6,750 (b)	$1,093, AU-50, Mar-10
1843C, Small Date, Crosslet 4	2,988	61	51.5	10	5,250	8,000	11,000	15,000	27,500	50,000		$3,220, MS-62, Jul-10
1843C, Large Date, Plain 4	23,076	196	47.2	9	2,000	3,250	5,500	6,500	8,500	15,000	21,500	$4,313, AU-58, Jun-10
1843D, Small Date, Crosslet 4	36,209	251	50.1	8	2,100	3,250	4,500	6,000	9,000	20,000	30,000	$7,475, MS-61, Apr-10
1843O, Small Date, Crosslet 4	288,002	388	53.8	20	385	575	800	1,150	2,250	3,250	8,500	$435, AU-53 CAC, Apr-10
1843O, Large Date, Plain 4	76,000	109	52.6	11	800	1,750	3,000	4,250	7,000	12,500	20,000	$863, AU-50, Oct-09
1844	6,784	61	52.8	7	850	2,000	3,500	4,500	7,500	12,500		$1,725, AU-53, Aug-08
1844C	11,622	103	47.9	11	2,400	6,000	9,000	12,000	17,500	27,500	40,000	$3,450, EF-40, Jul-10
1844D	17,332	147	52.4	14	2,400	3,000	4,250	5,500	8,000	15,000	25,000	$2,943, AU-55, Apr-10
1845	91,051	226	55.7	31	385	550	725	850	1,400	2,250	5,500 (c)	$1,093, MS-60, Jul-10
1845D	19,460	141	50.8	5	2,450	3,500	5,000	7,000	13,500	20,000	35,000	$63,250, MS-64, Mar-10
1845O	4,000	55	49.5	4	2,500	6,250	8,500	11,500	21,500	32,500	52,500	$7,188, AU-53, Jul-10
1846	21,598	121	55.3	15	710	1,300	1,850	2,750	5,750	15,000	23,500	$10,925, MS-62, Mar-10
1846C	4,808	59	49.1	10	2,750	8,000	11,000	12,500	18,500	25,000	37,500	$1,610, VF-25, Oct-09
1846D	19,303	177	51.6	8	2,500	3,250	5,500	7,500	11,000	13,500	28,500	$2,185, EF-45, Mar-10
1846D, D Over D	*	1	55.0	0	2,750	3,750	6,500	9,000	15,000			$6,613, AU-58, Apr-09
1846O	62,000	257	50.7	9	585	1,250	2,000	3,500	6,500	12,500	19,500	$863, EF-45, Jul-10
1847	29,814	123	54.2	17	435	900	1,400	2,000	3,750	5,500	9,500	$4,600, MS-62 CAC, Apr-10
1847C	23,226	212	51.5	15	2,450	3,000	4,000	5,000	6,500	8,000	15,000	$3,220, AU-58, May-10
1847D	15,784	145	51.4	13	2,500	3,000	4,500	5,500	10,000	13,500	24,500	$2,300, AU-50, Apr-10
1847O	124,000	290	48.9	10	510	1,050	2,000	2,750	4,000	9,500	15,000	$978, AU-53, Jun-10

* Included in number above. **a.** Value in MS-64 is $20,000. **b.** Value in MS-64 is $13,500. **c.** Value in MS-64 is $8,500.

1848, CAL. Above Eagle

1862, 2 Over 1

1873, Close 3

1873, Open 3

1891, Doubled-Die Reverse
FS-G2.5-1891-801.

Old Reverse (Pre-1859)

New Reverse

Shown 1.5x actual size.

	Mintage	Cert	Avg	%MS	AU-55	AU-58	MS-60	MS-62	MS-63	MS-64	MS-65	Recent Auction Record
1848	6,500	58	54.8	33	$2,750	$3,500	$5,500	$8,500	$16,000	$25,000		$2,175, AU-50, Mar-10
1848, CAL. Above Eagle	1,389	51	56.6	41	57,500	80,000	100,000	115,000	135,000	150,000	200,000	$27,600, VF-30, Jul-09
1848C	16,788	147	49.6	10	4,750	7,500	12,500	20,000				$4,152, AU-58, Mar-10
1848D	13,771	160	53.7	15	4,750	6,000	10,000	15,000	28,500			$2,875, AU-50, Apr-10
1849	23,294	135	55.2	15	1,350	2,000	2,500	4,500	8,000	14,000		$2,530, MS-61, Jul-10
1849C	10,220	85	50.7	11	7,500	10,000	20,000	45,000	65,000			$103,500, MS-65, Mar-10
1849D	10,945	141	53.5	9	5,500	8,500	15,000	25,000				$1,610, VF-20, Jun-10

Chart continued on next page.

	Mintage	Cert	Avg	%MS	AU-55	AU-58	MS-60	MS-62	MS-63	MS-64	MS-65	Recent Auction Record
1850	252,923	360	56.7	29	$560	$650	$1,250	$2,000	$3,500	$7,500		$2,875, MS-63, Jul-10
1850C	9,148	123	50.2	18	5,500	8,000	15,000	25,000	35,000			$2,530, EF-45 CAC, Mar-10
1850D	12,148	141	52.3	11	5,500	8,500	14,000	30,000	50,000			$4,888, AU-58, Apr-10
1850O	84,000	289	50.7	4	1,800	2,500	4,500	6,500	15,000			$1,725, AU-58, Jul-10
1851	1,372,748	643	59.5	61	375	410	560	1,100	1,725	2,500	$5,500	$299, AU-58, Jun-10
1851C	14,923	98	50.6	16	5,000	7,500	13,000	25,000	35,000			$7,475, MS-61, Jan-10
1851D	11,264	75	50.4	5	5,500	7,000	11,000	15,000	32,500	45,000		$3,335, AU-53, Mar-10
1851O	148,000	399	53.7	12	2,250	2,750	4,750	8,500	13,500	25,000		$633, AU-53, Jul-10
1852	1,159,681	786	60.1	65	375	385	560	950	1,725	2,500	5,500	$532, MS-62, Jul-10
1852C	9,772	90	52.6	13	6,500	10,000	16,000	25,000	35,000			$3,738, AU-55, Mar-10
1852D	4,078	57	53.2	11	8,500	10,000	17,500	35,000	45,000	65,000		$5,175, AU-55, Apr-10
1852O	140,000	419	52.8	7	1,500	2,500	5,250	8,500	13,500			$1,495, AU-58, Apr-10
1853	1,404,668	1,100	60.2	65	375	410	560	1,100	1,725	2,500	5,500	$518, MS-61, Jul-10
1853D	3,178	39	51.4	18	7,000	9,500	16,500	32,500				$6,325, AU-58, Jun-10
1854	596,258	513	59.7	58	375	410	560	1,100	1,900	2,750	6,500	$322, AU-58, Jul-10
1854C	7,295	91	53.5	21	7,000	9,500	15,000	22,500	37,500			$5,175, AU-58, Mar-10
1854D	1,760	20	49.8	20	16,500	20,000	30,000	40,000	75,000			$63,250, MS-63, Mar-10
1854O	153,000	458	53.9	12	710	900	1,750	4,500	9,000	15,000		$633, AU-58, Jul-10
1854S	246	8	32.8	0	400,000 (a)							$253,000, VF-35, Jul-09
1855	235,480	323	59.8	60	375	410	560	1,100	1,950	3,500	7,000	$1,150, MS-63, Apr-10
1855C	3,677	72	53.8	21	10,000	13,500	25,000	30,000	45,000			$4,313, AU-53, Mar-10
1855D	1,123	24	53.1	13	23,500	30,000	55,000					$6,325, EF-45, Mar-10
1856	384,240	487	59.7	59	375	385	560	1,050	2,000	3,500	6,500	$299, AU-53, Jun-10
1856C	7,913	87	52.2	16	7,000	8,500	14,000	22,500	35,000			$4,313, AU-55, Apr-10
1856D	874	16	52.6	31	35,000	40,000	75,000					$71,875, MS-61, Apr-06
1856O	21,100	138	53.5	10	2,000	3,000	7,500	20,000				$633, VF-25, Jun-10
1856S	72,120	179	52.6	16	1,500	2,250	4,500	8,000	12,500	16,000	27,500	$1,725, AU-55, Mar-10
1857	214,130	357	59.8	58	365	385	560	1,050	1,950	3,500	7,000	$633, MS-62, Apr-10
1857D	2,364	55	56.6	27	6,000	8,500	13,500	22,000	32,500			$21,850, MS-62, Mar-10
1857O	34,000	251	55.2	20	1,800	2,500	4,500	7,500	14,000	20,000		$2,070, AU-58, Jul-10
1857S	69,200	162	52.4	12	1,800	3,000	6,000	8,500	13,500	25,000		$748, AU-50, Apr-10
1858	47,377	178	58.3	36	560	800	1,400	1,850	3,500	6,000	12,000	$518, AU-58, Jul-10
1858C	9,056	122	54.2	30	4,750	6,000	9,500	15,000	32,500			$3,738, AU-58, Apr-10
1859, Old Reverse	39,364	107	58.0	34	1,300	1,600	3,500	5,500	9,500	13,500		$834, AU-58, Jan-10
1859, New Reverse	*	31	58.2	23	760	950	1,350	2,000	3,500	7,500	11,000	$526, AU-55, Jul-09
1859D	2,244	92	54.5	11	8,500	10,000	22,000	38,000				$3,220, AU-50, Mar-10
1859S	15,200	104	51.0	10	3,500	4,000	7,500	10,000	17,500			$8,050, MS-62, Mar-10
1860, Old Reverse	22,563	22	57.8	36	5,000	6,000	9,000	12,000	16,000			$2,990, AU-55, Aug-09
1860, New Reverse	*	29	58.9	48	610	650	1,100	1,600	2,750			$920, MS-61, Jun-10
1860C	7,469	122	51.1	8	7,000	10,000	21,000	26,000	40,000			$5,463, AU-58, Mar-10
1860S	35,600	114	48.9	11	1,850	2,250	3,750	7,000	15,000			$604, EF-45, Jul-10
1861, Old Reverse	1,283,788	89	58.8	44	2,500	3,000	4,750	7,500	10,000			$805, VF-35, Jul-10
1861, New Reverse	*	767	59.9	60	365	385	710	1,300	1,950			$2,185, MS-64, Jul-10
1861S	24,000	83	46.9	7	4,750	5,750	8,000	13,000				$6,325, AU-55, Mar-10
1862, 2 Over 1	**	50	55.2	20	4,750	5,750	9,000	12,500				$920, VF-25, Jun-10
1862	98,508	168	56.5	32	785	900	1,800	3,500	7,000	9,500		$3,335, AU-58, Jun-10
1862S	8,000	52	46.1	4	6,500	8,500	17,500	24,000				$6,325, AU-53, Jun-10
1863S	10,800	76	45.2	8	6,500	8,500	15,000	20,000	32,500			$4,888, AU-55, Jul-10
1864	2,824	7	52.4	29	35,000	40,000	50,000					$32,200, AU-53, Jul-09
1865	1,520	14	53.1	0	28,000	32,000	40,000	45,000	55,000			$18,400, AU-50, Jul-10
1865S	23,376	78	45.3	6	2,250	2,750	5,000	7,500	12,500			$1,955, AU-58, Jul-09
1866	3,080	32	51.3	19	8,500	10,500	15,000	20,000	26,000	32,500		$14,950, MS-62, Mar-10
1866S	38,960	169	46.8	4	3,250	4,000	7,500	12,000	20,000			$431, VF-35, Jul-10
1867	3,200	28	54.0	21	2,000	2,500	4,500	5,500	8,700	13,500	25,000	$1,955, AU-58, Mar-09
1867S	28,000	148	47.2	7	1,850	2,250	4,500	6,000	12,500	15,000		$403, EF-40, Mar-10
1868	3,600	137	56.9	19	935	1,150	2,500	4,500	8,000	12,000		$978, AU-58, Feb-10
1868S	34,000	216	51.9	10	1,500	2,000	4,500	6,500	11,000	16,000		$2,990, MS-61, Apr-10
1869	4,320	128	56.5	19	1,200	1,450	3,000	5,000	9,000			$4,600, MS-62, Mar-10

* Included in number above. ** Included in number below. **a.** Value in VF-20 is $175,000; in EF-40, $275,000; in AU-50, $375,000.

	Mintage	Cert	Avg	%MS	AU-55	AU-58	MS-60	MS-62	MS-63	MS-64	MS-65	Recent Auction Record
1869S	29,500	194	51.1	8	$1,600	$2,000	$4,250	$6,000	$10,000	$13,000		$403, EF-40, May-10
1870	4,520	81	56.7	19	1,200	1,500	3,250	5,500	8,500			$863, AU-55, Jan-10
1870S	16,000	116	49.4	10	1,600	2,250	4,750	6,500	14,000	17,500		$1,610, AU-58, Jul-10
1871	5,320	118	56.3	21	1,000	1,200	2,250	2,750	4,250	8,000		$460, EF-45, Oct-09
1871S	22,000	192	53.1	15	1,000	1,200	2,250	3,000	4,750	9,000	$17,500	$900, AU-58, Jul-10
1872	3,000	66	55.8	18	2,100	2,800	5,000	9,000	15,000	25,000		$2,300, AU-58, Jun-10
1872S	18,000	171	50.6	9	1,500	2,000	4,500	6,000	11,500	15,000		$6,325, MS-62, Jul-10
1873, Close 3	55,200	485	60.0	64	410	485	750	1,100	1,950	2,750	6,000	$431, MS-61, Jul-10
1873, Open 3	122,800	369	61.0	79	365	375	485	900	1,225	1,375	4,000	$1,150, MS-64, Apr-10
1873S	27,000	245	50.0	11	1,400	1,550	2,500	4,000	7,750	14,000		$748, AU-53, Apr-10
1874	3,920	120	57.0	25	1,050	1,200	2,100	4,500	6,750	9,500	25,000	$891, AU-58, Jan-10
1875	400	23	56.4	9	14,000	19,500	25,000	30,000	38,500			$10,925, AU-55, Jan-10
1875S	11,600	163	54.5	17	1,150	2,000	4,000	5,000	8,000	12,000		$1,265, AU-58, Mar-10
1876	4,176	113	53.6	13	1,800	2,250	3,250	4,000	6,500	12,000		$460, EF-40, Feb-10
1876S	5,000	137	54.3	19	1,600	2,000	3,500	4,500	8,500			$1,610, AU-58, Mar-10
1877	1,632	99	56.6	28	1,300	1,500	3,000	3,500	8,750	15,000		$1,725, AU-58, Apr-10
1877S	35,400	323	58.8	47	385	435	825	1,700	2,600	4,000	9,000	$345, AU-58, Jun-10
1878	286,240	1,790	61.0	77	365	375	535	900	1,225	1,325	2,600	$328, AU-55, Jun-10
1878S	178,000	529	59.6	59	365	375	635	1,050	2,050	3,500	12,000	$1,265, MS-63, Jul-10
1879	88,960	734	61.1	79	365	375	535	900	1,375	1,625	3,500	$489, MS-62, Mar-10
1879S	43,500	182	53.8	9	1,050	1,200	1,750	3,500	5,000	7,500		$633, AU-58, Jul-10
1880	2,960	126	58.9	49	900	1,100	1,550	2,000	3,750	6,000	12,500	$501, AU-55, Mar-10
1881	640	70	56.5	26	6,000	7,500	10,000	15,000	25,000	30,000		$5,463, AU-58, Feb-10
1882	4,000	160	59.8	56	750	800	1,000	1,700	3,000	4,000	9,000	$1,495, MS-62 CAC, Jun-10
1883	1,920	70	58.2	40	925	1,300	1,550	2,350	4,500	6,750	9,000	$3,450, MS-61, Jan-10
1884	1,950	103	60.1	62	800	900	1,150	1,900	2,400	3,500	5,000	$1,380, MS-60, Mar-10
1885	800	48	58.5	44	3,000	3,250	4,000	5,000	6,000	8,500	10,000	$4,773, MS-61, Jul-10
1886	4,000	125	59.8	55	610	800	1,000	1,450	2,025	3,000	6,000	$2,990, MS-63, Mar-10
1887	6,160	169	60.0	66	460	560	800	1,250	1,725	2,750	5,000	$21,850, MS-66, Jun-10
1888	16,001	378	61.9	89	385	410	550	850	1,150	1,475	2,250	$4,888, MS-65, Jun-10
1889	17,600	335	61.6	89	365	375	485	825	1,125	1,425	2,150	$1,323, MS-64, Jul-10
1890	8,720	187	60.9	71	385	415	550	900	1,125	1,475	2,750	$1,323, MS-63, Jun-10
1891	10,960	260	61.1	77	375	400	520	800	1,150	1,525	2,500	$8,338, MS-66, Jul-10
1891, Doubled-Die Reverse	*				410	450	650	900	1,225	1,775	3,000	$389, AU-55, Feb-10
1892	2,440	127	61.2	81	535	560	800	1,200	1,725	2,400	4,500	$604, MS-62, Jul-10
1893	30,000	737	62.2	90	365	375	485	800	1,100	1,275	2,050	$8,050, MS-67, Jul-10
1894	4,000	195	62.0	88	460	500	625	1,050	1,475	1,875	4,500	$2,760, MS-64, Mar-10
1895	6,000	238	62.6	92	365	390	500	800	1,225	1,425	2,100	$3,738, MS-65 CAC, Jun-10
1896	19,070	601	62.7	94	365	375	485	800	1,075	1,325	2,050	$3,335, MS-66, Jun-10
1897	29,768	861	62.8	95	365	375	485	775	1,075	1,175	2,050	$4,888, MS-67, Apr-10
1898	24,000	670	63.3	97	365	375	485	775	1,075	1,175	2,050	$1,975, MS-65, Jul-10
1899	27,200	696	62.9	98	365	375	485	775	1,075	1,175	2,050	$7,763, MS-67, Mar-10
1900	67,000	1,658	63.1	96	365	375	485	775	1,075	1,175	2,050	$1,610, MS-65, Jun-10
1901	91,100	1,962	63.0	96	365	375	485	775	1,075	1,175	2,050	$4,600, MS-66+ CAC, Jun-10
1902	133,540	2,809	63.0	97	365	375	485	775	1,075	1,175	2,050	$719, MS-63, Jul-10
1903	201,060	4,949	63.1	96	365	375	485	775	1,075	1,175	2,050	$2,070, MS-66, Jun-10
1904	160,790	3,681	63.0	96	365	375	485	775	1,075	1,175	2,050	$4,313, MS-67, Jul-10
1905 (b)	217,800	5,226	63.1	96	365	375	485	775	1,075	1,175	2,050	$518, MS-62, Jul-10
1906	176,330	4,419	63.0	96	365	375	485	775	1,075	1,175	2,050	$403, AU-55, Jul-10
1907	336,294	7,300	63.1	97	365	375	485	775	1,075	1,175	2,050	$5,319, MS-67, Jul-10

* Included in number above. **b.** Pieces dated 1905-S are counterfeit.

Proof Liberty Head Quarter Eagles

PF-60 to 70 (Proof). Proof Liberty Head quarter eagles exist in relation to their original mintages, with all issues prior to the 1890s being rare. Cameo contrast is the rule for Proofs prior to 1902. Beginning that year the portrait was polished in the die, although a few years later cameo-contrast coins were again made. *Obverse and Reverse:* PF-60 to 62 coins have extensive hairlines and

Continued on next page.

may have nicks and contact marks. At PF-63, hairlines are prominent, but the mirror surface is very reflective. PF-64 coins have fewer hairlines. At PF-65, hairlines should be minimal and mostly seen only under magnification. There should be no nicks or marks. PF-66 and higher coins should have no marks or hairlines visible to the unaided eye.

Proof Liberty Head Quarter Eagle
Shown 1.5x actual size.

	Mintage	Cert	Avg	PF-60	PF-63	PF-64	PF-65	Recent Auction Record
1840	3–6			(extremely rare; 3 known)				
1841	15–20	5	57.0	$150,000				$132,250, PF-58, Jul-09
1842	2–3			(unique, in the Smithsonian's National Numismatic Collection)				
1843	4–8	5	64.2	(extremely rare; 5–6 known)				
1844	3–6	1	66.0	(extremely rare; 4–5 known)				
1845	4–8	2	67.0	(extremely rare; 4–5 known)				
1846	4–8	1	64.0	(extremely rare; 4–5 known)				
1847	2–3			(unique, in the Smithsonian's National Numismatic Collection)				
1848	3–6			(extremely rare; 3–4 known)				$96,600, PF-64, Jan-08
1850	2–4			(extremely rare; 1–2 known)				$41,250, PF-62, Jun-95
1854	2–4			(unique, in the Bass Foundation Collection)				
1856	6–8			$37,500	65,000	$85,000	$125,000	
1857	6–8			35,000	55,000	75,000	125,000	
1858	6–8	3	65.0	25,000	45,000	65,000	115,000	$103,500, PF-66Cam, Aug-07
1859 (a)	80	7	65.0	15,000	27,500	45,000	75,000	$80,500, PF-66, Jul-05
1860 (b)	112	10	63.9	14,000	22,500	30,000	40,000	$11,550, PF-64Cam, Oct-93
1861 (c)	90	3	65.3	12,000	20,000	27,500	40,000	$44,850, PF-65DCam, Sep-05
1862	35	11	64.7	12,000	19,000	27,500	40,000	$46,000, PF-65UCam, Feb-07
1863 (d)	30	8	64.6	50,000	75,000	95,000	125,000	$57,500, PF-58, Apr-10
1864	50	15	64.9	12,000	20,000	27,500	40,000	$34,500, PF-65UCam, Jan-05
1865	25	13	63.9	13,500	20,000	27,500	40,000	$17,250, PF-62Cam, Jan-09
1866	30	13	63.8	10,000	15,000	20,000	32,500	$13,972, PF-61Cam, Nov-07
1867	50	11	64.4	10,000	15,000	20,000	30,000	$63,250, PF-67DCam, Aug-07
1868	25	4	63.3	9,500	16,000	22,500	35,000	$43,700, PF-65 CAC, Jan-09
1869	25	18	64.2	6,500	13,000	18,000	30,000	$20,700, PF-64UCam, Oct-09
1870	35	4	63.3	6,500	14,000	18,000	30,000	$11,550, PF-64, Aug-96
1871	30	8	64.1	6,500	13,000	18,000	27,500	$17,250, PF-64UCam, Jan-07
1872	30	7	64.9	6,500	13,000	18,000	27,500	$25,300, PF-65Cam, Feb-07
1873, Close 3	25	10	62.9	7,500	13,000	18,000	30,000	$9,200, PF-61, Aug-09
1874	20	7	64.3	7,500	15,000	25,000	40,000	$43,988, PF-65UCam, Jul-08
1875	20	11	63.6	13,500	30,000	40,000	55,000	$48,875, PF-65UCam, Sep-08
1876	45	16	64.5	6,500	12,000	18,000	27,500	$57,500, PF-65Cam, Aug-06
1877	20	5	64.6	6,500	12,000	18,000	27,500	$40,250, PF-66Cam, Feb-08
1878	20	10	64.4	6,500	12,000	18,000	27,500	$32,750, PF-65DCam, Aug-06
1879	30	8	65.0	6,000	12,000	18,000	27,500	$40,250, PF-65DCam, Nov-09
1880	36	14	63.9	6,500	12,000	18,000	27,500	$16,100, PF-64Cam, Feb-10
1881	51	17	64.1	6,500	13,000	19,000	27,500	$19,550, PF-64DCam, Jul-10
1882	67	15	65.2	4,500	9,000	14,000	22,500	$9,487, PF-64, May-06
1883	82	27	64.6	4,500	9,000	14,000	22,500	$32,200, PF-66Cam, Feb-10
1884	73	25	63.8	4,500	9,000	14,000	22,500	$17,250, PF-64, Dec-09
1885	87	22	64.3	5,000	9,000	14,000	25,000	$9,775, PF-63Cam CAC, Apr-10
1886	88	36	64.1	4,500	8,500	13,500	22,500	$4,313, PF-61Cam, Jul-10
1887	122	19	63.8	4,500	8,500	13,500	22,500	$2,300, PF-58, Oct-09
1888	97	31	64.4	4,500	8,000	13,500	22,500	$11,500, PF-64DCam, Aug-09
1889	48	13	64.9	4,500	8,000	13,500	22,500	$6,900, PF-63 CAC, Jan-10
1890	93	42	64.6	4,500	8,000	13,500	20,000	$2,990, PF-60, Oct-09

a. Nearly all 1859 Proofs are of the Old Reverse style. **b.** All known 1860 Proofs are of the New Reverse style. **c.** All 1861 Proofs were struck in the New Reverse style. **d.** Only Proofs were struck in 1863.

	Mintage	Cert	Avg	PF-60	PF-63	PF-64	PF-65	Recent Auction Record
1891	80	24	65.1	$4,500	$7,000	$12,500	$20,000	$9,200, PF-64DCam, Dec-08
1892	105	29	64.5	4,500	7,000	12,500	20,000	$3,881, PF-62Cam, Jan-10
1893	106	34	64.9	4,500	7,000	12,500	20,000	$9,200, PF-64DCam, Dec-09
1894	122	61	64.7	4,500	7,000	12,500	20,000	$37,375, PF-66, Jan-10
1895	119	65	65.0	4,500	7,000	12,500	20,000	$10,925, PF-64UCam, Nov-09
1896	132	57	64.8	4,500	7,000	12,500	20,000	$5,178, PF-62Cam, Mar-10
1897	136	71	64.8	4,500	7,000	12,500	20,000	$37,375, PF-67DCam, May-09
1898	165	104	64.6	4,500	7,000	12,500	20,000	$46,000, PF-68UCam CAC, Apr-10
1899	150	126	64.5	4,500	7,000	12,500	20,000	$4,600, PF-62DCam, Jan-10
1900	205	179	64.2	4,500	7,000	11,000	20,000	$8,050, PF-64Cam, Jun-10
1901	223	121	64.3	4,500	7,000	11,000	20,000	$13,800, PF-64Cam CAC, Apr-10
1902	193	92	64.0	4,500	7,000	11,000	20,000	$3,738, PF-62, Dec-09
1903	197	104	63.2	4,500	7,000	11,000	20,000	$6,900, PF-64, Jul-10
1904	170	117	64.0	4,500	7,000	11,000	20,000	$7,935, PF-64 CAC, Jan-10
1905	144	110	63.7	4,500	7,000	11,000	20,000	$3,450, PF-62, Nov-09
1906	160	130	64.5	4,500	7,000	11,000	20,000	$6,038, PF-64, Nov-09
1907	154	105	64.8	4,500	7,000	11,000	20,000	$14,375, PF-65Cam, Jun-10

INDIAN HEAD
(1908–1929)

Designer Bela Lyon Pratt; weight 4.18 grams; composition .900 gold, .100 copper (net weight .12094 oz. pure gold); diameter 18 mm; reeded edge; mints: Philadelphia, Denver.

Mintmark is on reverse, to left of arrows.

History. The Indian Head design—used on both the quarter eagle and the half eagle—is unusual in that the lettering and motifs are in sunken relief. (The design sometimes is erroneously described as *incuse*.) These coins circulated as money in the West, but not elsewhere. As the smallest gold denomination of the era, they were popular for use as souvenirs and gifts.

Striking and Sharpness. Striking varies. On many early issues the rims are flat, while on others, including most of the 1920s, they are slightly raised. Some have traces of a wire rim, usually on the reverse. Look for weakness on the high parts of the Indian's bonnet (particularly the garland of flowers) and in the feather details in the headdress. On the reverse, check the feathers on the highest area of the wing, the top of the shoulder. On some issues of the 1911-D, the D mintmark can be weak.

Availability. This design was not popular with collectors, and they saved relatively few of the coins. However, many coins were given as gifts and preserved in high quality. The survival of MS-63 and better coins is a matter of chance, especially for the issues dated from 1909 to 1915. The only scarce issue is 1911-D. Luster can range from deeply frosty to grainy. As the fields are the highest areas of the coin, luster diminished quickly as examples were circulated or jostled with others in bags. The Indian Head quarter eagle is one of the most challenging series for professional graders, and opinions can vary widely.

VF-20, 30 (Very Fine). *Obverse:* Many details of the ribbon above the forehead and the garland are worn away. Many feather vanes are blended together. The field is dull and has contact marks. *Reverse:* The neck and the upper part of the wing show extensive wear, other areas less so. The field is dull and has contact marks.

EF-40, 45 (Extremely Fine). *Obverse:* Light wear characterizes the portrait and headdress. Luster is gone.

Marks and tiny scratches are to be expected, but not distracting. *Reverse:* Light wear is most evident on the eagle's head and wing, although other areas are lightly worn as well. Luster is gone. Marks and tiny scratches are to be expected, but not distracting.

AU-50, 53, 55, 58 (About Uncirculated). *Obverse:* Friction on the cheek is very noticeable at AU-50, progressively less at higher levels to AU-58. The headdress shows light wear, most evident on the ribbon

above the forehead and on the garland. Luster is minimal at AU-50 and scattered and incomplete at AU-58. Nicks and contact marks are to be expected. *Reverse:* Friction on the wing and neck is very noticeable at AU-50, increasingly less at higher levels to AU-58. Otherwise, the same comments apply as for the obverse.

MS-60 to 70 (Mint State). *Obverse:* On MS-60 to 62 coins there is abrasion in the field, this representing

Continued on next page.

the highest part of the coin. Abrasion is also evident on the headdress. Marks and, occasionally, a microscopic pin scratch may be seen. At MS-63, there may be some abrasion and some tiny marks. Luster is

irregular. At MS-64, abrasion is less. Luster is rich. At MS-65 and above, luster is deep and frosty. No marks at all are visible without magnification at MS-66 and higher. *Reverse:* At MS-60 to 62, there is abrasion in

the field, this representing the highest part of the coin. Abrasion is also evident on the eagle's wing. Otherwise, the same comments apply as for the obverse.

	Mintage	Cert	Avg	%MS	EF-40	AU-50	MS-60	MS-62	MS-63	MS-64	MS-65	Recent Auction Record
1908	564,821	7,596	61.8	86	$355	$375	$450	$725	$1,400	$1,800	$4,750	$3,450, MS-65, Jul-10
1909	441,760	5,820	61.4	82	355	380	450	725	1,800	2,900	6,500	$4,888, MS-65, Jul-10
1910	492,000	6,665	61.5	86	355	380	450	825	1,500	2,750	7,500	$2,300, MS-64, Jul-10
1911	704,000	10,058	61.3	83	355	380	450	725	1,200	1,900	7,500	$7,475, MS-65 CAC, Jul-10
1911D (a)	55,680	4,234	60.0	59	3,750	4,750	8,500	11,000	18,500	25,000	75,000	$22,428, MS-64, Jul-10
1911D, Weak D	*	147	53.9	3	1,500	2,200	4,000					$2,243, AU-50, Jan-10
1912	616,000	6,862	60.9	77	355	380	450	825	1,800	3,000	11,000	$2,990, MS-64, Jul-10
1913	722,000	9,514	61.2	82	355	380	450	725	1,300	2,050	7,500	$1,840, MS-64 CAC, Jul-10
1914	240,000	6,044	60.9	77	380	525	650	1,825	5,000	12,000	32,500	$9,490, MS-64, Jul-10
1914D	448,000	8,519	61.3	83	355	380	450	825	1,750	4,000	32,500	$4,025, MS-64 CAC, Jul-10
1915	606,000	9,307	61.5	84	355	380	450	700	1,250	1,800	6,500	$1,380, MS-64, Jul-10
1925D	578,000	16,892	62.3	93	355	375	400	675	1,000	1,475	3,500	$1,265, MS-64 CAC, Jul-10
1926	446,000	15,231	62.3	95	355	375	400	675	1,000	1,475	3,500	$3,594, MS-65, Jul-10
1927	388,000	12,295	62.4	96	355	375	400	675	1,000	1,475	3,500	$1,380, MS-64, Jul-10
1928	416,000	13,287	62.4	97	355	375	400	675	1,000	1,475	3,500	$2,990, MS-65, Jul-10
1929	532,000	16,086	62.3	98	355	375	400	675	1,000	1,475	3,500	$4,890, MS-65, Jul-10

* Included in number above. **a.** Beware of counterfeit and altered pieces.

Proof Indian Head Quarter Eagles

PF-60 to 70 (Proof). Sand Blast (also called Matte) Proofs were made in 1908 and 1911 to 1915, while Satin (also called Roman Finish) Proofs were made in 1909 and 1910. The Sand Blast issues usually are somewhat dull, while the Satin Proofs usually are of a light-yellow gold. In their time the Proofs of both styles, made for all gold series, were not popular with numismatists.

Today, they are in strong demand. As a class these are significantly more readily available than half eagles of the same date and style of finish. Most are in grades from PF-63 upward. At lower levels coins can show light contact marks. Some microscopic bright flecks may be caused by the sandblasting process and, although they do not represent handling, usually result in a

coin being assigned a slightly lower grade. *Obverse and Reverse:* At PF-60 to 63, there is light abrasion and some contact marks; the lower the grade, the higher the quantity. On Sand Blast Proofs these show up as visually unappealing bright spots. At PF-64 and higher levels, marks are fewer, with magnification needed to see any at PF-65. At PF-66, there should be none at all.

Proof Indian Head Quarter Eagle
Shown 1.5x actual size.

	Mintage	Cert	Avg	PF-60	PF-63	PF-64	PF-65	Recent Auction Record
1908, Matte	236	135	65.1	$3,750	$8,500	$14,000	$25,000	$31,646, PF-67, Jan-10
1909, Roman Finish	139	39	64.4	4,000	9,000	15,000	25,000	$34,500, PF-66, Apr-10
1910, Roman Finish	682	101	65.1	4,000	9,000	15,000	25,000	$23,000, PF-66, Jan-10
1910, Matte (a)	unknown	1	66.0					
1911, Matte	191	94	65.8	3,750	8,500	13,500	25,000	$27,600, PF-65 CAC, Jun-10
1912, Matte	197	48	65.8	3,750	8,500	13,500	25,000	$27,600, PF-66, Aug-07
1913, Matte	165	55	65.9	3,750	8,500	13,500	25,000	$30,475, PF-67, Aug-09
1914, Matte	117	70	65.0	3,750	8,500	13,500	25,000	$30,475, PF-66, Aug-09
1915, Matte	100	46	65.1	4,000	10,000	17,500	30,000	$36,225, PF-67, Aug-09

a. Unique; part of a complete 1910 Matte Proof gold set. Others may exist, but have not yet been confirmed.

An Overview of
Three-Dollar Gold Pieces

The three-dollar gold coin denomination was conceived in 1853 and first produced for circulation in 1854. Although there were high hopes for it at the outset, and mintages were generous, the value was redundant given the $2.50 quarter eagle then in circulation. Mintages declined, and although pieces were struck each year through 1889, very few actually circulated after the 1850s.

Although many different three-dollar dates are available at reasonable prices, most numismatists opt to acquire either a circulated or Mint State 1854 (significant as the first year of issue; also, in this year the word DOLLARS is in smaller letters than on later issues) or a Mint State coin from the low-mintage era of 1879–1889. Similar to the situation for gold dollars, although the mintages of these later pieces were low, they were popularly saved at the time, and many more exist than might otherwise be the case.

For the Collector and Investor: Three-Dollar Gold Pieces as a Specialty

Collecting three-dollar pieces by date and mint would at first seem to be daunting, but it is less challenging than expected, outside of a handful of pieces. The 1870-S is unique (in the Harry W. Bass Jr. Collection on loan to the American Numismatic Association), the 1875 and 1876 were made only in Proof format to the extent of 20 and 45 pieces respectively, and the 1873 is quite rare. Beyond that, examples of coins in grades such as EF and AU (including some varieties with very low mintages) can be purchased for reasonable prices.

Choice examples can be elusive, this being particularly true of branch-mint issues of the 1854–1860 years. Generally, Mint State Philadelphia pieces are rare after 1855, but then come on the market with frequency for 1861 and later, with dates in the 1860s being scarcer than later issues. Coins of the years 1878 and 1879 were made in larger quantities, with the 1878 in particular being easy to find today, although examples usually are quite bagmarked. The low-mintage three-dollar pieces of 1879 through 1889 were popular at the time of issue, many were saved, and today Mint State pieces exist to a greater extent than would normally be the case.

Recommended Reading

Akers, David W. *Gold Dollars (and Other Gold Denominations)*, Englewood, OH, 1975–1982.
Bowers, Q. David. *United States Gold Coins: An Illustrated History*, Wolfeboro, NH, 1982.
Bowers, Q. David, and Winter, Douglas. *United States $3 Gold Pieces 1854–1889*, Wolfeboro, NH, 2005.
Breen, Walter. *Major Varieties of U.S. Gold Dollars (and Other Gold Denominations)*, Chicago, 1964.
Fivaz, Bill. *United States Gold Counterfeit Detection Guide*, Atlanta, GA, 2005.
Fivaz, Bill, and Stanton, J.T. *The Cherrypickers' Guide to Rare Die Varieties* (4th ed., vol. II), Atlanta, GA, 2006.
Garrett, Jeff, and Guth, Ron. *Encyclopedia of U.S. Gold Coins, 1795–1933* (2nd ed.), Atlanta, GA, 2008.

INDIAN PRINCESS HEAD
(1854–1889)

Designer James B. Longacre; weight 5.015 grams; composition .900 gold, .100 copper (net weight .14512 oz. pure gold); diameter 20.5 mm; reeded edge; mints: Philadelphia, Dahlonega, New Orleans, San Francisco.

Mintmark is below wreath.

History. The three-dollar gold coin was designed by chief engraver James B. Longacre, and first struck in 1854. The quarter eagle and half eagle had already been in use for a long time, and the reason for the creation of this odd new denomination is uncertain, although some numismatists note it could have been used to buy a sheet of current 3¢ stamps or a group of 100 silver trimes. After a large initial mintage in 1854, the coins were struck in smaller annual quantities.

Striking and Sharpness. Points to observe on the obverse include the tips of the feathers in the headdress, and the hair details below the band inscribed LIBERTY. Focal points on the reverse are the wreath details (especially the vertical division in the ribbon knot), and the two central date numerals. Many of the later issues—particularly those of the early 1880s—are prooflike.

Availability. In circulated grades the issues of 1854 to 1860 survive in approximate proportion to their mintages. MS coins are plentiful for the first-year Philadelphia issue, 1854, but are scarce to rare for other years and all branch-mint issues. For the 1860s and 1870s most are in grades such as EF, AU, and low MS, except for 1874 and in particular 1878, easily found in MS. Dates from 1879 to 1889 have a higher survival ratio and are mostly in MS, often at MS-65.

VF-20, 30 (Very Fine). *Obverse:* Most hair detail is gone, except at the back of the lower curls. The feather plume ends are flat. *Reverse:* The wreath and other areas show more wear. Most detail is gone on the higher-relief leaves.

EF-40, 45 (Extremely Fine). *Obverse:* Medium wear is seen on the hair below the coronet and on the feather plume tips. Detail is partially gone on the hair. Luster is gone on most coins. *Reverse:* Light wear is seen overall, and the highest parts of the leaves are flat, but detail remains elsewhere. Luster is gone on most coins.

AU-50, 53, 55, 58 (About Uncirculated). *Obverse:* Light wear on the hair below the coronet, the cheek, and the tips of the feather plumes is very noticeable at AU-50, increasingly less at higher levels to AU-58. Luster is minimal at AU-50 and scattered and incomplete at AU-58. Some tiny nicks and contact marks are to be expected and should be mentioned if they are distracting. *Reverse:* Light wear on the 1, the wreath, and the ribbon knot characterize an AU-50 coin, increasingly less at higher levels to 58. Otherwise, the same comments apply as for the obverse.

MS-60 to 70 (Mint State). *Obverse:* On MS-60 to 62 coins there is abrasion on the hair below the band lettered LIBERTY (an area that can be weakly struck, as well) and on tips of the feather plumes. At MS-63, there may be slight abrasion. Luster can be irregular. At MS-64, abrasion is less. Luster is rich on most coins, less so on the 1854-D (which often is overgraded). At MS-65 and above, luster is deep and frosty, with no marks at all visible without magnification at MS-66 and higher. *Reverse:* On MS-60 to 62 coins there is abrasion on the 1, the highest parts of the leaves, and the ribbon knot. Otherwise, the same comments apply as for the obverse.

	Mintage	Cert	Avg	%MS	AU-55	AU-58	MS-60	MS-62	MS-63	MS-64	MS-65	Recent Auction Record
1854	138,618	3,356	56.1	26	$2,100	$2,500	$3,500	$4,500	$8,500	$12,000	$25,000	$3,450, MS-62, Jul-10
1854D	1,120	97	51.4	9	50,000	65,000	95,000	155,000				$17,250, EF-45, Jan-10
1854O	24,000	712	49.0	3	12,000	16,000	28,500	60,000	95,000			$4,600, AU-50, Jul-10
1855	50,555	1,026	54.9	22	2,350	2,750	3,750	5,500	11,000	19,000	45,000	$518, G-6, Jun-10
1855S	6,600	146	41.9	2	15,000	18,000	27,500	55,000	95,000			$3,594, EF-45 CAC, Apr-10
1856	26,010	658	55.6	22	2,250	2,600	3,750	6,500	12,500	18,500		$8,625, MS-63 CAC, Apr-10
1856S (a)	34,500	482	46.6	5	4,500	7,500	12,500	18,000	32,500	48,000		$978, VF-35, Jun-10
1857	20,891	524	55.2	21	2,400	2,750	4,000	7,000	12,500	21,000	40,000	$6,900, MS-62, May-10
1857S	14,000	173	43.4	2	12,500	14,500	22,500	50,000	65,000			$3,335, EF-45, Apr-10
1858	2,133	114	52.4	8	6,750	8,500	13,500	15,000	25,000	40,000		$3,450, AU-53, Mar-10
1859	15,558	488	56.0	23	2,450	2,600	3,750	6,500	11,000	15,000	30,000	$4,888, MS-62, Jun-10
1860 (b)	7,036	301	56.0	27	2,750	3,000	4,000	7,500	12,500	16,000	27,500	$1,093, EF-40, Jul-10
1860S	7,000	134	42.5	4	13,500	16,000	32,500	50,000	72,500			$2,530, EF-40 CAC, Apr-10
1861	5,959	223	55.0	26	3,750	4,250	6,750	11,000	13,500	22,000	35,000	$3,335, AU-53, Mar-10
1862	5,750	182	55.4	25	3,850	4,250	6,750	11,000	13,500	24,000	40,000	$4,313, AU-55, Mar-10

a. Collectors recognize three mintmark sizes: Large (very rare); Medium (common), and Small (rare). **b.** Of the already low 1860 Philadelphia mintage, 2,592 coins were melted at the Mint.

	Mintage	Cert	Avg	%MS	AU-55	AU-58	MS-60	MS-62	MS-63	MS-64	MS-65	Recent Auction Record
1863	5,000	200	55.8	24	$3,850	$4,250	$6,750	$11,000	$13,500	$23,000	$35,000	$3,738, AU-55, Apr-10
1864	2,630	136	56.4	28	3,800	4,250	6,750	11,000	14,000	23,500	38,000	$11,500, MS-63, Jun-10
1865	1,140	61	57.6	38	10,000	12,500	15,000	20,000	30,000	35,000	55,000	$13,225, MS-61, Jan-10
1866	4,000	167	56.2	25	3,250	3,750	6,000	8,500	13,000	18,000	35,000	$6,728, MS-62, Jul-10
1867	2,600	120	56.8	21	3,250	3,750	5,500	8,500	13,000	19,000	35,000	$8,913, MS-64, Mar-10
1868 (e)	4,850	327	56.8	28	2,800	3,000	4,500	7,500	11,500	16,500	30,000	$11,500, MS-64, Apr-10
1869 (e)	2,500	151	54.4	15	3,000	3,250	4,750	9,000	13,500	25,000	45,000	$2,185, AU-53, Mar-10
1870	3,500	263	54.6	13	3,250	3,500	5,000	10,000	15,000	25,000		$19,550, MS-64, Jan-10
1870S (f)						*(unique, in Bass Foundation Collection)*						$687,500, EF-40, Oct-82
1871	1,300	157	56.7	25	3,250	3,600	5,000	8,500	12,500	20,000	35,000	$4,169, MS-61, Jul-09
1872	2,000	171	55.9	20	3,250	3,600	4,750	8,500	13,500	20,000		$7,475, MS-62, Mar-10
1873, Close 3	(g)	48	56.9	19	20,000	25,000	32,500	35,000	55,000	75,000		$20,828, AU-58, Jun-10
1874	41,800	2,412	57.2	33	2,100	2,350	2,750	3,500	8,000	10,000	18,000	$1,438, AU-58, Jul-10
1877	1,468	35	57.4	23	20,000	23,500	27,500	30,000	55,000	65,000		$11,213, AU-53, Jun-10
1878 (e)	82,304	4,969	60.0	62	2,000	2,300	2,850	3,500	5,750	7,500	16,000	$1,265, AU-58, Jul-10
1879	3,000	372	60.8	66	2,850	3,100	3,800	6,000	10,000	12,500	25,000	$15,525, MS-65, Jun-10
1880	1,000	142	62.7	90	3,850	4,200	5,500	8,000	11,000	15,000	30,000	$12,650, MS-64, Mar-10
1881	500	95	57.6	35	8,500	9,500	11,000	15,000	22,500	25,000		$13,225, MS-63, Nov-09
1882	1,500	233	58.9	55	3,000	3,400	4,250	7,000	11,000	15,000	28,000	$16,100, MS-64, Jul-10
1883	900	121	58.2	54	3,500	4,000	5,500	7,500	11,000	14,500	28,000	$20,125, MS-65, Jul-10
1884	1,000	54	60.9	70	4,000	4,250	5,500	7,500	11,000	14,500	28,000	$8,625, MS-61, Jul-10
1885	801	127	59.7	57	4,500	4,750	6,000	9,500	16,000	24,000	35,000	$4,313, AU-58, Jul-10
1886	1,000	147	57.7	41	4,000	4,250	5,500	7,500	11,500	14,000	35,000	$3,450, AU-55, Jul-10
1887	6,000	201	60.8	70	2,350	2,500	3,200	4,750	8,000	12,500	24,000	$9,200, MS-64, Jun-10
1888	5,000	491	61.2	76	2,100	2,350	2,950	4,500	6,000	8,000	18,000	$6,325, MS-63 CAC, Jun-10
1889	2,300	297	60.7	67	2,100	2,350	2,950	4,500	6,000	7,750	16,000	$1,840, AU-55, Mar-10

e. Varieties showing traces of possible overdating include 1868/7, 1869/8, and 1878/7. **f.** A second example of the 1870-S is rumored to exist in the cornerstone of the San Francisco Mint, but the cornerstone has never been located. **g.** The mintage of the 1873, Close 3, coins is unknown. Research suggests that only Proofs may have been struck (none for circulation), and those perhaps as late as 1879.

Proof Three-Dollar Gold Pieces

PF-60 to 70 (Proof). Three-dollar Proofs were struck of all years. All prior to the 1880s are very rare today, with issues of the 1850s exceedingly so. Coins of 1875 and 1876 were made only in Proof format, with no related circulation strikes. Most often seen in the marketplace are the higher-mintage Proofs of the 1880s. Some have patches of graininess or hints of non-Proof surface on the obverse, or an aura or "ghosting" near the portrait, an artifact of striking. *Obverse and Reverse:* PF-60 to 62 coins have extensive hairlines and may have nicks and contact marks. At PF-63, hairlines are prominent, but the mirror surface is very reflective. PF-64 coins have fewer hairlines. At PF-65, hairlines should be minimal and mostly seen only under magnification. There should be no nicks or marks. PF-66 and higher coins should have no marks or hairlines visible to the unaided eye.

Proof Three-Dollar Gold Piece
Shown 1.5x actual size.

	Est Mintage	Cert	Avg	PF-60	PF-63	PF-64	PF-65	Recent Auction Record
1854	15–20	7	62.0	$30,000	$80,000	$115,000	$175,000	$66,125, PF-63 CAC, Sep-09
1855	4–8	1	64.0	30,000	57,500	125,000	200,000	$75,900, PF-64Cam, Nov-03
1856	8–10	2	63.5	19,500	45,000	60,000	100,000	
1857	8–12	1	64.0	17,500	30,000	55,000	95,000	
1858	8–12	4	64.5	15,000	27,500	45,000	85,000	

Chart continued on next page.

	Mintage	Cert	Avg	PF-60	PF-63	PF-64	PF-65	Recent Auction Record
1859	80	12	64.3	$8,500	$20,000	$40,000	$60,000	$49,450, PF-65UCam, Jun-10
1860	119	15	64.5	7,000	15,000	30,000	55,000	$18,400, PF-64Cam, Nov-09
1861	113	5	64.4	7,000	15,000	30,000	55,000	
1862	35	8	64.9	7,000	15,000	30,000	55,000	$74,750, PF-66UCam, Aug-09
1863	39	10	63.3	7,000	15,000	30,000	50,000	$87,400, PF-65DCam, Sep-07
1864	50	22	63.5	7,000	15,000	30,000	47,500	$74,750, PF-66Cam, Feb-08
1865	25	6	63.8	8,500	19,500	32,500	50,000	$46,000, PF-64Cam, Mar-06
1865, Proof Restrike (a)	5			(extremely rare)				
1866	30	9	63.2	7,000	16,500	30,000	50,000	$4,888, PF-63, Oct-08
1867	50	10	63.7	7,000	16,500	30,000	50,000	$56,925, PF-66Cam, Aug-06
1868	25	10	64.3	7,000	16,500	30,000	50,000	$32,775, PF-65, Jan-00
1869	25	5	64.8	7,000	16,500	30,000	50,000	$57,500, PF-65UCam, Feb-09
1870	35	13	63.7	7,000	16,500	30,000	50,000	$19,435, PF-64Cam, Feb-09
1871	30	4	61.0	8,000	16,500	30,000	55,000	$19,550, PF-63, Sep-07
1872	30	15	62.9	8,000	16,500	30,000	47,500	$20,700, PF-64, Jan-07
1873, Open 3 (Original) (b)	25	6	64.0	19,500	32,000	45,000	70,000	$212,750, PF-65DCam, Sep-08
1873, Close 3	*			16,500	37,500	47,500	75,000	$40,250, PF-61, Jan-08
1874	20	14	64.1	12,500	26,500	40,000	60,000	$46,000, PF-65, Mar-05
1875, Proof only	20	6	64.7	80,000	135,000	155,000	200,000	$80,500, PF-65DCam, Feb-07
1876, Proof only	45	28	63.9	25,000	40,000	45,000	65,000	$86,250, PF-65DCam, Feb-09
1877	20	13	62.9	12,500	27,500	35,000	55,000	$8,050, PF-61Cam, Nov-03
1878	20	6	64.0	12,500	25,000	35,000	55,000	$48,300, PF-65UCam, Jan-05
1879	30	12	64.7	10,000	17,000	32,500	42,500	$80,500, PF-67UCam, Mar-07
1880	36	19	64.1	10,000	17,000	32,500	42,500	$25,300, PF-65Cam, Feb-09
1881	54	33	64.2	10,000	17,000	32,500	42,500	$20,700, PF-64DCam, Jan-09
1882	76	35	63.1	7,500	13,500	20,000	35,000	$37,375, PF-65UCam Star, May-09
1883	89	40	64.5	7,500	13,500	20,000	35,000	$6,325, PF-61 CAC, Feb-09
1884	106	37	63.9	7,500	13,500	20,000	35,000	$48,875, PF-66Cam, Jan-10
1885	109	61	63.6	7,500	15,000	20,000	35,000	$8,625, PF-62, Jan-09
1886	142	85	63.9	7,500	13,500	20,000	35,000	$11,500, PF-63Cam CAC, Apr-10
1887	160	72	63.8	7,500	13,500	20,000	35,000	$7,763, PF-62, Jul-10
1888	291	105	64.3	7,500	12,500	18,500	32,500	$9,488, PF-63Cam, Jan-10
1889	129	59	63.8	7,500	12,500	18,500	35,000	$13,225, PF-64 CAC, Sep-09

* Included in number above. **a.** Sometime around 1873, the Mint restruck a small number of 1865 three-dollar pieces using an obverse die of 1872 and a newly created reverse with the date slanting up to the right (previously listed in *United States Pattern Coins* as Judd-440). Two examples are known in gold. Versions were also made in copper (Judd-441) for interested collectors. **b.** Mint records report 25 Proof coins (with no reference to the style, Open or Close, of the number 3 in the date). The actual mintage may be as high as 100 to 1,000 coins. Value in PF-55 is $32,500; in PF-58, $40,000.

An Overview of Four-Dollar Gold Pieces

The four-dollar pattern gold coin, or Stella, is not widely collected, simply because of its rarity. For type-set purposes some numismatists opt to acquire a single example of the only issue readily available, Charles Barber's 1879 Flowing Hair, although these are expensive. However, the Coiled Hair style is a different type, much rarer, and a collector with the means might acquire an example of that design as well.

For the Collector and Investor: Four-Dollar Gold Pieces as a Specialty

Over the past century perhaps two dozen numismatists have put together complete sets of one of each gold striking of the 1879 and 1880 Flowing Hair and Coiled Hair Stella, this being made possible by collections being dispersed and sold to others, as it is unlikely that even as many as 20 complete sets could exist at one time.

Recommended Reading

Akers, David W. *Gold Dollars (and Other Gold Denominations),* Englewood, OH, 1975–1982.

Bowers, Q. David. *United States Gold Coins: An Illustrated History,* Wolfeboro, NH, 1982.

Breen, Walter. *Major Varieties of U.S. Gold Dollars (and Other Gold Denominations),* Chicago, 1964.

Garrett, Jeff, and Guth, Ron. *Encyclopedia of U.S. Gold Coins, 1795–1933* (2nd ed.), Atlanta, GA, 2008.

Judd, J. Hewitt. *United States Pattern Coins* (10th ed., Q. David Bowers, editor), Atlanta, GA, 2009.

Flowing Hair Obverse

Coiled Hair Obverse

STELLA, FLOWING HAIR AND COILED HAIR (1879–1880)

Designer Charles E. Barber (Flowing Hair), George T. Morgan (Coiled Hair); weight 7.0 grams; approx. composition .857 gold, .042 silver, .100 copper; diameter 22 mm; reeded edge.

Reverse
Shown 1.5x actual size.

History. The four-dollar gold Stellas of 1879 and 1880 are Proof-only patterns, not regular issues. However, as they have been listed in popular references for decades, collectors have adopted them into the regular gold series. The obverse inscription notes the coins' metallic content in proportions of gold, silver, and copper in the metric system, intended to facilitate their use in foreign countries, where the value could be quickly determined. The Stella was proposed by John A. Kasson (former chairman of the congressional Committee of Coinage, Weights, and Measures; in 1879 serving as envoy extraordinary and minister plenipotentiary to Austria-Hungary). Charles E. Barber designed the Flowing Hair type, and George T. Morgan the Coiled Hair. The only issue produced in quantity was the 1879 Flowing Hair. The others were made in secret and sold privately by Mint officers and employees. The Coiled Hair Stella was not generally known to the numismatic community until they were illustrated in *The Numismatist* in the early 20th century. Stellas are cataloged by their Judd numbers, assigned in the standard reference, *United States Pattern Coins*.

Striking and Sharpness. On nearly all examples the high parts of the hair are flat, often with striations. The other areas of the coin are typically well struck. Tiny planchet irregularities are common.

Availability. The 1879 Flowing Hair is often available on the market—usually in PF-61 to 64, although higher-condition examples come on the market with regularity (as do lightly handled and impaired coins). The 1880 Flowing Hair is typically found in PF-63 or higher. Both years of Coiled Hair Stellas are great rarities; typical grades are PF-63 to 65, with a flat strike on the head and with some tiny planchet flaws.

Proof Four-Dollar Gold Pieces

PF-60 to 70 (Proof). Striations are normally found on most pieces. *Obverse and Reverse:* PF-60 to 62 coins have extensive hairlines and may have nicks and contact marks. At PF-63, hairlines are prominent, but the mirror surface is very reflective. PF-64 coins have fewer hairlines. At PF-65, hairlines should be minimal and mostly seen only under magnification. There should be no nicks or marks. PF-66 and higher coins should have no marks or hairlines visible to the unaided eye.

	Est Mintage	Cert	Avg	PF-50	PF-60	PF-63	PF-64	PF-65	PF-66	PF-67	Recent Auction Record
1879, Flowing Hair	*425+*	207	63.9	$80,000	$100,000	$140,000	$160,000	$180,000	$235,000	$350,000	$115,000, PF-62 Cam, May-10
1879, Coiled Hair	*12 known*	12	64.9		250,000	375,000	450,000	550,000	675,000	850,000	$316,250, PF-63, Jan-07
1880, Flowing Hair	*17 known*	19	64.8		150,000	210,000	250,000	300,000	375,000	550,000	$431,250, PF-64, Jun-08
1880, Coiled Hair	*18 known*	11	65.0		500,000	600,000	750,000	900,000	1,000,000	1,500,000	$546,250, PF-62, Jul-09

The half eagle was the first gold coin actually struck for the United States. The five-dollar gold piece was authorized by the Act of April 2, 1792, and the first batch was minted in 1795.

Forming a type set of half eagles is a daunting but achievable challenge—if a collector has the finances and some determination. Examples of the first type, with Capped Bust to Right (conical cap obverse), and with an eagle on a palm branch on the reverse, readily come up on the market, usually of the date 1795. Typical grades range from EF to lower Mint State levels. Such pieces are scarce, and the demand for them is strong. The next type, the Heraldic Eagle motif, first struck in 1798, but also known from a 1795-dated die used later, was produced through 1807, and easily enough obtained today. Again, typical grades range from EF to Mint State. MS-63 and better coins are available, but are in the distinct minority.

The short-lived Capped Bust to Left style, 1807–1812, can be found in similar grades, although such pieces did not circulate as extensively, and AU and Mint State levels are the rule, with VF pieces scarce. Then follows the era of rarities. The Capped Head to Left, stars surrounding head, large diameter, 1813–1829 style is available courtesy of the first date of issue, 1813. This is the only date seen with some frequency. When available, examples tend to be choice. The later stretch of this series includes some formidable rarities, among which are the famous 1815 and the even rarer 1822, along with a whole string of other seldom-seen varieties in the 1820s. The same style, but of reduced diameter, 1829–1834, also is rare; examples of the 1830s turn up with some regularity, but these often lack eye appeal. For some reason, half eagles of the early 1830s are often heavily marked and abraded, which it not true at all for coins of the 1820s.

Classic Head half eagles, capless and without motto, first minted in August 1834, are easily enough obtained. They are usually of the first several dates, less frequently of 1837 or 1838. Grades range from VF upward, reflecting their extensive use in circulation. Mint State coins can be found on occasion and are scarce. Choice and gem pieces are rare.

With just a few exceptions, Liberty Head half eagles of the 1839–1866 type without motto are very plentiful in worn grades, including certain of the higher-mintage issues from the popular Charlotte and Dahlonega mints (permitting interesting varieties to be added to a type set). Mint State coins are scarce, and when seen are usually in lower levels such as MS-60 and MS-62. Gems of any date are rare. Then follow the Liberty Head pieces with the motto on the reverse, 1866 through 1908; the earlier years are mostly encountered in worn grades, the later ones are easy enough to find in Mint State. Proofs were made of all Liberty Head half eagle dates, and today they are generally collectible from about 1860 onward.

With two exceptions (1909-O and 1929), the Indian Head half eagles of 1908–1929 are common enough in worn grades as well as low Mint State levels, but true gems, accurately graded and with lustrous, frosty surfaces, are quite rare. The field is the highest area of the coin and thus is quite susceptible to scuffs and marks. Probably the most readily available dates in higher grades are 1908 and 1909, with the 1909-D being plentiful due to a hoard that came on the market a generation ago.

For the Collector and Investor: Gold Half Eagles as a Specialty

While in the annals of American numismatics dozens of old-time numismatists collected half eagles by date (or, less often, by date *and* mint), today rarities are so widely scattered and are so expensive that few collectors can rise to the challenge.

Early half eagles can be collected by dates and basic varieties, and also by die varieties. The year 1795 in particular is rich in the latter, and years ago several scholars described such varieties, beginning with J. Colvin Randall in the 1870s, continuing to William H. Woodin in the early 20th century, then Edgar H. Adams, Thomas Ollive Mabbott, and Walter Breen. In more recent times Robert Miller, Harry Bass, John Dannreuther, and others have added their research to the literature.

Among early half eagles there are two unique varieties: the 1797 with 16-star obverse, and 1797 with 15-star obverse, both with Heraldic Eagle reverse, likely struck in 1798. Of the later 1822, just three are known, two of which are at the Smithsonian Institution. Of all early half eagles the 1815 was far and away the most famous during the 19th century. (In the 1880s a publication on the Mint Collection stated that the two highlights there were the 1815 half eagle and the unique 1849 double eagle.) At the time the rarer 1822 had not been recognized for its elusive nature. Today an estimated 11 examples of the 1815 half eagles exist, mostly in higher circulated grades, including those in museums. The aforementioned 1822 is the rarity of rarities in the series, with just three known to exist, two of which are in the Smithsonian's National Numismatic Collection, with the third, the Eliasberg Collection coin, being a highlight of a private cabinet. There are only two known of the 1825, 5 Over 4 overdate, but it is not at all famous, probably because it is an overdate variety, not a single date on its own. Half eagles of 1826 through 1829 all are rare, with the 1829 being particularly well known. The latter date includes early pieces with regular diameter and later ones with the diameter reduced. Generally, all half eagles from 1815 through 1834 are scarce, some of them particularly so.

Classic Head half eagles of 1834–1838 include the scarce 1838-C and 1838-D, the first of the Charlotte and Dahlonega mints respectively; none are prohibitively rare. Generally, the higher-grade pieces are found toward the beginning of the Classic Head series, especially bearing the date 1834.

Liberty Head half eagles are readily available of most dates and mints from 1839 to 1908, save for the one great rarity, the 1854-S, of which just three are known (one is in the Smithsonian). There is a vast panorama of Charlotte and Dahlonega issues through 1861, most of which were made in fairly large quantities, as this was the highest denomination ever struck at each of these mints (larger-capacity presses were not on hand). Accordingly, they are highly collectible today. Some varieties are scarce, but none are out of reach. Typical grades range from VF to EF and AU, occasionally Mint State, though not often MS-63 or higher.

Among San Francisco half eagles most of the early issues are scarce, as such pieces circulated extensively and there was no thought to saving numismatic examples. However, there are not many specialists in the field, and for some varieties it can be said that collectors are harder to find than are the coins themselves, yielding the opportunity to purchase truly rare pieces for significantly less than would otherwise be the case. Carson City half eagles were minted beginning in 1870 and continuing intermittently through 1893. Most of the early issues range from scarce to rare, the 1870-CC being particularly well known in this regard. Proofs of the Liberty Head type are generally collectible from the 1860s onward, with most on the market being of the higher-mintage issues of the 1890s and 1900s.

Among Indian Head half eagles, 1908–1929, the 1909-O is the rarest of the early coins, and when seen is usually worn. A choice or gem Mint State 1909-O is an incredible rarity. However, enough worn 1909-O half eagles exist, including many brought from overseas hoards in recent decades, that a piece in VF or so grade presents no problem. Half eagles of 1929, of which just 662,000 were minted, were mostly melted, it seems. A couple hundred or so exist today, nearly all of which are Mint State, but nicked and with bagmarks, MS-60 to MS-62 or MS-63. Truly high-quality gems are exceedingly rare.

RECOMMENDED READING

Akers, David W. *Gold Dollars (and Other Gold Denominations)*, Englewood, OH, 1975–1982.

Bowers, Q. David. *United States Gold Coins: An Illustrated History*, Wolfeboro, NH, 1982.

Breen, Walter. *Major Varieties of U.S. Gold Dollars (and Other Gold Denominations)*, Chicago, 1964.

Dannreuther, John W., and Bass, Harry W. *Early U.S. Gold Coin Varieties*, Atlanta, GA, 2006.

Fivaz, Bill. *United States Gold Counterfeit Detection Guide*, Atlanta, GA, 2005.

Fivaz, Bill, and Stanton, J.T. *The Cherrypickers' Guide to Rare Die Varieties* (4th ed., vol. II), Atlanta, GA, 2006.

Garrett, Jeff, and Guth, Ron. *Encyclopedia of U.S. Gold Coins, 1795–1933* (2nd ed.), Atlanta, GA, 2008.

Miller, Robert W., Sr. *United States Half Eagle Gold Coins 1795–1834*, 1997.

CAPPED BUST TO RIGHT, SMALL EAGLE REVERSE (1795–1798)

Designer Robert Scot; weight 8.75 grams; composition .9167 gold, .0833 silver and copper; approx. diameter 25 mm; reeded edge.

Bass-Dannreuther-7.

History. Half eagles of this style, the first federal gold coins, were introduced in July 1795. The obverse features Miss Liberty wearing a conical cap, a design generally called Capped Bust to Right. The reverse depicts a "small" eagle perched on a palm branch. The same motif was used on contemporary $10 gold coins.

Striking and Sharpness. On the obverse, check the star centers and the hair details. On the reverse, check the feathers of the eagle, particularly on the breast. Examine the dentils on both sides.

Adjustment marks often are visible, but are not noted by the grading services.

Availability. Typical grades range from EF to AU and low MS. MS-63 and better coins are rare; when seen, they usually are of the 1795 date (of which many different die varieties exist). Certain varieties are rare, most famously the 1798 with Small Eagle reverse.

EF-40, 45 (Extremely Fine). *Obverse:* Wear is evident all over the portrait, with some loss of detail in the hair to the left of Miss Liberty's face. Excellent detail remains in low-relief areas of the hair, such as the front curl and at the back of her head. The stars show wear, as do the date and letters. Luster, if present at all, is minimal and in protected areas. *Reverse:* Wear is greater than at AU. The breast, neck, and legs of the eagle lack nearly all feather detail. More wear is seen on the edges of the wing. Some traces of luster may be seen, less so at EF-40 than at EF-45.

AU-50, 53, 55, 58 (About Uncirculated). *Obverse:* Light wear is seen on the cheek, the hair immediately to the left of the face, and the cap, more so at AU-50 than at 53 or 55. An AU-58 coin has minimal traces of wear. An AU-50 coin has luster in protected areas among the stars and letters, with little in the open fields or on the portrait. At AU-58, most luster is present in the fields, but is worn away on the highest parts of the motifs. *Reverse:* The eagle shows light wear on the breast and head in particular, but also at the tip of the wing on the left and elsewhere. Luster ranges from perhaps 40% remaining in protected areas (at AU-50) to nearly full mint bloom (at AU-58).

MS-60 to 70 (Mint State). *Obverse:* At MS-60, some abrasion and contact marks are evident, most notice-ably on the hair to the left of Miss Liberty's forehead and on the higher-relief areas of the cap. Luster is present, but may be dull or lifeless, and interrupted in patches. At MS-63, contact marks are few, and abrasion is very light. An MS-65 coin has hardly any abrasion, and contact marks are so minute as to require magnification. Luster should be full and rich. Grades above MS-65 for this type are more often theoretical than actual—but they do exist and are defined by having fewer marks as perfection is approached. *Reverse:* Comments apply as for the obverse, except that abrasion and contact marks are most noticeable on the breast and head of the eagle. The field area is mainly protected by the eagle, branch, and lettering.

1796, 6 Over 5

1797, 15-Star Obverse

1797, 16-Star Obverse

	Mintage	Cert	Avg	%MS	AU-50	AU-55	AU-58	MS-60	MS-62	MS-63	MS-64	Recent Auction Record
1795, Small Eagle	8,707	232	55.5	30	$40,000	$50,000	$55,000	$75,000	$115,000	$175,000	$300,000 (a)	$41,688, AU-50, Jun-10
1795, Small Eagle, S Over D in States (b)	*				42,000	52,500	57,000	75,000				$345,000, MS-65PL, Jul-09
1796, 6 Over 5	6,196	34	57.1	47	60,000	75,000	85,000	110,000	155,000	235,000	325,000	$40,250, EF-45, Jan-10
1797, All kinds	3,609											
1797, 15-Star Obverse		4	56.5	25	100,000	135,000	165,000	225,000				
1797, 16-Star Obverse		6	57.0	17	80,000	120,000	155,000	200,000				$109,250, AU-55, May-07
1798, Small Eagle (c) (7 known)	unknown	2	50.0	0	750,000	850,000		—				

* Included in number above. **a.** Value in MS-65 is $600,000. **b.** The final S in STATES is punched over an erroneous D. **c.** The reverse of the 1798, Small Eagle, was from a 1795 die. The obverse has an arched die crack or flaw beneath the date. The finest known example is an AU-55 from the collection of King Farouk of Egypt.

CAPPED BUST TO RIGHT, HERALDIC EAGLE REVERSE (1795–1807)

Designer Robert Scot; weight 8.75 grams; composition .9167 gold, .0833 silver and copper; approx. diameter 25 mm; reeded edge.

Bass-Dannreuther-13.

History. For this type, the obverse design is the same as that of the preceding. The reverse features a heraldic eagle, as used on other silver and gold coins of the era. Some half eagles of the Heraldic Eagle Reverse design are dated 1795, but these were actually struck in 1798, from a leftover obverse coinage die.

Striking and Sharpness. On the obverse, check the star centers and the hair details. On the reverse, check the upper part of the shield, the lower part of the eagle's neck, the eagle's wing, the stars above the eagle, and the clouds. Inspect the dentils on both sides. Adjustment marks can be a problem and are not identified by the grading services.

Availability. Although there are many rare die varieties, as a type this half eagle is plentiful. Typical grades are EF to lower MS. MS-63 and higher coins are seen with some frequency and usually are dated from 1802 to 1807. Sharply struck coins without adjustment marks are in the minority.

EF-40, 45 (Extremely Fine). *Obverse:* Wear is evident all over the portrait, with some loss of detail in the hair to the left of Miss Liberty's face. Excellent detail remains in low-relief areas of the hair, such as the front curl and at the back of her head. The stars show wear, as do the date and letters. Luster, if present at all, is minimal and in protected areas. *Reverse:* Wear is greater than at AU. The neck lacks feather detail on its highest points. Feathers have lost some detail near the edges of the wings, and some areas of the horizontal lines in the shield may be blended together. Some traces of luster may be seen, less so at EF-40 than at EF-45. Overall, the reverse appears to be in a slightly higher grade than the obverse.

AU-50, 53, 55, 58 (About Uncirculated). *Obverse:* Light wear is seen on the cheek, the hair immediately to the left of the face, and the cap, more so at AU-50 than at 53 or 55. An AU-58 coin has minimal traces of wear. An AU-50 coin has luster in protected areas among the stars and letters, with little in the open fields or on the portrait. At AU-58, most luster is present in the fields, but is worn away on the highest parts of the motifs. *Reverse:* The eagle's neck, the tips and top of the wings, the clouds, and the tail show noticeable wear, as do other features. Luster ranges from perhaps 40% remaining in protected areas (at AU-50) to nearly full mint bloom (at AU-58). Often the reverse of this type retains much more luster than the obverse.

MS-60 to 70 (Mint State). *Obverse:* At MS-60, some abrasion and contact marks are evident, most noticeably on the hair to the left of Miss Liberty's forehead and on the higher-relief areas of the cap. Luster is present, but may be dull or lifeless, and interrupted in patches. At MS-63, contact marks are few, and abrasion is very light. An MS-65 coin has hardly any abrasion, and contact marks are so minute as to require magnification. Luster should be full and rich. Grades above MS-65 are not often seen but are defined by having fewer marks as perfection is approached. *Reverse:* Comments apply as for the obverse, except that abrasion and contact marks are most noticeable on the upper part of the eagle and the clouds. The field area is complex, with not much open space, given the stars above the eagle, the arrows and olive branch, and other features. Accordingly, marks are not as noticeable as on the obverse.

1797, 7 Over 5

1797, 16-Star Obverse

1797, 15-Star Obverse

1798, Small 8

1798, Large 8

1798, 13-Star Reverse

1798, 14-Star Reverse

1799, Small Reverse Stars

1799, Large Reverse Stars

1800, Pointed 1

1800, Blunt 1

1800, 8 Arrows

1800, 9 Arrows

1802, 2 Over 1
FS-G5-1802/1-301.

1803, 3 Over 2

1804, Small 8

1804, Small 8 Over
Large 8

1806, Pointed-Top 6,
Stars 8 and 5

Closeup of
Pointed-Top 6

1806, Round-Top 6,
Stars 7 and 6

Closeup of
Round-Top 6

1807, Small Reverse Stars

1807, Large Reverse Stars

	Mintage	Cert	Avg	%MS	AU-50	AU-55	AU-58	MS-60	MS-62	MS-63	MS-64	Recent Auction Record
1795, Heraldic Eagle	(a)	18	60.0	67	$50,000	$60,000	$70,000	$90,000	$135,000	$180,000	$275,000	$22,425, AU-55, Aug-09
1797, 7 Over 5	(a)	4	58.0	25	70,000	95,000	120,000	185,000				$126,500, AU-58, Sep-05
1797, 16-Star Obverse	(a)				*(unique, in the Smithsonian's National Numismatic Collection)*							
1797, 15-Star Obverse	(a)				*(unique, in the Smithsonian's National Numismatic Collection)*							
1798, All kinds	24,867											
1798, Small 8		19	57.0	26	18,500	23,500	26,000	37,500	47,500	80,000		$20,700, AU-55, Jan-10
1798, Large 8, 13-Star Reverse		45	53.0	16	14,000	24,500	30,000	50,000				$21,850, AU-53, May-10
1798, Large 8, 14-Star Reverse		13	56.1	8	27,500	40,000	60,000	115,000				$16,100, AU-50, Mar-10
1799, All kinds	7,451											
1799, Small Reverse Stars		7	59.7	57	14,000	17,500	22,000	27,500	37,500	65,000	100,000	$11,615, AU-50 CAC, Feb-10
1799, Large Reverse Stars		20	57.8	60	14,000	17,500	22,000	27,500	37,500	65,000	100,000	$15,525, AU-55, Jan-09
1800	37,628	281	57.6	45	10,000	11,500	12,500	15,000	18,000	35,000	65,000	$9,488, AU-55, Apr-10
1800, Pointed 1 (b)	*				20,000	23,000	24,500	27,500				
1800, 9 Arrows (c)	*				16,500	20,000						
1802, 2 Over 1	53,176	273	57.5	36	10,000	11,500	12,500	15,000	18,500	30,000	55,000 (d)	$7,475, EF-40, Jun-10
1803, 3 Over 2	33,506	343	57.6	45	10,000	11,500	12,500	15,000	18,500	30,000	55,000 (d)	$9,775, AU-58, Jun-10
1804, All kinds	30,475											
1804, Small 8		24	60.6	67	10,000	13,500	15,000	18,000	22,000	30,000	60,000	$14,950, MS-62, Jun-10
1804, Small 8 Over Large 8 (e)		64	59.6	59	10,500	15,000	18,000	20,000	25,000	40,000	75,000	$19,550, MS-62, Apr-10
1805	33,183	193	60.3	66	10,000	11,500	12,500	16,500	19,000	30,000	60,000 (f)	$8,050, EF-45, Apr-10
1806, Pointed-Top 6	9,676	75	57.5	51	10,000	11,500	12,500	16,500	19,000	30,000	55,000 (f)	$8,625, AU-53, Apr-10
1806, Round-Top 6	54,417	160	59.6	63	10,000	11,500	12,500	15,500	19,000	30,000	55,000 (f)	$8,338, AU-50, Mar-10
1807, All kinds	32,488											
1807, Small Reverse Stars					10,000	11,500	12,500	15,000	18,000	28,000	55,000 (f)	$14,950, MS-61, Jul-10
1807, Large Reverse Stars					10,000	11,500	12,500	15,000	18,000	28,000	55,000 (f)	$9,488, AU-58, Jun-10

* Included in number above. **a.** The 1795 and 1797 Heraldic Eagle half eagles are thought to have been struck in 1798 and included in that year's mintage figure of 24,867. **b.** 4 to 6 specimens are known. **c.** 18 to 25 specimens are known. **d.** Value in MS-65 is $125,000. **e.** Created when the engraver mistakenly used an 8 punch intended for $10 gold coins, then corrected the error by overpunching with a much smaller 8. **f.** Value in MS-65 is $120,000.

CAPPED BUST TO LEFT
(1807–1812)

Designer John Reich; weight 8.75 grams; composition .9167 gold, .0833 silver and copper; approx. diameter 25 mm; reeded edge.

Bass-Dannreuther-8.

History. This half eagle motif, designed by John Reich and stylistically related to his Capped Bust half dollar of 1807, was used for several years in the early 1800s. Quantities minted were high, and the coins saw wide circulation.

Striking and Sharpness. The striking usually is quite good and is significantly better than on earlier half eagle types. Adjustment marks are seen only occasionally. On the obverse, check the star centers and the hair details. On the reverse, check the eagle, particularity at the shield and the lower left. Examine the dentils on both sides.

Availability. After 1821 gold coins of this standard no longer circulated, as their bullion value exceeded their face value. Accordingly, they never sustained extensive wear, and nearly all examples are in EF or higher grades (coins used as pocket pieces or jewelry are exceptions). As a type this issue is readily available in grades up to MS-63, although MS-64 and 65 coins are seen on occasion. Most have excellent eye appeal.

VF-20, 30 (Very Fine). *Obverse:* Wear on the portrait has reduced the hair detail, especially to the right of the face and the top of the head, but much can still be seen. *Reverse:* Wear on the eagle is greater, and details of feathers near the shield and near the top of the wings are weak or missing. All other features show wear, but most are fairly sharp. Generally, Capped Bust gold coins at this grade level lack eye appeal.

EF-40, 45 (Extremely Fine). *Obverse:* More wear than at AU is seen on the portrait, the hair, the cap, and the drapery near the clasp. Luster is minimal or nonexistent at EF-40, and may be slight at EF-45. *Reverse:* Wear is more extensive than at AU on the eagle, including the top of the wings, the head, the top of the shield, and the claws. Some traces of luster may be seen, less so at EF-40 than at EF-45.

AU-50, 53, 55, 58 (About Uncirculated). *Obverse:* Light wear is seen on the cheek and the higher-relief areas of the hair and cap. Friction and scattered marks are in the field, ranging from extensive at AU-50 to minimal at AU-58. Luster may be seen in protected areas, minimal at AU-50 but more evident at AU-58. On an AU-58 coin the field retains some luster as well. *Reverse:* The eagle's neck, the top of the wings, the leaves, and the arrowheads show noticeable wear, as do other features. Luster ranges from perhaps 40% remaining in protected areas (at AU-50) to nearly full mint bloom (at AU-58). Often the reverse of this type retains much more luster than the obverse, as the motto, eagle, and lettering protect the surrounding flat areas.

MS-60 to 70 (Mint State). *Obverse:* At MS-60, some abrasion and contact marks are seen on the cheek, the hair below the LIBERTY inscription, and the highest-relief folds of the cap. Luster is present, but may be dull or lifeless, and interrupted in patches. At MS-63, contact marks are few, and abrasion is very light. At MS-64, abrasion is even less. An MS-65 coin has hardly any abrasion, and contact marks are minute. Luster should be full and rich and is often more intense on the obverse. Grades above MS-65 are defined by having fewer marks as perfection is approached. *Reverse:* Comments apply as for the obverse, except that abrasion is most noticeable on the eagle's neck and the highest area of the wings.

| 1808, 8 Over 7 | 1808, Normal Date | 1809, 9 Over 8 | 1810, Small Date | 1810, Large Date |

| Small 5 | Large 5 | Tall 5 |

	Mintage	Cert	Avg	%MS	AU-50	AU-55	AU-58	MS-60	MS-62	MS-63	MS-64	Recent Auction Record
1807	51,605	272	59.1	59	$8,000	$9,000	$11,000	$13,500	$15,500	$25,000	$37,500 (a)	$14,950, MS-62, Jul-10
1808, All kinds	55,578											
1808, 8 Over 7		46	59.0	61	9,000	11,500	13,500	16,000	25,000	35,000	65,000	$16,388, MS-61, Jan-10
1808		215	58.8	58	8,000	9,000	11,000	13,500	15,500	25,000	37,500 (b)	$13,800, MS-61 CAC, Jun-10
1809, 9 Over 8	33,875	208	59.3	61	8,000	9,000	10,000	13,500	15,500	25,000	50,000	$77,050, MS-65, Jun-10
1810, All kinds	100,287											$138,000, MS-62, Jun-08
1810, Small Date, Small 5		6	54.8	33	95,000	135,000						$11,500, MS-61, Apr-10
1810, Small Date, Tall 5		79	58.8	56	8,000	9,000	11,000	14,000	16,000	25,000	55,000	
1810, Large Date, Small 5					90,000	110,000		175,000				
1810, Large Date, Large 5		272	59.6	65	8,000	9,000	11,000	13,500	15,500	25,000	37,500 (c)	$20,700, MS-63, Apr-10
1811, All kinds	99,581											
1811, Small 5		21	56.7	62	8,000	9,000	11,000	13,500	15,500	25,000	37,500 (c)	$11,500, MS-61, Jun-10
1811, Tall 5		41	60.0	61	8,000	9,000	11,000	13,500	15,500	25,000	37,500 (c)	$8,050, AU-53, Apr-10
1812	58,087	248	59.6	70	8,000	9,000	11,000	13,500	15,500	25,000	37,500 (c)	$71,875, MS-65, Jun-10

a. Value in MS-65 is $100,000. **b.** Value in MS-65 is $115,000. **c.** Value in MS-65 is $95,000.

CAPPED HEAD TO LEFT
(1813–1834)

Designer John Reich (design modified by William Kneass in 1829); weight 8.75 grams; composition .9167 gold, .0833 silver and copper; diameter 25 mm (reduced to 23.8 mm in 1829); reeded edge.

Bass-Dannreuther-1.

History. Half eagles of this design are divided into issues of 1813 to 1829 (with a larger diameter), and issues of 1829 to 1834 (with a smaller diameter, and smaller letters, dates, and stars). Those dated 1813 to 1815 are in bold relief and sometimes collected as a separate variety.

Striking and Sharpness. On the obverse, check the star centers and the hair details (these details are usually less distinct on the 1829–1834 smaller-diameter coins). On the reverse, check the eagle. Most examples are well struck. Adjustment marks are not often encountered.

Availability. The 1813 and 1814, 4 Over 3, are seen with some frequency and constitute the main supply available for assembling type sets. Other dates range from very rare to extremely rare, with the 1822 topping the list (just three are known, two of which are in the Smithsonian Institution). As gold coins did not circulate after 1821, issues of 1813 to 1820 are usually seen in high-level AU or in MS, and those of the 1820s in MS. The half eagles of the early 1830s are exceptions; these usually show light wear and are much rarer in high-level MS.

EF-40, 45 (Extremely Fine). *Obverse:* More wear than at AU is seen on the portrait, the hair, the cap, and the drapery near the clasp. Luster is minimal or nonexistent at EF-40, and may be slight at EF-45. *Reverse:* Wear is more extensive than at AU on the eagle, including the top of the wings, the head, the top of the shield, and the claws. Some traces of luster may be seen, less so at EF-40 than at EF-45.

AU-50, 53, 55, 58 (About Uncirculated). *Obverse:* Light wear is seen on the cheek and the higher-relief areas of the hair and cap. Friction and scattered marks are in the field, ranging from extensive at AU-50 to min-

imal at AU-58. Luster may be seen in protected areas, minimal at AU-50 but more evident at AU-58. On an AU-58 coin the field retains some luster as well. *Reverse:* The eagle's neck, the top of the wings, the leaves, and the arrowheads show noticeable wear, as do other features. Luster ranges from perhaps 40% remaining in protected areas (at AU-50) to nearly full mint bloom (at AU-58). Often the reverse of this type retains much more luster than the obverse, as the motto, eagle, and lettering protect the surrounding flat areas.

MS-60 to 70 (Mint State). *Obverse:* At MS-60, some abrasion and contact marks are seen on the cheek, the

hair below the LIBERTY inscription, and the highest-relief folds of the cap. Luster is present, but may be dull or lifeless, and interrupted in patches. At MS-63, contact marks are few, and abrasion is very light. At MS-64, abrasion is even less. An MS-65 coin has hardly any abrasion, and contact marks are minute. Luster should be full and rich and is often more intense on the obverse. Grades above MS-65 are defined by having fewer marks as perfection is approached. *Reverse:* Comments apply as for the obverse, except that abrasion is most noticeable on the eagle's neck and the highest area of the wings.

1820, Curved-Base 2

1820, Square-Base 2

1820, Small Letters

1820, Large Letters

1825, 5 Over
Partial 4

1825, 5 Over 4

1828, 8 Over 7

1829, Large Date
Bass-Dannreuther-1.

1829, Small Date
Bass-Dannreuther-2.

Small 5D

Large 5D

1832, Curved-Base 2,
12-Star Obverse

1832, Curved-Base 2,
13-Star Obverse

1833, Large Date

1833, Small Date

1834, Plain 4

1834, Crosslet 4

	Mintage	Cert	Avg	%MS	AU-50	AU-55	AU-58	MS-60	MS-62	MS-63	MS-64	Recent Auction Record
1813	95,428	333	59.5	60	$9,500	$10,000	$11,500	$13,000	$15,000	$23,500	$37,500 (a)	$8,625, AU-55, Jul-10
1814, 4 Over 3	15,454	67	59.9	72	10,000	12,000	13,500	18,500	25,000	37,500	55,000	$43,125, MS-63, Mar-10
1815 *(11 known)*	635	5	59.0	60	225,000	300,000	350,000	450,000	550,000	750,000		$460,000, MS-64, Jan-09
1818, All kinds	48,588											
1818		37	59.9	59	10,500	13,000	16,500	22,500	28,000	47,500	75,000 (b)	$13,800, AU-58, Nov-09
1818, STATESOF one word		43	60.3	72	10,500	13,000	16,500	22,500	28,000	47,500	75,000	$60,375, MS-63 CAC, Apr-10
1818, 5D Over 50		8	62.0	88	11,000	15,000	18,000	27,500	35,000	55,000	70,000 (c)	$63,250, MS-64, Jan-10
1819, All kinds	51,723											
1819		2	50.0	50	65,000	85,000	90,000	105,000				
1819, 5D Over 50		7	53.4	29	60,000	80,000	90,000	100,000				$92,000, MS-63, Aug-98
1820, All kinds	263,806											
1820, Curved-Base 2, Sm Ltr		1	62.0	100	13,250	15,500	17,500	20,000	30,000	45,000		$37,375, MS-61, Jan-07
1820, Curved-Base 2, Lg Ltr					10,500	12,500	14,500	18,000	25,000	40,000		$253,000, MS-65, Apr-08
1820, Square-Base 2		3	62.7	100	10,000	11,500	13,500	17,500	24,000	35,000		$21,850, MS-61, Apr-10
1821	34,641	7	56.4	43	55,000	75,000	85,000	110,000	135,000	185,000		$112,125, AU-53, Nov-09
1822 *(3 known)*	17,796	1	40.0	0								
1823	14,485	24	56.1	42	12,000	16,000	18,000	24,500	30,000	55,000	75,000	$15,525, AU-50, Jul-09
1824	17,340	17	60.4	65	35,000	50,000	55,000	60,000	85,000	100,000	135,000 (d)	$126,500, MS-63, Feb-09
1825, 5 Over Partial 4 (e)	29,060	8	61.6	88	37,500	47,500	55,000	67,500	80,000	100,000	125,000	$51,750, MS-61, Jan-07
1825, 5 Over 4 *(2 known)*	*	2	56.5	50								$690,000, AU-50, Jul-08
1826	18,069	8	63.3	100	25,000	35,000	40,000	45,000	55,000	75,000		$69,000, AU-55, Jul-08
1827	24,913	14	62.9	93	37,500	45,000	50,000	55,000	65,000	90,000		$126,500, MS-64, Apr-08

* Included in number above. **a.** Value in MS-65 is $95,000. **b.** Value in MS-65 is $135,000. **c.** Value in MS-65 is $135,000. **d.** Value in MS-65 is $250,000. **e.** Sometimes called 1825, 5 Over 1.

	Mintage	Cert	Avg	%MS	AU-50	AU-55	AU-58	MS-60	MS-62	MS-63	MS-64	Recent Auction Record
1828, 8 Over 7 *(5 known)*	**	3	63.3	100	$100,000	$150,000	$200,000	$250,000	$350,000	$500,000		
1828	28,029	6	60.8	67	45,000	65,000	80,000	100,000	125,000	175,000		
1829, Large Date	57,442	2	66.0	100				175,000	250,000	325,000		

** Included in number below.

	Mintage	Cert	Avg	%MS	EF-40	AU-50	AU-55	AU-58	MS-60	MS-62	MS-63	Recent Auction Record
1829, Small Date	*	4	61.3	100	$115,000	$165,000	$225,000	$250,000	$275,000	$325,000	$450,000	
1830, Small or Large 5D (a)	126,351	23	60.1	74	37,500	45,000	52,500	55,000	67,500	75,000	95,000	$241,500, MS-65, Nov-09
1831, Small or Large 5D (b)	140,594	14	60.4	57	37,500	45,000	52,500	55,000	67,500	75,000	95,000	$80,500, AU-58, Jan-06
1832, Curved-Base 2, 12 Stars												
(5 known)	**	2	60.5	50	350,000							$63,250, MS-62, Jan-09
1832, Square-Base 2, 13 Stars	157,487	15	61.8	80	37,500	45,000	55,000	60,000	70,000	75,000	95,000 (c)	$63,250, MS-62, Jan-09
1833, Large Date	193,630	12	60.8	75	37,500	45,000	52,500	55,000	67,500	72,500	95,000 (d)	$46,000, MS-61, Mar-09
1833, Small Date (e)	***	1	65.0	100	37,500	45,000	52,500	55,000	95,000	110,000	130,000 (f)	$126,500, MS-63 PQ, May-06
1834, All kinds	50,141											
1834, Plain 4		15	53.7	40	37,500	45,000	52,500	55,000	85,000	90,000	100,000	$1,265, AU-55, Mar-10
1834, Crosslet 4		9	58.8	67	40,000	47,500	55,000	60,000	100,000	110,000	125,000	$63,250, MS-62, Jan-10

* Included in "1829, Large Date" mintage. ** Included in number below. *** Included in number above. **a.** The 1830 Small 5D is slightly rarer than the Large 5D. Certified population reports are unclear, and auction-lot catalogers typically do not differentiate between the two varieties. **b.** The 1831 Small 5D is estimated to be three to four times rarer than the Large 5D. Both are extremely rare. **c.** Value in MS-64 is $125,000. **d.** Value in MS-64 is $120,000. **e.** The 1833 Small Date is slightly scarcer than the Large Date. **f.** Value in MS-64 is $150,000.

Proof Capped Head to Left Half Eagles

PF-60 to 70 (Proof). Proof coins were struck on a limited basis for inclusion in sets and for numismatists. All are exceedingly rare. Over the years some prooflike MS pieces have been classified as Proofs.

Obverse and Reverse: PF-60 to 62 coins have extensive hairlines and may have nicks and contact marks. At PF-63, hairlines are prominent, but the mirror surface is very reflective. PF-64 coins have fewer hairlines.

At PF-65, hairlines should be minimal and mostly seen only under magnification. There should be no nicks or marks. PF-66 and higher coins should have no marks or hairlines visible to the unaided eye.

Proof Capped Head to Left Half Eagle
Bass-Dannreuther-3.

	Est Mintage	Cert	Avg	PF-60	PF-63	PF-64	PF-65	Recent Auction Record
1820, Square-Base 2 (a)	2–3				*(unique, in the Bass Foundation Collection)*			
1821 *(2–3 known)* (b)	3–5				*(extremely rare)*			
1822 *(3 known)* (c)	unknown				*(extremely rare)*			
1823 (d)	unknown							
1824 (e)	unknown							
1825, 5 Over Partial 4 (f)	1–2				*(unique, in the Smithsonian's National Numismatic Collection)*			
1826	2–4				*(unique, in the Smithsonian's National Numismatic Collection)*			
1827 (g)	unknown							
1828	1–2				*(unique, in the Smithsonian's National Numismatic Collection)*			
1829, Small Date *(2–3 known)* (h)	2–4				*(extremely rare)*			
1830 *(2 known)* (i)	2–4	1	63.0		*(extremely rare)*			
1832, Square-Base 2, 13 Stars	2–3				*(extremely rare)*			
1833 *(4–5 known)*	4–6	3	60.7		*(extremely rare)*			$977,500, PF-67, Jan-05

a. Some experts have questioned the Proof status of this unique piece; the surface of the coin is reflective, but it is not as convincing as other true Proofs of the type. Prior claims that as many as four Proofs exist of this date have not been substantiated. **b.** One is in the Bass Foundation Collection, and another is in the Smithsonian's National Numismatic Collection. **c.** The Proof status of the 1822 half eagles has been questioned. **d.** The only auction references for a Proof 1823 half eagle are from 1885 and 1962. Neither coin (assuming they are not the same specimen) has been examined by today's standards to confirm its Proof status. **e.** No 1824 Proof half eagles are known to exist, despite previous claims that the Smithsonian's Mint collection specimen (actually an MS-62 circulation strike) is a Proof. **f.** The Smithsonian's example is a PF-67 with a mirrored obverse and frosty reverse. A second example, reported to have resided in King Farouk's collection, has not been confirmed. **g.** Two purported 1827 Proofs have been revealed to be circulation strikes: the Smithsonian's example is an MS-64, and the Bass example is prooflike. **h.** One 1829 Proof is in the Bass Foundation Collection, and another of equal quality (PF-66) is in the Smithsonian's National Numismatic Collection. **i.** One 1830 Proof is in the Byron Reed collection at the Durham Museum, Omaha, Nebraska.

CLASSIC HEAD
(1834–1838)

Designer William Kneass; weight 8.36 grams; composition (1834–1836) .8992 gold, .1008 silver and copper (1837–1838) .900 gold; diameter 22.5 mm; reeded edge; mints: Philadelphia, Charlotte, Dahlonega.

Breen-6518.

Mintmark is above date.

History. U.S. Mint chief engraver William Kneass based the half eagle's Classic Head design on John Reich's cent of 1808. Minted under the Act of June 28, 1834, the coins' reduced size and weight encouraged circulation over melting or export, and they served American commerce until hoarding became extensive during the Civil War. Accordingly, many show extensive wear.

Striking and Sharpness. On the obverse, weakness is often seen on the higher areas of the hair curls. Also check the star centers. On the reverse, check the rims. The dentils are usually well struck.

Availability. Most coins range from VF to AU or lower grades of MS. Most MS coins are dated 1834. MS-63 and better examples are rare. Good eye appeal can be elusive.

AU-50, 53, 55, 58 (About Uncirculated). *Obverse:* Friction is seen on the higher parts, particularly the cheek and the hair (under magnification) of Miss Liberty. Friction and scattered marks are in the field, ranging from extensive at AU-50 to minimal at AU-58. Luster may be seen in protected areas, minimal at AU-50, more evident at AU-58. On an AU-58 coin the field retains some luster as well. *Reverse:* The eagle's neck, the top of the wings, the leaves, and the arrowheads show noticeable wear, as do other features. Luster ranges from perhaps 40% remaining in protected areas (at AU-50) to nearly full mint bloom (at AU-58). Often the reverse of this type retains much more luster than the obverse.

MS-60 to 70 (Mint State). *Obverse:* At MS-60, some abrasion and contact marks are seen on the portrait, most noticeably on the cheek, as the hair details are complex on this type. Luster is present, but may be dull or lifeless, and interrupted in patches. Many low-level MS coins have grainy surfaces. At MS-63, contact marks are few, and abrasion is very light. Abrasion is even less at MS-64. An MS-65 coin will have hardly any abrasion, and contact marks are minute. Luster should be full and rich and is often more intense on the obverse. Grades above MS-65 are defined by having fewer marks as perfection is approached. *Reverse:* Comments apply as for the obverse, except that abrasion is most noticeable in the field, on the eagle's neck, and on the highest area of the wings. Most MS coins in the marketplace are graded liberally, with slight abrasion on both sides of MS-65 coins.

1834, Plain 4

1834, Crosslet 4

	Mintage	Cert	Avg	%MS	AU-55	AU-58	MS-60	MS-62	MS-63	MS-64	MS-65	Recent Auction Record
1834, Plain 4 (a)	657,460	1,771	51.9	16	$2,000	$2,500	$4,500	$7,000	$11,500	$16,500	$55,000	$661, EF-45, Jul-10
1834, Crosslet 4	*	69	45.8	13	10,000	15,000	24,500	30,000	65,000	100,000		$8,050, AU-55, Jun-10
1835 (a)	371,534	583	51.2	14	2,000	2,500	4,500	7,000	12,500	25,000	65,000	$1,265, AU-55, Jul-10
1836	553,147	969	50.6	14	2,000	2,500	4,500	7,000	12,000	25,000	70,000	$719, EF-40, Jun-10
1837 (a)	207,121	380	51.1	14	2,100	2,600	5,500	9,000	17,000	35,000	85,000	$4,025, MS-60, Jul-10
1838	286,588	564	52.5	15	2,050	2,650	5,000	7,500	13,500	25,000	65,000	$1,725, AU-50, Apr-10
1838C	17,179	93	43.1	4	22,500	27,500	47,500	65,000	100,000			$8,050, EF-40, Mar-10
1838D	20,583	115	49.0	10	15,000	22,000	32,500	42,500	65,000			$4,888, EF-40, Jul-09

* Included in number above. **a.** Varieties have either a script 8 or block-style 8 in the date. (See illustrations of similar quarter eagles on page 275.)

Proof Classic Head Half Eagles

PF-60 to 70 (Proof). Proofs of the Classic Head type were made in small quantities, and today probably only a couple dozen or so survive, most bearing the 1834 date. *Obverse and Reverse:* PF-60 to 62 coins have extensive hairlines and may have nicks and contact marks. At PF-63, hairlines are prominent, but the mirror surface is very reflective. PF-64 coins have fewer hairlines. At PF-65, hairlines should be minimal and mostly seen only under magnification. There should be no nicks or marks. PF-66 and higher coins should have no marks or hairlines visible to the unaided eye.

Proof Classic Head Half Eagle
Breen-6501, McCloskey-3B.

	Est Mintage	Cert	Avg	PF-60	PF-63	PF-64	PF-65	Recent Auction Record
1834, Plain 4	8–12	6	63.2	$35,000	$85,000	$135,000	$200,000	$92,000, PF-63Cam, Jan-07
1835 (3–4 known)	4–6	1	68.0	37,500	100,000	150,000	250,000	$690,000, PF-67, Jan-05
1836 (3–4 known)	4–6	3	67.0	(extremely rare)				
1837	4–6			(unique; in the Smithsonian's National Numismatic Collection)				
1838	2–3	1	65.0	(unique; in the Bass Foundation Collection)				

LIBERTY HEAD
(1839–1908)

Designer Christian Gobrecht; weight 8.359 grams; composition .900 gold, .100 copper (net weight .24187 oz. pure gold); diameter (1839–1840) 22.5 mm, (1840–1866) 21.6 mm; reeded edge; mints: Philadelphia, Charlotte, Dahlonega, Denver, New Orleans, San Francisco.

1839, mintmark is above date.

1840–1908, mintmark is below eagle.

History. Christian Gobrecht's Liberty Head half eagle design was introduced in 1839. The mintmark in that year was located on the obverse of branch-mint coins; for all later issues it was relocated to the reverse. The motto IN GOD WE TRUST was added to the reverse in 1866.

Striking and Sharpness. On the obverse, check the highest points of the hair and the star centers. On the reverse, check the eagle's neck, and the area to the lower left of the shield and the lower part of the eagle. Generally, the eagle on the $5 coins is better struck than on those of the $2.50 denomination. Examine the dentils on both sides. Branch-mint coins struck before the Civil War are often lightly struck in areas. San Francisco half eagles are in lower average grades than are those from the Philadelphia Mint, as Philadelphia coins did not circulate at par in the East and Midwest from late December 1861 until December 1878, and thus did not acquire as much wear. Most late 19th- and early 20th-century coins are sharp in all areas; for these issues, tiny copper staining spots can be a problem.

Availability. Early dates and mintmarks are generally scarce to rare in MS and very rare in MS-63 to MS-65, with only a few exceptions. Charlotte and Dahlonega coins are usually EF or AU, or overgraded as low MS, this situation paralleling that seen with quarter eagles. Rarities include 1854-S and several varieties in the 1860s and 1870s. Coins of the 1880s onward generally are seen in higher than average grades.

AU-50, 53, 55, 58 (About Uncirculated). *Obverse:* Light wear is seen on the face, the hair to the right of the face, and the highest area of the hair bun, more so at AU-50 than at 53 or 55. An AU-58 coin has minimal traces of wear. An AU-50 coin has luster in protected areas among the stars and letters, with little in the open fields or on the portrait. At AU-58, most luster is present in the fields, but is worn away on the highest parts of the motifs. Striking must be taken into consideration, for a lightly struck coin can be AU, but be weak in the central areas. *Reverse:* Abrasion and contact marks are most noticeable on the eagle's neck and to the lower left of the shield. The eagle shows wear in all of the higher areas, as well as the leaves and arrowheads. From 1866 to 1908 the motto IN GOD WE TRUST helped protect

Continued on next page.

the field, with the result that luster is more extensive on this side in comparison to the obverse. Luster ranges from perhaps 50% remaining in protected areas (at AU-50) to nearly full mint bloom (at AU-58).

MS-60 to 70 (Mint State). *Obverse:* At MS-60, some abrasion and contact marks are evident, most notice-

ably on the hair to the right of Miss Liberty's forehead and on the jaw. Luster is present, but may be dull or lifeless, and interrupted in patches. At MS-63, contact marks are few, and abrasion is very light. An MS-65 coin has only slight abrasion, and contact marks are so minute as to require magnification. Luster should be full and rich. Grades above MS-65 are defined by hav-

ing fewer marks as perfection is approached. *Reverse:* Comments apply as for the obverse, except that abrasion and contact marks are most noticeable on the eagle's neck and to the lower left of the shield.

     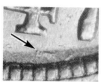

Small Letters   Large Letters   Small Date   Large Date   1846-D, High Second D Over D   1847, Top of Extra 7 Very Low at Border FS-G5-1847-301.

1848-D, D Over D   1850-C, Normal C   1850-C, Weak C   1851-D, Normal D   1851-D, Weak D   1854, Doubled-Die Obverse FS-G5-1854-101.

1854-C, Normal C   1854-C, Weak C   1854-D, Normal D   1854-D, Weak D

1873, Close 3   1873, Open 3   1881, Final 1 Over 0   1881, Recut 1881 Over 1881   1901-S, Final 1 Over 0 FS-G5-1901S-301.

	Mintage	Cert	Avg	%MS	AU-55	AU-58	MS-60	MS-62	MS-63	MS-64	MS-65	Recent Auction Record
1839	118,143	228	50.6	17	$1,500	$2,200	$4,000	$13,500	$20,000	$35,000		$1,121, AU-53, Apr-10
1839C	17,205	91	46.5	14	10,000	13,000	22,500	28,500	60,000			$126,500, MS-63, Mar-10
1839D	18,939	110	45.5	5	10,500	14,000	23,500	40,000				$5,175, EF-45, Jun-10
1840 (a)	137,382	302	50.9	8	1,850	2,300	3,500	4,500	11,000	23,000		$748, AU-50, Jul-10
1840C	18,992	80	45.9	6	10,500	14,500	25,000	35,000	57,500	95,000		$8,625, AU-58, Apr-10
1840D	22,896	66	50.4	20	9,500	13,000	16,000	26,000	45,000			$16,100, MS-61, Mar-10
1840O (a)	40,120	146	50.9	12	2,750	4,000	9,500	16,000	32,500			$1,495, AU-50, Jul-09
1841	15,833	88	54.4	26	1,850	2,500	4,500	6,500	10,000	17,500	$35,000	$1,610, AU-53, Dec-09
1841C	21,467	82	48.3	9	7,000	9,500	18,000	25,000	40,000	60,000		$23,000, MS-62 Secure, Jun-10
1841D	29,392	105	48.8	22	7,000	9,500	13,500	15,000	25,000	75,000		$1,610, VF-35, Mar-10
1841O (b)	50											
1842, All kinds	27,578											
1842, Small Letters		25	55.6	20	5,500	7,000	12,500	15,000	22,500	35,000	65,000	$1,842, AU-50, Apr-10
1842, Large Letters		22	49.8	0	6,500	8,000	13,500	16,000				$4,313, AU-58, Jun-10
1842C, All kinds	27,432											
1842C, Small Date		27	47.3	22	55,000	65,000	85,000	135,000				$92,000, MS-62, Jun-10
1842C, Large Date		92	49.2	10	5,500	7,500	14,000	18,500	35,000	47,500		$42,550, MS-64, Mar-10

a. Scarce varieties of the 1840 coins have the fine edge-reeding and wide rims of the 1839 issues. This is referred to as the broad-mill variety. **b.** Official Mint records report 8,350 coins struck at the New Orleans Mint in 1841. However, most—if not all—were actually dated 1840. No 1841-O half eagle has ever appeared on the market.

	Mintage	Cert	Avg	%MS	AU-55	AU-58	MS-60	MS-62	MS-63	MS-64	MS-65	Recent Auction Record
1842D, All kinds	59,608											
1842D, Small Date		143	45.4	6	$5,000	$6,500	$12,500	$17,500	$30,000			$1,955, VF-25, Dec-09
1842D, Large Date		24	44.3	8	21,500	25,000	40,000					$40,250, MS-61, Mar-10
1842O	16,400	46	43.1	4	15,000	17,000	22,500	30,000				$2,243, VF-30, Sep-09
1843	611,205	452	53.9	17	575	825	1,600	3,750	9,500	$17,500	$37,500	$504, AU-58, Jul-10
1843C	44,277	144	45.1	9	7,000	8,000	12,000	15,000	30,000	55,000		$3,105, AU-50, Apr-10
1843D	98,452	206	46.7	9	5,000	6,500	11,500	16,000	23,500	50,000		$1,955, VF-35, Jun-10
1843O, Small Letters	19,075	58	45.2	9	4,750	6,250	20,000	26,000	37,500	50,000	65,000	$1,495, EF-45, Sep-09
1843O, Large Letters	82,000	92	50.7	15	3,750	4,750	10,500	14,500	25,000	35,000		$21,850, MS-64, Sep-09
1844	340,330	284	53.7	12	625	875	1,950	3,500	8,000	18,000	55,000	$1,725, MS-61, Sep-09
1844C	23,631	67	46.0	9	10,000	12,500	17,500	25,000	35,000			$14,375, MS-61, Mar-10
1844D	88,982	207	47.0	10	5,000	6,500	9,500	12,500	27,500	40,000		$11,500, MS-62, Jul-10
1844O	364,600	608	50.7	9	1,400	2,200	4,250	6,000	13,500	23,500	45,000	$348, VG-8, May-10
1845	417,099	296	54.3	14	600	875	2,000	4,500	9,500	16,000		$805, AU-58, Jul-10
1845D	90,629	254	49.3	8	5,000	7,500	10,000	13,500	24,000	39,000	85,000	$4,888, AU-58, Mar-10
1845O	41,000	129	51.1	13	6,000	8,500	12,500	13,500	23,500			$1,265, EF-45, Jun-10
1846, All kinds	395,942											
1846, Large Date		147	55.1	17	1,350	2,250	3,500	3,750	13,500	18,500		$2,760, MS-61, Jul-10
1846, Small Date		67	55.6	18	700	875	2,750	3,500	12,500			$604, AU-53, Mar-10
1846C	12,995	63	50.2	13	10,000	14,000	21,000	26,000	57,500	85,000		$6,900, AU-58, Mar-10
1846D, All kinds	80,294											
1846D (c)		96	46.4	3	5,000	7,000	12,500	17,500				$14,950, MS-61, Jul-10
1846D, High Second D Over D		107	49.5	7	5,500	7,500	13,500	16,000	25,000			$6,325, AU-58, Mar-10
1846O	58,000	134	49.1	5	5,500	7,250	10,000	15,000	23,500			$3,450, AU-55, Dec-09
1847, All kinds	915,981											
1847		667	55.4	24	525	775	1,750	3,000	7,500	15,000		$404, AU-53, Apr-10
1847, Top of Extra 7 Very Low at Border		138	55.3	17	1,100	1,450	2,250	4,500	9,000	13,000		$920, AU-58, Jul-10
1847C	84,151	253	45.9	8	5,000	7,500	11,500	15,000	27,500	35,000	75,000	$2,013, EF-45, Jun-10
1847D	64,405	148	48.2	10	5,000	6,750	9,000	12,000	17,500			$2,473, AU-50, Jul-10
1847O	12,000	41	41.0	2	15,000	18,500	26,000	32,500				$1,265, VF-20, Jul-09
1848	260,775	324	54.0	13	700	875	1,600	3,500	9,500	25,000		$2,875, MS-62, Apr-10
1848C	64,472	164	45.1	4	6,750	9,000	16,500	25,000	45,000	67,500		$2,070, EF-45, Jul-10
1848D	47,465	107	49.0	7	6,750	9,000	12,500	17,500	25,000			$3,450, AU-50, Feb-10
1848D, D Over D	*				9,000	13,000	20,000	35,000				$29,900, MS-62, May-08
1849	133,070	168	53.7	16	1,050	1,350	2,750	5,500	12,500	15,000		$1,035, AU-58, Jun-10
1849C	64,823	201	50.4	15	5,250	7,500	11,000	14,000	26,000	40,000		$2,070, EF-40, Apr-10
1849D	39,036	138	49.0	6	5,000	7,500	12,000	17,500	34,000			$6,038, AU-58, Jun-10
1850	64,491	129	49.6	5	1,500	1,900	3,000	6,500	15,000	32,000	75,000	$805, AU-53, Apr-10
1850C	63,591	158	48.4	13	6,000	8,000	11,000	14,000	23,000	38,000		$8,625, MS-61, Jul-10
1850C, Weak C (d)	*	32	48.1	13	3,000	4,000						$3,738, AU-58, Oct-09
1850D	43,984	126	48.3	3	6,000	8,000	25,000	50,000				$6,900, AU-58, Apr-10
1851	377,505	366	55.4	19	575	875	2,750	4,500	9,000	23,000		$5,175, MS-62, Apr-10
1851C	49,176	135	47.7	9	5,500	8,000	13,000	24,000	40,000	60,000		$2,300, AU-50, Mar-10
1851D	62,710	112	49.5	8	6,000	8,000	11,500	15,000	25,000	45,000		$16,675, MS-62, Apr-10
1851D, Weak D (d)	*	9	56.8	44	3,000	4,000						$2,185, AU-50, Jul-09
1851O	41,000	129	46.2	1	6,000	8,000	11,000	16,000	21,000	60,000		$1,955, EF-45 CAC, Jul-09
1852	573,901	610	55.7	22	525	800	1,700	3,000	8,000	15,000	27,500	$1,668, MS-61, Apr-10
1852C	72,574	216	50.4	19	4,750	5,500	7,000	10,000	21,000	30,000		$1,898, EF-45, Mar-10
1852D	91,584	238	48.9	9	5,250	6,500	10,000	16,000	24,000			$3,881, AU-55, Jul-10
1853	305,770	432	55.1	18	550	800	1,800	3,500	7,750	15,000	65,000	$431, AU-55, Jun-10
1853C	65,571	150	48.6	17	4,750	5,000	7,500	11,000	25,000	50,000		$18,400, MS-63, Mar-10
1853D	89,678	327	51.5	11	4,500	5,000	7,500	11,500	19,000	55,000		$4,025, AU-58, Mar-10
1854	160,675	337	55.6	25	1,050	1,400	2,000	3,500	8,500	15,000		$633, AU-58, Jun-10
1854, Doubled-Die Obverse	*	15	53.0	13	1,350	1,850	2,500					$3,220, MS-62 CAC, Mar-09
1854C	39,283	108	49.8	13	6,000	8,000	11,500	22,500	36,000			$4,025, AU-58, Mar-10
1854C, Weak C (d)	*	27	49.3	15	3,000	4,000						$1,955, AU-55, Mar-10

* Included in number above. **c.** The 1846-D half eagle with a normal mintmark actually is rarer than the variety with a boldly repunched D Over D mintmark. The latter is in greater demand, however, because of its dramatic visual appeal; hence its higher market values in some grades. **d.** Several branch-mint half eagles of the early 1850s can exhibit weak (sometimes very weak or almost invisible) mintmarks; such coins generally trade at deep discounts.

Chart continued on next page.

	Mintage	Cert	Avg	%MS	AU-55	AU-58	MS-60	MS-62	MS-63	MS-64	MS-65	Recent Auction Record
1854D	56,413	225	53.5	24	$5,000	$7,500	$10,500	$14,000	$25,000	$42,500	$75,000	$9,775, MS-62, Jun-10
1854D, Weak D (d)	*	10	46.7	0	2,500	3,500						$1,475, AU-50, Oct-09
1854O	46,000	166	51.2	7	2,400	3,000	7,000	13,000	22,500			$1,265, AU-55, Jul-09
1854S (3 known)	268	1	58.0	0	3,000,000		—					
1855	117,098	210	54.7	13	650	875	1,850	3,500	7,500	16,000		$633, AU-55, Jun-10
1855C	39,788	144	48.8	10	5,500	8,000	13,500	17,500	40,000	65,000		$3,738, AU-55, Apr-10
1855D	22,432	74	50.1	8	5,500	7,500	15,000	17,500	37,500			$3,516, AU-53, Apr-10
1855O	11,100	64	48.7	5	6,000	8,000	20,000					$2,302, EF-45, Jul-09
1855S	61,000	115	47.2	3	4,750	6,000	12,500	22,000				$748, VF-35, Jul-10
1856	197,990	318	54.6	13	650	875	2,000	3,750	11,000	17,500	45,000	$403, AU-53, Apr-10
1856C	28,457	138	50.7	9	6,000	9,000	17,500	25,000	35,000			$1,898, EF-40, Jun-10
1856D	19,786	106	48.6	13	6,000	8,000	11,500	15,000	35,000	50,000		$2,990, AU-50, Jul-10
1856O	10,000	49	49.0	10	6,750	8,500	14,000	18,500				$4,744, AU-53 CAC, Oct-09
1856S	105,100	132	48.3	7	2,250	3,500	6,750	13,000	25,000	38,000		$3,335, AU-58, Jul-10
1857	98,188	268	55.5	16	550	800	1,900	4,000	8,000	16,000		$2,990, MS-62, Jun-10
1857C	31,360	171	53.3	13	5,000	6,000	8,500	16,000	27,500			$3,594, AU-58, Mar-10
1857D	17,046	102	51.5	12	6,250	7,500	11,500	16,000	34,000			$4,888, AU-55 CAC, Jun-10
1857O	13,000	86	49.5	3	6,500	7,750	12,500	25,000	42,500			$978, VF-30, Jul-10
1857S	87,000	115	48.9	5	2,500	4,000	10,500	14,000	21,000			$403, VG-10, Jul-10
1858	15,136	80	53.2	18	1,500	2,000	3,250	5,000	10,500	14,000	35,000	$690, EF-45, Jun-10
1858C	38,856	186	50.7	11	5,750	7,500	12,000	20,000	35,000			$18,400, MS-62 Secure, Jun-10
1858D	15,362	109	51.2	10	6,000	7,750	12,500	19,000	35,000	45,000		$5,175, AU-58, Mar-10
1858S	18,600	60	48.4	0	10,500	14,500	25,000					$5,463, AU-55, Aug-09
1859	16,734	92	49.6	8	1,500	3,000	6,000	7,500	12,500			$575, EF-45, Dec-09
1859C	31,847	129	50.7	10	6,000	8,500	15,000	23,000	40,000			$4,888, AU-58, Apr-10
1859D	10,366	118	52.3	9	6,000	8,000	14,000	27,000	37,500			$5,175, AU-58, Apr-10
1859S	13,220	30	47.7	7	10,000	13,500	22,500	30,000				$5,175, AU-55, Jul-10
1860	19,763	103	52.7	7	1,500	2,000	3,250	7,500	13,500	24,000		$633, EF-45, May-10
1860C	14,813	113	52.1	17	8,000	9,000	11,500	15,000	25,000	40,000		$1,725, VF-35, Jul-09
1860D	14,635	146	53.1	10	8,000	9,500	15,000	22,500	42,500	75,000		$5,463, AU-58, Jun-10
1860S	21,200	53	45.0	2	7,500	9,000	22,000	35,000				$690, VG-10, Jan-10
1861	688,084	1,382	56.1	20	500	800	1,600	3,500	7,500	12,000	30,000	$1,840, MS-61, Jul-10
1861C	6,879	89	51.1	7	12,500	15,000	27,500	45,000	85,000			$10,350, AU-55, Apr-10
1861D	1,597	37	51.5	14	37,500	45,000	65,000	100,000	185,000			$25,300, AU-53, Mar-08
1861S	18,000	46	42.2	0	10,000	15,000						$2,760, VF-30, Jul-09
1862	4,430	31	51.1	3	4,500	6,500	23,000					$4,313, EF-45, May-09
1862S	9,500	43	39.7	5	22,500	27,500	45,000					$1,495, VG-8, Jul-09
1863	2,442	17	51.9	12	12,000	16,000	24,000					$14,375, AU-58, May-08
1863S	17,000	57	43.4	0	16,000	20,000	30,000					$633, G-4, Feb-10
1864	4,170	52	52.5	8	7,000	8,500	12,500					$4,025, AU-53, Feb-10
1864S	3,888	10	37.6	0	35,000	45,000						$8,625, VF-35, Feb-09
1865	1,270	29	51.7	17	13,500	15,000	20,000					$8,050, AU-55, Jan-07
1865S	27,612	91	44.1	5	8,500	13,000	19,500	27,500	35,000	55,000		$4,313, AU-55, Apr-10
1866S, No Motto	9,000	50	34.5	0	16,000	21,000	35,000					$8,913, AU-53, May-10
1866, Motto Above Eagle	6,700	45	54.2	13	5,000	7,500	13,500	25,000	45,000			$2,875, AU-50, Apr-10
1866S, Motto Above Eagle	34,920	43	37.8	2	10,500	13,500	22,500					$2,760, EF-45, Dec-09
1867	6,870	54	49.4	4	4,500	6,000	10,000					$1,265, EF-45, Sep-09
1867S	29,000	78	40.4	0	15,000	20,000						$920, VF-20, Mar-10
1868	5,700	53	51.4	4	5,000	7,500	11,000	22,500				$4,600, AU-58, Feb-10
1868S	52,000	101	40.8	2	5,000	7,500	15,000					$1,035, EF-40, Apr-10
1869	1,760	42	52.5	10	5,000	7,500	12,500	21,000	27,000	37,500		$1,610, EF-40, Jul-09
1869S	31,000	118	40.9	2	7,000	10,000	20,000	25,000				$3,450, AU-55, Apr-10
1870	4,000	54	50.2	0	5,000	7,500	13,500					$1,748, EF-45, Dec-09
1870CC	7,675	42	35.8	2	47,500	65,000	115,000					$9,775, VF-20, Apr-10
1870S	17,000	101	39.9	0	11,000	13,500	22,500					$6,038, AU-53, Jul-10
1871	3,200	80	53.3	9	5,000	6,500	10,000					$2,530, EF-45, Jul-10
1871CC	20,770	82	36.7	2	18,500	25,000	50,000	65,000	90,000			$4,025, EF-40, Apr-10
1871S	25,000	107	45.5	2	7,000	8,500	12,000					$5,175, AU-58, Apr-10
1872	1,660				4,500	6,000	11,500	14,000	18,000	22,500		$3,220, AU-53, Jul-09

* Included in number above. **d.** Several branch-mint half eagles of the early 1850s can exhibit weak (sometimes very weak or almost invisible) mintmarks; such coins generally trade at deep discounts.

	Mintage	Cert	Avg	%MS	AU-55	AU-58	MS-60	MS-62	MS-63	MS-64	MS-65	Recent Auction Record
1872CC	16,980	58	36.0	0	$26,000	$37,500						$6,325, EF-45, Apr-10
1872S	36,400	137	43.5	2	6,750	8,000	$13,000					$2,875, AU-55, Mar-10
1873, Close 3	112,480	279	55.9	27	600	825	1,200	$2,500	$6,500	$10,000	$20,000	$978, MS-61, Jun-10
1873, Open 3	112,505	303	55.8	26	500	625	875	1,500	4,000	6,500	12,500	$354, AU-58, Mar-10
1873CC	7,416	31	34.4	3	30,000	35,000	50,000	65,000				$3,450, F-15, Jul-09
1873S	31,000	110	42.0	1	5,500	8,000	19,000					$863, EF-40, Jun-10
1874	3,488	52	49.8	10	3,500	5,000	11,000	15,000	22,500			$4,313, AU-58 CAC, Apr-10
1874CC	21,198	120	41.1	1	14,000	20,000	34,000	45,000				$13,800, AU-55, Mar-10
1874S	16,000	87	42.1	0	6,500	9,000						$3,738, AU-53, Jul-10
1875	200	4	52.5	0	100,000	125,000						$74,750, AU-55, Feb-07
1875CC	11,828	99	37.7	1	18,500	23,500	42,500	65,000	115,000			$4,025, VF-30, Jun-10
1875S	9,000	58	42.9	3	7,500	11,500	20,000	25,000	35,000			$2,530, EF-45, Jan-10
1876	1,432	24	55.5	21	6,000	8,000	11,000	16,000	19,000	25,000	40,000	$3,594, EF-40, Jun-10
1876CC	6,887	75	39.2	1	18,000	23,000	40,000	60,000				$34,500, MS-61, Jan-10
1876S	4,000	24	39.3	4	10,000	13,000	20,000					$1,955, VF-30, Jul-09
1877	1,132	44	54.9	23	4,750	6,500	12,500	17,500				$4,600, AU-53, May-09
1877CC	8,680	99	38.5	0	13,500	20,000	45,000	75,000				$5,750, EF-45, Jul-10
1877S	26,700	123	42.8	2	4,000	5,000	7,500	11,000	18,500	30,000		$1,380, AU-53, Feb-10
1878	131,720	342	59.0	54	475	490	550	950	2,000	6,500	12,000	$920, MS-62 Star, Jun-10
1878CC	9,054	47	40.6	4	27,500	35,000	75,000					$6,900, EF-40, Apr-10
1878S	144,700	445	56.4	26	525	625	900	1,500	4,000	7,000		$374, AU-58, Mar-10
1879	301,920	589	59.4	56	475	490	550	700	2,000	5,000	10,000	$4,744, MS-64, Jul-10
1879CC	17,281	153	44.4	3	6,000	8,000	20,000					$9,775, AU-58, Jul-10
1879S	426,200	659	57.1	27	490	625	900	1,500	3,000	6,000	20,000	$2,530, MS-63, Apr-10
1880	3,166,400	2,289	60.3	77	475	490	500	625	1,025	2,000	5,500	$374, EF-45, Jun-10
1880CC	51,017	280	46.3	4	4,250	6,500	11,500	23,500	36,000			$1,380, AU-50, Jul-10
1880S	1,348,900	1,618	61.0	84	475	490	500	625	1,025	1,800	6,000	$1,725, MS-64, Apr-10
1881, Final 1 Over 0 (e)	*	103	58.2	53	675	775	1,000	2,000	4,000	10,000		$3,738, MS-63, Jul-10
1881, Recut 1881 Over 1881	*				500	550	625	700	1,325			$518, MS-62, Apr-10
1881	5,708,802	12,418	61.5	92	475	490	500	625	1,025	1,600	4,000	$389, AU-58, Jul-10
1881CC	13,886	76	43.6	5	10,500	14,000	21,500	37,500	55,000			$805, F-15, Mar-10
1881S	969,000	1,531	61.4	90	475	490	500	625	1,025	1,650	5,000	$1,163, MS-64, Jun-10
1882	2,514,520	6,068	61.6	91	475	490	500	625	1,025	1,600	4,500	$1,265, MS-64, Jul-10
1882CC	82,817	499	51.4	6	2,300	4,500	10,000	18,000	35,000			$3,594, AU-58, Apr-10
1882S	969,000	1,880	61.7	92	475	490	500	625	1,025	1,600	4,250	$1,495, MS-64 CAC, Jul-10
1883	233,400	387	60.3	72	475	490	500	625	1,400	2,500	12,500	$575, MS-62, Feb-10
1883CC	12,598	128	50.2	4	6,500	8,500	18,500	25,000				$921, VG-10, Sep-09
1883S	83,200	199	57.6	47	475	490	875	1,500	3,250	7,000		$1,093, MS-62, Jun-10
1884	191,030	368	58.9	55	475	490	725	1,300	2,500	3,000	9,000	$1,035, MS-62, Jul-10
1884CC	16,402	174	50.3	3	6,000	9,000	20,000	27,500				$9,200, AU-58, Jul-10
1884S	177,000	420	59.9	68	475	490	500	625	1,750	3,500	10,000	$546, MS-62, Jun-10
1885	601,440	1,110	61.4	86	475	490	500	625	1,025	1,500	4,500	$863, MS-63, Jul-10
1885S	1,211,500	3,449	62.0	95	475	490	500	625	1,025	1,500	4,000	$690, MS-62, Jul-10
1886	388,360	524	60.0	65	475	490	500	625	1,025	1,500	7,000	$1,265, MS-63 CAC, Jun-10
1886S	3,268,000	6,149	61.4	93	475	490	500	625	1,025	1,500	4,250	$546, MS-62, Jul-10
1887S	1,912,000	2,669	61.3	92	475	490	500	625	1,025	1,800	5,000	$1,495, MS-64, Jul-10
1888	18,201	143	60.0	70	500	550	675	1,000	2,250	3,500	8,500	$1,006, MS-62, Jun-10
1888S	293,900	319	55.0	21	800	925	1,125	2,000	4,500			$1,265, MS-62, Jun-10
1889	7,520	136	58.1	42	700	825	1,050	1,800	3,000	6,000		$1,265, MS-61, Jun-10
1890	4,240	69	55.7	29	950	1,200	1,850	3,000	6,500	8,500	11,000	$1,955, MS-61, Jun-10
1890CC	53,800	536	57.5	50	900	1,100	1,500	3,000	9,000	15,000	45,000	$2,703, MS-62, May-10
1891	61,360	329	60.6	79	475	490	650	950	1,850	3,500	6,500	$2,070, MS-62 CAC, Mar-10
1891CC	208,000	1,634	58.3	56	950	1,350	2,500	3,000	4,000	7,000	25,000	$1,495, MS-61, Jul-10
1892	753,480	1,696	61.6	93	475	490	500	675	1,125	1,450	4,000	$863, MS-63, Jun-10
1892CC	82,968	607	54.1	23	1,050	1,250	2,000	3,000	8,250	13,500	28,000	$3,220, MS-62, Jul-10
1892O	10,000	43	57.9	49	1,750	2,000	3,250	6,500	12,500	16,000		$4,600, MS-60, Jun-10
1892S	298,400	392	57.7	44	475	490	675	950	2,500	4,000	7,500	$690, MS-62, Mar-10
1893	1,528,120	6,292	61.9	97	475	490	500	625	1,025	1,450	3,750	$1,610, MS-64, Jul-10
1893CC	60,000	556	55.8	30	1,250	1,400	2,000	3,500	8,500	16,000	25,000	$3,220, MS-62, Jun-10

* Included in number below. **e.** The last digit of the date is repunched over the remnants of a zero; this is easily visible with the naked eye, making the 1 Over 0 a popular variety.

Chart continued on next page.

	Mintage	Cert	Avg	%MS	AU-55	AU-58	MS-60	MS-62	MS-63	MS-64	MS-65	Recent Auction Record
18930	110,000	450	58.9	53	$650	$925	$1,250	$2,200	$6,250	$10,000		$1,093, MS-61, Apr-10
1893S	224,000	917	60.9	83	475	490	500	625	1,025	2,750	$8,500	$546, MS-62, Jul-10
1894	957,880	2,624	61.8	96	475	490	500	625	1,025	1,450	3,750	$805, MS-63, Jul-10
18940	16,600	293	57.7	37	800	975	1,500	2,200	7,000			$863, AU-58, Jun-10
1894S	55,900	201	52.6	12	900	1,200	2,500	3,500	8,500	16,000		$633, AU-58, Jun-10
1895	1,345,855	6,174	61.7	95	475	490	500	625	1,025	1,450	3,750	$805, MS-63, Jun-10
1895S	112,000	295	53.2	7	900	1,200	2,250	2,750	6,000	12,000	23,000	$446, AU-55, Jun-10
1896	58,960	428	61.9	94	475	490	500	625	1,025	1,450	3,750	$16,100, MS-65 CAC, Jun-10
1896S	155,400	353	54.3	18	700	925	1,250	2,500	6,000	7,500	20,000	$489, AU-58, Apr-10
1897	867,800	3,343	61.7	93	475	490	500	625	1,025	1,450	3,750	$489, MS-60, Jun-10
1897S	354,000	370	55.9	22	625	675	900	1,500	5,000	7,500		$748, MS-61, Apr-10
1898	633,420	1,937	61.6	94	475	490	500	625	1,025	1,600	3,750	$1,380, MS-64, Jul-10
1898S	1,397,400	553	59.6	70	475	490	500	625	1,100	2,750	7,500	$633, MS-62 Star, Jul-10
1899	1,710,630	10,610	62.5	98	475	490	500	625	1,025	1,450	3,750	$1,208, MS-64, Jul-10
1899S	1,545,000	762	59.8	73	475	490	500	625	1,100	1,750	8,500	$518, MS-62, Jun-10
1900	1,405,500	12,775	62.1	96	475	490	500	625	1,025	1,450	3,750	$984, MS-64, Jul-10
1900S	329,000	473	60.3	70	475	490	500	625	1,100	1,750	9,500	$546, MS-62, Jul-10
1901	615,900	4,260	61.9	93	475	490	500	625	1,025	1,600	3,750	$1,208, MS-64, Jun-10
1901S, All kinds	3,648,000											
1901S, Final 1 Over 0		325	60.8	73	500	525	575	700	1,500	2,000	6,000	$504, MS-62, Mar-10
1901S		5,910	62.1	92	475	490	500	625	1,025	1,450	3,750	$1,208, MS-64, Jun-10
1902	172,400	1,199	61.9	94	475	490	500	625	1,025	1,450	3,750	$3,738, MS-65, Apr-10
1902S	939,000	2,164	62.3	93	475	490	500	625	1,025	1,450	3,750	$1,840, MS-64 CAC, Jul-10
1903	226,870	1,500	61.7	92	475	490	500	625	1,025	1,450	3,750	$5,750, MS-66, Apr-10
1903S	1,855,000	3,630	62.2	93	475	490	500	625	1,025	1,450	3,750	$690, MS-63, Jul-10
1904	392,000	3,263	62.0	95	475	490	500	625	1,025	1,450	3,750	$6,325, MS-66, Apr-10
1904S	97,000	229	57.3	36	575	700	1,025	1,600	3,400	5,500	9,000	$360, AU-53, Mar-10
1905	302,200	2,221	62.0	94	475	490	500	625	1,025	1,450	3,750	$6,325, MS-66, Apr-10
1905S	880,700	808	57.3	30	490	525	675	1,025	2,000	3,500	8,000	$1,610, MS-63 CAC, Jul-10
1906	348,735	2,286	61.8	93	475	490	500	625	1,025	1,450	3,750	$417, MS-61, May-10
1906D	320,000	2,215	62.2	94	475	490	500	625	1,025	1,450	3,750	$489, MS-62, Apr-10
1906S	598,000	519	60.3	72	475	490	525	850	1,250	1,750	5,500	$1,610, MS-64, Mar-10
1907	626,100	7,204	62.1	96	475	490	500	625	1,025	1,450	3,750	$1,495, MS-64+, Jun-10
1907D	888,000	3,549	62.0	94	475	490	500	625	1,025	1,450	3,750	$4,025, MS-66, Apr-10
1908	421,874	5,108	62.4	96	475	490	500	625	1,025	1,450	3,750	$1,093, MS-64, Jul-10

Proof Liberty Head Half Eagles

PF-60 to 70 (Proof). Proof examples exist in relation to their original mintages, with all issues prior to the 1890s being rare. Cameo contrast is the rule for Proofs prior to 1902. Beginning that year the portrait was polished in the die, although a few years later cameo-contrast coins were again made. *Obverse and Reverse:* PF-60 to 62 coins have extensive hairlines and may have nicks and contact marks. At PF-63, hairlines are prominent, but the mirror surface is very reflective. PF-64 coins have fewer hairlines. At PF-65, hairlines should be minimal and mostly seen only under magnification. There should be no nicks or marks. PF-66 and higher coins should have no marks or hairlines visible to the unaided eye.

Proof Liberty Head Half Eagle

	Est Mintage	Cert	Avg	PF-60	PF-63	PF-64	PF-65	Recent Auction Record
1839 (2–3 known)	2–3	1	61.0	(extremely rare)				$184,000, PF-61, Jan-10
1840	2–3			(unique; in the Smithsonian's National Numismatic Collection)				
1841 (2 known) (a)	2–3	1	63.0	(extremely rare)				
1842, Small Letters (b)	4–6	1	64.0	(extremely rare)				$172,500, PF-64Cam Star, Jan-09

a. One is in the Smithsonian's National Numismatic Collection; the other is ex Eliasberg Collection. **b.** One is in the Smithsonian's National Numismatic Collection; the other is ex Pittman Collection.

	Mintage	Cert	Avg	PF-60	PF-63	PF-64	PF-65	Recent Auction Record
1843 (4–5 known)	4–8	4	64.0	(extremely rare)				$34,500, PF-58, Aug-09
1843D (c)	unknown	1	65.0				—	
1844 (2 known) (d)	3–5	1	64.0	(extremely rare)				
18440 (e)	1			(unique)				
1845 (4–5 known)	5–8	2	65.0	(extremely rare)				
1846 (4–5 known) (f)	6–10	1	64.0	(extremely rare)				
1847	2–3			(unique; in the Smithsonian's National Numismatic Collection)				
1848 (2 known) (g)	3–5			(extremely rare)				
1854 (h)	unknown							
1857 (2 known)	3–6	1	65.0	(extremely rare)				$230,000, PF-65Cam, Jan-07
1858 (4–5 known) (i)	4–6	5	65.6	$30,000	$75,000	$100,000	$150,000	$195,500, PF-66UCam, Mar-06
1859	80	4	63.5	22,500	42,500	75,000	125,000	
1860	62	5	64.6	20,000	40,000	65,000	100,000	$109,250, PF-66Cam, Jun-08
1861	66	2	65.0	18,500	35,000	55,000	87,500	
1862	35	10	64.4	17,000	35,000	55,000	87,500	$57,500, PF-64, Dec-08
1863	30	4	61.5	17,000	35,000	52,500	85,000	$69,000, PF-64DCam, Nov-05
1864	50	17	64.6	15,000	32,500	50,000	77,500	$86,250, PF-65DCam, Aug-09
1865	25	12	64.8	15,000	32,500	50,000	77,500	$14,375, PF-53, Apr-10
1866, Motto Above Eagle	30	5	61.0	12,500	25,000	35,000	60,000	
1867	50	6	63.3	12,500	25,000	35,000	60,000	$74,750, PF-66 CAC, Dec-09
1868	25	4	64.0	12,500	25,000	35,000	60,000	$69,000, PF-64DCam, Jun-08
1869	25	5	63.6	12,500	25,000	35,000	60,000	$47,150, PF-65Cam, Jan-07
1870	35	2	65.0	12,500	25,000	35,000	60,000	$109,250, PF-66Cam, Feb-07
1871	30	6	60.3	12,500	25,000	35,000	60,000	$65,500, PF-65Cam, Jan-08
1872	30	7	62.6	12,500	24,500	35,000	60,000	$21,275, PF-64, Jan-98
1873, Close 3	25	13	64.2	12,500	25,000	35,000	60,000	$59,800, PF-65UCam, Nov-09
1874	20	2	65.0	12,500	27,500	40,000	65,000	$57,500, PF-65Cam Star, Oct-08
1875 (j)	20	8	62.1	55,000	95,000	125,000	165,000	$161,000, PF-63, Mar-05
1876	45	16	64.3	10,000	18,500	25,000	47,500	$63,250, PF-66Cam, Aug-06
1877	20	3	65.3	10,000	22,500	32,500	57,500	$51,750, PF-63, Jun-05
1878	20	8	64.4	10,000	22,500	32,500	57,500	$60,375, PF-64, Mar-05
1879	30	5	64.4	10,000	20,000	30,000	55,000	$60,375, PFP-65Cam PQ, May-08
1880	36	7	65.7	8,500	17,500	30,000	52,500	$72,702, PF-67Cam, Aug-06
1881	42	8	65.6	7,500	16,500	25,000	40,000	$21,275, PF-64Cam, Feb-09
1882	48	13	64.4	7,500	15,500	25,000	40,000	$9,085, PF-63Cam, Feb-10
1883	61	9	64.2	7,500	15,500	25,000	40,000	$86,825, PF-67UCam, Nov-09
1884	48	8	64.5	7,500	15,500	25,000	40,000	$54,625, PF-65UCam, Mar-08
1885	66	21	64.3	7,500	15,000	25,000	40,000	$18,400, PF-64UCam, Mar-10
1886	72	9	64.1	7,500	15,000	25,000	40,000	$2,875, PF-55, Oct-06
1887 (Proof only)	87	11	62.4	37,500	62,500	80,000	115,000	$50,600, PF-64, Feb-09
1888	95	19	64.6	7,500	13,500	20,000	32,500	$34,500, PF-65DCam, Oct-08
1889	45	13	64.2	7,500	14,500	22,500	35,000	$16,100, PF-64Cam, Jan-10
1890	88	32	64.9	7,000	14,500	22,500	35,000	$35,650, PF-65DCam, May-08
1891	53	25	64.7	7,000	13,500	20,000	32,500	$19,550, PF-64DCam, Jan-10
1892	92	19	64.4	7,000	13,500	18,000	32,500	$16,738, PF-64DCam, May-09
1893	77	28	64.4	7,000	13,500	18,000	32,500	$51,750, PF-66DCam, Jun-07
1894	75	26	63.9	6,500	13,500	18,500	32,500	$37,375, PF-66Cam, Jun-10
1895	81	26	64.7	6,000	12,500	18,000	30,000	$16,675, PF-64UCam , Jul-09
1896	103	22	64.8	6,000	12,000	18,000	30,000	$17,250, PF-64UCam Star, Jan-10
1897	83	26	64.5	6,000	12,000	18,000	30,000	$47,294, PF-66UCam, Aug-07
1898	75	38	64.4	6,000	12,000	18,000	30,000	$60,375, PF-67UCam, Jul-09
1899	99	29	64.5	6,000	12,000	18,000	30,000	$13,800, PF-64Cam, May-10
1900	230	61	64.6	6,000	12,000	18,000	30,000	$69,000, PF-66Cam, Jan-10

c. One example of the 1843-D half eagle, probably a presentation strike of some sort, has been certified by NGC as a Specimen (rated Specimen-65). **d.** One is in the Smithsonian's National Numismatic Collection; the other is ex Pittman Collection. **e.** First sold in 1890; pedigree is ex Seavy, Parmelee, Woodin, Newcomer, Farouk, Kosoff; current location unknown. **f.** Of the 20 or so Proof sets made in 1846, experts believe only 4 or 5 contained the year's gold coinage. **g.** One is in the Smithsonian's National Numismatic Collection; the other is ex Pittman Collection. **h.** A complete 1854 Proof set was presented to the sovereign German city of Bremen at the time of issue. The set disappeared almost 100 years later, during World War II. **i.** One example resides in the Smithsonian's National Numismatic Collection, another in the collection of the American Numismatic Society. In recent decades the collections of Eliasberg, Trompeter, and Bass have included examples. **j.** The mintages of only 200 circulation strikes and 20 Proofs for the year 1875 combine to make the Proof a high-demand coin; hence its strong market value.

Chart continued on next page.

	Mintage	Cert	Avg	PF-60	PF-63	PF-64	PF-65	Recent Auction Record
1901	140	44	64.4	$6,000	$12,000	$18,000	$30,000	$74,750, PF-67Cam Star, Jun-07
1902	162	25	63.8	6,000	12,000	18,000	30,000	$2,200, PF-53 CAC, Dec-09
1903	154	58	63.7	6,000	12,000	18,000	30,000	$46,000, PF-67Cam, Feb-10
1904	136	63	63.8	6,000	12,000	18,000	30,000	$46,000, PF-67Cam, Dec-09
1905	108	32	63.1	6,000	12,000	18,000	30,000	$23,000, PF-65, Apr-07
1906	85	59	63.9	6,000	12,000	18,000	30,000	$16,100, PF-64, Jun-10
1907	92	42	64.2	6,000	12,000	18,000	30,000	$8,338, PF-63, May-09

INDIAN HEAD
(1908–1929)

Designer Bela Lyon Pratt; weight 8.359 grams; composition .900 gold, .100 copper (Net weight .24187 oz. pure gold); diameter 21.6 mm; reeded edge; mints: Philadelphia, Denver, New Orleans, San Francisco.

Mintmark is to left of arrows.

History. The Indian Head half eagle made its first appearance in 1908; it was minted continuously through 1916, and again in 1929. Its design elements are in sunken relief, like those of the similar quarter eagle; the mintmark is raised. On most examples the rims are flat, while on others they are slightly raised. These coins saw limited circulation in the West, and were rarely encountered elsewhere.

Striking and Sharpness. Striking varies. Look for weakness on the high parts of the Indian's bonnet and in the feather details in the headdress. On the reverse, check the feathers on the highest area of the wing.

Availability. These coins were not popular with numismatists of the time, who saved very few. Rare issues include the 1909-O, which usually is seen with evidence of circulation (often extensive) and the 1929, most of which are in MS. Luster can range from deeply frosty to grainy. Because the fields are the highest areas of the coin, luster diminished quickly as the coins were circulated or jostled with others in bags.

AU-50, 53, 55, 58 (About Uncirculated). *Obverse:* Friction on the cheek is very noticeable at AU-50, increasingly less at higher levels to AU-58. The headdress shows light wear, most evident on the ribbon above the forehead and on the garland. Luster is minimal at AU-50 and scattered and incomplete at AU-58. Nicks and contact marks are to be expected. *Reverse:* Friction on the wing and neck is very noticeable at AU-50, increasingly less noticeable at higher levels to 58. Otherwise, the same comments apply as for the obverse.

MS-60 to 70 (Mint State). *Obverse:* At MS-60 to 62, there is abrasion in the field, this representing the highest part of the coin. Abrasion is also evident on the headdress. Marks and, occasionally, a microscopic pin scratch may be seen. At MS-63, there may be some abrasion and some tiny marks. Luster is irregular. At MS-64, abrasion is less. Luster is rich. At MS-65 and above, luster is deep and frosty, with no marks at all visible without magnification at MS-66 and higher. *Reverse:* At MS-60 to 62 there is abrasion in the field, this representing the highest part of the coin. Abrasion is also evident on the eagle's wing. Otherwise, the same comments apply as for the obverse.

	Mintage	Cert	Avg	%MS	AU-55	AU-58	MS-60	MS-62	MS-63	MS-64	MS-65	Recent Auction Record
1908	577,845	5,611	61.5	85	$500	$525	$575	$1,025	$2,350	$4,000	$16,000	$3,450, MS-64, Jul-10
1908D	148,000	2,542	62.3	95	500	525	575	1,025	1,900	4,000	32,500	$1,725, MS-63, Jun-10
1908S	82,000	440	58.1	49	900	1,150	1,350	2,500	6,250	9,000	21,000	$9,200, MS-64, Apr-10
1909	627,060	4,542	61.0	81	500	525	575	1,025	2,000	4,000	15,000	$1,610, MS-63, Jul-10
1909D	3,423,560	26,668	61.6	88	500	525	575	975	1,775	3,500	15,000	$2,990, MS-64 CAC, Jul-10
1909O (a)	34,200	849	55.2	13	11,000	17,500	28,500	50,000	90,000	165,000	400,000	$5,319, EF-45, Jul-10
1909S	297,200	452	57.1	36	575	750	1,500	4,000	11,500	22,000	35,000	$920, AU-58, Jul-10
1910	604,000	4,518	60.7	77	500	525	600	1,050	2,000	3,600	16,000	$1,668, MS-63, Jun-10
1910D	193,600	855	60.5	77	500	525	600	1,050	3,500	7,500	35,000	$2,760, MS-63, Jun-10
1910S	770,200	897	57.1	26	725	900	1,150	3,500	6,500	23,500	37,500	$633, AU-58, Jul-10

a. Beware spurious "O" mintmark.

	Mintage	Cert	Avg	%MS	AU-55	AU-58	MS-60	MS-62	MS-63	MS-64	MS-65	Recent Auction Record
1911	915,000	7,830	60.7	76	$500	$525	$575	$1,025	$2,000	$3,600	$15,000	$719, MS-62, Jul-10
1911D	72,500	1,009	55.8	17	1,650	2,500	6,500	13,500	38,500	55,000	225,000	$9,775, MS-61 CAC, Jul-10
1911S	1,416,000	1,849	57.4	42	650	700	800	2,500	5,750	15,000	35,000	$5,031, MS-63 CAC, Jul-10
1912	790,000	7,427	60.9	79	500	525	575	1,025	2,000	3,600	15,000	$2,760, MS-64, Jul-10
1912S	392,000	1,031	56.2	17	700	950	1,800	5,000	13,500	25,000	95,000	$920, AU-58, Apr-10
1913	915,901	8,744	61.0	81	500	525	575	1,025	2,000	3,600	15,000	$3,738, MS-64 CAC, Jul-10
1913S	408,000	1,328	56.4	23	825	875	1,450	5,500	13,000	30,000	125,000	$9,200, MS-61, Jul-10
1914	247,000	2,216	61.0	80	500	525	600	1,075	2,100	3,600	16,000	$983, MS-62, Jul-10
1914D	247,000	1,988	60.6	72	500	525	600	1,075	2,100	3,750	22,000	$385, AU-58, Jul-10
1914S	263,000	1,085	58.0	37	700	900	1,400	4,500	12,500	45,000	100,000	$4,888, MS-62, Jul-10
1915 (b)	588,000	4,744	60.9	75	500	525	600	1,025	2,100	3,600	16,000	$1,955, MS-63, Jun-10
1915S	164,000	907	56.0	19	825	1,050	2,250	5,500	16,000	35,000	100,000	$1,265, AU-58, Jun-10
1916S	240,000	1,495	59.2	52	575	600	700	2,350	6,000	8,000	25,000	$690, AU-58, Jul-10
1929	662,000	210	62.6	93	15,500	16,500	18,000	22,500	28,500	37,500	55,000	$37,375, MS-63, Jun-10

b. Pieces dated 1915-D are counterfeit.

Proof Indian Head Half Eagles

PF-60 to 70 (Proof). Sand Blast (also called Matte) Proofs were made in 1908 and from 1911 to 1915, while Satin (also called Roman Finish) Proofs were made in 1909 and 1910. When seen, these are usually in higher Proof grades, PF-64 and above. As a class these are rarer than quarter eagles of the same date and style of finish. Most are in grades from PF-63 upward. At lower levels, coins can show light contact marks. Some microscopic bright flecks may be caused by the sandblasting process and, although they do not represent handling, usually result in a coin being assigned a slightly lower grade. *Obverse and Reverse:* At PF-60 to 63, there is light abrasion and some contact marks (the lower the grade, the higher the quantity). On Sand Blast Proofs these show up as visually unappealing bright spots. At PF-64 and higher levels, marks are fewer, with magnification needed to see any at PF-65. At PF-66, there should be none at all.

Proof Indian Head Half Eagle
Shown 1.5x actual size.

	Mintage	Cert	Avg	PF-60	PF-63	PF-64	PF-65	Recent Auction Record
1908, Matte	167	87	65.2	$6,000	$12,000	$18,000	$35,000	$37,375, PF-66 , May-10
1909, Roman Finish	78	34	65.4	7,000	13,000	20,000	37,500	$57,500, PF-67 Star, Feb-10
1909, Matte *(unique)* **(a)**	unknown	1	67.0					
1910, Roman Finish	250	44	65.3	7,000	13,000	20,000	37,500	$48,300, PF-67 Star, Aug-09
1910, Matte *(unique)* **(b)**	unknown	1	67.0					
1911, Matte	139	54	65.7	6,000	12,000	18,000	35,000	$18,400, PF-64, Mar-10
1912, Matte	144	34	66.5	6,000	12,000	18,000	35,000	$45,425, PF-66, Nov-09
1913, Matte	99	27	66.2	6,000	12,000	18,000	35,000	$46,000, PF-66, Sep-09
1914, Matte	125	33	65.8	6,000	12,000	18,000	35,000	$34,500, PF-66, Jan-10
1915, Matte	75	18	65.3	7,500	15,000	25,000	45,000	$86,250, PF-66, Mar-08

a. Certified by NGC as PF-67. **b.** Part of the unique complete 1910 Matte Proof gold set.

AN OVERVIEW OF GOLD EAGLES

The ten-dollar gold coin, or *eagle,* was first produced in 1795.

The Capped Bust to Right with Small Eagle reverse is the rarest of the early ten-dollar coin types. However, when seen they tend to be in higher grades such as EF, AU, or low levels of Mint State. The Heraldic Eagle reverse issues from 1797 through 1804 are much more readily available and in slightly higher average grade.

The Liberty Head eagles without motto, minted from 1838 through 1865, are elusive in any Mint State grade, although VF and EF pieces are plentiful, and there are enough AU coins to easily satisfy collector demands. Some collectors have considered the 1838 and 1839, 9 Over 8, with the head of Miss Liberty tilted forward in relation to the date, to be a separate date. Eagles with IN GOD WE TRUST on the reverse, from 1866 to 1907, are plentiful in high grades, including choice and gem Mint State. Some of these were repatriated from overseas bank vaults beginning in the second half of the 20th century.

The Saint-Gaudens eagles of 1907 With Periods, existing in the Wire Rim or Rounded Rim varieties, can be collected as a separate type, or not. Most readily available is the Wire Rim style, of which somewhat over 400 probably exist today, nearly all in Mint State, often choice or gem. These coins were made as regular issues but soon became numismatic delicacies for Treasury officials to distribute as they saw fit. Some were to have gone to museums, but in reality most were secretly filtered out through favored coin dealers. Then comes the 1907–1908 style, without periods, easily available in EF, AU, and lower Mint State levels, although gems are elusive.

The final eagle type, the 1908–1933 style with IN GOD WE TRUST on the reverse, is readily obtained in grades from EF through MS-63. Higher-grade pieces are elusive, and when seen are often dated 1932, a year in which 4,463,000 were struck—more than any other coin in the history of the denomination.

FOR THE COLLECTOR AND INVESTOR: GOLD EAGLES AS A SPECIALTY

Collecting ten-dollar gold coins by varieties is unusual, as the series includes so many scarce and rare coins. However, unlike other denominations, none is in the "impossible" category, and with some patience a full set of significant varieties, as listed in this book, can be obtained.

The early issues with Small Eagle reverse from 1795 through 1797, and those with Heraldic Eagle reverse from 1797 through 1804, can be collected and studied by die varieties, with *United States Ten Dollar Gold Eagles 1795–1804,* by Anthony Teraskza, being one useful guide. *Early U.S. Gold Coin Varieties: A Study of Die States, 1795–1834* (2006), by John W. Dannreuther and Harry W. Bass Jr., offers an abundance of information and enlarged photographs for study. In addition to the regular issues, a few 1804 *restrike* ten-dollar pieces exist from new 1804-dated dies created in 1834.

Liberty Head eagles from 1838 through 1866 (Without Motto) comprise many scarce dates and mintmarks. Years ago the 1858, of which only 2,521 were minted, was highly acclaimed as a landmark issue, but since then the publicity has faded. In any event, although certain date and mintmark varieties are rare, the number of numismatists collecting them by date sequence is very small, and thus opportunities exist to acquire very elusive pieces at a much smaller proportionate price than would be possible in, say, the gold dollar series. No full set of Mint State early eagles has ever been formed; probably none ever will be. EF and AU are typically the grades of choice, with Mint State pieces added where available.

Later Liberty Head eagles of the 1866–1907 style with motto include some low-mintage issues, but again these are not impossible. The most famous is the 1875 Philadelphia coin, of which just 100 circulation strikes were made. Although smaller numbers exist for Proof-only mintages, in terms of pieces made for commerce, the 1875 sets a record. The low-mintage 1879-O (1,500 made) and 1883-O (800) also have attracted much attention. Again, these pieces, while rare, are available to the specialist, as there is not a great deal of competition.

Among Indian Head eagles the 1907 With Periods style, Wire Rim, is famous, popular, and rare. Examples come on the market with regularity but are expensive due to the attention they attract. The Rounded Rim style is much rarer and when seen is usually in choice Mint State.

The regular without-periods 1907–1908 eagles are easy enough to obtain in Mint State, although gems are elusive. The varieties from 1908 through 1916 include no great rarities, although some are scarcer than others. Not many such pieces were saved at the time they were issued, and, accordingly, gems are elusive. However, grades such as AU and low Mint State will present no problem. Among later eagles, the 1920-S, 1930-S, and 1933 are rarities. In particular the 1920-S is difficult to find in choice and gem Mint State. The 1933 eagle is usually found in Mint State, but is expensive due to the publicity given to it. Readily available at reasonable prices are the 1926 and 1932.

RECOMMENDED READING

Akers, David W. *Gold Dollars (and Other Gold Denominations),* Englewood, OH, 1975–1982.

Bowers, Q. David. *United States Gold Coins: An Illustrated History,* Wolfeboro, NH, 1982.

Breen, Walter. *Major Varieties of U.S. Gold Dollars (and Other Gold Denominations),* Chicago, 1964.

Dannreuther, John W., and Bass, Harry W. *Early U.S. Gold Coin Varieties,* Atlanta, GA, 2006.

Fivaz, Bill. *United States Gold Counterfeit Detection Guide,* Atlanta, GA, 2005.

Fivaz, Bill, and Stanton, J.T. *The Cherrypickers' Guide to Rare Die Varieties* (4th ed., vol. II), Atlanta, GA, 2006.

Garrett, Jeff, and Guth, Ron. *Encyclopedia of U. S. Gold Coins, 1795–1933* (2nd ed.), Atlanta, GA, 2008.

Teraskza, Anthony. *United States Ten Dollar Gold Eagles 1795–1804.*

CAPPED BUST TO RIGHT, SMALL EAGLE REVERSE
(1795–1797)

Designer Robert Scot; weight 17.50 grams; composition .9167 gold, .0833 silver and copper; approx. diameter 33 mm; reeded edge.

Bass-Dannreuther-1.

History. Eagles of this style, the first in the denomination, debuted in the autumn of 1795. The obverse features Miss Liberty dressed in a conical cap. The reverse shows a "small" eagle perched on a palm branch and holding a laurel in his beak. The same motif was used on contemporary gold half eagles.

Striking and Sharpness. On the obverse, check the star centers and the hair details. On the reverse, check the feathers of the eagle. In particular, the breast feathers often are weakly struck. Examine the dentils on both sides. Planchet adjustment marks often are visible, but are not noted by the grading services.

Availability. Typical grades range from EF to AU and low MS. MS-63 and higher coins are rare, and when seen usually are of the 1795 or 1796 dates. Certain varieties are rare. Certain eagles of 1796 have prooflike surfaces and are particularly attractive if in high grades.

EF-40, 45 (Extremely Fine). *Obverse:* Wear is evident all over the portrait, with some loss of detail in the hair to the left of Miss Liberty's face. Excellent detail remains in low-relief areas of the hair, such as the front curl and at the back of her head. The stars show wear, as do the date and letters. Luster, if present at all, is minimal and in protected areas. *Reverse:* Wear is greater than at AU. The breast, neck, and legs of the eagle lack nearly all feather detail. More wear is seen on the edges of the wing. Some traces of luster may be seen, less so at EF-40 than at EF-45.

AU-50, 53, 55, 58 (About Uncirculated). *Obverse:* Light wear is seen on the cheek, the hair immediately to the left of the face, and the cap, more so at AU-50 than at 53 or 55. An AU-58 coin has minimal traces of wear. An AU-50 coin has luster in protected areas among the stars and letters, with little in the open fields or on the portrait. At AU-58, most luster is present in the fields, but is worn away on the highest parts of the motifs. *Reverse:* The eagle shows light wear on the breast and head in particular, but also at the tip of the wing on the left and elsewhere. Luster ranges from perhaps 40% remaining in protected areas (at AU-50) to nearly full mint bloom (at AU-58).

MS-60 to 70 (Mint State). *Obverse:* At MS-60, some abrasion and contact marks are evident, most noticeably on the hair to the left of Miss Liberty's forehead and on the higher-relief areas of the cap. Luster is present, but may be dull or lifeless, and interrupted in patches. At MS-63, contact marks are few, and abrasion is very light. An MS-65 coin has hardly any abrasion, and contact marks are so minute as to require magnification. Luster should be full and rich. On prooflike coins in any MS grade, abrasion and surface marks are much more noticeable. Coins above MS-65 exist more in theory than in reality for this type—but they do exist, and are defined by having fewer marks as perfection is approached. *Reverse:* Comments apply as for the obverse, except that abrasion and contact marks are most noticeable on the breast and head of the eagle. The field area is mainly protected by the eagle, branch, and lettering.

1795, 13 Leaves

1795, 9 Leaves

	Mintage	Cert	Avg	%MS	EF-40	AU-50	AU-55	AU-58	MS-60	MS-62	MS-63	Recent Auction Record
1795, 13 Leaves Below Eagle	5,583	30	53.9	20	$50,000	$65,000	$75,000	$80,000	$100,000	$155,000	$300,000 (a)	$48,875, AU-53, Feb-10
1795, 9 Leaves Below Eagle †	*	13	56.9	23	85,000	135,000	160,000	175,000	230,000	350,000		$161,000, AU-50, Jan-05
1796	4,146	69	56.5	25	55,000	67,500	80,000	90,000	125,000	185,000	325,000	$57,500, AU-53, Jun-10
1797, Small Eagle	3,615	27	54.7	33	65,000	105,000	140,000	160,000	225,000	300,000		$149,500, MS-61, Mar-09

* Included in number above. † Ranked in the *100 Greatest U.S. Coins* (third edition). **a.** Value in MS-64 is $550,000.

CAPPED BUST TO RIGHT, HERALDIC EAGLE REVERSE
(1797–1804)

Designer Robert Scot; weight 17.50 grams; composition .9167 gold, .0833 silver and copper; approx. diameter 33 mm; reeded edge.

Bass-Dannreuther-10.

History. Gold eagles of this type combine the previous obverse style with the Heraldic Eagle as used on other silver and gold coins of the era.

Striking and Sharpness. On the obverse, check the star centers and the hair details. On the reverse, check the upper part of the shield, the lower part of the eagle's neck, the eagle's wing, the stars above the eagle, and the clouds. Inspect the dentils on both sides. Planchet adjustment marks can be problematic; these are not identified by the grading services.

Availability. Eagles of 1797 appear in the market with some regularity. Those of 1798 are rare. Usually seen are the issues of 1799 through 1803. Typical grades range from EF to lower MS. MS-62 and higher coins are seen with some frequency and usually are dated 1799 and later. The 1804 is rare in true MS. Sharply struck coins without planchet adjustment marks are in the minority.

VF-20, 30 (Very Fine). *Obverse:* The higher-relief areas of hair are well worn at VF-20, less so at VF-30. *Reverse:* Wear is greater than at EF, including on the shield and wing feathers. The star centers are flat. Other areas have lost detail as well. E PLURIBUS UNUM may be faint in areas, but usually is sharp.

EF-40, 45 (Extremely Fine). *Obverse:* Wear is evident all over the portrait, with some loss of detail in the hair to the left of Miss Liberty's face. Excellent detail remains in low-relief areas of the hair, such as the front curl and at the back of her head. The stars show wear, as do the date and letters. Luster, if present at all, is minimal and in protected areas. *Reverse:* Wear is greater than at AU. The neck lacks some feather detail on its highest points. Feathers have lost some detail near the edges of the wings, and some areas of the horizontal lines in the shield may be blended together. Some traces of luster may be seen, less so at EF-40

than at EF-45. Overall, the reverse appears to be in a slightly higher grade than the obverse.

AU-50, 53, 55, 58 (About Uncirculated). *Obverse:* Light wear is seen on the cheek, the hair immediately to the left of the face, and the cap, more so at AU-50 than at 53 or 55. An AU-58 coin has minimal traces of wear. An AU-50 coin has luster in protected areas among the stars and letters, with little in the open fields or on the portrait. At AU-58, most luster is present in the fields, but is worn away on the highest parts of the motifs. *Reverse:* The eagle's neck, the tips and top of the wings, the clouds, and the tail show noticeable wear, as do other features. Luster ranges from perhaps 40% remaining in protected areas (at AU-50) to nearly full mint bloom (at AU-58). Often the reverse of this type retains much more luster than the obverse.

MS-60 to 70 (Mint State). *Obverse:* At MS-60, some abrasion and contact marks are evident, most notice-

ably on the hair to the left of Miss Liberty's forehead and on the higher-relief areas of the cap. Luster is present, but may be dull or lifeless, and interrupted in patches. At MS-63, contact marks are few, and abrasion is very light. An MS-65 coin has even less abrasion (most observable in the right field), and contact marks are so minute as to require magnification. Luster should be full and rich. Coins graded above MS-65 are more theoretical than actual for this type— but they do exist, and are defined by having fewer marks as perfection is approached. Gold eagles usually are graded with slightly less strictness than the smaller gold denominations of this design. *Reverse:* Comments apply as for the obverse, except that abrasion and contact marks are most noticeable on the upper part of the eagle and on the clouds. The field area is complex, without much open space, given the stars above the eagle, the arrows and olive branch, and other features. Accordingly, marks are not as noticeable as on the obverse.

1798, 8 Over 7, 9 Stars Left, 4 Right

1798, 8 Over 7, 7 Stars Left, 6 Right

1799, Small Obverse Stars

1799, Large Obverse Stars

1803, Small Reverse Stars   1803, Large Reverse Stars

	Mintage	Cert	Avg	%MS	AU-50	AU-55	AU-58	MS-60	MS-62	MS-63	MS-64	Recent Auction Record
1797, Large Eagle	10,940	169	56.4	33	$32,500	$37,500	$42,500	$52,500	$85,000	$125,000	$200,000	$23,000, AU-55, Jun-10
1798, 8 Over 7, 9 Stars Left, 4 Right †	900	29	56.9	31	55,000	80,000	90,000	125,000	215,000	300,000		$40,250, EF-45, Jan-10
1798, 8 Over 7, 7 Stars Left, 6 Right †	842	4	52.5	25	170,000	200,000	220,000	275,000	325,000			$161,000, AU-55, Jan-05
1799, Small Obverse Stars	37,449	15	59.5	47	21,000	24,000	26,000	32,500	42,500	65,000	135,000	$34,500, MS-61 CAC, Jun-10
1799, Large Obverse Stars	*	13	61.1	85	21,000	24,000	26,000	32,500	42,500	65,000	115,000	$31,625, MS-62, Jan-10
1800	5,999	106	57.5	42	22,500	26,000	29,000	38,500	52,500	72,500	150,000	$18,400, AU-58, Jun-10
1801	44,344	390	58.9	56	21,000	23,000	25,000	31,000	40,000	60,000	110,000	$20,700, AU-53, Jun-10
1803, Small Reverse Stars	15,017	11	53.3	36	22,000	25,000	27,000	37,500	50,000	72,500	135,000	$51,750, MS-61, Jul-10
1803, Large Reverse Stars (a)	*	6	59.0	50	22,000	25,000	27,000	37,500	50,000	72,500		$25,300, AU-53, Jul-10
1804	3,757	49	59.1	55	52,500	65,000	70,000	80,000	92,500	125,000		$48,875, AU-53, Apr-10

* Included in number above. † Ranked in the *100 Greatest U.S. Coins* (third edition). **a.** A variety without the tiny 14th star in the cloud is very rare; six or seven examples are known. It does not command a significant premium.

Proof Capped Bust to Right, Heraldic Eagle Reverse Eagles

PF-60 to 70 (Proof). There were no Proofs coined in the era in which this type was issued. Years later, in 1834, the Mint made up new dies with the 1804 date and struck an unknown number of Proofs, perhaps a dozen or so, for inclusion in presentation Proof sets for foreign dignitaries. A handful of these survive today. *Obverse and Reverse:* PF-60 to 62 coins have extensive hairlines and may have nicks and contact marks. At PF-63, hairlines are prominent, but the mirror surface is very reflective. PF-64 coins have fewer hairlines. At PF-65, hairlines should be minimal and mostly seen only under magnification. There should be no nicks or marks.

**Proof Capped Bust to Right,
Heraldic Eagle Reverse Eagle**
Bass-Dannreuther-2.

	Est Mintage	Cert	Avg	PF-60	PF-63	PF-64	PF-65	Recent Auction Record
1804, Plain 4, Restrike † *(3–4 known)*	5–8	1	65.0		$3,500,000	$5,000,000		

† Ranked in the *100 Greatest U.S. Coins* (third edition).

LIBERTY HEAD
(1838–1907)

Designer Christian Gobrecht; weight 16.718 grams; composition .900 gold, .100 copper (net weight: .48375 oz. pure gold); diameter 27 mm; reeded edge; mints: Philadelphia, Carson City, Denver, New Orleans, San Francisco.

No Motto Above Eagle
(1838–1866)

Motto Above Eagle
(1866–1907)

History. Production of the gold eagle, suspended after 1804, started up again in 1838, with the Liberty Head design. Midway through 1839 the style was modified slightly, including in the letters and Miss Liberty's portrait. In 1866 the motto IN GOD WE TRUST was placed on a banner above the eagle's head.

Striking and Sharpness. On the obverse, check the highest points of the hair and the star centers. On the reverse, check the eagle's neck, and the area to the lower left of the shield and the lower part of the eagle. Examine the dentils on both sides. Branch-mint coins issued before the Civil War often are lightly struck in areas, and some Carson City coins of the early 1870s can have areas of lightness. Most late 19th-century and early 20th-century coins are sharp in all areas. Tiny copper staining spots can be a problem for those issues.

Availability. Early dates and mintmarks are generally scarce to rare in MS and very rare in MS-63 and better grades, with only a few exceptions. These were workhorse coins in commerce; VF and EF grades are the rule for dates through the 1870s, and for some dates the finest known grade can be AU. In MS, Liberty Head eagles as a type are rarer than either quarter eagles or half eagles. Some varieties are not known to exist at this level. Eagles of the 1880s onward generally are seen in higher average grades.

AU-50, 53, 55, 58 (About Uncirculated). *Obverse:* Light wear is seen on the face, the hair to the right of the face, and the highest area of the hair bun, more so at AU-50 than at 53 or 55. An AU-58 coin has minimal traces of wear. An AU-50 coin has luster in protected areas among the stars and letters, with little in the open fields or on the portrait. At AU-58 most luster is present in the fields, but is worn away on the highest parts of the motifs. *Reverse:* The eagle shows wear in all of the higher areas, as well as the leaves and arrowheads.

Luster ranges from perhaps 40% remaining in protected areas (at AU-50) to nearly full mint bloom (at AU-58). Often the reverse of this type retains more luster than the obverse.

MS-60 to 70 (Mint State). *Obverse:* At MS-60, some abrasion and contact marks are evident, most noticeably on the hair to the right of Miss Liberty's forehead and on the jaw. Luster is present, but may be dull or lifeless, and interrupted in patches. At MS-63, contact marks are few, and abrasion is very light. An MS-65 coin has hardly any abrasion, and contact marks are so minute as to require magnification. Luster should be full and rich. For most dates, coins graded above MS-65 exist more in theory than in actuality—but they do exist, and are defined by having fewer marks as perfection is approached. *Reverse:* Comments apply as for the obverse, except that abrasion and contact marks are most noticeable on the eagle's neck and to the lower left of the shield.

1839, Large Letters
(Type of 1838)

1839, Small Letters
(Type of 1840)

1842, Small Date   **1842, Large Date**   **1846-O, 6 Over 5**   **1850, Large Date**   **1850, Small Date**

   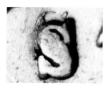

1853, 3 Over 2   **1854-O, Large Date**   **1854-O, Small Date**   **1865-S, 865 Over Inverted 186**   **1889-S, Repunched Mintmark**
FS-G10-1889S-501.

	Mintage	Cert	Avg	%MS	AU-55	AU-58	MS-60	MS-62	MS-63	MS-64	MS-65	Recent Auction Record
1838	7,200	47	47.0	4	$18,500	$25,000	$45,000	$55,000	$100,000			$6,325, EF-40, Apr-10
1839, Large Letters (a)	25,801	150	49.7	7	11,000	16,000	32,500	40,000	55,000	$95,000	$175,000	$3,738, EF-45, Apr-10
1839, Small Letters	12,447	38	45.4	3	11,000	18,000	40,000	50,000				$6,325, EF-45, Dec-08
1840	47,338	140	48.2	4	2,800	4,000	10,000					$1,725, AU-53, Mar-10
1841	63,131	184	49.3	7	2,500	4,000	8,500	17,500	30,000			$863, VF-35, Nov-09
18410	2,500	50	43.8	0	35,000	45,000						$5,463, VF-25, Apr-10
1842, Small Date	18,623	88	50.9	5	3,000	5,500	13,500	25,000				$6,325, AU-58, Jun-10
1842, Large Date	62,884	90	51.3	4	2,800	5,250	12,500	18,500	27,500	65,000	100,000	$1,006, AU-50, Feb-10
18420	27,400	220	47.7	2	7,250	13,000	26,000	40,000				$4,629, AU-55, May-10
1843	75,462	171	48.7	2	3,250	5,500	15,000					$5,175, AU-58, Jun-10
1843, Doubled Die	*											$1,265, AU-53, Jan-02
18430	175,162	389	49.5	2	3,250	5,500	12,500	30,000	45,000			$891, EF-40, Jul-10
1844	6,361	39	51.0	5	6,500	9,500	15,000					$2,990, EF-40, Jul-09
18440	118,700	345	50.2	5	3,400	6,000	15,000	30,000				$2,760, AU-55, Jul-10
1845	26,153	107	48.5	3	2,750	6,000	14,000	22,500				$805, VF-35, Dec-09
18450	47,500	228	49.4	6	5,250	8,500	15,500	32,500	50,000			$1,495, EF-45, Jun-10
1846	20,095	88	46.6	6	8,500	12,000	22,000	45,000				$8,050, AU-55, Mar-10
18460, All kinds	81,780											
18460		118	44.3	2	6,000	8,500	15,000	30,000				$978, EF-40, Feb-10
18460, 6 Over 5					7,000	9,500	18,000					$1,035, VF-30, Apr-10
1847	862,258	934	52.3	7	1,000	1,500	3,250	7,500	22,500	45,000		$1,093, AU-58, Mar-10
18470	571,500	800	49.9	3	1,250	2,500	6,000	10,000	22,500	35,000		$748, AU-53, Jun-10
1848	145,484	328	51.2	7	1,300	1,850	4,750	11,000	25,000	35,000		$2,013, EF-45, Apr-10
18480	35,850	170	47.2	4	7,000	9,500	15,000	22,000	27,500	40,000	75,000	$1,323, VF-30, May-10
1849	653,618	842	50.3	6	1,100	1,800	3,500	8,000	16,500	30,000		$719, AU-53, Jun-10
1849, Recut 1849 Over 849	*	4	56.8	0	1,350	2,100						$978, AU-50, Mar-09
18490	23,900	95	46.2	1	7,500	11,000	23,500					$8,625, AU-53, Mar-10
1850, All kinds	291,451											
1850, Large Date		416	49.8	5	1,000	1,500	3,800	8,000	17,500			$805, AU-55, Apr-10
1850, Small Date		125	47.1	5	3,750	5,000	8,500	16,000				$2,760, AU-55, Mar-10
18500	57,500	179	46.3	2	5,000	8,500	17,500	30,000				$1,840, EF-45, Jun-10
1851	176,328	262	51.8	8	1,300	1,800	4,250	8,500	32,500			$2,530, AU-55, Mar-10
18510	263,000	876	50.2	2	2,800	3,750	6,500	10,000	25,000	35,000		$4,025, AU-58, Jul-10
1852	263,106	577	52.8	6	1,050	1,500	5,000	8,000	23,500			$1,265, AU-58, Jun-10
18520	18,000	93	49.2	2	7,500	11,000	23,500					$4,888, AU-53, Feb-10
1853, All kinds	201,253											
1853, 3 Over 2		150	51.9	2	3,250	7,500						$4,313, AU-58, Apr-10
1853		608	53.6	7	1,050	1,500	3,500	7,500	18,500	30,000		$3,335, MS-61, Jun-10
18530	51,000	249	51.1	2	2,500	5,500	14,000					$1,380, AU-53, Jun-10
1854	54,250	250	52.3	6	1,300	1,900	5,750	15,000	21,500			$920, AU-53, Apr-10
18540, Large Date (b)	52,500	164	54.1	12	3,250	4,500	11,000	23,000				$978, EF-45, Mar-10
18540, Small Date (c)	*	126	53.7	0	3,000							$1,955, AU-55, Jul-10
1854S	123,826	431	50.0	1	1,850	3,000	9,500	18,500				$1,265, AU-53, Jan-10
1855	121,701	504	54.2	11	1,000	1,600	4,500	7,500	17,500	32,000		$1,955, AU-58 CAC, Jul-10
18550	18,000	105	48.8	0	8,000	11,000	23,500					$1,288, VF-25, May-10
1855S	9,000	36	46.7	0	9,000	16,500						$3,450, EF-45, Mar-10
1856	60,490	296	53.6	10	1,050	1,500	4,000	7,500	13,000	27,000		$4,888, MS-61, Apr-10
18560	14,500	111	48.9	3	7,000	9,500	16,500					$1,840, EF-40, Apr-10
1856S	68,000	261	49.9	1	2,500	4,000	9,000	19,500	26,000			$1,495, AU-55, Apr-10
1857	16,606	126	51.4	4	3,750	5,500	13,000	25,000				$1,955, AU-55, Apr-10
18570	5,500	61	51.7	0	6,250	9,500	26,000					$6,900, AU-55, Mar-10
1857S	26,000	69	45.6	3	4,000	5,500	10,500	14,000	23,500			$4,600, AU-55, Jan-10
1858 (d)	2,521	35	48.4	11	17,500	24,000	40,000	85,000				$12,075, AU-53, Jun-10
18580	20,000	192	51.1	3	3,250	4,500	9,500	17,500	32,500			$2,070, AU-55, Mar-10
1858S	11,800	61	50.6	0	12,000	27,500						$7,650, AU-55, Mar-10
1859	16,013	155	50.7	7	2,400	4,500	9,000	18,000				$1,380, AU-50, Jun-10
18590	2,300	22	51.0	5	39,000							$25,300, AU-58, Feb-09

* Included in number above. **a.** The Large Letters style is also known as the "Type of 1838," because of the distinct style of the 1838 Liberty Head motif. The Small Letters style (or "Type of 1840") was used on subsequent issues. **b.** The Large Date variety was made in error, when the diesinker used a date punch for a silver dollar on the much smaller $10 die. **c.** The Small Date variety is scarce in AU; only three or four MS examples are known, none finer than MS-60. **d.** Beware of fraudulently removed mintmark.

Chart continued on next page.

GOLD EAGLES, 1795–1933

	Mintage	Cert	Avg	%MS	AU-55	AU-58	MS-60	MS-62	MS-63	MS-64	MS-65	Recent Auction Record
1859S	7,000	42	41.3	2								$5,175, EF-45, Jul-09
1860	15,055	137	51.7	8	$2,750	$3,750	$8,000	$13,000	$20,000	$35,000		$2,300, AU-55, Jul-10
1860O	11,100	130	51.3	3	4,250	6,500	13,500	25,000				$2,760, EF-40, Feb-10
1860S	5,000	22	47.1	9	25,000							$3,220, F-12, May-09
1861	113,164	583	54.3	13	1,000	1,500	5,000	8,000	17,500	32,000		$1,265, AU-53, Apr-10
1861S	15,500	81	50.2	1	12,000	16,000	27,500					$2,645, VF-30, Aug-09
1862	10,960	101	51.4	11	3,000	4,500	12,000					$3,105, AU-55, Apr-10
1862S	12,500	54	47.1	0	9,500							$1,610, VF-20, Jul-09
1863	1,218	18	53.4	17	23,000	28,000	45,000	55,000	75,000			$28,750, AU-58, Jan-05
1863S	10,000	36	48.0	3	12,500	15,000	26,000					$1,380, F-12, Jul-09
1864	3,530	22	49.5	18	9,500	11,000	17,500					$8,625, AU-50, Jan-09
1864S	2,500	7	44.0	0	32,500							$50,600, EF-45, Jul-06
1865	3,980	31	47.7	3	9,000	14,500	36,000					$4,888, EF-45, Mar-10
1865S, All kinds	16,700											
1865S		30	37.7	3	23,500	32,000	47,500					$18,400, AU-55, Apr-10
1865S, 865 Over Inverted 186		31	39.5	3	17,500	22,500	35,000			85,000		$2,070, F-12, Jan-10
1866S, No Motto	8,500	33	45.2	3	17,500	24,000	47,500					$12,650, AU-50, May-09
1866, With Motto	3,750	50	49.1	8	8,500	11,000	23,500					$4,600, AU-53, Dec-09
1866S, With Motto	11,500	48	47.9	0	10,500	17,500						$3,220, VF-30, Mar-10
1867	3,090	73	49.7	3	8,000	14,000	27,500					$2,990, AU-50, Jan-09
1867S	9,000	35	44.5	0	15,000	25,000						$8,688, EF-45, May-09
1868	10,630	133	49.0	2	3,000	6,000	17,500					$4,744, AU-58, Jun-10
1868S	13,500	86	47.8	0	5,500	7,500						$920, F-15, Jul-10
1869	1,830	40	47.8	3	12,500	15,000	30,000	45,000				$3,220, EF-45, Jan-10
1869S	6,430	42	48.6	2	12,500	16,500	25,000					$6,325, AU-53, Mar-10
1870	3,990	83	48.5	1	6,000	11,000	17,500					$1,725, EF-45, Mar-10
1870CC	5,908	27	39.7	0	110,000							$40,250, EF-40, Jun-10
1870S	8,000	64	42.8	0	12,500	15,000	27,500					$1,380, VF-20, Mar-10
1871	1,790	39	49.0	0	8,500	13,000	20,000					$3,220, EF-40, Feb-10
1871CC	8,085	65	44.5	3	23,500	30,000	65,000					$17,250, AU-55, Jul-10
1871S	16,500	88	43.2	0	10,000	18,000						$9,200, AU-55, Sep-09
1872	1,620	24	50.5	4	11,000	12,500	17,500	22,000	32,000			$10,350, AU-55, Jun-08
1872CC	4,600	52	42.9	0	33,000							$16,675, AU-50, Jun-10
1872S	17,300	140	45.1	1	4,500	8,500	17,500					$1,756, AU-50, Mar-10
1873	800	19	50.3	0	18,500	27,500	40,000					$27,600, AU-58, Jun-10
1873CC	4,543	33	37.7	0	46,500							$63,250, AU-55 Star, Jul-09
1873S	12,000	85	42.5	0	7,500	12,000	21,500					$1,840, VF-35, Jun-10
1874	53,140	305	56.5	24	825	975	1,850	3,500	7,500			$1,610, MS-61, Feb-10
1874CC	16,767	196	42.6	1	12,500							$14,375, AU-55, May-10
1874S	10,000	86	40.8	0	10,000	16,000						$8,050, AU-55, Apr-10
1875	100	6	40.5	0	115,000							$48,875, VF-35, Jan-06
1875CC	7,715	59	38.1	3	30,000	38,500	72,500	95,000	115,000			$12,650, AU-50, Jun-10
1876	687	20	50.2	5	19,000							$3,738, VF-25, Oct-09
1876CC	4,696	89	40.0	0	30,000	40,000						$14,375, AU-53, Jun-10
1876S	5,000	52	42.9	0	8,500	18,500						$6,325, AU-55, Mar-10
1877	797	29	54.1	0	10,500	15,000	23,500					$10,350, AU-55, Jul-10
1877CC	3,332	44	38.2	0	23,500							$6,038, VF-35, Mar-10
1877S	17,000	168	46.5	1	4,500	11,000	26,000					$1,380, EF-45, Jul-10
1878	73,780	383	58.2	46	825	875	1,075	2,500	7,500	14,000		$690, EF-45, Apr-10
1878CC	3,244	46	46.4	2	28,500	37,500						$5,031, VF-20, Mar-10
1878S	26,100	218	47.3	2	3,250	4,500	13,500	16,500	29,500			$1,553, AU-55, Feb-10
1879	384,740	925	59.2	57	800	825	925	1,300	4,500			$690, AU-58, Apr-10
1879CC	1,762	37	40.6	3	32,000	40,000						$35,938, AU-53, Jun-08
1879O	1,500	49	48.8	2	14,500	19,000	37,500					$7,935, AU-50, Feb-09
1879S	224,000	434	57.0	27	800	825	1,125	2,350	6,500			$690, AU-55, Apr-10
1880	1,644,840	1,641	60.1	83	800	825	850	1,025	3,250	5,500		$2,185, MS-63, Apr-10
1880CC	11,190	182	50.0	7	3,850	5,000	14,500	25,000				$1,783, AU-50, Jun-10
1880O	9,200	154	51.6	7	2,650	4,500	8,500	15,000				$2,300, AU-53, Apr-10
1880S	506,250	877	60.3	79	800	825	850	1,075	4,250	12,000		$1,093, MS-62, Jul-10

	Mintage	Cert	Avg	%MS	AU-55	AU-58	MS-60	MS-62	MS-63	MS-64	MS-65	Recent Auction Record
1881	3,877,220	10,054	61.0	94	$800	$825	$850	$925	$1,500	$2,750	$10,000	$863, MS-61, Jul-10
1881CC	24,015	340	52.9	19	1,650	3,000	7,250	10,000	20,000			$11,500, MS-62, Jul-10
1881O	8,350	150	51.4	9	2,250	3,800	8,500					$1,725, AU-50, Jun-10
1881S	970,000	2,008	60.6	90	800	825	850	925	4,500			$2,990, MS-63 Star, Apr-10
1882	2,324,440	10,762	61.2	96	800	825	850	925	1,425	3,500		$748, MS-61, Jun-10
1882CC	6,764	146	52.3	3	7,250	9,500	17,500	30,000				$9,200, AU-58, Apr-10
1882O	10,820	168	52.3	11	2,200	3,500	6,750	12,000	23,500			$2,070, AU-58, May-10
1882S	132,000	302	60.5	84	800	825	850	1,075	4,500	9,500		$1,610, MS-62, Jul-10
1883	208,700	1,168	61.2	95	800	825	850	925	2,750	6,500		$1,625, MS-63, Jul-10
1883CC	12,000	167	46.8	2	5,000	8,500	17,500					$5,319, AU-58, Apr-10
1883O	800	17	51.9	6	27,500	45,000	65,000					$25,875, EF-45, Jan-10
1883S	38,000	129	56.0	40	800	825	1,175	3,500	9,750			$3,450, MS-62, Apr-10
1884	76,860	348	58.4	44	800	825	850	1,350	5,000	7,500		$1,093, MS-62, Apr-10
1884CC	9,925	190	51.0	4	4,500	7,000	13,500	20,000	50,000			$4,888, AU-58, Apr-10
1884S	124,250	447	59.2	64	800	825	850	1,400	6,000			$1,265, MS-62, Jun-10
1885	253,462	559	60.6	83	800	825	850	925	3,000	6,000	20,000	$1,150, MS-62, Apr-10
1885S	228,000	705	60.7	86	800	825	850	1,075	3,250	12,000		$2,530, MS-63, Jun-10
1886	236,100	576	59.2	62	800	825	850	1,075	4,250	6,500		$3,450, MS-63, Jul-10
1886S	826,000	2,498	61.2	95	800	825	850	925	1,425	6,000		$776, MS-62, Apr-10
1887	53,600	264	57.7	41	800	825	900	2,500	5,500	8,500		$920, MS-61, Apr-10
1887S	817,000	1,183	60.8	91	800	825	850	925	3,000	6,000		$1,955, MS-63, Jul-10
1888	132,921	427	58.6	54	800	825	900	2,400	5,500			$1,847, MS-62, Jun-10
1888O	21,335	523	60.2	80	875	975	1,025	1,600	5,750			$1,035, MS-61, Jun-10
1888S	648,700	1,457	60.8	90	800	825	850	1,075	2,400	6,000		$2,185, MS-63 CAC, Jul-10
1889	4,440	94	58.3	51	1,350	1,500	2,500	4,000	8,000			$4,313, MS-61 CAC, Jul-10
1889S	425,400	1,123	61.0	90	800	825	850	950	1,600	4,000		$1,840, MS-63, Jul-10
1889S, Repunched Mintmark	*				875	975	1,025	1,150	1,850			$1,035, MS-63, Aug-06
1890	57,980	397	58.8	60	800	825	975	1,600	5,000	8,000	14,000	$1,265, MS-62, Jun-10
1890CC	17,500	352	57.4	41	1,250	1,500	2,600	6,500	14,000			$3,220, MS-60, Jul-10
1891	91,820	604	61.1	95	800	825	850	925	4,000	6,500		$2,313, MS-63, Jul-10
1891CC	103,732	2,101	58.7	62	1,000	1,200	1,500	2,500	6,000	15,000		$1,725, MS-61, Jul-10
1892	797,480	6,865	61.4	98	800	825	850	925	1,425	2,500	8,500	$690, MS-60, Jul-10
1892CC	40,000	436	52.3	8	1,250	1,600	3,750	5,500	10,000	23,000		$1,208, AU-55, Jun-10
1892O	28,688	672	60.3	81	810	840	925	2,200	6,750			$1,783, MS-62, Jul-10
1892S	115,500	280	59.5	67	800	825	850	1,250	3,750	6,500		$2,760, MS-63, Apr-10
1893	1,840,840	28,828	61.8	99	800	825	850	925	1,425	2,500	5,500	$1,150, MS-62PL, Jul-10
1893CC	14,000	205	51.4	6	2,750	3,500	8,500	12,500	20,000			$2,875, AU-55, May-10
1893O	17,000	401	59.8	71	825	875	1,025	1,600	5,500			$1,380, MS-60, Jun-10
1893S	141,350	543	60.1	77	800	825	850	1,150	4,000	6,500		$2,875, MS-63, Jul-10
1894	2,470,735	29,867	61.7	99	800	825	850	925	1,425	2,500	5,500	$805, MS-62, Jul-10
1894O	107,500	716	57.5	36	825	875	1,225	1,650	5,000	8,500		$1,610, MS-62, Jul-10
1894S	25,000	143	53.3	13	1,000	1,800	3,500	8,000				$1,380, AU-58, Apr-10
1895	567,770	9,193	61.7	99	800	825	850	925	1,425	2,500	11,000	$1,840, MS-64, Jul-10
1895O	98,000	625	58.9	53	825	875	875	1,300	6,500	18,500		$920, MS-61, Jul-10
1895S	49,000	211	52.1	8	975	1,250	2,250	3,500	8,500	21,000		$2,990, MS-61, Jul-10
1896	76,270	1,187	61.7	98	800	825	850	925	2,200	3,500		$1,450, MS-63, Jul-10
1896S	123,750	455	53.8	15	810	925	2,250	3,500	10,500			$2,070, MS-61, Jul-10
1897	1,000,090	7,981	61.6	98	800	825	850	925	1,425	2,500	10,000	$5,750, MS-65, Jun-10
1897O	42,500	363	59.0	52	825	850	975	1,300	5,500	11,000	25,000	$1,610, MS-62, Jul-10
1897S	234,750	329	57.3	35	800	825	900	1,600	5,500	9,500	25,000	$5,175, MS-63, Jul-10
1898	812,130	3,151	61.3	94	800	825	850	925	1,425	2,500	7,500	$693, MS-62, Apr-10
1898S	473,600	384	60.5	87	800	825	850	925	1,800	2,750	7,000	$891, MS-62, Jul-10
1899	1,262,219	17,672	62.1	98	800	825	850	925	1,425	2,500	5,500	$2,300, MS-64 Star, Jul-10
1899O	37,047	193	59.1	49	810	840	925	1,500	5,500	13,000		$1,840, MS-62, Apr-10
1899S	841,000	487	59.9	78	800	825	850	925	3,500	6,000	12,000	$863, MS-61, Apr-10
1900	293,840	5,532	62.1	99	800	825	850	925	1,425	2,500	5,500	$8,914, MS-66, Jun-10
1900S	81,000	169	57.7	37	800	825	975	1,250	5,750	14,500		$1,380, MS-62, Apr-10
1901	1,718,740	20,795	62.3	98	800	825	850	925	1,425	2,500	5,500	$1,725, MS-64, Jul-10

* Included in number above.

Chart continued on next page.

	Mintage	Cert	Avg	%MS	AU-55	AU-58	MS-60	MS-62	MS-63	MS-64	MS-65	Recent Auction Record
1901O	72,041	369	60.0	68	$810	$840	$850	$1,250	$3,500	$6,500		$2,760, MS-63, Jul-10
1901S	2,812,750	15,092	62.9	99	800	825	850	925	1,425	2,500	$5,250	$2,185, MS-64+, Jul-10
1902	82,400	623	61.3	91	800	825	850	1,015	2,500	4,000	9,500	$863, MS-62, Jun-10
1902S	469,500	2,580	62.8	99	800	825	850	925	1,425	2,500	5,500	$2,070, MS-64, Apr-10
1903	125,830	958	61.5	93	800	825	850	925	2,500	3,850	11,000	$3,220, MS-64, Jul-10
1903O	112,771	1,009	60.3	74	810	840	875	950	3,250	6,500	17,500	$1,875, MS-63, Jun-10
1903S	538,000	941	62.5	93	800	825	850	925	1,425	2,500	5,500	$863, MS-62, Jun-10
1904	161,930	957	61.3	92	800	825	850	925	1,425	2,500	5,500	$1,725, MS-63, Jul-10
1904O	108,950	588	60.3	72	810	840	875	1,150	3,500	5,500	15,000	$1,380, MS-62, Jul-10
1905	200,992	1,821	61.6	94	800	825	850	925	1,425	2,500	5,500	$863, MS-62, Jul-10
1905S	369,250	532	56.9	26	810	925	1,175	2,000	5,500	8,500		$3,738, MS-62, Apr-10
1906	165,420	1,262	61.2	91	800	825	850	975	2,250	3,500	9,500	$1,495, MS-63, Jul-10
1906D	981,000	3,190	61.5	91	800	825	850	925	1,425	2,500	5,500	$1,495, MS-63, Jul-10
1906O	86,895	308	60.5	71	800	840	875	1,150	4,500	6,000	12,500	$1,840, MS-62, Apr-10
1906S	457,000	499	58.1	44	800	825	875	940	4,500	6,500	13,500	$863, MS-61, Jul-10
1907	1,203,899	20,214	62.0	98	800	825	850	925	1,425	2,500	7,500	$2,185, MS-64 CAC, Jul-10
1907D	1,030,000	464	61.6	90	800	825	850	925	2,000	3,500	11,000	$2,530, MS-64, Apr-10
1907S	210,500	323	58.9	55	800	825	900	1,150	5,500	6,500		$1,208, MS-62, Apr-10

Proof Liberty Head Eagles

PF-60 to 70 (Proof). Proof coins exist in relation to their original mintages, with all issues prior to the 1890s being very rare. Cameo contrast is the rule for Proofs prior to 1902. Beginning that year the portrait was polished in the die, although a few years later, cameo contrast coins were again made. *Obverse and Reverse:* PF-60 to 62 coins have extensive hairlines and may have nicks and contact marks. At PF-63, hairlines are prominent, but the mirror surface is very reflective. PF-64 coins have fewer hairlines. At PF-65, hairlines should be minimal and mostly seen only under magnification. There should be no nicks or marks. PF-66 and higher coins should have no marks or hairlines visible to the unaided eye.

Proof Liberty Head Eagle

	Est Mintage	Cert	Avg	PF-60	PF-63	PF-64	PF-65	Recent Auction Record
1838 † *(3 known)*	4–6	1	65.0		*(extremely rare)*			$550,000, CH. PF, May-98
1839, Large Letters *(3 known)*	4–6	1	67.0		*(extremely rare)*			$1,610,000, PF-67UCam, Jan-07
1840 **(a)**	1–2			*(unique; in the Smithsonian's National Numismatic Collection)*				
1841 *(3 known)*	4–6	1	61.0		*(extremely rare)*			
1842, Small Date *(2 known)*	2				*(extremely rare)*			
1843 *(5 known)*	6–8	3	62.7		*(extremely rare)*			
1844 *(3–4 known)*	6–8	1	63.0		*(extremely rare)*			
1844O †	1	1	65.0					
1845 *(4–5 known)*	6–8	1	65.0		*(extremely rare)*			$120,750, PF-64, Aug-99
1846 *(4 known)*	6–8	1	64.0		*(extremely rare)*			
1847	1–2			*(unique; in the Smithsonian's National Numismatic Collection)*				
1848 *(2 known)*	3–5	1	64.0		*(extremely rare)*			
1853O **(b)**	1	1	61.0					

† Ranked in the *100 Greatest U.S. Coins* (third edition). **a.** It is possible that other 1840 Proof eagles were made, given that duplicates are known of the quarter eagle and half eagle denominations. **b.** Not a true Proof from a technical standpoint, this unique coin has in the past been called a *presentation piece* and a *branch-mint Proof.* "Although the piece does not have the same convincing texture as the 1844-O Proof eagle, it is clearly different from the regular-issue eagles found for the year and mint" (*Encyclopedia of U.S. Gold Coins, 1795–1933,* second edition).

	Mintage	Cert	Avg	PF-60	PF-63	PF-64	PF-65	Recent Auction Record
1854 (c)	unknown							
1855 (d)	unknown							
1856 (d)	unknown							
1857	2–3	1	66.0					$396,000, PF-66, May-99
1858 (4–5 known)	4–6	2	64.0		(extremely rare)			
1859	80	3	64.3	$30,000	$70,000	$150,000	$200,000	
1860	50	5	63.6	15,000	47,500	75,000	125,000	$83,375, PF-64DCam, Jan-09
1861	69	6	64.2	15,000	45,000	65,000	115,000	$36,800, PF-64, Oct-99
1862	35	6	64.5	15,000	40,000	65,000	115,000	$115,000, PF-65UCam, Jan-07
1863	30	12	64.2	15,000	40,000	60,000	100,000	$138,000, PF-65UCam, Jan-08
1864	50	15	63.6	15,000	40,000	60,000	100,000	$161,000, PF-65Cam, Jan-10
1865	25	14	64.3	15,000	40,000	60,000	100,000	$32,200, PF-63, Oct-99
1866	30	7	64.1	10,000	32,500	50,000	85,000	$138,000, PF-65, Aug-07
1867	50	6	64.5	10,000	32,500	50,000	85,000	$92,000, PF-66Cam, Jan-05
1868	25	4	64.8	10,000	32,500	50,000	85,000	$24,150, PF-62Cam, Jun-05
1869	25	7	63.9	10,000	32,500	50,000	80,000	$132,250, PF-67UCam, Aug-06
1870	35	5	64.6	10,000	32,500	50,000	80,000	$77,625, PF-63Cam, May-06
1871	30	4	62.5	10,000	32,500	50,000	80,000	$3,220, PF-40, Jan-05
1872	30	6	64.8	10,000	32,500	50,000	80,000	$9,200, PF-64UCam, Mar-08
1873, Close 3	25	9	63.4	12,000	37,500	55,000	85,000	$80,500, PF-65UCam, Aug-06
1874	20	1	62.0	12,000	32,500	50,000	85,000	$29,900, PF-64Cam, Jun-06
1875	20	7	59.6	65,000	130,000	150,000	200,000	$172,500, PF-65UCam, Jan-07
1876	45	21	63.8	10,000	30,000	45,000	75,000	$57,500, PF-65Cam, Aug-06
1877	20	2	64.5	12,000	32,500	45,000	75,000	$39,100, PF-64Cam, Apr-02
1878	20	4	63.8	9,500	30,000	40,000	75,000	$89,125, PF-65Cam, Sep-08
1879	30	5	64.8	9,500	25,000	37,500	65,000	$50,313, PF-65Cam, Jan-07
1880	36	4	64.3	8,500	22,500	35,000	60,000	$32,200, PF-64, Oct-99
1881	40	4	65.0	8,500	22,500	32,500	55,000	$115,000, PF-66UCam , Jul-09
1882	40	9	64.0	8,500	20,000	32,500	55,000	$43,125, PF-65UCam, Oct-09
1883	40	10	64.3	8,500	20,000	32,500	55,000	$48,888, PF-65UCam, Jun-10
1884	45	6	64.3	8,500	20,000	32,500	55,000	$48,300, PF-65DCam, Jan-07
1885	65	11	63.6	7,500	18,500	32,500	52,500	$24,150, PF-64UCam, Jun-09
1886	60	9	64.4	7,500	18,500	32,500	52,500	$27,600, PF-64UCam, Sep-05
1887	80	12	64.3	7,500	18,500	32,500	52,500	$120,750, PF-67UCam Star, Jun-10
1888	75	14	64.0	7,500	18,500	32,500	52,500	$17,250, PF-63DCam, Feb-09
1889	45	3	64.0	7,500	18,000	32,500	52,500	$10,925, PF-63, Feb-09
1890	63	25	63.7	7,000	16,500	25,000	47,500	$52,388, PF-66UCam Star, Jan-10
1891	48	25	64.1	7,000	16,500	25,000	47,500	$12,075, PF-63 CAC, Feb-09
1892	72	12	63.7	7,000	16,500	25,000	47,500	$14,375, PF-62 CAC, May-09
1893	55	14	63.0	7,000	16,500	25,000	47,500	$27,600, PF-64DCam, Jun-08
1894	43	10	63.9	7,000	16,500	25,000	47,500	$80,500, PF-66Cam, Jan-05
1895	56	18	63.9	7,000	16,500	25,000	47,500	$54,625, PF-65, Jan-10
1896	78	22	64.3	7,000	16,500	25,000	47,500	$50,313, PF-65UCam, Jul-08
1897	69	12	64.3	7,000	16,500	25,000	47,500	$21,850, PF-64UCam, Jan-10
1898	67	29	65.2	7,000	16,500	25,000	47,500	$149,500, PF-68UCam, Jan-07
1899	86	38	64.3	7,000	13,500	23,500	45,000	$5,750, PF-60, Jun-10
1900	120	51	64.6	7,000	13,500	23,500	45,000	$54,625, PF-65DCam, Jan-10
1901	85	51	63.7	7,000	13,500	23,500	45,000	$54,625, PF-66UCam, Nov-09
1902	113	25	64.0	7,000	13,500	23,500	45,000	$28,750, PF-65, May-09
1903	96	47	64.3	7,000	13,500	23,500	45,000	$16,100, PF-64, Jun-09
1904	108	37	63.3	7,000	13,500	23,500	45,000	$9,488, PF-62Cam, Nov-09
1905	86	37	63.6	7,000	13,500	23,500	45,000	$27,600, PF-65Cam, Jul-09
1906	77	31	64.2	7,000	13,500	23,500	45,000	$63,250, PF-67Cam, Mar-10
1907	74	50	64.1	7,000	13,500	23,500	45,000	$34,500, PF-65, Jul-08

c. In July 1854 a set of Proof coins was given by the United States to the sovereign German city of Bremen. Various Proof 1854 gold dollars, quarter eagles, and three-dollar gold pieces have come to light, but the half eagle and eagle are unconfirmed. **d.** No Proof 1855 or 1856 eagles have been confirmed, but Wayte Raymond claimed to have seen one of each some time prior to 1949.

INDIAN HEAD
(1907–1933)

Designer Augustus Saint-Gaudens; weight 16.718 grams; composition .900 gold, .100 copper (net weight: .48375 oz. pure gold); diameter 27 mm; edge: (1907–1911) 46 raised stars, (1912–1933) 48 raised stars; mints: Philadelphia, Denver, San Francisco.

Mintmark at tip of branch on 1908-D, and left of arrow points thereafter.

History. The Indian Head eagle, designed by sculptor Augustus Saint-Gaudens, was struck from 1907 to 1916, and again in intermittent issues through the 1920s and early 1930s. The motto IN GOD WE TRUST was added to the reverse in July 1908, and remained to the end of the series. These coins were widely used until 1918, in the American West and for export.

Striking and Sharpness. On the obverse, check the hair details and the vanes in the feathers. On the reverse, check the shoulder of the eagle. As well-struck coins are available for all varieties, avoid those that are weakly struck. Luster varies, but is often deeply frosty. On other coins, particularly from 1910 to 1916, it may be grainy.

Availability. The rolled (or round) rim and wire rim 1907 coins, the 1920-S, 1930-S, and the 1933 are the key rarities. Others are generally available. MS-63 and higher coins are generally scarce to rare for the mintmarked issues. This is a very popular series. Most in collectors' hands are coins that were exported in their time, then brought back to America after World War II.

AU-50, 53, 55, 58 (About Uncirculated). *Obverse:* Light wear is seen on the cheek, the hair to the right of the face, and the headdress, more so at AU-50 coin than at 53 or 55. An AU-58 coin has minimal traces of wear. An AU-50 coin has luster in protected areas among the stars and in the small field area to the right. At AU-58, most luster is present in the fields but is worn away on the highest parts of the Indian. *Reverse:* The eagle's left wing, left leg, neck, and leg show light wear. Luster ranges from perhaps 40% (at AU-50) to nearly full mint bloom (at AU-58).

MS-60 to 70 (Mint State). *Obverse:* At MS-60, some abrasion and contact marks are evident, most noticeably on the hair to the left of Miss Liberty's forehead and in the left field. Luster is present, but may be dull or lifeless, and interrupted in patches. At MS-63, contact marks are few, and abrasion is very light. An MS-65 coin has hardly any abrasion, and contact marks are minute. Luster should be full and rich. Grades above MS-65 are defined by having fewer marks as perfection is approached. *Reverse:* Comments apply as for the obverse, except that abrasion and contact marks are most noticeable on the front of the left wing and in the left field.

No Periods

Periods

**No Motto
(1907–1908)**

**With Motto
(1908–1933)**

	Mintage	Cert	Avg	%MS	AU-58	MS-60	MS-62	MS-63	MS-64	MS-65	MS-66	Recent Auction Record
1907, Wire Rim, Periods	500	195	63.5	94	$27,500	$30,000	$34,000	$42,500	$50,000	$65,000	$75,000	$34,500, MS-62, Jul-10
1907, Rounded Rim, Periods Before and After •E•PLURIBUS•UNUM• † (a)	50	29	62.6	83	65,000	72,500	80,000	120,000	175,000	245,000	285,000	$233,450, MS-66, Jul-09
1907, No Periods	239,406	5,474	61.7	85	835	925	1,600	3,250	5,750	9,500	18,500	$8,050, MS-65, Jul-10
1908, No Motto	33,500	604	61.0	77	1,000	1,200	2,000	3,750	6,500	15,000	35,000	$1,265, MS-61, Jun-10
1908D, No Motto	210,000	721	59.7	55	835	950	2,450	6,000	17,500	37,500	100,000	$1,495, AU-58, Jul-10
1908, With Motto	341,370	3,410	60.9	79	810	835	1,500	2,500	4,000	11,500	17,500	$1,035, MS-62, Jul-10
1908D, With Motto	836,500	565	59.5	60	810	925	2,200	6,500	15,000	28,000	40,000	$23,000, MS-65, Jul-10
1908S	59,850	593	55.3	28	1,500	3,250	6,000	10,000	14,000	22,500	35,000	$1,495, AU-55, Jul-10
1909	184,789	1,581	60.6	74	810	835	1,450	3,500	6,000	15,000	32,500	$1,495, MS-62, Jul-10

† Ranked in the *100 Greatest U.S. Coins* (third edition). **a.** 31,500 were minted; all but 50 were melted at the mint.

	Mintage	Cert	Avg	%MS	AU-58	MS-60	MS-62	MS-63	MS-64	MS-65	MS-66	Recent Auction Record
1909D	121,540	775	59.5	59	$950	$1,000	$3,000	$6,000	$15,000	$27,500	$45,000	$6,038, MS-63, Jul-10
1909S	292,350	501	57.6	40	825	1,000	3,250	6,250	8,750	16,000	25,000	$13,800, MS-65, Jul-10
1910	318,500	4,794	61.6	88	810	835	1,125	1,600	2,750	9,500	16,000	$2,300, MS-64, Jul-10
1910D	2,356,640	9,446	61.7	90	810	835	1,050	1,600	2,500	8,000	16,000	$2,070, MS-64, Jul-10
1910S	811,000	1,145	57.1	35	825	1,000	2,750	8,000	17,500	50,000	85,000	$3,450, MS-62, Jul-10
1911	505,500	7,461	61.5	85	810	835	1,050	1,600	2,800	8,500	16,000	$6,325, MS-65, Jul-10
1911D	30,100	679	55.2	21	3,200	6,000	12,000	24,000	55,000	150,000		$27,600, MS-63, Jul-10
1911S	51,000	268	57.1	35	1,200	1,600	4,500	8,500	11,000	18,000	45,000	$2,990, MS-61, Jul-10
1912	405,000	5,053	61.3	85	810	835	1,050	1,700	3,000	11,000	18,000	$8,625, MS-65, Jul-10
1912S	300,000	725	57.3	31	900	1,200	3,200	7,000	11,000	37,500	120,000	$1,150, AU-58, Jul-10
1913	442,000	4,401	61.2	82	810	835	1,050	1,800	3,200	10,000	20,000	$8,050, MS-65, Jul-10
1913S	66,000	712	55.1	14	2,350	5,000	12,000	27,500	55,000	100,000		$28,750, MS-63, Jul-10
1914	151,000	1,725	61.3	82	810	835	1,050	2,000	3,500	12,000	22,000	$2,300, MS-63, Jun-10
1914D	343,500	2,166	60.7	74	810	835	1,050	1,800	4,000	15,000	21,000	$4,888, MS-64 CAC, Jul-10
1914S	208,000	754	59.2	49	825	865	3,000	7,000	12,000	28,000		$2,990, MS-61, Jul-10
1915	351,000	3,432	61.2	80	810	835	1,150	2,000	3,500	10,000	20,000	$3,335, MS-64, Jul-10
1915S	59,000	341	57.6	29	1,950	3,250	7,500	16,000	30,000	45,000	125,000	$2,760, AU-59, Jul-10
1916S	138,500	651	59.6	58	900	1,150	2,900	6,500	12,500	24,000	50,000	$2,990, MS-62, Jul-10
1920S	126,500	48	59.1	54	25,000	37,500	60,000	85,000	125,000	225,000	450,000	$46,000, MS-62, Oct-09
1926	1,014,000	28,937	62.5	99	810	825	1,025	1,400	2,350	5,000	13,500	$1,955, MS-64 CAC, Jul-10
1930S	96,000	76	63.8	97	16,500	20,000	32,000	40,000	55,000	67,500	90,000	$43,131, MS-64, Oct-09
1932	4,463,000	41,760	62.8	99	810	825	1,025	1,400	2,350	5,000	13,500	$8,050, MS-66,
1933 † (b)	312,500	12	64.3	100		275,000	300,000	350,000	400,000	500,000		$460,000, MS-65, Jul-09

† Ranked in the *100 Greatest U.S. Coins* (third edition). **b.** Nearly all were melted at the mint.

Proof Indian Head Eagles

PF-60 to 70 (Proof). Sand Blast (also called Matte) Proofs were made each year from 1907 through 1915. These have dull surfaces, much like fine-grained sandpaper. Satin (also called Roman Finish) Proofs were made in 1908, 1909, and 1910; they have satiny surfaces and are bright yellow. All are rare today. *Obverse and Reverse:* At PF-60 to 63, there is light abrasion and some contact marks (the lower the grade, the higher the quantity). On Sand Blast Proofs these show up as visually unappeal-ing bright spots. At PF-64 and higher levels, marks are fewer, with magnification needed to see any at PF-65. At PF-66, there should be none at all.

Proof Indian Head Eagle

	Mintage	Cert	Avg	PF-60	PF-63	PF-64	PF-65	Recent Auction Record
1907, Rounded Rim, Periods, Satin Finish	unknown	1	67.0					
1907, Matte *(2–3 known)*	unknown	1	64.0		*(extremely rare)*			
1908, Matte	116	63	65.2	$7,500	$16,500	$25,000	$50,000	$60,375, PF-67, Apr-10
1908, Satin Finish *(3–4 known)*	*	2	64.0		*(extremely rare)*			
1909, Satin Finish	74	48	65.0	8,000	17,500	25,000	55,000	$21,850, PF-64, Jan-10
1909, Matte *(2–3 known)*	*				*(extremely rare)*			
1910, Satin Finish	204	24	65.1	8,000	17,500	30,000	65,000	$60,375, PF-66, Nov-09
1910, Matte (a)	*	1	66.0					
1911	95	26	66.2	7,500	15,500	24,000	50,000	$63,250, PF-66, Sep-09
1912	83	27	65.5	7,000	15,500	24,000	50,000	$37,950, PF-65, Aug-09
1913	71	25	65.6	7,000	15,500	24,000	50,000	$40,250, PF-64, Jan-08
1914	50	29	65.6	7,000	16,500	24,000	50,000	$46,000, PF-66, Aug-09
1915	75	21	65.6	10,000	20,000	35,000	65,000	$43,700, PF-65, Aug-09

* Included in number above. **a.** Part of the unique complete 1910 Matte Proof gold set.

An Overview of Gold Double Eagles

The double eagle, or twenty-dollar coin—the largest denomination of all regular U.S. coinage issues—was authorized by the Act of March 3, 1849, in response to the huge amounts of gold coming from California.

Many gold collectors form a type set of the six major double eagle designs (with the 1861 Paquet added as a sub-type if desired). Double eagles are at once large and impressive to own. Thanks to overseas hoards repatriated since the 1950s, finding choice and gem Mint State examples is no problem at all for the later types.

The first double-eagle type, that of 1850–1866, is generally available in grades from VF up. Mint State pieces, while elusive, were greatly augmented by more than 5,000 pieces—including some gems— found in the discovery of the long-lost treasure ship SS *Central America*. The SS *Brother Jonathan,* lost at sea in 1865, was recovered and yielded hundreds of Mint State 1865-S double eagles, and some dated 1864 and a few earlier. The salvaged wreck of the SS *Republic,* lost in 1865 while on a voyage from New York City to New Orleans, has also yielded some very attractive Mint State double eagles of this first type.

The type from 1866 through 1876, with the motto IN GOD WE TRUST above the eagle and with the denomination expressed as TWENTY D., is the rarest in MS-63 and higher grades. Many EF and AU coins have been repatriated from overseas holdings, as have quite a few in such grades as MS-60 through MS-62. However, true gems are hardly ever seen.

Liberty Head double eagles of the 1877–1907 type with motto and with the denomination as TWENTY DOLLARS are exceedingly plentiful in just about any grade desired, with gems being available of certain issues of the early 20th century. While it is easy to obtain a gem of a common date, some collectors of type coins have opted to add a coin of special historical interest, such as a Carson City issue.

The famous MCMVII High Relief double eagle of 1907 was saved in quantity by the general public as well as by numismatists, and today it is likely that at least 5,000 to 6,000 exist, representing about half of the mintage. Most of these are in varying degrees of Mint State, with quite a few listed as MS-64 and MS-65. Lower grades such as VF and EF were often used for jewelry or polished, or have other problems. This particular design is a great favorite with collectors, and although the coins are not rarities, they are hardly inexpensive.

The so-called Arabic Numerals 1907–1908 Saint-Gaudens design is available in nearly any grade desired, with MS-60 through MS-63 or MS-64 pieces being plentiful and inexpensive. Double eagles of the final type, 1908–1933, are abundant in any grade desired, with choice and gem coins being plentiful.

For the Collector and Investor: Gold Double Eagles as a Specialty

Collecting double eagles by date and mint is more popular than one might think. Offhand, it would seem that these high denominations, laden with a number of rare dates, would attract few enthusiasts. However, over a long period of years more people have specialized in double eagles than have specialized in five-dollar or ten-dollar pieces.

Two particularly notable collections of double eagles by date and mint, from the earliest times to the latest, were formed by Louis E. Eliasberg of Baltimore, and Jeff Browning of Dallas. Both have been dispersed across the auction block. The first was cataloged by Bowers and Ruddy in 1982, and the second was offered by Stack's and Sotheby's in 2001. In addition, dozens of other collections over the years have had large numbers of double eagles, some specializing in the Liberty Head type of 1850–1907, others only with the Saint-Gaudens type from 1907 onward, and others addressing the entire range.

Among rarities in the double eagle series are the 1854-O and 1856-O, each known only to the extent of a few dozen pieces; the 1861 Philadelphia Mint coins with Paquet reverse (two known); the Proof-only issues of 1883, 1884, and 1887; several other low-mintage varieties of this era; the famous Carson City issue of 1870-CC; and various issues from 1920 onward, including 1920-S, 1921, mintmarks after 1923, and all dates after 1928. Punctuating these rarities are a number of readily available pieces, including the very common Philadelphia issues from 1922 through 1928 inclusive.

Recommended Reading

Akers, David W. *Gold Dollars (and Other Gold Denominations),* Englewood, OH, 1975–1982.

Bowers, Q. David. *A Guide Book of Double Eagle Gold Coins,* Atlanta, GA, 2004.

Bowers, Q. David. *United States Gold Coins: An Illustrated History,* Wolfeboro, NH, 1982.

Fivaz, Bill. *United States Gold Counterfeit Detection Guide,* Atlanta, GA, 2005.

Fivaz, Bill, and Stanton, J.T. *The Cherrypickers' Guide to Rare Die Varieties* (4th ed., vol. II), Atlanta, GA, 2006.

Garrett, Jeff, and Guth, Ron. *Encyclopedia of U.S. Gold Coins, 1795–1933* (2nd ed.), Atlanta, GA, 2008.

Moran, Michael. *Striking Change: The Great Artistic Collaboration of Theodore Roosevelt and Augustus Saint-Gaudens,* Atlanta, GA, 2008.

LIBERTY HEAD
(1849–1907)

Designer James B. Longacre; weight 33.436 grams; composition .900 gold, .100 copper (net weight: .96750 oz. pure gold); diameter 34 mm; reeded edge; mints: Philadelphia, Carson City, Denver, New Orleans, San Francisco.

Mintmark is below eagle.

History. The $20 denomination was introduced to circulation in 1850 (a unique pattern that currently resides in the Smithsonian was minted in 1849). The large new coin was ideal for converting the flood of California Gold Rush bullion into federal legal tender. U.S. Mint chief engraver James B. Longacre designed the coin. In 1866 the motto IN GOD WE TRUST was added to the reverse. In 1877 the denomination on the reverse, formerly given as TWENTY D., was changed to TWENTY DOLLARS. The double eagle denomination proved to be very popular, especially for export. By 1933, more than 75% of the American gold used to strike coins from the early days onward had been used to make double eagles.

Striking and Sharpness. On the obverse, check the star centers and the hair details. As made, the hair details are less distinct on many coins of 1859 (when a slight modification was made) through the 1890s, and knowledge of this is important. Later issues usually have exquisite detail. The reverse usually is well struck, but check the eagle and other features. The dentils are sharp on nearly all coins, but should be checked.

Availability. Basic dates and mintmarks are available in proportion to their mintages. The 1854-O, 1856-O, 1861 and 1861-S Paquet Reverse, 1866 No Motto, 1870-CC, 1879-O, and several Philadelphia Mint dates of the 1880s are key issues, but the vast majority of others are readily collectible. Among early coins, MS examples from about 1854 to 1857 are available, most notably the 1857-S and certain varieties of the 1860s. Most varieties of the 1880s onward, and particularly the 1890s and 1900s, are easily available in MS, due to the repatriation of millions of coins that had been exported.

AU-50, 53, 55, 58 (About Uncirculated). *Obverse:* Light wear is seen on the face, the hair to the right of the face, and the highest area of the hair behind the coronet, more so at AU-50 than at 53 or 55. An AU-58 coin has minimal traces of wear. An AU-50 coin has luster in protected areas among the stars and letters, with little in the open fields or on the portrait. At AU-58 most luster is present in the fields, but is worn away on the highest parts of the motifs. *Reverse:* The eagle and ornaments show wear in all of the higher areas. Luster ranges from perhaps 40% remaining in protected areas (at AU-50) to nearly full mint bloom (at AU-58). Often the reverse of this type retains more luster than the obverse.

MS-60 to 70 (Mint State). *Obverse:* At MS-60, some abrasion and contact marks are evident, most noticeably on the hair to the right of Miss Liberty's forehead and on the cheek. Luster is present, but may be dull or lifeless, and interrupted in patches. At MS-63, contact marks are few, and abrasion is light. An MS-65 coin has little abrasion, and contact marks are minute. Luster should be full and rich. Grades above MS-65 are defined by having fewer marks as perfection is approached. *Reverse:* Comments apply as for the obverse, except that abrasion and contact marks are most noticeable on eagle's neck, wingtips, and tail.

1853, So-called 3 Over 2
Note rust under LIBERTY.
FS-G20-1853-301.

1854, Small Date

1854, Large Date

1861-S, Normal Reverse

1861-S, Paquet Reverse
Note taller letters.

No Motto On Reverse

With Motto

1866, Doubled-Die Reverse
FS-G20-1866-801.

Open 3

Close 3

Value TWENTY D.
(1866–1876)

Value TWENTY DOLLARS
(1877–1907)

1888, Doubled-Die Reverse
FS-G20-1888-801.

	Mintage	Cert	Avg	%MS	AU-55	AU-58	MS-60	MS-62	MS-63	MS-64	MS-65	Recent Auction Record
1850	1,170,261	1,137	50.0	7	$4,500	$7,500	$10,500	$38,000	$55,000	$85,000	$150,000	$3,738, AU-53, Jul-10
1850O	141,000	321	46.1	2	18,500	38,000	55,000					$6,325, EF-45, Jul-10
1851	2,087,155	803	51.8	10	1,975	2,600	4,250	15,000	21,000	40,000		$1,955, AU-50, Jul-10
1851O	315,000	658	48.9	3	9,500	16,000	25,000	40,000	75,000			$6,038, AU-53, Apr-10
1852	2,053,026	1,368	52.2	9	2,025	2,550	4,250	12,000	16,500	35,000		$2,530, AU-53, Jul-10
1852O	190,000	566	50.7	3	8,500	14,500	27,500	42,500	62,500			$7,475, AU-53, Apr-10
1853, All kinds	1,261,326											
1853, So-called 3 Over 2 (a)		156	52.5	3	9,000	15,000	30,000					$4,313, AU-50, Jul-10
1853		1,025	52.4	5	2,050	2,750	6,000	18,000	25,000	40,000		$2,013, AU-53, Jul-10
1853O	71,000	237	49.5	2	13,500	22,500	37,500					$6,900, EF-45, Apr-10
1854, All kinds	757,899											
1854, Small Date		356	53.0	5	2,050	3,000	8,500	18,000	30,000			$2,300, AU-55, Jul-10
1854, Large Date		86	52.9	10	11,500	22,500	35,000	45,000	60,000	100,000		$23,000, AU-58 CAC, Apr-10
1854O † (b)	3,250	17	53.4	0	525,000	650,000	850,000					$603,750, AU-58, Oct-08
1854S	141,468	181	52.3	27	7,500	9,000	13,500	18,000	25,000	35,000	75,000	$4,888, XF-45, Jun-10
1855	364,666	309	52.9	6	2,800	4,500	10,000	20,000	60,000	125,000		$1,725, EF-45, Apr-10
1855O	8,000	45	49.2	7	55,000	75,000	100,000					$27,600, EF-45, Sep-09
1855S	879,675	787	51.8	4	2,500	3,500	7,250	12,000	18,500	35,000		$2,300, AU-55, Jul-10
1856	329,878	297	52.6	9	2,850	5,000	10,000	20,000	30,000			$3,220, AU-55, Apr-10
1856O † (c)	2,250	9	47.3	0	550,000							$460,000, AU-58, Jul-09
1856S	1,189,750	901	51.2	5	2,500	3,800	5,500	10,000	14,500			$4,600, AU-53, Jul-10
1857	439,375	428	53.9	12	2,050	2,800	4,500	13,000	27,500	45,000		$4,888, MS-60, Jun-10
1857O	30,000	114	51.7	6	17,500	25,000	37,500	65,000	150,000			$8,050, EF-45, Jul-10
1857S † (d)	970,500	1,197	55.5	34	2,075	2,550	4,500	6,500	8,500	9,500	15,000	$12,650, MS-65, Jul-10
1858	211,714	391	52.0	7	3,000	4,000	6,000	24,000	38,500			$1,898, EF-45, Jul-10
1858O	35,250	130	50.6	5	19,500	27,500	50,000					$9,200, AU-50, Jul-10
1858S	846,710	810	51.3	3	2,800	5,000	10,000	15,000	50,000			$4,600, AU-58, Jul-10
1859	43,597	131	51.6	5	9,500	14,000	30,000	45,000				$7,475, AU-50, Apr-10
1859O	9,100	65	50.1	2	62,500	85,000	135,000					$69,000, AU-58, Sep-09
1859S	636,445	698	50.7	3	2,900	6,000	8,000	25,000	47,500			$3,450, AU-55, Jul-10
1860	577,670	785	53.9	13	1,950	3,000	6,000		21,500	40,000		$6,900, MS-61, Jun-10
1860O	6,600	60	50.8	2	55,000	85,000	115,000					$51,750, AU-53, Mar-10
1860S	544,950	625	51.1	4	3,900	6,000	9,500		26,000			$5,463, AU-58, Dec-09
1861	2,976,453	2,739	54.4	18	1,800	2,550	4,000	8,500	14,500	25,000	40,000	$1,783, EF-45, Jul-10
1861O	17,741	114	47.1	5	55,000	80,000	115,000	135,000				$57,500, AU-55, Sep-09
1861S	768,000	782	50.5	3	4,000	6,000	12,500	22,000	45,000			$1,502, EF-45, Apr-10
1861, Paquet Rev (Tall Ltrs)												
(2 known) † (e)	unknown	1	67.0	100			2,000,000					$1,610,000, MS-61, Aug-06
1861S, Paquet Rev												
(Tall Ltrs) † (f)	19,250	71	47.4	0	145,000	175,000	250,000					$86,250, AU-50, Apr-10
1862	92,133	84	51.8	18	11,000	14,000	21,000	30,000	42,500	65,000		$8,050, EF-45, Feb-10

† Ranked in the *100 Greatest U.S. Coins* (third edition). **a.** In addition to the clearly visible remnants of a numeral beneath the 3 in the date, this variety shows a rust spot underneath the R of LIBERTY. **b.** Probably fewer than 35 exist, most in VF and EF. **c.** Probably fewer than 25 exist, most in VF and EF. **d.** The treasure of the shipwrecked SS *Central America* included thousands of 1857-S double eagles in high grades. **e.** Once thought to be a pattern; now known to have been intended for circulation. **f.** About 100 are known, most in VF and EF.

	Mintage	Cert	Avg	%MS	AU-55	AU-58	MS-60	MS-62	MS-63	MS-64	MS-65	Recent Auction Record
1862S	854,173	899	51.0	5	$4,500	$8,000	$13,500	$25,000	$40,000			$6,900, AU-58, Mar-10
1863	142,790	177	52.1	13	8,250	15,000	22,500	28,000	42,500			$3,738, EF-45, Apr-10
1863S	966,570	1,110	51.9	11	3,000	4,500	8,500	16,000	32,500			$3,450, AU-55, Jun-10
1864	204,235	265	52.2	10	5,000	7,500	16,500	25,000	42,500			$5,750, AU-55, Mar-10
1864S	793,660	846	51.1	14	3,500	6,500	10,000	16,000	32,500			$3,105, AU-55 CAC, Apr-10
1865	351,175	668	57.2	47	2,150	3,500	6,500	12,000	21,000	$27,000	$45,000	$2,530, AU-55, Jul-10
1865S	1,042,500	1,178	54.0	39	2,250	3,000	4,000	7,500	9,000	13,000	25,000	$3,220, AU-58, Jul-10
1866S	120,000	150	46.4	3	75,000	100,000	175,000					$31,635, AU-50, Oct-09

	Mintage	Cert	Avg	%MS	AU-50	AU-55	AU-58	MS-60	MS-62	MS-63	MS-64	Recent Auction Record
1866	698,745	501	53.3	8	$1,900	$2,750	$4,250	$9,250	$20,000	$45,000	$125,000	$8,050, AU-58+ CAC Secure, Jun-10
1866, Doubled-Die Reverse	*				2,500	3,500	5,000					$1,725, EF-40, Jun-10
1866S	842,250	679	48.9	3	2,000	8,000	13,000	18,500	35,000			$10,925, AU-58, Jul-10
1867	251,015	339	57.1	42	1,600	2,100	3,000	3,250	9,000	22,500		$8,625, MS-62, Jun-10
1867S	920,750	989	50.5	2	1,800	3,750	8,500	17,000	30,000			$2,996, AU-55, Jan-10
1868	98,575	176	51.9	6	2,500	5,000	7,250	16,000	30,000	60,000		$22,425, MS-61 CAC, Apr-10
1868S	837,500	1,238	51.6	3	1,700	3,000	6,000	12,500	27,500			$2,530, AU-55, Jun-10
1869	175,130	292	52.9	3	1,700	2,750	4,500	7,250	15,000	26,000	45,000	$1,392, EF-40, Apr-10
1869S	686,750	1,130	52.0	5	1,700	2,250	4,000	8,500	25,000	45,000	70,000	$3,450, AU-58, Apr-10
1870	155,150	239	53.6	14	2,250	3,250	5,500	11,000	25,000	45,000		$3,738, AU-50, Jun-10
1870CC † (a)	3,789	27	37.0	0	350,000	450,000						$230,000, EF-45, Jan-10
1870S	982,000	1,117	52.1	4	1,600	2,000	3,000	5,750	25,000	50,000		$33,350, MS-62, Apr-10
1871	80,120	218	52.6	5	2,000	3,000	4,000	6,500	25,000	50,000	75,000	$4,313, AU-55, Oct-09
1871CC	17,387	155	47.3	4	37,500	50,000	60,000	87,500				$40,250, AU-55, Jan-10
1871S	928,000	1,335	54.0	9	1,600	1,675	2,100	5,500	12,000	25,000	50,000	$2,070, AU-58, Jul-10
1872	251,850	616	55.3	12	1,600	1,775	2,300	4,250	15,000	28,500	75,000	$17,250, MS-62 Star, Apr-10
1872CC	26,900	398	49.3	3	8,500	14,500	22,000	37,500				$20,700, AU-58, Jul-10
1872S	780,000	1,210	54.4	9	1,600	1,625	2,100	3,750	13,500	25,000		$1,610, AU-55, Jun-10
1873, Close 3	1,709,825	320	54.5	12	1,675	1,875	2,150	3,500	10,000			$1,380, VF-30, Apr-10
1873, Open 3	*	6,398	59.0	55	1,600	1,625	1,675	1,725	3,200	12,000	38,000	$10,350, MS-63 CAC, Jul-10
1873CC, Close 3	22,410	371	51.7	5	10,000	16,500	24,000	42,500	85,000			$11,500, AU-55, Jun-10
1873S, Close 3	1,040,600	1,029	55.7	16	1,600	1,625	1,775	2,100	6,500	20,000		$2,990, MS-61 CAC, Jul-10
1873S, Open 3	*	633	54.3	10	1,600	2,500	3,500	8,000				$16,100, MS-61 CAC, Jul-10
1874	366,780	877	57.5	29	1,600	1,625	1,850	2,100	12,500	21,000	55,000	$4,313, MS-61 CAC, Jul-10
1874CC	115,085	1,200	48.4	1	3,250	5,000	8,500	13,000	25,000			$4,600, AU-55, Jul-10
1874S	1,214,000	2,467	56.8	22	1,600	1,625	1,900	2,300	10,000	25,000		$1,898, MS-60, Jun-10
1875	295,720	1,176	59.3	58	1,600	1,625	1,725	1,850	3,450	14,000	40,500	$3,450, MS-62 CAC, Jul-10
1875CC	111,151	1,490	53.0	28	2,200	2,500	3,000	3,850	12,000	25,000	65,000	$2,185, AU-50, Jun-10
1875S	1,230,000	3,008	57.6	31	1,600	1,625	1,725	1,850	3,750	22,000	40,500	$2,415, MS-61 CAC, Jul-10
1876	583,860	2,063	58.1	38	1,600	1,625	1,725	1,850	3,750	15,000	38,000	$9,775, MS-63, Jul-10
1876CC	138,441	1,752	51.8	13	2,200	2,900	3,500	6,750	16,000	35,000		$7,475, MS-60, Jun-10
1876S	1,597,000	4,739	57.9	34	1,600	1,625	1,725	1,850	3,750	14,000	35,500	$2,185, MS-61, Jun-10

* Included in number above. † Ranked in the *100 Greatest U.S. Coins* (third edition). a. An estimated 35 to 50 examples are believed to exist; most are in VF with extensive abrasions.

	Mintage	Cert	Avg	%MS	AU-55	AU-58	MS-60	MS-62	MS-63	MS-64	MS-65	Recent Auction Record
1877	397,650	838	59.4	66	$1,525	$1,550	$1,900	$3,500	$11,500	$25,000		$3,738, MS-62, Jun-10
1877CC	42,565	752	48.4	3	5,750	8,000	19,000	45,000				$2,530, XF-45, Jun-10
1877S	1,735,000	1,852	58.9	59	1,525	1,550	1,650	3,750	14,500	25,000	$30,000	$1,840, MS-61, Jul-10
1878	543,625	1,328	59.7	69	1,525	1,550	1,650	3,000	13,000	25,000		$2,875, MS-62, Jul-10
1878CC	13,180	297	45.5	2	15,000	20,000	32,500	55,000				$4,169, EF-40, Jul-10
1878S	1,739,000	1,274	58.2	55	1,525	1,600	1,800	5,500	19,500	45,000		$4,888, MS-62, Jul-10
1879	207,600	546	58.4	47	1,525	1,600	1,800	5,500	17,500			$2,645, MS-61, Jul-10
1879CC	10,708	281	49.3	3	16,000	21,000	37,500	55,000				$16,100, AU-55, Mar-10
1879O	2,325	73	49.8	12	47,500	55,000	85,000	125,000	150,000			$74,750, AU-58, Dec-09
1879S	1,223,800	1,157	57.2	27	1,525	1,700	2,100	15,000	40,000			$11,500, MS-62, Jul-10

Chart continued on next page.

	Mintage	Cert	Avg	%MS	AU-55	AU-58	MS-60	MS-62	MS-63	MS-64	MS-65	Recent Auction Record
1880	51,420	330	55.4	15	$1,525	$1,700	$4,000	$15,000	$25,000			$1,380, EF-40, Apr-10
1880S	836,000	793	58.0	38	1,525	1,550	1,900	6,000	20,000	$35,000		$3,220, MS-61, Jul-10
1881	2,199	18	53.9	17	25,000	55,000	85,000					$38,813, AU-53, Jan-10
1881S	727,000	667	58.5	52	1,525	1,550	1,600	4,500	20,000			$2,185, MS-61, Jul-10
1882	571	13	54.6	8	75,000	85,000	125,000	140,000	175,000			$57,500, EF-45, Feb-10
1882CC	39,140	814	53.1	7	3,950	5,500	10,000	22,000				$4,313, AU-55, Jun-10
1882S	1,125,000	1,199	58.9	60	1,525	1,550	1,600	4,000	17,500			$1,955, MS-61, Jul-10
1883CC	59,962	1,080	52.3	9	2,800	3,500	6,000	17,500	25,000			$9,200, MS-61, Jun-10
1883S	1,189,000	1,729	59.7	74	1,525	1,550	1,600	2,300	8,500	18,500		$1,495, AU-58, Jun-10
1884CC	81,139	1,448	53.8	18	2,600	3,000	3,750	15,000	22,500			$12,650, MS-62, Jul-10
1884S	916,000	2,267	60.6	83	1,525	1,550	1,600	2,350	6,500	15,000	$45,000	$3,738, MS-62, Jun-10
1885	751	48	55.3	27	37,500	42,000	65,000	85,000	100,000			$43,125, AU-58, Jan-10
1885CC	9,450	268	50.2	6	12,500	15,000	19,000	35,000	55,000			$12,650, AU-58, Jul-10
1885S	683,500	1,994	60.8	87	1,525	1,550	1,600	2,300	5,000	14,000		$2,530, MS-62+, Jun-10
1886	1,000	24	54.2	8	50,000	58,000	70,000	85,000	125,000			$86,263, AU-55, Oct-08
1887S	283,000	813	60.1	74	1,525	1,550	1,600	3,500	15,000	23,000		$4,313, MS-62 CAC, Jul-10
1888	226,161	973	60.1	73	1,525	1,550	1,600	2,500	12,000	15,000	30,000	$2,760, MS-62, Jul-10
1888, Doubled-Die Reverse	*	11	59.5	73	2,500	3,000	3,500					$10,350, MS-63, Apr-10
1888S	859,600	2,215	60.8	86	1,525	1,550	1,600	2,500	5,000	11,000		$2,530, MS-62, Jun-10
1889	44,070	471	60.5	81	1,525	1,550	1,950	3,500	13,000			$2,990, MS-62, Jun-10
1889CC	30,945	756	52.0	7	3,000	5,000	8,500	15,000	25,000			$4,888, AU-58, Jul-10
1889S	774,700	1,604	60.5	83	1,525	1,550	1,600	2,200	5,500	16,500		$2,070, MS-61, Jun-10
1890	75,940	555	60.5	81	1,525	1,550	1,600	2,300	10,000	22,000	30,000	$2,530, MS-62, Jun-10
1890CC	91,209	1,891	52.7	9	2,350	2,750	3,900	12,000	37,500			$5,468, AU-58, Jul-10
1890S	802,750	1,539	60.1	75	1,525	1,550	1,600	2,000	6,500	15,000		$2,530, MS-62, Jul-10
1891	1,390	36	55.7	11	25,000	42,000	62,500	95,000				$138,000, MS-63, Jan-10
1891CC	5,000	220	53.8	16	15,000	19,000	30,000	45,000	65,000			$10,350, AU-50, Jun-10
1891S	1,288,125	4,798	61.2	92	1,525	1,550	1,600	1,950	2,850	6,500		$2,760, MS-63 Star, Jul-10
1892	4,430	108	56.1	32	3,500	6,000	9,000	18,000	30,000	40,000	65,000	$8,050, AU-55 CAC, Jun-10
1892CC	27,265	716	54.2	22	3,500	5,000	7,250	20,000	35,000			$2,531, AU-50, Jul-10
1892S	930,150	3,673	61.1	90	1,525	1,550	1,600	2,000	3,250	7,500	28,500	$1,495, MS-62, Jul-10
1893	344,280	4,941	61.5	98	1,525	1,550	1,600	2,000	2,750	4,600		$1,610, MS-62, Jul-10
1893CC	18,402	639	57.4	49	3,250	5,000	6,250	15,000	27,500	35,000		$5,405, AU-58 CAC, Jul-10
1893S	996,175	4,403	61.0	92	1,525	1,550	1,600	2,000	3,500	12,000		$1,725, MS-62, Jul-10
1894	1,368,940	13,011	61.4	97	1,525	1,550	1,600	2,000	2,850	4,750	25,000	$2,185, MS-62PL, Apr-10
1894S	1,048,550	4,759	61.2	93	1,525	1,550	1,600	2,000	2,850	5,000	22,000	$2,530, MS-63, Jul-10
1895	1,114,605	18,406	61.7	98	1,525	1,550	1,600	2,000	2,750	3,500	17,000	$4,888, MS-64 CAC, Jul-10
1895S	1,143,500	5,904	61.3	94	1,525	1,550	1,600	1,800	2,850	4,750	17,500	$4,025, MS-64, Jul-10
1896	792,535	8,374	61.6	97	1,525	1,550	1,600	1,800	2,850	3,750	17,500	$2,760, MS-63 CAC, Jul-10
1896S	1,403,925	7,679	61.3	94	1,525	1,550	1,600	1,800	2,850	4,850	25,000	$1,610, MS-61, Jun-10
1897	1,383,175	15,185	61.7	98	1,525	1,550	1,600	1,800	2,650	3,650	16,000	$3,105, MS-64 CAC, Jul-10
1897S	1,470,250	10,822	61.6	95	1,525	1,550	1,600	1,800	2,550	3,750	16,000	$3,738, MS-64 CAC, Jul-10
1898	170,395	1,516	61.2	89	1,525	1,550	1,900	2,750	4,750	11,000		$4,025, MS-63, Jul-10
1898S	2,575,175	19,130	61.7	96	1,525	1,550	1,600	1,800	2,400	3,750	8,500	$2,645, MS-63PL, Jul-10
1899	1,669,300	19,767	62.0	98	1,525	1,550	1,600	1,800	2,300	3,000	9,000	$1,840, MS-62, Jun-10
1899S	2,010,300	7,890	61.3	92	1,525	1,550	1,600	1,800	2,300	3,250	17,500	$3,335, MS-64 CAC, Jul-10
1900	1,874,460	40,728	62.3	99	1,525	1,550	1,600	1,800	2,300	3,000	5,000	$2,760, MS-64, Jul-10
1900S	2,459,500	6,434	61.1	93	1,525	1,550	1,600	1,800	2,550	5,500	24,000	$1,725, MS-62 Star, Jul-10
1901	111,430	4,377	63.0	99	1,525	1,550	1,600	1,800	2,450	3,250	5,500	$2,128, MS-63, Jun-10
1901S	1,596,000	2,609	61.2	94	1,525	1,550	1,600	1,800	3,850	6,500	20,000	$1,495, MS-62, Jul-10
1902	31,140	434	59.9	68	1,525	1,550	1,700	2,000	11,000	15,000		$1,725, AU-58, Jul-10
1902S	1,753,625	3,814	61.0	94	1,525	1,550	1,600	2,000	3,500	10,000	23,000	$1,610, MS-62, Apr-10
1903	287,270	10,699	62.9	100	1,525	1,550	1,600	1,800	2,150	3,000	5,000	$4,600, MS-65, Jul-10
1903S	954,000	5,666	61.8	98	1,525	1,550	1,600	1,800	2,150	3,500	11,500	$2,300, MS-63, Jul-10
1904	6,256,699	194,357	62.6	99	1,525	1,550	1,600	1,800	2,150	3,000	5,000	$4,888, MS-65 CAC, Jul-10
1904S	5,134,175	21,787	62.4	98	1,525	1,550	1,600	1,800	2,150	2,750	4,750	$1,531, MS-61, Jul-10
1905	58,919	728	59.3	61	1,675	1,850	2,100	5,000	13,500	35,000	65,000	$4,888, MS-62 CAC, Jul-10
1905S	1,813,000	1,958	61.2	90	1,525	1,550	1,600	1,800	3,850	5,500	20,000	$6,325, MS-64, Jul-10

* Included in number above.

	Mintage	Cert	Avg	%MS	AU-55	AU-58	MS-60	MS-62	MS-63	MS-64	MS-65	Recent Auction Record
1906	69,596	605	60.4	76	$1,525	$1,550	$1,650	$3,500	$7,500	$12,500	$22,000	$2,760, MS-62, Jul-10
1906D	620,250	1,604	61.8	96	1,525	1,550	1,600	1,800	3,500	4,500	22,000	$3,594, MS-62, Mar-10
1906S	2,065,750	3,970	61.5	96	1,525	1,550	1,600	1,800	2,750	4,250	22,500	$1,438, MS-61, Jul-10
1907	1,451,786	26,198	61.9	99	1,525	1,550	1,600	1,800	2,150	3,000	7,500	$1,610, MS-62, Jul-10
1907D	842,250	1,971	62.4	96	1,525	1,550	1,600	1,800	2,850	3,500	6,500	$5,319, MS-64, Jul-10
1907S	2,165,800	3,047	61.8	96	1,525	1,550	1,600	1,800	2,550	4,500	25,000	$1,668, MS-62, Jul-10

Proof Liberty Head Double Eagles

PF-60 to 70 (Proof). Proofs were struck in all years from 1858 to 1907, and a few were made before then. Those dated through the 1870s are all very rare today; those of the 1880s are less so; and those of the 1890s and 1900s are scarce. Many have been mishandled. Dates that are Proof only (and those that are very rare in circulation-strike form) are in demand even if impaired; these include 1883, 1884, 1885, 1886, and 1887. Proofs of 1902 onward, particularly 1903, have the portrait polished in the die and lack the cameo contrast of earlier dates. *Obverse and Reverse:* PF-60 to 62 coins have extensive hairlines and may have nicks and contact marks. At PF-63, hairlines are prominent, but the mirror surface is very reflective. PF-64 coins have fewer hairlines. At PF-65, hairlines should be relatively few. These large and heavy coins reveal hairlines more readily than do the lower denominations, mostly seen only under magnification. PF-66 and higher coins should have no marks or hairlines visible to the unaided eye.

Proof Liberty Head Double Eagle

	Mintage	Cert	Avg	PF-60	PF-63	PF-64	PF-65	Recent Auction Record
1849 *(pattern)* **(a)**	1			*(unique; in the Smithsonian's National Numismatic Collection)*				
1850 **(b)**	1–2							
1854S † **(c)**	unknown			*(unique; in the Smithsonian's National Numismatic Collection)*				
1856O **(d)**	unknown	1	63.0					$1,437,500, SP-63, May-09
1858 *(3–4 known)*	unknown			*(extremely rare)*				
1859 *(7–8 known)*	80	5	63.0	$50,000	$125,000	$275,000	$400,000	$17,250, PF-58, Sep-06
1860 *(<10 known)*	59	7	64.1	45,000	100,000	185,000	350,000	$201,250, PF-64DCam, Apr-06
1861 *(5–6 known)*	66	3	65.0	40,000	95,000	185,000	325,000	$483,000, PF-67UCam, Aug-06
1862 *(about 12 known)*	35	6	64.2	40,000	85,000	150,000	300,000	$253,000, PF-65DCam, Jan-07
1863 *(about 12 known)*	30	9	64.2	40,000	85,000	150,000	300,000	$241,500, PF-65Cam, Sep-08
1864 *(12–15 known)*	50	12	64.3	40,000	85,000	150,000	300,000	$184,000, PF-64Cam, Jan-07
1865 *(<10 known)*	25	6	64.7	40,000	85,000	150,000	300,000	
1866, With Motto *(about 15 known)*	30	6	64.3	25,000	55,000	115,000	170,000	$126,500, PF-64, May-07
1867 *(10–12 known)*	50	4	64.5	25,000	52,500	115,000	170,000	$40,250, PF-61Cam, Jul-05

† Ranked in the *100 Greatest U.S. Coins* (third edition). **a.** An unknown quantity of 1849 double eagles was struck as patterns; all but two were melted. One (current location unknown) was sent to Treasury secretary W.M. Meredith; the other was placed in the Mint collection, and transferred with that collection to the Smithsonian in 1923. **b.** Although no examples currently are known, it is likely that a small number of Proof 1850 double eagles were struck. For the years 1851 to 1857, no Proofs are known. **c.** This unique coin, perhaps more accurately described as a *presentation strike* than a *Proof*, was sent to the Mint collection by superintendent Lewis A. Birdsall. It may have been the first coin struck for the year, set aside to recognize the opening of the San Francisco Mint. **d.** Fewer than 25 1856-O double eagles exist; of them, this prooflike presentation strike is unique.

Chart continued on next page.

	Mintage	Cert	Avg	PF-60	PF-63	PF-64	PF-65	Recent Auction Record
1868 (about 12 known)	25	7	64.4	$25,000	$52,500	$115,000	$170,000	$299,000, PF-66Cam, Apr-08
1869 (about 12 known)	25	7	65.0	25,000	52,500	115,000	170,000	$106,375, PF-64DCam, Feb-09
1870 (about 12 known)	35	5	65.2	25,000	52,500	115,000	170,000	$368,000, PF-66, Jan-07
1871 (<10 known)	30	5	63.6	25,000	50,000	115,000	170,000	$26,450, PF-62Cam, Aug-04
1872 (<12 known)	30	5	63.6	25,000	50,000	115,000	170,000	$71,875, PF-63DCam, Jul-09
1873, Close 3 (10–12 known)	25	7	63.9	25,000	50,000	115,000	170,000	$155,250, PF-65Cam, Jan-05
1874 (<10 known)	20	6	63.5	25,000	52,500	125,000	175,000	$103,500, PF-64UCam Star, Aug-04
1875 (10–12 known)	20	5	63.8	40,000	95,000	150,000	225,000	$115,000, PF-63Cam, Aug-07
1876 (about 15 known)	45	11	63.7					$43,125, PF-63, Aug-06
1877 (10–12 known)	20	11	63.5	20,000	37,500	75,000	125,000	$19,550, PF58Cam, Jun-10
1878 (<10 known)	20	8	64.5	20,000	39,500	65,000	115,000	$74,750, PF-64DCam, Jan-09
1879 (10–12 known)	30	5	64.0	20,000	39,500	65,000	115,000	$57,500, PF-64 CAC, Jul-09
1880 (10–12 known)	36	5	64.6	20,000	36,500	65,000	115,000	
1881 (<20 known)	61	8	63.9	20,000	37,500	75,000	115,000	$184,000, PF-66UCam, Apr-06
1882 (12–15 known)	59	6	63.5	20,000	37,500	75,000	115,000	$195,500, PF-66UCam Star, Sep-08
1883, Proof only (about 20 known)	92	15	64.1	45,000	110,000	150,000	200,000	$212,750, PF-65Cam, Jan-06
1884, Proof only (about 20 known)	71	10	63.1	45,000	105,000	150,000	200,000	$54,625, PF-53, Apr-09
1885 (15–20 known)	77	11	64.1	27,500	40,000	85,000	120,000	$37,375, PF-61UCam, Dec-09
1886 (20–25 known)	106	19	64.2	20,000	40,000	75,000	115,000	$62,100, PF-64, Jan-06
1887, Proof only (<30 known)	121	10	64.9	32,500	65,000	85,000	125,000	$155,250, PF-64DCam, Oct-08
1888 (20–30 known)	105	16	64.3	20,000	30,000	45,000	85,000	$103,500, PF-65UCam, Mar-08
1889 (10–12 known)	41	7	63.3	20,000	30,000	45,000	85,000	$64,400, PF-64UCam, Jul-05
1890 (about 15 known)	55	15	65.5	20,000	30,000	45,000	85,000	$86,250, PF-65UCam, Mar-07
1891 (20–25 known)	52	26	63.5	20,000	30,000	45,000	85,000	$158,125, PF-67UCam, Sep-09
1892 (about 25 known)	93	15	64.3	20,000	30,000	45,000	85,000	$120,750, PF-66DCam, Feb-10
1893 (15–20 known)	59	3	63.7	20,000	30,000	45,000	85,000	$15,525, PF-60Cam, Jul-05
1894 (15–20 known)	50	12	63.6	20,000	30,000	45,000	85,000	$54,625, PF-64Cam, Jan-05
1895	51	11	64.0	20,000	30,000	45,000	85,000	$48,875, PF-64Cam, Oct-08
1896 (45–50 known)	128	41	63.9	20,000	30,000	45,000	85,000	$126,500, PF-65, Jan-10
1897 (20–25 known)	86	23	64.0	20,000	30,000	45,000	85,000	$32,200, PF-63 CAC, Jul-09
1898 (35–40 known)	75	36	64.4	20,000	30,000	45,000	85,000	$80,500, PF-65DCam, Jan-09
1899 (<30 known)	84	26	64.1	20,000	30,000	45,000	85,000	$218,500, PF-67UCam, Mar-08
1900 (about 50 known)	124	34	64.5	20,000	30,000	45,000	85,000	$86,250, PF-65DCam, Jan-10
1901 (40–50 known)	96	41	63.0	20,000	30,000	45,000	85,000	$92,000, PF-66Cam, Apr-09
1902 (<50 known)	114	26	62.7	20,000	30,000	45,000	85,000	$57,500, PF-65, Sep-09
1903 (40–50 known)	158	32	63.1	20,000	30,000	45,000	85,000	$43,125, PF-64, Jul-10
1904 (about 50 known)	98	39	63.7	20,000	30,000	45,000	85,000	$15,525, PF-62, Mar-10
1905 (30–40 known)	92	23	63.0	20,000	30,000	45,000	85,000	$27,600, PF-63, Jan-10
1906 (45–50 known)	94	43	63.4	20,000	30,000	45,000	85,000	$80,500, PF-66, Jan-10
1906D (2 known) (e)	6			(extremely rare)				
1907 (40–50 known)	78	44	63.7	20,000	30,000	45,000	85,000	$24,150, PF-63Cam, Jan-10
1907D (f)	unknown	1	62.0					$71,875, PF-62, Jan-04

e. Six 1906 presentation strikes were made to commemorate the first coinage of double eagles at the Denver Mint. The coins were well documented at the time; however, at present only two are accounted for. **f.** Believed to have once been part of the King Farouk collection; cleaned.

SAINT-GAUDENS, HIGH RELIEF AND ULTRA HIGH RELIEF, MCMVII (1907)

Designer Augustus Saint-Gaudens; weight 33.436 grams; composition .900 gold, .100 copper (net weight: .96750 oz. pure gold); diameter 34 mm; edge: E PLURIBUS UNUM with words divided by stars (one specimen of the high-relief variety with plain edge is known); mints: Philadelphia, Denver, San Francisco.

History. Created by famous artist Augustus Saint-Gaudens under a commission arranged by President Theodore Roosevelt, this double eagle was first made (in pattern form) with sculptured-effect ultra high relief on both sides and the date in Roman numerals. The story of its production is well known and has been described in several books, notably *Renaissance of American Coinage, 1905–1908* (Burdette, 2006) and *Striking Change: The Great Artistic Collaboration of Theodore Roosevelt and August Saint-Gaudens* (Moran, 2008). After the Ultra High Relief patterns of 1907, a modified High Relief version was developed to facilitate production. Each coin required three blows of the press to strike up properly. They were made on a medal press in December 1907 and January 1908, to the extent of fewer than 13,000 pieces. In the meantime, production was under way for low-relief coins, easier to mint in quantities sufficient for commerce—these dated 1907 rather than MCMVII. Today, the MCMVII double eagle is a favorite, and when surveys are taken of beautiful and popular designs (as in *100 Greatest U.S. Coins,* by Garrett and Guth), it usually ranks at the top.

Striking and Sharpness. The striking usually is good. Check the left knee of the standing figure, which sometimes shows lightness of strike and, most often, shows flatness or wear (sometimes concealed by post-Mint etching or clever tooling). Check the Capitol at the lower left. On the reverse, check the high points at the top of the eagle. The surface on all is a delicate matte texture, grainy rather than deeply frosty. Under examination the fields show myriad tiny raised curlicues and other die-finish marks. There is no record of any being made as *Proofs,* nor is there any early numismatic record of any being sold as Proofs. Walter Breen in the 1960s made up some "guidelines" for Proofs, which some graders have adopted. Some homemade "Proofs" have been made by pickling or sandblasting the surface of regular coins—caveat emptor.

Availability. Half or more of the original mintage still exist today, as many were saved, and these grade mostly from AU-50 to MS-62. Circulated examples have often been cleaned, polished, or used in jewelry. Higher-grade coins are seen with some frequency, up to MS-65. Overgrading is common.

MS-60 to 70 (Mint State). *Obverse:* At MS-60, some abrasion and contact marks are seen on Liberty's chest. The left knee is flat on lower MS coins and all circulated coins. Scattered marks and abrasion are in the field. Satiny luster is present, but may be dull or lifeless, and interrupted in patches. Many coins at this level have been cleaned. At MS-63, contact marks are fewer, and abrasion is light, but the knee still has a flat spot. An MS-65 coin has little abrasion and few marks. Grades above MS-65 are defined by having fewer marks as perfection is approached. *Reverse:* Comments apply as for the obverse, except that abrasion and contact marks are most noticeable on the side of the eagle's body and the top of the left wing.

	Mintage	Cert	Avg	%MS	MS-60	MS-62	MS-63	MS-64	MS-65	MS-66	MS-67	Recent Auction Record
1907, High Relief, MCMVII, Wire Rim † (a)	12,367	1,060	62.5	91	$16,500	$22,000	$25,000	$30,000	$50,000	$85,000	$150,000	$32,200, MS-64 CAC, Jul-10
1907, Same, Flat Rim †	*	438	62.6	88	16,500	22,000	26,000	31,000	52,500	87,500	155,000	$46,000, MS-65, Jul-10

* Included in number above. † Ranked in the *100 Greatest U.S. Coins* (third edition). **a.** The Wire Rim and Flat Rim varieties were the result of different collars used in the minting process. The Flat Rim is considered slightly scarcer, but this has not led to large value differentials, as both varieties are very popular among collectors.

Proof Saint-Gaudens High Relief and Ultra High Relief Double Eagles

PF-60 to 70 (Proof). For all practical purposes the Ultra High Relief design of 1907 was unsuitable for production for circulation purposes. Between 16 and 22 Proof examples were struck. Among High Relief coins, NGC recognizes coins with certain characteristics as Proofs, while PCGS does not certify any High Relief examples as such. *Obverse and Reverse:* PF-60 to 62 coins have extensive hairlines and may have nicks and contact marks. At PF-63, hairlines are prominent, but the mirror surface is very reflective. PF-64 coins have fewer hairlines. At PF-65, hairlines should be relatively few. These large and heavy coins reveal hairlines more readily than do the lower denominations, mostly seen only under magnification. PF-66 and higher coins should have no marks or hairlines visible to the unaided eye.

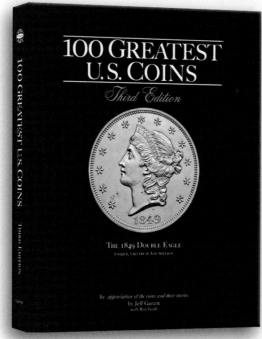

**Proof Saint-Gaudens MCMVII
Ultra High Relief Pattern Double Eagle**

	Est Mintage	Cert	Avg	PF-60	PF-63	PF-64	PF-65	PF-67	Recent Auction Record
1907, High Relief, MCMVII, Wire or Flat Rim	unknown	234	63.9	$25,000	$32,500	$40,000	$75,000		$20,700, PF-62, Apr-10
1907, Ultra High Relief, Plain Edge	*	2	63.0						
1907, Ultra High Relief, Inverted Edge	*	2	68.0						
1907, Ultra High Relief, Lettered Edge †	16–22	4	67.8				$2,250,000		$1,840,000, PF-68, Jan-07

* Included in number below. † Ranked in the *100 Greatest U.S. Coins* (third edition).

SAINT-GAUDENS, FLAT RELIEF, ARABIC NUMERALS
(1907–1933)

Designer Augustus Saint-Gaudens; weight 33.436 grams; composition .900 gold, .100 copper (net weight: .96750 oz. pure gold); diameter 34 mm; edge: E PLURIBUS UNUM with words divided by stars; mints: Philadelphia, Denver, San Francisco.

History. In autumn 1907 chief engraver Charles E. Barber modified Augustus Saint-Gaudens's design by lowering the relief and using Arabic (not roman) numerals. Coins of this type were struck in large quantities from 1907 to 1916 and again from 1920 to 1933. In July 1908 the motto IN GOD WE TRUST was added to the reverse. The vast majority of these coins were exported. Since World War II millions have been repatriated, supplying most of those in numismatic hands today. Coins dated 1907 to 1911 have 46 stars on the obverse; coins of 1912 to 1933 have 48 stars.

Striking and Sharpness. The details are often light on the obverse. Check the bosom of Miss Liberty, the covering of which tends to be weak on 1907 and, especially, 1908 No Motto coins. Check the Capitol building and its immediate area at the lower left. The reverse usually is well struck, but check the feathers on the eagle and the top of the wings.

Availability. Most dates and mintmarks range from very common to slightly scarce, punctuated with scarce to very rare issues such as 1908-S, 1920-S, 1921, mintmarks from 1924 to 1927, and all issues of 1929 to 1933.

From their initial mintages, most of the double eagles of the 1920s were returned to the Mint and melted in the 1930s. Some, however, were unofficially saved by Treasury employees. Estimates of the quantities saved range from a few dozen to several hundred thousand, depending on the date; this explains the high values for coins that, judged only by their initial mintages, should otherwise be more common.

Probably a million or more MS coins exist of certain dates, most notably 1908 No Motto, 1924, 1925, 1926, and 1928 (especially common). Quality varies, as many have contact marks. Philadelphia Mint coins from 1922 onward usually are seen with excellent eye appeal. Common varieties are not usually collected in grades below MS.

AU-50, 53, 55, 58 (About Uncirculated). *Obverse:* Light wear is seen on the chest, the left knee, the midriff, and across the field, more so at AU-50 than at 53 or 55. An AU-58 coin has minimal traces of wear. An AU-50 coin has luster in protected areas among the rays, with little in the open field above. At AU-58, most luster is present. *Reverse:* The side of the eagle below the front of the wing, the top of the wing, and the field show light wear. Luster ranges from perhaps 40% (at AU-50) to nearly full mint bloom (at AU-58).

MS-60 to 70 (Mint State). *Obverse:* At MS-60, some abrasion and contact marks are seen on Liberty's chest and left knee, and scattered marks and abrasion are in the field. Luster is present, but may be dull or lifeless, and interrupted in patches. At MS-63, contact marks are fewer, and abrasion is light. An MS-65 coin has little abrasion and few marks, although quality among certified coins can vary. On a conservatively graded coin the luster should be full and rich. Grades above MS-65 are defined by having fewer marks as perfection is approached. Generally, Mint State coins of 1922 onward are choicer and more attractive than the earlier issues. *Reverse:* Comments apply as for the obverse, except that abrasion and contact marks are most noticeable on the eagle's left wing.

No Motto   With Motto

1909, 9 Over 8   1922, Doubled-Die Reverse   1925, Doubled-Die Reverse

1933 Saint-Gaudens Double Eagle

	Mintage	Cert	Avg	%MS	AU-58	MS-60	MS-62	MS-63	MS-64	MS-65	MS-66	Recent Auction Record
1907, Arabic Numerals	361,667	9,585	62.7	98	$1,625	$1,650	$1,700	$1,825	$2,300	$4,000	$7,500	$6,617, MS-66, Jul-10
1908, No Motto	4,271,551	122,492	63.3	100	1,575	1,600	1,650	1,700	1,850	2,450	3,250	$8,050, MS-67, Jul-10
1908D, No Motto	663,750	3,978	62.4	97	1,600	1,625	1,675	1,775	2,500	9,500	25,000	$2,185, MS-64 CAC, Jul-10

	Mintage	Cert	Avg	%MS	AU-50	AU-55	MS-60	MS-62	MS-63	MS-64	MS-65	Recent Auction Record
1908, With Motto	156,258	1,854	62.0	95	$1,575	$1,600	$1,650	$1,800	$2,250	$5,000	$17,500	$6,325, MS-64 CAC, Jul-10
1908D, With Motto	349,500	1,996	62.5	94	1,525	1,550	1,600	1,650	1,750	2,500	5,000	$1,955, MS-64, Jul-10
1908S	22,000	443	55.9	32	6,000	6,750	11,000	17,500	23,500	27,500	50,000	$37,375, MS-65, Jul-10
1909, All kinds	161,282											
1909, 9 Over 8 (a)		1,406	59.3	58	1,475	1,550	1,650	3,500	6,000	20,000	40,000	$2,875, MS-62, Jul-10
1909		1,262	60.7	77	1,475	1,550	1,650	2,000	3,500	8,500	35,000	$6,900, MS-64, Jul-10
1909D	52,500	465	60.0	63	1,575	1,600	2,450	5,000	8,500	13,500	45,000	$27,600, MS-65, Jul-10
1909S	2,774,925	5,176	62.7	96	1,525	1,550	1,600	1,650	1,750	2,100	4,500	$4,888, MS-65, Jul-10
1910	482,000	7,005	62.3	98	1,525	1,550	1,600	1,650	1,800	2,300	9,500	$2,013, MS-64, Jul-10
1910D	429,000	6,122	62.9	98	1,525	1,550	1,600	1,650	1,750	2,100	3,250	$6,325, MS-66, Jul-10
1910S	2,128,250	3,848	61.9	91	1,525	1,550	1,600	1,650	1,800	2,250	7,500	$7,475, MS-65, Jul-10

a. This is one of the few Saint-Gaudens double eagle die varieties that commands a premium over the regular coin.

	Mintage	Cert	Avg	%MS	AU-50	AU-55	MS-60	MS-62	MS-63	MS-64	MS-65	Recent Auction Record
1911	197,250	2,410	61.9	90	$1,525	$1,550	$1,600	$1,650	$2,000	$3,500	$16,000	$3,450, MS-63 CAC, Jul-10
1911D	846,500	11,016	63.5	98	1,525	1,550	1,600	1,650	1,750	2,100	2,750	$12,650, MS-67, Jul-10
1911S	775,750	4,987	62.9	98	1,525	1,550	1,600	1,650	1,750	2,100	4,000	$10,350, MS-66, Jul-10
1912	149,750	2,306	61.5	89	1,525	1,550	1,600	1,650	1,900	5,500	22,000	$4,313, MS-64, Jul-10
1913	168,780	2,413	61.4	90	1,525	1,550	1,600	1,650	2,750	7,500	55,000	$5,750, MS-64, Jul-10
1913D	393,500	3,507	62.6	96	1,525	1,550	1,600	1,650	1,750	2,100	5,500	$2,300, MS-64, Jul-10
1913S	34,000	1,115	61.7	88	1,600	1,750	1,950	3,000	4,500	6,500	35,000	$6,325, MS-64, Jul-10
1914	95,250	1,595	62.0	92	1,525	1,550	1,600	1,650	3,500	5,500	20,000	$5,175, MS-64, Jul-10
1914D	453,000	6,016	63.1	98	1,525	1,550	1,600	1,650	1,750	1,900	3,250	$8,625, MS-66, Feb-10
1914S	1,498,000	19,685	63.1	99	1,525	1,550	1,600	1,650	1,750	1,900	2,450	$2,070, MS-65, Jul-10
1915	152,000	1,982	61.8	89	1,525	1,550	1,600	1,650	2,400	5,500	27,500	$1,840, MS-63, Jul-10
1915S	567,500	14,511	63.3	99	1,525	1,550	1,600	1,650	1,750	1,950	2,550	$6,325, MS-66, Jul-10
1916S	796,000	4,061	63.5	97	1,525	1,550	1,600	1,650	1,750	1,950	3,500	$2,473, MS-65, Jul-10
1920	228,250	5,703	62.1	99	1,525	1,550	1,600	1,650	1,750	4,250	65,000	$2,070, MS-63 CAC, Jul-10
1920S	558,000	79	61.1	75	27,500	35,000	55,000	75,000	100,000	165,000	275,000	$126,500, MS-64, Apr-10
1921	528,500	65	58.9	57	55,000	65,000	120,000	175,000	275,000	450,000	1,000,000	$218,500, MS-63, Apr-10
1922	1,375,500	45,854	62.6	100	1,525	1,550	1,600	1,650	1,750	1,900	4,750	$3,881, MS-65, Jul-10
1922, Doubled-Die Reverse	*				1,850	2,000	2,250	2,500	3,000			$1,840, MS-65, Nov-07
1922S	2,658,000	866	62.6	97	1,600	1,750	2,350	3,000	4,750	9,000	40,000	$9,775, MS-64 CAC, Jul-10
1923	566,000	25,277	62.4	100	1,525	1,550	1,600	1,650	1,750	1,900	4,750	$4,313, MS-65, Jul-10
1923D	1,702,250	5,636	64.3	100	1,525	1,550	1,600	1,650	1,750	1,900	2,450	$4,025, MS-66, Jul-10
1924	4,323,500	276,949	63.4	100	1,525	1,550	1,600	1,650	1,750	1,900	2,450	$4,888, MS-66 CAC, Jul-10
1924D	3,049,500	445	61.9	88	2,100	2,750	3,850	5,500	8,750	15,000	75,000	$4,888, MS-62, Jul-10
1924S	2,927,500	480	62.5	93	2,100	2,750	3,950	5,500	9,500	16,500	75,000	$10,350, MS-63, Jul-10
1925	2,831,750	46,558	63.2	100	1,525	1,550	1,600	1,650	1,750	1,900	2,450	$2,990, MS-66, Jul-10
1925, Doubled-Die Reverse (b)	*	5	64.4	100	1,850	2,000	2,250	2,500	3,000			$1,610, MS-65, Nov-07
1925D	2,938,500	302	62.6	98	2,850	3,000	4,750	7,500	11,500	20,000	75,000	$7,763, MS-62 CAC, Jun-10
1925S	3,776,500	374	59.4	57	3,000	4,500	9,250	15,000	23,500	60,000	150,000	$3,594, AU-55, Jul-10
1926	816,750	21,417	63.6	100	1,525	1,550	1,600	1,650	1,750	1,900	2,450	$3,450, MS-66, Jul-10
1926D	481,000	110	61.3	87	15,750	17,500	28,500	32,500	40,000	75,000	135,000	$18,400, MS-63, Apr-10
1926S	2,041,500	639	63.1	97	2,100	2,250	2,850	4,000	5,250	7,500	32,500	$6,900, MS-64, Jul-10
1927	2,946,750	127,110	63.5	100	1,525	1,550	1,600	1,650	1,750	1,900	2,450	$4,888, MS-66+, Jul-10
1927D †	180,000	5	64.2	80	525,000	625,000	775,000	850,000	1,100,000	1,350,000	1,500,000	$1,495,000, MS-66, Jan-10
1927S	3,107,000	122	61.4	76	14,000	16,500	27,000	37,500	55,000	75,000	150,000	$41,688, MS-63, Jun-10
1928	8,816,000	43,826	63.3	100	1,525	1,550	1,600	1,650	1,750	1,900	2,450	$2,645, MS-66, Jul-10
1929	1,779,750	129	63.2	97	13,500	15,500	20,000	30,000	40,000	55,000	75,000	$69,000, MS-65, Apr-10
1930S	74,000	20	63.8	95	42,500	45,000	57,500	75,000	115,000	150,000	195,000	$161,000, MS-65, Feb-10
1931	2,938,250	37	64.1	100	20,000	25,000	34,000	47,500	72,500	85,000	100,000	$92,000, MS-65, Apr-10
1931D	106,500	44	63.4	98	20,500	24,500	34,500	47,500	85,000	95,000	125,000	$66,125, MS-64, Apr-10
1932	1,101,750	68	64.0	100	20,500	23,500	33,500	55,000	80,000	85,000	100,000	$126,500, MS-66, Apr-10
1933 (13 known) † (c)	445,500						(extremely rare)					$7,590,000, Gem BU, Jul-02

* Included in number above. † Ranked in the *100 Greatest U.S. Coins* (third edition). **b.** Doubling is evident on the eagle's feathers, the rays, and IN GOD WE TRUST. **c.** All but a few 1933 double eagles were to have been melted at the mint. Today 13 examples are known to have survived. Only one, previously in the King Farouk collection, has ever been sold at auction.

Proof Saint-Gaudens, Flat Relief, Arabic Numerals, Double Eagles

PF-60 to 70 (Proof). Sand Blast (also called Matte) Proofs were made in 1908 and from 1911 to 1915. These have dull surfaces, much like fine-grained sandpaper. Satin (also called Roman Finish) Proofs were made in 1909 and 1910. They have satiny surfaces and are bright yellow. All are rare today. *Obverse and Reverse:* At PF-60 to 63, there is light abrasion and some contact marks (the lower the grade, the higher the quantity). On Sand Blast Proofs these show up as visually unappealing bright spots. At PF-64 and higher levels, marks are fewer, with magnification needed to see any at PF-65. At PF-66, there should be none at all.

GOLD DOUBLE EAGLES, 1850–1933

Proof Saint-Gaudens, Flat Relief, Arabic Numerals,
Double Eagle

	Mintage	Cert	Avg	PF-60	PF-63	PR-64	PF-65	Recent Auction Record
1907 *(2–3 known)*	*unknown*	4	67.0		*(extremely rare)*			$920,000, PF-68, Nov-05
1908, With Motto, Matte	101	73	65.3	$15,000	$30,000	$42,500	$75,000	$57,500, PF-66, Feb-10
1908, With Motto, Satin Finish								
(3–4 known)	*unknown*	6	64.5		*(extremely rare)*			$276,000, PF-64, Nov-05
1909	67	29	65.3	15,000	30,000	45,000	75,000	$77,625, PF-66, Jan-08
1910, Satin Finish	167	33	65.4	15,000	30,000	45,000	75,000	$60,375, PF-65, Jan-08
1910, Matte **(a)**	*unknown*	1	66.0					
1911	100	45	66.0	15,000	30,000	45,000	75,000	$54,625, PF-66, Jan-10
1912	74	54	66.0	15,000	30,000	45,000	75,000	$74,750, PF-67, Jan-10
1913	58	49	65.4	15,000	30,000	45,000	75,000	$86,250, PF-67, Jan-10
1914	70	27	65.4	15,000	30,000	45,000	75,000	$60,375, PF-66, Feb-10
1915	50	39	64.7	17,500	35,000	50,000	85,000	$43,125, PF-65, Jan-10
1921 *(2 known)* † **(b)**	*unknown*	1	64.0		*(extremely rare)*			

† Ranked in the *100 Greatest U.S. Coins* (third edition). **a.** Part of the unique complete 1910 Matte Proof gold set. **b.** Prior to the first public auction of a 1921 presentation-strike double eagle (a lightly cleaned specimen) in summer 2000, this variety was unknown to the numismatic community at large. That example reportedly was struck in 1921 to celebrate the birth of Joseph Baker, nephew of U.S. Mint director Raymond T. Baker. In 2006 a second example (this one with original, uncleaned surfaces) was discovered and subsequently auctioned.

AN OVERVIEW OF
CLASSIC COMMEMORATIVES

CLASSIC COMMEMORATIVES, 1892–1954

Commemorative coins have been popular since the time of ancient Greece and Rome. In the beginning they recorded and honored important events, and passed along the news of the day. Today commemorative coins, which are highly esteemed by collectors, have been issued by many modern nations—none of which has surpassed the United States when it comes to these impressive mementoes.

The unique position occupied by commemoratives in the United States coinage is largely due to the fact that, with few exceptions, all commemorative coins have real historical significance. The progress and advance of people in the New World are presented in an interesting and instructive manner on our commemorative coins. Such a record of history artistically presented on U.S. gold, silver, and other memorial issues appeals strongly to the collector who favors the romantic, storytelling side of numismatics. It is the historical features of our commemoratives, in fact, that create interest among many people who would otherwise have little interest in coins, and would not otherwise consider themselves collectors.

Concepts for commemorative issues are reviewed by two committees of Congress: the Committee on Banking, Housing, and Urban Affairs; and the Committee on Banking and Financial Services of the House; as well as by the Citizens Coinage Advisory Committee. Congress is guided to a great extent by the reports of these committees when considering bills authorizing commemorative coins.

These special coins are usually issued either to commemorate events or to help pay for monuments, programs, or celebrations that commemorate historical persons, places, or things. Pre-1982 commemorative coins were offered in most instances by a commission in charge of the event to be commemorated, and sold at a premium over face value.

Commemorative coins are popularly collected either by major types or in sets with mintmark varieties. The pieces covered here in the *Guide Book of United States Coins, Professional Edition,* are those of the "classic" era of U.S. commemoratives, 1892 to 1954. All commemoratives are of the standard weight and fineness of their regular-issue 20th-century gold and silver counterparts, and all are legal tender.

A note about mintages and distribution numbers. Unless otherwise stated, the coinage figures given in each "Distribution" column represent the total released mintage: the total mintage (including assay coins), minus the quantity of unsold coins. In many cases, larger quantities were minted but not all were sold. Unsold coins usually were returned to the mint and melted, although sometimes quantities were placed in circulation at face value. a limited number of Proof strikings or presentation pieces were made for some of the classic commemorative issues.

A note about price performance. It has mostly been in recent years that the general public has learned about commemorative coins. They have long been popular with coin collectors who enjoy the artistry and history associated with them, as well as the profit to be made from owning these rare pieces. Very few of them ever reached circulation because they were all originally sold above face value, and because they are all so rare. Most of the early issues were of the half dollar denomination, and were often made in quantities of fewer than 20,000 pieces. This is minuscule when compared to the regular half dollar coins that are made by the millions each year, and still rarely seen in circulation.

At the beginning of 1988, prices of classic commemoratives in MS-65 condition had risen so high that most collectors had to content themselves with pieces in lower grades. Investors continued to apply pressure to the high-quality pieces, driving prices even higher, while the collector community went after coins in grades from AU to MS-63. For several months the pressure from both influences caused prices to rise very rapidly (for all issues and grades) without even taking the price-adjustment breather that usually goes along with such activity.

By 1990, prices dropped to the point that several of the commemoratives began to look like bargains once again. Many of the MS-65 pieces held firm at price levels above the $3,000 mark, but others were still available at under $500 even for coins of similar mintage. Coins in MS-63 or MS-64 were priced at but a fraction of the MS-65 prices, which would seem to make them reasonably priced because the demand for these pieces is universal, and not keyed simply to grade, rarity, or speculator pressure.

Historically, the entire series of commemorative coins has frequently undergone a roller-coaster cycle of price adjustments. These cycles have usually been of short duration, lasting from months to years, with prices always recovering and eventually exceeding previous levels.

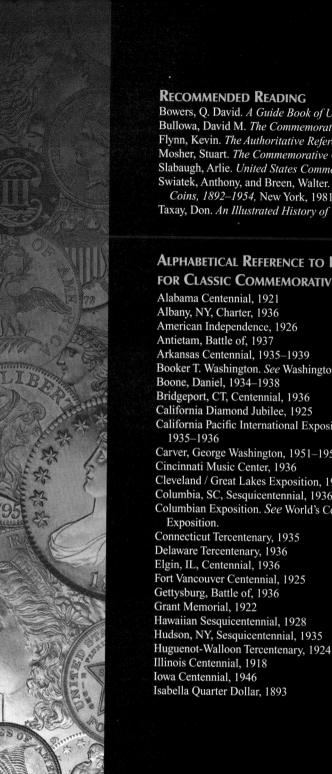

RECOMMENDED READING

Bowers, Q. David. *A Guide Book of United States Commemorative Coins,* Atlanta, GA, 2008.
Bullowa, David M. *The Commemorative Coinage of the United States, 1892–1938,* New York, 1938.
Flynn, Kevin. *The Authoritative Reference on Commemorative Coins, 1892–1954,* Roswell, GA, 2008.
Mosher, Stuart. *The Commemorative Coinage of the United States, 1892–1938,* New York, 1940.
Slabaugh, Arlie. *United States Commemorative Coinage,* Racine, WI, 1975.
Swiatek, Anthony, and Breen, Walter. *The Encyclopedia of United States Silver and Gold Commemorative Coins, 1892–1954,* New York, 1981.
Taxay, Don. *An Illustrated History of U.S. Commemorative Coinage,* New York, 1967.

ALPHABETICAL REFERENCE TO DATES FOR CLASSIC COMMEMORATIVES

Alabama Centennial, 1921
Albany, NY, Charter, 1936
American Independence, 1926
Antietam, Battle of, 1937
Arkansas Centennial, 1935–1939
Booker T. Washington. *See* Washington, Booker T.
Boone, Daniel, 1934–1938
Bridgeport, CT, Centennial, 1936
California Diamond Jubilee, 1925
California Pacific International Exposition, 1935–1936
Carver, George Washington, 1951–1954
Cincinnati Music Center, 1936
Cleveland / Great Lakes Exposition, 1936
Columbia, SC, Sesquicentennial, 1936
Columbian Exposition. *See* World's Columbian Exposition.
Connecticut Tercentenary, 1935
Delaware Tercentenary, 1936
Elgin, IL, Centennial, 1936
Fort Vancouver Centennial, 1925
Gettysburg, Battle of, 1936
Grant Memorial, 1922
Hawaiian Sesquicentennial, 1928
Hudson, NY, Sesquicentennial, 1935
Huguenot-Walloon Tercentenary, 1924
Illinois Centennial, 1918
Iowa Centennial, 1946
Isabella Quarter Dollar, 1893

Lafayette Dollar, 1900
Lewis and Clark Exposition, 1904–1905
Lexington-Concord Sesquicentennial, 1925
Long Island Tercentenary, 1936
Louisiana Purchase Exposition, 1903
Lynchburg, VA, Sesquicentennial, 1936
Maine Centennial, 1920
Maryland Tercentenary, 1934
McKinley Memorial, 1916–1917
Missouri Centennial, 1921
Monroe Doctrine Centennial, 1923
New Rochelle, NY, 250th Anniversary, 1938
Norfolk, VA, Bicentennial, 1936
Old Spanish Trail, 1935
Oregon Trail Memorial, 1926–1939
Panama-Pacific Exposition, 1915
Pilgrim Tercentenary, 1920–1921
Providence, RI, Tercentenary, 1936
Roanoke Island, NC, 350th Anniversary, 1937
Robinson–Arkansas Centennial, 1936
San Francisco–Oakland Bay Bridge, 1936
Spanish Trail, Old, 1935
Stone Mountain Memorial, 1925
Texas Centennial, 1934–1938
Vermont Sesquicentennial, 1927
Washington, Booker T., 1946–1951; 1951–1954
Wisconsin Territorial Centennial, 1936
World's Columbian Exposition, 1892–1893
York County, ME, Tercentenary, 1936

WORLD'S COLUMBIAN EXPOSITION HALF DOLLAR (1892–1893)

Designers Charles E. Barber (obv), George T. Morgan (rev); weight 12.50 grams; composition .900 silver, .100 copper; diameter 30.6 mm; reeded edge; mint: Philadelphia.

Designs. *Obverse:* Charles Barber's conception of Christopher Columbus, derived from a plaster model by Olin Levi Warner, taken from the explorer's portrait on an 1892 Spanish medal. The medal's portrait was inspired by a statue by Jeronimo Suñel, which itself was from an imagined likeness by Charles Legrand. *Reverse:* A sailing ship atop two globes representing the Old World and the New World. The vessel is from a plaster model by Olin Levi Warner, taken from a model made in Spain of Columbus's flagship, the *Santa Maria.*

Mintage and Melting Data. 1892: *Maximum authorized—* 5,000,000 (also includes coins dated 1893). *Number minted* (including an unknown number of assay coins)*—950,000.* Approximately 100 Proofs were struck. *Net distribution—950,000.* 1893: *Number minted* (including 2,105 assay coins)*—4,052,105. Number melted—2,501,700. Net distribution—1,550,405.*

Original Cost and Issuer. Sale price $1. Issued by the Exposition.

Key to Collecting. Both dates are common in all grades through MS-65, and are often available in MS-66 and higher. The typical high-grade coin is lustrous and frosty; some have attractive, original light-blue or iridescent toning. Well-worn examples are very common, as the Treasury Department eventually released large quantities into circulation at face value. Striking usually is good. Some coins can be weak at the center—on the higher areas of the portrait and, on the reverse, in the details of the ship's sails. Most have bagmarks from handling and distribution. High-grade 1892 coins typically are better struck than those of 1893. Approximately 100 brilliant Proofs were struck for each date; they vary widely in quality and eye appeal.

First Points of Wear. *Obverse:* The eyebrow, the cheek, and the hair at the back of the forehead. (The hair area sometimes is flatly struck.) *Reverse:* The top of the rear sail, and the right side of the Eastern Hemisphere.

	Distribution	Cert	Avg	%MS	MS-60	MS-62	MS-63	MS-64	MS-65	MS-66	Recent Auction Record
1892	950,000	4,993	63.4	96	$32	$45	$85	$140	$475	$1,050	$2,185, MS-66, Jul-10
1893	1,550,405	5,203	62.7	91	30	38	80	120	425	1,100	$805, MS-66, Jul-10

Note: Various repunched dates exist for both dates; these command little or no premium in the marketplace. For more information, see the *Cherrypickers' Guide to Rare Die Varieties,* fourth edition, volume II.

	Est Mintage	Cert	Finest	PF-60	PF-63	PF-64	PF-65	PF-66	Recent Auction Record
1892, Proof	100	32	PF-68	$2,750	$5,750	$7,000	$13,000	$19,500	$6,900, PF-64, Jan-10
1893, Proof	3–5	1	PF-63						$5,830, PF-64, Oct-93

WORLD'S COLUMBIAN EXPOSITION ISABELLA QUARTER (1893)

Designer Charles E. Barber; weight 6.25 grams; composition .900 silver, .100 copper; diameter 24.3 mm; reeded edge; mint: Philadelphia.

Designs. *Obverse:* Crowned profile portrait of Spain's Queen Isabella, who sponsored Christopher Columbus's voyages to the New World. *Reverse:* A lady kneeling with a distaff and spindle, symbolic of the industry of American women.

Mintage and Melting Data. Authorized on March 3, 1893. *Maximum authorized—40,000. Number minted* (including 23 assay coins)*—40,023. Number melted—15,809. Net distribution—* 24,214.

Original Cost and Issuer. Sale price $1. Sold by the Board of Lady Managers, World's Columbian Exposition.

Key to Collecting. Most examples in the marketplace are in Mint State, including many choice and gem pieces. Most are well struck and show full details, with richly lustrous fields. Connoisseurs avoid darkly toned, stained, and recolored coins. Many lower-grade Mint State examples have marks on Isabella's cheek and on the higher parts of the reverse design. The left obverse field often has bagmarks. The certification services have classified some coins with mirrored fields as Proofs, although no official records exist for the production of such.

First Points of Wear. *Obverse:* Isabella's cheekbone, and the center of the lower part of the crown. *Reverse:* The strand of wool at the lower left thigh.

	Distribution	Cert	Avg	%MS	MS-60	MS-62	MS-63	MS-64	MS-65	MS-66	Recent Auction Record
1893	24,214	3,176	62.9	92	$515	$575	$625	$825	$2,550	$4,300	$2,243, MS-65, Jul-10

	Est Mintage	Cert	Finest	PF-60	PF-63	PF-64	PF-65	PF-66	Recent Auction Record
1893, Proof	100–105	36	PF-66	$2,500	$4,750	$7,750	$13,000	$18,000	$4,888, PF-64, Jan-10

CLASSIC COMMEMORATIVES, 1892–1954

CLASSIC COMMEMORATIVES, 1892–1954

LAFAYETTE DOLLAR (1900)

Designer Charles E. Barber; weight 26.73 grams; composition .900 silver, .100 copper; diameter 38.1 mm; reeded edge; mint: Philadelphia.

Designs. *Obverse:* Conjoined portraits of the marquis de Lafayette and George Washington. *Reverse:* Side view of the equestrian statue erected by the youth of the United States in honor of Lafayette. This view was based on an early model of the statue; the final version that was erected in Paris is slightly different.

Mintage and Melting Data. Authorized March 3, 1899. *Maximum authorized*—50,000. *Number minted (including 26 assay coins)*—50,026. *Number melted*—14,000. *Net distribution*—36,026.

Original Cost and Issuer. Sale price $2. Sold by the Lafayette Memorial Commission through the American Trust & Savings Bank of Chicago.

Key to Collecting. Most surviving examples show evidence of circulation or other mishandling. The typical grade is AU. In Mint State, most are MS-60 to 63, and many are dull or unattractive, having been dipped or cleaned multiple times. Many have marks and dings. Properly graded MS-64 coins are very scarce, and MS-65 or higher gems are very rare, especially if with good eye appeal. Several die varieties exist and are collected by specialists.

Varieties. *Obverse varieties:* (1) Small point on the bust of Washington. The tip of Lafayette's bust is over the top of the L in DOL-LAR. The AT in STATES is cut high. (2) The left foot of the final A in AMERICA is recut, and the A in STATES is high. The second S in STATES is repunched (this is diagnostic). (3) The AT in STATES is recut and the final S is low. The letter F in OF and in LAFAYETTE is broken from the lower tip of the crossbar and to the right base extension, and AMERICA is spaced A ME RI C A. The period after OF is close to the A of AMERICA. The tip of Lafayette's vest falls to the right of the top of the first L in DOL-LAR. (4) The C in AMERICA is repunched at the inside top (this is diagnostic). The CA in AMERICA is spaced differently from the obverses previously described. *Reverse varieties:* (A) There are 14 long leaves and a long stem. The tip of the lowest leaf is over the 1 in 1900. (B) There are 14 shorter leaves and a short stem. The tip of the lowest leaf is over the space between the 1 and 9 in 1900. (C) There are 14 medium leaves and a short, bent stem. The tip of the lowest leaf is over the 9 in 1900. (D) There are 15 long leaves and a short, bent stem. The tip of the lowest leaf is over the 9 in 1900. (E) The tip of the lowest leaf is over the space to the left of the 1 in 1900.

First Points of Wear. *Obverse:* Washington's cheekbone, and Lafayette's lower hair curl. *Reverse:* The fringe of Lafayette's epaulet, and the horse's blinder and left rear leg bone.

	Distribution	Cert	Avg	%MS	MS-60	MS-62	MS-63	MS-64	MS-65	MS-66	Recent Auction Record
1900	36,026	2,166	62.5	91	$875	$1,100	$1,800	$2,850	$10,000	$18,500	$7,475, MS-65, Jul-10

LOUISIANA PURCHASE EXPOSITION GOLD DOLLAR (1903)

Designer Charles E. Barber (assisted by George T. Morgan); weight 1.672 grams; composition .900 gold, .100 copper; diameter 15 mm; reeded edge; mint: Philadelphia.

Designs, Jefferson. *Obverse:* Bewigged profile portrait of Thomas Jefferson, inspired by an early 19th-century medal by John Reich, after Houdon's bust. *Reverse:* Inscription and branch.

Designs, McKinley. *Obverse:* Bareheaded profile portrait of William McKinley, derived from his presidential medal (also designed by Barber). *Reverse:* Inscriptions and branch.

Mintage and Melting Data. Authorized June 28, 1902. *Maximum authorized*—250,000 (total for both varieties). *Number minted (including 258 assay coins comprising both varieties)*—250,258 (125,000 of each variety). *Number melted*—215,250 (total for both varieties; no account was kept of the portraits; 250 assay coins were melted). *Net distribution*—35,000; estimated at 17,500 of each variety.

Original Cost and Issuer. Sale price $3. Louisiana Purchase Exposition Company, St. Louis, Missouri (sales through Farran Zerbe). Some were sold as mounted in spoons, brooches, and stick pins; 100 certified Proofs of each design were made, mounted in an opening in a rectangular piece of imprinted cardboard.

Key to Collecting. Market demand is strong, from collectors and investors alike, as most surviving examples are in choice or gem Mint State, with strong eye appeal. Most specimens are very lustrous and frosty. An occasional coin is prooflike. Avoid any with copper stains (from improper mixing of the gold/copper alloy). Proofs enter the market rarely and garner much publicity.

First Points of Wear. *Obverse:* Portrait's cheekbone (usually more evident on the McKinley variety) and sideburn. *Reverse:* Date and denomination.

	Distribution	Cert	Avg	%MS	MS-60	MS-62	MS-63	MS-64	MS-65	MS-66	Recent Auction Record
1903, Jefferson	17,500	1,983	64.0	95	$665	$750	$875	$1,325	$1,875	$2,500	$6,325, MS-67, Jul-10
1903, McKinley	17,500	1,860	64.0	97	650	725	775	1,275	1,925	2,350	$1,495, MS-65, Jul-10

	Mintage	Cert	Finest	PF-60	PF-63	PF-64	PF-65	PF-66	Recent Auction Record
1903, Jefferson, Proof (a)	100	28	PF-67						$28,175, PF-66Cam, Mar-10
1903, McKinley, Proof (b)	100	28	PF-68						$10,925, PF-64Cam, Apr-10

a. The first 100 Jefferson gold dollars were struck in brilliant Proof format. True Proofs exhibit deeply mirrored fields and are sharply struck. Many also have frosted devices, giving them a cameo appearance. "Although many of the coins seen today have been certified and lack original packaging, they were originally housed in cardboard holders certifying each coin as having been one of the first 100 impressions from the dies. The original holders are quite interesting, with the coin covered by a small piece of wax paper and a piece of string sealed by dark red wax. The coins are difficult to see behind the wax paper, and the author has seen holders with a circulation-strike example substituted for the Proof piece. Caution should be used when purchasing an example of this extreme rarity" (*Encyclopedia of U.S. Gold Coins, 1795–1933*, second edition). **b.** Like the Jefferson issue, the first 100 McKinley gold dollars were struck as Proofs, and packaged as such. "Prooflike circulation strikes are quite common for the issue, and true Proofs can be distinguished by deeply mirrored surfaces and cameo devices. Certification is highly recommended" (*Encyclopedia of U.S. Gold Coins, 1795–1933*, second edition).

LEWIS AND CLARK EXPOSITION GOLD DOLLAR (1904–1905)

Designer Charles E. Barber; weight 1.672 grams; composition .900 gold, .100 copper; diameter 15 mm; reeded edge; mint: Philadelphia.

Designs. *Obverse:* Bareheaded profile portrait of Meriwether Lewis. *Reverse:* Bareheaded profile portrait of William Clark. These portraits were inspired by works of Charles Willson Peale.

Mintage and Melting Data. 1904: Authorized on April 13, 1904. *Maximum authorized*—250,000 (total for 1904- and 1905-dated coins). *Number minted* (including 28 assay coins)—25,028. *Number melted*—15,003. *Net distribution*—10,025. 1905: *Number minted* (including 41 assay coins)—35,041. *Number melted*—25,000. *Net distribution*—10,041.

Original Cost and Issuer. Sales price $2 (some at $2.50); many were probably discounted further. Lewis and Clark Centennial and American Pacific Exposition and Oriental Fair Company, Portland, Oregon (sales through Farran Zerbe and others).

Key to Collecting. Most surviving examples show evidence of handling. Some exhibit die problems (a rough raised area of irregularity at the dentils). Most range from AU-50 to 58, with an occasional MS-60 to 63. MS-64 coins are scarce, and MS-65 rare. Pristine examples are very rare. Most MS coins have areas of prooflike finish; some are deeply lustrous and frosty. The 1905-dated issue is noticeably scarcer than the 1904.

First Points of Wear. *Obverse:* Lewis's temple. *Reverse:* Clark's temple.

	Distribution	Cert	Avg	%MS	MS-60	MS-62	MS-63	MS-64	MS-65	MS-66	Recent Auction Record
1904	10,025	1,147	63.5	95	$1,075	$1,200	$1,675	$3,300	$7,500	$11,250	$7,475, MS-66, Jul-10
1905	10,041	1,118	62.9	93	1,300	1,550	1,950	3,700	14,000	24,000	$9,200, MS-65, Jul-10

	Est Mintage	Cert	Finest	PF-60	PF-63	PF-64	PF-65	PF-66	Recent Auction Record
1904, Proof	2–3	2	PF-64						

PANAMA-PACIFIC EXPOSITION HALF DOLLAR (1915)

Designers Charles E. Barber (obv), George T. Morgan (assisting Barber on rev); weight 12.50 grams; composition .900 silver, .100 copper; diameter 30.6 mm; reeded edge; mint: Philadelphia.

Designs. *Obverse:* Columbia scattering flowers, alongside a child holding a cornucopia, representing the bounty of the American West; the Golden Gate in the background. *Reverse:* A spread-winged eagle perched on a shield, with branches of oak and olive.

Mintage and Melting Data. Authorized by the Act of January 16, 1915. *Maximum authorized*—200,000. *Number minted* (including 30 assay coins)—60,030. *Number melted*—32,896, including 30 assay coins (29,876 were melted on September 7, 1916 and the balance on October 30, 1916). *Distribution*—27,134.

Original Cost and Issuer. Sale price $1. Coin and Medal Department (Farran Zerbe), Panama-Pacific International Exposition, San Francisco, California. (Combination offers included a set of four coins, including the buyer's choice of one $50, in a leather case, for $100; and a set of five coins in a copper frame for $200.)

Key to Collecting. The half dollar does not have the typical deep mint frost associated with earlier silver issues. Most are satiny in appearance with the high parts in particular having a microscopically grainy finish. Many pieces have an inner line around the perimeter near the rim, a die characteristic. On the reverse of all known coins, the eagle's breast feathers are indistinct, which sometimes gives MS coins the appearance of having light wear. Most surviving coins grade from AU-50 to MS-63.

First Points of Wear. *Obverse:* Columbia's left shoulder. *Reverse:* The eagle's breast.

	Distribution	Cert	Avg	%MS	MS-60	MS-62	MS-63	MS-64	MS-65	MS-66	Recent Auction Record
1915S	27,134	2,409	63.7	95	$515	$625	$725	$1,100	$2,400	$3,250	$2,990, MS-66, Jul-10

PANAMA-PACIFIC EXPOSITION GOLD DOLLAR (1915)

Designer Charles Keck; weight 1.672 grams; composition .900 gold, .100 copper; diameter 15 mm; reeded edge; mint: Philadelphia.

Designs. *Obverse:* Capped profile portrait of a Panama Canal laborer. *Reverse:* Two dolphins, symbolizing the Atlantic and Pacific oceans, and legends.

Mintage and Melting Data. Authorized by the Act of January 16, 1915. *Maximum authorized—25,000. Number minted (including 34 assay coins)—25,034. Number melted—10,034, including 34 assay coins (melted at the San Francisco Mint on October 30, 1916). Net distribution—15,000.*

Original Cost and Issuer. Sale price $2 (and a few at $2.25). Coin and Medal Department (Farran Zerbe), Panama-Pacific Interna-

tional Exposition, San Francisco, California. (Combination offers included, among others, a set of four coins, with the buyer's choice of one fifty-dollar coin, in a leather case, for $100; and a set of five coins in a copper frame for $200.)

Key to Collecting. Most examples are in Mint State. Many exhibit deep mint frost. Friction is common, especially on the obverse.

First Points of Wear. *Obverse:* The peak of the laborer's cap. *Reverse:* The heads of the dolphins, and the denomination.

	Distribution	Cert	Avg	%MS	MS-60	MS-62	MS-63	MS-64	MS-65	MS-66	Recent Auction Record
1915S	15,000	3,388	63.7	95	$640	$675	$725	$1,000	$1,550	$2,350	$9,775, MS-67 CAC, Jul-10

PANAMA-PACIFIC EXPOSITION QUARTER EAGLE (1915)

Designer Charles E. Barber (obv), George T. Morgan (rev); weight 4.18 grams; composition .900 gold, .100 copper; diameter 18 mm; reeded edge; mint: Philadelphia.

Designs. *Obverse:* Columbia seated on a hippocampus, holding a caduceus, symbolic of Medicine's triumph over yellow fever in Panama during the canal's construction. *Reverse:* An eagle, standing on a plaque inscribed E PLURIBUS UNUM, with raised wings.

Mintage and Melting Data. Authorized by the Act of January 16, 1915. *Maximum authorized—10,000. Number minted (including 17 assay coins)—10,017. Number melted—3,268, including 17 assay coins (melted at the San Francisco Mint on October 30, 1916). Distribution—6,749.*

Original Cost and Issuer. Sale price $4. Coin and Medal Department (Farran Zerbe), Panama-Pacific International Exposition,

San Francisco, California. (Combination offers included, among others, a set of four coins, with the buyer's choice of one fifty-dollar coin, in a leather case, for $100; and a set of five coins in a copper frame for $200.)

Key to Collecting. Most grade from AU-55 to MS-63. MS-64 coins are elusive, and MS-65 rare. Most MS pieces show a satiny, sometimes grainy luster.

First Points of Wear. *Obverse:* Columbia's head, breast, and knee. *Reverse:* The torch band and the eagle's leg.

	Distribution	Cert	Avg	%MS	MS-60	MS-62	MS-63	MS-64	MS-65	MS-66	Recent Auction Record
1915S	6,749	1,823	64.5	97	$1,850	$2,900	$3,850	$5,300	$6,600	$7,500	$6,325, MS-66 CAC, Jul-10

	Est Mintage	Cert	Finest	PF-60	PF-63	PF-64	PF-65	PF-66	Recent Auction Record
1915S, Proof (a)	unique	0	n/a						

a. This unique Roman Finish Proof resides in the National Numismatic Collection of the Smithsonian Institution.

PANAMA-PACIFIC EXPOSITION FIFTY-DOLLAR GOLD PIECE (1915)

Designer Robert Aitken; weight 83.59 grams; composition .900 gold, .100 copper; diameter 44 mm; reeded edge; mint: Philadelphia.

Designs. Round—*Obverse:* Helmeted profile portrait of Minerva, with shield and armor. *Reverse:* An owl, symbolic of wisdom, vigilant on a pine branch, with pinecones. Octagonal: *Obverse and reverse:* Same as the round coin, but with dolphins in the eight angled exergues on obverse and reverse.

Mintage and Melting Data. Authorized by the Act of January 16, 1915. Round: *Maximum authorized*—1,500. *Number minted* (including 10 assay coins)—1,510. *Number melted*—1,027. *Distribution*—483. Octagonal: *Maximum authorized*—1,500. *Number minted* (including 9 assay coins)—1,509. *Number melted*—864. *Distribution*—645.

Original Cost and Issuer. Round and octagonal: Sale price, each, $100. Coin and Medal Department (Farran Zerbe), Panama-Pacific

International Exposition, San Francisco, California. Combination offers included a set of four coins (buyer's choice of one fifty-dollar coin) in a leather case for $100, and a set of five coins in a copper frame for $200, this issued after the Exposition closed.

Key to Collecting. Because such small quantities were issued, these hefty gold commemoratives today are rare in any grade. The round coins trade hands slightly less frequently than the octagonal. Typical grades are MS-63 or 64 for coins kept in an original box or frame over the years, or AU-58 to MS-63 if removed. Coins that have been cleaned or lightly polished exhibit a multitude of tiny hairlines; such pieces are avoided by connoisseurs.

First Points of Wear. *Obverse:* Minerva's cheek. *Reverse:* The owl's upper breast.

	Distribution	Cert	Avg	%MS	MS-60	MS-62	MS-63	MS-64	MS-65	MS-66	Recent Auction Record
1915S, Round	483	374	63.3	95	$53,500	$65,000	$87,500	$115,000	$157,500	$200,000	$80,500, MS-64, May-10
1915S, Octagonal	645	438	63.1	95	50,000	63,000	79,500	110,000	150,000	225,000	$80,500, MS-64, May-10

MCKINLEY MEMORIAL GOLD DOLLAR (1916–1917)

Designers Charles E. Barber (obv) and George T. Morgan (rev); weight 1.672 grams; composition .900 gold, .100 copper; diameter 15 mm; reeded edge; mint: Philadelphia.

Designs. *Obverse:* Bareheaded profile portrait of William McKinley. *Reverse:* Artist's rendition of the proposed McKinley Birthplace Memorial intended to be erected in Niles, Ohio.

Mintage and Melting Data. Authorized February 23, 1916. *Maximum authorized*—100,000 (total for both years). 1916: *Number minted* (including 26 assay coins)—20,026 *Number melted*—5,000 (estimated). *Distribution*—15,000 (estimated). 1917: *Number minted* (including 14 assay coins)—10,014. *Number melted*—5,000 (estimated). *Distribution*—5,000 (estimated).

Original Cost and Issuer. Sale price $3. National McKinley Birthplace Memorial Association, Youngstown, Ohio.

Key to Collecting. The obverse of the 1916 issue often displays friction while its reverse can appear as choice Mint State. Prooflike fields are common. Some are highly prooflike on both sides. The 1917 issue is much harder to find than the 1916; examples usually are in higher grades with rich luster on both sides, and often exhibit a pale yellow color.

First Points of Wear. *Obverse:* McKinley's temple area, and the hair above his ear. *Reverse:* The pillar above the second 1 in the date; and the bottom of the flagpole.

	Distribution	Cert	Avg	%MS	MS-60	MS-62	MS-63	MS-64	MS-65	MS-66	Recent Auction Record
1916	15,000	2,320	63.8	97	$580	$625	$675	$950	$1,600	$2,150	$4,025, MS-67, Jul-10
1917	5,000	1,331	63.7	95	700	750	890	1,375	2,100	3,700	$1,610, MS-65, Jul-10

	Est Mintage	Cert	Finest	PF-60	PF-63	PF-64	PF-65	PF-66	Recent Auction Record
1916, Proof	3–6	0	n/a						$33,350, PF-63, Nov-08

ILLINOIS CENTENNIAL HALF DOLLAR (1918)

Designers George T. Morgan (obv) and John R. Sinnock (rev); weight 12.50 grams; composition .900 silver, .100 copper; diameter 30.6 mm; reeded edge; mint: Philadelphia.

Designs. *Obverse:* Bareheaded, beardless profile portrait of Abraham Lincoln, facing right. *Reverse:* A fierce eagle atop a crag, clutching a shield and carrying a banner; from the Illinois state seal.

Mintage Data. Authorized on June 1, 1918. *Maximum authorized*—100,000. *Number minted*—100,000 plus 58 for assay.

Original Cost and Issuer. Sale price $1. The Illinois Centennial Commission, through various outlets.

Key to Collecting. Examples were struck with deep, frosty finishes, giving Mint State pieces an unusually attractive appearance. The obverse typically shows contact marks or friction on Lincoln's cheek and on other high parts of his portrait. The field typically shows contact marks. The reverse usually grades from one to three points higher than the obverse, due to the protective nature of its complicated design. Most examples are lustrous and frosty, although a few are seen with partially prooflike fields.

First Points of Wear. *Obverse:* The hair above Lincoln's ear. *Reverse:* The eagle's breast. (Note that the breast was sometimes flatly struck; look for differences in texture or color of the metal.)

	Distribution	Cert	Avg	%MS	MS-60	MS-62	MS-63	MS-64	MS-65	MS-66	Recent Auction Record
1918	100,058	3,744	64.2	99	$135	$145	$160	$220	$475	$725	$633, MS-66 CAC, Jul-10

MAINE CENTENNIAL HALF DOLLAR (1920)

Designer Anthony de Francisci; weight 12.50 grams; composition .900 silver, .100 copper; diameter 30.6 mm; reeded edge; mint: Philadelphia.

Designs. *Obverse:* Arms of the state of Maine, with the Latin word DIRIGO ("I Direct"). *Reverse:* The centennial inscription enclosed by a wreath.

Mintage Data. Authorized on May 10, 1920. *Maximum authorized*—100,000. *Number minted*—50,028, including 28 for the U.S. Assay Commission.

Original Cost and Issuer. Sale price $1. Maine Centennial Commission.

Key to Collecting. Relatively few Maine half dollars were sold to the hobby community; the majority of coins distributed saw careless handling by the general public. Most examples show friction or handling marks on the center of the shield on the obverse. The fields were not completely finished in the dies and always show tiny raised lines or die finishing marks; at first glance these may appear to be hairlines or scratches, but they have no effect on the grade. Appealing examples in higher Mint State levels are much more elusive than the high mintage might suggest.

First Points of Wear. *Obverse:* The left hand of the scythe holder; the right hand of the anchor holder. (Note that the moose and the pine tree are weakly struck.) *Reverse:* The bow knot.

	Distribution	Cert	Avg	%MS	MS-60	MS-62	MS-63	MS-64	MS-65	MS-66	Recent Auction Record
1920	50,028	2,602	64.2	99	$150	$160	$185	$230	$435	$650	$633, MS-66, Jul-10

PILGRIM TERCENTENARY (1920–1921)

Designer Cyrus E. Dallin; weight 12.50 grams; composition .900 silver, .100 copper; diameter 30.6 mm; reeded edge; mint: Philadelphia.

Designs. *Obverse:* Artist's conception of a partial standing portrait of Governor William Bradford holding a book. *Reverse:* The *Mayflower* in full sail.

Mintage and Melting Data. Authorized May 12, 1920. *Maximum authorized*—300,000. 1920: *Number minted* (including 112 assay coins)—200,112. *Number melted*—48,000. *Net distribution*—152,112. 1921: *Number minted* (including 53 assay coins)—100,053. *Number melted*—80,000. *Net distribution*—20,053.

Original Cost and Issuer. Sale price $1. Pilgrim Tercentenary Commission.

Key to Collecting. The 1920 issue is common, and the 1921 slightly scarce. Coins grading MS-64 and higher usually have excellent eye appeal, though many exceptions exist. Most coins have scattered contact marks, particularly on the obverse. Nearly all 1921 coins are this way. Many coins (particularly coins which are early impressions from the dies) show tiny raised lines in the obverse field, represent-ing die finish marks; these are not to be confused with hairlines or other evidences of friction (which are recessed).

First Points of Wear. *Obverse:* Cheekbone, hair over ear, and the high areas of Governor Bradford's hat. *Reverse:* The ship's rigging and stern, the crow's nest, and the rim.

	Distribution	Cert	Avg	%MS	MS-60	MS-62	MS-63	MS-64	MS-65	MS-66	Recent Auction Record
1920	152,112	4,001	64.0	99	$90	$95	$105	$145	$315	$750	$518, MS-66, Jul-10
1921, With Added Date	20,053	1,859	64.3	99	190	200	215	250	410	900	$2,070, MS-67, Jul-10

MISSOURI CENTENNIAL HALF DOLLAR (1921)

Designer Robert Aitken; weight 12.50 grams; composition .900 silver, .100 copper; diameter 30.6 mm; reeded edge; mint: Philadelphia.

Designs. *Obverse:* Coonskin-capped profile portrait of a fron-tiersman. One variety has 2★4 in the field; the other is plain. *Reverse:* Standing figures of a frontiersman and an Indian look-ing westward, against a starry field; SEDALIA (the location of the Missouri centennial exposition) incused below.

Mintage and Melting Data. Authorized on March 4, 1921. *Max-imum authorized*—250,000 (combined for both types). *Number minted*—50,028 in all. *Number melted*—29,600. *Net distribu-tion*—20,428 (estimated), with 9,400 for 1921 2★4 and 11,400 for 1921 Plain. The 28 remaining were for the U.S. Assay Commission.

Original Cost and Issuer. Sale price $1. Missouri Centennial Committee, through the Sedalia Trust Company.

Key to Collecting. Most grade from AU-55 to MS-63; have fric-tion and contact marks on the higher areas of the design; and are lightly struck at the center of the portrait of Boone on the obverse, and at the torsos of the two figures on the reverse. MS-65 and higher coins with sharply struck centers are rarities.

First Points of Wear. *Obverse:* The hair in back of the ear. *Reverse:* The frontiersman's arm and shoulder.

	Distribution	Cert	Avg	%MS	MS-60	MS-62	MS-63	MS-64	MS-65	MS-66	Recent Auction Record
1921, "2★4" in Field	9,400	1,504	63.7	98	$650	$700	$1,025	$1,200	$3,100	$11,000	$2,530, MS-65, Jul-10
1921, Plain	11,400	1,803	63.5	97	550	650	800	1,100	3,200	9,250	$1,955, MS-65, Jul-10

	Est Mintage	Cert	Finest	PF-60	PF-63	PF-64	PF-65	PF-66	Recent Auction Record
1921, "2★4," Matte Proof	1–2	0	n/a						

ALABAMA CENTENNIAL HALF DOLLAR (1921)

Designer Laura Gardin Fraser; weight 12.50 grams; composition .900 silver, .100 copper; diameter 30.6 mm; reeded edge; mint: Philadelphia.

Designs. *Obverse:* Conjoined bareheaded profile portraits of William Wyatt Bibb, the first governor of Alabama, and T.E. Kilby, governor at the time of the centennial. *Reverse:* A dynamic eagle perched on a shield, clutching arrows and holding a banner; from the Alabama state seal.

Mintage and Melting Data. Authorized on May 10, 1920. *Maxi-mum authorized*—100,000. *Number minted*—70,044 (including 44 for assay). *Number melted*—5,000. *Net distribution*—2X2: esti-mated as 30,000. Plain: estimated as 35,000.

Original Cost and Issuer. Sale price $1. Alabama Centennial Commission.

Key to Collecting. Most of these coins were sold to citizens of Alabama, and of those, few were acquired by numismatists. Many are in circulated grades (typical being EF or AU), with most surviving pieces grading MS-63 or less. Those grading MS-65 or finer are rare. Nearly all show friction or contact marks on Governor Kilby's cheek on the obverse, and many are flatly struck on the eagle's left leg and talons on the reverse. These coins were produced carelessly, and many lack sharpness and luster (sharply struck examples are very rare). Nicks and marks from the original planchets are often found on the areas of light strik-ing. The eagle's upper leg is often lightly struck, particularly on the plain variety. The 2X2 coins usually are better struck than the plain variety.

First Points of Wear. *Obverse:* Kirby's forehead and the area to the left of his earlobe. *Reverse:* The eagle's lower neck and the top of its wings.

	Distribution	Cert	Avg	%MS	MS-60	MS-62	MS-63	MS-64	MS-65	MS-66	Recent Auction Record
1921, Plain	35,000	1,733	63.4	95	$185	$250	$390	$550	$1,275	$3,000	$1,265, MS-65 CAC, Jul-10
1921, "2X2" in Field	30,000	1,518	63.7	97	300	350	480	650	1,375	3,200	$2,070, MS-66, Jul-10

GRANT MEMORIAL HALF DOLLAR (1922)

Designer Laura Gardin Fraser; weight 1.672 grams; composition .900 gold, .100 copper; diameter 15 mm; reeded edge; mint: Philadelphia.

Designs. *Obverse:* Bareheaded profile portrait of Ulysses S. Grant in a military coat. One variety has a star above GRANT. *Reverse:* View of the house Grant was born in (Point Pleasant, Ohio), amidst a wooded setting.

Mintage and Melting Data. Authorized on February 2, 1922. *Maximum authorized*—250,000. No Star: *Number minted* (including 55 assay coins)—95,055. *Number melted*—27,650. *Net distribution*—67,405. With Star: *Number minted* (including 6 assay coins)—5,006. *Number melted*—750. *Net distribution*— 4,256.

Original Cost and Issuer. Sale price $1.50, later reduced to 75¢. U.S. Grant Centenary Memorial Commission (mail orders were serviced by Hugh L. Nichols, chairman, Batavia, Ohio).

Key to Collecting. The surface shows numerous raised die-finishing lines and other mint preparation marks (even on MS pieces). Most specimens are lightly struck on the center of the obverse. These factors combined make it very difficult to differentiate minute gradations among MS coins. A few are prooflike. The No Star variety is common, with typical grades ranging from MS-60 to 63 (MS-65 and higher coins are seen with some frequency, but are much scarcer). The With Star variety in MS is one of the very rarest pieces of U.S. commemoratives, because of the low mintage and the fact that few coins were sold to preservation-minded collectors.

First Points of Wear. *Obverse:* Grant's cheekbone. (Worn dies caused flatness in the hair above his ear.) *Reverse:* The leaves of the tree under the U in TRUST. (The coin often is weakly struck in the branches above the house.)

	Distribution	Cert	Avg	%MS	MS-60	MS-62	MS-63	MS-64	MS-65	MS-66	Recent Auction Record
1922, Star in Obv Field	4,256	1,175	63.7	98	$1,225	$1,400	$1,700	$2,500	$6,900	$13,000	$5,175, MS-65, Jul-10
1922, No Star in Field	67,405	3,230	63.8	97	115	125	150	250	650	1,150	$1,150, MS-66, Jul-10

GRANT MEMORIAL GOLD DOLLAR (1922)

Designer Laura Gardin Fraser; weight 1.672 grams; composition .900 gold, .100 copper; diameter 15 mm; reeded edge; mint: Philadelphia.

Designs. *Obverse:* Bareheaded profile portrait of Ulysses S. Grant in a military coat. One variety has a star above GRANT. *Reverse:* View of the house Grant was born in (Point Pleasant, Ohio), amidst a wooded setting.

Mintage Data. Authorized on February 2, 1922. No Star: *Number minted and distributed*—5,000. With Star: *Number minted and distributed*—5,016. Assay coins: 16.

Original Cost and Issuer. Sale price $3 for either variety. U.S. Grant Centenary Memorial Commission (mail orders were serviced by Hugh L. Nichols, chairman, Batavia, Ohio).

Key to Collecting. Almost all known specimens are MS-63 to 65 or better. MS-66 and 67 examples are easy to find. Some lower-grade coins show friction on Grant's cheek and hair. Some specimens have dull surfaces; these are avoided by connoisseurs.

First Points of Wear. *Obverse:* Grant's cheekbone and hair. *Reverse:* The leaves of the tree under the U in TRUST.

	Distribution	Cert	Avg	%MS	MS-60	MS-62	MS-63	MS-64	MS-65	MS-66	Recent Auction Record
1922, With Star	5,016	1,133	64.8	99	$1,575	$1,675	$1,950	$2,200	$2,650	$3,100	$3,450, MS-67, Jul-10
1922, No Star	5,016	1,114	64.4	97	1,650	1,775	1,975	2,150	2,750	3,350	$2,530, MS-65 CAC, Jul-10

MONROE DOCTRINE CENTENNIAL HALF DOLLAR (1923)

Designer Chester Beach; weight 12.50 grams; composition .900 silver, .100 copper; diameter 30.6 mm; reeded edge; mint: Philadelphia.

Designs. *Obverse:* Conjoined bareheaded profile portraits of presidents James Monroe and John Quincy Adams. *Reverse:* Stylized depiction of the continents of North and South America as female figures in the outlines of the two land masses.

Mintage Data. Authorized on January 24, 1923. *Maximum authorized*—300,000. *Number minted* (including 77 assay coins)—274,077. *Net distribution*—274,077.

Original Cost and Issuer. Sale price $1. Los Angeles Clearing House, representing backers of the First Annual American Historical Revue and Motion Picture Industry Exposition.

Key to Collecting. Most examples show friction or wear. MS coins are common. Evaluating the numerical grade of MS-60 to 63 coins is difficult because of the design's weak definition. Low-magnification inspection usually shows nicks and graininess at the highest point of the obverse center; these flaws are from the original planchets. Many examples of this coin have been doctored and artificially toned in attempts to earn higher grades upon certification; these are avoided by connoisseurs.

First Points of Wear. *Obverse:* Adams's cheekbone. *Reverse:* The upper figure, underneath CT in DOCTRINE.

	Distribution	Cert	Avg	%MS	MS-60	MS-62	MS-63	MS-64	MS-65	MS-66	Recent Auction Record
1923S	274,077	3,239	63.3	97	$75	$100	$140	$285	$1,600	$4,500	$1,840, MS-65, Jul-10

HUGUENOT-WALLOON TERCENTENARY HALF DOLLAR (1924)

Designer George T. Morgan (with model modifications by James Earle Fraser); weight 12.50 grams; composition .900 silver, .100 copper; diameter 30.6 mm; reeded edge; mint: Philadelphia.

Designs. *Obverse:* Hat-clad profile portraits representing Admiral Gaspard de Coligny and William the Silent, first stadtholder of the Netherlands. *Reverse:* The ship *Nieuw Nederland* in full sail.

Mintage Data. Authorized February 26, 1923. *Maximum authorized*—300,000. *Number minted* (including 80 assay coins)—142,080. *Net distribution*—142,080.

Original Cost and Issuer. Sale price $1. Huguenot-Walloon New Netherland Commission, Inc., and designated outlets.

Key to Collecting. This coin is readily available on the market, with most examples in MS-60 to 63. Those grading MS-64 and 65 are also found quite often; MS-66 coins are scarcer. Relatively few worn pieces exist. Friction and contact marks are sometimes seen on the cheek of Admiral Coligny on the obverse, and on the masts and ship's rigging on the reverse. Many coins have been cleaned or repeatedly dipped. Connoisseurs avoid deeply toned or stained coins, even those certified with high numerical grades. MS coins usually have satiny (rather than deeply lustrous or frosty) surfaces, and may have a gray appearance. High in the reverse field of most coins is a "bright" spot interrupting the luster, from a touch of polish in the die.

First Points of Wear. *Obverse:* Coligny's cheekbone. *Reverse:* The rim near the F in FOUNDING and over RY in TERCENTENARY; the lower part of the highest sail; the center of the ship's stern.

	Distribution	Cert	Avg	%MS	MS-60	MS-62	MS-63	MS-64	MS-65	MS-66	Recent Auction Record
1924	142,080	2,963	64.3	99	$125	$135	$145	$175	$375	$700	$546, MS-66, Jul-10

LEXINGTON-CONCORD SESQUICENTENNIAL HALF DOLLAR (1925)

Designer Chester Beach; weight 12.50 grams; composition .900 silver, .100 copper; diameter 30.6 mm; reeded edge; mint: Philadelphia.

Designs. *Obverse:* A view of the *Minute Man* statue, by Daniel Chester French, located in Concord, Massachusetts. *Reverse:* Lexington's Old Belfry, whose tolling bell roused the Minute Men to action in 1775.

Mintage and Melting Data. Authorized January 14, 1925. *Maximum authorized*—300,000. *Number minted* (including 99 assay coins)—162,099. *Number melted*—86. *Net distribution*—162,013.

Continued on next page.

Original Cost and Issuer. Sale price $1. U.S. Lexington-Concord Sesquicentennial Commission, through local banks.

Key to Collecting. Examples are easily found in all grades, with most being in high AU or low MS grades, although eye appeal can vary widely. MS-65 coins are scarce in comparison to those in MS-60 through 64. Some specimens are deeply frosty and lustrous, whereas others have partially prooflike fields.

First Points of Wear. *Obverse:* The thighs of the Minuteman. *Reverse:* The top edge of the belfry.

	Distribution	Cert	Avg	%MS	MS-60	MS-62	MS-63	MS-64	MS-65	MS-66	Recent Auction Record
1925	162,013	3,539	63.8	98	$100	$110	$120	$150	$600	$1,300	$863, MS-65, Jul-10

STONE MOUNTAIN MEMORIAL HALF DOLLAR (1925)

Designer Gutzon Borglum; weight 12.50 grams; composition .900 silver, .100 copper; diameter 30.6 mm; reeded edge; mint: Philadelphia..

Designs. *Obverse:* Equestrian portraits of Civil War generals Robert E. Lee and Thomas "Stonewall" Jackson. *Reverse:* An eagle perched on a cliff with wings in mid-spread.

Mintage and Melting Data. *Maximum authorized—5,000,000. Number minted* (including 4,709 assay coins)—2,314,709. *Number melted*—1,000,000. *Net distribution*—1,314,709.

Original Cost and Issuer. Sale price $1. Sold by the Stone Mountain Confederate Monumental Association through many outlets, including promotions involving pieces counterstamped with abbreviations for Southern states.

Key to Collecting. This is the most plentiful commemorative from the 1920s. Examples are easily found in grades ranging from lightly worn through gem Mint State (many with outstanding eye appeal). Circulated coins are also found, as well as those that were counterstamped for special fundraising sales. The typical coin has very lustrous and frosty surfaces, although the reverse field may be somewhat satiny.

First Points of Wear. *Obverse:* Lee's elbow and leg. *Reverse:* The eagle's breast.

	Distribution	Cert	Avg	%MS	MS-60	MS-62	MS-63	MS-64	MS-65	MS-66	Recent Auction Record
1925	1,314,709	6,585	64.2	98	$60	$70	$80	$125	$275	$375	$1,380, MS-67, Jul-10

CALIFORNIA DIAMOND JUBILEE HALF DOLLAR (1925)

Designer Jo Mora; weight 12.50 grams; composition .900 silver, .100 copper; diameter 30.6 mm; reeded edge; mint: Philadelphia.

Designs. *Obverse:* A rustic miner, squatting to pan for gold. *Reverse:* A grizzly bear, as taken from the state flag.

Mintage and Melting Data. Authorized February 24, 1925, part of the act also providing for the 1925 Fort Vancouver and 1927 Vermont half dollars. *Maximum authorized—300,000. Number minted* (including 200 assay coins)—150,200. *Number melted*—63,606. *Net distribution*—86,594.

Original Cost and Issuer. Sale price $1. Sold by the San Francisco Citizens' Committee through the San Francisco Clearing House Association and the Los Angeles Clearing House.

Key to Collecting. This coin's design is such that even a small amount of handling produces friction on the shoulder and high parts of the bear, in particular. As a result, most grade in the AU-55 to MS-62 range, and higher-level MS examples are rare. This issue exists in two finishes: frosty/lustrous, and the rarer "chrome-like" or prooflike. The frosty-finish pieces display some lack of die definition of the details. The prooflike pieces have heavily brushed and highly polished dies. Many specimens certified in high grades are toned, sometimes deeply, which can mask evidence of friction. Coins with no traces of friction are rarities.

First Points of Wear. *Obverse:* The folds of the miner's shirt sleeve. *Reverse:* The shoulder of the bear.

	Distribution	Cert	Avg	%MS	MS-60	MS-62	MS-63	MS-64	MS-65	MS-66	Recent Auction Record
1925S	86,594	3,694	64.1	97	$215	$225	$275	$440	$875	$1,250	$3,450, MS-67, Jul-10

	Est Mintage	Cert	Finest	PF-60	PF-63	PF-64	PF-65	PF-66	Recent Auction Record
1925S, Matte Proof	1–2	1	PF-65						

FORT VANCOUVER CENTENNIAL HALF DOLLAR (1925)
Designer Laura Gardin Fraser; weight 12.50 grams; composition .900 silver, .100 copper; diameter 30.6 mm; reeded edge; mint: Philadelphia.

Designs. *Obverse:* Bareheaded profile portrait of Dr. John McLoughlin, who built Fort Vancouver (Washington) on the Columbia River in 1825. *Reverse:* A pioneer in buckskin with a musket in his hands, with Fort Vancouver in the background.

Mintage and Melting Data. Authorized February 24, 1925. *Maximum authorized—300,000. Number minted (including 28 assay coins)—50,028. Number melted—35,034. Net distribution—14,994.*

Original Cost and Issuer. Sale price $1. The Fort Vancouver Centennial Corporation, Vancouver, Washington.

Key to Collecting. This coin's design is such that even a small amount of handling produced friction on the higher spots. As a result, higher-level MS examples are rare.

First Points of Wear. *Obverse:* McLaughlin's temple area. *Reverse:* The pioneer's right knee.

	Distribution	Cert	Avg	%MS	MS-60	MS-62	MS-63	MS-64	MS-65	MS-66	Recent Auction Record
1925 (a)	14,994	2,039	64.2	98	$350	$375	$400	$475	$1,000	$1,400	$690, MS-65, Jul-10

	Est Mintage	Cert	Finest	PF-60	PF-63	PF-64	PF-65	PF-66	Recent Auction Record
1925, Matte Proof	2–3	0	n/a						

SESQUICENTENNIAL OF AMERICAN INDEPENDENCE HALF DOLLAR (1926)
Designer John R. Sinnock; weight 12.50 grams; composition .900 silver, .100 copper; diameter 30.6 mm; reeded edge; mint: Philadelphia.

Designs. *Obverse:* Conjoined profile portraits of bewigged George Washington and bareheaded Calvin Coolidge. *Reverse:* The Liberty Bell.

Mintage and Melting Data. Authorized on March 23, 1925. *Maximum authorized—1,000,000. Number minted (including 528 assay coins)—1,000,528. Number melted—859,408. Net distribution—141,120.*

Original Cost and Issuer. Sale price $1. National Sesquicentennial Exhibition Association.

Key to Collecting. Accurate grading can be problematic for this coin. Many examples certified at high grades have mottled or deeply toned surfaces that obfuscate examination, and others have been recolored. Most have graininess—marks from the original planchet—on the highest part of the portrait.

First Points of Wear. *Obverse:* Washington's cheekbone. *Reverse:* The area below the lower inscription on the Liberty Bell.

	Distribution	Cert	Avg	%MS	MS-60	MS-62	MS-63	MS-64	MS-65	MS-66	Recent Auction Record
1926	141,120	3,920	63.2	97	$95	$105	$115	$300	$3,500	$17,000	$2,760, MS-65, Jul-10

SESQUICENTENNIAL OF AMERICAN INDEPENDENCE QUARTER EAGLE (1926)
Designer John R. Sinnock; weight 4.18 grams; composition .900 gold, .100 copper; diameter 18 mm; reeded edge; mint: Philadelphia.

Designs. *Obverse:* Miss Liberty standing, holding in one hand a scroll representing the Declaration of Independence and in the other, the Torch of Freedom. *Reverse:* A front view of Independence Hall in Philadelphia.

Mintage and Melting Data. Authorized on March 23, 1925. *Maximum authorized—200,000. Number minted (including 226*

assay coins)—200,226. Number melted—154,207. Net distribution—46,019.*

Original Cost and Issuer. Sale price $4. National Sesquicentennial Exhibition Association.

Key to Collecting. Nearly all examples show evidence of handling and contact from careless production at the Mint, and from later

Continued on next page.

indifference by their buyers. Most coins range from AU-55 to MS-62 in grade, and have scattered marks in the fields. MS-65 examples are rare. Well-struck coins are seldom seen. Some pieces show copper stains; connoisseurs avoid these.

First Points of Wear. *Obverse:* The bottom of the scroll held by Liberty. *Reverse:* The area below the top of the tower; and the central portion above the roof.

	Distribution	Cert	Avg	%MS	MS-60	MS-62	MS-63	MS-64	MS-65	MS-66	Recent Auction Record
1926	46,019	6,652	63.1	95	$465	$525	$765	$1,350	$3,200	$13,000	$3,002, MS-65 CAC, Jul-10

	Est Mintage	Cert	Finest	PF-60	PF-63	PF-64	PF-65	PF-66	Recent Auction Record
1926, Matte Proof (a)	*unique*	0	n/a						

a. "The coin is unique and displays a matte surface similar to the Proof gold coins of 1908 to 1915. The coin was reportedly from the estate of the designer, John R. Sinnock, who is best known for his Roosevelt dime and Franklin half dollar designs. The piece was in the possession of coin dealer David Bullowa in the 1950s. Another example is rumored by Breen, but the whereabouts or existence of the coin is unknown" (*Encyclopedia of U.S. Gold Coins, 1795–1933,* second edition).

OREGON TRAIL MEMORIAL HALF DOLLAR (1926–1939)

Designers James Earle Fraser and Laura Gardin Fraser; weight 12.50 grams; composition .900 silver, .100 copper; diameter 30.6 mm; reeded edge; mint: Philadelphia.

Designs. *Obverse:* A pioneer family in a Conestoga wagon, heading west into the sunset. *Reverse:* A standing Indian with a bow, arm outstretched, and a map of the United States in the background.

Mintage and Melting Data. *Maximum authorized*—6,000,000 (for the entire series from 1926 onward). 1926: *Number minted* (including 30 assay coins)—48,030. *Number melted*—75 (defective coins). *Net distribution*—47,955. 1926-S: *Number minted* (including 55 assay coins)—100,055. *Number melted*—17,000. *Net distribution*—83,055. 1928: *Number minted* (including 28 assay coins)—50,028. *Number melted*—44,000. *Net distribution*—6,028. 1933-D: *Number minted* (including unrecorded number of assay coins)—5,250. *Number melted*—242 (probably defective coins). *Net distribution*—5,008. 1934-D: *Number minted* (including 6 assay coins)—7,006. *Net distribution*—7,006. 1936: *Number minted* (including 6 assay coins)—10,006. *Net distribution*—10,006. 1936-S: *Number minted* (including 6 assay coins)—5,006. *Net distribution*—5,006. 1937-D: *Number minted* (including 8 assay coins)—12,008. *Net distribution*—12,008. 1938 P-D-S: *Number minted* (including 6, 5, and 6 assay coins)—6,006, 6,005, 6,006. *Net distribution*—6,006, 6,005, 6,006. 1939 P-D-S: *Number minted* (including 4, 4, and 5 assay coins)—3,004, 3,004, 3,005. *Net distribution*—3,004, 3,004, 3,005.

Original Cost and Issuer. Sale price $1 (with various increases). Oregon Trail Memorial Association, Inc., sold through Scott Stamp

& Coin Co., Inc., some sold through Whitman Centennial, Inc., Walla Walla, Washington. 1937 onward distributed by the Oregon Trail Memorial Association, Inc.

Key to Collecting. Although most of the later issues have low mintages, they are not rare in the marketplace, because the majority were originally sold to coin collectors and dealers. As a result, most surviving coins are in MS. The quality of the surface finish varies, with earlier issues tending to be frosty and lustrous and later issues (particularly those dated 1938 and 1939) having somewhat grainy or satiny fields. Grading requires care. Look for friction or contact marks on the high points of the Indian and the Conestoga wagon, but, more importantly, check both surfaces carefully for scattered cuts and marks. All three mints had difficulty in striking up the rims properly, causing many rejections. Those deemed acceptable and shipped out usually had full rims, but it is best to check when buying.

First Points of Wear. *Obverse:* The hip of the ox, and high points of the wagon (note that the top rear of the wagon was weakly struck in some years). *Reverse:* The Indian's left thumb and fingers (note that some pieces show flatness on the thumb and first finger, due to a weak strike).

	Distribution	Cert	Avg	%MS	MS-60	MS-62	MS-63	MS-64	MS-65	MS-66	Recent Auction Record
1926	47,955	1,854	64.4	98	$165	$170	$180	$195	$300	$475	$374, MS-66, Jul-10
1926S	83,055	2,547	64.8	99	165	170	180	195	300	425	$299, MS-66, Jul-10
1928 (same as 1926)	6,028	1,158	65.3	100	180	185	260	270	350	500	$374, MS-66, Jul-10
1933D (a)	5,008	926	65.0	100	345	360	365	390	435	700	$690, MS-66, Jul-10
1934D	7,006	1,193	64.8	100	200	205	210	215	360	550	$389, MS-66, Jul-10
1936	10,006	1,411	65.3	100	180	185	190	200	330	415	$633, MS-67, Jul-10
1936S	5,006	1,023	65.5	100	180	190	200	235	350	525	$374, MS-66, Jun-10
1937D	12,008	2,128	65.9	100	195	200	210	245	325	450	$299, MS-66, Jul-10
1938 (same as 1926)	6,006	1,090	65.4	100							$299, MS-66, Jul-10
1938D	6,005	1,299	65.8	100							$1,035, MS-67 Star, Mar-10
1938S	6,006	1,138	65.5	100							$276, MS-66, Jul-10
Set of 1938 P-D-S					500	600	625	650	975	1,300	$834, MS-66, Jun-10

	Distribution	Cert	Avg	%MS	MS-60	MS-62	MS-63	MS-64	MS-65	MS-66	Recent Auction Record
1939	3,004	709	65.5	100							$690, MS-66, Jul-10
1939D	3,004	738	65.8	100							$592, MS-66, Jul-10
1939S	3,005	727	65.5	100							$805, MS-66 CAC, Jul-10
Set of 1939 P-D-S					$1,600	$1,625	$1,650	$1,800	$2,000	$2,500	$2,530, MS-67, Mar-10

	Est Mintage	Cert	Finest	PF-60	PF-63	PF-64	PF-65	PF-66	Recent Auction Record
1926, Matte Proof	1–2	1	PF-65						

VERMONT SESQUICENTENNIAL HALF DOLLAR (1927)

Designer Charles Keck; weight 12.50 grams; composition .900 silver, .100 copper; diameter 30.6 mm; reeded edge; mint: Philadelphia.

Designs. *Obverse:* Profile portrait of a bewigged Ira Allen. *Reverse:* A catamount on a pedestal.

Mintage and Melting Data. Authorized by the Act of February 24, 1925. *Maximum authorized*—40,000. *Number minted* (including 34 assay coins)—40,034. *Number melted*—11,892. *Net distribution*—28,142.

Original Cost and Issuer. Sale price $1. Vermont Sesquicentennial Commission (Bennington Battle Monument and Historical Association).

Key to Collecting. The Vermont half dollar was struck with the highest relief of any commemorative issue. Despite the depth of the work in the dies, nearly all specimens were struck up properly and show excellent detail. Unfortunately, the height of the obverse portrait encourages evidence of contact at the central points, and nearly all coins show some friction on Allen's cheek. Most are in grades of MS-62 to 64 and are deeply lustrous and frosty. Cleaned examples are often seen—and are avoided by connoisseurs.

First Points of Wear. *Obverse:* Allen's cheek, and the hair above his ear and in the temple area. *Reverse:* The catamount's upper shoulder.

	Distribution	Cert	Avg	%MS	MS-60	MS-62	MS-63	MS-64	MS-65	MS-66	Recent Auction Record
1927	28,142	2,720	64.0	98	$260	$275	$300	$350	$850	$1,050	$805, MS-66, Jul-10

HAWAIIAN SESQUICENTENNIAL HALF DOLLAR (1928)

Designer Juliette M. Fraser; weight 12.50 grams; composition .900 silver, .100 copper; diameter 30.6 mm; reeded edge; mint: Philadelphia.

Designs. *Obverse:* Portrait of Captain James Cook. *Reverse:* A Hawaiian chieftain standing with arm outstretched and holding a spear.

Mintage and Melting Data. Authorized March 7, 1928. *Maximum authorized*—10,000. *Number minted* (including 8 assay coins and 50 Sandblast Proofs)—10,008. *Net distribution*—10,008.

Original Cost and Issuer. Sale price $2. Captain Cook Sesquicentennial Commission, through the Bank of Hawaii, Ltd.

Key to Collecting. This is the scarcest of U.S. commemorative coins. It is elusive in all grades, and highly prized. Most are

AU-55 to MS-62 or slightly finer; those grading MS-65 or above are especially difficult to find. Most examples show contact or friction on the higher design areas. Some coins have a somewhat satiny surface, whereas others are lustrous and frosty. Many undipped pieces have a yellowish tint. Beware of coins which have been repeatedly dipped or cleaned. Problem-free examples are rarer even than the low mintage would suggest. Fake "Sandblast Proofs" exist; these are coins dipped in acid.

First Points of Wear. *Obverse:* Cook's cheekbone. *Reverse:* The chieftain's legs; his fingers and the hand holding the spear.

	Distribution	Cert	Avg	%MS	MS-60	MS-62	MS-63	MS-64	MS-65	MS-66	Recent Auction Record
1928	10,008	1,556	63.8	99	$2,450	$2,700	$3,100	$3,600	$5,900	$11,500	$5,175, MS-65 CAC, Jul-10

	Est Mintage	Cert	Finest	PF-60	PF-63	PF-64	PF-65	PF-66	Recent Auction Record
1928, Proof (a)	50	23	PF-66						$21,850, PF-63, Oct-06

a. Sandblast Proof presentation pieces. "Of the production figure, 50 were Sandblast Proofs, made by a special process which imparted a dull, grainy finish to the pieces, similar to that used on certain Mint medals of the era as well as on gold Proof coins circa 1908–1915" (*Guide Book of United States Commemorative Coins*).

MARYLAND TERCENTENARY HALF DOLLAR (1934)

Designer Hans Schuler; weight 12.50 grams; composition .900 silver, .100 copper; diameter 30.6 mm; reeded edge; mint: Philadelphia.

Designs. *Obverse:* Three-quarters portrait of Cecil Calvert, Lord Baltimore. *Reverse:* The state seal and motto of Maryland.

Mintage and Melting Data. Authorized May 9, 1934. *Maximum authorized*—25,000. *Number minted* (including 15 assay coins)—25,015. *Net distribution*—25,015.

Original Cost and Issuer. Sale price $1. Maryland Tercentenary Commission, through various outlets.

Key to Collecting. The coin's field has an unusual "rippled" appearance, similar to a sculptured plaque, so nicks and other marks that

would be visible on a coin with flat fields are not as readily noticed. Most examples grade MS-62 to 64. Finer pieces, strictly graded, are elusive. This issue was not handled with care at the time of mintage and distribution, and nearly all show scattered contact marks. Some exist struck from a reverse die broken from the right side of the shield to a point opposite the upper right of the 4 in the date 1634.

First Points of Wear. *Obverse:* Lord Baltimore's nose (the nose usually appears flatly struck; also check the reverse for wear). *Reverse:* The top of the coronet on top of the shield, and the tops of the draperies.

	Distribution	Cert	Avg	%MS	MS-60	MS-62	MS-63	MS-64	MS-65	MS-66	Recent Auction Record
1934	25,015	3,095	64.7	100	$165	$175	$185	$200	$360	$575	$489, MS-66, Jul-10

	Est Mintage	Cert	Finest	PF-60	PF-63	PF-64	PF-65	PF-66	Recent Auction Record
1934, Matte Proof	2–4	2	PF-64						

TEXAS INDEPENDENCE CENTENNIAL HALF DOLLAR (1934–1938)

Designer Pompeo Coppini; weight 12.50 grams; composition .900 silver, .100 copper; diameter 30.6 mm; reeded edge; mint: Philadelphia.

Designs. *Obverse:* A perched eagle with a large five-pointed star in the background. *Reverse:* The goddess Victory kneeling, with medallions and portraits of General Sam Houston and Stephen Austin, founders of the republic and state of Texas, along with other Texan icons.

Mintage and Melting Data. Authorized June 15, 1933. *Maximum authorized*—1,500,000 (maximum total for all coins in the series 1934 onward). 1934: *Number minted* (including 113 assay coins)—205,113. *Number melted*—143,650. *Net distribution*—61,463. 1935-P-D-S: *Number minted* (including 8, 7, and 8 assay coins)—10,008; 10,007; 10,008. *Number melted*—12 Philadelphia (probably defective coins). *Net distribution*—9,996; 10,007; 10,008. 1936-P-D-S: *Number minted* (including 8, 7, and 8 assay coins)—10,008; 10,007; 10,008. *Number melted*—12 Philadelphia (probably defective coins). *Net distribution*—9,996; 10,007; 10,008. 1937-P-D-S: *Number minted* (including 5, 6, and 7 assay coins)—8,005; 8,006;8,007. *Number melted*—1,434; 1,401; 1,370. *Net distribu-

tion*—6,571; 6,605; 6,637. 1938-P-D-S: *Number minted* (including 5, 5, and 6 assay coins)—5,005; 5,005; 5,006. *Number melted*—1,225; 1,230; 1,192. *Net distribution*—3,780; 3,775; 3,814.

Original Cost and Issuer. 1934: Sale price $1. American Legion Texas Centennial Committee, Austin, Texas. 1935: Sale price $1.50 each; $4.50 per set of three. Issuer as preceding. 1936: Sale price $1.50 each; $4.50 per set of three. Texas Memorial Museum Centennial Coin Campaign. 1937: Sale price $1.50 each; $4.50 per set of three. Issuer as preceding. 1938: Sale price $2 each; $6 per set of three. Issuer as preceding.

Key to Collecting. The typical example grades MS-64 or 65. Early issues are very lustrous and frosty; those produced toward the end of the series are more satiny.

First Points of Wear. *Obverse:* The eagle's upper breast and upper leg. *Reverse:* The forehead and knee of Victory.

	Distribution	Cert	Avg	%MS	MS-60	MS-62	MS-63	MS-64	MS-65	MS-66	Recent Auction Record
1934	61,463	2,054	64.6	99	$135	$145	$155	$175	$290	$365	$322, MS-66, Jul-10
1935 (same as 1934)	9,996	1,391	65.6	100							$253, MS-66, Jul-10
1935D	10,007	1,437	65.5	100							$253, MS-66, Jul-10
1935S	10,008	1,193	65.2	100							$334, MS-66, Jul-10
Set of 1935 P-D-S					430	440	455	475	850	1,350	$1,495, MS-67 CAC, Sep-09

	Distribution	Cert	Avg	%MS	MS-60	MS-62	MS-63	MS-64	MS-65	MS-66	Recent Auction Record
1936 (same as 1934)	8,911	1,294	65.4	100							$1,610, MS-67 CAC, Jul-10
1936D	9,039	1,499	65.6	100							$805, MS-67 CAC, Jun-10
1936S	9,055	1,203	65.3	100							$403, MS-66, Jul-10
Set of 1936 P-D-S					$430	$440	$455	$480	$925	$1,375	$978, MS-66, May-09
1937 (same as 1934)	6,571	1,051	65.2	100							$300, MS-66 CAC, Jul-10
1937D	6,605	1,100	65.4	100							$345, MS-66, Jun-10
1937S	6,637	1,100	65.3	100							$230, MS-66, Jul-10
Set of 1937 P-D-S					430	440	455	500	900	1,125	$748, MS-66, Jul-09
1938 (same as 1934)	3,780	739	65.1	100							$575, MS-66, Jul-10
1938D	3,775	768	65.4	100							$805, MS-66, Jul-10
1938S	3,814	765	65.4	100							$575, MS-66, Jul-10
Set of 1938 P-D-S					700	750	785	875	1,275	2,200	$868, MS-64, Sep-09

DANIEL BOONE BICENTENNIAL HALF DOLLAR (1934–1938)

Designer Augustus Lukeman; weight 12.50 grams; composition .900 silver, .100 copper; diameter 30.6 mm; reeded edge; mint: Philadelphia.

Designs. *Obverse:* Artist's conception of Daniel Boone in a profile portrait. *Reverse:* Standing figures of Boone and Blackfish, war chief of the Chillicothe band of the Shawnee tribe. (In 1935 the date 1934 was added to the reverse design.)

Mintage and Melting Data. Authorized May 26, 1934 and, with "1934" added to modify the design, on August 26, 1935. *Maximum authorized*—600,000 (for total of all issues 1934 and onward). 1934: *Number minted* (including 7 assay coins)—10,007. *Net distribution*—10,007. 1935-P-D-S: *Number minted* (including 10, 5, and 5 assay coins): 10,010; 5,005; 5,005. Net distribution: 10,010; 5,005; 5,005. 1935 "small 1934" P-D-S: *Number minted* (including 8 assay coins)—10,008; 2,003; 2,004. *Net distribution*—10,008. 1936-P-D-S: *Number minted* (including 12, 5, and 6 assay coins)—12,012; 5,005; 5,006. *Net distribution*—12,012; 5,005; 5,006. 1937-P-D-S: *Number minted* (including 10, 6, and 6 assay coins)—15,010; 7,506; 5,006. Number melted: 5,200; 5,000; 2,500. *Net distribution*—9,810; 2,506; 2,506. 1938-P-D-S: *Number minted* (including 5, 5, and 6 assay coins)—5,005; 5,005; 5,006. Number melted: 2,905; 2,905; 2,906. *Net distribution*—2,100, 2,100, 2,100.

Original Cost and Issuer. 1934: Sale price $1.60. 1935: Sale price $1.10 for the Philadelphia issue; $1.60 each for the Denver and San Francisco coins. 1935, With 1934: Sale price $1.10 (raised to $1.60 on December 21, 1935); Denver and San Francisco $3.70 per pair. 1936: Sale price $1.10 Philadelphia; $1.60 each Denver and San Francisco. 1937: Sale price, Philadelphia, $1.60 singly; later as a pair with a Denver coin for $7.25 (Denver coins were not offered singly); P-D-S sets $12.40; San Francisco coins singly $5.15. 1938 P-D-S: Sale price $6.50 per set of three. Daniel Boone Bicentennial Commission (and its division, the Pioneer National Monument Association), Phoenix Hotel, Lexington, Kentucky (C. Frank Dunn, "sole distributor").

Key to Collecting. Most collectors desire just a single coin to represent the type, but there are enough specialists who want one of each date and mintmark to ensure a ready market whenever the scarcer sets come up for sale. Most surviving coins are in MS, with MS-64 to 66 pieces readily available for most issues. Early issues in the series are characterized by deep frosty mint luster, whereas issues toward the end of the run, particularly 1937 and 1938, often are seen with a satin finish and relatively little luster (because of the methods of die preparation and striking). The 1937-S is very often seen with prooflike surfaces, and the 1938-S occasionally so. In general, the Boone commemoratives were handled carefully at the time of minting and distribution, but scattered marks are often visible.

First Points of Wear. *Obverse:* The hair behind Boone's ear. *Reverse:* The left shoulder of the Indian.

	Distribution	Cert	Avg	%MS	MS-60	MS-62	MS-63	MS-64	MS-65	MS-66	Recent Auction Record
1934	10,007	908	64.8	100	$130	$135	$145	$155	$265	$410	$403, MS-66, Jul-10
1935	10,010	1,035	64.7	100							$276, MS-66, Jul-10
1935D	5,005	580	64.6	100							$127, MS-64, Jun-10
1935S	5,005	749	65.0	100							$1,955, MS-67, Jul-10
Set of 1935 P-D-S					400	410	425	460	825	1,550	$467, MS-65/65/66, May-09
1935, With Added Date	10,008	1,163	64.9	100							$265, MS-65, Jun-10
1935D, Same type	2,003	456	65.2	100							$604, MS-66, Jul-10
1935S, Same type	2,004	464	64.9	100							$3,738, MS-67, Jun-10
Set of 1935 P-D-S, With Added Date					900	935	985	1,100	2,000	3,750	$1,955, MS-66/67/66, Mar-10

Chart continued on next page.

	Distribution	Cert	Avg	%MS	MS-60	MS-62	MS-63	MS-64	MS-65	MS-66	Recent Auction Record
1936	12,012	1,325	64.8	100							$253, MS-66, Jul-10
1936D	5,005	757	65.0	100							$288, MS-66, Jul-10
1936S	5,006	808	65.1	100							$345, MS-66, Jul-10
Set of 1936 P-D-S					$400	$410	$425	$460	$815	$1,500	$1,093, MS-66, Aug-08
1937	9,810	1,232	64.9	100							$231, MS-66, Jul-10
1937D	2,506	502	64.9	100							$403, MS-66, Jul-10
1937S	2,506	615	65.0	100							$1,610, MS-67, Jul-10
Set of 1937 P-D-S					850	875	900	975	1,275	1,750	$4,600, MS-67, Jun-10
1938	2,100	410	64.8	100							$2,530, MS-67, Jul-10
1938D	2,100	439	65.1	100							$575, MS-66, Jul-10
1938S	2,100	438	64.9	100							$638, MS-66, Jul-10
Set of 1938 P-D-S					1,125	1,140	1,185	1,235	1,625	2,950	$1,840, MS-66, Sep-09

CONNECTICUT TERCENTENARY HALF DOLLAR (1935)

Designer Henry Kreiss; weight 12.50 grams; composition .900 silver, .100 copper; diameter 30.6 mm; reeded edge; mint: Philadelphia.

Designs. *Obverse:* A modernistic eagle, standing. *Reverse:* The Charter Oak.

Mintage Data. Authorized June 21, 1934. *Maximum authorized—25,000. Number minted* (including 18 assay coins)—25,018. *Net distribution*—25,018.

Original Cost and Issuer. Sale price $1. Connecticut Tercentenary Commission.

Key to Collecting. Most examples survive in upper AU and lower MS grades. Higher-grade coins such as MS-65 are elusive. Friction and/or marks are often obvious on the broad expanse of wing on the obverse, and, in particular, at the ground or baseline of the oak tree on the reverse. Examples that are otherwise lustrous, frosty, and very attractive, often have friction on the wing.

First Points of Wear. *Obverse:* The top of the eagle's wing. *Reverse:* The ground above ON and TI in CONNECTICUT.

	Distribution	Cert	Avg	%MS	MS-60	MS-62	MS-63	MS-64	MS-65	MS-66	Recent Auction Record
1935	25,018	3,127	64.5	99	$260	$270	$285	$300	$520	$875	$2,760, MS-67 Star, Jul-10

	Est Mintage	Cert	Finest	PF-60	PF-63	PF-64	PF-65	PF-66	Recent Auction Record
1935, Matte Proof	1–2	1	PF-65						

ARKANSAS CENTENNIAL HALF DOLLAR (1935–1939)

Designer Edward E. Burr; weight 12.50 grams; composition .900 silver, .100 copper; diameter 30.6 mm; reeded edge; mint: Philadelphia.

Designs. *Obverse:* An eagle with outstretched wings, stars, and other elements of the Arkansas state seal. *Reverse:* Portraits of an Arkansas youth of 1936 and an Indian chief of 1836.

Mintage and Melting Data. Authorized May 14, 1934. *Maximum authorized*—500,000 (maximum total for all issues 1935 onward). 1935-P-D-S: *Number minted* (including 5, 5, and 6 assay coins)—13,012; 5,505; 5,506. *Net distribution*—13,012; 5,505; 5,506. 1935-P-D-S: *Number minted* (including 10, 10, and 12 assay coins)—10,010; 10,010; 10,012. *Number melted*—350; 350; 350. *Net distribution*—9,660; 9,660; 9,662. 1937-P-D-S: *Number minted* (including 5, 5, and 6 assay coins)—5,505; 5,505; 5,506. *Net distribution*—5,505; 5,505; 5,506. 1938-P-D-S: *Number minted* (including 6, 5, and 6 assay coins)—6,006; 6,005; 6,006. *Number melted*—2,850; 2,850; 2,850. *Net distribution*—3,156; 3,155;

3,156. 1939-P-D-S: *Number minted* (including 4, 4, and 5 assay coins)—2,104; 2,104; 2,105. *Net distribution*—2,104; 2,104; 2,105.

Original Cost and Issuer. 1935: Sale price $1 per coin; however, few Denver and San Francisco coins were sold at this price as B. Max Mehl bought nearly the entire mintage and soon raised the "issue price" to $2.75 each. 1936: Sale price $1 per coin; then on February 1, 1936, $1.50 per coin; then $4.50 per set of three; then $6.75 per set of three; price for unsold sets was raised to $10 on March 1, 1940. 1937: $8.75 per set of three. 1938: $8.75 postpaid per set of three; $10 after July 1, 1938; $12 on and after March 1, 1940. 1939: $10 per set of three. Issuers: 1935, 1936, 1938, 1939: Arkansas Centennial Commission throughout. 1935: B. Max Mehl bought quantities and retailed them at higher prices. 1937: Stack's of New York City.

Key to Collecting. The coin sets were produced with a satiny, almost "greasy" finish; even freshly minted coins appeared as if they had been dipped or repeatedly cleaned. Issues of 193 to 1939 are usually more satisfactory but still are not deeply lustrous. The prominence of the girl's portrait on the center of the obverse renders that part of the coin prone to receiving bagmarks, scuffs, and other evidence of handling. As a result, relatively few pieces have great eye appeal. The obverse area where the ribbon crosses the eagle's breast is often very weak. Some examples are lightly struck on the eagle just behind its head.

First Points of Wear. *Obverse:* The eagle's head and the top of the left wing. *Reverse:* The band of the girl's cap, behind her eye.

	Distribution	Cert	Avg	%MS	MS-60	MS-62	MS-63	MS-64	MS-65	MS-66	Recent Auction Record
Single type coin	n/a	n/a	n/a	n/a	$110		$115		$235	$800	
1935	13,012	1,014	64.4	100							$460, MS-66, Jun-10
1935D	5,505	766	64.7	100							$345, MS-66, Jul-10
1935S	5,506	783	64.6	100							$347, MS-66, Jul-10
Set of 1935 P-D-S					290		335		700	2,400	$403, MS-65 , Mar-09
1936	9,660	841	64.3	100							$518, MS-66, Jan-10
1936D	9,660	816	64.5	100							$389, MS-66, Jul-10
1936S	9,662	843	64.5	100							$1,898, MS-67, Jul-10
Set of 1936 P-D-S					290		335		750	2,700	$1,150, MS-66/65/66, May-09
1937	5,505	645	64.3	100							$431, MS-66, Mar-10
1937D	5,505	718	64.5	100							$546, MS-66, Jul-10
1937S	5,506	578	64.2	100							$460, MS-66, Jan-10
Set of 1937 P-D-S					290		365		900	5,250	$1,840, MS-66, Feb-09
1938	3,156	459	64.3	100							$288, MS-65, Jul-10
1938D	3,155	502	64.4	100							$690, MS-66, Jul-10
1938S	3,156	439	64.3	100							$805, MS-66 CAC, Jul-10
Set of 1938 P-D-S					500		550		1,800	5,550	$403, MS-64, May-09
1939	2,104	392	64.2	100							$719, MS-65, Jul-10
1939D	2,104	403	64.4	100							$575, MS-65, Jul-10
1939S	2,105	445	64.4	100							$633, MS-65, Jul-10
Set of 1939 P-D-S					1,000		1,200		2,700	8,850	$2,243, MS-65 CAC, Mar-10

	Est Mintage	Cert	Finest	PF-60	PF-63	PF-64	PF-65	PF-66	Recent Auction Record
1938, set of P-D-S, Matte Proof	1–2								

ARKANSAS CENTENNIAL—ROBINSON HALF DOLLAR (1936)

Designers Henry Kreiss (obv) and Edward E. Burr (rev); weight 12.50 grams; composition .900 silver, .100 copper; diameter 30.6 mm; reeded edge; mint: Philadelphia.

Designs. *Obverse:* An eagle with outstretched wings, stars, and other elements of the Arkansas state seal. *Reverse:* Bareheaded profile portrait of Senator Joseph T. Robinson.

Mintage and Melting Data. Authorized June 26, 1936. *Maximum authorized*—50,000 (minimum 25,000). *Number minted* (including 15 assay coins)—25,265. *Net distribution*—25,265.

Original Cost and Issuer. Sale price $1.85. Stack's of New York City.

Key to Collecting. Most known coins are in MS, as most or all were originally sold to collectors and coin dealers. Examples are plentiful in the marketplace, usually grading MS-62 to 64. The coins were not handled with care during production, so many have contact marks on Robinson's portrait and elsewhere. Some examples are lightly struck on the eagle, just behind the head.

First Points of Wear. *Obverse:* The eagle's head and the top of the left wing. *Reverse:* Robinson's cheekbone.

	Distribution	Cert	Avg	%MS	MS-60	MS-62	MS-63	MS-64	MS-65	MS-66	Recent Auction Record
1936	25,265	2,372	64.3	100	$175	$195	$220	$230	$375	$675	$460, MS-66, Jul-10

HUDSON, NEW YORK, SESQUICENTENNIAL HALF DOLLAR (1935)

Designer Chester Beach; weight 12.50 grams; composition .900 silver, .100 copper; diameter 30.6 mm; reeded edge; mint: Philadelphia.

Designs. *Obverse:* The ship *Half Moon,* captained by Henry Hudson, in full sail. *Reverse:* The ocean god Neptune seated backward on a whale (derived from the seal of the city of Hudson); in the background, a mermaid blowing a shell.

Mintage Data. Approved May 2, 1935. *Maximum authorized—* 10,000. *Number minted* (including 8 assay coins)—10,008. *Net distribution*—10,008.

Original Cost and Issuer. Sale price $1. Hudson Sesquicentennial Committee, through the First National Bank & Trust Company of Hudson.

Key to Collecting. Examples are readily available in the marketplace. Note that deep or artificial toning, which can make close

inspection impossible, has led some certified coins to certified grades that are higher than they should be. True gems are very rare. These coins were struck at high speed and with little care to preserve their quality; by the time they were originally distributed most pieces showed nicks, contact marks, and other evidence of handling. Most are lustrous and frosty (except on the central devices), and grade in the lower MS levels. MS-62 to 64 are typical. Carefully graded MS-65 coins are scarce, and anything higher is very rare.

First Points of Wear. *Obverse:* The center of the lower middle sail. *Reverse:* The motto on the ribbon, and the figure of Neptune (both of which may also be lightly struck).

	Distribution	Cert	Avg	%MS	MS-60	MS-62	MS-63	MS-64	MS-65	MS-66	Recent Auction Record
1935	10,008	1,802	64.1	99	$860	$915	$1,065	$1,400	$2,025	$2,850	$1,610, MS-65, Jul-10

CALIFORNIA PACIFIC INTERNATIONAL EXPOSITION HALF DOLLAR (1935–1936)

Designer Robert Aitken; weight 12.50 grams; composition .900 silver, .100 copper; diameter 30.6 mm; reeded edge; mint: Philadelphia.

Designs. *Obverse:* Minerva seated, holding a spear and shield, with a grizzly bear to her right (from California's state seal). *Reverse:* The Chapel of St. Francis and the California Tower, at the California Pacific International Exposition.

Mintage and Melting Data. 1935-S: Authorized May 3, 1935. *Maximum authorized*—250,000. *Number minted* (including 132 assay coins)—250,132. *Number melted*—180,000. *Net distribution*—70,132. 1936-D: Authorized May 6, 1936 (special authorization for recoinage of melted 1935-S half dollars). *Maximum authorized*—180,000. *Number minted* (including 92 assay coins)—180,092. *Number melted*—150,000. *Net distribution*—30,092.

Original Cost and Issuer. 1935-S: Sale price $1 (increased to $3 in 1937; dropped to $2 in 1938). 1936-D: Sale price $1.50 (increased to $3 in 1937; reduced to $1 in 1938). California Pacific International Exposition Company.

Key to Collecting. Both the 1935-S and 1936-D issues were coined with deeply frosty and lustrous surfaces. The eye appeal usually is excellent. The design made these coins susceptible to bagmarks, and most survivors, even in higher MS grades, show evidence of handling. Minerva, in particular, usually displays some graininess or contact marks, even on coins given high numerical grades. Most coins are deeply lustrous and frosty. On the 1935 San Francisco coins the S mintmark usually is flat, and on the Denver coins the California Tower is often lightly struck at the top.

First Points of Wear. *Obverse:* The bosom and knees of Minerva. *Reverse:* The top right edge of the tower. (The 1936-D was flatly struck in this area; examine the texture of the surface to determine if actual wear exists.)

	Distribution	Cert	Avg	%MS	MS-60	MS-62	MS-63	MS-64	MS-65	MS-66	Recent Auction Record
1935S	70,132	4,295	64.9	100	$105	$110	$115	$130	$175	$215	$776, MS-67, Jun-10
1936D	30,092	2,518	64.9	100	120	125	135	155	200	255	$322, MS-66, May-10

OLD SPANISH TRAIL HALF DOLLAR (1935)

Designer L.W. Hoffecker; weight 12.50 grams; composition .900 silver, .100 copper; diameter 30.6 mm; reeded edge; mint: Philadelphia.

Designs. *Obverse:* The head of a steer. *Reverse:* A map of the Southeastern states and a yucca tree.

Mintage Data. Authorized June 5, 1935. *Maximum authorized*— 10,000. *Number minted*—10,008.

Original Cost and Issuer. Sale price $2. L.W. Hoffecker, trading as the El Paso Museum Coin Committee.

Key to Collecting. These coins were handled with care during their production and shipping—still, most show scattered contact marks.

They typical grade is MS-65 and higher. The fields are usually somewhat satiny and gray, not deeply lustrous and frosty.

First Points of Wear. *Obverse:* The top of the cow's head. *Reverse:* The lettering at the top.

	Distribution	Cert	Avg	%MS	MS-60	MS-62	MS-63	MS-64	MS-65	MS-66	Recent Auction Record
1935	10,008	1,622	65.0	100	$1,320	$1,375	$1,550	$1,650	$2,025	$2,350	$3,738, MS-67 CAC, Jul-10

PROVIDENCE, RHODE ISLAND, TERCENTENARY HALF DOLLAR (1936)

Designers Arthur G. Carey and John H. Benson; weight 12.50 grams; composition .900 silver, .100 copper; diameter 30.6 mm; reeded edge; mint: Philadelphia.

Designs. *Obverse:* Roger Williams, the founder of Rhode Island, being welcomed by an Indian. *Reverse:* Elements from the Rhode Island state seal, including the anchor of Hope and a shield.

Mintage and Melting Data. Authorized May 2, 1935. *Maximum authorized*—50,000. 1936-P-D-S: *Number minted and distribution*—20,013; 15,010; 15,011. Assay coins: 13; 10; 11.

Original Cost and Issuer. Sale price $1. Rhode Island and Providence Plantations Tercentenary Committee, Inc.

Key to Collecting. These coins are readily available singly and in sets, with typical grades being MS-63 to 65. Contact marks are common. Higher-level coins, such as MS-66 and 67, are not hard to find, but are elusive in comparison to the lesser-condition pieces. The 1936 (in particular) and 1936-S are sometimes found with prooflike surfaces. Most specimens have a combination of satiny/frosty surface. Many are light gray in color.

First Points of Wear. *Obverse:* The prow of the canoe, and the Indian's right shoulder. *Reverse:* The center of the anchor, and surrounding areas.

	Distribution	Cert	Avg	%MS	MS-60	MS-62	MS-63	MS-64	MS-65	MS-66	Recent Auction Record
Single type coin	n/a	n/a	n/a	n/a	$110	$115	$125	$135	$275	$425	
1936	20,013	2,176	64.7	100							$1,208, MS-67, Jul-10
1936D	15,010	1,621	64.7	100							$299, MS-66, Jul-10
1936S	15,011	1,366	64.6	100							$299, MS-66, Jul-10
Set of 1936 P-D-S					340	345	375	410	835	1,700	$347, MS-64, Jul-10

CLEVELAND CENTENNIAL / GREAT LAKES EXPOSITION HALF DOLLAR (1936)

Designer Brenda Putnam; weight 12.50 grams; composition .900 silver, .100 copper; diameter 30.6 mm; reeded edge; mint: Philadelphia.

Designs. *Obverse:* Bewigged profile portrait of Moses Cleaveland. *Reverse:* A map of the Great Lakes region with nine stars marking various cities, and a compass point at the city of Cleveland.

Mintage Data. Authorized May 5, 1936. *Minimum authorized*—25,000, *Maximum authorized*—50,000. *Number minted (including 30 assay coins)*—50,030. *Net distribution*—50,030.

Original Cost and Issuer. Sale price: one coin for $1.65; two for $1.60 each; three for $1.58 each; five for $1.56 each; ten for $1.55 each; twenty for $1.54 each; fifty for $1.53 each; one hundred for $1.52 each. Cleveland Centennial Commemorative Coin Association (Thomas G. Melish, Cleveland).

Key to Collecting. The Cleveland half dollar is the most readily available issue from 1936—a bumper-crop year for U.S. commemoratives. Nearly all coins are in Mint State, typically from MS-63 to 65, and most are very lustrous and frosty. This issue was not handled with care at the Mint, and scattered contact marks are typically found on both obverse and reverse.

First Points of Wear. *Obverse:* The hair behind Cleaveland's ear. *Reverse:* The top of the compass, and the land (non-lake) areas of the map.

	Distribution	Cert	Avg	%MS	MS-60	MS-62	MS-63	MS-64	MS-65	MS-66	Recent Auction Record
1936	50,030	4,340	64.6	100	$120	$125	$130	$135	$200	$390	$374, MS-66, Jul-10

WISCONSIN TERRITORIAL CENTENNIAL HALF DOLLAR (1936)

Designer David Parsons; weight 12.50 grams; composition .900 silver, .100 copper; diameter 30.6 mm; reeded edge; mint: Philadelphia.

Designs. *Obverse:* A badger on a log, from the state emblem; and arrows representing the Black Hawk War of the 1830s. *Reverse:* A miner's arm holding a pickaxe over a mound of lead ore, derived from Wisconsin's territorial seal.

Mintage Data. Authorized May 15, 1936. *Minimum authorized*— 25,000 (unlimited maximum). *Number minted* (including 15 assay coins)—25,015. *Net distribution*—25,015.

Original Cost and Issuer. Sale price $1.50 plus 7¢ postage for the first coin, 2¢ postage for each additional coin (later sold for $1.25 each in lots of 10 coins, and still later sold for $3 per coin). Wis-

consin Centennial Coin Committee (also known as the Coinage Committee of the Wisconsin Centennial Commission). Unsold remainders were distributed, into the 1950s, by the State Historical Society.

Key to Collecting. Examples are readily available in the marketplace. Most grade MS-62 to 64– although higher grades are not rare—and are very lustrous and frosty, except for the higher areas of the design (which often have a slightly polished appearance).

First Points of Wear. *Obverse:* The flank and shoulder of the badger. *Reverse:* The miner's hand.

	Distribution	Cert	Avg	%MS	MS-60	MS-62	MS-63	MS-64	MS-65	MS-66	Recent Auction Record
1936	25,015	3,498	65.3	100	$255	$265	$270	$290	$375	$425	$863, MS-67 CAC, Jul-10

CINCINNATI MUSIC CENTER HALF DOLLAR (1936)

Designer Constance Ortmayer; weight 12.50 grams; composition .900 silver, .100 copper; diameter 30.6 mm; reeded edge; mint: Philadelphia.

Designs. *Obverse:* Bareheaded profile portrait of Stephen Foster, "America's Troubadour." *Reverse:* A woman playing a lyre, personifying Music.

Mintage Data. Authorized March 31, 1936. *Maximum authorized*— 15,000. 1936-P-D-S: *Number minted* (including 5, 5, and 6 assay coins)—5,005; 5,005; 5,006. *Net distribution*—5,005; 5,005; 5,006.

Original Cost and Issuer. Sale price $7.75 per set of three (actually $7.50 plus 25¢ for the display container with cellophane slide front). Cincinnati Musical Center Commemorative Coin Association, Ohio (Thomas G. Melish).

Key to Collecting. Nearly all sets of these coins were bought by collectors and investors, thus most still exist in Mint State, primarily MS-63 to 65. Conservatively graded MS-65 and finer specimens are rare. Most coins were carelessly handled at the mints, and nearly all show scattered contact marks. This issue has a somewhat satiny or "greasy" surface, instead of fields with deep luster and frost. Denver Mint coins are typically found in slightly higher grades than their Philadelphia and San Francisco Mint companions.

First Points of Wear. *Obverse:* The hair at Foster's temple. *Reverse:* The left breast, and the skirt, of the female figure.

	Distribution	Cert	Avg	%MS	MS-60	MS-62	MS-63	MS-64	MS-65	MS-66	Recent Auction Record
Single type coin	n/a	n/a	n/a	n/a	$310	$315	$340	$365	$675	$975	
1936	5,005	758	64.3	100							$748, MS-66, Mar-10
1936D	5,005	1,119	64.9	100							$1,025, MS-66 CAC, Jul-10
1936S	5,006	800	64.1	100							$385, MS-65, Mar-10
Set of 1936 P-D-S					925	940	1,025	1,200	2,100	5,350	$13,800, MS-66, Feb-10

LONG ISLAND TERCENTENARY HALF DOLLAR (1936)

Designer Howard K. Weinman; weight 12.50 grams; composition .900 silver, .100 copper; diameter 30.6 mm; reeded edge; mint: Philadelphia.

Designs. *Obverse:* Conjoined profile portraits of a Dutch settler and an Algonquin Indian. *Reverse:* A Dutch vessel with full-blown sails.

Mintage and Melting Data. Authorized April 13, 1936. *Maximum authorized*—100,000. *Number minted* (including 53 assay coins)— 100,053. *Number melted*—18,227. *Net distribution*—81,826.

Original Cost and Issuer. Sale price $1. Long Island Tercentenary Committee, through various banks and other outlets.

Key to Collecting. These are among the most plentiful survivors from the commemorative issues of the 1930s, and examples grading MS-64 to 66 are readily obtainable. The coins were minted and handled carelessly, and at the time of distribution most showed nicks, bagmarks, and other evidence of contact; these grade from AU-50 to MS-60. Most coins have, as struck, a satiny or slightly "greasy" luster and are not deeply frosty.

First Points of Wear. *Obverse:* The hair and the cheekbone of the Dutch settler. *Reverse:* The center of the lower middle sail.

	Distribution	Cert	Avg	%MS	MS-60	MS-62	MS-63	MS-64	MS-65	MS-66	Recent Auction Record
1936	81,826	3,795	64.2	100	$100	$105	$120	$125	$375	$835	$489, MS-66, Jul-10

YORK COUNTY, MAINE, TERCENTENARY HALF DOLLAR (1936)

Designer Walter H. Rich; weight 12.50 grams; composition .900 silver, .100 copper; diameter 30.6 mm; reeded edge; mint: Philadelphia.

Designs. *Obverse:* Brown's Garrison, on the Saco River (site of a town settled in 1636). *Reverse:* An adaptation of the seal of York County.

Mintage Data. *Maximum authorized—30,000. Number minted* (including 15 assay coins)—25,015.

Original Cost and Issuer. Sale price $1.50 ($1.65 postpaid by mail to out-of-state buyers). York County Tercentenary Commemorative Coin Commission, York National Bank, Saco, Maine.

Key to Collecting. This issue was well handled at the Mint and in distribution, so most examples are in higher grades and are relatively free of marks. On the reverse, the top of the shield is a key point. Some coins have been brushed and have a myriad of fine hairlines; these can be detected by examining the coin at various angles to the light. MS-64 and 65 coins are readily found in the marketplace.

First Points of Wear. *Obverse:* The mounted sentry near the corner of the fort; the stockade; and the rim of the coin. *Reverse:* The pine tree in the shield; the top-right area of the shield; and the rim.

	Distribution	Cert	Avg	%MS	MS-60	MS-62	MS-63	MS-64	MS-65	MS-66	Recent Auction Record
1936	25,015	3,097	65.4	100	$220	$225	$230	$240	$320	$365	$374, MS-67, Jul-10

BRIDGEPORT, CONNECTICUT, CENTENNIAL HALF DOLLAR (1936)

Designer Henry Kreiss; weight 12.50 grams; composition .900 silver, .100 copper; diameter 30.6 mm; reeded edge; mint: Philadelphia.

Designs. *Obverse:* Bareheaded profile portrait of P.T. Barnum, Bridgeport's most famous citizen. *Reverse:* An art deco eagle, standing.

Mintage Data. Authorized May 15, 1936. *Minimum authorized—* 25,000 (unlimited maximum). *Number minted* (including 15 assay coins)—25,015. *Net distribution—25,015.*

Original Cost and Issuer. Sale price $2. Bridgeport Centennial, Inc., through the First National Bank and Trust Co. and other banks.

Key to Collecting. These coins are readily available in the marketplace. Most grade from MS-62 to 64. Many have been cleaned or lightly polished, but pristine MS-65 pieces are readily available. Obvious friction rub and/or marks are often seen. Some coins were struck from dies with lightly polished fields and have a prooflike or partially prooflike appearance in those areas.

First Points of Wear. *Obverse:* Barnum's cheek. *Reverse:* The eagle's wing.

	Distribution	Cert	Avg	%MS	MS-60	MS-62	MS-63	MS-64	MS-65	MS-66	Recent Auction Record
1936	25,015	2,686	64.6	100	$150	$155	$170	$185	$315	$425	$299, MS-66, Jul-10

LYNCHBURG, VIRGINIA, SESQUICENTENNIAL HALF DOLLAR (1936)

Designer Charles Keck; weight 12.50 grams; composition .900 silver, .100 copper; diameter 30.6 mm; reeded edge; mint: Philadelphia.

Designs. *Obverse:* Bareheaded profile portrait of Senator Carter Glass, a native of Lynchburg and former secretary of the Treasury. *Reverse:* A figure of Miss Liberty standing before the old Lynchburg courthouse.

Continued on next page.

Mintage Data. Authorized May 28, 1936. *Maximum authorized—* 20,000. *Number minted* (including 13 assay coins)—20,013. *Net distribution*—20,013.

Original Cost and Issuer. Sale price $1. Lynchburg Sesqui-Centennial Association.

Key to Collecting. Most of these half dollars are in higher grades; MS-65 and 66 examples are readily available in the marketplace.

Some show graininess (from striking) on the high areas of the obverse portrait and on the bosom and skirt of Miss Liberty, or show evidences of handling or contact in the same areas. Surfaces are often somewhat satiny, instead of deeply lustrous and frosty. Often the reverse field is semi-prooflike. This issue must have been handled with particular care at the Mint.

First Points of Wear. *Obverse:* The hair above Glass's ear. *Reverse:* The hair of Miss Liberty, the folds of her gown, and her bosom.

	Distribution	Cert	Avg	%MS	MS-60	MS-62	MS-63	MS-64	MS-65	MS-66	Recent Auction Record
1936	20,013	2,301	64.8	100	$265	$270	$285	$295	$365	$490	$374, MS-66, Jul-10

ELGIN, ILLINOIS, CENTENNIAL HALF DOLLAR (1936)

Designer Trygve Rovelstad; weight 12.50 grams; composition .900 silver, .100 copper; diameter 30.6 mm; reeded edge; mint: Philadelphia.

Designs. *Obverse:* The fur-capped profile of a bearded pioneer (a closeup view of the statue depicted on the reverse). *Reverse:* The *Pioneer Memorial* statuary group, whose creation was financed by the sale of these coins.

Mintage and Melting Data. Authorized June 16, 1936. *Maximum authorized*—25,000. *Number minted* (including 15 assay coins)— 25,015. *Number melted*—5,000. *Net distribution*—20,015.

Original Cost and Issuer. Sale price $1.50. Elgin Centennial Monumental Committee, El Paso, Texas (L.W. Hoffecker in charge); banks in and near Elgin, including the First National Bank of Elgin, the Elgin National Bank, and the Union National Bank.

Key to Collecting. Elgin half dollars are fairly plentiful in today's marketplace. They seem to have been handled with particular

care at the time of minting, as most have fewer bagmarks than many other commemoratives of the same era. Typical coins grade MS-64 to 66. The surfaces often have a matte-like appearance (seemingly a combination of a lustrous circulation strike and a Matte Proof) quite different from other commemorative issues of 1936. Some coins are fairly frosty. On many a bright spot is evident on the reverse below the A of AMERICA, the result of an inadvertent polishing on a small area of the die. Chief Engraver John Sinnock made a few Matte Proofs, perhaps as many as 10, by pickling coins in acid at the Mint.

First Points of Wear. *Obverse:* The cheek of the pioneer. *Reverse:* The rifleman's left shoulder. (Note that a lack of detailed facial features is the result of striking, not wear, and that the infant is always weakly struck.)

	Distribution	Cert	Avg	%MS	MS-60	MS-62	MS-63	MS-64	MS-65	MS-66	Recent Auction Record
1936	20,015	2,998	65.0	100	$225	$230	$250	$260	$365	$550	$748, MS-67, Jul-10

ALBANY, NEW YORK, CHARTER HALF DOLLAR (1936)

Designer Gertrude K. Lathrop; weight 12.50 grams; composition .900 silver, .100 copper; diameter 30.6 mm; reeded edge; mint: Philadelphia.

Designs. *Obverse:* A plump beaver gnawing on a maple branch— fauna and flora evocative of Albany and New York State, respectively. *Reverse:* A scene with Albany's first mayor, Peter Schuyler, and his secretary, Robert Livingston, accepting the city's charter in 1686 from Governor Thomas Dongan of New York.

Mintage and Melting Data. Authorized on June 16, 1936. *Maximum authorized*—25,000. *Number minted* (including 13 assay coins)— 25,013. *Number melted*—7,342. *Net distribution*—17,671.

Original Cost and Issuer. Sale price $1. Albany Dongan Charter Coin Committee.

Key to Collecting. This issue was fairly carefully handled during production and distribution, and most examples are relatively free of marks in the fields. Most specimens are lustrous and frosty, although the frost has satiny aspects. Albany half dollars are readily available on the market. The typical example grades from MS-63 to 65 and has at least minor friction and marks.

First Points of Wear. *Obverse:* The hip of the beaver (nearly all coins show at least minor evidence of contact here). *Reverse:* The sleeve of Dongan (the figure at left).

	Distribution	Cert	Avg	%MS	MS-60	MS-62	MS-63	MS-64	MS-65	MS-66	Recent Auction Record
1936	17,671	2,663	64.8	100	$320	$325	$340	$350	$430	$575	$546, MS-66, Jul-10

SAN FRANCISCO–OAKLAND BAY BRIDGE OPENING HALF DOLLAR (1936)

Designer Jacques Schnier; weight 12.50 grams; composition .900 silver, .100 copper; diameter 30.6 mm; reeded edge; mint: Philadelphia.

Designs. *Obverse:* A stylized grizzly bear standing on all fours and facing the viewer. *Reverse:* A fading-to-the-horizon view of the San Francisco–Oakland Bay Bridge and part of San Francisco.

Mintage and Melting Data. Authorized June 26, 1936. *Maximum authorized*—200,000. *Number minted (including 55 assay coins)*—100,055. *Number melted*—28,631. *Net distribution*—71,424.

Original Cost and Issuer. Sale price $1.50. Coin Committee of the San Francisco-Oakland Bay Bridge Celebration.

Key to Collecting. These coins are readily available in today's marketplace, with most grading MS-62 to 64, typically with contact marks on the grizzly bear. The reverse design, being complex with many protective devices, normally appears free of marks, unless viewed at an angle under a strong light. The grade of the reverse for a given coin often is a point or two higher than that of the obverse. The fields of this coin often have a "greasy" appearance, rather than being deeply lustrous and frosty.

First Points of Wear. *Obverse:* The bear's body, in particular the left shoulder. *Reverse:* The clouds.

	Distribution	Cert	Avg	%MS	MS-60	MS-62	MS-63	MS-64	MS-65	MS-66	Recent Auction Record
1936S	71,424	3,176	64.7	99	$175	$180	$200	$225	$370	$465	$1,438, MS-67, Jul-10

COLUMBIA, SOUTH CAROLINA, SESQUICENTENNIAL HALF DOLLAR (1936)

Designer A. Wolfe Davidson; weight 12.50 grams; composition .900 silver, .100 copper; diameter 30.6 mm; reeded edge; mint: Philadelphia.

Designs. *Obverse:* Justice, with sword and scales, standing before the state capitol of 1786 and the capitol of 1936. *Reverse:* A palmetto tree, the state emblem, with stars encircling.

Mintage Data. Authorized March 18, 1936. *Maximum authorized*—25,000. *1936-P-D-S: Number minted and distribution*—9,007; 8,009; 8,007.

Original Cost and Issuer. Sale price $6.45 per set of three (single coins $2.15 each). Columbia Sesqui-Centennial Commission.

Key to Collecting. These coins were widely distributed at the time of issue, and examples are readily obtainable today. Most grade from MS-63 to 65. They were treated carefully in their minting and distribution, so most coins exhibit lustrous surfaces with very few handling marks. Nearly all, however, show friction on the bosom of Justice and, to a lesser extent, on the high areas of the palmetto tree foliage on the reverse.

First Points of Wear. *Obverse:* The right breast of Justice. *Reverse:* The top of the palmetto tree.

	Distribution	Cert	Avg	%MS	MS-60	MS-62	MS-63	MS-64	MS-65	MS-66	Recent Auction Record
Single type coin	n/a	n/a	n/a	n/a	$260	$265	$275	$285	$320	$360	
1936	9,007	1,393	65.2	100							$374, MS-66, May-10
1936D	8,009	1,474	65.7	100							$974, MS-67, Jun-10
1936S	8,007	1,407	65.4	100							$276, MS-66, Mar-10
Set of 1936 P-D-S					800	810	840	860	975	1,150	$805, MS-66, Jul-09

DELAWARE TERCENTENARY HALF DOLLAR (1936)

Designer Carl L. Schmitz; weight 12.50 grams; composition .900 silver, .100 copper; diameter 30.6 mm; reeded edge; mint: Philadelphia.

Designs. *Obverse:* Old Swedes Church, the oldest Protestant church in the United States still used for worship. *Reverse:* The ship *Kalmar Nyckel.*

Mintage and Melting Data. Authorized May 15, 1936. *Minimum authorized*—25,000 (unlimited maximum). *Number minted (including 15 assay coins)*—25,015. *Number melted*—4,022. *Net distribution*—20,993.

Original Cost and Issuer. Sale price $1.75. Delaware Swedish Tercentenary Commission, through the Equitable Trust Company of Wilmington.

Key to Collecting. Most examples in today's marketplace grade MS-64 or 65, though they typically exhibit numerous original planchet nicks and marks. Most coins are very lustrous and frosty.

Continued on next page.

First Points of Wear. *Obverse:* The roof above the church entrance. (Note that the triangular section at the top of the entrance is weakly struck, giving an appearance of wear.) *Reverse:* The center of the lower middle sail (also often shows graininess and nicks from the original planchet).

	Distribution	Cert	Avg	%MS	MS-60	MS-62	MS-63	MS-64	MS-65	MS-66	Recent Auction Record
1936	20,993	2,619	64.7	100	$265	$270	$285	$300	$455	$685	$389, MS-66, Jul-10

BATTLE OF GETTYSBURG ANNIVERSARY HALF DOLLAR (1936)

Designer Frank Vittor; weight 12.50 grams; composition .900 silver, .100 copper; diameter 30.6 mm; reeded edge; mint: Philadelphia.

Designs. *Obverse:* Uniformed profile portraits of a Union soldier and a Confederate soldier. *Reverse:* Union and Confederate shields separated by a fasces.

Mintage and Melting Data. Authorized June 16, 1936. *Maximum authorized*—50,000. *Number minted (including 28 assay coins)*— 50,028. *Number melted*—23,100. *Net distribution*—26,928.

Original Cost and Issuer. Sale price $1.65. The Pennsylvania State Commission, Hotel Gettysburg, Gettysburg. The price was later raised to $2.65 for coins offered by the American Legion, Department of Pennsylvania.

Key to Collecting. Examples are fairly plentiful in the marketplace. The typical coin grades from MS-63 to 65, is deeply frosty and lustrous, and shows scattered contact marks, which are most evident on the cheeks of the soldiers on the obverse and, on the reverse, on the two shields (particularly at the top of the Union shield on the left side of the coin).

First Points of Wear. *Obverse:* The cheekbones of each soldier. *Reverse:* The three ribbons on the fasces, and the top of the Union shield.

	Distribution	Cert	Avg	%MS	MS-60	MS-62	MS-63	MS-64	MS-65	MS-66	Recent Auction Record
1936	26,928	2,869	64.5	100	$465	$470	$485	$535	$820	$1,075	$891, MS-66, Jul-10

NORFOLK, VIRGINIA, BICENTENNIAL HALF DOLLAR (1936)

Designers William M. and Marjorie E. Simpson; weight 12.50 grams; composition .900 silver, .100 copper; diameter 30.6 mm; reeded edge; mint: Philadelphia.

Designs. *Obverse:* The seal of the city of Norfolk, with a three-masted ship at center. *Reverse:* The city's royal mace, presented by Lieutenant Governor Dinwiddie in 1753.

Mintage and Melting Data. Authorized June 28, 1937. *Maximum authorized*—25,000. *Number minted (including 13 assay coins)*— 25,013. *Number melted*—8,077. *Net distribution*—16,936.

Original Cost and Issuer. Sale price $1.50 locally ($1.65 by mail for the first coin, $1.55 for each additional). Norfolk Advertising Board, Norfolk Association of Commerce.

Key to Collecting. Examples are fairly plentiful in today's marketplace, with most in high MS grades. The cluttered nature of the design had a positive effect: all of the lettering served to protect the fields and devices from nicks and marks, with the result that MS-65 and 66 coins are plentiful.

First Points of Wear. *Obverse:* The sails of the ship, especially the lower rear sail. *Reverse:* The area below the crown on the royal mace.

	Distribution	Cert	Avg	%MS	MS-60	MS-62	MS-63	MS-64	MS-65	MS-66	Recent Auction Record
1936	16,936	2,458	65.9	100	$435	$440	$450	$460	$550	$615	$518, MS-65, Jul-10

ROANOKE ISLAND, NORTH CAROLINA, 350TH ANNIVERSARY HALF DOLLAR (1937)

Designer William M. Simpson; weight 12.50 grams; composition .900 silver, .100 copper; diameter 30.6 mm; reeded edge; mint: Philadelphia.

Designs. *Obverse:* Profile portrait of Sir Walter Raleigh in plumed hat and fancy collar. *Reverse:* Ellinor Dare and her baby, Virginia, the first white child born in the Americas to English parents.

Mintage and Melting Data. *Minimum authorized*—25,000 (unlimited maximum). *Number minted (including 30 assay coins)*— 50,030. *Number melted*—21,000. *Net distribution*—29,030.

Original Cost and Issuer. Sale price $1.65. Roanoke Colony Memorial Association of Manteo.

Key to Collecting. Most of these coins were handled with care during their minting, and today are in high grades. MS-65 pieces are plentiful. Most coins are lustrous and frosty. Partially prooflike pieces are occasionally seen (sometimes offered as "presentation pieces" or "prooflike presentation pieces").

First Points of Wear. *Obverse:* Raleigh's cheek and the brim of his hat. *Reverse:* The head of Ellinor Dare.

	Distribution	Cert	Avg	%MS	MS-60	MS-62	MS-63	MS-64	MS-65	MS-66	Recent Auction Record
1937	29,030	3,446	65.1	100	$220	$225	$230	$245	$325	$390	$1,495, MS-67, Jul-10

BATTLE OF ANTIETAM ANNIVERSARY HALF DOLLAR (1937)

Designer William M. Simpson; weight 12.50 grams; composition .900 silver, .100 copper; diameter 30.6 mm; reeded edge; mint: Philadelphia.

Designs. *Obverse:* Uniformed profile portraits of generals Robert E. Lee and George B. McClellan, opponent commanders during the Battle of Antietam. *Reverse:* Burnside Bridge, an important tactical objective of the battle.

Mintage and Melting Data. Authorized June 24, 1937. *Maximum authorized—50,000. Number minted (including 28 assay coins)—50,028. Number melted—32,000. Net distribution—18,028.*

Original Cost and Issuer. Sale price $1.65. Washington County Historical Society, Hagerstown, Maryland.

Key to Collecting. Antietam half dollars were handled with care during production. More often seen are scattered small marks, particularly on the upper part of the obverse. Most examples are very lustrous and frosty. MS-65 and finer coins are plentiful in the marketplace.

First Points of Wear. *Obverse:* Lee's cheekbone. *Reverse:* The leaves of the trees; the bridge; and the rim of the coin.

	Distribution	Cert	Avg	%MS	MS-60	MS-62	MS-63	MS-64	MS-65	MS-66	Recent Auction Record
1937	18,028	2,354	65.1	100	$660	$670	$680	$700	$930	$1,175	$805, MS-65, Jul-10

NEW ROCHELLE, NEW YORK, 250TH ANNIVERSARY HALF DOLLAR (1938)

Designer Gertrude K. Lathrop; weight 12.50 grams; composition .900 silver, .100 copper; diameter 30.6 mm; reeded edge; mint: Philadelphia.

Designs. *Obverse:* John Pell, who sold the French Huguenots the land for New Rochelle, and a fatted calf, an annual provision of the sale. *Reverse:* A fleur-de-lis, adapted from the seal of the city.

Mintage and Melting Data. Authorized May 5, 1936. *Maximum authorized—25,000. Number minted (including 15 assay coins)—25,015. Number melted—9,749. Net distribution—15,266.*

Original Cost and Issuer. Sale price $2. New Rochelle Commemorative Coin Committee, through the First National Bank of New Rochelle, New Rochelle, New York.

Key to Collecting. These half dollars received better-than-average care and handling during the minting and distribution process. The typical coin grades MS-64 or higher. Some examples show very light handling marks, but most are relatively problem-free. Some show areas of graininess or light striking on the high spots of the calf on the obverse, and on the highest area of the iris on the reverse. The majority of pieces have lustrous, frosty surfaces, and a few are prooflike (the latter are sometimes offered as "presentation pieces").

First Points of Wear. *Obverse:* The hip of the calf. *Reverse:* The bulbous part of the fleur-de-lis. (Note that on the central petal the midrib is flatly struck.)

	Distribution	Cert	Avg	%MS	MS-60	MS-62	MS-63	MS-64	MS-65	MS-66	Recent Auction Record
1938	15,266	2,283	65.0	100	$385	$390	$400	$415	$580	$740	$431, MS-65, Jul-10

	Est Mintage	Cert	Finest	PF-60	PF-63	PF-64	PF-65	PF-66	Recent Auction Record
1938, Proof	*1–2*	11	PF-68						

IOWA CENTENNIAL HALF DOLLAR (1946)

Designer Adam Pietz; weight 12.50 grams; composition .900 silver, .100 copper; diameter 30.6 mm; reeded edge; mint: Philadelphia.

Designs. *Obverse:* The Old Stone Capitol building at Iowa City. *Reverse:* An eagle with wings spreading, adapted from the Iowa state seal.

Mintage Data. Authorized August 7, 1946. *Maximum authorized*—100,000. *Number minted* (including 57 assay coins)—100,057.

Original Cost and Issuer. Sale price $2.50 to in-state buyers, $3 to those out of state. Iowa Centennial Committee, Des Moines, Iowa.

Key to Collecting. Most specimens are in varying degrees of Mint State, and are lustrous and frosty. MS-63 to 66 are typical grades. The nature of the design, without open field areas, is such that a slight amount of friction and contact is usually not noticeable.

First Points of Wear. *Obverse:* The clouds above the Capitol, and the shafts of the building near the upper-left and upper-right windows. *Reverse:* The back of the eagle's head and neck. (Note that the head sometimes is flatly struck.)

	Distribution	Cert	Avg	%MS	MS-60	MS-62	MS-63	MS-64	MS-65	MS-66	Recent Auction Record
1946	100,057	5,162	65.5	100	$120	$125	$130	$135	$150	$185	$408, MS-67, Jul-10

BOOKER T. WASHINGTON MEMORIAL HALF DOLLAR (1946–1951)

Designer Isaac S. Hathaway; weight 12.50 grams; composition .900 silver, .100 copper; diameter 30.6 mm; reeded edge; mint: Philadelphia.

Designs. *Obverse:* Bareheaded three-quarters profile portrait of Booker T. Washington. *Reverse:* The Hall of Fame at New York University and a slave cabin.

Mintage and Melting Data. Signed into law by President Harry S Truman on August 7, 1946. *Maximum authorized*—5,000,000, with dates not specified. 1946-P-D-S: *Number minted* (including 546, 113, and 279 assay coins)—1,000,546; 200,113; 500,279. *Net distribution*—700,546 (estimated); 50,000 (estimated); 500,279 (estimated). 1947-P-D-S: *Number minted* (including 17 assay coins each mint)—100,017; 100,017; 100,017. *Net distribution*—6,000 (estimated); 6,000 (estimated); 6,000 (estimated). 1948-P-D-S: *Number minted* (including 5 assay coins each mint): 20,005; 20,005; 20,005. *Net distribution*—8,005; 8,005; 8,005. 1949-P-D-S: *Number minted* (including 4 assay coins each mint)—12,004; 12,004; 12,004. *Net distribution*—6,004; 6,004; 6,004. 1950-P-D-S: *Number minted* (including 4, 4, and 91 assay coins)—12,004; 12,004; 512,091. *Net distribution*—6,004; 6,004; 62,091 (estimated). 1951-P-D-S: *Number minted* (including 82, 4, and 4 assay coins)—510,082; 12,004; 12,004. *Net distribution*—210,082 (estimated); 7,004; 7,004.

Original Cost and Issuer. 1946: Sale price $1 per coin for Philadelphia and San Francisco, $1.50 for Denver, plus 10¢ postage per coin. Booker T. Washington Birthplace Memorial Commission, Inc., Rocky Mount, Virginia (Dr. S.J. Phillips in charge), Stack's of New York City, Bebee Stamp & Coin Company (a.k.a. Bebee's). Later issues: Costs and distributors varied.

Key to Collecting. Of all commemorative half dollar issues produced up to this point, the Booker T. Washington half dollars were made with the least amount of care during the coining process at the mints. At the time of release, nearly all were poorly struck on the obverse and were marked with abrasions and nicks. Many have graininess and marks on Washington's cheek, from the original planchet surface that did not strike up fully. Many coins grade from MS-60 to (liberally graded) 65. Some have natural or artificial toning that masks the true condition and facilitates gem certification. Prooflike coins are sometimes seen, including for 1947-S (in particular), 1948-S, 1949, and 1951-S. These are not at all mirrorlike, but still have surfaces different from the normal mint frost.

First Points of Wear. *Obverse:* Washington's cheekbone. *Reverse:* The center lettering (FROM SLAVE CABIN, etc.).

	Distribution	Cert	Avg	%MS	MS-60	MS-62	MS-63	MS-64	MS-65	MS-66	Recent Auction Record
Single type coin	n/a	n/a	n/a	n/a	$20	$21	$23	$24	$67	$180	
1946	700,546	2,203	64.8	100							$748, MS-67, Jun-10
1946D	50,000	1,303	64.9	100							$863, MS-67, Jul-10
1946S	500,279	1,870	65.0	100							$1,150, MS-67, Jun-10
Set of 1946 P-D-S					65	70	90	100	190	585	$5,750, MS-66 Star, Jan-10
1947	6,000	665	64.9	100							$374, MS-66, Jul-10
1947D	6,000	523	65.0	100							$633, MS-66, Jul-10
1947S	6,000	730	65.1	100							$276, MS-66, Jul-10

	Distribution	Cert	Avg	%MS	MS-60	MS-62	MS-63	MS-64	MS-65	MS-66	Recent Auction Record
Set of 1947 P-D-S					$125	$130	$185	$195	$285	$2,050	$1,495, MS-66, Jan-08
1948	8,005	661	65.1	100							$213, MS-66, Mar-10
1948D	8,005	669	65.2	100							$219, MS-66, Jul-10
1948S	8,005	824	65.3	100							$207, MS-66, Jun-10
Set of 1948 P-D-S					190	200	245	255	290	1,175	$460, MS-66, Mar-10
1949	6,004	668	65.2	100							$253, MS-66 CAC, Jul-10
1949D	6,004	643	65.1	100							$219, MS-66, Jul-10
1949S	6,004	715	65.5	100							$155, MS-66, Jul-10
Set of 1949 P-D-S					240	250	270	295	330	650	$7,475, MS-67/67/66, Jan-08
1950	6,004	496	65.1	100							$150, MS-66, May-10
1950D	6,004	489	65.1	100							$403, MS-66 CAC, Jan-10
1950S	62,091	1,034	65.2	100							$104, MS-66, Jul-10
Set of 1950 P-D-S					160	170	180	190	250	1,500	$1,150, MS-66, Aug-07
1951	210,082	1,018	64.7	100							$299, MS-66 CAC, Jul-10
1951D	7,004	571	65.2	100							$748, MS-67, Jul-10
1951S	7,004	637	65.5	100							$196, MS-66, Jul-10
Set of 1951 P-D-S					160	170	180	200	225	1,025	$288, MS-65/66/65, May-09

CARVER/WASHINGTON COMMEMORATIVE HALF DOLLAR (1951–1954)

Designer Isaac S. Hathaway; weight 12.50 grams; composition .900 silver, .100 copper; diameter 30.6 mm; reeded edge; mint: Philadelphia.

Designs. *Obverse:* Conjoined bareheaded profile portraits of George Washington Carver and Booker T. Washington. *Reverse:* A map of the United States, with legends.

Mintage Data. Signed into law by President Harry S Truman on September 21, 1951. *Maximum authorized*—3,415,631 (total for all issues 1951 onward; consisting of 1,581,631 undistributed Booker T. Washington coins which could be converted into Carver-Washington coins, plus the unused 1,834,000 earlier authorization for Booker T. Washington coins). The following include author's estimates: 1951-P-D-S: *Number minted* (including 18, 4, and 4 assay coins)—110,018; 10,004; 10,004. *Net distribution*—20,018 (estimated); 10,004 (estimated); 10,004 (estimated). 1952-P-D-S: *Number minted* (including 292, 6, and 6 assay coins)—2,006,292; 8,006; 8,006. *Net distribution*—1,106,292 (estimated); 8,006 (estimated); 8,006 (estimated). 1953-P-D-S: *Number minted* (including 3, 3, and 20 assay coins)—8,003; 8,003; 108,020. *Net distribution*—8,003 (estimated); 8,003 (estimated); 88,020 (estimated). 1954-P-D-S: *Number minted* (including 6, 6, and 24 assay coins)—12,006; 12,006; 122,024. *Net distribution*—12,006 (estimated); 12,006 (estimated); 42,024 (estimated).

Original Cost and Issuer. 1951-P-D-S: $10 per set. 1952-P-D-S: $10 per set; many Philadelphia coins were sold at or near face

value through banks. 1953-P-D-S: $10 per set; some 1953-S coins were distributed at or near face value (Bebee's prices $9 until January 15, 1952, $10 after that date). 1954-P-D-S: Official sale price: $10 per set; some 1954-S coins were paid out at face value (Bebee's prices for sets $9 until January 20, 1954, $12 after that date). Issued mainly by the Carver-Washington Coin Commission acting for the Booker T. Washington Birthplace Memorial Foundation (Booker Washington Birthplace, Virginia) and the George Washington Carver National Monument Foundation (Diamond, Missouri). Also, for some issues, these dealers: Stack's, Bebee Stamp & Coin Company, Sol Kaplan, and R. Green.

Key to Collecting. Nearly all coins of this issue were handled casually at the mints and also during the distribution process. Most were not fully struck up, with the result that under magnification many tiny nicks and marks can be seen on the higher parts, originating from planchet marks that were not obliterated during the striking process. Many MS examples are available on the market.

First Points of Wear. *Obverse:* Carver's cheekbone. (Note that some pieces were struck poorly in this area; check the reverse also for wear.) *Reverse:* The lettering U.S.A. on the map.

	Distribution	Cert	Avg	%MS	MS-60	MS-62	MS-63	MS-64	MS-65	MS-66	Recent Auction Record
Single type coin	n/a	n/a	n/a	n/a	$21	$22	$24	$40	$75	$320	
1951	20,018	703	64.2	100							$863, MS-66 CAC, Apr-10
1951D	10,004	524	64.6	100							$374, MS-66, Mar-10
1951S	10,004	711	65.1	100							$253, MS-66, Jul-10
Set of 1951 P-D-S					135	145	205	215	540	3,750	$403, MS-65, Aug-09
1952	1,106,292	2,859	64.4	99							$161, MS-66, Jul-10
1952D	8,006	435	64.4	100							$863, MS-67, Jan-10

Chart continued on next page.

	Distribution	Cert	Avg	%MS	MS-60	MS-62	MS-63	MS-64	MS-65	MS-66	Recent Auction Record
1952S	8,006	550	65.0	100							$253, MS-66, Jul-10
Set of 1952 P-D-S					$140	$150	$180	$190	$385	$1,650	$196, MS-65, Aug-09
1953	8,003	435	64.6	100							$1,265, MS-66 CAC, Feb-10
1953D	8,003	381	64.4	100							$805, MS-66, Jan-10
1953S	88,020	983	64.8	100							$242, MS-66, Jul-10
Set of 1953 P-D-S					140	150	210	230	540	1,650	$334, MS-65, Dec-08
1954	12,006	651	64.6	100							$431, MS-66, Jun-10
1954D	12,006	566	64.4	100							$575, MS-66, Jun-10
1954S	42,024	930	64.6	100							$150, MS-66, Jul-10
Set of 1954 P-D-S					135	145	180	190	390	1,650	$374, MS-65, Jul-09

AN OVERVIEW OF PROOF AND MINT SETS

PROOF COINS AND SETS

A Proof is a specimen coin struck for presentation, souvenir, exhibition, or numismatic purposes. Before 1968, Proofs were made only at the Philadelphia Mint, except in a few rare instances in which presentation pieces were struck at branch mints. Today Proofs are made at the San Francisco and West Point mints.

The term *Proof* refers not to the condition of a coin, but to its method of manufacture. Regular-production coins in Mint State have coruscating, frosty luster; soft details; and minor imperfections. A Proof coin can usually be distinguished by its sharpness of detail, high wire edge, and extremely brilliant, mirrorlike surface. All Proofs are originally sold by the Mint at a premium.

Very few Proof coins were made prior to 1856. Because of their rarity and infrequent sales, they are not all listed in the regular edition of the *Guide Book of United States Coins.* However, here, in the Professional Edition, you will find them listed individually within their respective denominations.

Frosted Proofs were issued prior to 1936 and starting again in the late 1970s. These have a brilliant, mirrorlike field with contrasting dull or frosted design.

Matte Proofs have a granular, "sandblast" surface instead of the mirror finish. Matte Proof cents, nickels, and gold coins were issued from 1908 to 1916; a few 1921 and 1922 silver dollars and a 1998-S half dollar were also struck in this manner.

Brilliant Proofs have been issued from 1936 to date. These have a uniformly brilliant, mirrorlike surface and sharp, high-relief details.

"Prooflike" coins are occasionally seen. These are examples from dies that have been lightly polished, often inadvertently during the removal of lines, contact marks, and other marks in the fields. In other instances, such as with certain New Orleans gold coins of the 1850s, the dies were polished in the machine shop of the mint. They are not true Proofs, but may have most of the characteristics of a Proof coin and generally command a premium. Collectors should beware of coins that have been buffed to look like Proofs; magnification will reveal polishing lines and lack of detail.

HOW MODERN PROOF COINS ARE MADE

Selected dies are inspected for perfection and are highly polished and cleaned. They are again wiped clean or polished after every 15 to 25 impressions and are replaced frequently to avoid imperfections from worn dies. Coinage blanks are polished and cleaned to ensure high quality in striking. They are then hand fed into the coinage press one at a time, each blank receiving two or more blows from the dies to bring up sharp, high-relief details. The coinage operation is done at slow speed with extra pressure. Finished Proofs are individually inspected and are handed with gloves or tongs. They also receive a final inspection by packers before being sonically sealed in special plastic cases.

After a lapse of 20 years, Proof coins were struck at the Philadelphia Mint from 1936 to 1942, inclusive. In 1942, when the composition of the five-cent piece was changed, there were two types of this denomination available to collectors. The striking of Proof coins was temporarily suspended from 1943 through 1949, and again from 1965 through 1967; during the latter period, Special Mint Sets were struck (see page 361). Proof sets were resumed in 1968.

Sets from 1936 through 1972 include the cent, nickel, dime, quarter, and half dollar; from 1973 through 1981 the dollar was also included, and again from 2000 on. Regular Proof sets issued from 1982 to 1998 contain the cent through the half dollar. Specially packaged Prestige sets containing commemorative coins were sold from 1983 through 1997 at an additional premium. From 1999 to 2009, sets contain five different Statehood or Territorial quarters, and from 2010 to 2021, different National Parks quarters. In 1999 Proof dollars were sold separately. Four-piece Presidential dollar sets have been issued since 2007.

The above-mentioned modern Proof sets, as well as Legacy Collection sets containing Proof and commemorative coins, are covered annually in the regular edition of the *Guide Book of United States Coins.* Here, in the Professional Edition, the Proof sets of 1936 to 1942 (sometimes called *vintage*) and those of 1950 to 1964 (sometimes called *classic*) are studied.

A note about values listed: The Proof set values listed here are not for average coins in their original government packaging. Rather, they are for sets of individually certified (encapsulated) coins in the Proof levels indicated, with coins that are brilliant or only very lightly toned. Coins with blotches, specks, or other aspects that negatively affect eye appeal are worth less.

1936 Proof Set
*Liberty Walking half dollar, Washington quarter dollar, Mercury or Winged Liberty dime,
Buffalo nickel, and Lincoln cent with Wheat Ears reverse.*

1938 Proof Set
Buffalo nickel replaced with the new Jefferson nickel.

1950 Proof Set
*There was a seven-year hiatus (1943–1949) before Proof sets were issued again after World War II. By 1950 the Liberty Walking half dollar
had been replaced by the Franklin half dollar (introduced 1948), and the Mercury dime by the Roosevelt dime (introduced 1946).*

1955 Proof Set
*Issued in traditional individual envelopes, or in the new pliofilm package (pictured),
with a Philadelphia Mint embossed paper seal with a metallic finish.*

1964 Proof Set
*Franklin half dollar replaced with the new Kennedy half dollar; includes Lincoln cent with
Memorial reverse, which had replaced the Lincoln cent with Wheat Ears reverse in 1959.*

	Mintage	Issue Price	PF-65	PF-66	PF-67
1936	3,837	$1.89	$14,000	$22,000	$52,000
1937	5,542	1.89	4,650	6,250	13,500
1938	8,045	1.89	2,200	3,000	8,300
1939	8,795	1.89	2,250	3,500	9,850
1940	11,246	1.89	2,100	3,200	10,500
1941	15,287	1.89	1,500	2,200	17,500
1942, Both nickels	21,120	1.89	1,650	2,800	7,800
1942, One nickel	*	1.89	1,500	2,600	7,400

* Included in number above.

	Mintage	Issue Price	PF-66	PF-66Cam	PF-66UC	PF-67	PF-67Cam	PF-67UC
1950	51,386	$2.10	$1,050	$7,200	$77,000	$3,700	$26,000	$200,000
1951	57,500	2.10	800	3,750	34,000	1,600	9,500	83,000
1952	81,980	2.10	575	2,750	25,000	950	8,000	50,000
1953	128,800	2.10	425	1,025	13,000	700	4,000	26,500
1954	233,300	2.10	275	575	4,600	375	1,125	14,250
1955, Box pack	378,200	2.10	225	525	2,225	350	650	7,000
1955, Flat pack	*	2.10	225	525	2,225	350	650	7,000
1956	669,384	2.10	140	325	1,725	225	575	5,250
1957	1,247,952	2.10	140	500	6,850	225	1,600	11,000
1958	875,652	2.10	160	425	4,225	235	710	8,875
1959	1,149,291	2.10	120	600	6,900	205	825	20,500
1960, With Large Date cent	1,691,602	2.10	115	250	525	160	350	900
1960, With Small Date cent	*	2.10	125	275	700	195	400	1,125
1961	3,028,244	2.10	110	200	675	160	275	950
1962	3,218,019	2.10	120	185	350	155	275	535
1963	3,075,645	2.10	110	175	295	150	260	400
1964	3,950,762	2.10	60	95	225	90	175	350

* Included in number above.

Uncirculated Mint Sets

Official Uncirculated Mint sets are specially packaged by the government for sale to collectors. They contain Uncirculated specimens of each year's coins for every denomination issued from each mint. Before 2005, the coins were the same as those normally intended for circulation and were not minted with any special consideration for quality. Since 2005, however, Mint sets have been made with a satin finish rather than the traditional Uncirculated luster. As in the past, coins struck only as Proofs are not included.

Uncirculated Mint sets sold by the Treasury from 1947 through 1958 contained two examples of each regular-issue coin. These were packaged in cardboard holders that did not protect the coins from tarnish. Nicely preserved early sets generally command a 10 to 20% premium above listed values. No official Uncirculated Mint sets were produced in 1950, 1982, or 1983.

Since 1959, sets have been sealed in protective plastic envelopes. In 1965, 1966, and 1967, Special Mint Sets (see next section) of higher-than-normal quality were made to substitute for Proof sets, which were not being made during that period. Similar sets dated 1964 are reported to exist.

Privately assembled Mint sets, and Souvenir sets produced for sale at the Philadelphia or Denver mints for special occasions, are valued according to the individual pieces they contain. Only the official, government-packaged full sets are included in the following list.

A note about values listed: Valuations are for average MS-63 coin sets, with cents that are brilliant or only very lightly toned. Coins with blotches, specks, or other aspects that negatively affect eye appeal are worth less.

	Mintage	Issue Price	Face Value	MS-63
1947 P-D-S	5,000	$4.87	$4.46	$1,500
1948 P-D-S	6,000	4.92	4.46	775
1949 P-D-S	5,000	5.45	4.96	1,000
1951 P-D-S	8,654	6.75	5.46	950
1952 P-D-S	11,499	14	5.46	850
1953 P-D-S	15,538	6.14	5.46	600
1954 P-D-S	25,599	6.19	5.46	275
1955 P-D-S	49,656	3.57	2.86	180
1956 P-D	45,475	3.34	2.64	175
1957 P-D	34,324	4.40	3.64	285
1958 P-D	50,314	4.43	3.64	150
1959 P-D	187,000	2.40	1.82	60
1960 P-D	260,485	2.40	1.82	35
1961 P-D	223,704	2.40	1.82	45
1962 P-D	385,285	2.40	1.82	33
1963 P-D	606,612	2.40	1.82	33
1964 P-D	1,008,108	2.40	1.82	33

Special Mint Sets

In mid-1964 the Treasury department announced that the Mint would not offer Proof sets or Mint sets the following year. This was prompted by a nationwide shortage of circulating coins, which was wrongly blamed on coin collectors.

In 1966 the San Francisco Assay Office began striking coins dated 1965, for inclusion in so-called United States Special Mint Sets. These were issued in pliofilm packaging similar to that of recent Proof sets. The coins in early 1965 Special Mint Sets are semi-brilliant or satiny (distinctive, but not equal in quality to Proofs); the coins in later 1965 sets feature very brilliant fields (but again not reaching Proof brilliance).

The San Francisco Assay Office started striking 1966-dated coins in August of that year, and its Special Mint Sets were packaged in rigid, sonically sealed plastic holders. The coins were struck once on unpolished planchets, unlike Proof coins (which are struck at least twice on polished planchets). Also unlike Proofs,

the SMS coins were allowed to come into contact with each other during their production, which accounts for minor contact marks and abrasions. To achieve a brilliant finish, Mint technicians over-polished the coinage dies. The result was a tradeoff: most of the coins have prooflike brilliance, but many are missing polished-off design details, such as Frank Gasparro's initials on the half dollar.

All 1967-dated coinage was struck in that calendar year. Nearly all SMS coins of 1967 have fully brilliant, prooflike finishes. This brilliance was achieved without overpolishing the dies, resulting in coins that approach the quality of true Proofs. Sales of the 1967 sets were lackluster, however. The popularity of coin collecting had dropped from its peak in 1964. Also, collectors and speculators did not anticipate much secondary-market profit from the sets, which had an issue price of $4.00, compared to $2.10 for a 1964 Proof set. As a result, fewer collectors bought multiples of the 1967 sets, and today they are generally worth more than those of 1965 and 1966.

	Mintage	Issue Price	Face Value	MS-66	MS-66Cam	MS-66UC	MS-67	MS-67Cam	MS-67UC
1965	2,360,000	$4.00	$0.91	$75	$1,800	$9,000	$275	$6,250	$18,000
1966	2,261,583	4.00	0.91	100	600	7,000	225	2,400	10,500
1967	1,863,344	4.00	0.91	110	625	3,250	255	2,750	4,750

AN OVERVIEW OF
U.S. MINT BULLION COINS

The United States' bullion-coin program was launched in 1986. Since then, American Eagle and other U.S. silver, gold, and platinum coins have provided investors with convenient vehicles to add physical bullion to their investment portfolios.

In addition to regular investment-grade strikes, the U.S. Mint offers its bullion coins in various collectible formats. Proofs are created in a specialized minting process: a polished coin blank is manually fed into a press fitted with special dies; the blank is struck multiple times "so the softly frosted yet detailed images seem to float above a mirror-like field" (per Mint literature); a white-gloved inspector scrutinizes the coin; and it is then sealed in a protective plastic capsule and mounted in a satin-lined velvet presentation case along with a certificate of authenticity. Members of the public can purchase Proofs directly from the Mint, at fixed prices.

From 2006 to 2008, Burnished (called Uncirculated by the Mint) coins were also sold directly to the public. These coins are distinguished from regular bullion strikes by a W mintmark (for West Point), and by their distinctive finish (the result of burnished coin blanks). Their blanks were individually fed by hand into specially adapted coining presses. After striking, each Burnished specimen was carefully inspected, encapsulated in plastic, and packaged in a satin-lined velvet presentation case, along with a certificate of authenticity.

Regular bullion-strike coins are bought in bulk by Mint-authorized purchasers (wholesalers, brokerage companies, precious-metal firms, coin dealers, and participating banks). These authorized purchasers in turn sell them to secondary retailers, who then make them available to the general public. Authorized purchasers are required to meet financial and professional criteria, attested to by an internationally accepted accounting firm. They must be an experienced and established market-maker in bullion coins; provide a liquid two-way market for the coins; be audited annually; have an established and broad retail-customer base for distribution; and have a tangible net worth of $5 million (for American Silver Eagles) or $50 million (for gold and platinum American Eagles). Authorized purchasers of gold must have sold more than 100,000 ounces of gold bullion coins over any 12-month period since 1990. For gold and platinum, the initial order must be for at least 1,000 ounces, with reorders in increments of 500 ounces. For American Eagles, an authorized purchaser's cost is based on the market value of the bullion, plus a premium to cover minting, distribution, and other overhead expenses. For ASEs, the premium is $1.50 per coin. For gold, the premiums are 3% (for the one-ounce coin), 5% (1/2 ounce), 7% (1/4 ounce), and 9% (1/10 ounce). For platinum: 4% (for the one-ounce coin), 6% (1/2 ounce), 10% (1/4 ounce), and 15% (1/10 ounce).

Note that the U.S. Mint does not release bullion mintage data on a regular basis; the numbers given herein reflect the most recently available official data.

The listed values of uncertified, average Mint State coins have been based on current bullion prices of silver ($27 per ounce), gold ($1,370 per ounce), and platinum ($1,660 per ounce).

Mintmark location.

AMERICAN SILVER EAGLES
(1986 TO DATE)

Designers Adolph A. Weinman (obverse) and John Mercanti (reverse); weight 31.101 grams; composition .9993 silver, .0007 copper (net weight 1 oz. pure silver); diameter 40.6 mm; reeded edge; mints: Philadelphia, San Francisco, West Point.

History. The American Silver Eagle (face value $1, actual silver weight one ounce) is a legal-tender bullion coin with weight, content, and purity guaranteed by the federal government. It is the only silver coin allowed in individual retirement accounts (IRAs).The obverse design features Adolph A. Weinman's Liberty Walking, as used on the circulating half dollar of 1916 to 1947. Weinman's initials appear on the hem of Miss Liberty's gown. The reverse design, by John Mercanti, is a rendition of a heraldic eagle.

From 1986 to 1999 all American Silver Eagles were struck at the Philadelphia and San Francisco mints (with the exception of the 1995 West Point Proof). In 2000 they were struck at both Philadelphia (Proofs) and the U.S. Mint's West Point facility (bullion strikes). Since 2001, West Point has been their sole producer (with one exception), making regular bullion strikes (without mintmarks) and Proof and "Burnished" specimens (with mintmarks). (The exception is the 2006 Reverse Proof, which was struck in Philadelphia.)

In addition to the individual coins listed below, American Silver Eagles were issued in two 2006 "20th Anniversary" sets (see page 374) and in several of the bullion coin sets (see pages 369 and 374).

Striking and Sharpness. Striking is generally sharp. The key elements to check on the obverse are Miss Liberty's left hand, the higher parts and lines of her skirt, and her head. On the reverse, the eagle's breast is a main focal point.

Availability. The American Silver Eagle is one of the most popular silver-investment vehicles in the world. Between the bullion coins and various collectible formats, more than 220 million have been sold since 1986. The coins are readily available in the numismatic marketplace and from some banks, investment firms, and other non-numismatic channels.

MS-60 to 70 (Mint State). *Obverse and reverse:* At MS-60, some abrasion and contact marks are evident on the higher design areas (Miss Liberty's left arm, her hand, and the areas of the skirt covering her left leg). Luster may be dull or lifeless at MS-60 to 62, but there should be deep frost at MS-63 and better, particularly in the lower-relief areas. At MS-65 and above, the luster should be full and rich. These guidelines are more academic than practical, as American Silver Eagles are not intended for circulation, and nearly all are in high Mint State grades.

Regular Finish

Burnished Finish

Reverse Lettering Style of 1986–2007
Note the sans-serif U.

Reverse Lettering Style of 2008 to Date
Note the serif U.

	Mintage	Unc.	MS-69	MS-70
1986 (a)	5,393,005	$36	$42	$700
1987 (a)	11,442,335	34	39	1,500
1988 (a)	5,004,646	34	39	1,900
1989 (a)	5,203,327	32	37	700
1990 (a)	5,840,210	36	41	1,000
1991 (a)	7,191,066	34	39	1,800
1992 (a)	5,540,068	34	39	1,200
1993 (a)	6,763,762	34	39	2,200
1994 (a)	4,227,319	36	41	900
1995 (a)	4,672,051	37	42	700

	Mintage	Unc.	MS-69	MS-70
1996 (a)	3,603,386	$67	$72	$4,000
1997 (a)	4,295,004	35	40	425
1998 (a)	4,847,549	36	41	650
1999 (a)	7,408,640	36	41	4,000
2000 (b)	9,239,132	35	40	1,350
2001 (b)	9,001,711	32	37	475
2002 (b)	10,539,026	32	37	195
2003 (b)	8,495,008	32	37	165
2004 (b)	8,882,754	32	37	165
2005 (b)	8,891,025	32	37	165

	Mintage	Unc.	MS-69	MS-70
2006 (b)	10,676,522	$32	$39	$140
2006W, Burnished (c)	468,020	97	102	230
2007 (b)	9,028,036	32	37	150
2007W, Burnished	621,333	32	37	82
2008 (b)	20,583,000	32	37	97
2008W, Burnished	533,757	35	40	100
2008W, Burnished, Reverse of 2007 (d)	*	500	550	750
2009 (b)	30,459,000	32	37	97
2010 (b)		32	37	90

Note: Values in the Unc. column are for uncertified, average Mint State coins. * Included in number above. **a.** Minted at Philadelphia, without mintmark. **b.** Minted at West Point, without mintmark. **c.** In celebration of the 20th anniversary of the Bullion Coinage Program, in 2006 the W mintmark was used on bullion coins produced in sets at West Point. **d.** Reverse dies of 2007 and earlier have a plain (sans serif) U in UNITED. Modified dies of 2008 and later have a small serif at the bottom right of the U.

PROOF AMERICAN SILVER EAGLES

PF-60 to 70 (Proof). Proofs that are extensively cleaned and have many hairlines are lower level, such as PF-60 to 62. Those with fewer hairlines or flaws are deemed PF-63 to 65. (These exist more in theory than actuality, as nearly all Proof ASEs have been maintained in their original high condition by collectors and investors.) Given the quality of modern U.S. Mint products, even PF-66 and 67 are unusually low levels for ASE Proofs.

2006-P, Reverse Proof

	Mintage	PF	PF-69	PF-70
1986S	1,446,778	$62	$82	$1,000
1987S	904,732	62	82	2,000
1988S	557,370	67	87	900
1989S	617,694	67	87	500
1990S	695,510	62	82	400
1991S	511,925	62	82	600
1992S	498,654	67	87	575
1993P	405,913	150	170	3,500
1994P	372,168	230	250	2,200

	Mintage	PF	PF-69	PF-70
1995P	438,511	$150	$170	$500
1995W	30,125	3,500	3,700	14,000
1996P	500,000	100	120	450
1997P	435,368	150	170	650
1998P	450,000	67	87	300
1999P	549,769	67	87	400
2000P	600,000	62	82	575
2001W	746,398	62	82	150
2002W	647,342	62	82	150

	Mintage	PF	PF-69	PF-70
2003W	747,831	$62	$82	$100
2004W	801,602	62	82	100
2005W	816,663	62	82	100
2006W	1,092,477	62	82	150
2006P, Reverse Proof (a)	248,875	210	230	450
2007W	821,759	62	82	102
2008W	700,979	87	100	115
2010W (b)		90	115	130

Note: Values in the PF column are for uncertified Proof coins of average quality. **a.** The 2006-P Reverse Proof coins were issued to mark the 20th anniversary of the Bullion Coinage Program. They have brilliant devices, and their background fields are frosted (rather than the typical Proof format of frosted devices and mirror-like backgrounds). **b.** The U.S. Mint did not strike any Proof American Silver Eagles in 2009.

	Uncert	69	70
2006 Silver Dollars. Uncirculated, Proof, Reverse Proof	$350	$400	$830
2006W 1-oz. Gold- and Silver-Dollar Set. Uncirculated	1,300	1,395	1,780

Note: Values in the Uncert column are for uncertified sets of average quality.

AMERICA THE BEAUTIFUL SILVER BULLION COINS (2010–2021)

Designers various; weight 155.517 grams; composition .999 silver, .001 copper (net weight 5 oz. pure silver); diameter 76.2 mm; lettered edge; mint: Philadelphia.

History. In conjunction with the National Park quarter dollars, the U.S. Mint issues silver-bullion coins based on each of the "America the Beautiful" program's circulation-strike coins. The coinage dies are cut on a CNC milling machine, bypassing a hubbing operation, which results in finer details than seen on the smaller quarter dollars. The bullion coins are made of .999 fine silver, have a diameter of three inches, weigh five ounces, and carry a face value of 25 cents. The fineness and weight are incused on each coin's edge. The Mint's German-made Gräbener press strikes 22 coins per minute, with two strikes per coin at 450 to 500 metric tons of pressure. In December 2010 the Mint announced it would produce Uncirculated and Proof versions for collectors.

Striking and Sharpness. Striking is generally sharp.

Availability. The National Park silver bullion coins are distributed through commercial channels similar to those for the Mint's American Silver Eagle coins. Production of the 2010 coins was delayed (finally starting September 21) as the Mint worked out the technical details of striking such a large product. Production and distribution are expected to be smooth, and the Mint anticipates striking up to 500,000 of the coins annually, divided equally between each year's issues, through the program's duration.

MS-60 to 70 (Mint State). *Obverse and reverse:* At MS-60, some abrasion and contact marks are evident on the higher design areas. Luster may be dull or lifeless at MS-60 to 62, but there should be deep frost at MS-63 and better, particularly in the lower-relief areas. At MS-65 and above, the luster should be full and rich. These guidelines are more academic than practical, as these coins are not intended for circulation, and nearly all are in high Mint State grades.

	Mintage	Unc.	MS-69	MS-70
2010, Hot Springs National Park		$150	$175	$250
2010, Yellowstone National Park		150	175	250
2010, Yosemite National Park		150	175	250

	Mintage	Unc.	MS-69	MS-70
2010, Grand Canyon National Park		$150	$175	$250
2010, Mt. Hood National Forest		150	175	250

Note: Values in the Unc. column are for uncertified, average Mint State coins.

AMERICAN EAGLE GOLD BULLION COINS
(1986 TO DATE)

Designers Augustus Saint-Gaudens (obverse) and Miley Busiek (reverse); composition .9167 gold, .03 silver, .0533 copper; reeded edge; mints: Philadelphia, West Point. Weights and diameters: $5 1/10 oz., 3.393 grams, 16.5 mm; $10 1/4 oz., 8.483 grams, 22 mm; $25 1/2 oz., 16.966 grams, 27 mm; $50 1 oz., 33.931 grams, 32.7 mm.

Design common to all denominations.

Mintmark location.

History. American Eagle gold bullion coins are made in four denominations: $5 (1/10 ounce pure gold), $10 (1/4 ounce), $25 (1/2 ounce), and $50 (1 ounce). Each shares the same obverse and reverse designs: a modified rendition of Augustus Saint-Gaudens's famous Liberty (as depicted on the double eagle of 1907 to 1933), and a "family of eagles" motif by sculptor Miley Tucker-Frost (nee Busiek). From 1986 to 1991 the obverse bore a Roman numeral date, similar to the first Saint-Gaudens double eagles of 1907; this was changed to Arabic dating in 1992. The coins are legal tender—with weight, content, and purity guaranteed by the federal government—and are produced from gold mined in the United States. Investors can include them in their individual retirement accounts.

"American Eagles use the durable 22-karat standard established for gold circulating coinage over 350 years ago," notes the U.S. Mint. "They contain their stated amount of pure gold, plus small amounts of alloy. This creates harder coins that resist scratching and marring, which can diminish resale value."

Since the Bullion Coin Program started in 1986, these gold pieces have been struck in Philadelphia and West Point, in various formats similar to those of the American Silver Eagles—regular bullion strikes, Burnished, Proof, and Reverse Proof. Unlike their silver counterparts, none of the American Eagle gold coins have been struck at San Francisco.

In addition to the individual coins listed below, American Eagle gold bullion coins have been issued in various sets (see page 374).

Striking and Sharpness. Striking is generally sharp. The key elements to check on the obverse are Liberty's chest and left knee, and the open fields.

Availability. American Eagles are the most popular gold-coin investment vehicle in the United States. The coins are readily available in the numismatic marketplace as well as from participating banks, investment firms, and other non-numismatic channels.

MS-60 to 70 (Mint State). *Obverse and reverse:* At MS-60, some abrasion and contact marks are evident on the higher design areas (in particular, Miss Liberty's chest and left knee) and the open fields. Luster may be dull or lifeless at MS-60 to 62, but there should be deep frost at MS-63 and better, particularly in the lower-relief areas. At MS-65 and above, the luster should be full and rich. Contact marks and abrasion are less and less evident at higher grades. These guidelines are more academic than practical, as these coins are not intended for circulation, and nearly all are in high Mint State grades.

Regular Finish

$5 1/10-OUNCE AMERICAN EAGLE GOLD BULLION COINS

	Mintage	Unc.	MS-69	MS-70		Mintage	Unc.	MS-69	MS-70		Mintage	Unc.	MS-69	MS-70
$5 MCMLXXXVI (1986)	912,609	$170	$185	$400	$5 1997	528,266	$160	$170	$250	$5 2005	300,043	$160	$165	$185
$5 MCMLXXXVII (1987)	580,266	160	175	500	$5 1998	1,344,520	160	170	200	$5 2006	285,006	160	165	185
$5 MCMLXXXVIII (1988)	159,500	235	250	3,300	$5 1999	2,750,338	160	170	200	$5 2006W, Burnished	20,643	175	180	190
$5 MCMLXXXIX (1989)	264,790	165	180	3,000	$5 1999W, Unc made					$5 2007	190,010	160	165	185
$5 MCMXC (1990)	210,210	165	180	2,750	from unpolished					$5 2007W, Burnished	22,501	165	170	185
$5 MCMXCI (1991)	165,200	170	185	700	Proof dies (a)	14,500	600	650	1,800	$5 2008	305,000	165	170	185
$5 1992	209,300	160	170	2,000	$5 2000	569,153	165	170	185	$5 2008W, Burnished	12,657	160	165	185
$5 1993	210,709	165	175	900	$5 2001	269,147	160	165	185	$5 2009	270,000	160	165	220
$5 1994	206,380	165	175	300	$5 2002	230,027	160	165	185	$5 2010		160	165	255
$5 1995	223,025	160	170	1,000	$5 2003	245,029	160	165	185					
$5 1996	401,964	160	170	250	$5 2004	250,016	160	165	185					

Note: Values in the Unc. column are for uncertified, average Mint State coins. **a.** Unpolished Proof dies were used to mint some 1999 $5 gold coins, resulting in a regular bullion-strike issue bearing a W mintmark (usually reserved for Proofs). A similar error exists in the $10 (1/4-ounce) series. The mintage listed is an estimate. Other estimates range from 6,000 to 30,000 pieces.

$10 1/4-OUNCE AMERICAN EAGLE GOLD BULLION COINS

	Mintage	Unc.	MS-69	MS-70		Mintage	Unc.	MS-69	MS-70		Mintage	Unc.	MS-69	MS-70
$10 MCMLXXXVI (1986)	726,031	$380	$405	$1,200	$10 1997	108,805	$380	$405	$2,000	$10 2005	72,015	$380	$395	$455
$10 MCMLXXXVII (1987)	269,255	380	405	1,000	$10 1998	309,829	380	405	2,000	$10 2006	60,004	380	395	455
$10 MCMLXXXVIII (1988)	49,000	380	405	1,800	$10 1999	564,232	380	405	1,500	$10 2006W, Burnished	15,188	480	550	650
$10 MCMLXXXIX (1989)	81,789	380	405	1,000	$10 1999W, Unc. Made					$10 2007	34,004	380	395	455
$10 MCMXC (1990)	41,000	380	405	4,000	from unpolished					$10 2007W, Burnished	12,766	525	600	700
$10 MCMXCI (1991)	36,100	455	480	2,500	Proof dies (a)	10,000	800	1,000	9,000	$10 2008	70,000	380	395	455
$10 1992	59,546	380	405	1,100	$10 2000	128,964	380	395	550	$10 2008W, Burnished	8,883	600	700	1,100
$10 1993	71,864	380	405	2,500	$10 2001	71,280	380	395	455	$10 2009	110,000	380	395	455
$10 1994	72,650	380	405	1,800	$10 2002	62,027	380	395	505	$10 2010		380	395	455
$10 1995	83,752	380	405	2,000	$10 2003	74,029	380	395	455					
$10 1996	60,318	380	405	1,000	$10 2004	72,014	380	395	455					

Note: Values in the Unc. column are for uncertified, average Mint State coins. **a.** Unpolished Proof dies were used to mint some 1999 $10 gold coins, resulting in a regular bullion-strike issue bearing a W mint-mark (usually reserved for Proofs). A similar error exists in the $5 (1/10-ounce) series. The mintage listed is an estimate. Other estimates range from 6,000 to 30,000 pieces.

$25 1/2-OUNCE AMERICAN EAGLE GOLD BULLION COINS

	Mintages	Unc.	MS-69	MS-70		Mintages	Unc.	MS-69	MS-70		Mintages	Unc.	MS-69	MS-70
$25 MCMLXXXVI (1986)	599,566	$730	$795	$1,200	$25 1996	39,287	$770	$895	$3,000	$25 2006	66,005	$730	$765	$895
$25 MCMLXXXVII (1987)	131,255	730	795	2,000	$25 1997	79,605	730	765	2,600	$25 2006W, Burnished	15,164	895	1,000	1,200
$25 MCMLXXXVIII (1988)	45,000	795	995	3,500	$25 1998	169,029	730	765	895	$25 2007	47,002	730	765	895
$25 MCMLXXXIX (1989)	44,829	895	1,300	4,500	$25 1999	263,013	730	765	2,800	$25 2007W, Burnished	11,455	1,045	1,150	1,400
$25 MCMXC (1990)	31,000	1,045	1,400	5,000	$25 2000	79,287	730	765	1,000	$25 2008	61,000	730	765	895
$25 MCMXCI (1991)	24,100	1,600	2,000	3,500	$25 2001	48,047	730	795	995	$25 2008W, Burnished	15,682	1,150	1,350	1,700
$25 1992	54,404	770	805	2,500	$25 2002	70,027	730	765	845	$25 2009	110,000	730	765	895
$25 1993	73,324	730	765	2,000	$25 2003	79,029	730	765	895	$25 2010		730	765	895
$25 1994	62,400	730	765	2,000	$25 2004	98,040	730	765	895					
$25 1995	53,474	730	765	4,500	$25 2005	80,023	730	765	895					

Note: Values in the Unc. column are for uncertified, average Mint State coins.

$50 1-OUNCE AMERICAN EAGLE GOLD BULLION COINS

	Mintage	Unc.	MS-69	MS-70		Mintage	Unc.	MS-69	MS-70		Mintage	Unc.	MS-69	MS-70
$50 MCMLXXXVI (1986)	1,362,650	$1,425	$1,450	$1,800	$50 1996	189,148	$1,425	$1,450	$1,600	$50 2006	237,510	$1,425	$1,450	$1,600
$50 MCMLXXXVII (1987)	1,045,500	1,425	1,450	1,800	$50 1997	664,508	1,425	1,450	1,600	$50 2006W, Burnished	45,053	1,425	1,480	1,650
$50 MCMLXXXVIII (1988)	465,000	1,425	1,450	1,600	$50 1998	1,468,530	1,425	1,450	1,600	$50 2007	140,016	1,425	1,450	1,600
$50 MCMLXXXIX (1989)	415,790	1,425	1,450	7,000	$50 1999	1,505,026	1,425	1,450	1,600	$50 2007W, Burnished	18,066	1,425	1,480	1,650
$50 MCMXC (1990)	373,210	1,425	1,450	1,600	$50 2000	433,319	1,425	1,450	1,600	$50 2008	710,000	1,425	1,450	1,600
$50 MCMXCI (1991)	243,100	1,425	1,480	1,600	$50 2001	143,605	1,425	1,450	1,600	$50 2008W, Burnished	11,908	1,425	1,480	1,750
$50 1992	275,000	1,425	1,450	2,000	$50 2002	222,029	1,425	1,450	1,600	$50 2009	1,493,000	1,425	1,450	1,600
$50 1993	480,192	1,425	1,450	1,600	$50 2003	416,032	1,425	1,450	1,600	$50 2010		1,425	1,450	1,600
$50 1994	221,633	1,425	1,450	6,500	$50 2004	417,019	1,425	1,450	1,600					
$50 1995	200,636	1,425	1,450	1,600	$50 2005	356,555	1,425	1,450	1,600					

Note: Values in the Unc. column are for uncertified, average Mint State coins.

PROOF AMERICAN EAGLE GOLD BULLION COINS

PF-60 to 70 (Proof). Proofs that are extensively cleaned and have many hairlines are lower level, such as PF-60 to 62. Those with fewer hairlines or flaws are deemed PF-63 to 65. (These exist more in theory than actuality, as nearly all Proof American Eagle gold bullion coins have been maintained in their original high condition by collectors and investors.) Given the quality of modern U.S. Mint products, even PF-66 and 67 are unusually low levels for these Proofs.

$5 1/10-OUNCE PROOF AMERICAN EAGLE GOLD BULLION COINS

	Mintage	PF	PF-69	PF-70		Mintage	PF	PF-69	PF-70		Mintage	PF	PF-69	PF-70
$5 MCMLXXXVIII (1988)P	143,881	$200	$220	$350	$5 1996W	57,047	$200	$220	$350	$5 2004W	35,131	$200	$220	$350
$5 MCMLXXXIX (1989)P	84,647	200	220	350	$5 1997W	34,977	200	220	500	$5 2005W	49,265	200	220	350
$5 MCMXC (1990)P	99,349	200	220	350	$5 1998W	39,395	200	220	450	$5 2006W	47,277	200	220	300
$5 MCMXCI (1991)P	70,334	200	220	350	$5 1999W	48,428	200	220	750	$5 2007W	58,553	210	230	300
$5 1992P	64,874	200	220	350	$5 2000W	49,971	200	220	350	$5 2008W	28,116	200	220	350
$5 1993P	58,649	200	220	400	$5 2001W	37,530	200	220	350	$5 2010W		200	200	350
$5 1994W	62,849	200	220	400	$5 2002W	40,864	200	220	350					
$5 1995W	62,667	200	220	500	$5 2003W	40,027	200	220	350					

Note: Values in the PF column are for uncertified Proof coins of average quality, in their complete original U.S. Mint packaging.

$10 1/4-OUNCE PROOF AMERICAN EAGLE GOLD BULLION COINS

	Mintage	PF	PF-69	PF-70		Mintage	PF	PF-69	PF-70		Mintage	PF	PF-69	PF-70
$10 MCMLXXXVIII (1988)P	98,028	$400	$425	$550	$10 1996W	38,219	$400	$425	$550	$10 2004W	28,839	$400	$450	$600
$10 MCMLXXXIX (1989)P	54,170	400	425	550	$10 1997W	29,805	400	425	600	$10 2005W	37,207	400	450	600
$10 MCMXC (1990)P	62,674	400	425	550	$10 1998W	29,503	400	425	600	$10 2006W	36,127	425	450	550
$10 MCMXCI (1991)P	50,839	400	425	550	$10 1999W	34,417	400	425	600	$10 2007W	46,189	475	500	550
$10 1992P	46,269	400	425	550	$10 2000W	36,036	400	425	550	$10 2008W	18,877	475	500	550
$10 1993P	46,464	400	425	1,400	$10 2001W	25,613	400	425	550	$10 2010W		475	500	550
$10 1994W	48,172	400	425	550	$10 2002W	29,242	400	425	550					
$10 1995W	47,526	400	425	550	$10 2003W	30,292	400	425	550					

Note: Values in the PF column are for uncertified Proof coins of average quality, in their complete original U.S. Mint packaging.

$25 1/2-OUNCE PROOF AMERICAN EAGLE GOLD BULLION COINS

	Mintages	PF	PF-69	PF-70		Mintages	PF	PF-69	PF-70		Mintages	PF	PF-69	PF-70
$25 MCMLXXXVII (1987)P	143,398	$925	$975	$1,050	$25 1995W	45,388	$925	$975	$1,050	$25 2003W	28,270	$925	$975	$1,050
$25 MCMLXXXVIII (1988)P	76,528	925	975	1,050	$25 1996W	35,058	925	975	1,050	$25 2004W	27,330	925	975	1,050
$25 MCMLXXXIX (1989)P	44,798	925	975	1,050	$25 1997W	26,344	925	975	1,050	$25 2005W	34,311	925	975	1,050
$25 MCMXC (1990)P	51,636	925	975	1,050	$25 1998W	25,374	925	975	1,000	$25 2006W	34,322	925	975	1,050
$25 MCMXCI (1991)P	53,125	925	975	2,500	$25 1999W	30,427	925	975	1,300	$25 2007W	44,025	925	975	1,050
$25 1992P	40,976	925	975	1,050	$25 2000W	32,028	925	975	1,100	$25 2008W	22,602	925	975	1,050
$25 1993P	43,819	925	975	1,050	$25 2001W	23,240	925	975	1,050	$25 2010W		925	975	1,050
$25 1994W	44,584	925	975	6,500	$25 2002W	26,646	925	975	1,050					

Note: Values in the PF column are for uncertified Proof coins of average quality, in their complete original U.S. Mint packaging.

$50 1-OUNCE PROOF AMERICAN EAGLE GOLD BULLION COINS

	Mintage	PF	PF-69	PF-70		Mintage	PF	PF-69	PF-70		Mintage	PF	PF-69	PF-70
$50 MCMLXXXVI (1986)W	446,290	$1,800	$1,850	$2,200	$50 1995W	46,368	$1,800	$1,850	$2,200	$50 2004W	28,215	$1,800	$1,850	$2,200
$50 MCMLXXXVII (1987)W	147,498	1,800	1,850	2,200	$50 1996W	36,153	1,800	1,850	2,200	$50 2005W	35,246	1,800	1,850	2,200
$50 MCMLXXXVIII (1988)W	87,133	1,800	1,850	2,200	$50 1997W	32,999	1,800	1,900	2,300	$50 2006W	47,092	1,800	1,850	2,200
$50 MCMLXXXIX (1989)W	54,570	1,800	1,850	2,200	$50 1998W	25,886	1,800	2,050	2,800	$50 2006W, Rev Proof (a)	9,996	2,800	2,850	3,500
$50 MCMXC (1990)W	62,401	1,800	1,850	2,200	$50 1999W	31,427	1,800	2,100	2,900	$50 2007W	51,810	1,800	1,850	2,200
$50 MCMXCI (1991)W	50,411	1,800	1,850	2,200	$50 2000W	33,007	1,800	1,850	2,200	$50 2008W	30,237	1,800	1,900	2,250
$50 1992W	44,826	1,800	1,850	2,200	$50 2001W	24,555	1,800	1,950	2,500	$50 2010W		1,800	1,900	2,250
$50 1993W	34,369	1,800	2,000	2,500	$50 2002W	27,499	1,800	1,850	2,200					
$50 1994W	46,674	1,800	1,850	2,200	$50 2003W	28,344	1,800	1,850	2,200					

Note: Values in the PF column are for uncertified Proof coins of average quality, in their complete original U.S. Mint packaging. **a.** The 2006-W Reverse Proof coins were issued to mark the 20th anniversary of the Bullion Coinage Program. They have brilliant devices, and their background fields are frosted (rather than the typical Proof format of frosted devices and mirror-like backgrounds).

AMERICAN EAGLE BULLION COIN SETS

	PF	PF-69	PF-70
1987 Gold Set. $50, $25	$2,750	$2,825	$3,250
1988 Gold Set. $50, $25, $10, $5	3,350	3,470	4,150
1989 Gold Set. $50, $25, $10, $5	3,350	3,470	4,150
1990 Gold Set. $50, $25, $10, $5	3,350	3,470	4,150
1991 Gold Set. $50, $25, $10, $5	3,350	3,470	5,600
1992 Gold Set. $50, $25, $10, $5	3,350	3,470	4,150
1993 Gold Set. $50, $25, $10, $5	3,350	3,620	5,350
1993 Bicentennial Gold Set. $25, $10, $5, Silver Eagle, and medal (a)	1,425	1,790	6,350
1994 Gold Set. $50, $25, $10, $5	3,350	3,470	4,300
1995 Gold Set. $50, $25, $10, $5	3,350	3,470	4,150

	PF	PF-69	PF-70
1995 Anniversary Gold Set. $50, $25, $10, $5, and Silver Eagle (b)	$6,000	$7,170	$18,300
1996 Gold Set. $50, $25, $10, $5	3,350	3,470	4,150
1997 Gold Set. $50, $25, $10, $5	3,350	3,520	4,450
1997 Impressions of Liberty Set. $100 platinum, $50 gold, Silver Eagle (c)	3,700	4,120	5,950
1998 Gold Set. $50, $25, $10, $5	3,350	3,670	5,550
1999 Gold Set. $50, $25, $10, $5	3,350	3,720	4,200
2000 Gold Set. $50, $25, $10, $5	3,350	3,470	4,450

	PF	PF-69	PF-70
2001 Gold Set. $50, $25, $10, $5	$3,350	$3,570	$4,150
2002 Gold Set. $50, $25, $10, $5	3,350	3,470	4,150
2003 Gold Set. $50, $25, $10, $5	3,350	3,470	4,200
2004 Gold Set. $50, $25, $10, $5	3,350	3,495	4,200
2005 Gold Set. $50, $25, $10, $5	3,350	3,495	4,100
2006 Gold Set. $50, $25, $10, $5	3,350	3,495	4,100
2007 Gold Set. $50, $25, $10, $5	3,375	3,495	4,100
2008 Gold Set. $50, $25, $10, $5	3,375	3,495	4,100
2010 Gold Set. $50, $25, $10, $5 (d)	3,375	3,495	4,100

Note: Values in the PF column are for uncertified Proof coins of average quality, in their complete original U.S. Mint packaging. **a.** The 1993 set was issued to commemorate the bicentennial of the first coins struck by the U.S. Mint in Philadelphia. **b.** The 1995 set marked the 10th anniversary of the passage of the Liberty Coin Act, which authorized the nation's new bullion coinage program. **c.** The Impressions of Liberty set was issued in the first year that platinum coins were added to the Mint's bullion offerings. **d.** The U.S. Mint did not issue a 2009 gold set.

	Uncert	69	70
2006W $50 Gold Set. Uncirculated, Proof, and Reverse Proof	$5,000	$6,000	$7,250
2006W 1-oz. Gold- and Silver-Dollar Set. Uncirculated	1,515	1,575	1,880

Note: Values in the Uncert column are for uncertified sets of average quality.

AMERICAN BUFFALO .9999 FINE GOLD BULLION COINS (2006 TO DATE)

Designer James Earle Fraser; composition .9999 gold; reeded edge; mint: West Point. Weights and diameters: $5 1/10 oz., 3.393 grams, 16.5 mm; $10 1/4 oz., 8.483 grams, 22 mm; $25 1/2 oz., 16.966 grams, 27 mm; $50 1 oz., 31.108 grams, 32.7 mm.

Design common to all denominations.

History. American Buffalo gold bullion coins, authorized by Congress in 2005 and produced since 2006, are the first 24-karat (.9999 fine) gold coins made by the U.S. Mint. They are coined, by mandate, of gold derived from newly mined sources in America. They feature an adaptation of James Earle Fraser's iconic Indian Head / Buffalo design, first used on circulating five-cent pieces of 1913 to 1938.

Only 1-ounce ($50 face value) coins were struck in the American Buffalo program's first two years, 2006 and 2007. For 2008, the Mint expanded the coinage to include fractional pieces of 1/2 ounce ($25), 1/4 ounce ($10), and 1/10-ounce ($5), in various finishes, individually and in sets.

The coins are legal tender, with weight, content, and purity guaranteed by the federal government. Investors can include them in some individual retirement accounts. Proofs and Burnished (*Uncirculated,* in the Mint's wording) pieces undergo special production processes, similar to the American Eagle gold-bullion coinage, and can be purchased directly from the Mint. As with other products in the Mint's bullion program, regular bullion-strike pieces are distributed through a network of authorized distributors.

All American Buffalo gold bullion coins (Proofs, Burnished, and regular bullion pieces) are struck at the U.S. Mint's West Point facility.

Striking and Sharpness. Striking is generally sharp.

Availability. American Buffalo .9999 fine gold bullion coins are a popular way to buy and sell 24-karat gold. The coins are readily available in the numismatic marketplace as well as from participating banks, investment firms, and other non-numismatic channels.

MS-60 to 70 (Mint State). *Obverse and reverse:* At MS-60, some abrasion and contact marks are evident on the higher design areas and the open areas of the design. Luster may be dull or lifeless at MS-60 to 62, but there should be deep frost at MS-63 and better, particularly in the lower-relief areas. At MS-65 and above, the luster should be full and rich. Contact marks and abrasion are less and less evident at higher grades. These guidelines are more academic than practical, as these coins are not intended for circulation, and nearly all are in high Mint State grades, as struck.

Regular Finish   Burnished Finish

	Mintage	Unc.	MS-69	MS-70
$5 2008W, Burnished	17,429	$450	$550	$600
$10 2008W, Burnished	9,949	800	1,200	1,300
$25 2008W, Burnished	16,908	1,200	1,400	1,700

	Mintage	Unc.	MS-69	MS-70
$50 2006	337,012	$1,425	$1,500	$1,600
$50 2007	136,503	1,425	1,500	1,600
$50 2008	189,500	1,450	1,550	1,700

	Mintage	Unc.	MS-69	MS-70
$50 2008W, Burnished	9,074	$2,900	$3,100	$3,500
$50 2009	200,000	1,425	1,500	1,600
$50 2010		1,425	1,500	1,600

Note: Values in the Unc. column are for uncertified, average Mint State coins.

PROOF AMERICAN BUFFALO .9999 FINE GOLD BULLION COINS

PF-60 to 70 (Proof). Proofs that are extensively cleaned and have many hairlines are lower level, such as PF-60 to 62. Those with fewer hairlines or flaws are deemed PF-63 to 65. (These exist more in theory than actuality, as nearly all Proof American Buffalo gold coins have been maintained in their original high condition by collectors and investors.) Given the quality of modern U.S. Mint products, even PF-66 and 67 are unusually low levels for these Proofs.

	Mintage	PF	PF-69	PF-70
$5 2008W	18,884	$550	$600	$800
$10 2008W	13,125	850	1,100	1,700
$25 2008W	12,169	1,300	1,400	1,800
$50 2006W	246,267	1,550	1,600	1,700

	Mintage	PF	PF-69	PF-70
$50 2007W	58,998	$1,550	$1,600	$1,700
$50 2008W	18,863	3,300	3,500	4,000
$50 2009W	49,388	1,550	1,600	1,700
$50 2010W		1,600	1,700	1,800

Note: Values in the PF column are for uncertified Proof coins of average quality, in their complete original U.S. Mint packaging.

AMERICAN BUFFALO .9999 FINE GOLD BULLION COIN SETS

	Mintage	MS-69	MS-70	PF-69	PF-70
2008W Four-coin set ($5, $10, $25, $50)				$6,700	$7,100
2008W Four-coin set ($5, $10, $25, $50), Burnished		$6,250	$7,100		
2008W Double Prosperity set (Unc. $25 Buffalo gold and $25 American Eagle coins)		2,750	3,400		

FIRST SPOUSE $10 GOLD BULLION COINS (2007 TO DATE)

Weight 8.483 grams; composition .9999 gold; diameter 22 mm; reeded edge; mint: West Point. Designers: Martha Washington—*Joseph Menna (obv), Susan Gamble (rev);* Abigail Adams—*Joseph Menna (obv), Thomas Cleveland (rev);* Thomas Jefferson's Liberty—*Robert Scot / Phebe Hemphill (obv), Charles Vickers (rev);* Dolley Madison—*Don Everhart (obv), Joel Iskowitz (rev);* Elizabeth Monroe—*Joel Iskowitz (obv), Donna Weaver (rev);* Louisa Adams—*Susan Gamble (obv), Donna Weaver (rev);* Andrew Jackson's Liberty—*John Reich (obv), Justin Kunz (rev);* Martin Van Buren's Liberty—*Christian Gobrecht (obv), Thomas Cleveland (rev);* Anna Harrison—*Donna Weaver (obv), Thomas Cleveland (rev);* Letitia Tyler—*Phebe Hemphill (obv), Susan Gamble (rev);* Julia Tyler—*Joel Iskowitz;* Sarah Polk—*Phebe Hemphill;* Margaret Taylor—*Phebe Hemphill (obv), Mary Beth Zeitz (rev);* Abigail Fillmore—*Phebe Hemphill(obv), Susan Gamble (rev);* Jane Pierce—*Donna Weaver;* James Buchanan's Liberty—*Christian Gobrecht (obv), David Westwood (rev);* Mary Todd Lincoln—*Phebe Hemphill (obv), Joel Iskowitz).*

Martha Washington
The first coin in the series.

History. The U.S. Mint's First Spouse bullion coins are struck in .9999 fine (24-karat) gold. Each weighs one-half ounce and bears a face value of $10. The coins honor the nation's first spouses on the same schedule as the Mint's Presidential dollars program. Each features a portrait on the obverse, and on the reverse a unique design symbolic of the spouse's life and work. In cases where a president held office widowed or unmarried, the coin bears "an obverse image emblematic of Liberty as depicted on a circulating coin of that era and a reverse image emblematic of themes of that president's life." All First Spouse gold bullion coins (Proofs and regular bullion pieces) are struck at the U.S. Mint's West Point facility.

Note that the Mint does not release bullion mintage data on a regular basis; the numbers given herein reflect the most recently available official data.

Striking and Sharpness. Striking is generally sharp.

Availability. These coins are readily available in the numismatic marketplace. They can be purchased by the public, in both bullion-strike and Proof formats, directly from the U.S. Mint.

MS-60 to 70 (Mint State). *Obverse and reverse:* At MS-60, some abrasion and contact marks are evident on the higher design areas and the open areas of the design. Luster may be dull or lifeless at MS-60 to 62, but there should be deep frost at MS-63 and better, particularly in the lower-relief areas. At MS-65 and above, the luster should be full and rich. Contact marks and abrasion are less and less evident at higher grades. These guidelines are more academic than practical, as these coins are not intended for circulation, and nearly all are in high Mint State grades, as struck.

	Mintage	Unc.	MS-69	MS-70
$10 2007W, M. Washington	17,661	$750	$765	$800
$10 2007W, A. Adams	17,142	750	765	800
$10 2007W, Jefferson's Liberty	19,823	750	765	800
$10 2007W, D. Madison	11,813	750	765	800
$10 2008W, E. Monroe	4,519	875	925	1,500
$10 2008W, L. Adams	4,223	875	925	1,500
$10 2008W, Jackson's Liberty	4,281	1,100	1,150	1,500
$10 2008W, Van Buren's Liberty	3,443	1,150	1,200	1,500
$10 2009W, A. Harrison	2,993	890	950	1,300

	Mintage	Unc.	MS-69	MS-70
$10 2009W, L. Tyler	2,381	$1,100	$1,150	$1,500
$10 2009W, J. Tyler	2,188	1,250	1,300	1,750
$10 2009W, S. Polk	1,893	850	900	1,200
$10 2009W, M. Taylor		850	900	1,200
$10 2010W, A. Fillmore		840	890	950
$10 2010W, J. Pierce		840	890	950
$10 2010W, Buchanan's Liberty		840	890	950
$10 2010W, M. Lincoln		840	890	950

Note: Values in the Unc. column are for uncertified, average Mint State coins.

PROOF FIRST SPOUSE GOLD BULLION COINS

PF-60 to 70 (Proof). Proofs that are extensively cleaned and have many hairlines are lower level, such as PF-60 to 62. Those with fewer hairlines or flaws are deemed PF-63 to 65. (These exist more in theory than actuality, as nearly all Proof First Spouse gold coins have been maintained in their original high condition by collectors and investors.) Given the quality of modern U.S. Mint products, even PF-66 and 67 are unusually low levels for these Proofs.

	Mintage	PF	PF-69	PF-70
$10 2007W, M. Washington	19,169	$750	$765	$800
$10 2007W, A. Adams	17,149	750	765	800
$10 2007W, Jefferson's Liberty	19,815	750	765	800
$10 2007W, D. Madison	17,661	750	765	800
$10 2008W, E. Monroe	7,933	925	975	1,500
$10 2008W, L. Adams	7,454	850	900	1,400
$10 2008W, Jackson's Liberty	7,454	1,000	1,050	1,400
$10 2008W, Van Buren's Liberty	6,187	1,150	1,200	1,500
$10 2009W, A. Harrison	5,801	1,050	1,100	1,300

	Mintage	PF	PF-69	PF-70
$10 2009W, L. Tyler	4,341	$1,100	$1,200	$1,400
$10 2009W, J. Tyler	3,878	1,250	1,300	1,750
$10 2009W, S. Polk	3,512	900	950	1,100
$10 2009W, M. Taylor		900	950	1,100
$10 2010W, A. Fillmore		840	890	925
$10 2010W, J. Pierce		840	890	1,000
$10 2010W, Buchanan's Liberty		840	890	925
$10 2010W, M. Lincoln		840	890	925

Note: Values in the PF column are for uncertified Proof coins of average quality, in their complete original U.S. Mint packaging.

MMIX ULTRA HIGH RELIEF GOLD COIN
(2009)

Designer Augustus Saint-Gaudens; weight 31.101 grams; composition .9999 gold (actual gold weight 1 oz.); diameter 27 mm; lettered edge; mint: Philadelphia.

MMIX Ultra High Relief Gold Coin
Photographed at an angle to show the edge (lettered E PLURIBUS UNUM), the thickness (4 mm), and the depth of relief.

History. In 2009 the U.S. Mint produced a modern collector's version of the first Saint-Gaudens double eagle. When the original debuted in 1907, the Mint had been unable to strike large quantities for circulation—the ultra high relief design was artistic, but difficult to coin. (It was modified later in 1907 to a lower relief suitable for commercial production.) Just over 100 years later, the 2009 version was a showcase coin: a tangible demonstration of the Mint's 21st-century ability to combine artistry and technology to make an outstanding numismatic treasure.

Like its predecessor, the new coin was dated in Roman numerals (with 2009 as MMIX). The Mint digitally mapped Saint-Gaudens's original plasters and used the results in the die-making process. The date was changed, and four additional stars were inserted, to represent the nation's current 50 states. Augustus Saint-Gaudens's striding Liberty occupied the obverse. On the reverse was his flying eagle, with the addition of IN GOD WE TRUST, a motto not used in the original design. The 2009 version was made in a smaller diameter (27 mm instead of 34) and composed of 24-karat (.9999 fine) gold, thus making it easier to strike and stay true to the ultra high relief design.

As with other bullion products of the U.S. Mint, the coins are legal tender and their weight, content, and purity are guaranteed by the federal government. They were packaged in a fancy mahogany box and sold directly to the public, instead of through a network of distributors.

Note that the Mint does not release bullion mintage data on a regular basis; the number given here reflects the most recently available official data.

Striking and Sharpness. Striking is sharp.

Availability. The coins are available in the numismatic marketplace for a premium above their gold bullion value.

MS-60 to 70 (Mint State). *Obverse and reverse:* At MS-60, some abrasion and contact marks are evident on the higher design areas and the open areas of the design. Luster may be dull or lifeless at MS-60 to 62, but there should be deep frost at MS-63 and better, particularly in the lower-relief areas. At MS-65 and above, the luster should be full and rich. Contact marks and abrasion are less and less evident at higher grades. These guidelines are more academic than practical, as these coins are not intended for circulation, and presumably all are in high Mint State grades, as struck.

	Mintage	Unc.	MS-69	MS-70
MMIX Ultra High Relief $20 Gold Coin	115,178	$1,850	$1,900	$2,600

Note: Values in the Unc. column are for uncertified, average Mint State coins.

AMERICAN EAGLE PLATINUM BULLION COINS
(1997 TO DATE)

Designers John M. Mercanti (obverse), Thomas D. Rogers Sr. (original reverse) (see image captions for other reverse designers); composition .9995 platinum; reeded edge; mints: Philadelphia, West Point. Weights and diameters: $10 1/10 oz., 16.5 mm; $25 1/4 oz., 22 mm; $50 1/2 oz., 27 mm; $100 1 oz., 32.7 mm.

Common obverse and original reverse design.

History. Platinum American Eagles (face values of $10 to $100) are legal-tender bullion coins with weight, content, and purity guaranteed by the federal government. They were added to the U.S. Mint's program of silver and gold bullion coinage in 1997.

In their debut year, Proofs had the same reverse design as regular bullion strikes. Since then, the regular strikes have continued with the 1997 reverse, while the Proofs have featured new reverse designs each year. From 1998 through 2002, these special Proof designs comprised a "Vistas of Liberty" subset, with eagles flying through various American scenes. Since 2003, they have featured patriotic allegories and symbolism. From 2006 to 2008 the reverse designs honored "The Foundations of Democracy"—the nation's legislative branch (2006), executive branch (2007), and judicial branch (2008). In 2009 the Mint introduced a new six-year program of reverse designs, exploring the core concepts of American democracy as embodied in the preamble to the Constitution. The first design is *To Form a More Perfect Union* (2009), featuring four faces representing the nation's diversity, with the hair and clothing interweaving symbolically. The tiny eagle privy mark is from an original coin punch from the Philadelphia Mint's archives. This design is followed by *To Establish Justice* (2010), *To Insure Domestic Tranquility* (2011), *To Provide for the Common Defence* (2012), *To Promote the General Welfare* (2013), and *To Secure the Blessings of Liberty to Ourselves and our Posterity* (2014). The themes for the reverse designs are inspired by narratives prepared by the chief justice of the United States.

The Philadelphia Mint strikes regular bullion issues, which are sold to the public by a network of Mint-authorized precious-metal firms, coin dealers, banks, and brokerages. The West Point facility strikes Burnished pieces (called *Uncirculated* by the Mint), which are sold directly to collectors. Proofs are also struck at West Point and, like the Burnished coins, are sold by the Mint to the public, without middlemen. Similar to their gold-bullion cousins, the platinum Proofs and Burnished coins bear a W mintmark and are specially packaged in plastic capsules and fancy presentation cases.

In addition to the individual coins listed below, platinum American Eagles were issued in the 1997 "Impressions of Liberty" bullion coin set (see page 374); in 2007 "10th Anniversary" sets; and in annual platinum-coin sets.

Striking and Sharpness. Striking is generally sharp.

Availability. The platinum American Eagle is one of the most popular platinum-investment vehicles in the world. The coins are readily available in the numismatic marketplace and through some banks, investment firms, and other non-numismatic channels.

MS-60 to 70 (Mint State). *Obverse and reverse:* At MS-60, some abrasion and contact marks are evident on the higher design areas. Luster may be dull or lifeless at MS-60 to 62, but there should be deep frost at MS-63 and better, particularly in the lower-relief areas. At MS-65 and above, the luster should be full and rich. These guidelines are more academic than practical, as platinum American Eagles are not intended for circulation, and nearly all are in high Mint State grades.

Regular Finish

$10 1/10-OUNCE AMERICAN EAGLE PLATINUM BULLION COINS

	Mintage	Unc.	MS-69	MS-70		Mintage	Unc.	MS-69	MS-70		Mintage	Unc.	MS-69	MS-70
$10 1997	70,250	$200	$220	$950	$10 2002	23,005	$200	$220	$300	$10 2006W, Burnished	3,544	$425	$450	$550
$10 1998	39,525	200	220	1,450	$10 2003	22,007	200	220	350	$10 2007	13,003	200	220	250
$10 1999	55,955	200	220	500	$10 2004	15,010	200	220	275	$10 2007W, Burnished	5,556	225	250	300
$10 2000	34,027	200	220	400	$10 2005	14,013	200	220	275	$10 2008	17,000	200	225	275
$10 2001	52,017	200	220	400	$10 2006	11,001	200	220	275	$10 2008W, Burnished	3,706	225	325	400

Note: Values in the Unc. column are for uncertified, average Mint State coins.

$25 1/4-OUNCE AMERICAN EAGLE PLATINUM BULLION COINS

	Mintage	Unc.	MS-69	MS-70		Mintage	Unc.	MS-69	MS-70		Mintage	Unc.	MS-69	MS-70
$25 1997	27,100	$490	$520	$3,000	$25 2002	27,405	$490	$520	$625	$25 2006W, Burnished	2,676	$565	$600	$900
$25 1998	38,887	490	520	1,300	$25 2003	25,207	490	520	625	$25 2007	8,402	490	520	625
$25 1999	39,734	490	520	3,000	$25 2004	18,010	490	520	625	$25 2007W, Burnished	3,690	515	520	675
$25 2000	20,054	490	520	900	$25 2005	12,013	490	520	625	$25 2008	22,800	490	520	625
$25 2001	21,815	490	520	2,400	$25 2006	12,001	490	520	625	$25 2008W, Burnished	2,481	515	520	900

Note: Values in the Unc. column are for uncertified, average Mint State coins.

$50 1/2-OUNCE AMERICAN EAGLE PLATINUM BULLION COINS

	Mintage	Unc.	MS-69	MS-70		Mintage	Unc.	MS-69	MS-70		Mintage	Unc.	MS-69	MS-70
$50 1997	20,500	$925	$990	$1,700	$50 2002	24,005	$925	$990	$2,000	$50 2006W, Burnished	2,577	$950	$990	$1,500
$50 1998	32,415	925	990	3,000	$50 2003	17,409	925	990	1,300	$50 2007	7,001	925	990	1,050
$50 1999	32,309	925	990	3,500	$50 2004	13,236	925	990	1,300	$50 2007W, Burnished	3,635	950	990	1,150
$50 2000	18,892	925	990	4,000	$50 2005	9,013	925	990	1,300	$50 2008	14,000	925	990	1,050
$50 2001	12,815	925	990	3,500	$50 2006	9,602	925	990	1,050	$50 2008W, Burnished	2,253	950	990	1,700

Note: Values in the Unc. column are for uncertified, average Mint State coins.

$100 1-OUNCE AMERICAN EAGLE PLATINUM BULLION COINS

	Mintage	Unc.	MS-69	MS-70		Mintage	Unc.	MS-69	MS-70		Mintage	Unc.	MS-69	MS-70
$100 1997	56,000	$1,775	$1,950	$9,000	$100 2002	11,502	$1,775	$1,950	$9,000	$100 2006W, Burnished	3,068	$1,875	$2,100	$2,300
$100 1998	133,002	1,775	1,950	9,000	$100 2003	8,007	1,775	1,950	4,000	$100 2007	7,202	1,775	1,950	2,200
$100 1999	56,707	1,775	1,950	10,000	$100 2004	7,009	1,775	1,950	2,500	$100 2007W, Burnished	4,177	1,875	2,100	2,300
$100 2000	10,003	1,775	1,950	10,000	$100 2005	6,310	1,775	1,950	2,500	$100 2008	21,800	1,775	1,950	2,200
$100 2001	14,070	1,775	1,950	10,000	$100 2006	6,000	1,775	1,950	2,200	$100 2008W, Burnished	2,876	1,875	2,200	2,300

Note: Values in the Unc. column are for uncertified, average Mint State coins.

AMERICAN EAGLE PLATINUM BULLION COIN SETS

	Unc.	MS-69	MS-70		Unc.	MS-69	MS-70
1997 Platinum Set. $100, $50, $25, $10	$3,400	$3,695	$14,100	2006 Platinum Set. $100, $50, $25, $10	$3,400	$3,725	$3,700
1998 Platinum Set. $100, $50, $25, $10	3,400	3,695	13,750	2007 Platinum Set. $100, $50, $25, $10	3,400	3,725	3,700
1999 Platinum Set. $100, $50, $25, $10	3,400	3,695	16,850	2008 Platinum Set. $100, $50, $25, $10	3,400	3,725	3,700
2000 Platinum Set. $100, $50, $25, $10	3,400	3,695	15,300	2006W Platinum Burnished Set.			
2001 Platinum Set. $100, $50, $25, $10	3,400	3,695	16,350	$100, $50, $25, $10	3,900	4,200	5,150
2002 Platinum Set. $100, $50, $25, $10	3,400	3,695	11,950	2007W Platinum Burnished Set.			
2003 Platinum Set. $100, $50, $25, $10	3,400	3,725	6,500	$100, $50, $25, $10	3,650	3,860	4,375
2004 Platinum Set. $100, $50, $25, $10	3,400	3,725	3,900	2008W Platinum Burnished Set.			
2005 Platinum Set. $100, $50, $25, $10	3,400	3,725	3,900	$100, $50, $25, $10	3,650	3,960	5,300

Note: Values in the Unc. column are for uncertified Mint State coins of average quality, in their complete original U.S. Mint packaging.

PROOF AMERICAN EAGLE PLATINUM BULLION COINS

PF-60 to 70 (Proof). Proofs that are extensively cleaned and have many hairlines are lower level, such as PF-60 to 62. Those with fewer hairlines or flaws are deemed PF-63 to 65. (These exist more in theory than actuality, as nearly all Proof American Eagle platinum bullion coins have been maintained in their original high condition by collectors and investors.) Given the quality of modern U.S. Mint products, even PF-66 and 67 are unusually low levels for these Proofs.

Common Proof Obverse

Proof Reverse, 1998: Eagle Over New England Vistas of Liberty series. Designer: John Mercanti.

Proof Reverse, 1999: Eagle Above Southeastern Wetlands Vistas of Liberty series. Designer: John Mercanti.

Proof Reverse, 2000: Eagle Above America's Heartland Vistas of Liberty series. Designer: Alfred Maletsky.

Proof Reverse, 2001: Eagle Above America's Southwest Vistas of Liberty series. Designer: Thomas D. Rogers Sr.

Proof Reverse, 2002: Eagle Fishing in America's Northwest Vistas of Liberty series. Designer: Alfred Maletsky.

Proof Reverse, 2003 Designer: Alfred Maletsky.

Proof Reverse, 2004 "America," after Daniel Chester French.

Proof Reverse, 2005 Designer: Donna Weaver.

Proof Reverse, 2006 "Legislative Branch," designed by Joel Iskowitz.

Proof Reverse, 2007 "Executive Branch," designed by Thomas Cleveland.

Proof Reverse, 2008 "Judicial Branch," designed by Joel Iskowitz.

Proof Reverse, 2009 "To Form a More Perfect Union," designed by Susan Gamble.

$10 1/10-OUNCE PROOF AMERICAN EAGLE PLATINUM BULLION COINS

	Mintage	PF	PF-69	PF-70		Mintage	PF	PF-69	PF-70
$10 1997W	36,993	$225	$235	$400	$10 2003W	9,534	$275	$300	$600
$10 1998W	19,847	225	235	450	$10 2004W	7,161	625	675	1,000
$10 1999W	19,133	225	235	350	$10 2005W	8,104	225	325	500
$10 2000W	15,651	225	235	400	$10 2006W	10,205	225	235	400
$10 2001W	12,174	225	235	450	$10 2007W	8,176	225	235	300
$10 2002W	12,365	225	235	350	$10 2008W	5,138	225	275	625

Note: Values in the PF column are for uncertified Proof coins of average quality, in their complete original U.S. Mint packaging.

$25 1/4-OUNCE PROOF AMERICAN EAGLE PLATINUM BULLION COINS

	Mintage	PF	PF-69	PF-70		Mintage	PF	PF-69	PF-70
$25 1997W	18,628	$500	$525	$800	$25 2003W	7,044	$500	$525	$700
$25 1998W	14,873	500	525	700	$25 2004W	5,193	1,400	1,470	2,500
$25 1999W	13,507	500	525	700	$25 2005W	6,592	650	685	1,000
$25 2000W	11,995	500	525	650	$25 2006W	7,813	500	525	750
$25 2001W	8,847	500	525	700	$25 2007W	6,017	500	525	600
$25 2002W	9,282	500	525	650	$25 2008W	4,153	500	525	600

Note: Values in the PF column are for uncertified Proof coins of average quality, in their complete original U.S. Mint packaging.

$50 1/2-OUNCE PROOF AMERICAN EAGLE PLATINUM BULLION COINS

	Mintage	PF	PF-69	PF-70		Mintage	PF	PF-69	PF-70
$50 1997W	15,431	$975	$1,050	$1,400	$50 2003W	7,131	$975	$1,050	$1,750
$50 1998W	13,836	975	1,050	1,250	$50 2004W	5,063	1,875	1,900	3,400
$50 1999W	11,103	975	1,050	1,400	$50 2005W	5,942	1,075	1,100	1,400
$50 2000W	11,049	975	1,050	1,350	$50 2006W	7,649	975	1,050	1,500
$50 2001W	8,254	975	1,050	1,500	$50 2007W	25,519	975	1,050	1,400
$50 2002W	8,772	975	1,050	1,500	$50 2008W	4,020	1,275	1,300	1,400

Note: Values in the PF column are for uncertified Proof coins of average quality, in their complete original U.S. Mint packaging.

$100 1-OUNCE PROOF AMERICAN EAGLE PLATINUM BULLION COINS

	Mintage	PF	PF-69	PF-70		Mintage	PF	PF-69	PF-70
$100 1997W	20,851	$1,900	$2,050	$3,000	$100 2004W	6,007	$2,500	$2,700	$4,500
$100 1998W	14,912	1,900	2,050	2,800	$100 2005W	6,602	1,900	2,050	3,000
$100 1999W	12,363	1,900	2,050	2,900	$100 2006W	9,152	1,900	2,050	2,700
$100 2000W	12,453	1,900	2,050	2,700	$100 2007W	8,363	1,900	2,050	2,300
$100 2001W	8,969	1,900	2,050	2,900	$100 2008W	4,769	2,400	2,600	2,400
$100 2002W	9,834	1,900	2,050	2,800	$100 2009W	8,000	2,400	2,550	2,850
$100 2003W	8,246	1,900	2,050	2,800	$100 2010W		2,150	2,300	2,500

Note: Values in the PF column are for uncertified Proof coins of average quality, in their complete original U.S. Mint packaging.

PROOF AMERICAN EAGLE PLATINUM BULLION COIN SETS

	PF	PF-69	PF-70		PF	PF-69	PF-70
1998 Platinum Set. $100, $50, $25, $10	$3,750	$3,860	$5,600	2005W Platinum Set. $100, $50, $25, $10	$3,850	$3,860	$5,300
1999 Platinum Set. $100, $50, $25, $10	3,750	3,860	5,200	2006W Platinum Set. $100, $50, $25, $10	3,750	3,890	5,850
2000 Platinum Set. $100, $50, $25, $10	3,750	3,860	5,350	2007W Platinum Set. $100, $50, $25, $10	3,750	6,475	11,400
2003 Platinum Set. $100, $50, $25, $10	3,850	3,860	5,100	2008W Platinum Set. $100, $50, $25, $10	3,850	4,125	5,900
2004W Platinum Set. $100, $50, $25, $10	3,950	3,900	5,550				

Note: Values in the PF column are for uncertified Proof coins of average quality, in their complete original U.S. Mint packaging.

2007 10TH-ANNIVERSARY PLATINUM BULLION COIN SETS

	Mintage	Price	PF-69	PF-70
2007W Two-Coin Set (a)	19,583	$2,100	$2,250	$2,400

a. This two-coin set, housed in a mahogany-finish hardwood box, includes one half-ounce Proof (with the standard cameo-finish background and frosted design elements) and one half-ounce Reverse Proof (with frosted background fields and mirrored raised elements) dated 2007-W.

APPENDIX:
2009–2010 MARKET REVIEW, AND LOOKING AT 2011

THE ECONOMY AS A MARKET FACTOR

Taken as a whole, 2009 and 2010 were dynamic in the numismatic market—the buying and selling of coins, tokens, medals, and paper money. The American economy cast uncertainty over this and most other markets, but overall numismatics did well.

The U.S. economy hummed along mid-decade until 2008, when unexpected problems combined to create a financial crisis. Certain areas—most notably banking and real estate—entered difficult times, and many enterprises collapsed. Who would have dreamed that large banks would fail or be forced to merge, that some securities companies would experience the same situations, that national unemployment would rise to levels not seen in recent times, and that hundreds of billions of dollars of private and commercial real estate would go into foreclosure?

As if this were not enough, many investors and other citizens holding cash grew very conservative, electing to place their money into Treasury bonds, FDIC-insured money-market accounts, and the like. The infusion of funds was so great that interest rates dropped below 1%—another situation that would have been considered impossible several years earlier. Moreover, the federal government essentially wrote hundreds of billions of dollars in checks on an empty bank account, in an effort to strengthen the economy, including bailing out huge banks and the insurance company AIG. The government also helped distressed semi-federal agencies including the Federal National Mortgage Association (FNMA, known as Fannie Mae) and the Federal Home Loan Mortgage Corporation (FHLMC, known as Freddie Mac). Complicating matters further, the recession, aspects of deflation, and monetary troubles spread around the globe.

There were many unintended consequences to the federal government's relief efforts. Bailout funds given to large banks enabled them to borrow money less expensively than community and regional banks, causing, in part, many fine smaller institutions to fail, as they could not be competitive. Real-estate woes contributed more to the distress. For many important pieces of legislation, Congress was deadlocked, as Republicans resisted Democrats, and Democrats resisted Republicans, leading to inaction for many programs. The approval rate of President Barack Obama, high at the time of his inauguration in January 2009, fell below 50% by early 2010.

All Eyes on Gold!

The aforementioned uncertainties combined to make intense worldwide demand for *gold*. American Eagles, Canadian Maple Leafs, and other bullion-type coins saw unprecedented demand. The price of gold was featured on television, on the radio and Internet, and in print, and excitement prevailed. The enthusiasm had been building for two years. On January 3, 2008, a new record of $865.35 per troy ounce (a.m. London spot price) was set. This was a long time coming, as the previous peak had been a generation earlier, in January 1980. "Gold bugs," as enthusiasts are sometimes called, were delighted. Another record was set on March 17, 2008, at $1,023.50 per ounce.

In 2009 gold was active from the outset, fueled by media attention as well as advertisements encouraging the public to sell gold jewelry and other items to raise money and, conversely, to buy gold coins as a hedge against the falling American dollar, which seemed to be in danger due to unprecedented deficit spending by the government. Gold's zenith was attained on December 2, 2009, at $1,215 per ounce.

The price subsided in early 2010, as did demand, but only slightly. In the meantime, as uncertainty and economic conditions worsened in many areas, interest in acquiring gold as a hedge against deflation of the dollar and for its basic feeling of comfort continued unabated. Before year's end, gold had exceeded $1,400.

Meanwhile in Numismatics

Meanwhile, in the traditional rare-coin market and in all of numismatics, collectors continued collecting and dealers continued dealing. Fortunately for the hobby, few people had assembled collections or investment "portfolios" using borrowed funds. Accordingly, there was no rash of foreclosures or liquidations. In fact, scarcely any mention of such was made in the trade. Still, a collector or investor whose house or commercial property was in foreclosure, or who had taken a hit in the stock market, was not likely to increase his coin-buying budget. Similarly, those who in the past had substantial interest income to invest from bonds, money-market accounts, and other sources found themselves with smaller returns. The result was that overall sales volume was somewhat less in 2009 and 2010 than in previous years, but for the most part retail prices held steady.

There were exceptions, of course, and some big-ticket items (particularly coins that are common enough in grades such as MS-65 and 66, but are perceived to be "rare" if certified as MS-69 or MS-70) experienced price reductions. Many of these originally had been sold as promotions to people who do not know much about coins, and who did not realize that, for example, nearly all current products of the U.S. Mint are in grades such as 69 or 70 and are common. Moreover, the population reports put out by the leading certification services—ANACS, the Numismatic Guaranty Corporation of America (NGC), and the Professional Coin Grading Service (PCGS)—always *increase* in the number of pieces certified, never decrease. Newcomers forget (or don't realize) that 500 examples of a modern coin might today be certified as MS-70, but a year from now there might be 3,000 pieces. Comparing the rarity of a common modern coin in high Mint State or Proof grade with the rarity of a 19th-century or early 20th-century coin simply has no logic.

At the 2009 summer convention of the American Numismatic Association, held in Los Angeles in August, attendance slumped to only about 7,000, including dealers—the lowest figure in many years. Business was slow. Most professionals attributed the poor showing to the downtown location of the show, requiring an expensive taxi ride from the airport and long walks from hotels to the show venue. In contrast, the Florida United Numismatists (FUN) conventions in Florida in January 2009 and January 2010 were well attended and saw active trading. The three Whitman Coin and Collectibles Expos in Baltimore and one in Philadelphia in 2009 were successes as well, and the Expo held in Baltimore in March 2010 registered a 30% increase in attendance over the preceding year. The inaugural Nashville Expo, held in May 2010, saw brisk wholesale and retail business being done.

The 2009 auction market was very strong, but with a lower volume overall than for 2008. Leading firms included Heritage,

Stack's, Bowers & Merena, Ira and Larry Goldberg, and several others. The spotlight shone most brightly in September 2009 on the Goldbergs' sale of the Daniel Holmes and Ted Naftzger collections of large copper cents, in which just about every record in the book was smashed, amid a great deal of excitement. Many of the coins had been off the market for years.

In January 2010, one of five known examples of the 1913 Liberty Head nickel crossed the auction block at a Heritage sale, for $3,737,500. The 64th edition of the *Guide Book of United States Coins* (published in spring 2010) included an appendix of the top 250 auction prices for U.S. coins. This appendix had a jump of nearly $12,000 compared to the same chart in the 63rd edition. (The 250-ranked coin sold for $356,500, compared to $345,000 the year before.) In addition, six more individual coins broke the $1 million auction mark, for a total of 40.

In general, though, rarities and expensive coins at $100,000-plus were not as active as in preceding years, although there were exceptions. Die varieties continued to be a focus for many collectors, with interest ranging from issues of the 1790s down to the latest differences and features of modern Lincoln cents and golden dollars.

Tokens and medals saw much action in the auction arena, including with the Alan Bleviss Collection of Civil War tokens and in the seemingly obscure field of Betts medals (illustrating aspects of American history prior to the Revolution). Many records were set in the field of obsolete paper money, including among the reference collection of Chester Krause (founder of Krause Publications), sold by Stack's. The *collector* has been more important than ever in maintaining the integrity of such markets.

The Internet has taken an increasingly important role in the market, with one auction house reporting that only 17% of its sales volume went to bidders actually attending an event—the rest selling to Internet (in particular) and telephone bidders. Security delays, reduction of flight schedules, and the overall expense of traveling has placed greater focus on buying, selling, and trading coins on the Internet. This is not without its hazards. In 2009, with the lead being taken by the "About.com Guide to Coins," researcher Gregory V. DuBay, and hobby journal *Coin World,* publicity was given to the vast numbers of American coins being counterfeited in China. There is no Chinese regulation against such counterfeiting as long as the replicated coin is dated pre-1949 (the year the People's Republic of China was founded). Large numbers of forgeries, many of them deceptive, have been sold on the Internet, including on eBay. Unless you are an expert, if you are buying a scarce or rare coin of significant value, insist upon certification by a leading service such as ANACS, NGC, or PCGS. The chances of finding an *authentic* rare coin at a bargain price, offered on the Internet by someone who is not a well-established professional numismatist, are almost nil.

New Coin Issues

The U.S. Mint scored a signal success with the release of the Ultra High Relief MMIX (2009) double eagle, copying the design (issued in 1907 with the MCMVII date) of noted sculptor Augustus Saint-Gaudens. The modern version is slightly smaller in diameter, compensated by extra thickness. The resultant coins are beautiful, and they were (and are) widely admired.

The Statehood Quarter Program expired in 2008, and was followed by production in 2009 of quarter dollars for the District of Columbia and five U.S. territories, keeping up the appeal of new designs reaching circulation. However, public interest had subsided somewhat, and not as much notice was taken of them. A new program, honoring national parks, historic sites, and other locations, one for each state and territory, was launched in 2010.

Golden dollars of the Sacagawea type were discontinued in 2008, with the mini-dollar format next being occupied by Native American dollars (with a similar obverse design, and annually changing reverse designs). Presidential dollars, honoring each chief executive from Washington onward, continued in production, as did gold bullion coins featuring presidential wives. Most of the golden dollars went to collectors, with very few reaching circulation and use in commerce. The Treasury Department reported that nearly a billion of them are in storage, while mintage continues. The Mint's Direct Ship Program offers the coins to citizens at face value, free of shipping charges, as an effort to encourage their circulation.

In 2007 there had been much publicity about the production expenses of the cent and nickel, each of which cost more than face value to make. In 2009 not much was said on this subject. The Mint issued four new reverse designs for the Lincoln cent, for the 200th anniversary of Abraham Lincoln's birth and the centennial of the introduction of the Lincoln cent in 1909. Unfortunately, the slump in the national economy reduced the need for coins in circulation, the Mint laid off many employees, and coin production was lower in 2009 than in any recent year. This had a dampening effect in the mintage and distribution of the new cents. Fewer were made than anticipated, and although numismatists eagerly bought them (at a premium) from the Mint, the coins remained elusive in general circulation. The situation was similar for the 2010 Lincoln cents with the new "Union Shield" reverse. Slowly the 2009 and 2010 cents are entering normal commercial channels.

Summary and a Look At 2011

Dealers and collectors consulted during the preparation of this market review uniformly felt that the coin market has performed well in the past two years, and they are grateful this is the case. Collectors and dealers alike are pleased that the coin market maintains its overall strength, that there is a ready demand for most items offered at direct sale or crossing the auction block, and that activity will be robust in 2011.

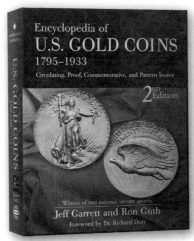
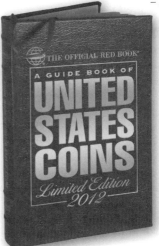
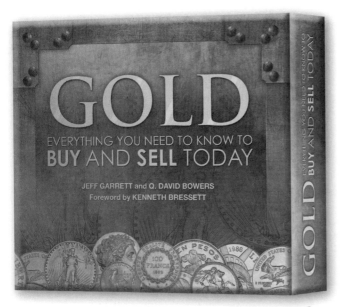
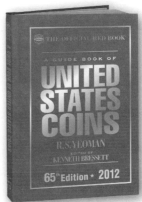